John Willis

WITH ASSOCIATE EDITOR **Barry Monush**

SCREEN WORLD

2005 FILM ANNUAL

VOLUME 56

APPLAUSE
THEATRE & CINEMA BOOKS

SCREEN WORLD
Volume 56

Art Direction: Mark Lerner
Book design by Pearl Chang **Cover design** by Pearl Chang

ISBN (hardcover): 1-55783-667-1
ISBN (paperback): 1-55783-668-X
ISSN: 1545-9020

Applause Theatre & Cinema Books
19 West 21st Street, Suite 201
New York, NY 10010
Phone: (212) 575-9265
Fax: (212) 575-9270
Email: info@applausepub.com
Internet: www.applausepub.com

Applause books are available through your local bookstore, or you may order at www.applausepub.com or call Music Dispatch at 800-637-2852

Sales & Distribution
North America:
  Hal Leonard Corp.
  7777 West Bluemound Road
  P.O. Box 13819
  Milwaukee, WI 53213
  Phone: (414) 774-3630
  Fax: (414) 774-3259
  Email: halinfo@halleonard.com
  Internet: www.halleonard.com
Europe:
  Roundhouse Publishing Ltd.
  Millstone, Limers Lane
  Northam, North Devon EX 39 2RG
  Phone: (0) 1237-474-474
  Fax: (0) 1237-474-774
  Email: roundhouse.group@ukgateway.net

CONTENTS

EDITOR   John Willis

ASSOCIATE EDITOR   Barry Monush

ACKNOWLEDGEMENTS:

Anthology Film Archives, Bazan Entertainment, Brian Black,

Thomas Buxereau, Castle Hill Films, Pearl Chang, David Christopher,

The Cinema Guild, Columbia Pictures, Consolidated Poster Service,

Samantha Dean and Associates, DreamWorks, Film Forum, First Look

Pictures, First Run Features, Focus Features, Fox Searchlight, IFC Films,

Kino International, Leisure Time Features, Lions Gate Films, Tom Lynch,

MGM, Mike Maggiore, Magnolia Pictures, Michael Messina, Miramax Films,

David Munro, New Line Cinema/Fine Line Features, New Yorker Films,

Newmarket Films, Susan Norget, Palm Pictures, Paramount Pictures,

Paramount Classics, Haley Pierson, 7th Art Releasing, Samuel Goldwyn Films,

Kallie Shimek, Sony Classics, Sony Pictures Entertainment, Sheldon Stone,

Strand Releasing, TLA Entertainment, ThinkFilm, Twentieth Century Fox,

Universal Pictures, Walt Disney Pictures, Vitagraph,

Warner Independent Pictures, Wellspring, Zeitgeist Films

Easy Rider

A Safe Place

The Last Detail

Chinatown

One Flew Over the Cuckoo's Nest

Goin' South

The Postman Always Rings Twice

As Good As It Gets

Something's Gotta Give

To **JACK NICHOLSON**

A uniquely gifted, often eccentrically charismatic performer who has ascended to the very top of his profession, being both an outstanding actor and a giant among modern film stars.

FILMS: 1958: The Cry Baby Killer; **1960:** Too Soon to Love; The Wild Ride; Studs Lonigan; The Little Shop of Horrors; **1962:** The Broken Land; **1963:** The Raven; The Terror; Thunder Island (writer only); **1964:** Ensign Pulver; Flight to Fury; Back Door to Hell; **1965:** Ride in the Whirlwind (also writer, producer); **1967:** The Shooting (also producer); Hell's Angels on Wheels; The St. Valentine's Day Massacre; The Trip (writer only); **1968:** Psych-Out; Head (also writer, producer); **1969:** Easy Rider (Academy Award nomination); **1970:** Rebel Rousers; On a Clear Day You Can See Forever; Five Easy Pieces (Academy Award nomination); **1971:** Drive, He Said (director, writer, producer only); Carnal Knowledge; A Safe Place; **1972:** The King of Marvin Gardens; **1973:** The Last Detail (Academy Award nomination); **1974:** Chinatown (Academy Award nomination); **1975:** Tommy; The Fortune; The Passenger; One Flew Over the Cuckoo's Nest (Academy Award for Best Actor); **1976:** The Missouri Breaks; The Last Tycoon; **1978:** Goin' South (also director); **1980:** The Shining; **1981:** The Postman Always Rings Twice; Reds (Academy Award nomination); **1982:** The Border; **1983:** Terms of Endearment (Academy Award for Best Supporting Actor); **1985:** Prizzi's Honor (Academy Award nomination); **1986:** Heartburn; **1987:** The Witches of Eastwick; Broadcast News; Ironweed (Academy Award nomination); **1989:** Batman; **1990:** The Two Jakes (also director); **1992:** Man Trouble; A Few Good Men (Academy Award nomination); Hoffa; **1994:** Wolf; **1995:** The Crossing Guard; **1996:** Mars Attacks!; The Evening Star; **1997:** Blood and Wine; As Good as It Gets (Academy Award for Best Actor); **2000:** The Pledge; **2002:** About Schmidt (Academy Award nomination); **2003:** Anger Management; Something's Gotta Give; **2006:** The Departed.

SCREEN HIGHLIGHTS OF 2004

THE AVIATOR
Right: Leonardo DiCaprio
PHOTOS COURTESY OF WARNER BROS./ MIRAMAX

A VERY LONG ENGAGEMENT
Left: Audrey Tautou
Bottom: Audrey Tautou
PHOTOS COURTESY OF WARNER BROS.

MILLION DOLLAR BABY
Above: Hilary Swank, Clint Eastwood

PHOTOS COURTESY OF WARNER BROS.

CLOSER
Right: Clive Owen, Natalie Portman,
Julia Roberts, Jude Law

PHOTOS COURTESY OF COLUMBIA PICTURES

KINSEY
Left: Laura Linney, Liam Neeson
PHOTOS COURTESY OF FOX SEARCHLIGHT

RAY
Below: Jamie Foxx, Kerry Washington,
Eric O'Neal Jr., Harry Lennix
PHOTOS COURTESY OF UNIVERSAL

SIDEWAYS
Right: Paul Giamatti, Virginia Madsen
Below: Sandra Oh, Thomas Haden Church

PHOTO COURTESY OF FOX SEARCHLIGHT

**ETERNAL SUNSHINE
OF THE SPOTLESS MIND**
Above: Jim Carrey, Kate Winslet
PHOTO COURTESY OF FOCUS FEATURES

GARDEN STATE
Left: Peter Sarsgaard,
Natalie Portman, Zach Braff
PHOTO COURTESY OF FOX SEARCHLIGHT

THE SEA INSIDE
Top, right: Belén Rueda
PHOTOS COURTESY OF FINE LINE FEATURES

**ANDREW LLOYD WEBBER'S
THE PHANTOM OF THE OPERA**
Left: Patrick Wilson, Emmy Rossum
PHOTOS COURTESY OF WARNER BROS. PICTURES

THE MANCHURIAN CANDIDATE
Bottom, right: Liev Schreiber
PHOTOS COURTESY OF NEW LINE CINEMA

DE-LOVELY
Above: Kevin Kline, Ashley Judd
PHOTO COURTESY OF MGM

VERA DRAKE
Left: Imelda Staunton
PHOTO COURTESY OF FINE LINE FEATURES

**LEMONY SNICKET'S A SERIES OF
UNFORTUNATE OF EVENTS**
Above: Liam Aiken,
Shelby Hoffman/Kara Hoffman, Emily Browning
PHOTO COURTESY OF PARAMOUNT/ DREAMWORKS

KILL BILL: VOLUME 2
Right: Uma Thurman, Gordon Liu
PHOTO COURTESY OF MIRAMAX

ALEXANDER
Left: Angelina Jolie, Connor Paolo
PHOTO COURTESY OF WARNER BROS.

THE PASSION OF THE CHRIST
Above: Maia Morgenstern
PHOTO COURTESY OF NEW MARKET FILMS

TROY
Left: Eric Bana
PHOTO COURTESY OF WARNER BROS.

THE INCREDIBLES
Right: Violet, Dash, Mr. Incredible, Elastigirl
PHOTO COURTESY OF WALT DISNEY PICTURES

FINDING NEVERLAND
Below: Freddie Highmore, Joe Prospero, Johnny
Depp, Nick Roud, Kate Winslet, Luke Spill
PHOTO COURTESY OF MIRAMAX

HOTEL RWANDA
Above: Don Cheadle, Sophie Okonedo
PHOTO COURTESY OF UNITED ARTIST/MGM

THE TERMINAL
Left: Zoë Saldana, Tom Hanks
PHOTO COURTESY OF DREAMWORKS PICTURES

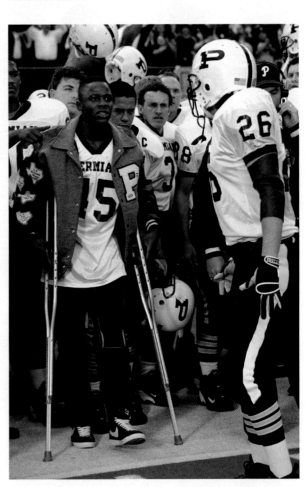

FAHRENHEIT 911
Top, left: Sgt. Abdul Henderson, Michael Moore
PHOTO COURTESY OF LIONS GATE FILMS

THE DOOR IN THE FLOOR
Center: Kim Basinger
PHOTO COURTESY OF FOCUS FEATURES

FRIDAY NIGHT LIGHTS
Above: Derek Luke
PHOTO COURTESY OF UNIVERSAL

BAD EDUCATION
Bottom, left: Gael García Bernal, Javier Cámara
PHOTO COURTESY OF SONY CLASSICS

13 GOING ON 30
Left: Jennifer Garner, Lucy Greer
Below, right: Mark Ruffalo, Jennifer Garner
PHOTO COURTESY OF COLUMBIA TRISTAR

THE NOTEBOOK
Bottom: Rachel McAdams, Ryan Gosling
PHOTO COURTESY OF NEW LINE CINEMA

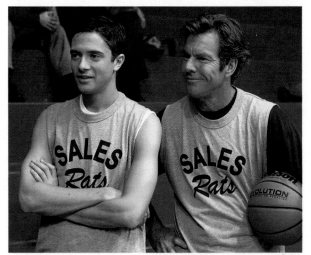

MEAN GIRLS
Top, Left: Tina Fey
Bottom, left: Lacey Chabert, Rachel McAdams,
Lindsay Lohan, Amanda Seyfried
PHOTO COURTESY OF PARAMOUNT

IN GOOD COMPANY
Top, right: Topher Grace, Dennis Quaid
Bottom, right: Scarlett Johansson
PHOTO COURTESY OF UNIVERSAL

DOMESTIC FILMS

2004 RELEASES

ALONG CAME POLLY

(UNIVERSAL) Producers, Danny DeVito, Michael Shamberg, Stacey Sher; Executive Producers, Jane Bartelme, Dan Levine; Director/Screenplay, John Hamburg; Photography, Seamus McGarvey; Designer, Andrew Laws; Costumes, Cindy Evans; Music, Theodore Shapiro; Music Supervisor, Randall Poster; Editors, William Kerr, Nick Moore; Choreographer, Joann Fregalette Jansen; Casting, Kathleen Chopin; a Jersey Films production; Dolby; Technicolor; Rated PG-13; 90 minutes; Release date: January 16, 2004

Hank Azaria

Philip Seymour Hoffman, Ben Stiller

Cast

Reuben Feffer **Ben Stiller**
Polly Prince **Jennifer Aniston**
Sandy Lyle **Philip Seymour Hoffman**
Lisa Kramer **Debra Messing**
Stan Indursky **Alec Baldwin**
Claude **Hank Azaria**
Leland Van Lew **Bryan Brown**
Javier **Jsu Garcia**
Vivian Feffer **Michele Lee**
Irving Feffer **Bob Dishy**
Roxanne **Missi Pyle**

and Judah Friedlander (Dustin), Kevin Hart (Vic), Masi Oka (Wonsuk), Kym E. Whitley (Gladys), Amy Hohn (Cheryl), Nathan Dean (Mitch), Cheryl Hines (Catering Manager), Caroline Aaron (Wedding Coordinator), Christina Kirk (Party Hostess), Todd Stashwick (Security Officer), Robb Skyler, Eddie Conna (Basketball Player), Bruce Nozick (Executive Chief), Mark Adair-Rios (Cake Decorator), Michael Shamberg, Nick Jameson (Van Lew Executives), Richard Willgrubs (AFLAC Executive), Richard Assad (Indian Waiter), Ronald Hunter (Peanut Vendor), Rabbi David Baron (Rabbi), James Dumont (Larry), Nicholas Benevento (Wedding Photographer), Jeffrey Ross (Wedding Band Leader), Mitch Silpa (J.C. Superstar Director), Robert M. Koch (Partygoer), Mark Ramos Nishita (Salsa Band Leader), Theodor Shapiro (Hector), Claudio Tenorio Gonzales (Salsa Singer), Carmit Bachar, Marco de la Cruz, Alison Faulk, Tomasina Parrott, Gustavo Vargas, Allen Walls, Rudy Zalez (Salsa Dancers), Paul Blazeak, Richard Barron, George Balmaseda, Leslie Drayton, Jose Espinosa, Walter Miranda, Alfredo Ortiz, Phillip Ranelin, Michael Wong

Ben Stiller, Jennifer Aniston PHOTOS COURTESY OF UNIVERSAL

(Salsa Band), Adrienne Ash, Christine Barger, Toni Blair, Eugenia Care, Mari Endo, Mike Fujimoto, Gustavo Hernandez, Monique "Nikki" Jongs, Anjulie Marriott, Jeffrey Sherrard (J.C. Superstar Singers), Ryan Cross, Anthony King, Vernon Neilly, Stu Silverstein (J.C. Superstar Band)

Having lost his wife to another man while on his honeymoon, hapless Reuben Feffer returns to New York where he falls in love with ditsy Polly Prince.

Leonard, Spot

DISNEY'S TEACHER'S PET

(WALT DISNEY PICTURES) Producer, Stephen Swofford; Director, Timothy Björklund; Creators/Executive Producers, Gary Baseman, Bill & Cheri Steinkellner; Screenplay, Bill & Cheri Steinkellner; Art Director, Gary Baseman; Voice Casting/Dialogue Director, Jamie Thomason; Music, Stephen James Taylor; Songs, Randy Petersen, Kevin Quinn, Cheri Steinkellner, Brian Woodbury, Peter Lurye; Supervising Film Editor, Nancy Frazen; Technical Director, Andy Schoentag; Unit Animation Director, Dante Clemente; Consulting Layout Supervisor, Greg Hill; Line Producer, Michael Karafilis; Associate Producer, Melina Carrillo; Animation Production, Toon City Animation, Inc.; a Walt Disney Television Animation production; Dolby; Techincolor; Rated PG; 73 minutes; Release date: January 16, 2004

Voice Cast

Spot/Scott **Nathan Lane**
Dr. Krank **Kelsey Grammer**
Leonard Helperman **Shaun Fleming**
Mrs. Helperman **Debra Jo Rupp**
Jolly **David Ogden Stiers**
Pretty Boy **Jerry Stiller**
Dennis **Paul Reubens**
Adele **Megan Mullally**
Ian **Rob Paulsen**
Principal Stickler **Wallace Shawn**
Mrs. Boogin **Estelle Harris**
Barry Anger **Jay Thomas**
Marsha/Marcia **Genie Ann Francis**
John/Juan **Anthony Geary**
Blue Fairy **Rosalyn Landor**
Beefeater **David Maples**
Trevor/Taylor/Tyler **Pamela S. Adlon**
Daddy **Timothy Stack**
Little Girl **Emma Steinkellner**

Leonard, Spot, Mrs. Helperman

Spot

and Ken Swofford (Officer White), Lauren Tom (Younghee), Mae Whitman (Leslie), Kevin M. Richardson (Conductor)

Determined to be accepted as a human, Leonard Helperman's dog Spot follows his master to school, passing himself as the newest kid in the fourth grade. Based on the ABC-TV Saturday morning series that debuted in 2000.

Pretty Boy, Mr.Jolly PHOTOS COURTESY OF WALT DISNEY PICTURES

WIN A DATE WITH TAD HAMILTON!

(DREAMWORKS) Producers, Douglas Wick, Lucy Fisher; Executive Producers, William S. Beasley, Gail Lyon; Director, Robert Luketic; Screenplay, Victor Levin; Photography Peter Collister; Designer, Missy Stewart; Costumes, Catherine Adair; Editor, Scott Hill; Music, Edward Shearmur; Music Supervisors, Laura Wasserman, Darren Higman; Casting, Joseph Middleton; a Lucy Fisher/Douglas Wick production; Dolby; Color; Rated PG-13; 91 minutes; Release date: January 23, 2004

Kate Bosworth, Ginnifer Goodwin, Topher Grace

Sean Hayes, Josh Duhamel, Nathan Lane

Gary Cole, Kate Bosworth, Josh Duhamel

Cast

Rosalee Futch **Kate Bosworth**
Pete Monash **Topher Grace**
Tad Hamilton **Josh Duhamel**
Richard Levy, The Driven **Nathan Lane**
Richard Levy, The Shameless **Sean Hayes**
Henry Futch **Gary Cole**
Cathy Feely **Ginnifer Goodwin**
Angelica **Kathryn Hahn**
Janine **Octavia Spencer**
Nurse **Amy Smart**
Porsche Woman **Ren Trostle**
Customer **Wendy Worthington**
George Ruddy **Stephen Tobolowsky**

and Moon Bloodgood (Gorgeous Woman), Mary Jo Smith (Sonja), Joseph Convery (Mickey—Tad's Driver), Deena Dill (Reporter), Bob Glouberman (Rosalee's Limo Driver), Sam Pancake (Hotel Clerk), Jay Underwood (Policeman Tom), Patrick O'Brien (Father Newell), Larry Agney (90 Year Old Man), Willow Bay, Jessy Moss, Marshall Goodman, Danny Weissfeld, Caleb Spier (Themselves), Todd Eckert (Maitre D'), David Wolrod (Roger Bodger), Peter Iovino (Paparrazi)

Small town grocery clerk Rosalee Futch wins a date with screen idol Tad Hamilton, much to the dismay of her best friend and co-worker Pete Monash, who harbors a secret crush on her.

Topher Grace PHOTOS COURTESY OF DREAMWORKS

THE BUTTERFLY EFFECT

(NEW LINE CINEMA) Producers, Chris Bender, A.J. Dix, Anthony Rhulen, JC Spink; Executive Producers, Toby Emmerich, Richard Brener, Cale Boyter, William Shively, David Krintzman, Jason Goldberg, Ashton Kutcher; Directors/Screenplay, Eric Bress, J. Mackye Gruber; Photography, Matthew F. Leonetti; Designer, Douglas Higgins; Costumes, Carla Hetland; Co-Producer, Lisa Richardson; Editor, Peter Amundson; Music, Michael Suby; Music Supervisor, Kevin J. Edelman; Casting, Carmen Cuba; a Benderspink and FilmEngine production presented in association with Katalyst; Dolby; Deluxe color; Rated R; 113 minutes; Release date: January 23, 2004

Cast

Evan Treborn **Ashton Kutcher**
Andrea Treborn **Melora Walters**
Kayleigh Miller **Amy Smart**
Lenny Kagan **Elden Henson**
Tommy Miller **William Lee Scott**
George Miller **Eric Stoltz**
Evan Treborn at 13 **John Patrick Amedori**
Kayleigh Miller at 13 **Irene Gorovaia**
Lenny at 13 **Kevin G. Schmidt**
Tommy Miller at 13 **Jesse James**

Logan Lerman, Melora Walters

and Logan Lerman (Evan Treborn at 7), Sarah Widdows (Kayleigh Miller at 7),Jake Kaese (Lenny Kagan at 7), Cameron Bright (Tommy Miller at 7), Callum Keith Rennie (Jason Treborn), Lorena Gale (Mrs. Boswell), Nathaniel DeVeaux (Dr. Redfield), John Tierney (Priest), Kendall Cross (Mrs. Kagan), Ted Friend (Anchor), John B. Lowe (Prof. Carter), Ethan Suplee (Thumper), Camille Sullivan (Cricket), Tara Wilson (Heidi), Jesse Hutch (Spencer), Jacqueline J. Stewart (Gwen), Grant Thompson (Hunter), Sadie Lawrence (Mrs. Halpern), Bill Croft (Boss), Glenn Richards (Pinching Customer), Sam Easton (Theta Chi Pledge), Daniel Spink (Senior Brother), Daniel J. Arthurs (Karl), Kevin Durand (Carlos), Paul Lazenby (Rick), Kimani Smith (Orderly), June B. Wilde (Waitress), Trevor Jones (Sunnyvale Guard), Colby Chartrand (Teen Punk), Shelly Schiavoni (Mrs. Miller), Brandy Heidrick (Kristen), Chapelle Jaffe (Madame Helga), Scottt Swanson (Obstetrician), Kevan Ohtsji (Anesthesiologist), Melanie Hall (Gesela), Amy Esterle (Gothic Co-Ed), David Cook (Movieoger), Magda Apanowicz (Teen Punk Girl), Garry Little (Wedding Priest), J. Jackson Kocela (Evan at 3), Andrew Olcott (Andrea's New Husband)

Having been emotionally damaged while a child, a young man hopes to summon up these repressed bad memories in order to go back in time and change his life, and those of his friends, for the better.

Wiliam Lee Scott, Ashton Kutcher (on ground)

Ashton Kutcher, Amy Smart PHOTOS COURTESY OF NEW LINE CINEMA

Steve Sandvoss, Joseph Gordon-Levitt

LATTER DAYS

(TLA RELEASING) Producers, Kirkland Tibbels, Jennifer Schaefer; Executive Producers, Scott Zimmerman, J. Todd Harris; Co-Producer, George Bendele; Co-Executive Producers, Kermit Johns, G. Sterling Zinsmeyer, Michael Wool, Tom Soto; Director/Screenplay, C. Jay Cox; Photography, Carl F. Bartels; Designer, Chris Anthony Miller; Costumes, Lisa Lesniak; Music, Eric Allaman; Music Supervisor, Michael Lloyd; Editor, John Keitel; Casting, Dan Shaner, Michael Testa; a Funny Boy production; Dolby; Color; Rated R; 107 minutes; Release date: January 30, 2004

Cast

Aaron Davis **Steve Sandvoss**
Christian Markelli **Wes Ramsey**
Julie Taylor **Rebekah Jordan**
Traci Levine **Amber Benson**
Andrew **Khary Payton**
Lila Montague **Jacqueline Bisset**
Paul Ryder **Joseph Gordon-Levitt**
Harmon **Rob McElhenney**
Gilford **Dave Power**
Keith Griffin **Erik Palladino**
Gladys Davis **Mary Kay Place**
Farron Davis **Jim Ortlieb**
Susan Davis **Linda Pine**
Susan's Husband **Bob Gray**
Noreen **Judith Morton Fraser**
Quinn, Elizabeth's Date **Robert LaCroix**

and Terry Simpson (Dirk), Brian Patrick Wade (Stacy), Kurt Hargan (Stacy's Husband), Mik Scriba (Maintenance Man), Jason-Shane Scott (Christian's Sublet), John Giansiracusa, Robert Ramirez (Men in Black), Hilary Bell (Hollywood Starlet), Michael Moriarty, Matthew Mertens (Bodyguards), Doyle Wolfgang, Trudi Wolfgang (Couple Waiting for Table), Oneil Cespedes (Christian's Hook Up), Rick Moriarty (Man Taking Picture), Joseph Dipippa (New Mormon), Laurent Weber (Mormon at Airport), Ed Cha (Itchy the Cook), Daisy Lewis (Hostess), Rob Gunnerson

Wes Ramsey, Jacqueline Bisset, Rebekah Jordan

(Bartender at Club), Andre Araujo, Bill Gill, Marc-Allen Barker (Project Angel Food Volunteers), Alexandra Swanland (Nurse), Dale Hawes (Doctor), Charles Edwards (Cher Impersonator), Leora Lutz (Angel Impersonator), Roger Dertinger (Devil Impersonator)

Aaron Davis arrives in Los Angeles to begin his work as a Mormon missionary only to realize that he is having very strong feelings for his openly gay neighbor Christian.

Steve Sandvoss, Wes Ramsey

Steve Sandvoss, Wes Ramsey PHOTOS COURTESY OF TLA RELEASING

Jarell Houston, Marques Houston, Omari Grandberry (bottom center)

YOU GOT SERVED

(SCREEN GEMS) Producers, Marcus Morton, Cassius Vernon Westhersby, Billy Pollina; Executive Producers, Ketrina "Taz" Askew, Max Gousse; Director/Screenplay, Christopher B. Stokes; Photography, David Hennings; Designer, Maxine Shepard; Costumes, Ca-Trece Mas'sey; Music, Tyler Bates; Music Supervisor, Barry Cole; Editor, Earl Watson; Choreographers, Dave Scott, Shane Sparks; Line Producer, Kevin Halloran; Casting, Monica Swann; an Ultimate Group Films production in association with Melee Entertainment; Dolby; Color; Rated PG-13; 94 minutes; Release date: January 30, 2004

Cast

Elgin **Marques Houston**
David **Omari Grandberry**
Rico **Jarell Houston**
Vick **DeMario Thornton**
Rashaan **Dreux Frederic**

and Jennifer Freeman (Liyah), Lil' Kim, Alani "La La" Vasquez, Wade Robson (Themselves)**,** Michael "Bear" Taliferro (Emerald), Christopher Jones (Wade), Meagan Good (Beautiful), Steve Harvey (Mr. Red), Marty Dew (Marty), Jerome James (Sonny), Tuere "Tanee" McCall (Toya), Amanda Rodrigues (Keke), Malcolm David Kelley (Lil Saint), Robert James Hoffman III (Max), Esther Scott (Grandma), Irene Stokes (Nurse), Dorien Wilson (Doctor), Juanita Charles (Waitress), Oscar Orosco (Oscar), Jackée Harry (Mama), Brenda J. Crawford-Bee (Woman in Stands), Skip Cheatham, Dwight Crossfield, Troy "DJ Trouble T" Ewing, Don Gibbs, Darryl Huckaby, Dejai Jeffries, Mohamed Moretta, Big Nat (Themselves), David "Elsewhere" Bernal, Donnie "Crumbs" Counts, Jon "Do Knock"

Dreux Frederic, Jennifer Freeman, Omari Grandberry PHOTOS COURTESY OF SCREEN GEMS

Cruz, Jason "Easy Roc" Geoffrey, Lamonte "Tails" Goode, Gabriel "Wicket" Joachico, Garland Spencer, Allen "French Twist" Tepper, Ivan "Flipz" Velez, Isaiah Vest (B-Boys), Julie "Jules" Urich (B-Girl)

Two L.A. street dancers find themselves involved with a crime boss just as they are about to enter a big MTV dance-off.

Charlie Sheen, Morgan Freeman, Owen Wilson PHOTO COURTESY OF WARNER BROS.

THE BIG BOUNCE

(WARNER BROS.) Producers, Steve Bing, Jorge Saralegui; Executive Producers, Zan Winer, Brent Armitage; Co-Producer, Channing Dungee; Director, George Armitage; Screenplay, Sebastian Gutierrez; Based on the novel by Elmore Leonard; Photography, Jeffrey L. Kimball; Designer, Stephen Altman; Costumes, Betsy Cox, Tracy Tynan; Music, George S. Clinton; Music Supervisor, Dana Sano; Editors, Brian Berdan, Barry Malkin; Casting, Mali Finn; a Shangri-La Entertainment presentation of a Material Films production; Dolby; Super 35 Widescreen; FotoKem color; Rated PG-13; 89 minutes; Release date: January 30, 2004

Cast

Jack Ryan **Owen Wilson**
Walter Crewes **Morgan Freeman**
Ray Ritchie **Gary Sinise**
Nancy Hayes **Sara Foster**
Joe Lurie **Willie Nelson**
Lou Harris **Vinnie Jones**
Alison Ritchie **Bebe Neuwirth**
Bob Rogers, Jr. **Charlie Sheen**

and Harry Dean Stanton (Bob Rogers, Sr.), Andrew Wilson (Ned Coleman), Steve Jones (Dick, Coleman's Lover), Anahit Minasyan (Virginia No. 9), Butch Helemano (Hawaiian Priest), Gregory Sproleder (Frank Pizzarro), Terry L. Ahue (Jimmy Opono), Pete Johnson (Con Nuuiwa), Mike Renfro, Tony Dorsett (Workers), Brian Keaulana (Barry Salu), Wendy Thorlakson (Wendy the Party Planner), Beate Antares (Celia, PBN Girl), John John Florence, Kala Alexander, Kelly Slater (Themselves), Lita Weidenbach, Leigh French (Rell), Brian Costa (Waimea Willy)

Layabout Jack Ryan arrives in Hawaii where he is approached by the mistress of real estate tycoon Ray Ritchie to rob her lover of $200,000. Remake of 1969 Warner Bros. film starring Ryan O'Neal, Leigh Taylor Young, and Van Heflin.

Scarlett Johansson, Leonard Nam, Chris Evans

Erika Christensen, Darius Miles, Chris Evans

Leonard Nam, Scarlett Johansson, Chris Evans, Erika Christensen, Bryan Greenberg, Darius Miles PHOTOS COURTESY OF PARAMOUNT

THE PERFECT SCORE

(PARAMOUNT) Producers, Roger Birnbaum, Jonathan Glickman, Brian Robbins, Mike Tollin; Executive Producer, Donald J. Lee, Jr.; Director, Brian Robbins; Screenplay, Mark Schwahn, Marc Hyman, Jon Zack; Story, Marc Hyman, Jon Zack; Photography, Clark Mathis; Designer, James Hinkle; Costumes, Melissa Toth; Editor, Ned Bastille; Music, John Murphy; Music Supervisors, Jennfier Pyken, Madonna Wade-Reed; Casting, Amanda Mackey Johnson, Cathy Sandrich Gelfond; a Roger Birnbaum Tollin/Robbins production, presented in association with MTV Films; Dolby; Deluxe color; Rated PG-13; 93 minutes; Release date: January 30, 2004

Chris Evans, Bryan Greenberg PHOTOS COURTESY OF PARAMOUNT

Cast
Anna **Erika Christensen**
Kyle **Chris Evans**
Matty **Bryan Greenberg**
Francesca **Scarlett Johansson**
Desmond **Darius Miles**
Roy **Leonard Nam**
Desmond's Mother **Tyra Ferrell**
Larry **Matthew Lillard**
Attractive Woman **Vanessa Angel**
Lobby Guard **Bill Mackenzie**

and Dan Zukovic (Mr. G), Iris Quinn (Kyle's Mother), Lorena Gale (Proctor), Patricia Idlette (Receptionist), Lynda Boyd (Anna's Mother), Michael Ryan (Anna's Father), Robert Clarke (Arnie Branch), Serge Houde (Kurt Dooling), Kyle Labine (Dave), Dee Jay Jackson (ETS Lobby Guard), Alfred E. Humphreys (Tom Helton), Fulvio Cecere (Francesca's Father), Mike Jarvis (Illinois Coach), Steve Makaj (Kyle's Father), Kurt Max Runte (SWAT Captain), Jay Brazeau (Test Instructor), Rebecca Robbins (Tiffany), Jessica May (ETS Woman), Miriam Smith (ETS Reception), Alex Green (Security Guard), Samuel Scantlebury (Keyon), Sonja Bennett (Pregnant Girl), Sarah Afful (Girl), Alex Corr (Preppy Boy), Nikolas Malenovic (Boy), John Shaw (ETS Man), Jaime Yochlowitz (Man in Jail)

Worried that his low SAT scores will not allow him to get into the Ivy League school he desires, high school senior Kyle gathers together some friends to help him break into the building that houses the answers to the exam.

MIRACLE

(WALT DISNEY PICTURES) Producers, Mark Ciardi, Gordon Gray; Executive Producers, Justis Greene, Ross Greenburg; Director, Gavin O'Connor; Screenplay, Eric Guggenheim; Co-Producer, Greg O'Connor; Photography, Daniel Stoloff; Designer, John Willett; Costumes, Tom Bronson; Music, Mark Isham; Music Supervisor, Brian Ross; Editor, John Gilroy; Associate Producer, Jonathan Mone; Casting, Randi Hiller, Sarah Halley Finn; a Mayhem Pictures production; Dolby; Super 35 Widescreen; Color; Rated PG; 135 minutes; Release date: February 6, 2004

Cast

Herb Brooks **Kurt Russell**
Patty Brooks **Patricia Clarkson**
Craig Patrick **Noah Emmerich**
Walter Bush **Sean McCann**
Doc Nagobads **Kenneth Welsh**
Jim Craig **Eddie Cahill**
Mike Eruzione **Patrick O'Brien Demsey**
Jack O'Callahan **Michael Mantenuto**
Rob McCallahan **Nathan West**
Ralph Cox **Kenneth Mitchell**

and Eric Peter-Kaiser (Mark Johnson), Bobby Hanson (Dave Silk), Joseph Cure (Mike Ramsey), Billy Schneider (Buzz Schneider), Nate Miller (John "Bah" Harrington), Chris Koch (Mark Pavelich), Kris Wilson (Phil Verchota), Steve Kovalcik (Dave Christian), Sam Skoryna (Steve Janaszak), Pete Duffy (Bob Suter), Nick Postle (Bill Baker), Casey Burnette (Ken Morrow), Scott Johnson (Steve Christoff), Trevor Alto (Neal Broten), Robbie MacGregor (Eric Strobel), Joe Hemsworth (Mark Wells), Adam Knight (Tim Harrer), Sarah Anne Hepher (Kelly Brooks), Evan Smith (Danny Brooks), Bill Mondy (Lou Nanne), Tom Butler (Bob Allen), Don S. Davis (Bob Fleming), Michael Kopsa (Bruce Norris), Lisa Marie Caruk (Disco Girl), Malcolm Stewart (Donald Craig), Ellie Harvie (Margie), Mark McConchie, Mark Burgess (Olympic Officials), Fred Keating (Party Husband), Andrew Johnston (Peter Grace), Susan Astley (Receptionist), Kurt Evans, Igor Morozov, Peter Kelamis, Daniel Bacon, Julius Chapple, Kwesi Ameyaw (Reporters), Philip Maurice Hayes (TV Reporter), Tatiana Loutchaninova (Doc's Wife), Brent Chapman (Equipment Manager), Peter Shinkoda (Japanese Athlete), Mariko Kage (Japanese Interpreter), L. Harvey Gold (MSG Announcer), Beverley Bereuer (Party Wife), Mike Cleven, Michael Ronnekleiv (Norway Rink Managers), Bill Finck, Sarah Hayward, Wanda Sturtevant, Alvie Leeper (Try-Outs Organizers), Richard Yee (Team Photographer), Garry Monahan (Colorado Coach), Ty Olsson (State Trooper), John Ashbridge (American Announcer), Alexander Kalugin (Russian Announcer), Ted Friend (Thief River Falls Sportscaster), Steve Pascal (The Cop), Terry Lemky (Angry Driver), Rob Morton (Lake Placid Head of Security), Ryan Walter (Referee), David Short (I.O.C. Presenter), Birchana Caldwell (Girl on Ice), Al Michaels, Ken Dryden, Jim McKay (Themselves)

The true story of how Coach Herb Brooks whipped a college hockey team into shape to challenge the Russians at the 1980 Winter Olympics.

Kurt Russell (center)

Nathan West, Patrick O'Brien Demsey

Eddie Cahill PHOTOS COURTESY OF WALT DISNEY PICTURES

Willis (Johnny), T'Shaun Laren, Tai'Isha "Tai" Davis (Nappy Cuts Video Couple), Cory S. Stewart, Olumiji "Miji" Olawumi (Guys), Susan Yoo (Japanese Woman), Joe Yau (Japanese Man), Dick Johnson (News Anchor), Cynthia Maddox (Angry Woman), Deon Cole (Customer Dante), Vanessa Fraction (Monisha), Janina Gavankar (Field Reporter), DeAnna N.J. Brooks (Pauline), Charla Agers (Gina's Customer), Talia Toms (Talia), Corey L. Hemingway, Sr. (Customer Corey), Nicole L. Sullivan (Double Dutch Girl), Mario K.P. Wilson (Calvin Sr.'s Customer)

Worried about the regentrification of their South Chicago neighborhood, Calvin and his barbershop employees take a stand against the money-hungry corporation that threatens their business. Sequel to the 2002 MGM film *Barbershop* with most of the principals repeating their roles.

Cedric the Entertainer, Queen Latifah, Ice Cube in *Barbershop 2* PHOTO COURTESY OF MGM

BARBERSHOP 2: BACK IN BUSINESS

(MGM) Producers, Robert Teitel, George Tillman, Jr., Alex Gartner; Director, Kevin Rodney Sullivan; Screenplay, Don D. Scott; Based on the characters created by Mark Brown; Executive Producers, Mark Brown, Ice Cube, Matt Alvarez; Photography, Tom Priestley; Designer, Robb Wilson King; Costumes, Jennifer Bryan; Editor, Paul Seydor; Music, Richard Gibbs, Wu-Tang Clan, featuring The RZA; Line Producer, Thomas J. Busch; Casting, Mary Vernieu, Felicia Fasano; a State Street Pictures production, a CubeVision production; Dolby; Color; Rated PG-13; 98 minutes; Release date: February 6, 2004

Cast

Calvin **Ice Cube**
Eddie **Cedric the Entertainer**
Jimmy **Sean Patrick Thomas**
Terri **Eve**
Isaac **Troy Garity**
Ricky **Michael Ealy**
Dinka **Leonard Earl Howze**

and Harry Lennix (Quentin Leroux), Robert Wisdom (Alderman Brown), Jazsmin Lewis (Jennifer), Carl Wright (Checkers Fred), DeRay Davis (Hustle Guy), Kenan Thompson (Kenard), Queen Latifah (Gina), Garcelle Beauvais-Milon (Loretta), Sam Sanders (Mr. Johnson), Jackie Taylor (Miss Emma), Julanne Chidi Hill (Shawna), Linara Washington (Keisha), Marcia Wright (Joyce), Javon Johnson (Calvin Palmer, Sr.), Parvesh Cheena (Samir), Tom Wright (Det. Williams), Chris Tinsey (Artis), Brian Weddington (Benny), Jay Deep (Horace), Tamara Anderson (Jiwanda), Leon S. Rogers, Jr. (Kwame), James David Shanks (Lamar), Allen Edge (Lloyd), David Newman (Muhammad), Mark Simmons (Rodney), Norm Van Lier (Sam), Rome Anthony (Tyrone), Maximino Arciniega, Jr., Llou Johnson (Customers), Ray Thompson (Calvin's Customer), Ronnel Taylor ("I" Customer), Pierre S. Reed, Barrie D. Buckern Jr, Devan Jones (Isaac's Customers), Rich Pierrelouis (Ricky's Customer), Marvin Nelson, David Pompeii (Terri's Customers), Ron OJ Parson (Mr. Stewart), Phillip Edward VanLear (Mr. Diggs), Paul Christopher Hobbs (Hank), Chavez Ravine (Tanya), E.J. Murray (Maggie), Bradley Armacost (City Council President), Tiffany L. Addison (Attractive Female), Mike McNamara (Yuppie), Clifton Wiliams, Antonio Polk (Black Panthers), Lauren "Keke" Palmer (Gina's Niece), China L. Colston (Five Kid Woman), Avant (Dexter), Byron Glenn

Buster Keaton, Charles Chaplin in *Limelight*, from *Charlie: The Life and Times of Charlie Chaplin* PHOTOS COURTESY OF WARNER BROS.

CHARLIE: THE LIFE AND TIMES OF CHARLES CHAPLIN

(WARNER BROS.) Producers, Richard Schickel, Douglas Freeman, Bryan McKenzie; Executive Producer in Charge of Production Brian Jamieson; Director/Screenplay, Richard Schickel; Photography, Kris Denton, Thomas Albrecht, Rob Godlie, Simon Fanthorpe, John Halliday, Ross Keith; Music, José Padilla, Charles Chaplin; Editor, Bryan McKenzie; Narrator, Sydney Pollack; a Lorac Productions, MK2 Difussion production; Dolby; Color; Not rated; Black and white/color; Not rated; 132 minutes; Release date: February 13, 2004. Documentary on silent film comedian and pioneering filmmaker Charles Chaplin.

With

Woody Allen, Richard Attenborough, Jeanine Basinger, Claire Bloom, Geraldine Chaplin, Michael Chaplin, Sydney Chaplin, Johnny Depp, Robert Downey Jr., Milos Forman, Bill Irwin, Norman Lloyd, Marcel Marceau, David Raksin, David Robinson, Andrew Sarris, Martin Scorsese, Jeffrey Vance

50 FIRST DATES

(COLUMBIA) Producers, Jack Giarraputo, Steve Golin, Nancy Juvonen; Executive Producers, Daniel Lupi, Michael Ewing, M. Jay Roach; Director, Peter Segal; Screenplay, George Wing; Photography, Jack Green; Designer, Alan Au; Costumes, Ellen Lutter; Editor, Jeff Gourson; Co-Producers, Larry Kennar, Scott Bankston; Music, Teddy Castellucci; Music Supervision, Michael Dilbeck; Casting, Roger Mussenden; a Happy Madison, Anonymous Content and Flower Films production; Dolby; Panavision; Deluxe color; Rated PG-13; 99 minutes; Release date: February 13, 2004

Cast

Henry Roth **Adam Sandler**
Lucy Whitmore **Drew Barrymore**
Ula **Rob Schneider**
Doug Whitmore **Sean Astin**
Alexa **Lusia Strus**
Dr. Keats **Dan Aykroyd**
Sue **Amy Hill**
Ten Second Tom **Allen Covert**
Marlin Whitmore **Blake Clark**
Stacy **Maya Rudolph**
Nick **Nephi Pomaikai Brown**
Old Hawaiian Man **Joe Nakashima**
Security Guards **Peter Dante, Dom Magwili**
Jennifer **Jonathan Loughran**
Young Man **J.D. Donaruma**
Patient **Wayne Federman**
Cooks Helper **Kent Avenido**

and Sharon Omi, Glen Chin, Aukuso Gus Puluti Sr. (Cafe Regulars), Christian Gutierrez, James Lee, Kylie Moore, Keali'i Olmos, Tache Uesugi (Ula's Kids), Lynn Collins (Attractive Woman), Esmond Chung (Sheriff), Kristin Bauer (Firefighter), Ishtar Uhvana (Salon Worker), Brenda Vivian, Chantell D. Christopher, Shenika Williams (Salon Patrons), Nectar Rose (Blonde in Office), Jackie Titone (Dentist), Yan Lin (Coroner), Nicola Hersh (Woman in Car), Viriginia Reece (Red Head), Melissa Lawyner (Tan Friend), Katheryn Winnick (Young Woman), David Suapaia (Stacy's

Drew Barrymore, Adam Sandler PHOTOS COURTESY OF COLUMBIA

Rob Schneider, Adam Sandler

Sean Astin, Dan Aykroyd, Adam Sandler

Drew Barrymore, Adam Sandler

Boyfriend), Peter Chen (Caddy), Julianne Morris (Noreen), Marguerite Cazin (Henry & Lucy's Daughter), Kevin James (Factory Worker), Michael Osborn (Sean Lion Trainer), Denise Bee (Ula's Wife), Albert Chi (Waiter), Brian L. Keaulana (Jet Skier)

Veterinarian Henry Roth falls in love with Lucy Whitmore, a beautiful young woman who suffers from short-term memory loss, which means he must continually woo her again and again.

EUROTRIP

(DREAMWORKS) Producers, Daniel Goldberg, Jackie Marcus, Alec Berg, David Mandel; Executive Producers, Ivan Reitman, Tom Pollock, Joe Medjuck; Co-Producer, Tom Karnowski; Director, Jeff Schaffer; Screenplay, Alec Berg, David Mandel, Jeff Schaffer; Photography, David Egby; Designer, Allan Starski; Costumes, Vanessa Vogel; Editor, Roger Bondelli; Music, James L. Venable; Music Supervisor, Patrick Houlihan; Visual Effects Supervisor, Kevin Blank; Casting, Meg Liberman, Cami Patton, Nelia Morago; a Montecito Picture Co. production; Dolby; Technicolor; Rated R; 89 minutes; Release date: February 20, 2004

Travis Wester, Scott Mechlowicz. Jacob Pitts

Michelle Trachtenberg

Vinnie Jones, Jacob Pitts, Scott Mechlowicz PHOTO COURTESY OF DREAMWORKS

Cast

Scott Thomas **Scott Mechlowicz**
Cooper Harris **Jacob Pitts**
Jenny **Michelle Trachtenberg**
Jamie **Travis Wester**
Mieke **Jessica Boehrs**
Madame Vandersexxx **Lucy Lawless**
Mad Maynard **Vinnie Jones**
Creepy Italian Guy **Fred Armisen**
Fiona **Kristin Kreuk**
Mrs. Thomas **Cathy Meils**
Bert **Nial Iskhakov**

and Matt Damon (Donny), Molly Schade (Candy), Jakki Degg (Missy), Lenka Vomocilova (Sissy), Andrea Stuart (Courier Clerk), Petr Jakl (Gunter), Jakub Kohak (French Soccer Fan), J.P. Manoux (Robot Man), Patrick Rapold (Christoph), Jana Pallaske (Anna, The Camera Store Girl), Rade Sherbedgia (Tibor), Steve Hytner (Green Fairy), Jeffrey Tambor (Scott's Dad), J. Adams, Christoph Baird, Nicholas J.M. Cloutman, Bruce Fulford (Lustra, Donny's Band), Paul Oldham, Mike McGuffie, John Comer, Jeff Smith, Mike Cella, David Fisher, Christian Dunckley Clark (Hooligans), Eric Moscoso Veritz (Naked Spanish Guy), Labass Kanoute (Naked African Guy), Sota Sakuma (Naked Tiny Asian Guy), Edita Deveroux, Petra Tomankova (Nude Beach Ladies), Barbora Navratilova, Lucie Kachtikova, Tereza Zimova, Zuzana Kocova (Vandersexxx Girls), Go GO Dyei Jen-Michel (Rasta Waiter), Helder Cambolo (Rasta Chef), Vilem Holy (Hans), Jiri Maria Sieber (Gruber), Diedrich Bader (Mugger), Roger Denesha (Bakery Man), Amy Huck (Bakery Woman), Dominic Raacke (Trucker), Jan Nemejovsky (Manager at Opulent Hotel), Miroslav Táborsky (Waiter at Opulent Hotel), Tereza Brettschneiderova (Girl in Orange Juice), Kristyna Simova (Girl in Orange Juice Ad), Vitezslav Bouchner (Orange Juice Ad Voice Over), Walter Sittler (Mieke's Father), Adam Dotlacil (Heinrich), Joel Kirby (Swiss Guard), Andrea Miltnerova (Vatican Tour Guide), Patrick Malahide (Arthur Frommer), Ellen Savaria (Tourist Woman in Vatican), Pedja Bjelac (Italian Guy at Vatican), Nick Jameson (Reporter), Jack Marston (Pope), Pat Kilbrane (American Robot Guy), Joanna Lumley (Hostel Clerk)

Scott Thomas convinces his friends to join him on a trip to Europe, where he hopes to make ammends with the Internet contact he had severed ties with.

Petr Jakl, Jessica Boehrs

WELCOME TO MOOSEPORT

(20TH CENTURY FOX) Producers, Tom Schulman, Basil Iwanyk; Executive Producers, Rory Rosegarten, David Coatsworth, Moritz Borman, Doug Richardson; Director, Donald Petrie; Screenplay, Tom Schulman; Story, Doug Richardson; Photography, Victor Hammer; Designer, David Chapman; Costumes, Vicki Graef; Music, John Debney; Editor, Debra Neil-Fisher; Casting, Sheila Jaffe, Georgianne Walken; an Intermedia production, presented in association with Mediastream IV; Dolby; Deluxe color; Rated PG-13; 110 minutes; Release date: February 20, 2004

Maura Tierney, Ray Romano

Cast

Monroe Cole **Gene Hackman**
Handy Harrison **Ray Romano**
Grace Sutherland **Marcia Gay Harden**
Sally Mannis **Maura Tierney**
Charlotte Cole **Christine Baranski**
Bullard **Fred Savage**
Bert Langdon **Rip Torn**
Irma **June Squibb**
Morris Gutman **Wayne Robson**

and John Rothman (Stu), Karl Pruner (Dyer), David MacNiven (Cloud), Jackie Richardson (Martha), Paul Bates (Bob), Reagan Pasternak (Mandy), Philip Williams (Kent), Jim Feather (Reuben), Ed Fielding (Harve), Denis Akyama (Izuki Nami), Jessica Holmes (Dina), Natalie Bowen (Laurie Smith), Paul McGuire (Local Reporter Chip), Heather Allin (Local Reporter Heather), JC Kenny (Local Reporter JC), Diana Platts (Fox Newscaster Jane), Peter Snider (Fox Newscaster Bill), Dan Duran (Local News Anchor Faryl), Lee Taylor (Local News Anchor Leah), Pat Moffatt (Council Woman), James Barrett (Jim), Colleen Reynolds (Rebecca), Bill Lynn (Clay), Colleen Williams (Francis), Jayne Eastwood (Lucy Decker), Diane Gordon (Elderly Woman on Street), Angelo Tsarouchas (Grizzled Tatooed Driver), Chi Chi Rodriguez (Himself), Carly Street (Pig and Whistle Waitress), Richard A. Romano (Handy's Bar Buddy), Catherine Burdon (Flight Representative), Enis Esmer, Deborah Grover (Airport Passengers), Adam Bramble (Smitty the Cook), Mike Kinney (Secret Service Agent),

Gene Hackman (right)

Jon Manfrellotti (Reporter), Mark Kersey (One Man Band), Sam Moses (Hardware Store Customer), Krista Sutton (Live Newscaster), Dawn Greenhalgh (Coffee Shop Waitress), Jeff Gruich, Andrew Moodie, Doug Murray (Bar Patrons), Denise Desrochers, Jackie Laidlaw (Townspersons), Tim Eddis (Stage Manager), Leslie M. Richardson (Assistant to Grace), Danny Mijovich, Bernard Keir Smith, Louis Strezos (Golfers), Andy Hirsch (Radio DJ "Danny"), Arlin Miller (Radio DJ "Jim")

Jealous that the retired U.S. President has not only decided to run for mayor of Mooseport but has taken an interest in his girlfriend, hardware store proprietor Handy Harrison decides to run against the former Chief Executive.

Christine Baranski, Gene Hackman

Rip Torn, Marcia Gay Harden, Fred Savage PHOTOS COURTESY OF 20TH CENTURY FOX

Alison Pill, Lindsay Lohan

Ashley Leggat, Megan Fox, Barbara Mamabolo

Eli Marienthal, Lindsay Lohan PHOTOS COURTESY OF WALT DISNEY PICTURES

CONFESSIONS OF A TEENAGE DRAMA QUEEN

(WALT DISNEY PICTURES) Producers, Robert Shapiro, Jerry Leider; Director, Sara Sugarman; Screenplay, Gail Parent; Based on the book by Dyan Sheldon; Photography, Stephen H. Burum; Designer, Leslie McDonald; Costumes, David C. Robinson; Editor, Anita Brandt Burgoyne; Music, Mark Mothersbaugh; Music Supervisor, Dawn Solér; Choreographer, Marguerite Derricks; Line Producer, Mathew Hart; Casting, Marcia Ross, Donna Morong; Dolby; Technicolor; Rated PG; 89 minutes; Release date: February 20, 2004

Lindsay Lohan, Adam Garcia

Cast
Lola Cep **Lindsay Lohan**
Stu Wolff **Adam Garcia**
Karen Cep **Glenne Headley**
Ella Gerrard **Alison Pill**
Sam **Eli Marienthal**
Miss Baggoli **Carol Kane**
Carla Santini **Megan Fox**
Mrs. Gerard **Sheila McCarthy**
Calum **Tom McCamus**
Mr. Gerard **Richard Fitzpatrick**
Sgt. Rose **Alison Sealy-Smith**
Marcia **Ashley Leggat**

and Barbara Mamabolo (Robin), Maggie Oskam (Paige), Rachael Oskam (Paula), Adam MacDonald (Steve), Gerry Quigley (Slimy Guy), Kyle Massardjian (Andy), Connor Lynch (Colonel Pickering), Pedro Miguel Arce (Ticket Taker), Kevin Brown (Doorman), Bruce McFee (Lentigo), Diane Douglass (Waitress), Courtney Alan Taylor (Man at Party), Zoe (Negus the Dog), Tracey Armstrong, Amanda Balen, Julia Carnevale, Lisa Jennings, Jerilyn Low, Christine Micelli, Kelly Phillippe, Rochelle Labrecque, Matt Carroll, Greg Farkas, Graeme Goodhall, Christopher Robinson, Jesse Weafer, Carlos Bustamante, Joshua Feldman, Michael Peter Piccio (Chorus Dancers), Melissa Bathory, Megan Barker, Janee Reid, Lauren Boutette, Sheldon Smith, Stephen Davis (Chorus)

Teenager Lola Cep worries that the life she loves has been destroyed when her family moves from New York City to suburban New Jersey.

THE PASSION OF THE CHRIST

(NEWMARKET) Producers, Mel Gibson, Bruce Davey, Stephen McEveety; Executive Producer, Enzo Sisti; Director, Mel Gibson; Screenplay, Benedict Fitzgerald, Mel Gibson; Photography, Caleb Deschanel; Designer, Francesco Frigeri; Costumes, Maurizio Millenotti; Music, John Debney; Editor, John Wright; Special Makeup and Visual Effects Designer and Producer, Keith Vanderlaan; Casting, Shaila Rubin; an Icon Prods. presentation in association with Newmarket Films of an Icon production; Dolby; Deluxe color; Rated R; 126 minutes; Release date: February 25, 2004

Cast

Jesus **James Caviezel**
Mary Magdalene **Monica Bellucci**
Claudia Procles **Claudia Gerini**
Mary **Maia Morgenstern**
Dismas **Sergio Rubini**
Annas **Toni Bertorelli**
Malchus **Roberto Bestazzoni**
Gesmas **Francesco Cabras**
Cassius **Giovanni Capalbo**
Satan **Rosalinda Celentano**
Peter **Francesco De Vito**
John **Hristo Jivkov**
Judas **Luca Lionello**
Simon of Cyrene **Jarreth Merz**
Janus **Matt Patresi**
Abenader **Fabio Sartor**
Caiphas **Mattia Sbragia**
Pontius Pilate **Hristo Naumov Shopov**
Joseph of Arimathea **Giancinto Ferro**
Nicodemus **Olek Mincer**
Thomas **Adel Ben Ayed**
James **Chokri Ben Zagden**
Herod **Luca De Dominicis**
Barabbas **Pedro Sarubbi**

and Sheila Mokhtari (Woman in Audience), Lucio Allocca (Old Temple

James Caviezel

Guard), Paco Reconti (Whipping Guard), Adel Bakri (Temple Guard), Luciano Dragone (Second Man), Franco Costanzo, Lino Salemme, Emanuele Gullotto, Francsco De Rosa (Accusers), Maurizio Di Carmine, Francesco Gabriele, Angelo Di Loreta, Federico Pacifici, Robert Santi, Giovanni Vettorazzo, Ted Rusoff (Elders), Tom Shaker (Eyepatch), Andrea Coppola (Grizzled Beard), Emilio De Marchi, Roberto Visconti (Scournful Romans), Lello Giulivo (Brutish Roman), Romuald Klos, Giuseppe Lo Console, Dario D'Ambrosi (Roman Soldiers), Luciano Federico (Man in Audience), Omar Capalbo, Valerio Esposito, Antonello Iacovone, Nicola Tagarelli, Ivan Gaudiano (Boys), Abel Jafry (2nd Temple Officer), Andrea Ivan Refuto (Young Jesus), Sabrina Impacciatore (Seraphia), Daniela Poti (Young Girl), Noemi Marotta, Rossella Longo (Women), Davide Marotta (Baby), Danilo Di Ruzza (Pilate's Servant), Vincenzo Monti, Danilo Maria Valli, Nuot Arquint, Abraam Fontana, Valerio Isidori (Hero'd Courter), Paolo Dos Santos (Herod's Boy), Arianna Vitolo, Gabriella Barbuti, Ornella Giusto, Michelle Bonev, Lucia Stara, Evelina Meghangi (Herod's Court Women), Francis Dokyi Baffour (Herod's Servant)

Monica Bellucci, Maia Morgenstern, Hristo Jivkov

A look at the brutality suffered by Jesus in the final hours of his life, leading up to his crucifixion. Previous films about Jesus include *The King of Kings* (MGM, 1927), with H.B. Warner; *King of Kings* (MGM, 1961), with Jeffrey Hunter; *The Greatest Story Ever Told* (UA, 1965), with Max von Sydow; *The Gospel According to St. Matthew* (Continental, 1966), with Enrique Irazoqui; *Jesus Christ Superstar* (Univ., 1973), with Ted Nealy, and *The Last Temptation of Christ* (Univ., 1988), with Willem Dafoe.

This film received Oscar nominations for cinematography, makeup, and music score.

(third) James Caviezel, (fourth) Hristo Jivkov PHOTOS COURTESY OF NEWMARKET

TWISTED

(PARAMOUNT) Producers, Arnold Kopelson, Anne Kopelson, Barry Baeres, Linne Radmin; Executive Producers, Stephen Brown, Robyn Meisinger, Michael Flynn; Director, Philip Kaufman; Screenplay, Sarah Thorp; Photography, Peter Deming; Designer, Dennis Washington; Costumes, Ellen Mirojnick; Music, Mark Isham; Editor, Peter Boyle; Co-Producers, Peter Kaufman, Sherryl Clark; a Kopelson Entertainment production, presented in association with Interntainment; Dolby; Color; Rated R; 97 minutes; Release date: February 27, 2004

Cast

Jessica Shepard **Ashley Judd**
John Mills **Samuel L. Jackson**
Mike Delmarco **Andy Garcia**
Dr. Melvin Frank **David Strathairn**
Lieutenant Tong **Russell Wong**
Lisa **Camryn Manheim**
Jimmy Schmidt **Mark Pellegrino**
Dale Becker **Titus Welliver**
Ray Porter **D.W. Moffett**
Wilson Jefferson **Richard T. Jones**
Edmund Cutler **Leland Orser**
John Flanagan **James Oliver Bullock**
Chip Marshall **William Hall**

and Joe Duer (Larry Geber), James Hechim (Bob Sherman), Drew Letchworth (Bartender), Diane Amos (Jones), Anni Long, David Tenenbaum (Cops), Leonard Thomas (Mills' Aide), Joe Drago (Man at Bar), Bruce F. Marovich (Lt. Marovich), Danny Lopez (Sgt. Lopez), Lyn Tomioka (Yawara Instructor), Leslie Kaye, Angela Tse (Forensic Lab Technicians), Ofri Fuchs (Girl at Saloon), Angelo Miller (Saloon Bouncer), Peter Ridet (Cop Bar Bartender), Garrett Townsend (Man at Saloon), Victor Vallejo (Inspector Vallejo), Carola Zertuche (Flamenco Dancer), Veronica Cartwright (Landlady)

Police woman Jessica Shepard is put in charge of tracking down a killer, despite the fact that one of the victims had ended up dead after spending a drunken night with her.

Ashley Judd, Leland Orser

Andy Garcia, Ashley Judd

Samuel L. Jackson PHOTOS COURTESY OF PARAMOUNT

Mark Pellegrino, Ashley Judd, Samuel L. Jackson

Adam Alexi-Malle, Peter Mensah, Viggo Mortensen

Viggo Mortensen

Silas Carson, Louise Lombard PHOTOS COURTESY OF TOUCHSTONE

HIDALGO

(TOUCHSTONE) Producer, Casey Silver; Executive Producer, Don Zepfel; Director, Joe Johnston; Screenplay, John Fusco; Photography, Shelly Johnson; Designer, Barry Robison; Costumes, Jeffrey Kurland; Music, James Newton Howard; Editor, Robert Dalva; Visual Effects Supervisor, Tim Alexander; Casting, Nancy Foy; Distributed by Buena Vista; Dolby; Panavision; Technicolor; Rated PG-13; 135 minutes; Release date: March 5, 2004

Omar Sharif, Viggo Mortensen

Cast

Frank Hopkins **Viggo Mortensen**
Jazira **Zuleikha Robinson**
Sheikh Riyadh **Omar Sharif**
Lady Anne Davenport **Louise Lombard**
Aziz **Adam Alexi-Malle**
Prince Bin Al Reeh **Said Taghmaoui**
Katib **Silas Carson**
Yusef **Harsh Nayyar**
Buffalo Bill Cody **J.K. Simmons**

and Adoni Maropis (Sakr), Victor Talmadge (Rau Rasmussen), Peter Mensah (Jaffa), Joshua Wolf Coleman (The Kurd), Franky Mwangi (Slave Boy), Floyd Red Crow Westerman (Chief Eagle Horn), Elizabeth Berridge (Annie Oakley), C. Thomas Howell (Preston Webb), Lt. Steven Rimkus (Military Cistern), Jerry Hardin (Nate Salisbury), Frank Collison (Texas Jack), Chris Owen (First Soldier), Marshall Manesh (Camel Skinner), Philip Sounding Sides (Chief Big Foot), George Gerdes (Maj. Whitside), Todd Kimsey (Corpoal at Wounded Knee), Ed Nah New Rider Weber (Old Lakota Woman), Adam Ozturk (Bedouin Rider), John Prosky (Officer at Horse Corral), Michael Canavan (Cattleman), David Midthunder (Black Coyote), Lee Trotter (Soldier at Wounded Knee), Dave Florek (Sentry at Wounded Knee), Jeff Kober (Sergeant at Wounded Knee), Sam Sako (Call to Prayer Singer), Te'Amir Sweeney (Tower Boy), Jake Miller (Ghost Dance Singer), Mary Ellis (Mary), Clement Richareds (Lakota Wagon Driver), Kimberly Norris Guerrero (Frank's Mother), Zachary Badasci (Young Frank Hopkins), Malcolm McDowell (Maj. Davenport)

Former cowboy Frank Hopkins becomes the first American invited to participate in the Ocean of Fire, a gruelling 3,000 mile horse race across the Arabian Desert.

STARSKY & HUTCH

(WARNER BROS.) Producers, William Blinn, Stuart Cornfeld, Akiva Goldsman, Tony Ludwig, Alan Riche; Executive Producer, Gilbert Adler; Director, Todd Phillips; Screenplay, John O'Brien, Todd Phillips, Scot Armstrong; Story, Stevie Long, John O'Brien, based on characters created by William Blinn; Photography, Barry Peterson; Designer, Edward Verreaux; Costumes, Louise Mingenbach; Music, Theodore Shapiro; Music Supervisors, Randall Poster, George Drakoulias; Associate Producers, Scott Budnick, David A. Siegel; Stunts, Dennis R. Scott; Casting, Juel Bestrop, Jeanne McCarthy; Dolby; Panavision; Technicolor; Rated PG-13; 101 minutes; Release date: March 5, 2004

Cast

David Starsky **Ben Stiller**
Ken Hutchinson **Owen Wilson**
Huggy Bear **Snoop Dogg**
Captain Doby **Fred Williamson**
Reese Feldman **Vince Vaughn**
Kitty **Juliette Lewis**
Kevin **Jason Bateman**
Holly **Amy Smart**
Staci **Carmen Electra**
Chau **George Kee Cheung**
Manetti **Chris Penn**
Heather **Brande Roderick**
Mrs. Feldman **Molly Sims**
Eddie **Matt Walsh**

and G.T. Holme (Bartender), Jeffrey Lorenzo (Willis), Har Mar Superstar (Dancin' Rick), Patton Oswalt (Disco DJ), Brigette Romanek (Banquet Singer), Paul Michael Glaser (Original Starsky), David Soul (Original Hutch), Dan Finnerty (Bat Mitzvah Singer), Jernard Burks (Leon), Omar Dorsey (Lamell), Pramod Kumar (Indian Shopkeeper), Rod Tate (Bee Bee), Richard Edson (Monix), Raymond Ma (Marks), Terry Crews (Porter), Richie Nathanson (Drug Dealer), David Pressman (Terrence Meyers), Scott L. Schwartz (Fat Ron), Judah Friedlander (Ice Cream Man), Akerin Suksawat Premwattana (Toby), Amber Meade (Banquet Waitress), Archbishop Don "Magic" Juan (Himself), Darlena Tejeiro (Lorraine), Harry O'Reilly (Cop in Shower), Tangie Ambrose (Kiki), Sara Swain (Elizabeth), Delores Gilbeaux

Ben Stiller, David Soul, Paul Michael Glaser, Owen Wilson

Jason Bateman, Vince Vaughn

Snoop Dogg, Ben Stiller, Owen Wilson

(Sexy Bartender), Kimberly Brickland (Diner Waitress), Minnie Lagrimas, Rachel Harris (Mrs. Feldman's Friends), David Burton (Rooftop Bad Guy), Ton Suckhasem, Henry T. Yamada (Bookies), Charles Edward Townsend (Smokey), Will Ferrell (Big Earl)

A pair of cops, by-the-book David Starsky and ne'er-do-well Ken Hutchinson, are teamed to track down drug dealer Reese Feldman. Based on the ABC-TV series (1975–79), with the stars of the show, Paul Michael Glaser and David Soul, making cameo appearances.

Carmen Electra, Amy Smart PHOTOS COURTESY OF WARNER BROS.

John Turturro, Johnny Depp

Johnny Depp

SECRET WINDOW

(COLUMBIA) Producer, Gavin Polone; Executive Producer, Ezra Swerdlow; Director/Screenplay, David Koepp; Based upon the story "Secret Window, Secret Garden" by Stephen King; Photography, Fred Murphy; Designer, Howard Cummings; Costumes, Odette Gadoury; Music, Philip Glass; Editor, Jill Savitt; Visual Effects Supervisor, Gray Marshall; Casting, John Papsidera, Pat McCorkle; a Pariah production; Dolby; Super 35 Widescreen; Deluxe color; Rated PG-13; 96 minutes; Release date: March 12, 2004

Cast

Mort Rainey **Johnny Depp**
John Shooter **John Turturro**
Amy Rainey **Maria Bello**
Ted Milner **Timothy Hutton**
Ken Karsch **Charles S. Dutton**
Sheriff Dave Newsome **Len Cariou**
Mrs. Garvey **Joan Heney**
Tom Greenleaf **John Dunn Hill**
Fire Chief Wickersham **Vlasta Vrana**
Detective Bradley **Matt Holland**
Fran Evans **Gillian Ferrabee**
Greta Bowie **Bronwen Mantel**
Juliet **Elizabeth Marleau**
Busboy **Kyle Allatt**
Motel Manager **Richard Jutras**
Public Works Guys **Kevin Woodhouse, Vito De Filippo**
Sheriff's Niece **Sarah Allen**
Himself **Chico**

Mort Rainey, a successful author facing a messy divorce and having trouble writing his newest novel, is contronted by a stranger named John Shooter, who accuses him of having plagiarized his story.

Charles S. Dutton, Johnny Depp PHOTOS COURTESY OF COLUMBIA

Johnny Depp, Timothy Hutton, Maria Bello

SPARTAN

(WARNER BROS.) Producers, Art Linson, Moshe Diamant, Elie Samaha, David Bergstein; Executive Producers, Frank Huebner, Tracee Stanley, James Holt; Director/Screenplay, David Mamet; Photography, Juan Ruiz Anchia; Designer, Gemma Jackson; Costumes, Shay Cunliffe; Music, Mark Isham; Editor, Barbara Tulliver; Co-Producers, Jan Fanti, Joseph Mehri; a Franchise Pictures presentation of an Apollo Media/Apollo Promedia/Quality Intl.co-produciton in association with Signature Pictures; Dolby; Panavision; Deluxe color; Rated R; 107 minutes; Release date: March 12, 2004

Val Kilmer, Derek Luke

Cast
Scott **Val Kilmer**
Curtis **Derek Luke**
Stoddard **William H. Macy**

and Ed O'Neill (Burch), Kristen Bell (Laura Newton), Said Taghmaoui (Tariq Asani), Linda Kimbrough (Donny), Tia Texada (Jackie Black), Jeremie Campbell (Cadre Candidate), Bob Jennings (Grace's Aide), Lionel Mark Smith (Col. Blane), Johnny Messner (Grace), Chris J. Lacentra (Cpl. Sattler), Renato Magno (Grossler), Mark FitzGerald (Training Facility Guard), Tony Mamet (Parker), Clark Gregg (Miller), Ron Butler (Headquarters Agent), Stephen Culp (Gaines), Vincent Guastaferro (Naylor), Robert Bella (Davio), Lana Bilzerian (Undercover Agent), Aaron Stanford (Michael Blake), Ann Morgan (Secret Service Agent), Geoff Pierson (Pearce), Sophia Luke (Agent), Alexandra Kerry (Bartender), Andy Davoli (Zimmer), J.J. Johnston (Night Club Manager), Natalija Nogulich (Nadya), Margot Farley (Young Whore), Ricky Levy (Sedan Man), Jim Frangione (Stakeout Agent), Dan Hovanesian (Stakeout Driver), Norm Compton, Chino Binamo (Essex House Men), Mark Pellegrino (Convict), Mordechai Finley (Cadre Operator), Jonathan Rossetti (Medic), Gail Silver (Pharmacist), Scott Barry (Cadre Team Leader), Robert Castro (State Police Liaison Officer), Deb Martin (Debriefer), Dick Friedman (Crew Chief), David Aranovich (Cadre Technician), Jody Snider (Harvard Square Reporter), Virginia Pereira (TV Anchor Woman), Morris Lamore (Billy), Clara Mamet (Billy's Daughter), Matt Malloy (Mr. Reese), Deborah Bartlett (Mrs. Newton), Linda Kimbrough (Donny), Moshe Ivgy (Avi), Christopher Kaldor (Yitzik), Ektimal Shbib (Stewardess), Al Faris (Customs

Ed O'Neill, William H. Macy

Official), Zosia Mamet (Bedouin Woman), Kick Gurry (Jones), Damon Caro (Balcony Shooter), Ken Moreno, JJ Perry (Bodyguards), Michael Hilow (Perimeter Guard), Steve Martinez, Max Daniels (Gate Keepers), Sandra Lindquist (Swedish Reporter), Neil Pepe (News Cameraman), Tim Fleming (Night Sun Operator), Marc-Allen Barker (Pilot), Chelle Cerceo (Marine Flight Crew Chief), Jennifer Ritchkoff (Martin Captain), Stephen Greif (Business Man), Michael Kuroiwa (Swat Team Member), Lauren Bowles (Entertainment Reprter), David Paymer (TV News Anchor), Christopher Tandon (Prof. Gerald Sloan)

A pair of military operations specialitists are recruited to help rescue the President of the United States' kidnapped daughter, who has ended up in the hands of slave traders in Dubai.

Kristen Bell, Val Kilmer PHOTOS COURTESY OF WARNER BROS.

Kirsten Dunst, Tom Wilkinson

Jim Carrey, Kate Winslet

Jim Carrey, Kate Winslet

ETERNAL SUNSHINE OF THE SPOTLESS MIND

(DREAMWORKS) Producers, Steve Golin, Anthony Bregman; Executive Producers, David Bushell, Charlie Kaufman, Glenn Williamson, George S. Bermann; Director, Michel Gondry; Screenplay, Charlie Kaufman; Story, Charlie Kaufman, Michel Gondry, Pierre Bismuth; Photography, Ellen Kuras; Designer, Dan Leigh; Costumes, Melissa Toth; Music, Jon Brion; Editor, Valdis Oskarsdottir; Casting, Jeanne McCarthy; Dolby; Color; Rated R; 108 minutes; Release date: March 19, 2004

Kate Winslet, Jim Carrey

Cast

Joel Barish **Jim Carrey**
Clementine Kruczynski **Kate Winslet**
Mary **Kirsten Dunst**
Stan **Mark Ruffalo**
Patrick **Elijah Wood**
Dr. Howard Mierzwiak **Tom Wilkinson**
Train Conductor **Gerry Robert Byrne**
Frank **Thomas Jay Ryan**
Carrie **Jane Adams**
Rob **David Cross**
Young Joel **Ryan Whitney**
Joel's Mother **Debbon Ayer**
Young Bullies **Amir Ali Said, Brian Price, Paul Litowsky, Josh Flitter**
Young Clementine **Lola Daehler**
Hollis **Deirdre O'Connell**

Jim Carrey

Finding out that the girl he loves has subjected herself to an experiment that allows her to erase him from her mind, Joel Barish agrees to undergo the treatment himself.

Academy Award Winner for Best Original Screenplay. This film received an additional nomination for actress (Winslet).

Jim Carrey, Kate Winslet

Kirsten Dunst, Mark Ruffalo, Tom Wilkinson

Elijah Wood

Mark Ruffalo

Kate Winslet, Jim Carrey   PHOTOS COURTESY OF DREAMWORKS

DAWN OF THE DEAD

(UNIVERSAL) Producers, Richard P. Rubinstein, Marc Abraham, Eric Newman; Executive Producers, Thomas A. Bliss, Dennis E. Jones, Armyan Bernstein; Director, Zack Snyder; Screenplay, James Gunn; Based on a screenplay by George A. Romero; Photography, Matthew F. Leonetti; Designer, Andrew Neskoromny; Costumes, Denise Cronenberg; Editor, Niven Howie; Music Supervisor, G. Marq Roswell; Co-Producer, Michael Messina; Special Makeup Effects, David Leroy Anderson; Casting, Joseph Middleton; Stunts, John Stoneham, Jr.; Zombie Fight Choreographer, Damon Caro; a Strike Entertainment/New Amsterdam Entertainment production; Dolby; Deluxe color; Rated R; 100 minutes; Release date: March 19, 2004

Jake Webber, Sarah Polley, Ving Rhames, Mekhi Phifer, Inna Korobkina

Cast

Ana	**Sarah Polley**
Kenneth	**Ving Rhames**
Michael	**Jake Weber**
Andre	**Mekhi Phifer**
Steve	**Ty Burrell**
CJ	**Michael Kelly**
Terry	**Kevin Zegers**
Bart	**Michael Barry**

and Lindy Booth (Nicole), Jayne Eastwood (Norma), Boyd Banks (Tucker), Inna Korbkina (Luda), R.D. Reid (Glen), Kim Poirier (Monica), Matt Frewer (Frank), Justin Louis (Luis), Hannah Lochner (Vivian), Bruce Bohne (Andy), Ermes Blarasin (Bloated Woman), Sanjay Talwar (Dr. Rosen), Kim Roberts (Cora), Tim Post (Reviving Doctor), Matt Austin, Philip DeWilde (EMS Technicians), Colm Magner (Armed Neighbor), Luigia Zucaro (Naked Woman), Geoff Williams (Metro Bus Driver), Mike Realba (Maintenance Man), David Campbell (Squished Zombie), Philip MacKenzie (Thrashing Zombie), Laura DeCarteret (Washington Politician), Georgia Craig (Anchorwoman), Tino Monte (Istanbul Reporter), Chris Gillett (Older Anchorman), Derek Keurvorst (Scienist), Dan Duran (Confused Reporter), Neville Edwards (CDC Spokesman), Sandy Jobin-Bevans, Natalie Brown, Liz West (CDC Reporters), Blu (Chips the Dog), Scott Reiniger (General), Tom Savini (Sheriff), Ken Foree (Televangelist)

Mekhi Phifer

A group of people barricade themselves inside of a suburban shopping mall in order to escape the onslaught of raging, flesh-eating zombies. Remake of the 1979 film, with appearances here from three participants from that film: Scott Reiniger, Tom Savini, Ken Foree.

Zombies

Sarah Polley, Ving Rhames PHOTOS COURTESY OF UNIVERSAL

TAKING LIVES

(WARNER BROS.) Producers, Mark Canton, Bernie Goldmann; Executive Producers, Bruce Berman, Dana Goldberg, David Heyman; Co-Producers, Alan C. Blomquist, Anna DeRoy; Director, DJ Caruso; Screenplay/Screen Story, Jon Bokenkamp; Based on the novel by Michael Pye; Photography, Amir Mokri; Designer, Tom Southwell; Costumes, Marie-Sylvie Denveau; Music, Philip Glass; Editor, Anne V. Coates; Associate Producer, Josette Perrotta; Stunts, Guy Bews; Casting, Deborah Aquila, Tricia Wood; a Mark Canton production, presented in association with Village Roadshow Pictures; Dolby; Panavision; Technicolor; Rated R; 103 minutes; Release date: March 19, 2004

Ethan Hawke, Angelina Jolie

Tcheky Karyo, Angelina Jolie

Cast

Illeana Scott **Angelina Jolie**
James Costa **Ethan Hawke**
Hart **Kiefer Sutherland**
Joseph Paquette **Olivier Martinez**
Hugo Leclair **Tcheky Karyo**
Emil Duval **Jean-Hugues Anglade**
Mrs. Asher **Gena Rowlands**
Young Asher **Paul Dano**
Matt Soulsby **Justin Chatwin**
Cashier **André Lacoste**

Angelina Jolie

Special FBI agent Illeana Scott is called on by the Quebec police to help investigate a series of murders in which the killer seems to take on the identity of each man he kills.

and Billy Two Rivers (Car Salesman), Richard Lemire (Quebec City Cop), Julien Poulin (Quebec City Inspector), Marie-Josée Croze (Medical Examiner), Christian Tessier (Interrogation Officer), Brigitte Bedard (French Reporter), Dominique Briand (Bartender), Alex Sol (Hotel Manager), Shawn Roberts (Desk Clerk), Martin Brisebois (Henri Bisonette), Gabriel Charland-Gagné, Nathalie Matteau, Hugh Probyn (Victims), Henri Pardo (Officer Mann), Fabiano Amato (Waiter), Judith Baribeau (Mr. Costa's Assistant), Anne Marineau (Woman in Gallery), Eugenio "Kiko" Osorio, Jesus Alejandro Nino, Lisandro Martinez, Sandra Campanelli (Sandra & the Latin Groove), Emmanuel Bilodeau (Doctor), Vince Grant (Illeana's Hotel Manager), Freddy Bessa (Det. Roch), Andy Bradshaw (Officer Darabont), Steven Wallace Lowe (Man at Moncton Street), Marcel Jeannin (Train Man), Brett Watson (Clive Morin), David Eisner (Committee Head), Lois Dellar (Postal Clerk)

Ethan Hawke, Kiefer Sutherland PHOTOS COURTESY OF WARNER BROS.

THE LADYKILLERS

(TOUCHSTONE) Producers, Ethan Coen, Joel Coen, Tom Jacobson, Barry Sonnenfeld, Barry Josephson; Directors/Screenplay, Joel Coen, Ethan Coen; Based upon the motion picture *The Ladykillers* written by William Rose; Photography, Roger Deakins; Designer, Dennis Gassner; Costumes, Mary Zophres; Editor, Roderick Jaynes; Music, Carter Burwell; Executive Music Producer, T Bone Burnett; Co-Producer, John Cameron; Associate Producers, Robert Graf, David Diliberto; Visual Effects Supervisor, Janek Sirrs; Casting, Ellen Chenoweth; Dolby; Color; Rated R; 104 minutes; Release date: March 26, 2004

Cast

Professor Goldthwait Higginson Dorr **Tom Hanks**
Marva Munson **Irma P. Hall**
Gawain MacSam **Marlon Wayans**
Garth Pancake **J.K. Simmons**
The General **Tzi Ma**
Lump **Ryan Hurst**
Mountain Girl **Diane Delano**
Sheriff Wyner **George Wallace**
Deputy Sheriff **John McConnell**
Weemack Funthes **Jason Weaver**
Fernand Gudge **Stephen Root**
Rosalie Funthes **Baadja-Lyne Odums**
Elron **Walter Jordan**
Preacher **George Anthony Bell**

and Greg Grunberg (TV Commercial Director), Hallie Singleton (Craft Service), Robert Baker (Quarterback), Blake Clark (Football Coach), Amada Jackson, Aldis Hodge (Doughnut Gangsters), Freda Foh Shen (Doughnut Woman), Paula Martin (Gawain's Mama), Jeremy Suarez (Li'l Gawain), Te Te Benn (Gawain's Sister), Khalil East (Gawain's Brother), Jennifer Echols (Waffle Hut Waitress), Nita Norris, Vivian Smallwood, Maryn Tasco, Muriel Whitaker, Jessie Bailey (Tea Ladies), Louisa Abernathy, Mildred Dumas, Al Fann, Mi Mi Green-Fann (Church Voices)

Ryan Hurst, Tom Hanks, J.K. Simmons, Tzi Ma

Irma P. Hall, Marlon Wayans

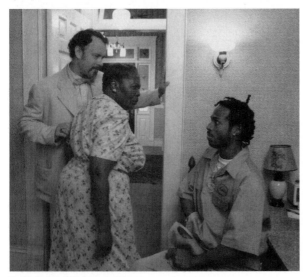

Tom Hanks, Irma P. Hall, Marlon Wayans PHOTOS COURTESY OF TOUCHSTONE

An eccentric thief gathers together a motley collection of criminals to help him rob a casino, using the root cellar of an unsuspecting church-going old lady as their base of operations. Remake of the 1955 British film *The Ladykillers* which was released in the U.S. in 1956 by Continental Distributing and starred Alec Guinness, Herbert Lom, Peter Sellers, and Katie Johnson.

JERSEY GIRL

(MIRAMAX) Producer, Scott Mosier; Executive Producer, Bob Weinstein, Harvey Weinstein, Jonathan Gordon; Director/Screenplay, Kevin Smith; Photography, Vilmos Zsigmond; Designer, Robert Holtzman; Costumes, Juliet Polcsa; Co-Producer, Laura Greenlee; Editors, Kevin Smith, Scott Mosier; Music, James Venable; Associate Producer, Phil Benson; Casting, Amy Kaufman; a View Askew production; Dolby; Deluxe color; Rated PG-13; 102 minutes; Release date: March 26, 2004

Liv Tyler, Raquel Castro, Ben Affleck

Liv Tyler, Ben Affleck

Cast

Ollie Trinke **Ben Affleck**
Maya **Liv Tyler**
Bart Trinke **George Carlin**
Arthur Brickman **Jason Biggs**
Gertie Trinke **Raquel Castro**
Block **Mike Starr**
Greenie **Stephen Root**
Gertrude **Jennifer Lopez**
PR Execs **Jason Lee, Matt Damon**
Himself **Will Smith**
Teacher **Betty Aberlin**
Bryan **Paulie Litowsky**
Susan **Jennifer Schwalbach**

and Matt McFarland, Christian Fan, Victor Chavez, William Mace (Boys), Sarah Stafford (Girl), S. Ephatha Merkerson, Carol Florence (Doctors), Jada Copeland Goodman (ER Nurse), Alice Schaerer, Brian T. Delaney (Nurses), Matt Maher (Delivery Guy), Robert McKay, Ernie O'Donnell, Cymande Lewis, Dan Etheridge, Mark Jwayad (Press), Charles Gilbert ("Sweeney Todd"), Charles McCloskey ("Sweeney Todd Victim"), Matthew Cloran (Anthony), Tom Cleary (Comptroller), John Willyung (Townie), Edward Janda (Town Clapper)

Raquel Castro, George Carlin

After his wife dies in childbirth and he loses his job as a high-power music publicist, Ollie Trinke finds himself having to adapt to his new life as a single father.

Jason Biggs, Ben Affleck PHOTOS COURTESY OF MIRAMAX

HOME ON THE RANGE

(WALT DISNEY PICTURES) Producer, Alice Dewey Goldstone; Director/Screenplay, Will Finn, John Sanford; Additional Dialogue, Shirley Pierce; Music, Alan Menken; Original songs by Alan Menken (music) and Glenn Slater (lyrics); Story, Will Finn, John Sanford, Michael LaBash, Sam Levine, Mark Kennedy, Robert Lence; Associate Producer, David J. Steinberg; Art Director, David Cutler; Editor, H. Lee Peterson; Artistic Supervisors: Layout, Jean-Christophe Poulain; Background, Cristy Maltese Lynch; Clean-Up, Marshall Lee Toomey; Visual Effects, Marlon West; Artistic Coordinator, Dennis M. Blakey; Distributed by Buena Vista Pictures; Dolby; Digial Widescreen; Technicolor; Rated PG; 76 minutes; Release date: April 2, 2004

Ollie, Maggie

Mrs. Caloway, Maggie, Grace

Wesley, Alameda Slim

Mrs. Caloway, Maggie, Grace, Lucky Jack

Voice Cast

Maggie **Roseanne Barr**
Mrs. Caloway **Judi Dench**
Grace **Jennifer Tilly**
Wesley **Steve Buscemi**
Rusty **G.W. Bailey**
Buck **Cuba Gooding, Jr.**
Alameda Slim **Randy Quaid**
Junior **Lance Legault**
Rico **Charles Dennis**
Willie Brothers **Sam J. Levine**
Jeb, the Goat **Joe Flaherty**
Sheriff **Richard Riehle**
Pearl **Carole Cook**
Lucky Jack **Charles Haid**
Barry & Bob **Mark Walton**
Audrey, the Chicken **Estelle Harris**
Ollie, the Pig **Charlie Dell**
Piggies **Bobby Block, Keaton Savage, Ross Simanteris**
Larry, the Duck **Marshall Efron**

Maggie, the newest cow at the Patch of Heaven dairy farm, rallies the other animals to action when greedy outlaw Alameda Slim threatens to take possession of their home.

Rico, Buck, Sheriff PHOTOS COURTESY OF WALT DISNEY PICTURES

HELLBOY

(COLUMBIA) Producers, Lawrence Gordon, Mike Richardson, Lloyd Levin; Executive Producer, Patrick Palmer; Co-Executive Producer, Mike Mignola; Director/Screenplay, Guillermo del Toro; Screen Story, Guillermo del Toro, Peter Briggs; Based upon the Dark Horse Comic created by Mike Mignola; Photography, Guillermo Navarro; Designer, Stephen Scott; Costumes, Wendy Partridge; Music, Marco Beltrami; Editor, Peter Amundson; Hellboy Makeup Consultant, Rick Baker; Visual Effects Supervisor, Edward Irastorza; Casting, Jeremy Zimmerman; Stunts, Monty Simons; a Revolution Studios presentation of a Lawrence Gordon/Lloyd Levin production in association with Dark Horse Entertainment; Dolby; Deluxe color; Rated PG-13; 125 minutes; Release date: April 2, 2004

Rupert Evans, Selma Blair

Agent Moss **James Babson**
Agent Quarry **Stephen Fisher**
Agent Stone **Garth Cooper**
Sgt. Whitman **Angus MacInnes**
Cpl. Matlin **Jim Howick**

and Mark Taylor (Truck Driver), Daniel Aarsman, Bettina Ask, Alvaro Navarro, Emilio Navarro (Kids), Rory Copus (Kid on Rooftop), Tara Hugo (Dr. Jenkins), Richard Haas (Second Doctor), Andrea Miltner (Dr. Marsh), Jo Eastwood (Down's Patient), Charles Grisham, Jan Holicek (Museum Guards), Jeremy Zimmerman (Lobby Guard), Monty Simons (Orderly), Pavel Cajzl (Sherpa Guide), Andrea Stuart (Girl with Kittens), William Hoyland (Von Krupt), Millie Wilkie (Young Liz), Bob Sherman (Television Host), Ellen Savaria (Blonde Television Reporter), Petr Sekanina, Alesa Kosnar (German Scientists), Justin Svoboda (Young Guy), Ave Zoli (Girlfriend Winter), Santiago Segura, Albert May (Train Drivers), David Hyde Pierce (Voice of Abe Sapien)

Hellboy, a deformed creature with paranormal gifts, joins forces with other members of the Bureau for Paranormal Research and Defense to battle the evil Rasputin, who hopes to reclaim Hellboy for his own means and bring on the destruction of mankind.

Ron Perlman

Cast

Hellboy **Ron Perlman**
Trevor "Broom" Bruttenholm **John Hurt**
Liz Sherman **Selma Blair**
John Myers **Rupert Evans**
Grigori Rasputin **Karel Roden**
Tom Manning **Jeffrey Tambor**
Abe Sapien **Doug Jones**
Sammael **Brian Steele**
Kroenen **Ladislav Beran**
Ilsa **Bridget Hodson**
Agent Clay **John William Johnson**
Young Broom **Kevin Trainor**
Agent Lime **Brian Caspe**

Doug Jones, John Hurt PHOTOS COURTESY OF COLUMBIA

THE PRINCE & ME

(PARAMOUNT) Producer, Mark Amin; Executive Producers, Cami Winikoff, Robin Schorr; Director, Martha Coolidge; Screenplay, Jack Amiel, Michael Begler, Katherine Fugate; Story, Mark Amin, Katherine Fugate; Photography, Alex Nepomniaschy; Designer, James Spencer; Costumes, Magali Guidasci; Music, Jennie Muskett; Music Supervisor, Robin Urdang; Editor, Steven Cohen; Co-Producer, Jeffrey Lampert; Casting, Hopkins Smith Barden & Bennett; a Sobini Films production, presented in association with Lions Gate Entertainment; Dolby; Deluxe color; Rated PG; 110 minutes; Release date: April 2, 2004

Julia Stiles, Luke Mably

James Fox, Miranda Richardson PHOTOS COURTESY OF PARAMOUNT

Cast

Paige Morgan **Julia Stiles**
Prince Edvard (Eddie) **Luke Mably**
Soren **Ben Miller**
King Haraald **James Fox**
Queen Rosalind **Miranda Richardson**
Amy Morgan **Alberta Watson**
Ben Morgan **John Bourgeois**
Princess Arabella **Eliza Bennett**
John Morgan **Zachary Knighton**
Mike Morgan **Stephen O'Reilly**
Beth Curtis **Elisabeth Waterston**
Scotty **Devin Ratray**
Stacey **Clare Preuss**

Eliza Bennett, Luke Mably

and Yaani King (Amanda), Eddie Irvine (Himself), Angelo Tsarouchas (Stu), Jacques Tourangeau (Prof. Amiel), Joanne Baron (Marguerite), Stephen Singer (Prof. Begler), Sarah Manninen (Krista), Tony Munch (Keith Kopetsky), John E. Nelles (Race Announcer), Claus Bue (Lutheran Archbishop), James McGowan, Jean Pearson (Photographers), Dasha Blahova (Lady in Waiting), Henrik Jandorf (Prime Minister), Niels Anders Thorn (Thomas Anderson), Jesper Asholt (Cab Driver), Andrea Veresova, Winter Ave Zoli (Eddie's Girlfriends), Jennifer Roberts Smith (John's Wife), Zdeneke Maryskya (Corporation Negotiator), Vladimir Kulhavy (Union Negotiator), Garth Hewitt (Desperate Dan), Dana Reznik (Wild Girl), Amy Stewart (Rathskeller Servere), Richard Lee (Deli Patron), Barbora Kodetová, Klára Issová, Eva Docolomanska (English Teacher Assistants), Philip Craig (Doctor), Dinah Watts (Nurse), David O'Kelly (TV Reporter), Robert Russel (Royal Herald), Go Go Jean Michel Francis (Ambassador Koskel), Jan Nemejvosky (Parliamentary Herald), Lenka Termerova (Danish Woman in Crowd), Emil Helt (Little Kid), Daniel Petronijevic, Jason Burke (Rathskeller Bouncers), Michael McLachlan (Gopher Fan), Patricia Netzer (Brigett, Palace Maid), Andrea Milterova (Anna, Palace Maid), Jennifer Vey (The Bride)

Pre-med student Paige Morgan falls in love with classmate Eddie, not realizing that he is the Crown Prince of Denmark, attending university incognito.

THE UNITED STATES OF LELAND

(PARAMOUNT CLASSICS) Producers, Kevin Spacey, Bernie Morris, Palmer West, Jonah Smith; Executive Producers, Mark Damon, Sammy Lee, Stewart Hall; Director/Screenplay, Matthew Ryan Hope; Photography, James Glennon; Designer, Edward T. McAvoy; Costumes, Genevieve Tyrrell; Music, Jeremy Enigk; Editor, Jeff Betancourt; Casting, Emily Schweber; a Thousand Words presentation in association with MDP Worldwide of a Trigger Street production; Dolby; Color; Rated R; 108 minutes; Release date: April 2, 2004

Michelle Williams, Jena Malone

Cast

Pearl Madison **Don Cheadle**
Leland P. Fitzgerald **Ryan Gosling**
Allen Harris **Chris Klein**
Becky Pollard **Jena Malone**
Marybeth Fitzgerald **Lena Olin**
Albert T. Fitzgerald **Kevin Spacey**
Julie Pollard **Michelle Williams**
Harry Pollard **Martin Donovan**
Karen Pollard **Ann Magnuson**

Don Cheadle PHOTOS COURTESY OF PARAMOUNT CLASSICS

Ryan Gosling, Jena Malone

Kevin Spacey

Ayesha **Kerry Washington**
Mrs. Calderon **Sherilyn Fenn**
Charlie **Matt Malloy**
Bengel **Wesley Jonathan**

and Michael Peña (Guillermo), Michael Welch (Ryan Polalrd), Ron Canada (Elden), Troy Winbush (Dave), Nick Kokich (Kevin), Yolonda Ross (Miranda), Leyna Nguyen (TV Reporter), Jim Haynie (Ben), Randall Bosley (Sheriff Donaldson), Jody Wood (Cop One), Robert Peters (Security Guard), Kathleen Dunn (Doris), Tony McEwing (News Anchor), Lawrence Lowe (Detention Specialist), Charles Hess (Main Entrance Guard), Kimberly Scott (Myra), Angela Paton (Airplane Woman), Ryan Malgarini (6-Year-Old Leland), Maria Arcé (Bethany), Dell Yount (Court Officer), Clyde Kusatsu (Judge), Melanie Lora (Hotel Waitress), Rene Rivera, Michael McCleery (Mechanics), Alec Medlock (12-Year-Old Leland), Jim Metzler (Cemetery Reporter), David Barrera (First Officer), Sheeri Rappaport (Second Officer), Kevin Kelly (Doctor), Evan Helmuth (Grocery Guy), Eric Ty Hodges (Student), Edward T. McAvoy (Creepy Man)

A teacher at a correctional facility tries to understand why young Leland Fitzgerald brutally murdered a retarded boy.

WALKING TALL

(MGM) Producers, Ashok Amritraj, David Hoberman, Jim Burke, Lucas Foster, Paul Schiff; Executive Producers, Keith Samples, Vince McMahon; Director, Kevin Bray; Screenplay, David Klass, Channing Gibson, David Levien, Brian Koppleman; Based on a screenplay by Mort Briskin; Photography, Glen MacPherson; Designer, Brent Thomas; Costumes, Gersha Phillips; Music, Graeme Revell; Music Supervisor, G. Marq Roswell; Editors, George Bowers, Robert Ivison; Co-Producer, Bill Bannerman; Casting, Sarah Halley Finn, Randi Hiller; Stunts, Jeff Habberstad; a Hyde Park Entertainment/Mandeville Films production in association with Burke/Samples/Foster Productions and WWE Films; Dolby; Super 35 Widescreen; Deluxe color; Rated PG-13; 87 minutes; Release date: April 2, 2004

Cast

Chris Vaughn **The Rock**
Ray Templeton **Johnny Knoxville**
Jay Hamilton **Neal McDonough**
Michelle Vaughn **Kristen Wilson**
Deni **Ashley Scott**
Pete Vaughn **Khleo Thomas**
Chris Vaughn, Sr. **John Beasley**

and Connie Vaughn (Barbara Tarbuck), Michael Bowen (Sheriff Stan Watkins), Kevin Durand (Booth), Andrew Tarbet (Jimmy), Patrick Gallagher (Keith), John Stewart (Rusty), Eric Breker (Deputy Ralston), Ryan Robbins (Travis), Michael Adamthwaite (Burke), Darcy Laurie (Smitty), Fred Keating (Doctor), Ben Cardinal (Michelle's Partner), Kett Turton (Kenner), Terence Kelly (Judge L. Powell), Tom Scholte (Merle Crowe), Mark Houghton (County Prosecutor), James Ashcroft (Bailiff), Eric Kennlyeside (Dan Stadler), Aaron Douglas (Casino Stickman), Michael Soltis (Casino Maintenance Worker), April Amber Telek (Casino Waitress), Sandra Steier (Addict Mother), Ben Cotton (Drug Dealer), Cobie Smulders (Exotic Beauty), Chelsie Amber McEachnie, Kaja Gjesdal, Melody Tinesa Cherpaw (Lap Dancers), Alana Drozduke, Sandra Higueras (Casino Trashy Women), Ty Olsson (Deputy), Ana Mirkovic (Blackjack Dealer), David Purvis (Ray's AA Sponsor), Beverley Elliott (Nurse), Rita Theresa Edwards,Sarah Smith (Wet T-Shirt Girls), Douglas Sheridan (Boxman), Katina Robillard (Dollar Bill Girl), Jacqueline Stewart (Girl on Platform)

Khleo Thomas, The Rock

Johnny Knoxville, The Rock

When retired special forces soldier Chris Vaughn returns home to find that Jay Hamilton has turned his hometown into a community run by crime, he gets himself elected sheriff in order to shut down Hamilton's operations. Semi-remake of the 1973 Cinerama film of the same name that starred Joe Don Baker.

Kristen Wilson, The Rock PHOTOS COURTESY OF MGM

Gabby Soleil, Vanessa Williams, Solange Knowles, Bow Wow, Cedric the Entertainer

Vanessa Williams, Cedric the Entertainer, Solange Knowles, Bow Wow, Gabby Soleil

JOHNSON FAMILY VACATION

(FOX SEARCHLIGHT) Producers, Paul Hall, Eric C. Rhone, Cedric the Entertainer, Wendy Park; Executive Producers, Andrew Sugerman; Director, Christopher Erskin; Screenplay, Todd R. Jones, Earl Richey Jones; Photography, Shawn Maurer; Designer, Keith Brian Burns; Costumes, Dana M. Campbell; Music, Richard Gibbs; Editor, John Carter; Casting, Reuben Cannon, Kim Williams; a Hallway Pictures/A Bird and a Bear Entertainment production; Dolby; Deluxe color; Rated PG-13; 97 minutes; Release date: April 7, 2004

Cast
Nate Johnson/Uncle Earl **Cedric the Entertainer**
Dorothy Johnson **Vanessa Williams**
Nikki Johnson **Solange Knowles**
D.J. Johnson **Bow Wow**
Destiny Johnson **Gabby Soleil**
Chrishelle Rene Babineau **Shannon Elizabeth**
Mack Johnson **Steve Harvey**
Glorietta Johnson **Aloma Wright**
Jacqueline **Shari Headley**
Jill **Jennifer Freeman**
Mack, Jr. **Philip Daniel Bolden**
Cousin Lump **Rodney Perry**
Stan **Christopher B. Duncan**
Gladys **Lorna Scott**
Stall Guy **Kevin Farley**
Betty Sue **Lee Garlington**
Angus **Shane Woodson**
Navarro **Jason Momoa**

and DeRay Davis (Jamaican Stoner), Jonathan Joss (Casino Host), Godfrey Danchimah (Motorcycle Cop), Kurupt (Himself), Masasa, Chana Ylahne Orr (Thetas), Chris Hardwick (Arson Investigator), Gabriel Corbin, Tracie Burton, Katerina Graham, Jamil Morgan (Dancers), Jeremiah "J.J." Williams, Jr. (Cousin Bodie), Tanjareen Martin (Tangerine), Lichelli Lazar-Lea (Navi Computer Voice)

Nate Johnson, his wife, and their three kids travel from California to Missouri so Nate can compete with his brother Mack for a "family of the year" trophy.

Cedric the Entertainer, Steve Harvey

Cedric the Entertainer PHOTOS COURTESY OF FOX SEARCHLIGHT

THE ALAMO

(TOUCHSTONE) Producers, Mark Johnson, Ron Howard; Executive Producers, Todd Hallowell, Philip Steuer; Director, John Lee Hancock; Screenplay, Leslie Bohem, Stephen Gaghan, John Lee Hancock; Photography, Dean Semler; Designer, Michael Corenblith; Costumes, Daniel Orlandi; Music, Carter Burwell; Editor, Eric L. Beason; Stunts, Philip Neilson; Casting, Ronna Kress; an Imagine Entertainment presetnation of a Mark Johnson production; Dolby; Panavision; Technicolor; Rated PG-13; 137 minutes; Release date: April 9, 2004

Patrick Wilson, Billy Bob Thornton, Jason Patric

Cast

Sam Houston **Dennis Quaid**
Davy Crockett **Billy Bob Thornton**
Jim Bowie **Jason Patric**
William Travis **Patrick Wilson**
Antonio López de Santa Anna **Emilio Echevarria**
Juan Seguin **Jordi Mollá**
Sgt. William Ward **Leon Rippy**
Col. Green Jameson **Tom Davidson**
James Bonham **Marc Blucas**

and Robert Prentiss (Albert Grimes), Kevin Page (Micajah Autry), Joe Stevens (Mial Scurlock), Stephen Bruton (Capt. Almeron Dickinson), Laura Clifton (Susanna Dickinson), Ricardo A. Chavira (Pvt. Gregorio Esparza), Steven Chester Prince (Lt. John Forsythe), Craig Erickson (Tom Waters), Nick Kokich (Daniel Coud), Richard Nance, Jett Garner (Greys), Estephania Lebaron (Juana), Afemo Omilami (Sam), Edwin Hodge (Joe), Emily Deschanel (Rosanna Travis), Blue Deckert (Colorado Smith), Turk Pipkin (Isaac Millsaps), Brandon Smith (Lt. Col. J.C. Neill), Tommy G. Kendrick (T.J. Rusk), W. Earl Brown (David Burnet), Tom Everett (Mosley Baker), Rance Howard (Gov. Smith), Stewart Finlay-McLennan (James Grant), Matt O'Leary (Boy in Store), John S. Davies (Store Owner), Kit Gwin (Mrs. Ayres), Castulo Guerra (Gen. Castrillon), Francisco Philibert (Gen. Cos), Mauricio Zatarain (Col. Jose Batres), Flavio Hinojosa (Col. Juan Almonte), Hugo Perez (Charging Mexican Soldier), Jesus Mayorga (Battery Private), Hector Garcia (Battery Sergeant), Roland Uribe (Col.

Emilio Echevarria

Duque), Ruben G. Rojas (Francisco Esparza), Lanell Pena (Ana Esparza), Michael Crabtree (Deaf Smith), Anna Reyes (Tejano Child), Sonia Montoya (Stunning Tejana's Mother), Elena Hurst (Stunning Tejana), Lynn Mathis (James Hackett), Charles Sanders (Stage Manager), Rutherford Cravens (Mr. Smith), Dameon Clarke (Mr. Jones), Tim Mateer (Bill the Rider), Nathan Price (Charlie Travis), Don Javier Castillo (Don Jose Palaez), Lonnie Rodriguez (Mexican Scout), Julio Cesar Cedillo (Cos' Messenger), Buck Taylor (Settler), Oscar D. Silva (Firing Squad Ist Lt.), Marc Menchaca (Fifer), Safia Gray (Ursula Veramendi), Eirc Montoya (Enrique Esparza), Michael Clossin (Tennessean #1), Robert Bassetti (Bowie Man in Street), Nathan Walker (Goliad Man)

The true story of how fewer than 200 Texans attempted to hold the Alamo against an onslaught of thousands of Mexican soldiers under the command of General Santa Ana. Previous film version (UA, 1960) starred John Wayne and Richard Widmark

Dennis Quaid PHOTOS COURTESY OF TOUCHSTONE

THE GIRL NEXT DOOR

(20TH CENTURY FOX) Producers, Charles Gordon, Harry Gittes, Marc Sternberg; Executive Producers, Arnon Milchan, Guy Riedel; Director, Luke Greenfield; Screenplay, Stuart Blumberg, David T. Wagner, Brent Goldberg; Story, David T. Wagner, Brent Goldberg; Photography, Jamie Anderson; Designer, Stephen Lineweaver; Costumes, Marilyn Vance; Editor, Mark Livolsi; Music, Paul Haslinger; Music Supervisor, Peter Afterman; Co-Producer, Richard Wenk; Casting, Mali Finn; a Regenecy Enterprises presentation of a New Regency/Gordon/Gittes production from Lakeshore Entertainment; Dolby; Panavision; Deluxe color; Rated R; 109 minutes; Release date: April 9, 2004

Elisha Cuthbert

Cast

Matthew Kidman **Emile Hirsch**
Danielle **Elisha Cuthbert**
Kelly **Timothy Olyphant**
Hugo Posh **James Remar**
Eli **Chris Marquette**
Klitz **Paul Dano**
Mr. Kidman **Timothy Bottoms**
Mrs. Kidman **Donna Bullock**
Hunter **Jacob Young**
Derek **Brian Kolodziej**
Troy **Brandon Irons**
April **Amanda Swisten**
Ferrari **Sung Hi Lee**
Samnang **Ulysses Lee**

and Harri Laskawy (Dr. Salinger), Julie Osburn (Jeannie), Laird Stuart (Mr. Ruether), Dane A. Garretson (Ryan Winger), Richard Fancy (Mr. Peterson), Catherine McGoohan (Mrs. Peterson), Josh Henderson (Pep Rally Jock), Nicholas Thomas (Glen), John-Clay Scott (Rent-A-Cop), Matt "Horshu" Wiese (Mule), Maria Arce (Chloe), Alonzo Bodden (Steel), Ellis E. Williams (Scholarship President), Stephanie Fabian (Mina Lopez), Michael Villani (TV Talk Show Host), Dan Klass (School Photographer), Benjamin Banks (Karate Guy in Porn Film), Tomas Herrera (Film School Student), John Harrington Bland (Fan at Convention), Shulan Tuan (Samnang's Mother), Kayla Tabish (Kathy), Nicholas Downs (Bob in 70's Sex-Ed Film), Danny Seckel (Bob's Friend in '70s Sex-Ed Film), Katie Stuart (Jennie), Olivia Wilde (Kellie), Autumn Reeser (Jane), Reda Beebe (Cocktail Waitress), Rudy Mettia (Limo Driver), Christ Verdiglione (Responsible Media Minion), Martin Pierron, Freddy Smith, Ray Mono, Ricardo Amaya, Hector Garcia (Media Minions), Paul Aluicino (Voice of Parrot), Beth Buck (Attractive Woman at Scholarship Banquet)

Elisha Cuthbert, Emile Hirsch

Paul Dano, Emile Hirsch, Chris Marquette

An overachieving teen believes his high school years have been uneventful until he falls in love with his new next door neighbor, who just happens to have been a former porn star.

Timothy Olyphant, Elisha Cuthbert PHOTOS COURTESY OF 20TH CENTURY FOX

ELLA ENCHANTED

(MIRAMAX) Producer, Jane Startz; Executive Producer, Bob Weinstein, Harvey Weinstein, Julie Goldstein, Su Armstrong; Director, Tommy O'Haver; Screenplay, Laurie Craig, Karen McCullah Lutz, Kirsten Smith, Jennifer Heath, Michelle J. Wolff; Based on the novel by Gail Carson Levine; Photography, John de Borman; Designer, Norman Garwood; Costumes, Ruth Myers; Music, Shaun Davey; Choreographer, Bruno Tonioli; Editor, Masahiro Hirakubo; Special Effects Supervisor, Angus Bickerton; Casting, Susie Figgis; a Jane Startz production; Dolby; Deluxe color; Rated PG; 101 minutes; Release date: April 9, 2004

Anne Hathaway, Hugh Dancy

Ella tries to remove the obedience curse placed upon her at birth, in order to battle her cruel stepsisters and the wicked Sir Edgar.

Anne Hathaway

Cast

Ella of Frell **Anne Hathaway**
Prince Charmont **Hugh Dancy**
Sir Edgar **Cary Elwes**
Lucinda Perriweather **Vivica A. Fox**
Dame Olga **Joanna Lumley**
Mandy **Minnie Driver**
Narrator **Eric Idle**
Slannen of Pim **Aidan McArdle**
Sir Peter **Patrick Bergin**
Benny **Jimi Mistry**
Areida **Parminder K. Nagra**
Hattie **Lucy Punch**
Olive **Jennifer Higham**
Voice of Heston the Snake **Steve Coogan**
Nish the Ogre **Jim Carter**
Ella's Mother **Donna Dent**

and Ankita Malkan (Young Areida), Sally-Ann Tingle (Mean Little Girl), Aimee Brigg (Ella, aged 8), Helen Norton (Prof. Edith), Emmet Kirwen (Vendor), Christopher Kelly (Salesman), Audrey Hamm (Perfume Sprayer), Mikel Murfi (Mall Cop), Rory Keenan (Otto), Aonghus Og McAnally (Bluto), Aaron Monaghan (Pug), Heidi Klum (Brumhilda), Alvaro Lucchesi (Koopooduk), Paraic Breathnach, Daniel Naprous (Ogres), Nora Jane Noone (Fairy No. 1), Pat Kinevane (Make-Up Artist), Andrea Irvine (Castle Tour Guide), Merrina Millsapp (Hall of Records Attendant), Amelia Crowley (Fairy Administrator), Pat McGrath (Dungeon Guard), Susan Ward (Fan Club Girl), Tommy O'Haver (Squirrel-on-a-Stick Vendor)

Jim Carter, Anne Hathaway, Aidan McArdle PHOTOS COURTESY OF MIRAMAX

CONNIE AND CARLA

(UNIVERSAL) Producers, Roger Birnbaum, Gary Barber, Jonathan Glickman; Executive Producers, Nia Vardalos, Rita Wilson, Peter Safran; Director, Michael Lembeck; Screenplay, Nia Vardalos; Photography, Richard Greatrex; Designer, Jasna Stefanovic; Costumes, Ruth Myers; Music, Randy Edelman; Music Supervisor, Paul Bogaev; Choreographer, Cynthia Onrubia; Editor, David Finfer; Co-Producer, Warren Carr; Casting, Francine Maisler, Kathy Driscoll-Mohler; a Spyglass Entertainment presentation of a Birnbaum/Barber production; Dolby; Deluxe color; Rated PG-13; 98 minutes; Release date: April 16, 2004.

Nia Vardalos, Toni Collette

After witnessing a murder, two lounge singers flee to West Hollywood, where they get jobs performing as drag queens.

Stephen Spinella, Robert Kaiser, Toni Collette, Nia Vardalos, Christopher Logan, Alec Mapa PHOTOS COURTESY OF UNIVERSAL

Cast

Connie **Nia Vardalos**
Carla **Toni Collette**
Jeff **David Duchovny**
Robert/Peaches **Stephen Spinella**
Lee/N' Cream **Alec Mapa**
Brian/Brianna **Christopher Logan**

and Robert Kaiser (Paul), Ian Gomez (Stanley), Nick Sandow (Al), Dash Mihok (Mikey), Robert John Burke (Rudy), Boris McGiver (Tibor), Don Ackerman (Super Fey Guy), Debbie Reynolds (Herself), Veena Sood (Mrs. Morse), Babz Chula (Carla's Mom), Linda Darlow (Connie's Mom), Linda Darlow (Connie's Mom), Charles Payne (Hollywood Policeman), Michael Roberds (Frank), Guy Fauchon (Another Super Fey Guy), Gary Jones (Bartender), Fiona Hogan (Natasha), Ryf Van Rij, Adam Harrington (Cute Guys), D. Neil Mark (Crooked Cop), Krista Rae (Mary), Brittney Wilson (Young Carla), Danielle Woodman (Young Connie), Kristi Angus (Woman in Crowd), Douglas Baird (Cameraman), Nicola Crosbie (Repter), Fred Keating, Bart Anderson (Men in Airport), June B. Wilde (Woman in Airport), Kristina Copeland (Botox Woman), Chelah Horsdal (Botox's Friend), Carl McDonald (Dressing Room Guy), Elanie Kliner (Snoring Woman in Airport), Douglas McLeod (Bass Player), Stephen Cottrill (Guitar Player), Lloyd Nicholson (Pianist), Gordon Roberts (Drummer)

Debbie Reynolds (center)

David Duchovny, Nia Vardalos

KILL BILL VOL. 2

(MIRAMAX) Producer, Lawrence Bender; Executive Producers, Bob Weinstein, Harvey Weinstein, Erica Steinberg, E. Bennett Walsh; Director/Screenplay, Quentin Tarantino; Photography, Robert Richardson; Designers, David Wasco, Cao Jui Ping; Costumes, Catherine Thomas, Kumiko Ogawa; Music, The RZA, Robert Rodriguez; Music Supervisor, Mary Ramos; Visual Effects, Centro Digital Pictures; Martial Arts Adviser, Yuen Wo-Ping; Stunts, Keith Adams; Casting, Johanna Ray; a Band Apart production; Dolby; Panavision; Deluxe color/Black and white; Rated R; 137 minutes; Release date: April 16, 2004

Uma Thurman, Gordon Liu

Uma Thurman

Cast
The Bride (Beatrix Kiddo) **Uma Thurman**
Bill **David Carradine**
Budd **Michael Madsen**
Elle Driver **Daryl Hannah**
Pai Mei **Gordon Liu**
Esteban Vihaio **Michael Parks**
B.B. Kiddo **Perla Haney-Jardine**
Karen **Helen Kim**
Clarita **Claire Smithies**
Ernie **Clark Middleton**
Rocket **Laura Cayouette**
Larry Gomez **Larry Bishop**
Jay **Sid Haig**
Lucky **Reda Beebe**
Rufus **Samuel L. Jackson**
Tommy Plympton **Chris Nelson**
Janeen **Caitlin Keats**
Mrs. Harmony **Jeannie Epper**
Reverend Harmony **Bo Svenson**
Joleen **Stephanie L. Moore**
Erica **Shana Stein**
1st Grade Teacher **Venessia Valentino**
Melanie Harrhouse **Thea Rose**

Daryl Hannah PHOTOS COURTESY OF MIRAMAX

David Carradine, Uma Thurman

Soda Jerk **William P. Clark**
Trixie **Vicki Lucai**
Tim **Steveo Polyi**
Marty Kitrosser **Al Manuel Douglas**
Bartender/Pimp **Jorge Silva**

and Patricia Silva, Maria Del Rosario Gutiérrez, Sonia Angelia Padilla Curiel, Veronica Janet Martinez, Lucia Cruz Marroquin, Citlati Guadaluipe Bojorquez, Graciela Salazar Mendoza, Maria de Lourdes Lombera (Hookers)

Left for dead at her wedding, the Bride continues to seek revenge on the hit-squad responsible. The first part of the film, *Kill Bill Vol. 1* premiered on October 10, 2003

Michael Madsen

Uma Thurman, Gordon Liu

THE PUNISHER

(LIONS GATE) Producers, Avi Arad, Gale Anne Hurd; Executive Producers, Stan Lee, Kevin Feige, John Starke, Amir Malin, Richard Saperstein, Andrew Golov, Patrick Gunn, Andreas Schmid, Christopher Roberts, Christopher Eberts; Director, Jonathan Hensleigh, Michael France; Based on the Marvel comic book character; Photography, Conrad W. Hall; Designer, Michael Z. Hanan; Costumes, Lisa Tomczeszyn; Editor, Steven Kemper; Second Unit/Stunts, Gary Hymes; a Valhalla Motion Pictures production in association with VIP2/VIP3 and Artisan Entertainment, in association with Marvel Enterprises; Dolby; Super 35 Widescreen; Deluxe color; Rated R; 124 minutes; Release date: April 16, 2004

Tom Jane, Rebecca Romijn-Stamos in *The Punisher* PHOTOS COURTESY OF LIONS GATE

Cast
Frank Castle/The Punisher **Tom Jane**
Howard Saint **John Travolta**
Quentin Glass **Will Patton**
Frank Castle, Sr. **Roy Scheider**
Livia Saint **Laura Harring**
Spacker Dave **Ben Foster**
Maria Castle **Samantha Mathis**
John Saint/Bobby Saint **James Carpinello**
Jimmy Weeks **Russell Andrews**

and Eddie Andrews (Micky Duka), John Pinette (Mr. Bumpo), Rebecca Romijn-Stamos (Joan), Mark Collie (Harry Heck), Eduardo Yanez (Mike Toro), Omar Avila (Joe Toro), Kevin Nash (The Russian), Marcus Johns (Will Castle), Russ Comegys (Tattooed Mike), Antoni Corone (T.J.), Rick Elmhurst (Bay News 9 Newscaster), Michael Francis (Toro Croupier), Will Hasenzahl (EMT), Marco St. John (Police Chief Morris), Marcus Johns (Will Castle), Bonnie Johnson (Betty Castle), Veryl Jones (Candelaria), Carleth Keys (Bay News 9 Newscaster), Jim Meskimen, Alan Lilly, Jack Swanson (Accountants), Terry Loughlin (Spoon), Marc Macaulay (Dante), Tom Nowicki (Lincoln), Robin O'Dell (Field Reporter), Yamil Piedra (Toro Pit Boss), Steve Raulerson (Yuri Astrov), Hank Stone (Cutter), Sonny Surowiec (Saint Puerto Rico Enforcer), Josh Thomas (NBC Newscaster)

FBI Agent Frank Castle swears vengeance on the mobster who has killed his family in retaliation for the death of his own son during a sting operation gone wrong.

Kett Turton, Sara Rue in *Gypsy 83* PHOTOS COURTESY OF SMALL PLANET

GYPSY 83

(SMALL PLANET) Producers, Todd Stephens, Karen Jaroneski; Executive Producer, Michael Wolfson; Line Producer, Christine McAndrews; Co-Producer, Judith Zarin; Director/Screenplay, Todd Stephens; Story, Todd Stephens, Tim Katltenecker; Photography, Gina Degirolamo; Designer, Nancy Arons; Costumes, Kitty Boots; Music, Marty Beller; Editor, Annette Davey; Casting, Eve Battaglia; Color; Not rated; 94 minutes; Release date: April 23, 2004

Cast
Gypsy **Sara Rue**
Clive **Kett Turton**
Bambi LeBleau **Karen Black**
Ray **Joe Doe**
Lois **Carolyn Lois**
Zachariah **Anson Scoville**

and Paulo Costanzo (Troy), Stephanie McVay (Polly Pearl), Nancy Arons (White Trash Mommy), Vera Beren (Chi Chi Valenti), Andersen Gabrych (Banning), Bear Sheppard (Twirling Stevie), Matthew Faust (Frat Boy)

Goth misfits Gypsy and her gay friend Clive leave their Ohio town and head for New York, where Gypsy hopes to find success as a singer.

Kett Turton, Paulo Costanzo in *Gypsy 83* PHOTOS COURTESY OF SMALL PLANET

MAN ON FIRE

(20TH CENTURY FOX) Producers, Arnon Milchan, Tony Scott, Lucas Foster; Executive Producers, Lance Hool, James W. Skotchdopole; Director, Tony Scott; Screenplay, Brian Helgeland; Based on the novel by A.J. Quinnell; Photography, Paul Cameron; Production Designers, Benjamin Fernandez, Chris Seagers; Costumes, Louise Frogley; Music, Harry Gregson-Williams; Editor, Christian Wagner; Co-Producer, Conrad Hool; Casting, Bonnie Timmermann; a Fox 2000 Pictures and Regency Enterprises presentation of a New Regency/Scott Free production; Dolby; Panavision; Deluxe color; Rated R; 146 minutes; Release date: April 21, 2004

Denzel Washington, Christopher Walken

Cast

John Creasy **Denzel Washington**
Pita Ramos **Dakota Fanning**
Samuel Ramos **Marc Anthony**
Lisa Ramos **Radha Mitchell**
Rayburn **Christopher Walken**
Manzano **Giancarlo Giannini**
Mariana **Rachel Ticotin**
Fuentes **Jesus Ochoa**
Jordan **Mickey Rourke**
Sister Anna **Angelina Pelaez**
Daniel Sanchez **Gustavo Sanchez Parra**
Aurelio Sanchez **Gero Camilo**

and Rosa Maria Hernandez (Maria), Heriberto del Castillo (Bruno), Mario Zaragoza (Jorge Ramirez), Javier Torres Zaragoza (Sandri), Itzel Navarro Vazquez (Sandri's Girl), Esteban de la Trinidad, Charles Paraventi, Carmen Salinas (Guardians), Rodrigo Zurita (Eighteen), Marizol Cal y Mayor (Eighteen's Girlfriend), Hector Hernandez Zertuche (Chauffer), Rene Campero (Father), Angelica Rosado (Mother), Norma Pablo (Reina Rosas), Georgina Gonzalez (Rayburn's Wife), Abraham Sandoval (Rayburn's Kid), Itati Cantoral (Evelyn), Jorge Zarate (Customs Official), Hugo Pelaez (Pedro), Alejandro Camps, Jorge Almada, Carlos Barada, Eduardo Yanez (Bodyguards), Jose de Jesus Hernandez, Takanori Takena, Jorge yu Lee, Ryoji Ishiguro, Ryoirchiro Yoshida, Roberto Kwok (Japanese Businessmen), Jorge Victoria (Comandande Judicial), Ariane Pellicer

Dakota Fanning, Radha Mitchell

(Reporter #1), Stacy Perskie (Cynical Reporter), Adrian Grunberg (Docile Reporter), Raul Zermeno (Highranking Government Official), Jorge Merlo (Judicial Police), Jorge Picont (Piano Teacher), Steve Gonzalez (Insurance Lawyer), Alberto Pineda, Rodrigo Chavez (Fuentes Men), Jesus Gonzalez (Jesus Gonzalez), Fernando Arvizu, Ghalil Elhateb Estrada (Thug Cops), Alberto Estrella (Adjutant AFI), Gerardo Taracena (Executive Adjutant), Hugo Genesio, Gonzalo Alvarez (Plainclothes), Fernando Moya (Doctor), Nydia A. Trujillo, Maria Hall Rueda (Nurses), Andres Pardave (Vet), Elvira Richards (Vet Assistant), Valentina Garcia Contreras (Camila), Enrique Cimet (Eldery Man), Sparkle (Eldery Woman), Dunia Alvarez (AFI Plainclothes #1), Beatriz Pina (Undercover AFI), Hector Tagle (Mariana's Driver), Jose Montini (Restaurant Owner), Jose Jesus Garcia, Guadalupe Flores Garcia, Daniela Martinez (Sanchez Kids), Ruben Santana, Fernando Berzosa (AFI Trailer Techs), Eduardo Rivera (AFI Operator on Radio), Ofelia Aguirre (Interviewer), Rosanna Fuentes (Newscaster), Victor de Pascual, Norma Martinez (Arms Dealers), Aram Cardenas (Nephew), Jorge Guerrero (Priest), Enrique Gonzalez (Taxi Driver), Rafael Gaucin (Customs Official #2), Manuel Poncelis (School Clerk), Arturo Farfan (Bartender)

A disillusioned former CIA operative/assassin reluctantly forms a bond with the nine-year-old girl he is hired to guard only to have her kidnapped on his watch.

Giancarlo Giannini, Rachel Ticotin PHOTOS COURTESY OF 20TH CENTURY FOX

13 GOING ON 30

(COLUMBIA) Producers, Susan Arnold, Donna Arkoff Roth, Gina Matthews; Executive Producers, Todd Garner, Dan Kolsrud; Director, Gary Winick; Screenplay, Josh Goldsmith, Cathy Yuspa; Photography, Don Burgess; Designer, Garreth Stover; Costumes, Susie DeSanto; Music, Theodore Shapiro; Music Supervision, John Houlihan; Co-Producer, Allegra Clegg; Casting, Ellen Lewis, Terri Taylor; a Revolution Studios presentation of a Roth/Arnold production, a Gina Matthews production; Dolby; Deluxe color; Rated PG-13; 98 minutes; Release date: April 23, 2004

Christa B. Allen, Sean Marquette

Jennifer Garner, Marcia DeBonis, Susan Egan PHOTOS COURTESY OF COLUMBIA

Cast

Jenna Rink **Jennifer Garner**
Matt Flamhaff **Mark Ruffalo**
Lucy Wyman **Judy Greer**
Richard Kneeland **Andy Serkis**
Bev Rink **Kathy Baker**
Wayne Rink **Phil Reeves**
Alex Carlson **Samuel Ball**
Arlene **Marcia DeBonis**
Young Jenna **Christa B. Allen**
Young Matt **Sean Marquette**
Trish Sackett **Kiersten Warren**

Jennifer Garner

Jennifer Garner, Mark Ruffalo

and Joe Grifasi (Mr. Flamhaff), Mary Pat Gleason (Mrs. Flamhaff), Susan Egan (Tracy Hansen), Lynn Collins (Wendy), Renee Olstead (Becky), Alexandra Kyle (Young Tom-Tom), Alex Black (Young Chris Grandy), Ashley Benson, Brittany Curran, Brie Larson, Megan Lusk, Julia Roth (Six Chicks), Jeffrey Shane Cohn, George Hine (Grandy's Friends), Philip Pavel (Phil), Sarah Loew (Carla), Maz Jobrani (Glenn), Ian Barford (Pete Hansen), Benita Krista Nall (Waitress at Party), Robinne Lee (Rachel), Justin Burke (13-Year-Old Boy in Bar), Sara Swain (Sara), Catherine Combs (Catherine), Gina Mantegna (Gina), Sydni Beaudoin (Sydni), Jim Gaffigan (Chris Grandy), Corena Chase (Poise Employee), Crystal Michelle (Poise Secretary), Madeline Sprung-Keyser (Maddy), Swoop Whitebear (DJ), Shambo Pfaff, John Grant, Fabrice Calmettes, Eron Otcasek (Band Members), Kevin D. White (Yearbook Photographer), Timothy Anderson, Adrian Armas, Carmit Bachar, Rita Maye Bland, Douglas Caldwell, Keith Diorio, Nadine Ellis, Janina N. Garraway, Stacey Harper, Brandon Nicholas Henschel, Michael William Higgins, Katie Miller, Nancy O'Meara, Bubba Dean Rambo, Caroline A. Rice, Kevin Stea, Michon Suyama, Kadee Sweeney, Natalie Willes, Darrel Wright, Kimberly Wyatt, Jason Yribar (Dancers)

Jenna Rink, a 13-year-old, unhappy with her high school life, gets her wish to become an adult, waking up 17 years in the future to discover that she has become a rich and successful New York magazine editor.

ENVY

(DREAMWORKS/COLUMBIA) Producers, Barry Levinson, Paul Weinstein; Executive Producer, Mary McLaglen; Director, Barry Levinson; Screenplay, Steve Adams; Photography, Tim Maurice Jones; Designer, Victor Kempster; Costumes, Glorai Gresham; Music, Mark Mothersbaugh; Editors, Stu Linder, Blair Daily; Casting, Ellen Lewis; a Baltimore/Spring Creek Pictures production, presented in association with Castle Rock Entertainment; Dolby; Technicolor; Rated PG-13; 99 minutes; Release date: April 30, 2004

Christopher Walken, Ben Stiller

Cast

Tim Dingman **Ben Stiller**
Nick Vanderpark **Jack Black**
Debbie Dingman **Rachel Weisz**
Natalie Vanderpark **Amy Poehler**
J-Man **Christopher Walken**
Lula Dingman **Ariel Gade**
Nellie Vanderpark **Lily Jackson**
Nathan Vanderpark **Connor Matheus**
Eduardo **Hector Elias**

Amy Poehler, Jack Black PHOTOS COURTESY OF DREAMWORKS/COLUMBIA

Jack Black, Ben Stiller

Woman at Play **Angee Hughes**
Dimitriov **Manny Kleinmuntz**
Cal **Blue Deckert**
Les **John Gavigan**
3M Worker **Terry Bozeman**
Mr. Parmenter **Brian Reddy**

and E.J. Callahan (Bartender), Edith Jefferson (Mable), Tom McCleister (Bosco), Tumbleweed (Lester), John Marrott (State Trooper), Ofer Marrott (Pete), Daniel Lugo (Italian Minister), Frank Roman (Translator), Randall Bosley (Oscar), Amy D. Higgins (Vanderpark Nanny), Curtis Andersen (Young Kissing Man), Maricela Ochoa (Dr. Fernandez), Tara Karsian (Lab Assistant), Ted Rooney (Upscale Announcer), Douglas Roberts (Downscale Auctioneer), Melissa Polik (Girl at Play, Bee), Ashlynn Rose (Girl at Play, Butterfly), Hannah Rosenberg (Girl at Play, Flower), Atiana Coons-Parker (Girl at Play, Rock), Jacob Greenblatt (Boy at Play, Duck), Cayden Boyd (Boy at Play, Wolf), Nicholas Sugimoto (Boy at Play, Worm), Jaye K. Danford (Campaign Emcee), Gustavo Hernandez (Pool Worker), Kent Shockenk (Newscaster), Tracy Dixon (Teacher at Play)

Ben Stiller, Rachel Weisz

Tim Dingman is tortured by the fact that he decided not to invest in his friend Nick Vanderpark's invention, the Vapoorizer, a spray that dissolves animal droppings, and has made Nick enormously wealthy.

MEAN GIRLS

(PARAMOUNT) Producer, Lorne Michaels; Executive Producer, Jill Messick; Director, Mark Waters; Screenplay, Tina Fey; Based on the book *Queen of the Wannabes* by Rosalind Wiseman; Photography, Daryn Okada; Designer, Cary White; Costumes, Mary Jane Fort; Dance Choreographer, Donna Feore; Music, Rolfe Kent; Music Supervisor, Amanda Scheer Demme; Editor, Wendy Greene Bricmont; Co-Producer, Louise Rosner; Casting, Marci Liroff; Dolby; Deluxe color; Rated PG-13; 97 minutes; Release date: April 30, 2004

Tim Meadows, Tina Fey

Cast

Cady Heron **Lindsay Lohan**
Regina George **Rachel McAdams**
Ms. Norbury **Tina Fey**
Mr. Duvall **Tim Meadows**
Mrs. George **Amy Poehler**
Cady's Mom **Ana Gasteyer**
Gretchen Wieners **Lacey Chabert**
Janis Ian **Lizzy Caplan**
Damian **Daniel Franzese**
Cady's Dad **Neil Flynn**
Aaran Samuels **Jonathan Bennett**
Karen Smith **Amanda Seyfried**
Kevin Gnapoor **Rajiv Surendra**
Spelling Girl **Elana Shilling**
Homeschooled Boys **Graham Kartna, Ely Henry**
African Warrior **Ayo Agbonkpolo**
Kristen Hadley **Molly Shanahan**
Kristen's Boyfriend **Jonathan Malen**
"Farting" Guy **Jeff Moser**
Michigan Girl **Miranda Edwards**
Chemistry Teacher **Les Porter**
English Teacher **Eve Crawford**
History Teacher **Jack Newman**
Music Teacher **Michelyn Emelle**
German Teacher **Bathsheba Garnett**

Lindsay Lohan, Lizzy Caplan, Daniel Franzese

and Ky Pham (Trang Pak), Danielle Nguyen (Sun Jin Dinh), Daniel Desanto (Jason), Alisha Morrison (Lea Edwards), Chris Poszczansky (Huge Guy), Dwayne Hill (Coach Carr), Diego Klattenhoff (Shane Oman), Jan Caruana (Emma Gerber), Wai Choy (Mathlete Tim Pak), Julia Chantrey (Amber D'Alessio), Jacky Chamberlain (Giselle Sgro), Olympia Lukis (Jessica Lopez), Stefanie Drummond (Bethany Byrd), Kristen Bone (Short Girl),

Amy Poehler PHOTOS COURTESY OF PARAMOUNT

Amanda Seyfried, Rachel McAdams, Lacey Chabert, Lindsay Lohan

Lindsay Lohan, Lizzy Caplan, Daniel Franzese

Jessie Wright (Cady 5 Years Old), Tyson Fennell (Nfume), Stephan Dixon, Andreja Punkris, Noelle Boggio, Jordan Dawe (Animal Dancers), Alexandra Stapley (Taylor Wedell), Laura Decarteret (Taylor Wedell's Mom), Nicole Crimi (Kylie George), Erin Thompson (Dawn Schweitzer), Dan Willmott (Mr. George), Michelle Hoffmann, Valerie Casault (Kissing Girls), Sharron Matthews (Joan the Secretary), Jo Chim (Salesperson), Randi Lee Butcher, Erin Jarvis (Skater Girls), Kaylen Christensen (Jock Girl), Jill Morrison (Crying Girl), David Sazant (Marymount Captain), Clare Preuss (Caroline Krafft), Bruce Hunter (Mathlete Moderator), Megan Millington, Tara Shelley, Shannon Todd (Junior Plastics)

A newcomer to high school finds herself accepted by a vicious clique of popular and self-involved girls calling themselves the Queen Bees.

Jonathan Bennett, Lindsay Lohan

Lacey Chabert, Rachel McAdams, Lindsay Lohan, Amanda Seyfried

VAN HELSING

(UNIVERSAL) Producers, Stephen Sommers, Bob Ducsay; Executive Producer, Sam Mercer; Director/Screenplay, Stephen Sommers; Photography, Allen Daviau; Designer, Allan Cameron; Costumes, Gabriella Pescucci, Carlo Poggioli; Music, Alan Silvestri; Editors, Bob Ducsay, Kelly Matsumoto; Special Visual Effects & Animation, Industrial Light & Magic; Visual Effects Supervisors, Ben Snow, Scott Squires; Animation Supervisor, Daniel Jeannette; Special Makeup Creator, Greg Cannom; Casting, Priscilla John, Ellen Lewis, Joanna Colbert; Stunts, R.A. Rondell; a Sommers Company production; Dolby; Technicolor; Rated PG-13; 132 minutes; Release date: May 7, 2004

Hugh Jackman, Kate Beckinsale

Cast
Gabriel Van Helsing **Hugh Jackman**
Anna Valerious **Kate Beckinsale**
Count Vladislaus Dracula **Richard Roxburgh**
Carl **David Wenham**
Frankenstein's Monster **Shuler Hensley**
Aleera **Elena Anaya**
Velkan **Will Kemp**
Igor **Kevin J. O'Connor**
Cardinal Jinette **Alun Armstrong**
Verona **Silvia Colloca**
Marishka **Josie Maran**
Top Hat **Tom Fisher**
Dr. Victor Frankenstein **Samuel West**
Mr. Hyde **Robbie Coltrane**
Doctor Jekyll **Stephen H. Fisher**
Barmaid **Dana Moravkova**
Opera Singer **Zuzana Durdinova**
Gendarme **Jaroslav Vizner**
Villager **Marek Vasut**
Vampire Child **Samantha Sommers**
Dracula's Ball Performers **Dorel Mois, Marianna Mois,
   Laurence Racine, Patrice Wojciechowski**

Gabriel Van Helsing travels to Transylvania to put a stop to the nefarious vampire Count Dracula before he can kill off the last descendent of a powerful royal family.

David Wenham, Hugh Jackman, Shuler Hensley

Will Kemp, Kate Beckinsale

Elena Anaya, Richard Roxburgh, Silvia Colloca PHOTOS COURTESY OF UNIVERSAL

Morgan Spurlock

SUPER SIZE ME

(SAMUEL GOLDWYN CO.) Producer/Director, Morgan Spurlock; Executive Producers, J.R. Morley, Heather Winters; Photography, Scot Ambrozy; Music, Steve Horowitz, Michael Parrish; Editors, Stela Guerguieva, Julie "Bob" Lombardi; Art Director/Animations, Joe the Artist; Color; HD camera; 98 minutes; Release date: May 7, 2004. Documentary in which filmmaker Morgan Spurlock decides to eat only from the McDonald's menu for a thirty-day period.

Morgan Spurlock

Morgan Spurlock

With

Morgan Spurlock, John F. Banzhaf III, Bridget Bennett, Kelly Brownell, Ron English, Jared Fogle, Dr. Lisa Ganjhu, Don Gorske, Mary Gorske, Samuel Hirsch, Dr. Daryl Isaacs, "Healthy Chef" Alex Jamieson, William Kirsh, Marion Nestle, John Robbins, Ashley Sandy, Kacie Sandy, Laura Sandy, Dr. David Satcher, Dr. Stephen Siegel, Kymme Simchak, Jacob Sullum, Tommy Thompson, Dr. Lisa Young

This film received an Oscar nomination for documentary feature.

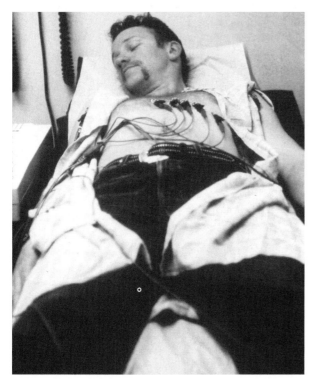

Morgan Spurlock

Morgan Spurlock PHOTOS COURTESY OF ROADSIDE ATTRACTIONS AND SAMUEL GOLDWYN

THE MUDGE BOY

(STRAND) Producers, Elizabeth W. Alexander, Alison Benson, Randy Ostrow; Executive Producer, Stanley Tucci; Director/Screenplay, Michael Burke; Photography, Vajna Cernjul; Designer, David Doernberg; Costumes, Toni Fusco; Music, Marcelo Zarvos; Editor, Alfonso Goncalves; Line Producer, George Paaswell; Associate Producer, Kevin Burke; Casting, Kathleen Choipin, Michele Ortlip; a Showtime presentation of a First Cold Press production; Dolby; Color; Not rated; 94 minutes; Release date: May 7, 2004

Emile Hirsch

Emile Hirsch

Tom Guiry

Cast

Duncan Mudge **Emile Hirsch**
Perry Foley **Tom Guiry**
Edgar Mudge **Richard Jenkins**
Brent **Pablo Schreiber**
Travis **Zachary Knighton**
Scotty **Ryan Donowho**
Tonya **Meredith Handerhan**
April **Beckie King**
Juster **John Alexander**
Drunken Teen **Macklen Makhloghi**
Hay Bailer **Joshua J. Masters**

A sensitive farm boy tries to cope with the unexpected death of his mother, falling in with some wayward teens, including Perry Foley, on whom he develops a crush.

Tom Guiry, Emile Hirsch PHOTOS COURTESY OF STRAND

COFFEE AND CIGARETTES

(UNITED ARTISTS) Producers, Joana Vicente, Jason Kliot; Not the Executive Producer, Bart Walker; Co-Producers, Stacey Smith, Gretchen McGowan; Director/Screenplay, Jim Jarmusch; Photography, Frederick Elmes, Ellen Kuras, Robby Müller, Tom DiCillo; Designers, Mark Friedberg, Tom Jarmusch, Dan Bishop; Editors, Jay Rabinowitz, Melody London, Terry Katz, Jim Jarmusch; Associate Producer, Rachel Dengiz; a Smokescreen presentation in association with Asmik Ace and BIM Distribuzione; Dolby; Black and white; Rated R; 96 minutes; Release date: May 14, 2004

Steven Wright, Roberto Benigni

Cast

Roberto **Roberto Benigni**
Steven **Steven Wright**
Good Twin **Joie Lee**
Evil Twin/Kitchen Guy **Cinqué Lee**
Waiter **Steve Buscemi**
Iggy **Iggy Pop**
Tom **Tom Waits**
Joe **Joe Rigano**
Vinny **Vinny Vella**
Vinny Jr. **Vinny Vella, Jr.**
Renée **Renée French**
Waiter **E.J. Rodriguez**
Alex **Alex Descas**
Isaach **Isaach De Bankolé**
Cate/Shelly **Cate Blanchett**
Waiter **Mike Hogan**
Jack **Jack White**
Meg **Meg White**
Alfred **Alfred Molina**
Steve **Steve Coogan**
Katy **Katy Hansz**
GZA **GZA**
RZA **RZA**
Bill Murray **Bill Murray**
Bill **Bill Rice**
Taylor **Taylor Mead**

Alfred Molina, Steve Coogan

Cate Blanchett

A series of offbeat discussions and vignettes revolving around coffee and cigarettes, each segment filmed at varying times since 1986.

GZA, RZA, Bill Murray PHOTOS COURTESY OF UNITED ARTISTS

Shrek, Puss in Boots

SHREK 2

(DREAMWORKS) Producers, Aron Warner, David Lipman, John H. Williams; Executive Producer, Jeffrey Katzenberg; Directors, Andrew Adamson, Kelly Asbury, Conrad Vernon; Screenplay, Andrew Adamson, Joe Stillman, J. David Stern, David N. Weiss; Story, Andrew Adamson; Based upon the book *Shrek* by William Steig; Music, Harry Gregson-Williams; Music Supervisor, Chris Douridas; Editors, Michael Andrews, Sim Evan-Jones; Designer, Guillaume Aretos; Visual Effects Supervisor, Ken Bielenberg; Art Director, Steve Pilcher; Supervising Animators, Raman Hui, Tim Cheung, James Baxter; Character Design, Tom Hester; Casting, Leslee Feldman; a PDI/DreamWorks production; Dolby; Technicolor; Rated PG; 88 minutes; Release date: May 19, 2004

Voice Cast
Shrek **Mike Myers**
Donkey **Eddie Murphy**
Princess Fiona **Cameron Diaz**
Queen **Julie Andrews**
Puss in Boots **Antonio Banderas**
King **John Cleese**
Prince Charming **Rupert Everett**
Fairy Godmother **Jennifer Saunders**
Wolf **Aron Warner**
Page/Elf/Nobleman/Nobleman's Son **Kelly Asbury**
Pinocchio/Three Pigs **Cody Cameron**
Gingerbread Man/Cedric/Announcer/
  MuffinMan/Mongo **Conrad Vernon**
Blind Mouse **Christopher Knights**
Herald/Man with Box **David P. Smith**
Mirror/Dresser **Mark Moseley**
Fast Food Clerk **Kelly Cooney**
Bar Frog **Wendy Bilanski**

Prince Charming, Fairy Godmother

and Larry King (Ugly Stepsister), Guillaume Aretos (Receptionist), Chris Miller (Humphries/Magic Mirror), Latifa Ouaou (Doll/Jill), Alina Phelan (Maiden #1/Generic Female #2), Erika Thomas (Maiden #2), Joan Rivers (Herself), Andrew Adamson (Captain of the Guards)

Queen, King

Shocked that his daughter and her new husband are both ogres, the King enlists the aide of Fairy Godmother, Prince Charming, and Puss in Boots to set things right. Sequel to the 2001 film *Shrek* (DreamWorks), with Myers, Murphy, and Diaz repeating their roles.

This film received Oscar nominations for animated feature and original song ("Accidentally in Love").

Shrek, Princess Fiona, Donkey PHOTOS COURTESY OF DREAMWORKS

CONTROL ROOM

(MAGNOLIA) Producers, Rosadel Varela, Hani Salama; Executive Producers, Noujaim Varela, Abdullah Schleifer; Director, Jehane Noujaim; Photography, Jehane Noujaim, Hani Salama; Music Supervisor, Mona Eldaief; Associate Producer, Bent-Jorgen Perlmutt; Editor, Julia Bacha; a Noujaim Films production; Color; Not rated; 85 minutes; Release date: May 21, 2004.

Documentary on independent Arab news service Al-Jazeera, featuring Samir Khader, Lt. Josh Rushing, Hassan Ibrahim, Deema Khatib, Tom Mintier, David Shuster

Al-Jazeera anchorwoman PHOTO COURTESY OF AL JEZEERA SATELLITE NETWORK

Lt. Josh Rushing

Samir Khader

Hassan Ibrahim PHOTOS COURTESY OF MAGNOLIA PICTURES

Deema Khatib

Hayden Panettiere, Abigail Breslin, Kate Hudson, Spencer Breslin

RAISING HELEN

(TOUCHSTONE) Producers, Ashok Amritraj, David Hoberman; Executive Producers, Mario Iscovich, Ellen H. Schwartz; Director, Garry Marshall; Screenplay, Jack Amiel, Michael Begler; Story, Patrick J. Clifton, Beth Rigazo; Photography, Charles Minsky; Designer, Steven Jordan; Costumes, Gary Jones; Music, John Debney; Music Supervisor, Dawn Soler; Editors, Bruce Green, Tara Timpone; Co-Producers, Todd Lieberman, Karen Stirgwolt; Casting, Mali Finn; a Beacon Pictures presentation; Distributed by Buena Vista; Dolby; Technicolor; Rated PG-13; 119 minutes; Release date: May 28, 2004

Cast

Helen Harris **Kate Hudson**
Pastor Dan Parker **John Corbett**
Jenny Portman **Joan Cusack**
Audrey Davis **Hayden Panettiere**
Henry Davis **Spencer Breslin**
Sarah Davis **Abigail Breslin**
Dominique **Helen Mirren**
Mickey Massey **Hector Elizondo**
Lindsay **Felicity Huffman**

and Sakina Jaffrey (Nilma Prasad), Ed Portman (Kevin Kilner), Sean O'Bryan (Paul Davis), Amber Valletta (Martina), Ethan Browne (Devon), Michael Esparza (BZ), Katie Carr (Caitlin), Shakara Ledard (Tinka), Jane Morris (Landlord), Joseph Mazzello (Prom Date Peter), Catherine Tayrien (Jasmine Portman), Evan Sabara (Oliver Portman), Paris Hilton (Amber); Sandra Taylor (Lacey), Wesley Horton (Gary Hagelnick), Bernie Hiller (Jean Paul), Shanda Renee (Intern Mary), Brigitta Lauren (Simone), Shannon Wilcox (Photographer), Matthew Walker (Fashion Show Security), Kelli Clendion, Jacki Tenerelli, Erinn Bartlett, Tonje Larsgard (Fashion Show Models), Daru Kawalkowski (Martina's Agent); *New York Life*: Alec Nemser (Hippo Waiter), James Hanlon (Restaurant Maitre'd), Sunny Hawks (Kyra), Jason Olive (Chip), Anthony Mangano (Club Doorman), Scott Marshall (Club DJ), Ellen H. Schwartz (Club Line Girl), Joseph Leo Bwarie (Club Bartender), Sarina Ranftl (Restaurant Waitress), Erica Lookadoo (Devon's Friend), Marvin Braverman (Hot Dog Vendor Aaron), Rio Hackford (Brunch Maitre'd), Joy Rosenthal, Isadora O'Boto (Brunch Patrons), Karina Calabro (Brunch Waitress), Matias Masucci (Karaoke MC), Julie Schubert (Karaoke Bartender), Tracy Reiner, Marlyn Mason, Steve Totland, Eric J. Olson (Job Interviewers), Catherine McCord (Lola Model), Micky Hoogen (Make-Up Trailer Model); *New Jersey Life*:

Julie Paris (Real Estate Woman), Larry J. Robbins, Made Miller (Lawyers), Joe Allen Price, Peggy Crosby, Ronny Hallin, Barbara Nabozny, Frank Campanella, Herbert Malina, Steve Nave, Kamilla Bjorlin, Ron Rogge, Norma Jean Jahn (Mourners), Barbara Marshall, Terry Brown (Neighbors); *Queens Life*: Bob Jacobs, Artir Sax (Bridge Chair Guys), Alan Thicke (Hockey Cantor), Gary Jones (Hockey Ref "Scotty Buttons"), Mark DeCarlo (Hockey Rabbi), Joe Unitas (Hockey Announcer), Charles Guardino (News Vendor), Steve Restivo (Motel Manager), Lisa Roberts Gillan (Zoo Reporter), Jared Brown (Zoo Tour Guide), John Cooney (Zoo Cameraman), Cassius Wilkinson, Jamila Wilkinson (Nilma's Kids); *Queens School*: Kathleen Marshall (Mrs. LaGambina), Tom Hines (Pastor Wells), David Scharf (Prom DJ), Ira Glick (Basketball Referee), Lauri Labeau (Basketball Coach), Cassie Rowell (Basketball Nurse), Gwenda Perez (Basketball Parent), Spencer Perez (Basketball Student), Brady Woods, Erik Bragg, Emily Hart, Claudia Vazquez (Audrey's Friends), Joie Shttler (Vesper's Mom), Lori Marshall (Brownie Mom), Lily Marshall-Fricker, Charlotte Marshall-Fricker (Kindergarten Kids), Kerry Palmisano, Blake Ewing, Sterling Jennings, Pamela Kilroy, Daniel Cathers, Jenna Reni Zuccari, Dedzidi Ladzekpo, Allison Norton, Kelly Durban, Sarah Hahn, Emily Alonson, Michael Ullerick, Aaron Anderson, Josiah Bartel (Church Choir), Mark Vogel (Choir Director); *Massey Motors*: Bernard White (Ravi), Rowan Joseph (Ralphy), Pamela Zane (Renee DeCarlo), Scott Crumly (Car Washer), Grace Nassar (New Receptionist), Larry Miller (car buyer)

John Corbett, Kate Hudson

Helen Harris's whirlwind life working for one of Manhattan's top modelling agencies comes to a halt when she is made the guardian of her late sister's three children.

Felicity Huffman, Kate Hudson, Joan Cusack PHOTOS COURTESY OF TOUCHSTONE

SAVED!

(UNITED ARTISTS) Producers, Michael Stipe, Sandy Stern, Michael Ohoven, William Vince; Director, Brian Dannelly; Screenplay, Brian Dannelly, Michael Urban; Photography, Bobby Bukowski; Designer, Tony Devenyi; Costumes, Wendy Chuck; Music, Christophe Beck; Music Supervisor, Jon Leshay; Co-Executive Producers, Kerry Rock, David Prybil, Kaye Dyal, Steven Gagnon; Line Producer, Cal Shumiatcher; Canadian Casting, Coreen Mayrs, Heike Brandstatter; a Single Cell Pictures and Infinity Media production; Distributed by MGM Distribution Co.; Dolby; Deluxe color; Rated PG-13; 92 minutes; Release date: May 28, 2004

Chad Faust, Kett Turton

Martin Donovan, Mary-Louise Parker

Cast

Mary	**Jena Malone**
Hilary Faye	**Mandy Moore**
Roland	**Macaulay Culkin**
Patrick	**Patrick Fugit**
Tia	**Heather Matarazzo**
Cassandra	**Eva Amurri**
Dean	**Chad Faust**
Veronica	**Elizabeth Thai**
Pastor Skip	**Martin Donovan**
Lillian	**Mary-Louise Parker**
Mitch	**Kett Turton**
PE Coach	**Julia Arkos**
Trudy Mason	**Donna White**
Hairdresser	**James Caldwell**
Guitar Player	**Nicki Clyne**
Paramedic	**Aaron Douglas**
Dean's Mother	**Patricia Drake**
Church Man	**Brent Fidler**

and Jay Hilliker (Waiter/Host), John Innes (Pastor), Greg Kean (Dean's Father), Joe MacLeod (Lead Singer), Althea McAdam (Church Wife), Thomas Plustwik (Carpenter/Jesus), Syndie Skeeles (3-Year Old Mary), Susan Wilkey (Pink Bouffant Lady), Valerie Bertinelli (Herself)

Mary enters her senior year at American Eagle Christian High School with the news that her boyfriend is gay and she's pregnant.

Jena Malone, Macaulay Culkin, Mandy Moore

Jena Malone, Patrick Fugit PHOTOS COURTESY OF UNITED ARTISTS

THE DAY AFTER TOMORROW

(20TH CENTURY FOX) Producers, Mark Gordon, Roland Emmerich; Executive Producers, Ute Emmerich, Kelly Van Horn, Stephanie Germain; Director/Story, Roland Emmerich; Screenplay, Roland Emmerich, Jeffrey Nachmanoff; Suggested in part by the book *The Coming Global Superstorm* by Art Bell & Whitley Strieber; Photography, Ueli Steiger; Designer, Barry Chusid; Costumes, Renee April; Film Editor, David Brenner; Co-Producer, Thomas M. Hammel; Visual Effects Supervisor, Karen E. Goulekas; Music, Harald Kloser; Stunts, Charlie Breweer, Branko Racki; a Centropolis Entertainment/Lions Gate/Mark Gordon Company production; Dolby; Deluxe color; Rated PG-13; 124 minutes; Release date: May 28, 2004

Dennis Quaid, Dash Miho

Cast

Jack Hall	**Dennis Quaid**
Sam Hall	**Jake Gyllenhaal**
Laura Chapman	**Emmy Rossum**
Jason Evans	**Dash Mihok**
Frank Harris	**Jay O. Sanders**
Dr. Lucy Hall	**Sela Ward**
J.D.	**Austin Nichols**
Brian Parks	**Arjay Smith**
Janet Tokada	**Tamlyn Tomita**
Parker	**Sasha Roiz**
Terry Rapson	**Ian Holm**
Saudi Delegate	**Nassim Sharara**
Venezuelan Delegate	**Carl Alacchi**
Vice President Becker	**Kenneth Welsh**
Saudi Translator	**Michael A. Samah**
Tony	**Robin Wilcock**
Paul	**Jason Blicker**
Bob	**Kenneth Moskow**
Taka	**Tim Hamaguchi**

and Glenn Plummer (Luther), Adrian Lester (Simon), Richard McMillan (Dennis), Nester Serrano (Gomez), Sylvain Landry (Science Officer), Chris Britton (Vorsteen), Vlasta Vrana (Booker, MPC), Pauline Little (Lanson, SSL), Alan Fawcett (Commander Daniels, Hurricane Hunter), Howard Bilerman (Rookie Scientist, Hurricane Hunter), John MacLaren (Veteran Scientist, Hurrican Hunter), Frank Schoprion (DC Fireman), Rachelle Glait (Pinehurst Academy Teacher), Pierre LeBlanc (International Reporter—New Delhi), Richard Zeman (Fight Director), Perry King (President Blake), Frank Fontaine (Caddy "Cooper"), Mimi Kuzyk (Secretary of State), Al Vandecruys (Scholastic Decathlon Referee), Vitali Makarov (Yuri, Russian Astronaut), Russell Yuen (Hideki, Japanese Astronaut), Tim Bagley (Tommy), Pierre Lenoir (J.D.'s Doorman), Don Kirk (Victor, J.D.'s Driver), Lisa Canning (L.A. Anchorwoman), Terry Rhoads (L.A. Anchorman), Nicolas Feller (Shop Owner Grandson), J.P. Manoux (LA Cameraman), Chuck Shamata (General Pierce), Phillip Jarrett (Campbell), Tetchena Bellange (Jama), Tony Calabretta (Cabbie), Vivian Winther (Noel, Frozen Woman), Sheila McCarthy (Judith), Tom Rooney (Jeremy), Amy Sloan (Elsa), David Schaap (Financial Reporter), Marylou Belugou (Binata), Nobuya Shimamoto (Japanese Policeman), Bunrey Miyake (Japanese Shop Owner), Karen Glave (Maria), Jennifer Morehouse (French Reporter), Christian Tessier (Aaron), Joe Cobden (Zack), Caroline Kennan-Wiseman (Tina), Aaron Lustig (Bernie), Sam Woods (Mr. Walden), Jesús "Choy" Pérez (Mexican, NWS Janitor), Jack Laufer (Jeff Baffin), Luke Letourneau (Peter), John Moore (New York Reporter), William Francis McGuire (Bart Chopper Reporter), Michael McNally (Buckingham Palace Reporter), Anne Day-Jones (Jeanette), Emanuel Hoss-Desmarais (Cecil), Lynne Debel (Old Frozen Woman), Mikio Owaki (Noodle Chef), Terry Simpson (Cesar), Alvin Tam (Japanese Reporter), Joey Elias (Library Security Guard), Ron Darling (Hawaiian News Anchor), Jose Ramon Rosario (Cabbie, "Crazy Weather"), Kwasi Songui (Statue of Liberty Guard), John C. Colton, Dilva Henry (Fox Newscasters), Mark Thompson (News Reporter), Wendy L. Walsh, Mark Pfister (Weather Channel Newscasters), Ana Garcia (Headline Reporter), Lauren Sanchez (International Newscaster), Rob Fukuzaki (National Newscaster), Ross King (British Reporter), Robert Holguin, Suzanne Michaels (Reporters), Leyna Nguyen, Lina Patel (Newscasters), Rosey Edeh (New York Reporter), Lori Graham (Grocery Store Reporter), Jesse Todd (Scientist in Hallway), Gordon Masten (New York Bus Driver), Matt Adler (Truck Radio Announcer), Ray Légaré (Construction Man), Matt Holland, Greg Kramer, Joel McNichol (RAFs)

Global warming causes a cataclysmic shift in the planet's climate, bringing on a new Ice Age as half the Earth begins to freeze.

Emmy Rossum, Arjay Smith, Austin Nichols, Jake Gyllenhaal PHOTOS COURTESY OF 20TH CENTURY FOX

Rainn Wilson, Karimah Westbrook, Mario Van Peebles, Kate Krystowiak

BAADASSSSS!

(SONY CLASSICS) formerly *How to Get the Man's Foot Outta Your Ass*; Producer/Director, Mario Van Peebles; Screenplay, Mario Van Peebles, Dennis Haggerty; Based on the original book by Melvin Van Peebles; Executive Producers, Jerry Offsay, Michael Mann; Line Producer, Bruce Wayne Gillies; Co-Producer, Dennis Haggerty; Co-Executive Producer, Tobie Haggerty; Photography, Robert Primes; Designer, Alan E. Muraoka; Costumes, Kara Saun; Music, Tyler Bates; Music Supervisors, G. Marq Roswell, Garth Trinidad; Editors, Anthony Miller, Nneka Goforth; Casting, Anya Colloff, Amy McIntyre Britt; an MPVP Filmz production; Dolby; Color; Rated R; 108 minutes; Release date: May 28, 2004

Cast

Melvin Van Peebles **Mario Van Peebles**
Priscilla **Joy Bryant**
Bill Cosby **T.K. Carter**
Big T **Terry Crews**
Granddad **Ossie Davis**
Clyde **David Alan Grier**
Sandra **Nia Long**
Jose Garcia **Paul Rodriguez**
Howard "Howie" Kaufman **Saul Rubinek**
Jerry **Vincent Schiavelli**
Mario **Khleo Thomas**
Bill Harris **Rainn Wilson**
Ginnie **Karimah Westbrook**
Manny & Mort Goldberg **Len Lesser**
Roz **Sally Struthers**
Working Girl **Jazsmin Lewis**
Bert **Adam West**

and Ralph Martin (Tommy David), Robert Peters (Bob Maxwell), Glenn Plummer (Angry Brother), Khalil Kain (Maurice), Pamela Gordon (Ethel), Wesley Jonathan (Panther), Joseph Culp (Attorney), John Singleton (Detroit J), Joan Blair (Brenda), Penny Bae Bridges (Megan), Mandela Van Peebles (Angel Muse), E.J. Callahan (Bartender), Keith Diamond (Large Brother), Don Dowe (Officer), Brent Schaffer, Brian "Skinny B" Lewis

(Panthers), Mickey Mello (David), Christopher Michael (Journalist), Tyrone M. Mitchell, Alan James Morgan (Josh), David Alan Smith (Brewster), Nathan Wetherington (Jimmy), Robin Wilson (Excited Lady), Paul Roach (Pimpy Paul), Marley Van Peebles, Maya Van Peebles, Bridget Avildsen, Craig Jones (Trick or Treaters), Kate Krystowiak (Moonbeam), Anthony Rodriguez (Fernando), Thomas Longo (Camera Assistant), Robert Yosses (Script Supervisor), Danny Hebert (Crew Member), Michele Hill (Biker Girl), Les Miller (Nora), Bill Cosby, Melvin Van Peebles (Themselves), Troy Garity (Donovan)

Saul Rubinek, Mario Van Peebles

The true story of how filmmaker Melvin Van Peebles beat the odds to make the independent film *Sweet Sweetback's Baadasssss Song*, which became one of the seminal hits in the black film movement.

Joy Bryant, Terry Crews PHOTOS COURTESY OF SONY CLASSICS

HARRY POTTER
AND THE PRISONER OF AZKABAN

(WARNER BROS.) Producers, David Heyman, Chris Columbus, Mark Radcliffe; Executive Producers, Michael Barnathan, Callum McDougall, Tanya Seghatchian; Director, Alfonso Cuarón; Screenplay, Steve Kloves; Based on the novel by J.K. Rowling; Photography, Michael Seresin; Designer, Stuart Craig; Costumes, Jany Temime; Music, John Williams; Editor, Steven Weisberg; Visual Effects Supervisors, Roger Guyett, Tim Burke; Creature & Makeup Effects Designer, Nick Dudman; Casting, Jina Jay; a Heyday Films/1492 Pictures production; Dolby; Widescreen; Technicolor; Rated PG; 141 minutes; Release date: June 4, 2004

Daniel Radcliffe

Gary Oldman

Cast

Harry Potter **Daniel Radcliffe**
Ron Weasley **Rupert Grint**
Hermione Granger **Emma Watson**
Rubeus Hagrid **Robbie Coltrane**
Albus Dumbledore **Michael Gambon**
Sirius Black **Gary Oldman**
Professor Severus Snape **Alan Rickman**
Aunt Petunia **Fiona Shaw**
Professor Minerva McGonagall **Maggie Smith**
Peter Pettigrew **Timothy Spall**
Professor Lupin **David Thewlis**
Professor Sybil Trelawney **Emma Thompson**
Mrs. Molly Weasley **Julie Walters**
Uncle Vernon **Richard Griffiths**
Draco Malfoy **Tom Felton**
Cornelius Fudge **Robert Hardy**
Wizard **Warwick Davis**
Argus Filch **David Bradley**
Neville Longbottom **Matthew Lewis**
Madame Rosmerta **Julie Christie**
Aunt Marge **Pam Ferris**
Dudley Dursley **Harry Melling**

Michael Gambon

Emma Watson, Rupert Grint, Alan Rickman, Daniel Radcliffe

Daniel Radcliffe, Rupert Grint

David Thewlis

James Potter **Adrian Rawlins**
Lily Potter **Geraldine Somerville**
Stan Shunpike **Lee Ingleby**
Shrunken Head **Lenny Henry**
Ernie the Bus Driver **Jimmy Gardner**
Tom the Innkeeper **Jim Tavare**
Young Witch Maid **Abby Ford**
George Weasley **Oliver Phelps**
Fred Weasley **James Phelps**
Percy Weasley **Chris Rankin**
Ginny Weasley **Bonnie Wright**
Mr. Arthur Weasley **Mark Williams**
Seamus Finnegan **Devon Murray**
Parvati Patel **Sitara Shah**
Lavender Brown **Jennifer Smith**
Slytherin Boy **Bronson Webb**
Gregory Goyle **Josh Herdman**
Pansy Parkinson **Genevieve Gaunt**

and Kandice Morris, Sharon Sandhu (Girls), Alfred Enoch (Dean Thomas), Dawn French (Fat Lady in Painting), Annalisa Bugliani (Mother in Portrait), Tess Bu Cuarón (Baby in Portrait), Violet Columbus (Girl with Flowers), Paul Whitehouse (Sir Cadogan), Ekow Quartey, Rick Sahota (Boys), Jamie Waylett (Vincent Crabbe), Danielle Tabor (Angelina Johnson), Freddie Davis (Old Man in Portrait), Peter Best (The Executioner)

Emma Watson, Daniel Radcliffe, Rupert Grint

Boy wizard Harry Potter is told that his life is in danger when a dangerous wizard, Sirius Black, escapes from Azkaban Prison. Third in the WB series following *Harry Potter and the Sorcerer's Stone/Harry Potter and the Philosopher's Stone* (2001) and *Harry Potter and the Chamber of Secrets* (2002), with most of the cast repeating their roles. Michael Gambon replaces the late Richard Harris as Dumbledore.

This film received Oscar nominations for score and special visual effects.

Emma Watson, Emma Thompson PHOTOS COURTESY OF WARNER BROS.

THE CHRONICLES OF RIDDICK

(UNIVERSAL) Producers, Scott Kroopf, Vin Diesel; Executive Producers, Ted Field, George Zakk, David Womark; Director/Screenplay, David Twohy; Based on characters created by Jim & Ken Wheat; Photography, Hugh Johnson; Designer, Holger Gross; Costumes, Ellen Mirojnick, Michael Dennison; Editors, Martin Hunter, Dennis Virkler; Music, Graeme Revell; Co-Executive Producer, Tom Engelman; Visual Effects Supervisor, Peter Chiang; Visual Effects Producer, Kimberly Nelson Locascio; Casting, Anne McCarthy; a Radar Pictures/One Race Films production; Dolby; Panavision; Techincolor; Rated PG-13; 119 minutes; Release date: June 11, 2004

Cast

Riddick **Vin Diesel**
Lord Marshall **Colm Feore**
Dame Vaako **Thandie Newton**
Aereon **Judi Dench**
Vaako **Karl Urban**
Kyra **Alexa Davalos**
Purifier **Linus Roache**
The Guv **Yorick van Wageningen**
Toombs **Nick Chinlund**
Imam **Keith David**

and Mark Gibbon (Irgun), Terry Chen (Merc Pilot), Christina Cox (Eve Logan), Nigle Vonas, Shawn Reis, Fabian Gujral, Ty Olsson (Mercs), Peter Williams, Darcy Laurie, John Mann, P. Adrien Dorval (Convicts), Alexander Kalugin (Slam Boss), Douglas H. Arthurs, Vitaliy Kravchenko, Ron Selmour, Raoul Ganeev, Mark Acheson, Shohan Felber, Ben Cotton (Slam Guards), Kim Hawthorne (Lajjun), Alexis Llewellyn (Ziza), Charles Zuckermann (Scales), Andy Thompson (Scalp Taker), Cedric de Souza (Black Robed/Meccan Cleric), Ahmad Sharmrou, Stefano Colacitti (Black Robed Clerics), Mina Erian Mina (Coptic Cleric), John Prowse (Bump Pilot), Lorena Gale (Defense Minister), Christopher Heyerdahl, Rob Daly (Helion Politicos), Micasha Armstrong (Lead Meccan Officer), Aaron Douglas (Young Meccan Soldier), Colin Corrigan (Vault Officer)

Richard Riddick tries to stop the evil Lord Marshall from turning all humans into Necromongers and conquering the universe. Sequel to the 2000 film *Pitch Black* (USA) with Vin Diesel and Keith David repeating their roles.

Thandie Newton, Vin Diesel, Linus Roache PHOTO COURTESY OF UNIVERSAL

Breckin Meyer, Odie, Garfield, Jennifer Love Hewitt PHOTOS COURTESY OF 20TH CENTURY FOX

GARFIELD: THE MOVIE

(20TH CENTURY FOX) Producer, John Davis; Executive Producer, Neil Machlis; Director, Pete Hewitt; Screenplay, Joel Cohen, Alec Sokolow; Based on the comic strip created by Jim Davis; Photography, Dean Cundey; Designer, Alexander Hammond; Costumes, Marie France; Music, Christophe Beck; Music Supervisor, Spring Aspers; Editor, Peter Berger; Co-Producers, Michele Imperato Stabile, Brian Manis; Animation Supervisor, Chris Bailey; Casting, Risa Bramon Garcia, Brennan du Fresne; a David Entertainment Company production; Dolby; Deluxe color; Rated PG; 80 minutes; Release date: June 11, 2004

Cast

Jon **Breckin Meyer**
Liz **Jennifer Love Hewitt**
Happy Chapman **Stephen Tobolowsky**
Voice of Garfield **Bill Murray**
Wendell **Evan Arnold**
Christopher Mello **Mark Christopher Lawrence**
Miss True-Value **Vanessa Christelle**

and Daamen Krall (Announcer), Rufus Gifford, Randee Reicher, Ryan McKasson, Susan Moore (Dog Owners), Eve Brent (Mrs. Baker), Bill Hoag (Roy the Lodge Member), Michael Monks (Deputy Hopkins), Mel Rodriguez (Security Officer), Juliette Goglia (Little Girl), Ben Kronen (Older Man), Fabio Serafini (Red Cap), Jerry Hauck (Cop), Jerry Giles (Conductor), Evan Helmuth (Steward), Annalea Rawicz (Information Agent), Danny Gil, Frank Payne, Joe Ochman (Engineers), Leyna Nguyen (News Reporter), Joe Bays (Racoon Lodge Member), Danna Hansen (Older Woman), Joseph Edward Taylor (Frank), John F. Schaffer (Larry), Ariel Joseph Towne (Technician), Joseph Hale (Little Girl's Dad); VOICES: Nick Cannon (Louis), Alan Cumming (Persnikitty), David Eigenberg (Nermal), Brad Garrett (Luca), Jimmy Kimmel (Spanky), Debra Messing (Arelen), Richard Kind (Dad), Debra Jo Rupp (Mom Rat), Jordan Kaiser, Yatt Smith, Alyson Stoner (Kid Rats)

Garfield, a lazy, self-involved cat is horrified when his owner decides to purchase a dog to impress a veterinarian he hopes to date.

Glenn Close, Christopher Walken

CENTER: Matthew Broderick, Christopher Walken, Jon Lovitz

THE STEPFORD WIVES

(PARAMOUNT/DREAMWORKS) Producers, Scott Rudin, Donald De Line, Edgar J. Sherick, Gabriel Grunfeld; Executive Producers, Ron Bozman, Keri Lyn Selig; Director, Frank Oz; Screenplay, Paul Rudnick; Based on the book by Ira Levin; Photography, Rob Hahn; Designer, Jackson DeGovia; Costumes, Ann Roth; Editor, Jay Rabinowitz; Music, David Arnold; Music Supervisor, Randall Poster; Choreographer, Patricia Birch; Special Effects Coordinator, Steve Kirschoff; Casting, Juliet Taylor, Laura Rosenthal; a Scott Rudin/De Line Pictures production; Dolby; Deluxe color; Rated PG-13; 93 minutes; Release date: June 11, 2004

Cast

Joanna Eberhart **Nicole Kidman**
Walter Kresby **Matthew Broderick**
Bobbie Markowitz **Bette Midler**
Claire Wellington **Glenn Close**
Mike Wellington **Christopher Walken**
Roger Bannister **Roger Bart**
Jerry Harmon **David Marshall Grant**
Dave Markowitz **Jon Lovitz**

Pete Kresby **Dylan Hartigan**
Kimberly Kresby **Fallon Brooking**
Sarah Sunderson **Faith Hill**
Herb Sunderson **Matt Malloy**

and Kate Shindle (Beth Peters), Tom Riis Farrell (Stan Peters), Lorri Bagley (Charmaine Van Sant), Robert Stanton (Ted Van Sant), Lisa Masters (Carol Wainwright), Christopher Evan Welch (Ed Wainwright), Colleen Dunn (Marianne Stevens), Jason Kravits (Vic Stevens), Emily Wing (Additional Stepford Wife), C.S. Lee, Tony Torn (Additional Stepford Husbands), Mary Beth Peil (Helen Devlin), Andrea Anders (Heather), Mike White (Hank), Carrie Preston (Barbara), Billy Bush ("I Can Do Better" Host), Tyler McGuckin (Adam Markowitz), Nick Reidy (Ben Markowitz), Sebastian Rand (Max Markowitz), Tanoai Reed (Tonkiro), Blaise Corrigan, George Aguilar (Security Guards), Meredith Vieira ("Balance of Power" Host), Rick Holmes (Bob), KaDee Strickland (Tara), Larry King (Himself), Munro M. Bonnell (Stepford Guard), Michelle Durning (Nurse), Kenny Kosek, Will Woodard (Square Dance Musicians), Elizabeth Austin, Deanna Dys, Joanne DiMauro, Digene Farrar, Bernard Ferstenberg, James Peter Lynch, Shannon McGain, Cristin Mortenson, Elizabeth A. Patek, David Purves, Joseph Ricci, Mark Vaughn (Dancers)

Nicole Kidman, Bette Midler

FRONT ROW: Faith Hill, Roger Bart, Nicole Kidman   PHOTOS COURTESY OF PARAMOUNT/DREAMWORKS

Joanna Eberhart and Walter Kresby move to the suburban town of Stepford, where all the housewives seem eerily perfect and content to be subservient to their husbands. Remake of the 1975 Columbia film of the same name that starred Katharine Ross, Paula Prentiss, and Patrick O'Neal.

NAPOLEON DYNAMITE

(FOX SEARCHLIGHT) Producers, Jeremy Coon, Sean C. Covel, Chris Wyatt; Executive Producers, Jeremy Coon, Jory Weitz; Director, Jared Hess; Screenplay, Jared Hess, Jerusha Hess; Photography, Munn Powell; Designer, Cory Lorenzen; Costumes, Jerusha Hess; Music, John Swihart; Editor, Jeremy Coon; Casting, Jory Weitz; Dolby; Deluxe color; Rated PG ; 86 minutes; Release date: June 11, 2004

Emily Kennard, Haylie Duff

Jon Heder, Efren Ramirez

Cast

Napoleon Dynamite **Jon Heder**
Uncle Rico **Jon Gries**
Kip **Aaron Ruell**
Pedro Sanchez **Efren Ramirez**
Rex **Diedrich Bader**
Deb **Tina Majorino**
Grandma **Sandy Martin**
Summer **Haylie Duff**
Don **Trevor Snarr**
LaFawnduh Lucas **Shondrella Avery**
Randy **Bracken Johnson**
Starla **Carmen Brady**
Ilene **Ellen Dubin**
Jocks **J.C. Cunningham, James Smooth**
Lance **Brian Petersen**
Nathan **Brett Taylor**

and Tom Lefler (Principal Svadean), Elizabeth Miklavcic (Renae), Scott Thomas (Sheldon), Loria Badelli (Shoney), Emily Kennard (Trisha), Jamen Gunnell (Vern), Nanette Young (Corrina), Nano De Silva, Arturo De Silva (Cholos), Pat Donahue (Farmer), Dale Critchlow (Lyle), Tom Adams, Eldean Holliday, Arlando Larsen (FFA Judges), Mary Heers (Teacher), T.J. Adams, Jake Visser, Brady Stokes (Farm Boys), Thedora Peeterborg, Becky Demke (Secretaries), Julia Ruell (Girl on Bike), Tara Roach (Good Hand Club Dancer)

Tina Majorino, Jon Heder

Socially inept nerd Napoleon Dynamite goes through life on his own terms, oblivious to the gracelessness of his efforts, while his equally wimpy brother Kip attempts to romance a girl online and his misfit new friend Pedro is encouraged against all odds to run for class president.

Aaron Ruell, Jon Heder PHOTOS COURTESY OF FOX SEARCHLIGHT

Jerry Orbach

Carole Cook

Barbara Cook PHOTOS COURTESY OF DADA FILMS

BROADWAY: THE GOLDEN AGE BY THE LEGENDS WHO WERE THERE

(DADA FILMS) Producers, Rick McKay, Albert M. Tapper; Director/Screenplay/ Photography/Editor/Narrator, Rick McKay; Executive Producer, Georgia Frontiere; Co-Producers, Jamie deRoy, Anne L. Bernstein; Associate Producers, Jack Coco, Sandi Durell, Jane Klain, Richard Weigle; an Albert M. Tapper in association with Georgia Frontiere presentation; Dolby; Color; Not rated; 111 minutes; Release date: June 11, 2004. Documentary in which several performers and figures from the theatre community reminisce about Broadway from the 1930s to 1960s.

Carol Burnett

With

Edie Adams, Bea Arthur, Elizabeth Ashley, Alec Baldwin, Kaye Ballard, Betsy Blair, Tom Bosley, Carol Burnett, Kitty Carlisle Hart, Carol Channing, Betty Comden, Barbara Cook, Carole Cook, Hume Cronyn, Arlene Dahl, Charles Durning, Fred Ebb, Nanette Fabray, Cy Feuer, Betty Garrett, Ben Gazzara, Robert Goulet, Farley Granger, Adolph Green, Tammy Grimes, Uta Hagen, Julie Harris, Rosemary Harris, June Havoc, Jerry Herman, Mimi Hines, Al Hirschfeld, Celeste Holm, Sally Ann Howes, Kim Hunter, Jeremy Irons, Anne Jackson, Derek Jacobi, Lainie Kazan, John Kenley, Joan Kobin, Miles Kreuger, Martin Landau, Frank Langella, Angela Lansbury, Arthur Laurents, Carol Lawrence, Michele Lee, Hal Linden, Shirley MacLaine, Karl Malden, Donna McKechnie, Ann Miller, Liliane Montevecchi, Patricia Morison, Robert Morse, James Naughton, Patricia Neal, Phyllis Newman, Fayard Nicholas, Harold Nicholas, Jerry Orbach, Janis Paige, Don Pippin, Jane Powell, Hal Prince, John Raitt, Rex Reed, Elliott Reid, Charles Nelson Reilly, Diana Rigg, Chita Rivera, Tony Roberts, Mary Rodgers, Gena Rowlands, Eva Marie Saint, Marian Seldes, Vincent Sherman, Stephen Sondheim, Maureen Stapleton, Kim Stanley, Elaine Stritch, Tommy Tune, Leslie Uggams, Gwen Verdon, Betsy von Furstenberg, Eli Wallach, Fay Wray, Gretchen Wyler

Tom Hanks

Kennedy International Airport

Barry Shabaka Henley, Stanley Tucci, Tom Hanks, Corey Reynolds

Diego Luna, Tom Hanks, Kumar Pallana, Chi McBride

Tom Hanks (far right) PHOTOS COURTESY OF DREAMWORKS

THE TERMINAL

(DREAMWORKS) Producers, Walter F. Parkes, Laurie MacDonald, Steven Spielberg; Executive Producers, Patricia Whitcher, Jason Hoffs, Andrew Niccol; Director, Steven Spielberg; Screenplay, Sacha Gervasi, Jeff Nathanson; Story, Andrew Niccol, Sacha Gervasi; Photography, Janusz Kaminski; Designer, Alex McDowell; Costumes, Mary Zophres; Music, John Williams; Editor, Michael Kahn; Co-Producer, Sergio Mimica-Gezzan; Casting, Debra Zane; a Parkes/MacDonald presentation; Dolby; Technicolor; Rated PG-13; 128 minutes; Release date: June 18, 2004

Barry Shabaka Henley, Tom Hanks, Chi McBride, Diego Luna, Zoë Saldana

Cast

Viktor Navorski **Tom Hanks**
Amelia Warren **Catherine Zeta-Jones**
Frank Dixon **Stanley Tucci**
Mulroy **Chi McBride**
Enrique Cruz **Diego Luna**
Thurman **Barry Shabaka Henley**
Gupta Rajan **Kumar Pallana**
Torres **Zoë Saldana**
Salchak **Eddie Jones**
Karl Iverson **Jude Ciccolella**
Waylin **Corey Reynolds**

and Guillermo Diaz (Bobby Alima), Rini Bell (Nadia), Stephen Mendel (First Class Steward), Valera Nikolaev (Milodragovich), Michael Nouri (Max), Ana Maria Quintana, Bob Morrisey (Government Inspectors), Sasha Spielberg (Lucy), Susan Slome (Woman with Cart), Mik Scriba (Transportation Liaison), James Ishida (Yoshinoya Manager), Carlease Burke (Brookstone Manager), Stephon Fuller (Swatch Manager), Dan Finnerty (Discovery Store Manager), Anastasia Basil (La Perla Employee Julie), Lydia Blanco, Joseph Davis (Burger King Employees), Tonya Ivey (Godiva Employee), Kevin Mukherji (Soundworks Dave), John Eddins, Kenneth Choi, Cas Anvar, Conrad Pla, Danette MacKay, Ian Finlay, Janique Kearns (CBP Officers), Eddie Santiago (Man on Phone), Kevin Ryder (Businessman), Dusan Dukic (Young Drug Trafficker), Matt Holland (Ramada Inn Clerk), Benny Golson (Himself), Buster Williams (Bass), Mike

Tom Hanks

Catherine Zeta-Jones

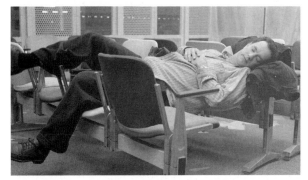

Tom Hanks

Ledonne (Piano), Carl Allen (Drums), Scott Adsit (Cab Driver), Robert Covarrubias (Janitor), Terry Haig (CPB Inspector), Jeff Michael, Dilva Henry (Anchors), Michelle Arthur (Field Reporter), Thinh Truong, Sandrine Kwan, Carl Alacchi, Tanya Van Blokland, Evelyen de la Chenelière (Passengers), Laurie Meghan Phelps (Homeland Security Officer)

After his homeland falls during a coup, Eastern European Viktor Navorski finds himself stranded at Kennedy International Airport, being unauthorized to actually set foot in the United States.

Vince Vaughn, Alan Tudyk, Chris Williams, Christine Taylor, Stephen Root, Justin Long

LB Denberg, Justin Long

Rip Torn, Stephen Root, Vince Vaughn, Alan Tudyk, Joel David Moore, Chris Williams, Justin Long PHOTOS COURTESY OF 20TH CENTURY FOX

DODGEBALL: A TRUE UNDERDOG STORY

(20TH CENTURY FOX) Producers, Ben Stiller, Stuart Cornfeld; Executive Producers, Mary McLaglen, Rhoades Rader; Director/Screenplay, Rawson Marshall Thurber; Photography, Jerzy Zielinski; Designer, Maher Ahmad; Costumes, Carol Ramsey; Editor, Alan Baumgarten; Music, Theodore Shapiro; Music Supervisor, George Drakoulias; Casting, Juel Bestrop, Jeanne McCarthy, Blythe Cappello; Stunts, Alex Daniels; a Red Hour production, presented in association with Mediastream IV; Dolby; Panavision; Deluxe color; Rated PG-13; 92 minutes; Release date: June 18, 2004

Vince Vaughn

Cast

Peter La Fleur **Vince Vaughn**
Kate Veatch **Christine Taylor**
White Goodman **Ben Stiller**
Patches O'Houlihan **Rip Torn**
Justin **Justin Long**
Gordon **Stephen Root**
Owen **Joel David Moore**
Dwight **Chris Williams**
Steve the Pirate **Alan Tudyk**
Fran **Missi Pyle**
Me'Shell Jones **Jamal E. Duff**
Cotton McKnight **Gary Cole**
Pepper Brooks **Jason Bateman**
Young Patches **Hank Azaria**
Tournament Referee **Al Kaplon**
Themselves **Lance Armstrong, Chuck Norris**
Dodgeball Chancellor **William Shatner**
German Coach **David Hasselhoff**
Amber **Julie Gonzalo**
Derek **Trever O'Brien**
Timmy **Cayden Boyd**
Blade **Rusty Joiner**
Lazer **Kevin Porter**
Blazer **Brandon Molale**

Gordon's Wife **Suzy Nakamura**
Martha Johnstone **LB Denberg**
Cheerleaders **Julia Ensign, David Boyd, Bowd J. Beal**
Mr. Ralph **Curtis Armstrong**
Waldorff Referee **Tate Chalk**
Angry Troop #417 Girl **Jordyn Colemon**
Crying Troop #417 Girl **Hayley Rosales**
Homeless Man **Bix Barnaba**
Elderly S&M Enthusiast **Earl Schuman**
S&M Man **Robert "Duckie" Carpenter**
Ronnie **Tony Daly**
Keno Waitress **Amy Stiller**
Weird Guy with Monster Truck **Jim Cody Williams**
Alec **John Kesler**
Bartender **Doug Grimes**
Joyce **Scarlett Chorvat**
Casino Worker #1 **Matt Levin**
High School Jerk **Rawson Thurber**
Friendly Bondage Master **Sik End**

Ben Stiller

Missi Pyle, Ben Stiller, Jamal E. Duff

Frustrated Cougars **Stephen B. Turner**, **Tim Soergel**
Uber Film Narrator **Andy Chanley**

In order to save his rundown gym from being purchased by egomaniacal fitness guru White Goodman, Peter La Fleur agrees to a showdown dodgeball competition.

Ben Stiller

Ben Stiller, Christine Taylor

FAHRENHEIT 9/11

(LIONS GATE/IFC) Producers, Jim Czarnecki, Kathleen Glynn, Michael Moore; Co-Producers, Jeff Gibbs, Kurt Engfehr; Supervising Producer, Tia Lessin; Director/Screenplay, Michael Moore; Photography, Mike Desjarlais; Music, Jeff Gibbs; Editors, Kurt Engfehr, Christopher Seward, T. Woody Richman; Chief Archivist/Field Producer, Carl Deal; a Dog Eat Dog and Wild Bunch presentation; Dolby; Technicolor; Rated R; 121 minutes; Release date: June 22, 2004. Documentary on George W. Bush's questionable handling of the terrorist attacks of September 11, 2001, and the subsequent war in Iraq.

George W. Bush

John Tanner, Michael Moore

Featuring

Michael Moore, Byron Dorgan, Abdul Henderson, Lila Lipscomb, Jim McDermott, Craig Unger, Helen Thomas, John T. Dolittle, John Tanner

George W. Bush

Michael Moore, Lila Lipscomb

George W. Bush PHOTOS COURTESY OF LIONS GATE/IFC

Secret Serviceman, Michael Moore

George W. Bush (center)

George W. Bush

Military recruiter

Sgt. Abdul Henderson, Michael Moore

WHITE CHICKS

(COLUMBIA) Producers, Keenen Ivory Wayans, Shawn Wayans, Marlon Wayans, Rick Alvarez, Lee R. Mayes; Director, Keenen Ivory Wayans; Screenplay, Keenen Ivory Wayans, Shawn Wayans, Marlon Wayans, Andy McElfresh, Michael Anthony Snowden, Xavier Cook; Story, Keenen Ivory Wayans, Shawn Wayans, Marlon Wayans; Photography, Steven Bernstein; Designer, Paul R. Peters; Costumes, Jori Woodman; Music, Teddy Castellucci; Music Supervision, Lisa Brown; Make-Up Effects Creators, Greg Cannom, Keith Vanderlaan; Casting, Lisa Beach, Sarah Katzman; a Revolution Studios presentation of a Wayan Bros. production; Dolby; Deluxe color; Rated PG-13; 108 minutes; Release date: June 22, 2004

Cast

Kevin Copeland **Shawn Wayans**
Marcus Copeland **Marlon Wayans**
Heather Vandergeld **Jaime King**
Section Chief Elliott Gordon **Frankie Faison**
Agent Jake Harper **Lochlyn Munro**
Warren Vandergeld **John Heard**
Karen **Busy Philipps**
Latrell Spencer **Terry Crews**
Megan Vandergeld **Brittany Daniel**
Agent Vincent Gomez **Eddie Velez**
Tori **Jessica Cauffiel**
Brittany Wilson **Maitland Ward**
Tiffany Wilson **Anne Dudek**
Denise Porter **Rochelle Aytes**
Lisa **Jennifer Carpenter**
Gina Copeland **Faune Chambers**
Heath **John Reardon**

and Steven Grayhm (Party Boy, Russ), Drew Sidora (Shaunice), Casey Lee (Tony), Heather McDonald (Saleswoman), Kevin Blatch (Aubrey), Taras Kostyuk (Russian), Zoltan Barabas (Drug Dealer), Brad Loree, Paul Lazenby (Dealer Henchmen), David Lewis (Josh), Suzy Joachim (Elaine Vandergeld), Kerbie O'Neill, Shannon Dagg, Jennifer Berry (Hamptons Girls), Patrick Baynham (Hamptons Guy), Kristi Angus (Wheelchair Girl),

Shawn Wayans, Marlon Wayans, Frankie Faison

Shawn Wayans, Anne Dudek, Maitland Ward, Marlon Wayans

Marshall Virtue (Purse Snatcher), Ryan Hesp, Dan Kelly (Young Men at Auction), Ricardo Scarabelli (FBI Agent), Fraser Aitcheson, James Michalopoulos (Strippers), Liam Ranger, Zack Nicholson (Young Boys), Luciana Carro (Waitress), Michael Shore (Waiter at Hamptons Restaurant), Lilliane Lee (Housekeeper), Melissa Panton, Kathryn Schellenberg (Karen's Backup Dancers), Heather Robertson, Joanne Pesusich, Jennifer Oleksiuk (Vandergeld Dance Team), David Manske (Fashion Critic), Ben Nemtin (Guy), Charlie (Baby the Dog)

A pair of FBI agents disguise themselves as a pair of high society Hamptons debutantes in order to investigate a kidnapping ring.

Drew Sidora PHOTOS COURTESY OF COLUMBIA

THE NOTEBOOK

(NEW LINE CINEMA) Producers, Mark Johnson, Lynn Harris; Executive Producers, Toby Emmerich, Avram Butch Kaplan; Director, Nick Cassavetes; Screenplay, Jeremy Leven; Adaptation, Jan Sardi; Based on the novel by Nicholas Sparks; Photography Robert Fraisse; Designer, Sarah Knowles; Costumes, Karyn Wagner; Music, Aaron Zigman; Editor, Alan Heim; Casting, Matthew Barry, Nancy Green-Keyes; a Gran Via production; Dolby; Panavision; Deluxe color; Rated PG-13; 123 minutes; Release date: June 25, 2004

James Garner, Gena Rowlands

Cast

Noah Calhoun **Ryan Gosling**
Allie Hamilton **Rachel McAdams**
Duke **James Garner**
Allie Calhoun **Gena Rowlands**
Lon Hammond **James Marsden**
Fin **Kevin Connolly**
John Hamilton **David Thornton**
Martha Shaw **Jamie Anne Brown**
Sara Tuffington **Heather Wahlquist**
Frank Calhoun **Sam Shepard**
Anne Hamilton **Joan Allen**
Rower **Tim Ivey**
Nurse Esther **Starletta DuPois**
Nurse Keith **Anthony-Michael Q. Thomas**
Harry **Ed Grady**
Nurse at Counter **Renée Amber**
Nurse Selma **Jennifer Echols**
Barker **Geoffrey Knight**
Matthew Jamison III **Andrew Schaff**
Seabrook Boys **Matt Shelly, Michael D. Fuller, Jonathan Parks Jordan**
Seabrook Girl **Leslea Fisher**
Tommy, the Ferris Wheel Operator **Jude Kitchens**
Mr. Tuffington **Tim O'Brien**
Mrs. Tuffington **Meredith O'Brien**
Bodee **Cullen Moss**

Rachel McAdams

and Traci Dinwiddie (Veronica), Pat Leonard (Lieutenant Davis), Kweli Leapart (Willa), James Middleton (Aaron), Frederick Bingham (Postman), Daniel Czekalski (Recruitment Officer), Peter Rosenfeld (Professor), Bradley D. Capshaw, James Scott Deaton (Injured Soldiers), Eve Kagan, Stephanie Wheeler, Erin Guzowski (Sarah Lawrence Girls), Obba Babatunde (Band Leader), Chuck Pacheco (Bus Driver), John A. Cundari (Maitre d'), Hugh Robertson (Pastor), Robert Washington (Elgin), Todd Lewis (Reporter), Mark Johnson (Photographer), Robert Fraisse, Barbara Weetman, Dan Chamblin (Buyers), Sasha Azevedo (Wife of Buyer #3), Robert Ivey (Dressmaker), Rebecca Koon (Aunt Georgia), Sandra W. Van Natta (Aunt Jeanette), Deborah Hobart (Aunt Kitty), Lindy Newton (Heather Lynn), Sherrill Turner (Linda Jean), Sylvia Jefferies (Rosemary), Mark Garner, Scott Ritenour, Milton Buras (Lon's Employees), Elizabeth Bond (Lon's Secretary), Matt Barry (Dr. Barnwell), Nancy De Mayo (Mary Allen), Meredith Zealy (Maggie), Julianne Keller Lewis (Davanee), Madison Wayne Ellis (Noah, Jr.), Riley Novak (Edmond), Ronald Betts (Male Nurse)

At a nursing home an elderly man reads a faded notebook to a woman whose memory has faded, relating the story of how well-to-do Allie Hamilton fell in love with local boy Noah Calhoun, despite the objections of her parents.

Ryan Gosling PHOTOS COURTESY OF NEW LINE CINEMA

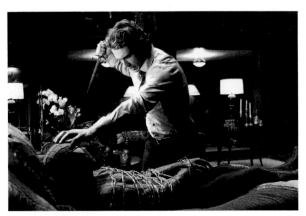

Tobey Maguire, James Franco

SPIDER-MAN 2

(COLUMBIA) Producers, Laura Ziskin, Avi Arad; Executive Producers, Joseph M. Carraciolo, Stan Lee, Kevin Feige; Director, Sam Raimi; Screenplay, Alvin Sargent; Screen Story, Alfred Gough, Miles Millar, Michael Chabon; Based on the Marvel Comic Book by Stan Lee and Steve Ditko; Co-Producer, Grant Curtis; Photography, Bill Pope; Designer, Neil Spisak; Costumes, James Acheson, Gary Jones; Music, Danny Elfman; Editor, Bob Murawski; Visual Effects Designer, John Dykstra; Casting, Dianne Crittenden; Fight Choreographer, Dion Lam; Stunts, Dan Bradley, Scott Rodgers; a Marvel Enterprises/Laura Ziskin production; Dolby; Panavision; Deluxe color; Rated PG-13; 127 minutes; Release date: June 30, 2004

Cast

Peter Parker (Spider-Man) **Tobey Maguire**
Mary Jane Watson **Kirsten Dunst**
Harry Osborn **James Franco**
Dr. Otto Octavius (Doc Ock) **Alfred Molina**
Mary Parker **Rosemary Harris**
J. Jonah Jameson **J.K. Simmons**
Rosalie Octavius **Donna Murphy**
John Jameson **Daniel Gillies**
Dr. Curt Connors **Dylan Baker**
Joseph "Robbie" Robertson **Bill Nunn**
Louise **Vanessa Felito**
Mr. Aziz **Aasif Mandvi**
Norman Osborn (Green Goblin) **Willem Dafoe**
Ben Parker **Cliff Robertson**
Hoffman **Ted Raimi**
Miss Brant **Elizabeth Banks**
Snooty Usher **Bruce Campbell**
Dr. Davis **Gregg Edelman**
Mr. Ditkovitch **Elya Baskin**

and Mageina Tovah (Ursula), Daniel Dae Kim (Raymond), Hal Sparks (Elevator Passenger), Joel McHale (Mr. Jacks), Stan Lee (Man Dodging Debris), Kelly Connell (Dr. Isaacs), Brent Briscoe (Garbage Man), Emily Deschanel (Receptionist), Jason Fiore-Ortiz (Henry Jackson), Scott Spiegel (Man on Balcony), Andrew Bale (OsCorp Executive), Christine Estabrook (Mrs. Jamseon), Molly Cheek (Society Woman), John Paxton (Houseman), Joy Brant (Woman at Web), Joane Baron (Skeptical Scientist), Peter McRobbie (OsCorp Representative), Tim Jerome (Injured Scientist), Taylor Gilbert (Mrs. Watson), Peter Vouras (Stage Manger), Donnell Rawlings (Pizza "Heist" Witness), Zachry Rogers (Girl Saved by Spider-Man), Ella Rogers (Girl Saved by Spider-Man), Louis Lombardi (Poker Player), Marc John Jefferies, Roshon Fegan (Amazed Kids), Brenand Connor (Theater Traffic Cop), Reed Diamond ("Algernon"), Dan Callahan ("Jack"), Elyse Dinh (Violinist), John Landis (Doctor), Tim Storms (Chainsaw Doctor), Susie Park, Christina Delia Rose, Tricia Peters (Clawing Nurse), Michael Edward Thomas (Man at Fire), Anne Betancourt (Woman at Fire), Venus Larn (Child in Burning Building), Bill E. Rogers, Joe Virzi (Firemen), Tom Carey (Train Conductor), Jopaul Epp, Weston Ep (Boys with Mask), Peter Allas, Brianna Lynn Brown, William Calvert, Tony Campisi, Joey Coco Diaz, Chloe Dykstra, Simone Gordon, Danny Hicks, Julia Max, Savannah Pope, Timothy Patrick Quill, Jill Sayre, Rickey G. Williams (Train Passengers)

Peter Parker is called back into duty as Spider-Man in order to battle brilliant scientist Otto Octavius whose fusion experimentation has caused him to mutate into the deadly, multi-tentacled Doc Ock. Sequel to the 2002 Columbia film *Spider-Man* with several principals repeating their roles.

2004 Academy Award-winner for Best Special Visual Effects.
This film received additional Oscar nominations for sound and sound editing.

Alfred Molina

Kirsten Dunst, Tobey Maguire PHOTOS COURTESY OF COLUMBIA

BEFORE SUNSET

(WARNER INDEPEDENT) Producer, Anne Walker-McBay; Executive Producer, John Sloss; Director, Richard Linklater; Screenplay, Richard Linklater, Julie Delpy, Ethan Hawke; Story, Richard Linklater, Kim Krizan, based on their characters; Co-Producer, Isabelle Coulet; Photography, Lee Daniel; Designer, Baptiste Glaymann; Costumes, Thierry Delettre; Editor, Sandra Adair; a Castle Rock presentation of a Detour Filmproduction; Dolby; Color; Rated R; 80 minutes; Release date: July 2, 2004

Ethan Hawke, Julie Delpy

Ethan Hawke

Cast

Jesse **Ethan Hawke**
Celine **Julie Delpy**
Bookstore Manager **Vernon Dobtcheff**
Journalists **Louise Lemoine Torres, Rodolphe Pauly**
Waitress **Mariane Plasteig**
Philippe **Diabolo**
Boat Attendant **Denis Evrard**
Man at Grill **Albert Delpy**
Woman in Courtyard **Marie Pillett**

Ethan Hawke, Julie Delpy

Nine years after they had spent one day together in Vienna, Jesse and Celine are reunited in Paris where they converse about their lives since then. Sequel to the 1995 film *Before Sunrise* (Columbia), with Hawke and Delpy repeating their roles.

This film received an Oscar nomination for adapted screenplay.

Julie Delpy

Ethan Hawke, Julie Delpy PHOTOS COURTESY OF WARNER INDEPENDENT

Kevin Kline

Jonathan Pryce PHOTOS COURTESY OF MGM

Ashley Judd, Kevin Kline

DE-LOVELY

(MGM) Producers, Irwin Winkler, Rob Cowan, Charles Winkler; Executive Producers, Simon Channing Williams, Gail Egan; Director, Irwin Winkler; Screenplay, Jay Cocks; Photography, Tony Pierce-Roberts; Designer, Eve Stewart; Costumes, Janty Yates; Editor, Julie Monroe; Music & Lyrics, Cole Porter; Music Arranger/Producer, Stephen Endelman; Choreographer, Francesca Jaynes; Make-Up, Sarah Monzani; Line Producer, Georgina Lowe; Casting, Nina Gold; Dolby; Super 35 Widescreen; Deluxe color; Rated PG-13; 125 minutes; Release date: July 2, 2004

John Barrowman, Kevin Kline

Elvis Costello

Peter Polycarpou, Kevin Kline

Robbie Williams

Sheryl Crow

Cast

Cole Porter **Kevin Kline**
Linda Porter **Ashley Judd**
Gabe **Jonathan Pryce**
Gerald Murphy **Kevin McNally**
Sara Murphy **Sandra Nelson**
Monty Woolley **Allan Corduner**
L.B. Mayer **Peter Polycarpou**
Irving Berlin **Keith Allen**
Edward Thomas **James Wilby**
Bobby Reed **Kevin McKidd**
Bill Wrather **Richard Dillane**
Boris Kochno **Edward Baker-Duly**
Ellin Berlin **Angie Hill**
Dr. Moorhead **Harry Ditson**
Honoria Murphy **Tayler Hamilton**
Patrick Murphy **Lexie Peel**
Boath Murphy **Greg Sheffield**
Diaghilev **Peter Jessop**
Cody **Jeff Harding**
Mrs. L.B. Mayer **Susannah Fellows**
Stage Manager **Teddy Kempner**

Musical Performers

"It's De-Lovely" **Robbie Williams**
"What is This Thing Called Love?" **Lemar**
"Let's Misbehave" **Elvis Costello**
"Let's Do It, Let's Fall in Love" **Alanis Morissette**
"Night and Day" **John Barrowman**
"Anything Goes" **Caroline O'Connor**
"Begin the Beguine" **Sheryl Crow**
"I Love You" **Mick Hucknall**
"Just One of Those Things" **Diana Krall**
"Love for Sale" **Vivian Green**
"So in Love" **Lara Fabian, Mario Frangoulis**
"Ev'ry Time We Say Goodbye" **Natalie Cole**

The story of Broadway songwriter Cole Porter and his unconventional relationship with his wife Linda. Previous film about Porter was the 1946 WB release *Night and Day*, starring Cary Grant and Alexis Smith.

Kevin McNally, Ashley Judd, Kevin Kline, Sandra Nelson

THE CLEARING

(FOX SEARCHLIGHT) Producers, Palmer West, Jonah Smith, Pieter Jan Brugge; Executive Producers, Karen Tenkehoff; Co-Producer, Dara Weintraub; Director, Pieter Jan Brugge; Screenplay, Justin Haythe; Story, Pieter Jan Brugge, Justin Haythe; Photography, Denis Lenoir; Designer, Chris Gorak; Costumes, Florence-Isabelle Megginson; Music, Craig Armstrong; Editor, Kevin Tent; Casting, Vickie Thomas; a Thousand Words presentation in association with Mediastream III of a Thousand Words/Wildwood production; Dolby; Deluxe color; Rated R; 95 minutes; Release date: July 2, 2004

Cast

Wayne Hayes **Robert Redford**
Eileen Hayes **Helen Mirren**
Arnold Mack **Willem Dafoe**
Tim Hayes **Alessandro Nivola**
Agent Ray Fuller **Matt Craven**
Jill Hayes **Melissa Sagemiller**
Louise Miller **Wendy Crewson**
Tom Finch **Larry Pine**
Eva Finch **Diana Scarwid**
Cindy Mack **Elizabeth Ruscio**
Agent Kathleen Duggan **Gwen McGee**
Lane Hayes **Sarah Koskoff**
Graciela **Graciela Marin**
Det. Kyle Woodward **Mike Pniewski**
John Devitt **Geoff McKnight**
Mr. Schmidt **Tom Arcuragi**
Lisa **Audrey Wasilewski**

and Peter Gannon (Agent Elkins), Jacqui Loewy (Agent Crew), Matt Miller (Another Agent), Mark Emery Moore (Agent Sullivan), Joel S. Nunley (Waiter), Ted Manson (Robert Gidden), Blake Law, Noah Law (Oscar Hayes), John Rifchard Fairchild, Ken Meverden (FBI Agents)

A wealthy businessman is kidnapped at gunpoint from his driveway and taken deep into the wilderness by his kidnapper, causing panic to his wife who begins to question her feelings for her absent husband.

Willem Dafoe

Robert Redford, Willem Dafoe

Robert Redford, Helen Mirren <small>PHOTOS COURTESY OF FOX SEARCHLIGHT</small>

ANCHORMAN:
THE LEGEND OF RON BURGUNDY

(DREAMWORKS) Producer, Judd Apatow; Executive Producers, Shauna Robertson, David O. Russell; Director, Adam McKay; Screenplay, Wille Ferrell, Adam McKay; Photography, Thomas Ackerman; Designer, Clayton R. Hartley; Costumes, Debra McGuire; Editor, Brent White; Music, Alex Wurman; Co-Producer, David Householter; Casting, Juel Bestrop, Jeanne McCarthy; an Apatow production; Dolby; Technicolor; Rated PG-13; 94 minutes; Release date: July 9, 2004

Will Ferrell (center)

(Bum), Chuck Poynter (Announcer), Esmeralda McQuillan (Middle Class Mother), Angela Grillo (Elderly Woman), Lionel Allen, Trina D. Johnson, Mary Alice G. Goodin, Jasmine Nicole Jackson (Wealthy Family), Fred Dresch (Doctor), Glen Hambly (Middle Class Dad), Stuart Gold (Nursing Room Resident), Bill Kurtis (Bill Lawson), Luke Wilson (Frank Vitchard), Vince Vaughn (Wes Mantooth), Jack Black (Angry Biker), Tim Robbins (Public News Anchor), Ben Stiller (Hispanic News Anchor)

In 1970s San Diego, arrogant anchorman Ron Burgundy and his all-male news team are appalled to discover that a female newswoman will be co-anchoring.

Paul Rudd, Will Ferrell, David Koechner, Steve Carell

Cast

Ron Burgundy **Will Ferrell**
Veronica Corningstone **Christina Applegate**
Brian Fantana **Paul Rudd**
Brick Tamland **Steve Carell**
Champ Kind **David Koechner**
Ed Harken **Fred Willard**
Garth Holliday **Chris Parnell**
Helen **Kathryn Hahn**
Tino **Fred Armisen**
Eager Cameraman **Seth Rogen**
MC **Paul F. Tompkins**
Bartender **Danny Trejo**
Waiter at Tino's **Scot Robinson**
Stage Manager **Ian Roberts**
Hot Blonde **Darcy Donavan**
Petite Brunette **Renee Weldon**
Tino's Bassist **Jerry Minor**
Director **Holmes Osborne**

and Charles Walker (Security Guard), Shira Piven (Mother), Lili Rose McKay (Child), Thomas E. Mastrolia (Biker Guy), Jay Johnston (Eyewitness News Member), Peter Hulne (Man in Kitchen), Laura Kightlinger (Donna), Adam McKay, Joseph T. Mastrolia (Custodians), Judd Apatow, Debra McGuire (News Station Employees), Kent Shocknek (Network Reporter), Monique McIntyre (Yelling Woman), Bob Rummler

Christina Applegate PHOTOS COURTESY OF DREAMWORKS

THE DOOR IN THE FLOOR

(FOCUS) Producers, Ted Hope, Anne Carey, Michael Corrente; Executive Producers, Amy J. Kaufman, Roger Marino; Co-Producer, Marisa Polvino; Director/Screenplay, Tod Williams; Based on the novel *A Widow for One Year* by John Irving; Photography, Terry Stacey; Designer, Therese DePrez; Costumes, Eric Daman; Music, Marcelo Zarvos; Music Supervisor, Beth Amy Rosenblatt; Casting, Ann Goulder; a Revere Pictures presentation of a This Is That production; Dolby; Super 35 Widescreen; Technicolor; Rated R; 111 minutes; Release date: July 14, 2004

Jeff Bridges, Mimi Rogers

Kim Basinger, Jon Foster

Cast

Ted Cole **Jeff Bridges**
Marion Cole **Kim Basinger**
Eddie O'Hare **Jon Foster**
Evelyn Vaughn **Mimi Rogers**
Ruth Cole **Elle Fanning**
Alice **Bijou Philips**
Eduardo Gomez **Louis Arcella**
Interviewer **Larry Pine**
Minty O'Hare **John Rothman**
Dr. Loomis **Harvey Loomis**
Mendelssohn **Robert LuPone**
Frame Shop Owner **Donna Murphy**
Thomas **Tod Harrison Williams**
Timothy **Carter Williams**

and Mike S. Ryan (Reception Fan), Libby Langdon (Woman at Reception), Rachel Style (Bookstore Assistant), Amanda Posner (Frame Shop Clerk), Marion McCorry (Bookstore Customer), Kristina Valada-Viars (Effie), LeAnna Croom (Glorie Moutsier), Claire Beckman (Mrs. Mountsier).

Jon Foster, Kim Basinger

Young Eddie O'Hare comes to the East Hampton home of children's author Ted Cole and his wife Marion to work as a writer's assistant and becomes deeply involved in the couple's strained and tragedy-ridden relationship.

Jeff Bridges, Elle Fanning PHOTOS COURTESY OF FOCUS

Will Smith, Bridget Moynahan, Sonny

Will Smith

I, ROBOT

(20TH CENTURY FOX) Producers, Laurence Mark, John Davis, Topher Dow, Wyck Godfrey; Executive Producers, Will Smith, James Lassiter, Michel Shane, Anthony Romano; Director, Alex Proyas; Screenplay, Jeff Vintar, Akiva Goldsman; Screen Story, Jeff Vintar; Suggested by Isaac Asimov's book; Photography, Simon Duggan; Designer, Patrick Tatopoulos; Costumes, Elizabeth Keogh Palmer; Editors, Richard Learoyd, Armen Minasian, William Hoy; Co-Producer, Steven R. McGlothen; Music, Marco Beltrami; Visual Effects Supervisor, John Nelson; Visual Effects Supervisor—Digital Domain, Erik Nash; Animation Supervisors—Weta Digital, Joe Letteri, Brian Van't Hul; Associate Producer, John Kilkenny; Casting, Juel Bestrop, Jeanne McCarthy, Coreen Mayrs, Heike Brandstatter; Stunts, Glenn Boswell, Scott Ateah; a Davis Entertainment Company/Laurence Mark/Overbrook Films production, presented in association with Mediastream IV; Dolby; Super 35 Widescreen; Deluxe color; Rated PG-13; 115 minutes; Release date: July 16, 2004

Cast
Det. Del Spooner **Will Smith**
Dr. Susan Calvin **Bridget Moynahan**
Sonny **Alan Tudyk**
Dr. Alfred Lanning **James Cromwell**
Lawrence Robertson **Bruce Greenwood**
Granny **Adrian L. Ricard**
Lt. John Bergin **Chi McBride**
Baldez **Jerry Wasserman**
V.I.K.I. **Fiona Hogan**
Chin **Peter Shinkoda, Terry Chen**
NS4 & NS5 Robots **David Haysom, Scott Heindl**
Woman **Sharon Wilkins**
Detective **Craig March**
Girl **Kyanna Cox**
Homeless Man **Darren Moore**
USR Attorneys **Aaron Douglas, Michael St. John Smith**
Laughing Girl **Shayla Dyson**
Girl's Dad **Bobby L. Stewart**
TV Anchor Person **Nicola Crosbie**
Farber **Shia LaBeouf**

Shia LaBeouf, Will Smith

and Travis Webster (Guy with a Pie), Roger Haskett (Mob Man), Tiffany Knight (Mob Woman), Angela Moore (Wife), Ryan Zwick, Essra Vischon, Kenyan Lewis, Aaron Joseph, Simon R. Baker (Farber Posse), Marrett Green (News Reporter)

In the year 2035, Detective Del Spooner's distrust of the rampant dependency on robots leads him to believe that a robot is responsible for the death of scientist Alfred Lanning, despite the law that states that robots cannot possibly harm a human being.

This film received an Oscar nomination for visual effects.

Chi McBride, Will Smith, Bruce Greenwood PHOTOS COURTESY OF 20TH CENTURY FOX

Madeline Zima, Andrea Avery, Jennifer Coolidge

A CINDERELLA STORY

(WARNER BROS.) Producers, Clifford Werber, Ilyssa Goodman, Hunt Lowry, Dylan Sellers; Executive Producers, E.K. Gaylord II, Michael Rachmil, Peter Greene, Keith Giglio; Co-Executive Producer, Susan Duff; Director, Mark Rosman; Screenplay, Leigh Dunlap; Photography, Anthony P. Richmond; Designer, Charles Breen; Costumes, Denise Wingate; Music, Christophe Beck; Music Supervisor, Debra A. Baum; Associate Producer, Troy Rowland; Casting, Randi Hiller, Sarah Halley Finn; a Clifford Werber production in association with Dylan Sellers Prods.; Dolby; Technicolor; Rated PG; 95 minutes; Release date: July 16, 2004

Cast
Sam Montgomery **Hilary Duff**
Fiona **Jennifer Coolidge**
Austin **Chad Michael Murray**
Carter **Dan Byrd**
Rhonda **Regina King**
Shelby **Julie Gonzalo**
Mrs. Wells **Lin Shaye**
Brianna **Madeline Zima**
Gabriella **Andrea Avery**
Eleanor **Mary Pat Gleason**
Bobby **Paul Rodriguez**
Sam's Dad **Whip Hubley**

and Kevin Kilner (Austin's Dad), Erica Hubbard (Madison), Simon Helberg (Terry), Brad Bufanda (David), JD Pardo (Ryan), Aimee Lynn Chadwick (D.J.), Kady Cole (Caitlin), Hannah Robinson (Young Sam), Josh Prince (Swim Coach), Art La Fleur (Coach), James Eckhouse (Mr. Farrell), Vernon Slavin (Vernon), John Billingsley (Mr. Rothman), Lilli Babb (Young Gabriella), Carlie Westerman (Young Brianna), Mike Randleman (Chuck), Christie Herring, Lindsay Hollister, Brittany Weber (Bachelorettes), Taylor Hoover (Beautiful Bachelorette), Darryl Sivad (District Attorney), Rita Maye Bland, Keli Murphy (Rollerskating Waitresses), Alexis Raich (Girl at Car Wash), Sabin Rich (Locker Guy), Sandra McCoy, Julianne Waters, Karen Elmore, Stella Choe, Jessie Rice-Holiday, Cricket Hamar, Shannon Novak (Cheerleaders), Oscar Orosco (Fighting Frog Mascot), Jason Beitel,

Hilary Duff, Chad Michael Murray

Erica Hubbard, Julie Gonzalo, Kady Cole

Hillary Duff, Dan Byrd PHOTOS COURTESY OF WARNER BROS.

Kato Bonner, Carol Borjas, Reshma Gajjar, Molly Gosline, Hunter Hamilton, Richard Jackson, Trey Knight, Jonathan Ritter, Jenny Seeger, Becca Sweitzer (Halloween Dancers), Jonathan Slavin (Vernon)

Stuck living with her shrewish stepmother and stepsisters, Sam Montgomery finds sollace in an e-mail correspondence with a mysterious guy who calls himself "Nomad."

MARIA FULL OF GRACE

(FINE LINE FEATURES) Producer, Paul Mezey; Co-Producer, Jaime Osorio Gomez; Director/Screenplay, Joshua Marston; Photography, Jim Denault; Designer, Monica Marulanda, Debbie De Villa; Costumes, Lauren Press, Sarah Beers; Music, Jacobo Lieberman, Leonardo Heiblum; Music Supervisor, Lynn Fainchtein; Associate Producers, Orlando Tobon, Rodrigo Guerrero; Casting, Maria E. Nelson, Ellyn Long Marshall; an HBO Films presentation of a Journeyman production in association with Tucan Producciones; U.S.-Columbian; Dolby; Color; Rated R; 101 minutes; Release date: July 16, 2004

John Alex Toro, Catalina Sandino Moreno

Pregnant and having quit her job, Maria Alvarez heads to Bolivia with the intention of finding work as a domestic and ends up smuggling drugs into the United States.

This film received an Oscar nomination for actress (Catalina Sandino Moreno).

Catalina Sandino Moreno, Selenis Leyva

Cast
Maria Alvarez **Catalina Sandino Moreno**
Blanca **Yenny Paola Vega**
Lucy Diaz **Giulied Lopez**
Franklin **John Alex Toro**
Carla Aristizabal **Patricia Rae**
Juan **Wilson Guerrero**
Javier **Jaime Osorio Gomez**
Diana Alvarez **Johanna Andrea Mora**
Don Fernando **Orlando Tobon**
Pablo Aristizcibal **Fernando Velasquez**
Juana **Virgina Ariza**
Baby Pancho **Mateo Suarez, Fabricio Suarez**
Pharmacists **Juana Guarderas, Hugo Ferro**
Supervisor **Rodrigo Sanchez Borhorquez**
Felipe Charles **Albert Patino**
Rosita **Evangelina Morales**
Pellet Maker **Victor Macias**
Stewardess **Ana Maria Acosta**
Carolina Ada **Vergara De Solano**
Constanza **Maria Consuelo Perez**

Catalina Sandino Moreno

and Ed Trucco, Selenis Leyva (Customs Inspectors), Juan Porras Hincapie (Wilson), Oscar Bejarano (Carlos), Singkhan Bandit (Gas Attendant), Patrick Rameau (Taxi Driver), Monique Curnen (Receptionist), Lourdes Martin (Doctor), Osvaldo Plasencia (Enrique)

Catalina Sandino Moreno, Yenny Paola Vega PHOTOS COURTESY OF FINE LINE FEATURES

THE BOURNE SUPREMACY

(UNIVERSAL) Producers, Frank Marshall, Patrick Crowley, Paul L. Sandberg; Executive Producers, Doug Liman, Jeffrey M. Weiner, Henry Morrison; Director, Paul Greengrass; Screenplay, Tony Gilroy; Based on the novel by Robert Ludlum; Photography, Oliver Wood; Designer, Dominic Watkins; Costumes, Dinah Collin; Music, John Powell; Editors, Christopher Rouse, Richard Pearson; Casting, Joseph Middleton, John Hubbard, Dan Hubbard; Stunt Coordinator (2nd Unit), Darrin Prescott; Fight Stunt Coordinator, Jeff Imada; a Kennedy/Marshall production in association with Ludlum Entertainment; Dolby; Super 35 Widescreen; Technicolor; Rated PG-13; 108 minutes; Release date: July 23, 2004

Matt Damon, Franka Potente

Joan Allen, Brian Cox

Gabriel Mann PHOTOS COURTESY OF UNIVERSAL

Matt Damon, Julia Stiles

Cast

Jason Bourne **Matt Damon**
Marie **Franka Potente**
Ward Abbott **Brian Cox**
Nicky **Julia Stiles**
Kirill **Karl Urban**
Danny Zorn **Gabriel Mann**
Pamela Landy **Joan Allen**
Jarda **Morton Csokas**
Tom Cronin **Tom Gallop**
Teddy **John Bedford Lloyd**
Kurt **Ethan Sandler**
Kim **Michelle Monaghan**
Gretkov **Karel Roden**
Martin Marshall **Tomas Arana**

and Oksana Akinshina (Irena Neski), Jevgeni Sitochin (Mr. Neski), Marina Weis-Burgaslieva (Mrs. Neski), Tim Griffin (Nevins), Sean Smith (Vic), Maxim Kovalevski (Ivan), Maxim Kovalevski (Ivan), Patrick Crowley (Jack Weller), Jon Collin, Sam Brown, Shane Sinutko (Jarheads), Barnaby P. Smith, Jr. (CIA Techie), Dominique Chiout (Waitress), Wanja Mues (Night Clerk), Aleksey Shmarinov (Moscow Taxi Driver), Stephan Wolf-Schónburg (Suspicious Cop), Olov Ludwig (Market Security Guard), Keshav Nadkarni (Mr. Mohan), Violetta Gráfin Tarnowska Bronner (Neski Neighbor), Aleksey Medvedev (Young Cop), Aleksander Doobina (2nd Cop), Alexander Boyev (2nd Taxi Driver), Claudio Maniscalco (Immigration Officer), Manfred Witt (Doorman), Aleksey Trotsenko (Vodka Police Passenger), Victoria Unikel (Mercedes Driver), Oksana Semenova (Mercedes Passenger), Vitalei Abdulov (Volga Taxi Owner), Dirk Schoeden (Berlin Taxi Driver), Ivan Shvedoff, Denis Burgazliev (Moscow Policemen), Nick Wilder (Delta C.O.)

Former assassin Jason Bourne, believing he has escaped from his past, finds himself on the run once again when an operative is assigned to kill him. Sequel to the 2002 Universal film *The Bourne Identity* with Damon, Potente, and Mann repeating their roles.

A HOME AT THE END OF THE WORLD

(WARNER INDEPENDENT) Producers, Tom Hulce, Christine Vachon, Katie Roumel, Pamela Koffler, John Wells, John N. Hart Jr., Jeffrey Sharp; Executive Producers, John Sloss, Michael Hogan; Director, Michael Mayer; Screenplay, Michael Cunningham, based on his novel; Photography, Enrique Chediak; Designer, Michael Shaw; Costumes, Beth Pasternak; Music, Duncan Shiek; Music Supervision, Linda Cohen; Editor, Lee Percy; Casting, Jim Carnahan; a Killer Films/John Wells/Plymouth Projects/Hart Sharp Entertainment production; Dolby; Super 35 Widescreen; Color; Rated R; 95 minutes; Release date: July 24, 2004

Sissy Spacek, Dallas Roberts

Erik Smith, Harris Allan

Colin Farrell, Robin Wright Penn

Cast

Bobby Morrow (1982) **Colin Farrell**
Clare **Robin Wright Penn**
Jonathan Glover (1982) **Dallas Roberts**
Bobby Morrow (1967) **Andrew Chalmers**
Carlton Morrow **Ryan Donowho**
Emily **Asia Vieira**
Dancing Party Guest **Quancetia Hamilton**
Frank **Jeffrey Authors**
Frank's Date **Lisa Merchant**
Burt Morrow **Ron Lea**
Bobby Morrow (1974) **Erik Smith**
Jonathan Glover (1974) **Harris Allan**
Ned Glover **Matt Frewer**
Alice Glover **Sissy Spacek**
Club Boy **Shawn Roberts**
Jonathan's Co-Worker **Michael Mayer**
Wes **Barna Moricz**
Woman at Home Cafe **Viriginia Reh**

Two young men, who had experimented sexually as kids, hook up again in early 1980s New York, where they end up sharing an apartment with free-spirited Clare.

Colin Farrell   PHOTOS COURTESY OF WARNER INDEPENDENT

Lambert Wilson, Sharon Stone

CATWOMAN

(WARNER BROS.) Producers, Denise Di Novi, Edward L. McDonnell; Executive Producers, Michael Fottrell, Benjamin Melniker, Michael E. Uslan, Robert Kirby, Bruce Berman; Co-Producer, Alison Greenspan; Director, Pitof; Screenplay, John Brancato, Michael Ferris, John Rogers; Story, Theresa Rebeck, John Brancato, Michael Ferris; Based on characters created by Bob Kane and published in DC Comics; Photography, Thierry Arbogast; Costumes, Angus Strathie; Music, Klaus Badelt; Music Supervisor, Dawn Soler; Editor, Sylvie Landra; Visual Effects Supervisor, Ed Jones; Stunts, Steve M. Davison, Jacob Rupp; Fight Coordinators, Mike Gunther, Kirk Caouette; Casting, John Papsidera, Coreen Mayrs, Heike Brandstatter; Dolby; Super 35 Widescreen; Technicolor; Rated PG-13; 101 minutes; Release date: July 24, 2004

Cast

Patience Philips (Catwoman) **Halle Berry**
Tom Lone **Benjamin Bratt**
Laurel Hedare **Sharon Stone**
George Hedare **Lambert Wilson**
Ophelia Powers **Frances Conroy**
Sally **Alex Borstein**
Armando **Michael Massee**
Wesley **Byron Mann**
Drina **Kim Smith**
Rocker **Christopher Heyerdahl**
Dr. Ivan Slavicky **Peter Wingfield**
Lance **Berend McKenzie**

and Chase Nelson-Murray, Manny Petruzzelli, Harley Reiner (Kids), Ona Grauer (Sandy), Landy Cannon (Randy), Judith Maxie (Jeweler), Michael Dangerfield (Forensics Cop), Benita Ha (Forensics Technician), James Lloyd Reynolds (Hottie Doctor), Jill Krop (Newscaster), Dagmar Midcap (Television Reporter), Ryan Robbins (Bartender), John Cassini (Graphologist), Patricia Mayan Salazar (Housekeeper), Diego Del Mar (Barker), Connor Crash Dunn (Little Boy), Michael P. Northey (Jail Guard), Aaron Douglas, Peter Williams (Detectives), Janet Varney (Party Girl), John Mann (Bouncer), Brooke Theiss (Ferris Wheel Man), Michasha Armstrong (Ferris Wheel Operator), James Ashcroft (Janitor), Herbert Duncanson (Security Guard), Larry Sullivan (Warehouse Supervisor), Ashlea Earl, Lori Fung, Ursula Haczkiewicz, Alisoun Payne, Lawrence Racine Choiniere (Preformance Dancers)

Halle Berry

Benjamin Bratt, Halle Berry

Left for dead after uncovering an unethical plot within the Hedare cosmetics empire, Patience Philips is brought back to life by an Egyptian Mau cat and discovers that she possesses unusual feline powers.

Frances Conroy, Halle Berry   PHOTOS COURTESY OF WARNER BROS.

SHE HATE ME

(SONY CLASSICS) Producers, Spike Lee, Preston Holmes, Fernando Sulchin; Director, Spike Lee; Screenplay, Michael Genet, Spike Lee; Co-Producer, Craig Spitzer; Photography, Matthew Libatique; Designer, Brigitte Broch; Costumes, Donna Berwick; Music, Terence Blanchard; Editor, Barry Alexander Brown; Casting, Kim Coleman; a 40 Acres and a Mule Filmworks Production in association with Pathe and with Rule 8 Productions; Dolby; Color; Rated R; 138 minutes; Release date: July 28, 2004

Michole Briana White, Bai Ling, Paula Jai Parker, Savannah Haske, Sarita Choudhury

Cast

John Henry "Jack" Armstrong **Anthony Mackie**
Fatima Goodrich **Kerry Washington**
Margo Chadwick **Ellen Barkin**
Simona Bonasera **Monica Bellucci**
Geronimo **Jim Brown**
Judge Buchanan **Ossie Davis**
Doak **Jamel Debbouze**
Chairman Church **Brian Dennehy**
Leland Powell **Woody Harrelson**
Oni **Bai Ling**
Lottie Armstrong **Lonette McKee**
Evelyn **Paula Jai Parker**
Vada Huff **Q-Tip**
Alex Guerrero **Dania Ramirez**
Don Angelo Bonasera **John Turturro**
Frank Wills **Chiwetel Ejiofor**
Dr. Herman Schiller **David Bennent**
Agent Flood **Isiah Whitlock**
Nadiyah **Michole Briana White**
Song **Sarita Choudhury**
Rachel **Savannah Haske**
Gloria Reid **Joie Lee**
Jamal Armstrong **Michael Genet**
Lucy Armstrong **Roslyn Tate**
Gia **Christine Pepe**

and Kym Hampton (Leilani), Angela Forrest (Ruby), Martha Williams (Fifi), Aura Grimolyte (Ticha), Chris Magna (Nino Bonasera), Rick Aiello (Rocco Bonasera), Chris Tardio (Franco Bonasera), Samrat Chakrabarti (Ahmad), Kandiss Edmundson (Millie), Kristina Klebe (Ruth Lacey), Jamilah Rutherford (Terri), Marion McCorry (Senator Jacobs), Hal Sherman (Detective Boyd), Reynaldo Rosales (Jimmy), James McCaffrey (Bob), Kim Director (Grace), T.V. Carpio (Gail), Gerald Anthony (Mr. Jennings), Peter Michael Marino (John Dean), Don Harvey (G. Gordon Liddy), Gary Evans (H.R. Haldeman), Murphy Guyer (John Erlichman), Keith Jochim (Richard Nixon), Brian Simons (Jeb Stuart Magruder), Jeff Hughes (Oliver North), Richard Kelly (Klansman), Wynne Anders (Nurse), Jade Wu (Midwife), P.J. Brown (Sgt. Leper), Paul Albe (James McCord), Wass Stevens (Frank Sturgis), Lemon (Eugeni Martinez), Carlos Leon (Virgilio Gonzalez), Christopher Wynkoop (Bernard Baker), Kendra Day (Karen), Laura Goodwin (Norma), Kisha Batista (Jo), Sope Phang (Michelle), Alison Folland (Doris), Tristan Taormino (Olga), Muriel Hurtado Herrera (Lorna), Jim Ward (Det. Sholler), Lars Hanson (Det. Barrett), Tim Miller (Bank President), Albert Zihenni (Flood's Partner), Sandra Endo (NY1 Field Reporter), Martin Murphy, Michael Devine (Officers), Peter Kybart (German Pastor), Patrick Reale (Bodyguard), Rodney Bear Jackson, Bradley C. Williams (Federal Correction Officers), Charles Santy (Police Officer), Alice Liu (Oni's Girlfriend), Naja Hill (Nadiyah's Girlfriend), Shakara Singh (Evelyn's Girlfriend), Zakiya (Ruby's Girlfriend), Poorna (Song's Girlfriend), Sarah Desage (Fifi's Girlfriend), Neisha Butler (Stacey's Girlfriend), Catherine Rogers (Jo's Girlfriend), Natasha Carabello (Michelle's Girlfriend), Connie Freestone (Karen's Girlfriend), Piper Corbett (Norma's Girlfriend), Wynn Hall (Doris' Girlfriend), Shira Bocar (Rachel's Girlfriend)

A fired business executive, desperate to make a living, offers to impregnate lesbians desiring motherhood.

Dania Ramirez, Kerry Washington PHOTOS COURTESY OF SONY CLASSICS

GARDEN STATE

(FOX SEARCHLIGHT) Producers, Pamela Abdy, Richard Klubeck, Gary Gilbert, Dan Halsted; Executive Producers, Danny DeVito, Michael Shamberg, Stacey Sher; Co-Producer, Bill Brown; Director/Screenplay, Zach Braff; Photography, Lawrence Sher; Designer, Judy Becker; Costumes, Michael Wilkinson; Music, Chad Fisher; Music Supervisors, Amanda Scheer Demme, Buck Damon; Line Producer, Ann Ruark; Casting, Avy Kaufman; a Camelot Pictures presentation of a Jersey Films/Double Feature Films production; Dolby; Panavision; Deluxe color; Rated R; 109 minutes; Release date: July 28, 2004

Cast

Andrew Largeman **Zach Braff**
Sam **Natalie Portman**
Mark **Peter Sarsgaard**
Gideon Largeman **Ian Holm**
Dr. Cohen **Ron Liebman**
Diego **Method Man**
Olivia **Ann Dowd**
Albert **Denis O'Hare**
Kenny **Michael Weston**
Carol **Jean Smart**
Tim **Jim Parsons**
Aunt Sylvia Largeman **Jackie Hoffman**
Dana **Amy Ferguson**
Titembay **Ato Essandoh**
Restaurant Manager **George C. Wolfe**

and Kennth Graymez (Busboy), Austin Lusy (Waiter), Gary Gilbert (Young Hollywood Guy), Jill Flint (Obnoxious Girl), Alex Burns (Dave), Chris Carley (Gleason Party Drunk), Armando Riesco (Jesse), Trisha LaFrache (Kelly), Yvette Mercedes (Neurology Receptionist), Jayne Houdy Shell (Mrs. Lubin), Wunter Kullman (Pam), Geoffrey Arend (Karl Benson), Soara-Joy Ross (Handi-World Cashier), Ryan B. Moschetti (Teen in Hallway), Joe Bacino (Man Having Sex), Tracey Antosiwiecz (Hooker), Seth Michael May (Peeping Tom), Debbon Ayer (Faye)

Natalie Portman, Zach Braff

Andrew Largeman, a marginally successful actor who has become emotionally numbed from all the meds fed into his system since childhood, returns to his New Jersey hometown for the first time in years, experiencing the quirky and often dead-end lives of those he left behind.

Zach Braff, Natalie Portman

Peter Sarsgaard, Natalie Portman, Zach Braff PHOTOS COURTESY OF FOX SEARCHLIGHT

Peter Sarsgaard (center)

Bryce Dallas Howard, Judy Greer

THE VILLAGE

(TOUCHSTONE) Producers, M. Night Shyamalan, Scott Rudin, Sam Mercer; Director/Screenplay, M. Night Shyamalan; Photography, Roger Deakins; Designer, Tom Foden; Costumes, Ann Roth; Music, James Newton Howard; Editor, Christopher Tellefsen; Casting, Douglas Aibel; a Blinding Edge Pictures/Scott Rudin production; Dolby; DuArt color; Rated PG-13; 108 minutes; Release date: July 30, 2004

Cast

Ivy Walker **Bryce Dallas Howard**
Lucius Hunt **Joaquin Phoenix**
Noah Percy **Adrien Brody**
Edward Walker **William Hurt**
Alice Hunt **Sigourney Weaver**
August Nicholson **Brendan Gleeson**
Mrs. Clack **Cherry Jones**
Vivian Percy **Celia Weston**
Robert Percy **John Christopher Jones**
Victor **Frank Collison**
Tabitha Walker **Jayne Atkinson**
Kitty Walker **Judy Greer**
Christop Crane **Fran Kranz**
Finton Coin **Michael Pitt**
Jamison **Jesse Eisenberg**

and Charlie Hofheimer, Robert Lenzi (Young Men), Scott Sowers (Man with the Raised Eyebrows), Zach Wall (Donald), Pascale Renate Smith (Marybeth), Jordan Burt (12-Year-Old Boy), Jane Lowe (Brown-Eyed Girl), Charlie McDermott (10-Year-Old Boy), William Zuur (Gerald), Liz Stauber (Beatrice), Tim Moyer (Flustered Man), Sydney Shapiro (Oldest Walker Daughter), Mia Rose Colona (Middle Walker Daughter), Chloe Wieczkowski, Sydney Wieczkowski (Youngest Walker Daughters), John Rusk (Town Crier), Joey Anaya, Kevin Foster (Those We Don't Speak Of), M. Night Shyamalan (Trooper)

The inhabitants of a 19th century village keep close watch on each other as they are constantly threatened by mysterious creatures in the surrounding woods.

This film received an Oscar nomination for music score.

Joaquin Phoenix

Bryce Dallas Howard

Sigourney Weaver, William Hurt PHOTOS COURTESY OF TOUCHSTONE

Denzel Washington

Denzel Washington, Meryl Streep

THE MANCHURIAN CANDIDATE

(PARAMOUNT) Producers, Tina Sinatra, Scott Rudin, Jonathan Demme, Ilona Herzberg; Director, Jonathan Demme; Screenplay, Daniel Pyne, Dean Georgaris; Based on the novel by Richard Condon and the screenplay by George Axelrod; Executive Producers, Scott Aversano; Music, Rachel Portman, Wyclef Jean; a Scott Rudin/Tina Sinatra production in association with Clinica Estetico; Dolby; Deluxe color; Rated R; 130 minutes; Release date: July 30, 2004

Cast
Major Ben Marco **Denzel Washington**
Senator Eleanor Prentiss Shaw **Meryl Streep**
Raymond Shaw **Liev Schreiber**
Senator Thomas Jordan **Jon Voight**
Rosie **Kimberly Elise**
Al Melvin **Jeffrey Wright**
Colonel Howard **Ted Levine**
Richard Delp **Bruno Ganz**
Dr. Atticus Noyle **Simon McBurney**
Jocelyn Jordan **Vera Farmiga**
Lauren Tokar **Robyn Hitchcock**
Eddie Ingram **Pablo Schreiber**
Robert Baker **Anthony Mackie**
Owens **Dorian Missick**
Villalobos **Jose Pablo Cantillo**
Atkins **Joaquin Perez-Campbell**
Jameson **Tim Artz**
Boy Scouts **Antoine Taylor, Joseph Alessi**
Scout Dad **Ray Anthony Thomas**
Scoutmaster **Bill Irwin**

and Al Franken (TV Commentator), Paul Lazar (Gillespie), Danny Darst (Elle's Mysterious Aide), Stephanie McBride, Molly Hickcock, Victoria Haynes (Political Aides), Adam LeFevre (Congressman Healy), Roger Corman (Mr. Secretary), Leona E. Sondreal (Green Room Official), Zeljko

Denzel Washington, Liev Schreiber PHOTOS COURTESY OF PARAMOUNT

Ivanek (Vaughn Utly), Jim Roche (Senator from Florida), Ann Dowd (Congresswoman Becket), Obba Babatundé (Senator Wells), Harry Northup (Congressman Flores), James Beattie Howard (Himself), Walter Mosley (Congressman Rawlins), Gordon Brummer ("Gordy"), Gayle King (Media Icon), Brad Holbrook, Stacey Newsome Santiago, Krstien Shaughnessy, Prue Lewarne, Forrest Sawyer, Ukee Washington, Ed Crane, Kaity Tong, Roma Torre-Lopez (Newscasters), William Meisle (Tyler Prentiss), Dan Olmstead (Senator John Shaw), Sakina Jaffrey

Liev Schreiber, Vera Farmiga

Denzel Washington, Jeffrey Wright

(Mysterious Arabic Woman), Charles Napier (General Sloan), Robert Castle (General Wilson), John Aprea (Rear Admiral Glick), Tom Stechschulte (Robert Arthur), Jane DeNoble (Robert Arthur's Wife), Jude Ciccolella (David Donovan), Dean Stockwell (Mark Whiting), John Bedford Lloyd (Jay "J.B." Johnston), David Keeley (Agent Evan Anderson), Christopher M. Russo, Michael C. Pierce (Secret Service Agents), Miguel Ferrer (Colonel Garret), Marin Ireland, Glen Hartell (Army Transcribers), Tracey Walter (Night Clerk), Alyson Reynaldo (Mirella Freeman), Edwidge Danticat (Rosie's Cousin), Kenny Utt (Rosie's Cousin's Mentor), Enrique Correa, David Neumann, Neda Armian (Reporters), Paul Johnson (Campaign Security), James McCauley (FBI Agent Jonas), Be Be Winans (FBI Agent Williams), Darrell Larson (FBI Agent Ramirez), Kate Valk ("Shadow" Agent Volk), Beau Sia (Late Night Comedian), Duana

Meryl Streep

Butler (Library Clerk), Big Jim Wheeler (Library Patron), Lauren Roselli, Stephen Richardson (Jordan's Aides), Sing Ka (Rosie's Sidekick), Malcolm Simpson (Yelling Kid), Cassius Wilkinson ("Abe Lincoln"), Josephine Demme ("Statue of Liberty"), Gabriela Fung ("Betsy Ross"), Denzel Dellahoussaye ("George Washington"), Aaron Schoenfeld ("Uncle Sam"), Geovonne Long ("MLK"), Jonathan Borst ("JFK"), Michael Shehata ("American Eagle"), Tom Chapin (Governor Edward Nelson), Lewis "Jiggs" Walker (Churchgoer), Joey Perillo (Jimmy), Buzz Kilman (The Guy with the Shades), Marie Runyon (Arthur's Mother), Eliza Simpson, Julie Adamy (Arthur's Children), Andre Blake (Victory Party Director), Tymberly Canale Harris (Victory Party Celebrity Soldier), Lilly McDowell, Josh Elrod (Shaw's Aides), Craig Branam (Klaus Bachman), Sidney Lumet, Reno, Anna Devere Smith, Roy Blount Jr., Fab 5 Freddy (Political Pundits)

Denzel Washington, Kimberly Elise

Major Ben Marco realizes that the nightmares he's been having are connected to a vague incident involving his sergeant's supposedly heroic behavior during an ambush in the Kuwait desert. Ben comes to worry that that same sergeant is now inching close to attaining the vice presidential nomination. Remake of the 1962 United Artists film which starred Frank Sinatra (Marco), Laurence Harvey (Shaw), and Angela Lansbury (Mrs. Shaw).

HAROLD & KUMAR GO TO WHITE CASTLE

(NEW LINE CINEMA) Producers, Greg Shapiro, Nathan Kahane; Executive Producers, J. David Brewington, Jr., Luke Ryan, Joe Drake, Carsten Lorenz, Hanno Huth; Director, Danny Leiner; Screenplay, Jon Hurwitz, Hayden Schlossberg; Co-Producer, J. Miles Dale; Photography, Bruce Douglas Johnson; Designer, Steve Rosenzweig; Music, David Kitay; Music Supervisor, Dave Jordan; Editor, Jeff Betancourt; Casting, Cassandra Kulukundis; Stunts, Jamie Jones; a Senator International/Kingsgate production in association with Endgame Entertainment; Dolby; Fotokem color; Rated R; 88 minutes; Release date: July 30, 2004

Cast
Harold Lee **John Cho**
Kumar Patel **Kal Penn**
Maria **Paula Garces**
Himself **Neil Patrick Harris**
Goldstein **David Krumholtz**
Rosenberg **Eddie Kaye Thomas**
Freakshow **Christopher Meloni**
Male Nurse **Ryan Reynolds**
Dr. Willoughby **Fred Willard**
Officer Palumbo **Sandy Jobin-Bevans**
Billy Carver **Ethan Embry**
J.D. **Robert Tinkler**
Cole **Steve Braun**
Extreme Sports Punk #1 **Dan Bochart**
"I'm So High" Kid **Mike Sheer**
"Don't You Wanna Be Cool" Kid **Christopher Thompson**
Mean Tollbooth Guy **Angelo Tsachouras**
Burger Shack Employee **Anthony Anderson**
Cindy Kim **Siu Ta**
Kenneth Park **Bobby Lee**
Hippie Student **Dov Tiefenbach**
Christy **Kate Kelton**
Clarissa **Brooke D'Orsay**

Paula Garces, John Cho

Kal Penn, John Cho PHOTOS COURTESY OF NEW LINE CINEMA

John Cho, Neil Patrick Harris, Kal Penn

and Albert Howell (Security Guard), Errol Sitahal (Dr. Patel), Shaun Majumder (Saikat Patel), Boyd Banks (E.R. Patient), Malin Akerman (Liane), Rick Sood (Indian Cashier), Gary Anthony Williams (Tarik), Brad Borbridge (Officer Martone), Frank Spadone (Officer Reilly), Jordan Prentice (Giant Bag of Weed), Gary Achibald (Nathaniel Brooks), John Boylan (Officer Brucks), Dan Warry-Smith (White Castle Teenager), Thea Andrews (Anchor), Jamie Kennedy (Urinating Guy)

After getting high, Harold and Kumar develop such a severe case of the "munchies," that they go on an all-night quest through New Jersey to find a White Castle restaurant to satisfy their cravings.

LITTLE BLACK BOOK

(COLUMBIA) Producers, Elaine Goldsmith-Thomas, Deborah Schindler, William Sherak, Jason Shuman; Executive Producers, Herbert W. Gains, Rachel Horovitz, Warren Zide, Craig Perry; Director, Nick Hurran; Screenplay, Melissa Carter, Elisa Bell; Story, Melissa Carter; Photography, Theo Van de Sande; Designer, Bob Ziembicki; Costumes, Susie DeSanto; Music, Christophe Beck; Music Supervision, Randall Poster; Editor, John Richards; Casting, Nancy Nayor Battino; a Revolution Studios presentation of a Blue Star Pictures production; Dolby; Super 35 Widescreen; Deluxe color; Rated PG-13; 106 minutes; Release date: August 6, 2004

Ron Livingston, Brittany Murphy

Brittany Murphy, Julianne Nicholson

Cast

Stacy **Brittany Murphy**
Barb **Holly Hunter**
Kippie Kann **Kathy Bates**
Derek **Ron Livingston**
Joyce **Julianne Nicholson**
Carl **Stephen Tobolowsky**
Ira **Kevin Sussman**
Dr. Rachel Keyes **Rashida Jones**
Lulu Fritz **Josie Maran**

Brittany Murphy, Holly Hunter

(Midget), Louis Bernstein (Neighbor), Norma Lee Resnick, Irene Goostein (Themselves), Keram Malicki-Sanchez (Waiter), Chad Holland (Chef), Natalie Denise Sperl (Natalie)

and Jason Antoon (Larry), Sharon Lawrence (Mom), Gavin Rossdale (Random), Cress Williams (Phil), Dave Annable (Bean), Yvette Nicole Brown (Production Assistant), Vivian Bang (Katie), Ron Pearons (Warm Up Guy), Matthew Frauman (Backstage Production Assistant), Katie Murphy (Stacy at 7), Emma Thaler (Emma Greer), Mercedes Mercado (Honey Squeeze), Lee Cherry (Rapper Taye), Ross Gottstein (Sound Guy), Alex S. Alexander (Nurse Kisilevsky), Marjorie Loomis (Grandma), Lucy Lee Flippin (Daughter) Sarah Chase (Colleen, Bean's Wife), Stephanie Langhoff (Jane), Gary Dubin (Father), Dan Benson (Phillip), Guy Wilson (Sean), Joey Capone (Bruce), Shawnacy Patrick Todd (Jeremy), Benjamin Caya (Gideon), Jason Cowles (Noah), Chris Dotson (Mudfoot), Trent Gill (Dan), Marshall Allman (Trotsky), Noah Smith (John), Mat Botuchis (Earl), Ben Ziff (Frank), Zach Cole (Brian), Kory Alden (Vic), Brendan Bonner (Bartender), Nick Vallelonga (Tough Guy at Bar), Greg Baker, Noah Harpster (Guys at Bar), Mary C. Firestone (Receptionist), Jon Simanton

Eager to find out about her current boyfriend's past girlfriends, Stacy is encouraged by her co-worker Barb to delve into his Palm pilot, an act which opens an unexpected can of worms.

Josie Maran, Brittany Murphy PHOTOS COURTESY OF COLUMBIA

Tom Cruise, Jamie Foxx, Barry Shabaka Henley

Tom Cruise

Tom Cruise, Jamie Foxx PHOTOS COURTESY OF DREAMWORKS/PARAMOUNT

COLLATERAL

(DREAMWORKS/PARAMOUNT) Producers, Michael Mann, Julie Richardson; Executive Producers, Frank Darabont, Rob Fried, Chuck Russell, Peter Giuliano; Director, Michael Mann; Screenplay, Stuart Beattie; Photography, Dion Beebe, Paul Cameron; Designer, David Wasco; Costumes, Jeffrey Kurland; Music, James Newton Howard; Editors, Jim Miller, Paul Rubell; Stunts, Joel Kramer; Casting, Francine Maisler; a Parkes/MacDonald production, an Edge City Production; Dolby; Panavision; Technicolor; Rated R; 120 minutes; Release date: August 6, 2004

Javier Bardem

Cast

Vincent **Tom Cruise**
Max Durocher **Jamie Foxx**
Annie Farrell **Jada Pinkett Smith**
Fanning **Mark Ruffalo**
Richard Weidner **Peter Berg**
Pedrosa **Bruce McGill**
Ida Durocher **Irma P. Hall**
Daniel **Barry Shabaka Henley**
Traffic Cops **Richard T. Jones, Jamie McBride**
Feds **Klea Scott, Wade Andrew Williams, Paul Adelstein**
Young Professional Man **Bodhi Elfman**
Young Professional Woman **Debi Mazar**
Felix **Javier Bardem**
Paco **Emilio Rivera**
FBI Agents **Kenver Cammen, Charlie E. Schmidt, Jr.**
Fever Bouncer **Michael A. Bentt**
Cell Phone Partier **Ian Hannin**
Sergeant **Robert Deamer**
Crime Scene Cops **David Mersault, Anthony Ochoa**
El Rodeo Doormen **Omar Orozco, Edgar Sanchez, Cosme Urquiola**
Ramone **Thomas Rosales, Jr.**
Criminalist **Jessica Ferrarone**
Morgue Attendant **Troy Blendell**
Peter Lim **Inmo**

Pissed Off Driver **Howard Bacharach**
Plainclothes Cop **Chic Daniel**
Waitresses **Corinne Chooey, Jonell Kennedy**

and Steven Kozlowski, Roger Stoneburner, Rodney Sandberg, George Petrina (White Guys), Donald Dean, Elliott Newman, Trevor Ware, Bobby English, Auggie Cavanagh, Ronald Muldrow (Jazz Musicians), Peter McKernan, Jr. (Police Helicopter Pilot), Ivor Shier (News Helicopter Pilot), Daniel Luján, Eddie Diaz (Rubios), Joey Burns, John Convertino, Josh Cruze, Martin Flores, Rick Garcia, Lawrence Goldman, Maurilio Pineda, Daniel Sistos, Jacob Valenzuela, Luis Villegas, Yussi Wenger (El Rodeo Band Members), Jason Statham (Airport Man), Angelo Tiffe (Sylvester Clarke), Ismael Vidrio (Gas Station Attendant), Ron Eckert (Hotel Security Desk Guard), Manuel Urrego (Direction Asking Businessman), Jessie Bernard (Nurse), Luis Moncada (Cold Eyed Killer), Dyna Teal, Sandi Schroeder (Sylvester Clarke Girls), Michael-John Wolfe (Hotel Clerk), Addie Yungmee, J.D. McElroy, Megan Hiratzka (Fever Dancers), Kate Gopaoco, Christy Yi, Lisa Marie Basada (Young Girls), Wilson Wong (Tactical Sergeant), Mark Stainbrook (Tactical), Brandon Molale (Limo Driver)

Mark Ruffalo, Paul Adelstein, Peter Berg, Bruce McGill

L.A. taxi driver Max Durocher finds himself in jeopardy when he unwittingly picks up a hit man who expects Max to drive him around for the evening so he can eliminate five key witnesses.

This film received an Oscar nomination for supporting actor (Jamie Foxx).

Tom Cruise

Jamie Foxx

Jamie Foxx, Jada Pinkett Smith

Daniel Travis, Blanchard Ryan

Blanchard Ryan, Daniel Travis

Blanchard Ryan, Daniel Travis PHOTOS COURTESY OF LIONS GATE

OPEN WATER

(LIONS GATE) Producer, Laura Lau; Director/Screenplay/Editor, Chris Kentis; Photography, Chris Kentis, Laura Lau; Music, Graeme Revell; Associate Producer; Dolby; Color; Rated R; 79 minutes; Release date: August 6, 2004

Daniel Travis, Blanchard Ryan

Cast
Susan **Blanchard Ryan**
Daniel **Daniel Travis**
Seth **Saul Stein**
Estelle **Estelle Lau**
Davis **Michael E. Williamson**
Linda **Cristina Zenarro**
Junior **John Charles**

Vacationing couple Susan and Daniel are accidentally left behind by their scuba diving team and realize they now must face hours in shark infested waters, hoping for rescue.

Anne Hathaway, Chris Pine   PHOTO COURTESY OF WALT DISNEY PICTURES

THE PRINCESS DIARIES 2: ROYAL ENGAGEMENT

(WALT DISNEY PICTURES) Producers, Debra Martin Chase, Whitney Houston, Mario Iscovich; Executive Producer, Ellen H. Schwartz; Director, Garry Marshall; Screenplay, Shonda Rhimes; Story, Gina Wendkos, Shonda Rhimes; Based on characters created by Meg Cabot; Photography, Charles Minsky; Designer, Albert Brenner; Costumes, Gary Jones; Music, John Debney; Editor, Bruce Green; Co-Producer, David Scharf; Casting, Marcia Ross, Donna Morong, Gail Goldberg; a Brownhouse and Debra Martin Chase production; Dolby; Technicolor; Rated G; 113 minutes; Release date: August 11, 2004

Cast

Mia Thermopolis **Anne Hathaway**
Queen Clarisse Renaldi **Julie Andrews**
Joe **Hector Elizondo**
Viscount Mabrey **John Rhys-Davies**
Lilly Moscovitz **Heather Matarazzo**
Nicholas Devereaux **Chris Pine**
Andrew Jacoby **Callum Blue**

and Kathleen Marshall (Charlotte Kutaway), Tom Poston (Lord Palimore), Joel McCrary (Prime Minister Motaz), Kim Thomson (Repoter Elsie), Raven (Asana), Larry Miller (Paolo), Caroline Goodall (Mia's Mom Helen), Sean O'Bryan (Mia's Stepfather Patrick), Matthew Walker (Captain Kip Kelly); Princeton University Campus: Larry Robbins (Dean), Beth Anne Garrison (Anna), Cristi Andrews (Cristi), Lauren Davidson (Lauren); The Birthday Ball: Spencer Breslin (Prince Jacques), Tom Hines (Majordomo), Allan Kent (Bracelet Footman), Wesley Horton (Tiara Footman), Clare Sera (Mrs. Motaz), Elinor Donahue (Lady Palimore), Barbara Marshall (Lady Jerome), Sam Denoff (Lord Jerome), Amy Edwards (Lady Blake), Daru Kawalkowski (Countess Puck), Steve Restivo (Count Vitello), Hope Alexander (Lady Caroline), Susan Elizabeth Jackson (Teresa), Madison Dunaway (Friend

Nyla), Kazumi Nakamura (Keiko), Daston Kalili (Greek Dancer), Joe Smith (Clumsy Dancer), Jess Rowland (Tall Dancer), Chris Wynne (Arm Pump Dancer), Jacki Tenerelli (Lady Sprint), Peggy Crosby (Duchess Quincey), Shannon Wilcox (Lady Salsa), Kamilla Bjorlin (Countess Elan), Dale Hikawa Silverman (Viola Player); The Palace: Jane Morris (Mabrey's Servant, Gretchen), Shea Curry (Lady's Maid Brigitte), Anna White (Lady's Maid Brigitta), Cassie Rowell (Lady's Maid Olivia), Erik Bragg (Security Guard Lionel), Scott Marshall (Security Guard Shades), Alec Nemser (Dancing Footman Felix), Claudia Katz (Housekeeper Freda), Tracy Reiner (Lady Anthony), Julie Paris (Lady Palisades), Jennifer Jackson (Lady's Maid Priscilla), Mark McDaniels (Squire Tom), Brian Klugman (Military Guard), Aldric A. Horton (Palace Guard), Bruce Hall (Palace Chef); Parliament: Paul Vogt (Lord Crawley), Rowan Joseph (Lord Peroit), Paul Williams (Lord Harmony), Bernie Hiller (Parliament Member Hiller), Herb Malina (Parliament Member Bishop), Peter Allen Vogt (Lord Crawley's Brother), Greg Lewis (Baron Von Troken), Bonnie Aarons (Baroness Von Troken); The Press: Sandra Taylor (Suki Sanchez), David Rockwell (Elsie's Cameraman), Shane Partlow (Suki's Cameraman), Greg Vojtanek (Lip Reader George), Keisuke Hoashi (Japanese Reporter); The Genovians: Larrs Jackson (Shepherd), Kate Albrecht (French Citizen), Neal Kaz (Italian Citizen), David Powledge (Tiny Duval), Charles Guardino (Mia's Limo Driver), Jeffrey Scott Jensen (Cafe Owner), Shanda Renee, Gwenda Perez, Rajia Baroudi (Cafe Patrons), Diane Frazen, Stanley Frazen (Citizens), Bud Markowitz (Pear Juggler); The Tea Party: Meredith Patterson (Lady Elissa), Anna Netrebko (Opera Singer Anna), Jonny Blu ("Miracles" Singer), Brad Golden (Henry), Brigitta Lauren (Lady Lindenlaub), Zrinka Domic, Grace Nassar (Guests), Joe Ross (Butler), Darwood Chung (Emperor Sakamoto), Joe Wilson (Sleeping Guest); The Parade: Abigail Breslin (Carolina), Joseph Leo Bwarie (Monsieur Dupont), Isabella Hoffmann (Miss Genovia Hildegard), Marvin Braverman (Tiara Vendor), Blake Davidson, John Carlo Kensinger (Boys), Rosie Krieger (Spectator), Lori Marshall (Teacher Seacliff), Scott Grossman, Joaquin Escamilla, Darrel Wright, Donna Dunmire, Susan Carr George, Karen Russell Budge (Folk Dancers); Bridal Shower Slumber Party: Lauren Bell (DJ), Hannah Schneider (Dancing Princess Hannah), Lorraine Nicholson, Charlee Corra Disney, Alexandra Guthy, Aimee Adams Hall, Brady Woods, Jordan Wright, Claudia Vazquez, Nadege August, Maui Vang (Princesses), Charlotte Marshall-Fricker (Princess Grace), Lily Marshall-Fricker (Princess Camille); The Wedding: Joe Allen Price (Archbishop), Kate McCauley (Choir Director), Tanya Callau (Spanish Guest), Stan Lee (Three Stooges Guest), Sparrow Heatley, Ali Gage (Paolo's Assistants), Marty Nadler (Rabbi), Jeff Michalski (Bouquet Guest), Judy Baldwin, Anina Lincoln, Sarina Ranftl, Patrick Price (Guests), Regina Spencer Sipple (Andrew's Mother), Luana Jackman, Clydene Jackson-Edwards, Karen Harper, Bobbi Page, Teri Koide, John West, Rick Logan, Kevin Dorsey, Dwayne Condon, Gerald White, Oren Waters (Church Choir), Sam Marshall (Cherub-Cheeked Ring Bearer); The Coronation: Sol Rosenthal (Chancellor of Venice), Harvey Keenan (Lord Apparel), Joe Straus (Lord Skylar), Leon Dewayne Cozy (Captain Kip's Assistant), Fat Louie, Maurice (Themselves)

Mia is told that she must be crowned ruler of Genovia sooner than expected, an act which according to law means that she must also be married in time for the coronation. Sequel to the 2001 Disney film *The Princess Diaries* with most of the principals repeating their roles.

WE DON'T LIVE HERE ANYMORE

(WARNER INDEPENDENT) Producers, Harvey Kahn, Naomi Watts, Jonas Goodman; Executive Producers, Ruth Epstein, Mark Ruffalo, Larry Gross; Co-Producers, Ken Lawson, Robert Lee, Sanford Rosenberg; Director, John Curran; Screenplay, Larry Gross; Based on the short stories *We Don't Live Here Anymore* and *Adultery* by Andre Dubus; Photography, Maryse Alberti; Designer, Tony Devenyi; Costumes, Katia Stano; Music, Lesley Barber; Music Supervisor, Laurie Parker; Casting, Ellen Lewis, Audrey Skalbania; a Renaissance Films presentation of a Front Street Pictures presentation; Dolby; Panavision; Color; Rated R; 101 minutes; Release date: August 13, 2004

Cast

Jack Linden **Mark Ruffalo**
Terry Linden **Laura Dern**
Hank Evans **Peter Krause**
Edith Evans **Naomi Watts**
Sean Linden **Sam Charles**
Natasha Linden **Halli Page**
Sharon Evans **Jennifer Bishop**
Audrey **Jennifer Mawhinney**
Lauren **Amber Rothwell**
Lollipop Girl **Meg Roe**
Joe Ritchie **Jim Francis**
Plumber **Marc Baur**
Jim **Patrick Earley**

Mark Ruffalo, Peter Krause

Jack Linden causes a destructive rift in his marriage and in his friendship with fellow teacher Hank Evans when he begins having an affair with Hank's wife, Edith.

Mark Ruffalo, Peter Krause, Naomi Watts, Laura Dern

Mark Ruffalo PHOTOS COURTESY OF WARNER INDEPENDENT

Laura Dern

Christina Moore, Rachel Blanchard, Matthew Lillard, Dax Shepard, Seth Green in *Without a Paddle* PHOTO COURTESY OF PARAMOUNT

WITHOUT A PADDLE

(PARAMOUNT) Producer, Donald De Line; Executive Producers, Richard Vane, Andrew Haas, Wendy Japhet; Director, Steven Brill; Screenplay, Jay Leggett, Mitch Rouse; Story, Fred Wolf, Harris Goldberg, Tom Nursall; Photography, Jonathan Brown; Designer, Perry Andelin Blake; Costumes, Ngila Dickson; Music, Christophe Beck; Music Supervisor, Julianne Jordan; Editor, Debra Neil-Fisher, Peck Prior; Casting, Sheila Jaffe; a De Line Pictures production; Dolby; Super 35 Widescreen, Color; Rated PG-13; 99 minutes; Release date: August 20, 2004

Cast
Dr. Dan Mott **Seth Green**
Jerr Conlaine **Matthew Lillard**
Tom Marshall **Dax Shepard**
Elwood **Ethan Suplee**
Dennis **Abraham Benrubi**
Flower **Rachel Blanchard**
Del Knox **Burt Reynolds**
Bear **Bart the Bear**
Young Tom **Matthew Price**
Young Jerry **Andrew Hampton**
Young Dan **Jarred Rumbold**
Young Billy **Carl Snell**
Billy Newwood **Anthony Starr**
Angie **Nadine Bernecker**
Tony **Danielle Cormack**
Dick Stark **David Stott**
Denise **Bonnie Somerville**

and Scott Adsit (Greasy Man), Morgan Reese Fairhead (Sandi), Liddy Holloway (Bonnie Newwood), Mia Blake (Giselle), Bruce Phillips (Minister), Kate Harcourt (Old Woman), Ray Baker (Sheriff Briggs), Gregory Norman Cruz (River Guide), Christina Moore (Butterfly), Susan Brady (Leslie), Connor Carty-Squires (Boy Scout)

Three childhood friends reunite as adults and decide to fulfill their dream of finding the lost treasure of hijacker D.B. Cooper by canoeing in the Pacific Northwest.

EXORCIST: THE BEGINNING

(WARNER BROS.) Producers, James G. Robinson; Executive Producers, Guy McElwaine, David C. Robinson; Co-Produce, Wayne Morris; Director, Renny Harlin; Screenplay, Alexi Hawley; Story, William Wisher, Caleb Carr, based on character created by William Peter Blatty; Photography, Vittorio Storaro; Designer, Stefano Ortolani; Costumes, Luke Reichle; Music, Trevor Rabin; Editor, Mark Goldblatt; Special Effects Supervisor, Danilo Bollettini; Special Makeup Effects, Gary Tunnicliffe; Casting, Pam Dixon; a James G. Robinson presentation of a Morgan Creek production; Dolby; Univision; Technicolor; Rated R; 114 minutes; Release date: August 20, 2004

Cast
Father Lankester Merrin **Stellan Skarsgård**
Father Francis **James D'Arcy**
Dr. Sarah Novack **Izabella Scorupco**
Joseph **Remy Sweeney**
Major Granville **Julian Wadham**
Chuma **Andrew French**
Sergeant Major **Ralph Brown**
Semelier **Ben Cross**
Father Gionetti **David Bradley**

and Alan Ford (Jeffries), Antonie Kamerling (Lt. Kessel), Eddie Osei (Emekwi), Israel Aduramo (Jomo), Patrick O'Kane (Bession), James Bellamy (James), Cecilia Amati (Little Dutch Girl), Matti Ristinen (Medieval Priest), Lidia Darly (Sebutuana's Wife), James Paparella (Boy in Market), Silvio Jimenez Hernandez (Stricken Turkana Worker), Yemi Goodman Ajibade (Turkana Shaman), Michel Leroy (Tribesman in Hospital), John Sesay, Sayoh Lahai (Turkana Warriors), Alessandro Casula (Preacher with Pazuzu), Roberto Purvis (Cpl. Finn)

Disenchanted clergyman Lankester Merrin finds himself working as an archaeologist in Cairo where a church is mysteriously unearthed, bringing forth supernatural events. This is the third sequel to the 1973 Warner Bros. film *The Exorcist* , following *Exorcist II: The Heretic* (WB, 1977), and *The Exorcist III* (WB, 1990). Skarsgard plays the role of Father Merrin, acted in the first film by Max von Sydow. An alternate version of this film, directed by Paul Schrader, was released by WB on May 20, 2005 under the title *Dominion: Prequel to the Exorcist*.

James D'Arcy, Stellan Skarsgård in *Exorcist: The Beginning* PHOTO COURTESY OF WARNER BROS.

MEAN CREEK

(PARAMOUNT CLASSICS) Producers, Rick Rosenthal, Susan Johnson, Hagai Shaham; Executive Producers, Nancy Stephens, Gig Pritzker, Deborah Del Prete; Co-Producer, Jacob Mosler; Director/Screenplay, Jacob Estes; Photography, Sharone Meir; Designer, Greg McMickle; Costumes, Cynthia Morrill; Music, tomandandy; Music Supervisor, Robin Urdang; Associate Producers, Ryan Peterson, Dessie Markovsky; Casting, Matthew Lessall; a Whitewater Films presentation; Dolby; Fotokem color; Rated R; 89 minutes; Release date: August 20, 2004

Josh Peck, Carly Schroeder, Rory Culkin

Rory Culkin, Trevor Morgan, Carly Schroeder, Scott Mechlowicz, Ryan Kelley, Josh Peck

Josh Peck, Carly Schroeder, Scott Mechlowicz, Rory Culkin, Ryan Kelley, Trevor Morgan

Cast
Sam **Rory Culkin**
Clyde **Ryan Kelley**
Marty Blank **Scott Mechlowicz**
Rocky **Trevor Morgan**
George **Josh Peck**
Millie **Carly Schroeder**
Tom **J.W. Crawford**
Mr. Levinworth **Michael Fisher-Welsh**
Maggie Tooney **Raissa Fleming**
Detective Wright **Kaz Garas**
Mr. Merric **Shelly Lipkin**
Jasper **Heath Lourwood**
Cashier **Ryan Peterson**
Police Officer **Hagai Shaham**
Kile **Brandon Williams**

Scott Mechlowicz, Rory Culkin

Tired of being picked on by the bullying George, Sam agrees to his brother's plan to take the boy on a boating trip with the intention of humiliating him, a plan that goes awry with unexpected consequences.

Trevor Morgan, Scott Mechlowicz PHOTOS COURTESY OF PARAMOUNT CLASSICS

VANITY FAIR

(FOCUS) Producers, Janette Day, Donna Gigliotti, Lydia Dean Pilcher; Executive Producers, Howard Cohen, Pippa Cross, Jonathan Lynn; Director, Mira Nair; Screenplay, Julian Fellowes; Based on the novel by William Makepeace Thackeray; Photography, Declan Quinn; Designer, Maria Djurkovic; Costumes, Beatrix Aruna Pasztor; Music, Mychael Danna; Editor, Allyson C. Johnson; Makeup/Hair Designer, Jenny Shircore; Associate Producers, Matthew Faulk, Mark Skeet; Co-Producer, Jane Frazer; Casting, Mary Selway; a Tempesta Films/Granada Films production, produced in association with Inside Track Films 2 LLP; U.S.-British; Dolby; Super 35 Widescreen; Deluxe color; Rated PG-13; 140 minutes; Release date: September 1, 2004

Jonathan Rhys Meyers, Rhys Ifans, James Purefoy

Eileen Atkins, Reese Witherspoon

Cast

Becky Sharp **Reese Witherspoon**
Miss Matilda Crawley **Eileen Atkins**
Mr. Osborne **Jim Broadbent**
The Marquess of Steyne **Gabriel Byrne**
Amelia Sedley **Romola Garai**
Sir Pitt Crawley **Bob Hoskins**
William Dobbin **Rhys Ifans**
Lady Southdown **Geraldine McEwan**
Rawdon Crawley **James Purefoy**
George Osborne **Jonathan Rhys Meyers**
Pitt Crawley **Douglas Hodge**
Lady Jane Sheepshanks **Natasha Little**
Joseph Sedley **Tony Maudsley**
Young Becky **Angelica Mandy**
Francis Sharp **Roger Lloyd Pack**
Miss Pinkerton **Ruth Sheen**
Miss Pinkerton's Crone **Kate Fleetwood**
Mrs. Dubey **Lillette Dubey**
Mrs. Sedley **Deborah Findlay**
Mr. Sedley **John Franklyn-Robbins**
Biju **Paul Bazely**
Gambler **Charlie Beall**
Lady Crawley **Meg Wynn Owen**

and Georgina Edmonds (Young Rose Crawley), Emilie Richardson (Young Celia Crawley), Tim Preece (Horrocks), Helene Coker (Firkin), Sophie Hunter (Maria Osborne), Tim Seely (Doctor), Paul Bentall (Coalman), David Sterne (Queen's Crawley Mail Coach Driver), Sean McKenzie (Auctioneer), Kathryn Drysdale (Rhoda Swartz), John Woodvine (Lord Bareacres), Barbara Leigh-Hunt (Lady Bareacres), Nicholas Jones (Lord Darlington), Sian Thomas (Lady Darlington), Trevor Cooper (General Tufto), Brian Pettifer (Mr. Raggles), Steven Elder (Curzon Street Footman), Gabrielle Lloyd (Nursemaid), William Melling (Rawdy), Daniel Hay (Georgy), Niall O'Brien (Mr. Moss), Anu Gopalakrishnan (Desert Beauty), Tom Beard (Officer), Roma Edmonds (Rose Crawley), Gledis Cimque (Celia Crawley), Thomas Grant (Little Pitt), Kelly Hunter (Lady Steyne), Camilla Rutherford (Lady Gaunt), Alexandra Staden (Lady George), Jonny Phillips (Mr. Wenham), Richard McCabe (The King), Virendra Saxena (Coventry Island Man), Bruce Mackinnon, Matthew Horne (Casino Boys), Timothy Bentinck (German Official), Andrew Price (Casino Stranger), Tom Sturridge (Young Georgy), Chloe Treend, Stefane Sauer, Nicole Forbes, Amanda Courtney-Davies, Louise Weekley, Lene Langgaard, Sarah Mogg, Tracey Lushington, Sandy Borne, Stephanie McMillan, Suzanne Thomas, Mari Baade, K. Knight, Sylvano Clarke (Slave Dancers)

Having endured an impoverished upbringing Becky Sharp makes it her goal to climb to the top of high society and live a life of wealth and leisure.

Previous version of the novel was *Becky Sharp* (UA, 1935) starring Miriam Hopkins.

Tony Maudsley, Reese Witherspoon PHOTOS COURTESY OF FOCUS

CELLULAR

(NEW LINE CINEMA) Producers, Dean Devlin, Lauren Lloyd; Executive Producers, Douglas Curtis, Toby Emmerich, Richard Brener, Keith Goldberg; Co-Producer, Marc Roskin; Director, David R. Ellis; Screenplay, Chris Morgan; Story, Larry Cohen; Photography, Gary Capo; Designer, Jaymes Hinkle; Costumes, Christopher Lawrence; Music, John Ottman; Editor, Eric Sears; Stunts, Freddie Hice; Associate Producers, Tawny Ellis, Caroline Hynes Rault; Casting, Roger Mussenden; an Electric Entertainment production; Dolby; Panavision; Deluxe color; Rated PG-13; 92 minutes; Release date: September 10, 2004

Chris Evans

William H. Macy, Chris Evans

Kim Basinger PHOTOS COURTESY OF NEW LINE CINEMA

Cast

Jessica Martin **Kim Basinger**
Ryan **Chris Evans**
Ethan **Jason Statham**
Chad **Eric Christian Olsen**
Deason **Matt McColm**
Jack Tanner **Noah Emmerich**
Mooney **William H. Macy**
Mad Dog **Brendan Kelly**
Dmitri **Eric Etebari**

and Caroline Aaron (Marilyn Mooney), Adam Taylor Gordon (Ricky Martin), Richard Burgi (Craig), Rick Hoffman (Lawyer), Dan Ballard, Adam Lieberman (Irate Customers), Will Beinbrink (Young Security Guard), Jessica Biel (Chloe), Chase Bloch (Timid Boy), Chelsea Bloch (Surf Girl's Friend), Chantille Bouousque (Chloe's Chilly Friend), Robin Brenner (Excitable Customer), Paige Cannon (Girl at Concert), Nikki Christian (Porsche Girl), John Churchill (Young Guard), Greg Collins (Aging Security Guard), Valerie Cruz (Bayback), Marco DiMaio (Superior Officer), Eddie Driscoll (Crewcut Officer), Tagert Ellis (Kid in Phone Store), John Ennis, Noe Gonzale (Rent a Cops), Erin Foster (Surf Girl), Willie Gault (Detector Operator), Ernie Grunwald (Busy Salesman), James Hinkle (Skater Boy), Summer Hubbell (Beach Girl's Friend), Lenore Kasdorf (Ticket Checker), Chuck Kelley (Tense Guard), Mark Kubr (Eurotrash Man), Robert Lawrence (Auto Theft Detective), Lexi Lieth (Beach Girl), Kate London (Newscaster at 457 Store), Matt McColm (Deason), Esther "Tita" Mercado (Rosario), L.E. Moko/Robert Shaye (Detective-Looking Guy), Mircea Monroe (Chloe's Friend), Rob Nagle (Paramedic), Dat Phan (Vietnamese Artist), Rachel Reynolds (Videogame Babe), Ron Rogge (Athletic Officer), Lara Romanoff (Eurotrash Girlfriend), Paul Sunderland, Lauren Sanchez (News Anchors), Al Sapienza (False Craig), Lorna Scott (Bank Teller), Lin Shaye (Exotice Car Driver), Sherri Shepherd (Jaded Cashier), Sean Smith (Perky Salesman), Bobb'e J. Turner-Thompson (Lil Rapper), Ishtar Uhvana (Busy Saleswoman), Afsoun Yazdian (Airline Passenger), Dean Devlin (Cab Driver)

Ryan desperately attempts to save a kidnapped woman who has randomly contacted him on her cell phone.

Maggie Gyllenhaal, John C. Reilly, Diego Luna

John C. Reilly, Diego Luna PHOTOS COURTESY OF WARNER INDEPENDENT

CRIMINAL

(WARNER INDEPENDENT PICTURES) Producers, George Clooney, Gregory Jacobs, Steven Soderbergh; Executive Producers, Jennifer Fox, Ben Cosgrove, George Kacandes, Todd Wagner, Mark Cuban; Director, Gregory Jacobs; Screenplay, Gregory Jacobs, Sam Lowry (Steven Soderbergh); Based on the film *Nine Queens* written by Fabian Bielinsky; Photography, Chris Menges; Designer, Philip Messina; Costumes, Jeffrey Kurland; Music, Alex Wurman; Editor, Stephen Mirrione; a Section Eight production, presented in association with 2929 Entertainment; Dolby; Color; Rated R; 87 minutes; Release date: September 10, 2004

Maggie Gyllenhaal, Peter Mullan

Cast

Richard Gaddis **John C. Reilly**
Rodrigo **Diego Luna**
Valerie **Maggie Gyllenhaal**
William Hannigan **Peter Mullan**
Ochoa **Zitto Kazann**
Michael **Jonathan Tucker**
Grandma **Ellen Geer**

and Laura Ceron, Soledad St. Hilaire (Waitresses), Brandon Keener (Daniel, Waiter), Nick Anavio (Cafe Manager), Deborah Van Valkenburgh (Woman in Elevator), Maeve Quinlan (Heather), Brent Sexton (Ron), Malik Yoba (Frank Hill), Lillian Hurst (Mrs. Ochoa), Jack Conley (Henry the Angry Man), Juan Carlos Cantu (Rodrigo's Dad), Enrico Colantoni (Bookish Man), Manuel G. Jimenez (Briefcase Thief), Luis Contreras (Carlos), Michael Shannon (Gene), Patricia Belcher (Bank Executive), Paul Norwood (Bank Manager), Gary Mack (Security Guard)

Scam artist Richard Gaddis enlists the aid of novice con man Rodrigo to help him pass off a counterfeit silver certificate. Remake of the Agentinian film *Nine Queens*, which was distributed in the U.S. in 2001 by Sony Classics.

SKY CAPTAIN AND THE WORLD OF TOMORROW

(PARAMOUNT) Producers, Jon Avnet, Marsha Oglesby, Sadie Frost, Jude Law; Executive Producers, Aurelio De Laurentiis, Raffaella De Laurentiis, Bill Haber; Director/Screenplay/Designer/Costumes, Kerry Conran; Photography, Eric Adkins; Costumes for Gwyneth Paltrow and Jude Law, Stella McCartney; Music, Edward Shearmur; Editor, Sabrina Plisco; Co-Producers, Hester Hargett-Aupetit, Brooke Breton; Special Photographic Process, Stephen Lawes; Senior Visual Effects Supervisor, Scott E. Anderson; Visual Effects Supervisor, Darin Hollings; Animation Director/Digital Effects Supervisor, Michael Sean Foley; Casting, Rick Pagano, Sheila Trezise; an Aurelio De Laurentiis and Jon Avnet presentation of a Brooklyn Films II/Riff Raff-Blue Flower/Filmauro production; Dolby; Deluxe color; Rated PG; 107 minutes; Release date: September 17, 2004

The World of Tomorrow

Cast

Polly Perkins **Gwyneth Paltrow**
Joe Sullivan (Sky Captain) **Jude Law**
Capt. Francesca "Franky" Cook **Angelina Jolie**
Dex Dearborn **Giovanni Ribisi**
Editor Paley **Michael Gambon**
Mysterious Woman **Bai Ling**
Kaji **Omid Djalili**
Dr. Totenkopf **Sir Laurence Olivier**
Dr. Walter Jennings **Trevor Baxter**
Dr. Jorge Vargas **Julian Curry**
Dr. Arler Kessler **Peter Law**
German Scientist **Jon Rumney**
Creepy **Khan Bonfils**
Scary **Samta Gyatso**
Executive Officer **Louis Hilyer**
Communications Engineer **Mark Wells**
Uniformed Officer **James Cash**
Kalacakra Priest **Tenzin Bhagen**

and Thupten Tsondru (Dying Old Man), Matthew Grant, Steve Morphew (Crewmen), Nancy Crane (Receptionist), Stuart Milligan (Police Sergeant), Paul Canter (Police Officer), Demetri Goritsas (Radio Operator), William Hope (American Broadcaster), Jonathan Keeble (British

Giovanni Ribisi

Broadcaster), Stephan Cornicard (French Broadcaster), Stephen Ballantyne (German Broadcaster), Victor Sobchak (Russian Broadcaster), Mido Himadi (Soldier), Gerard Monaco (Technician), Chris Robson (Hindenburg Porter), Matthew Coulter (Hindenburg Boy), Merritt Yohnka (Construction Worker), Sky Soleil (Officer)

When a group of key German scientists are abducted and a horde of gigantic robots are unleashed on the city, mercenary flier Sky Captain is summoned to the rescue. This was the first film to incorporate live action into a digitally created background.

Angelina Jolie

Jude Law, Gwyneth Paltrow PHOTOS COURTESY OF PARAMOUNT

SILVER CITY

(NEWMARKET) Producer, Maggie Renzi; Co-Producer, Lansing Parker; Director/Screenplay/Editor, John Sayles; Photography, Haskell Wexler; Designer, Toby Corbett; Costumes, Shay Cunliffe; Music, Mason Daring; Associate Producer, Suzanne Ceresco; Casting, John and Ros Hubbard; an Anarchists' Convention production; Dolby; Color; Rated R; 128 minutes; Release date: September 17, 2004

Cast

Danny O'Brien **Danny Huston**
Nora Allardyce **Maria Bello**
Chandler Tyson **Billy Zane**
Dickie Pilager **Chris Cooper**
Chuck Raven **Richard Dreyfuss**
Sen. Jud Pilager **Michael Murphy**
Maddy Pilager **Daryl Hannah**
Wes Benteen **Kris Kristofferson**
Grace Seymour **Mary Kay Place**
Mort Seymour **David Clennon**
Cliff Castleton **Miguel Ferrer**

Richard Dreyfuss, James Gammon

Mary Kay Place, Danny Huston

Casey Lyle **Ralph Waite**
Tony Guerra **Sal Lopez**
Sheriff Joe Skaggs **James Gammon**
Mitch Paine **Tim Roth**
Karen Cross **Thora Birch**
Vince Esparza **Luis Saguar**
Lupe Montoya **Alma Delfina**

and Aaron Vieyra (Frito Lopez), Hugo E. Carbajal (Rafi Quinones), Cajardo Lindsey (Lloyd), Elizabeth Rainer (Leslie), Donevon Martinez (Laxaro Huerta), Benjamin Kroger (Deputy Davis), Charles Mitchell (Henry), Roslyn Washington (Hilary), James Van Sickle, Patty Calhoun (Reporters), Denis Berkfeldt (Rev. Tubbs), Maggie Roswell (Ellie Hastings), Paul Rohrer (Phil Ross), Richard Beall (Freddy Mondragon), Mare Trevathan Philpott (Rebecca Zeller), David Russell (Foreman), Gary Sirchia (Preacher), Rodney Lizcano (Yanez), Stephen Brackett (Dewey Jr.), Michael Shalhoub (Leo), Amie MacKenzie (Marcy), Larry Gallegos (Contreras)

When a corpse is accidentally pulled from the river by a dim-witted, Bush-like Colorado gubernatorial candidate, an investigation is called to find out who might have tried to sabotage his election chances.

Kris Kristofferson, Chris Cooper PHOTOS COURTESY OF NEWMARKET

Danny Huston, Sal Lopez

MR. 3000

(TOUCHSTONE/DIMENSION) Producers, Gary Barber, Roger Birnbaum, Maggie Wilde; Executive Producers, Jonathan Glickman, Frank Marshall, Steven Greener, Timothy M. Bourne; Director, Charles Stone III; Screenplay, Eric Champnella, Keith Mitchell, Howard Michael Gould; Story, Eric Champnella, Keith Mitchell; Photography, Shane Hurlbut; Designer, Maher Ahmad; Costumes, Salvador Perez; Editor, Bill Pankow; Co-Producer, Derek Evans; Music, John Powell; Casting, Marcia Ross, Gail Goldberg; a Barber and Birnbaum/Kennedy Marshall production; Dolby; Technicolor; Rated PG-13; 104 minutes; Release date: September 17, 2004

Bernie Mac, Angela Bassett

Cast

Stan Ross **Bernie Mac**
Mo Simmons **Angela Bassett**
Boco **Michael Rispoli**
T-Rex Pennebaker **Brian White**
Fukuda **Ian Anthony Doyle**
Fryman **Evan Jones**
Minadeo **Amaury Nolasco**
Skillett **Dondré Whitfield**
Gus Panas **Paul Sorvino**
Lenny Koron **Earl Billings**
General Manager Shembri **Chris Noth**

and Neil Brown, Jr. (Clubhouse Assistant), Scott Brooks (Eddie Richling), Rich Komwnich (Big Horse Borelli), David Devey (Gervis), John McConnell (HOF President), Ric Reitz (HOF President's Assistant), Jaqueline C. Fleming (Young Woman), Travis Kerber (Earl), Phil Ridarelli (Dad), J. David Ruby (Kid), Beth Lacke (Pilates Instructor), Liz Kaschak (Spinning Instructor), Charlie Kaugk (Man in Stands), Greg Bond (Young), Tom Arnold, Ron Darling, Larry King, Tony Kornheiser, John Salley, Stuart Scott, Michael Wilbon, Jay Leno, Chris Rose, Peter Gammons (Themselves), Bronzell Miller (Red Sox First Baseman), John D. Vodenlich (Astros Catcher), Andrew Prater (Red Sox Catcher), Steve Guden (Giants Catcher), Bert Beatson (Braves Catcher), Gerald M. Davis, Jr. (Brewers Player), J. Anthony Brown, Jeff Stern, Allen Beranek, Bob Still (First Base

Brian White (center)

Umpries), Larry Palmer, David Furru, James Cranston, John Schwab (Umpires), Dick Enberg (Brewers Sportscaster), John G. Connoll, Matt DeCaro, Keegan Michael Key, Chris Marrs, Mykel Shannon, Marco St. John, Christian Stolte (Reporters), John Judd, Scott Benjaminson (Executives), Larry Larson, Douglas Torres (Barflies), John O'Neal, Antonio Paone (Bar Patrons)

On the eve of being inducted into the Hall of Fame, egotistical former ballplayer Stan Ross realizes that he has actually fallen three short of his 3,000 hits record and must return to his old team to bring the score up to the correct figure.

Chris Noth, Bernie Mac

Scott Brooks, Bernie Mac, Michael Rispoli   PHOTOS COURTESY OF TOUCHSTONE PICTURES

WIMBELDON

(UNIVERSAL) Producers, Tim Bevan, Eric Fellner, Liza Chasin, Mary Richards; Executive Producers, Debra Hayward, David Livingstone; Director, Richard Loncraine; Screenplay, Adam Brooks, Jennifer Flackett, Mark Levin; Photography, Darius Khondji; Designer, Brian Morris; Costumes, Louise Stjernsward; Music, Edward Shearmur; Music Supervisor, Nick Angel; Editor, Humphrey Dixon; Tennis Consultant, Pat Cash; Casting, Irene Lamb; a Studio Canal presentation of a Working Title production; Dolby; Widescreen; Technicolor; Rated PG-13; 97 minutes; Release date: September 17, 2004

Kirsten Dunst, Paul Bettany

Sam Neill, Kirsten Dunst

Cast

Lizzie Bradbury **Kirsten Dunst**
Peter Colt **Paul Bettany**
Dennis Bradbury **Sam Neill**
Ron Roth **Jon Favreau**
Edward Colt **Bernard Hill**
Augusta Colt **Eleanor Bron**
Dieter Prohl **Nikolaj Coster-Waldau**
Jake Hammond **Austin Nichols**
Ian Frazier **Robert Lindsay**
Carl Colt **James McAvoy**
Themselves **John McEnore, Chris Evert,
        Mary Carillo, John Barrett**

and Kyle Hyde (Monte Carlo Opponent), Celia Imrie (Mrs. Kenwood), Penny Ryder (Mrs. Littlejohn), Annabel Leventon (Mrs. Rossdale), Amanda Walker (Country Club Tennis Lady), Marina Morgan (Hotel Receptionist), Barry Jackson (Danny Oldham), Beti Sekulovski (Lizzie's 1st Opponent), Vikas Punna (Ajay Bhatt), Abhin Galeya (Vijay), John McGlynn (Bookmaker), Jonathan Timmins (Ball Boy), Martin O'Brien, John Warnaby, Tam Hoskyns (Reporters), Peter Cartwright (Elderly Man in Lift), Eve Pearce (Elderly Woman in Lift), Murphy Jensen (Ivan Dragomir), Jeremy Child (Fred Pilger), Cecilia Dazzi (Billi Clementi), Ulla Dirscherl Van Zeller (Sophia Eri), Jess Loncraine (Tennis Player), Kellie Shirley (Betting Shop Girl), Gemma Catlin (Betting Shop Girl's Friend), Alun Jones (Tom Cavendish), Simon Greenall (Chauffeur), Laura Morley (Lizzie's 2nd Opponent), Danny Baker (Radio London DJ), Hamed Madani (Pierre Maroux), Rebecca Dandeniya (Arliyia Rupersindhe), Sam Bond (TV Reporter), Laurence Kennedy (TV Interviewer), Alan David (Dr. Taylor), Helen Blatch (Mrs. Biggins), Chris Moyles (Radio 1 DJ), Azucena Duran (Dorchester Maid), Gareth Llewelyn (Dochester Bellhop), Geoff Leesley (Dorchester Doorman), Barry-Lee Thomas (Umpire—Final), Ryan McCluskey (Outside Broadcast Director), Maggie McCormack (Peter and Lizzie's Daughter), Thomas Blore (Peter and Lizzie's Son)

Paul Bettany, Jonathan Timmins PHOTOS COURTESY OF UNIVERSAL

Aging British tennis pro Pete Colt gets his final chance to compete at Wimbledon and finds himself falling in love with upcoming American player Lizzie Bradbury.

FIRST DAUGHTER

(20TH CENTURY FOX) Producers, John Davis, Mike Karz, Wyck Godfrey; Executive Producers, Arnon Milchan, Forest Whitaker, Jerry O'Connell, Jeffrey Downer; Director, Forest Whitaker; Screenplay, Jessica Bendinger, Kate Kondell; Story, Jessica Bendinger, Jerry O'Connell; Photography, Toyomichi Kurita; Designer, Alexander Hammond; Costumes, Francine Jamison-Tanchuck; Music, Michael Kamen, Blake Neely; Music Supervisor, Liza Richardson; Editor, Richard Chew; Casting, Denise Chamian; a Regency Enterprises presentation of a New Regency/Davis Entertainment/Spirit Dance production; Dolby; Deluxe color; Rated PG; 105 minutes; Release date: September 24, 2004

Katie Holmes, Michael Keaton

Katie Holmes, Amerie PHOTOS COURTESY OF 20TH CENTURY FOX

Katie Holmes, Marc Blucas

Cast

Samantha Mackenzie **Katie Holmes**
James **Marc Blucas**
Mia **Amerie**
President John Mackenzie **Michael Keaton**
Melanie Mackenzie **Margaret Colin**
Liz Pappas **Lela Rochon Fuqua**
Agent Bock **Michael Milhoan**

and Dwayne Adway (Agent Dylan), Hollis Hill (Agent Colvin), Ken Moreno (Agent Mercer), Andrew Caple-Shaw (Agent Dryer), Alex Avant (Shift Leader), Barry Livingston (Press Secretary), Piper Cochrane (Communications Director), Adam Donshik (First Lady's Chief of Staff), Damon Whitaker (Charles), Steve Tom (Senator Downer), Peter White (College Dean), Parry Shen (Rally Leader), Johnny Sneed (English Professor), Marilyn McIntyre (Teacher at Party), Ryan Raddatz, Toby Moore (Frat Guys), Freddy Bouciegues, Austin Priester (Dancing Frat Guys), Scott Hamm (Frat Guy with Water Gun), Philip Boyd (Frank), Katrina Connor, Sophia Chang (Sorority Gals), Natalie Core (Lady with Camera), Teck Holmes (Mia's Flame), Justine Wachsberger (Passing Student), Andrea Avery (Linda Patterson), Sheila Shaw (Health Center Receptionist), Ann Ryerson (Nurse Practitioner), Andy Umberger (Secret Service Supervisor), Mane Andrew (Mia's Visitor), Jeff Michael (News Reporter), Kent Shocknek (Contentious Reporter), Maria Quiban, Ted Garcia (White House Reporters), Tim Liles (Reporter on Street), Dan Brinkle (Caucus Host), Michael Connor, Nicole Avant (Protestors), Brian A. Smith (Guy on Street), Tore Birkedal (Pizza Guy), Gunther Jensen (Football Coach), Vera Wang, Joan Rivers, Melissa Rivers, Jay Leno (Themselves), Forest Whitaker (Narrator), Sonnet Noel Whitaker (Laughing Girl), Grecco Buratto, Sean Householder, Ed Delmark, Bryan Kelling (Band at Frat Party), Enoch Asmuth, Drew Harrah, Guy Maeda, Scott Dicken, Oren Waters, Tonoccus McClain, Tim Davis, Bobbi Page (Singers at White House)

Hoping to escape from the limelight and live like a normal girl, Samantha Mackenzie, the daughter of the President of the United States, enrolls at a West Coast university where she falls in love with the resident advisor at her dorm.

THE LAST SHOT

(TOUCHSTONE) Producers, Larry Brezner, David Hoberman; Executive Producers, Stan Wlodkowski, Todd Lieberman; Director/Screenplay, Jeff Nathanson; Based upon the article *What's Wrong with This Picture?* by Steve Fishman; Photography, John Lindley; Designer, William Arnold; Costumes, Gloria Gresham; Music, Rolfe Kent; Editor, David Rosenbloom; Co-Producer, Ellen Erwin; Casting, Deborah Aquila, Tricia Wood; a Morra, Brezner, Steinberg and Tenebaum production in association with a Madeville Films production; Dolby; Color; Rated R; 93 minutes; Release date: September 24, 2004

Joan Cusack

Cast

Steven Schats **Matthew Broderick**
Joe Devine **Alec Baldwin**
Emily French **Toni Collette**
Tommy Sanz **Tony Shalhoub**
Valerie Weston **Calista Flockhart**
Marshal Paris **Tim Blake Nelson**
Lonnie Bosco **Buck Henry**
Jack Devine **Ray Liotta**

and Ian Gomez (Agent Nance), Troy Winbush (Agent Ray Dawson), Tom McCarthy (Agent Pike), W. Earl Brown (Willie Gratzo), Evan Jones (Troy Haines), Glenn Morshower (Agent McCaffrey), James Rebhorn (Abe White), Amy Smallman (Heidi Katz), Michael Papajohn (Ed Rossi, Jr.), Jon Polito (Wally Kamin), Valeria Hernandez (Delores), Richard Penn (Funeral Director), Stanley Anderson (Howard Schats, "Ben Cartwright"), Solaria Trent (Monica), Bob Colonna (Farmer), Abel Soto (Valet Parker), Stephanie Venditto (Producer), Ross Canter (Man with Couch), Blue Deckert (Criminal #1), Robert Lee (Mayor Delaney), Kelly McNair (Receptionist), Sean Whalen (P.A.), Gina Doctor (Costume Designer), Chris Kelley (FBI Agent), Yorgo Constantine (First A.D.), Alan Selka (Butler), Shoshannah Stern (Steven's Girlfriend), Sybyl Walker (Reporter), John Prosky (Hotel Manger), Robert Axelrod (Man), Tava Smiley (Nicky's Wife/Widow), Michael Glover, Robyn Rosenkrantz (Steven's Friends), Peter Sherayko (Show Announcer), Buck Damon (Little Joe), Jim Murphy (Hoss), James McCombie (Hop Sing), Barbara Orson (Hysterical Woman), Jamie Freeman, Dustin Fuller (Theatre Employees), Art Olsen, Teddy M. Haggarty, Markus Baldwin, Jess Burch, Casey McCarthy, Kimberly DeMarse, Scott Chase, Gary Levy, Dan Lewk (Hollywood Boulevard Types), Miguel A. Vazquez, Dimas Arellano, Felipe De La Rosa (Mariachi Singers), Theadell Brown (Bat Guy), William Belli (Bus Stop Drag Queen), Sally Insul (Lonnie's Wife), Jasmine Arnold (13-Year-Old Girl), Adam McCarthy (Doorman), Russell Means, Pat Morita (Themselves), Joan Cusack (Fanny Nash)

An aspiring Hollywood filmmaker believes he is getting his big break when he is approached to direct his script when in fact the whole arrangement is a secret FBI operation set up to ferret out the mob.

Matthew Broderick, Alec Baldwin

Matthew Broderick, Calista Flockhart PHOTOS COURTESY OF TOUCHSTONE

A DIRTY SHAME

(FINE LINE FEATURES) Producers, Christine Vachon, Ted Hope; Executive Producers, Mark Ordesky, Mark Kaufman, Merideth Finn, John Wells, The Fisher Brothers; Director/Screenplay, John Waters; Photography, Steve Gainer; Designer, Vincent Peranio; Costumes, Van Smith; Music, George S. Clinton; Music Supervisor, Tracy McKnight; Editor, Jeffrey Wolf; Co-Producer, Ann Ruark; Co-Executive Producers, Michael Almog, Bob Jason; Special Effects Coordinator, Drew Jiritano; Casting/Associate Producer, Pat Moran; a This Is That, Killer Films, John Wells production in association with City Lights Pictures; Dolby; Color; Rated NC-17; 89 minutes; Release date: September 24, 2004

Tracey Ullman, Chris Isaak

Cast

Sylvia Stickles **Tracey Ullman**
Ray-Ray Perkins **Johnny Knoxville**
Caprice Stickles **Selma Blair**
Vaughn Stickles **Chris Isaak**
Big Ethel **Suzanne Shepherd**
Marge the Neuter **Mink Stole**
Paige **Patty Hearst**
Dora **Jackie Hoffman**
Weird Paperboy **Nicholas E.I. Noble**

and Wes Johnson (Fat Fuck Frank), David A. Dunham (Mama Bear), Jeffrey Auerbach (Baby Bear), Susan Allenbach (Betty Doggett), Paul DeBoy (Wendell Doggett), Channing Wilroy, Rosemary Knower (Motorists), Jewel Orem (Loose Linda), Richard Pelzman (Paw Paw), Shirleyann Kaladjian, Hari Leigh (Gay Women), Ricki Lake, David Hasselhoff (Themselves), James Ransome (Dingy Dave), Alan J. Wendl (Officer Alvin), Jonas Grey (Warren the Mailman), Richard DeAngelis (Neuter Man with Sub-Titles), Susan Rome (Messy Melinda), Gwendolyn Briley-Strand (Anti "Oral Sex" Neuter), Kate Kiley (Anti "Bear" Neuter), Grace Nalls (Vaughn's Mother), Ty Ford (Taxi Driver), Randall Boffman (Neuter Businessman), Patsy Grady Abrams (Neuter Old Maid), Doug Roberts (Driving Neuter Husband), Joyce Flick Wendl (Driving Neuter Wife),Jean Schertler (Neuter Grandmother on Bus), Carlos Juan Gonzalez (Bus Driver), Brilane Bowman (Cow Patty), David DeBoy (Dr. Arlington), Kevin Reese (Ronnie the Rimmer), Michael Willis (Tony the Tickler), Lance

Selma Blair

Johnny Knoxville

Baldwin (Larry), Kosha Engler (Lu Ann), Mary Vivian Pearce (Unjudgmental Ex-Sex Addict), Michael Gabel (Mr. Pay Day), John Shields (Chesapeake Cooking Man), Gaelan Alexander Connell (Horny Kid), Frederick Strother ("Strange" Sex Addict), Jean Hill (Woman on Fire Escape), Richard Salamanca, Britt Prentice (Fat Boys), Nathan Fulford (Tire Lick Boy), Christopher Glenn Wilson (Tire Lick Dad), Lynn McCune (Neuter Mom #4), Liam Hughes (Coffee Sex Addict), Steve Mack, Don Hewitt (Injured Neuter Men), Jeanette Chivvas (Fan on Airplane)

After a conk on the head, pruddish, repressed housewife Sylvia Stickles finds herself joining a cult of sex addicts who express their carnal lust without control.

Tracey Ullman PHOTOS COURTESY OF FINE LINE FEATURES

THE FORGOTTEN

(COLUMBIA) Producers, Joe Roth, Bruce Cohen, Dan Jinks; Executive Producers, Steve Nicolaides, Todd Garner; Director, Joseph Ruben; Screenplay, Gerald Di Pego; Photography, Anastas Michos; Designer, Bill Groom; Costumes, Cindy Evans; Music, James Horner; Editor, Richard Francis-Bruce; Visual Effects Supervisor, Carey Villegas; Stunts, Terry J. Leonard; Casting, Margery Simkin; a Jinks/Cohen Company production, from Revolution Studios; Dolby; Deluxe color; Rated PG-13; 91 minutes; Release date: September 24, 2004

Cast

Telly Paretta **Julianne Moore**
Sam **Christopher Kovaleski**
Sam at 5 **Matthew Pleszewicz**
Jim **Anthony Edwards**
Eliot **Jessica Hecht**
A Friendly Man **Linus Roache**
Dr. Jack Munce **Gary Sinise**
Ash **Dominic West**
Library Clerk **Katie Cooper**
Cops **Scott Nicholson, PJ Morrison**
Carl Dayton **Robert Wisdom**
Agent Alec Wong **Tim Kang**
Lauren **Kathryn Faughnan**
Anne Pope **Alfre Woodard**
Brasher **Felix Solis**
Agent Lisa Franks **Susan Misner**
Al Petalis **Lisa Tergesen**
Gas Station Attendant **Ken Abraham**
Sheriff Houwell **J. Tucker Smith**
Eileen the Accountant **Ann Dowd**

A woman, devastated by the death of her son in an airplane crash fourteen months earlier, is told by her psychiatrist that they boy never existed, prompting her to form an alliance with the father of another crash victim to find the answers to this puzzle.

Julianne Moore, Dominic West

Alfre Woodard, Gary Sinise

Julianne Moore PHOTOS COURTESY OF COLUMBIA

Julianne Moore, Dominic West

Lily Tomlin, Jason Schwartzman, Dustin Hoffman, Mark Wahlberg

Jude Law, Naomi Watts

Mark Wahlberg, Jude Law, Jason Schwartzman PHOTOS COURTESY OF FOX SEARCHLIGHT

I ♥ HUCKABEES

(FOX SEARCHLIGHT) Producers, David O. Russell, Gregory Goodman, Scott Rudin; Executive Producer, Michael Kuhn; Director, David O. Russell; Screenplay, David O. Russell, Jeff Baena; Photography, Peter Deming; Designer, K.K. Barrett; Costumes, Mark Bridges; Music, Jon Brion; Editor, Robert K. Lambert; Co-Producer, Dara L. Weintraub; Visual Effects Supervisor, Russell Barrett; Casting, Mary Vernieu; A Kanzeon, Scott Rudin, N1 European Film Produktions production, presented in association with Qwerty Films; Dolby; Panavision; Deluxe color; Rated R; 106 minutes; Release date: October 4, 2004

Jason Schwartzman, Mark Wahlberg

Cast

Albert Markovski **Jason Schwartzman**
Caterine Vauban **Isabelle Huppert**
Bernard Jaffe **Dustin Hoffman**
Vivian Jaffe **Lily Tomlin**
Brad Stand **Jude Law**
Tommy Corn **Mark Wahlberg**
Dawn Campbell **Naomi Watts**
Angela Franco **Angela Grillo**
Mr. Nimieri **Ger Duany**
Darlene **Darlene Hunt**
Marty **Kevin Dunn**
Davy **Benny Hernandez**
Josh **Richard Appel**

and Benjamin Nurick (Harrison), Jake Muxworthy (Tim), Pablo Davanzo (Bobby), Matthew Muzio (Construction Worker), Shawn Patrick, Patrick Walsh, Michael Randall Lovan (Firemen), Tippi Hedren (Mary Jane Hutchinson), Ashley A. Fondrevay, Lisa Guzman (Frosh Girls), Scott Wannberg (Bik Schottinger), Altagracia Guzman (Mrs. Echevarria), Saïd Taghmaoui (Translator), Jean Smart (Mrs. Hooten), Sydney Zarp (Cricket), Jonah Hill (Bret), Denis Hayes (Orrin Spencer), Matthew Grillo-Russell (Boy at Mancala Hour), Janet Grillo (Boy's Mother), Adam Clinton, Antonio Evans (Security Guards), Robert Lambert (Daryl), Isla Fisher (Heather), Kimberly Cutter, John Rothman (Corporate Board), Talia Shire (Mrs. Silver), Bob Gunton (Mr. Silver), Kamala Lopez-Dawson (Molly

Jason Schwartzman, Jude Law

Jason Schwartzman, Jude Law (right)

Isabelle Huppert, Jason Schwartzman

Corn), Saige Ryan Campbell (Caitlin Corn), Kaied Hussan (Turkish Man), Chuck Saftler (Dexicorp Attorney), James J. McCoy (Medic), Shania Twain (Herself), George Meyer, Maria Semple (Formal Couple), Jerry Schumacher (Corporate Man), Julie Ann Johnson, Jeannie Epper-Kimack (Ladies in Gowns), Keith Barrett (Maitre'd), Jake Hoffman (Valet), Meredith Mines (Girl in Elevator), Richard Jenkins (Mr. Hooten)

Hoping to find out what is missing from his life, environmental activist/poet Bernard Markovksi seeks help from a team of professional existential detectives.

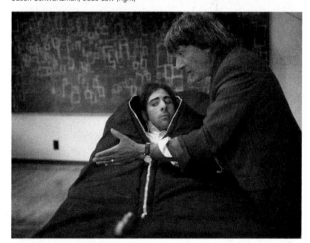

Jason Schwartzman, Dustin Hoffman

Dustin Hoffman, Lily Tomlin

Jason Schwartzman, Dustin Hoffman, Lily Tomlin

LADDER 49

(TOUCHSTONE) Producer, Casey Silver; Executive Producers, Armyan Bernstein, Marty Eewin; Director, Jay Russell; Screenplay, Lewis Colick; Photography, James L. Carter; Designer, Tony Burrough; Costumes, Reneé Enrlich Kalfus; Editors, Bud Smith, Scott Smith; Music, William Ross; Visual Effects Supervisor, Peter Donen; Co-Producer, Chris Salvaterra; Music Supervisor, John Bissell; Associate Producers, Manny Chavez, Anson Downes, Linda Favila; Casting, Nancy Foy; Stunts, G.A. Aguilar; a Beacon Pictures presentation of a Casey Silver production; Dolby; Panavision; Technicolor; Rated PG-13; 115 minutes; Release date: October 1, 2004

Joaquin Phoenix, John Travolta PHOTOS COURTESY OF TOUCHSTONE

Cast

Jack Morrison **Joaquin Phoenix**
Captain Mike Kennedy **John Travolta**
Linda Morrison **Jacinda Barrett**
Lenny Richter **Robert Patrick**
Tommy Drake **Morris Chestnut**
Dennis Gauquin **Billy Burke**
Ray Gauquin **Balthazar Getty**
Tony Corrigan **Tim Guinee**
Frank McKinney **Kevin Chapman**
Keith Perez **Jay Hernandez**
Don Miller **Kevin Daniels**
Pete Lamb **Steve Maye**
Ed Reilly **Robert Logan Lewis**
Katie Morrison **Brooke Hamlin**
Nicky Morrison **Spencer Berglund**
Opal **Karen Vicks**
Maria **Desiree Care**
Marlene **Deidra LaWan Starnes**
Julia **Peggy Cafferty**
Margarita Soto **Marja Allen**
Roseleen Morrison **Leslie Lyles**
Kevin Morrison **Robert Keiper**
Battalion Chief **Robert McKay**
Lt. Yant **Mark Yant**
P.I.O. **Richard Pilcher**

Brooke Hamlin, Joaquin Phoenix, Spencer Berglund, Jacinda Barrett

Fire Captain **John Lumia**
Paramedics **Lynn Filusch, Todd Cahoon, Jess King**
Father Hogan **Robert O'Neill**
Chaplain **Reverend J. Kevin Farmer**

and Delaney Williams (Fireman), Charlene Williams, Barbara Ward (Nurses), Rori D. Godsey (Jenny),Dakota Lee Holloway (Kid), Carol Florence (Delivery Room Nurse), Kyle Prue (Plant Manager), Stan Stovall (TV News Reporter), Sean Pratt (Bartender), Andrea LaBelle (Blonde), Yvonne Erickson (Alice), Dane Anton Aska III (Waiter), Heather Seidle (Girl in Bar), Donna Dundon (Woman with Dog), Tony Rizzoli (Man at Wedding), Frank F. Snyder (Happy Guest), Edward B. Grant (Wedding DJ), Nick Loren (Man at Bar), Carrie Wilson (Sexy Bartender), Patricia DiZebba (Coffee Shop Waitress), Michael Mack (Truck Officer), Paul M. Novak, Jr. (Radio Dispatcher), William Goodwin (Fire Chief), Mayor Martin O'Malley (Mayor), Beau Russel (Birthday Boy)

During a raging fire, while his life hangs in the balance, firefighter Jack Morrison looks back on the path that led him here from his first day with the Baltimore Fire Department.

Balthazar Getty, John Travolta, Kevin Daniels, Morris Chestnut, Joaquin Phoenix, Kevin Chapman, Robert Logan Lewis, Robert Patrick, Jay Hernandez

Oscar, Angie

SHARK TALE

(DREAMWORKS) Producers, Bill Damaschke, Janet Healy, Allison Lyon Segan; Executive Producer, Jeffrey Katzenberg; Directors, Vicky Jenson, Bibo Bergeron, Rob Letterman; Screenplay, Michael J. Wilson, Rob Letterman; Designer, Daniel St. Pierre; Music, Hans Zimmer; Music Supervisors, Darren Higman, Laura Wasserman; Supervising Editor, Nick Fletcher; Visual Effects Supervisor, Doug Cooper; Associate Producer, Mark Swift; Casting, Leslee Feldman; Supervising Animators, Ken Stuart Duncan, Lionel Gallat, Fabrice Joubert, Fabio Lignini, William Salazar; a DreamWorks Animation production; Dolby; Technicolor; Rated PG; 90 minutes; Release date: October 4, 2004

Voice Cast
Oscar **Will Smith**
Don Lino **Robert De Niro**
Angie **Renée Zellweger**
Lenny **Jack Black**
Lola **Angelina Jolie**
Sykes **Martin Scorsese**
Ernie **Ziggy Marley**
Bernie **Doug E. Doug**
Frankie **Michael Imperioli**
Luca **Vincent Pastore**
Don Feinberg **Peter Falk**
Katie Current **Katie Couric**

and David Soren (Shrimp/Worm/Starfish #1/Killer Whale #2), David P. Smith (Crazy Joe), Bobb'e J. Thompson, Kamali Minter, Emily Lyon Segan (Shorties), Lenny Venito (Giuseppe/Great White #1), Saverio Guerra (Pontrelli), Shelley Morrison (Mrs. Sanchez), Mark Swift (Announcer), James Madio (Great White #2/Hammerhead), Frank Vincent, Joseph Siravo (Great Whites), Steve Alterman (Messenger Fish/Tip Fish #2), Phil LaMarr (Prawn Shop Owner), Jenifer Lewis (Motown Turtle), Sean Bishop (Tip Fish #1/Great White #4/Whale/Killer Whale #1), James Ryan (Cashier/Starfish #2/Starfish #3/Oyster/Clown Whale), Latifa Ouaou (Whale Wash Co-Worker), David Yanover (Taxi Fish)

Oscar, Lenny

Oscar, Lola

Oscar, a boastful whale wash employee, forms an unlikely friendship with a sensitive shark named Lenny, who just happens to be the misfit son of powerful mob boss Don Lino.

This film received an Oscar nomination for Animation Feature.

Sykes PHOTOS COURTESY OF DREAMWORKS

TAXI

(20TH CENTURY FOX) Producer, Luc Besson; Executive Producers, Robert Simonds, Ira Shuman; Director, Tim Story; Screenplay, Robert Ben Garant, Thomas Lennon, Jim Kouf; Based upon the film written by Luc Besson; Photography, Vance Burberry; Designer, Mayne Berke; Costumes, Sanja Milkovic Hays; Music, Christophe Beck; Music Supervisor, Spring Aspers; Co-Producer, Steve Chasman; Editor, Stuart Levy; Casting, Donna Isaacson, Christian Kaplan, Ilene Starger; a Europacorp/Robert Simonds production; Dolby; Arriflex Widescreen; Deluxe color; Rated PG-13; 97 minutes; Release date: October 6, 2004

Queen Latifah, Jimmy Fallon in *Taxi* PHOTOS COURTESY OF 20TH CENTURY FOX

New York cop Andy Washburn convinces speed-demon cab driver Belle Williams to help him catch a team of beautiful Brazlian bank robbers. Remake of the 1998 French film of the same name by Luc Besson, which had no distribution in the U.S.

Jennifer Esposito, Jimmy Fallon

Cast

Belle Williams **Queen Latifah**
Andy Washburn **Jimmy Fallon**
Jesse **Henry Simmons**
Lt. Marta Robbins **Jennifer Esposito**
Vanessa **Gisele Bündchen**
Redhead **Ana Cristina de Oliveira**
Third Robber **Ingrid Vandebosch**
Fourth Robber **Magali Amadei**
Washburn's Mom **Ann-Margret**
Agent Mullins **Christian Kane**
Franklin **Boris McGiver**

and Adrian Martinez (Brazlian Man), Joe Lisi (Mr. Scalia), Bryna Weiss (Mrs. Scalia), GQ (Stopwatch Messenger), Joey "CoCo" Diaz (Freddy), Rick Overton (Man at Taxi Commission), John Rothman (Businessman), Mike Santana (Young Dealer), Herman Chaves (Undercover Domino Player), Lou Torres (Sweaty Dealer), Sixto Ramos (Twitchy Dealer), Mario Roberts (Third Dealer), Jamie Mahoney (Kid), Amanda Anka (Officer), John Duerler (Uniformed Cop), Patton Oswalt (Clerk at Impound Office), John Sierros (Fat Cop), Earl Schumann (Old Janitor), Will Cote, Riley G. Matthews, Jr. (Cops at Airport), Adam LeFevre (Big Cop), Kevin Carolan (Cop at Bank #3), Edward Conna (Lou's Garage Cop), Victor Isaac, Ramon Fernandez, John Krasinski (Messengers), Jay Sparado (Bodega Owner), Shirell Furgeson (Nurse), Nashawan Kearse (Cop in Harlem), Alli Danziger (Girl at Bank), Tanner Schwartz (The Hostage)

Jonathan Caouette in *Tarnation* PHOTO COURTESY OF WELLSPRING

TARNATION

(WELLSPRING) Producers, Stephen Winter, Jonathan Caouette; Executive Producer, Gus Van Sant; Co-Executive Producer, John Cameron Mitchell, Vanessa Arteaga, Marie Therese Guirgis, Ryan Werner; Director/Screenplay/Photography/Music Supervisor/Editor, Jonathan Caouette; Music, Max Avery Lichtenstein, John Califra; a Jonathan Couette production; Color/Black & white; Not rated; 87 minutes; Release date: October 6, 2004. Documentary in which filmmaker traces his mother's mental deterioration through personal artifacts and old footage.

With

Jonathan Caouette, Renee Leblanc, Adolph Davis, Rosemary Davis, David Sanin Paz, Dagon James, Shanna King

AROUND THE BEND

(WARNER INDEPENDENT PICTURES) Producers, Elliott Lewitt, Julie Kirkham; Executive Producer, Ronald G. Smith; Director/Screenplay, Jordan Roberts; Photography, Michael Grady; Designer, Sarah Knowles; Costumes, Alix Friedberg; Music, David Baerwald; Editor, Francoise Bonnot; Casting, Mali Finn, Darlene Hansen; a Kirkham-Lewitt production; Dolby; Color; Rated R; 83 minutes; Release date: October 8, 2004

Cast
Turner Lair **Christopher Walken**
Jason Lair **Josh Lucas**
Henry Lair **Michael Caine**
Katrina **Glenne Headly**
Zach Lair **Jonah Bobo**
John **David Eigenberg**
College Student **Robert Douglas**
KFC Counterman **Carlos Cabarcas**
Albert **Gerry Bamman**
Albert's Mother **Jean Effron**
Tiffany's Saleswoman **Lily Knight**
KFC Manager **Rick Negron**
Detective **David Marciano**
Walter **Norbert Weisser**
Ruth **Laurie O'Brien**
Sarah **Kathryn Hahn**
Cowboy **Michael O'Neill**

Glenne Headly, Michael Caine in *Around the Bend*

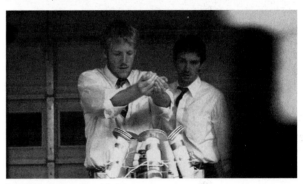

David Sullivan, Shane Carruth in *Primer* PHOTO COURTESY OF THINKFILM

PRIMER

(THINKFILM) Producer/Director/Screenplay/Editor/Music/Designer, Shane Carruth; Photography, Anand Upadhyaya, Daniel Bueche; a Primer Movie Ltd. production; Color; Not rated; 78 minutes; Release date: October 8, 2004

Cast
Aaron **Shane Carruth**
Abe **David Sullivan**
Robert **Casey Gooden**
Phillip **Annad Upadhyaya**
Kara **Carrie Crawford**

and Jay Butler (Metalshop Worker), John Carruth, Juan Tapia (Men on Couch), Ashley Warren (Hostess), Samantha Thomson (Rachel Granger), Chip Carruth (Thomas Granger), Delaney Price (Laney), Jack Pyland (Aaron's Co-Worker), Ketih Bradshaw (Clean Room Technician), Asok Upadhyaya (Laboratory Technician), Brandon Blagg (Will), Jon Cook (Will's Cousin), David Joyner (Rachel's Date), Eric De Soualhat (Translator)

A quartet of engineers create a time traveling aparatus capable of unusual powers.

Michael Caine, Josh Lucas, Jonah Bobo, Christopher Walken PHOTOS COURTESY OF WARNER INDEPENDENT

Turner Lair returns to his estranged family and takes off on a road trip with his son and grandson with the intention of carrying out the bizarre funeral request of Turner's dad.

Garrett Hedlund, Jay Hernandez, Lucas Black, Lee Jackson

Billy Bob Thornton, Lee Thompson Young, Lucas Black

Jay Hernandez, Derek Luke, Garrett Hedlund, Lucas Black

Tim McGraw, Garrett Hedlund PHOTOS COURTESY OF UNIVERSAL

FRIDAY NIGHT LIGHTS

(UNIVERSAL) Producer, Brian Grazer; Executive Producers, James Whitaker, John Cameron; Director, Peter Berg; Screenplay, David Aaron Cohen, Peter Berg; Based on the book by H.G. Bissinger; Photography, Tobias Schliessler; Designer, Sharon Seymour; Costumes, Susan Matheson; Music Producer, Brian Reitzell; Editors, David Rosenbloom, Colby Parker, Jr.; Associate Producer, David Bernardi; Co-Producers, Robert Graf, Sarah Aubrey; Second Unit Director/Stunts, Allan Graf; Casting, Janet Hirshenson, Jane Jenkins; an Imagine Entertainment presentation of a Brian Grazer production; Dolby; Panavision; Technicolor; Rated PG-13; 117 minutes; Release date: October 8, 2004

Billy Bob Thorton (center)

Cast

Coach Gary Gaines **Billy Bob Thornton**
Mike Winchell **Lucas Black**
Don Billingsley **Garrett Hedlund**
Boobie Miles **Derek Luke**
Brian Chavez **Jay Hernandez**
Ivory Christian **Lee Jackson**
Chris Comer **Lee Thompson Young**
Charles Billingsley **Tim McGraw**
L.V. Miles **Grover Coulson**
Sharon Gaines **Connie Britton**
Mrs. Winchell **Connie Cooper**
Flippy **Kasey Stevens**
Melissa **Ryanne Duzich**
Maria **Amber Heard**
Jennifer Gaines **Morgan Farris**
Come's Girlfriend **Laine Kelly**
Trapper **Gavin Grazer**
Skip Baldwin **Turk Pipkin**
Dr. Rogers **Dr. Carey Windler**

and Tommy G. Kendrick (Odessa Doctor), Brad Leland (John Aubrey), Lillian Langford (Nancy Aubrey), Christian Kane (Brian), Buddy Hale, Ken Farmer, Marco Perella, Eloise Dejoria, Robert Weaver (Boosters), Katherine Willis, Angie Bolling (Booster Wives), Charles Sanders

Jay Hernandez, Lucas Black

(Buddy's Burgers Manager), Barry Sykes (Permian Play-by-Play Announcer), Clay Kennedy (Permian Color Announcer), Lewis B. Johnson, J.D. Hawkins (Carter Play-by-Play Announcers), B.T. Stone (Slammin' Sammy), Wade Johnston (Coach Miller), Rick Herod (Coach McCutcheon), Paul Mitchell Wright (Coach Belew), Julius Tennon (Coach James), Dennis Hill (Coach Harper), Timothy Walter (Coach Vonner), Robert Scott Smith (Coach Smith), Kenneth Plunk (Coach Plunk), Josh Berry (Coach Campbell), Branson Washburn (Coach Washburn), David Johnson (Coach Johnson), John Hayden, Chris Palmer (Permian Booth Coaches), Kyle Scott Jackson, C. Anthony "Charles" Jackson, Kippy Brown, Cleveland "Chick" Harris (Carter Booth Coaches), Billy Melvin Thomas, Kammerin Hunt (Carter Assistant Coaches), Roy Williams (Midland Lee Assistant Coach), Gary Mack Griffin (Marshall High School Coach), Randy Brinlee (Marshall Game Referee), Dan Rankin (Cooper Game End Zone Official), Tim Crowley (Carter Game Referee), Harvey L. Jeffries (Carter Game Official), Tiki Davis (Carter Co-Captain—Baird), Everett Smith (Carter Quarterback—Whitaker), Ty Law (Carter Wide Receiver—Graf), Chris Dahlberg (Clancy Kent), Peter Harrell, Jr. (C.C. Russeau), Kevin Page (John Wilkins), Brady Coleman (Jerald McClary), Stephen Bishop (Loie Harris), Bob Richardson (Marvin Edwards), Mark

Derek Luke, Billy Bob Thornton, Grover Coulson

Donaldson (State Trooper), Aisha Schliessler (Cheerleader), Evan Bernard (Drunk Driver), Rutherford Cravens, Wayne Hanawalt (Kansas Wesleyan Recruiters), Brian Thornton, Sam Austin, Mark Nutter (Recruiters), Jeff Gibbs (Journalist Jim), Richard Dillard, Robert Flores (Reporters), Terry Parks (Skip Baldwin's Cameraman), Talon Smith, Taylor Sawyers, Bradley Lisman (Young Kids), Richard Nance (Buzzard), Arron Babino, Dean Baldwin, Ben Bronson, Sunny Byrd, John Clark, Bobby Doherty, Chris Fisher, Cedric Foster, Corey Hargers, Tavis Harvey, Deshaun Hill, Ryan Jacobs, Nick Jester, Mike Jones, Tyrone Jones, Mark Llewellyn, Jon Luke, O.J. McClintock, Robert Nguyen, Joseph Norman, Dewayne Patmon, Everick Rawls, Brett Robin, Steven Rogers, Ray Ross, Chad L. Stevens, Travis Thompson, Matt Trissell, Brandon Tully, Darrick Wallace (Football Players)

Derek Luke, Jay Hernandez, Lucas Black, Garrett Hedlund, Lee Thompson Young

True story of how, in 1988, the Permian Panthers of Odessa, Texas, the most successful high school football team in the country, set their goal on winning their fifth state championship.

SHALL WE DANCE

(MIRAMAX) Producer, Simon Fields; Executive Producers, Bob Weinstein, Harvey Weinstein, Julie Goldstein; Co-Producer, Mari Jo Winkler-Ioffreda; Co-Executive Producers, Jennifer Berman, Amy Israel; Director, Peter Chelsom; Screenplay, Audrey Wells; Based on the Altimira Pictures film of the same name written by Masayuki Suo; Photography, John de Borman; Designer, Caroline Hanania; Costumes, Sophie de Rakoff; Music, Gabriel Yared, John Altman; Music Producer, Randy Spendlove; Choreographer, John O'Connell; Editors, Charles Ireland, Roebrt Leighton; Casting, Richard Hicks, Ross Clydesdale; a Simon Fields production; Dolby; Deluxe color; Rated PG-13; 106 minutes; Release date: October 15, 2004

Stanley Tucci, Susan Sarandon, Richard Gere, Jennifer Lopez

Cast

John Clark	**Richard Gere**
Paulina	**Jennifer Lopez**
Beverly Clark	**Susan Sarandon**
Link	**Stanley Tucci**
Bobbie	**Lisa Ann Walter**
Devine	**Richard Jenkins**
Miss Mitzi	**Anita Gillette**
Chic	**Bobby Canavale**
Vern	**Omar Miller**
Jenna Clark	**Tamara Hope**
Evan Clark	**Stark Sands**
Scott	**Nick Cannon**

and Sarah Lafleur (Carolyn), Onalee Ames (Diane), Diana Salvatore (Tina), Daphne Korol (Daphne), Driton "Tony" Dovolani (Slick Willy), Keti Virshilas (Perky Girl), Dave Sparrow (Louis), Matt Gordon (Frank), Candace Smith (Betsy), Sandra Caldwell (Elise), Mairi Babb (Patty), Ann Margaret Clements (Commuter), Karina Smirnoff (Link's Pouty Dance Partner), Diane Marquis (Tanya), Beatriz Pizano (Paulina's Mother), Deborah Yates (Winking Dancer), Mya Harrison (Vern's Fiance), Holly Johnson (Chic's Cute Dance Partner), Gio Tropea (D.J.), James Sermons (Chic's Young Man), Barre W. Hall (Silver Fox), Nicholas Kosovich (Winking Dancer's Partner), Chantelle Leonardo (Christie), Steven Martin (Emcee), John

Richard Gere, Jennifer Lopez

O'Connell (Judge), Caitlynn Taczynski (Young Paulina), Denis Tremblay, Brian Torner, Pierre Allaire (Pauline's Students), Jean Marc Genereux (Smarmy Old Man), Francesco Flumiani (Young Teacher), Gary McDonald (Paulina's Blackpool Partner—Flashback), Vyacheslav "Slavik" Kryklyvyy (Paulina's Blackpool Partner—Present), Geri Hall (Bemused Co-Worker), Sean O'Brian (Parking Attendant), Brian Drader (Competitor in Parking Lot), Ja Rule (Hip Hop Bar Performer), Alison Black (Jackstage "De-Trainer"), Kim Kindrick (Officer Girl)

Attorney John Clark, feeling that there is something missing from his life, decides to take up dance lessons, a fact he withholds from his wife.

Remake of the 1996 Japanese film of the same name which was released here in 1997 by Miramax.

Lisa Ann Walter, Jennifer Lopez PHOTOS COURTESY OF MIRAMAX

Laura Linney, Topher Grace in *P.S.*

P.S.

(NEWMARKET) Producers, Robert Kessel, Anne Chaisson, John Hart, Jeff Sharp; Executive Producer, Michael Hogan; Co-Producer, Allen Bain; Director, Dylan Kidd; Screenplay, Dylan Kidd, Helen Schulman; Based on the novel *P.S. I Love You* by Helen Schulman; Photography, Joaquin Baca-Asay; Designer, Stephen Beatrice; Costumes, Amy Westcott; Music, Craig Wedren; Editor, Kate Sanford; Associate Producer, Nina Wolarsky; Casting, Mackey, Sandrich, Weidman & De Miguel; a Hart Sharp Entertainment production in association with Fortissimo Film Sales; Dolby; Color; Rated R; 97 minutes; Release date: October 15, 2004

Cast

Louise Harrington **Laura Linney**
F. Scott Feinstadt **Topher Grace**
Sammy Silverstein **Paul Rudd**
Elie Silverstein **Lois Smith**
Peter Harrington **Gabriel Byrne**
Missy Goldberg **Marcia Gay Harden**

and Jennifer Carta (Work-Study), Ross A. McIntyre (Jimmy), Chris Meyer (Ricky), Becki Newton (Rebecca), Stacy Lynn Spierer (Stacey)

Against her better instincts, college admissions officer Louise Harrington has an affair with a promising incoming student whom she believes resembles her long dead first love.

Gabriel Byrne, Laura Linney in *P.S.* PHOTOS COURTESY OF NEWMARKET

TEAM AMERICA: WORLD POLICE

(PARAMOUNT) Producers, Scott Rudin, Trey Parker, Matt Stone; Executive Producers, Scott Aversano, Anne Garefino; Director, Trey Parker; Screenplay, Trey Parker, Matt Stone, Pam Brady; Photography, Bill Pope; Designer, Jim Dultz; Costumes, Karen Patch; Music, Harry Gregson-Williams; Original Songs, George Drakoulias; Editor, Tom Vogt; Visual Consultant, David Rockwell; Co-Producers, Michael Polaire, Frank Agnone; Puppet Designer, Norman Tempia; Puppet Producers, Chiodo Bros.; Special Effects, Joe Viskocil; a Scott Rudin/Matt Stone production; Dolby; Panavision; Deluxe color; Rated R; 98 minutes; Release date: October 15, 2004

Joe, Gary, Chris, Lisa, Sarah PHOTO COURTESY OF PARAMOUNT

Voice Cast

Gary Johnston/Joe/Hans Prix/Kim Jong Il/ Carson/Drunk/ Tim Robbins/Sean Penn/Michael Moore/Helen Hunt/ Matt Damon/Susan Sarandon **Trey Parker**
Chris/George Clooney/Danny Glover/ Ethan Hawke/Matt Damon **Matt Stone**
Lisa **Kristen Miller**
Sarah **Masasa**
Spottswoode **Daran Norris**
Intelligence/Chechnian Terrorist **Phil Hendrie**
Alec Baldwin **Maurice LaMarche**
French Mother **Chelsea Marguerite**
Jean Francois **Jeremy Shada**
Fred Tatasciore **Samuel L. Jackson**

An elite anti-terrorist group sets out to stop crazed North Korean dictator Kim Jong Il from world domination.

Paul Giamatti, Virginia Madsen

Paul Giamatti, Thomas Haden Church

Virginia Madsen, Paul Giamatti, Thomas Haden Church, Sandra Oh

Paul Giamatti, Thomas Haden Church

SIDEWAYS

(FOX SEARCHLIGHT) Producer, Michael London; Co-Producer, George Parra; Director, Alexander Payne; Screenplay, Alexander Payne, Jim Taylor; Based on the novel by Rex Pickett; Photography, Phedon Papamichael; Designer, Jane Ann Stewart; Costumes, Wendy Chuck; Music, Rolfe Kent; Editor, Kevin Tent; Casting, John Jackson; a Michael London production; Dolby; Deluxe color; Rated R; 126 minutes; Release date: October 22, 2004

Cast
Miles Raymond **Paul Giamatti**
Jack Lopate **Thomas Haden Church**
Maya **Virginia Madsen**
Stephanie **Sandra Oh**
Miles' Mother **Marylouise Burke**
Victoria **Jessica Hecht**
Cammi **Missy Doty**
Cammi's Husband **M.C. Gainey**
Christine Erganian **Alysia Reiner**
Mrs. Erganian **Shaké Toukhmanian**

Paul Giamatti, Virginia Madsen

Sandra Oh, Thomas Haden Church

Mike Erganian **Duke Moosekian**
Mike's Building Manager **Robert Covarrubias**
Gary the Bartender **Patrick Gallagher**
Stephanie's Mother **Stephanie Faracy**
Frass Canyon Pourer **Joe Marinelli**
Chris at Stanford **Chris Burroughs**
Voice of Evelyn Berman-Silverman **Toni Howard**
Armenian Priest **Rev. Fr. Khoren Babouchian**
Ken Cortland **Lee Brooks**
Leslie Brough **Peter Dennis**
Foxen Winery Pourer **Alison Herson**
Vacationing Dr. Walt Hendricks **Phil Reeves**
Obnoxious Golfer **Rob Trow**
Los Olivos Waitress **Lacey Rae**
Barista **Cesar "Cheeser" Ramos**
Reciting Eighth Grader **Daniel Rogers**
Siena **Natalie Carter**
Mini-Mart Owner **Simon Kassis**
Armenian Deacon **Sevag Kendirjian**
Acoustic Guitarist **Jaren Coler**

Still hurting after being dumped by his wife, teacher and aspiring novelist Miles Raymond takes his friend Jack on a weeklong trip through California's wine country prior to the latter's upcoming marriage.

Paul Giamatti, Thomas Haden Church   PHOTOS COURTESY OF FOX SEARCHLIGHT

Paul Giamatti, Thomas Haden Church

2004 Academy Award-winner for Best Screenplay Adaptation.
This film received additional Oscar nominations for picture, director, supporting actor (Church), and supporting actress (Madsen),.

Sandra Oh, Thomas Haden Church, Virginia Madsen, Paul Giamatti

Thomas Haden Church, Paul Giamatti

Dermot Mulroney

Jamie Bell, Devon Alan

UNDERTOW

(UNITED ARTISTS) Producers, Lisa Muskat, Terrence Malick, Edward R. Pressman; Executive Producers, John Schmidt, Alessandro Camon, Saar Klein; Director, David Gordon Green; Screenplay, Joe Conway, David Gordon Green; Story, Lingard Jervey; Photography, Tim Orr; Designer, Richard Wright; Costumes, Jill Newell; Music, Philip Glass; Editors, Zene Baker, Steven Gonzales; Casting, Mali Finn; a ContentFilm presentation of a Sunflower production; Distributed by MGM Distribution Co.; Dolby; Color; Rated R; 108 minutes; Release date: October 22, 2004

Cast
Chris Munn **Jamie Bell**
Deel Munn **Josh Lucas**
Tim Munn **Devon Alan**
Violet **Shiri Appleby**
John Munn **Dermot Mulroney**
Grant the Mechanic **Pat Healy**
Grandfather **Bill McKinney**
Lila **Kristen Stewart**
Bern **Robert Longstreet**
Officer Clayton **Terry Loughlin**
Wadsworth Pela **Eddie Rouse**
Amica Pela **Patrice Johnson**

and Charles "Jester" Poston (Hard Hat Dandy), Mark Darby Robinson (Conway), Leigh Hill (Muriel the Cashier), Alfred M. Jackson, William D. Turner (Dock Workers), Michael Bacall (Jacob), Carla Bessey (Violet's Friend), Damien Jewan Lee (Gus)

A pair of dirt poor brothers find themselves on the run from their psychotic uncle after he murders the boys' father.

Josh Lucas PHOTOS COURTESY OF UNITED ARTISTS

THE GRUDGE

(COLUMBIA) Producers, Sam Raimi, Rob Tapert, Taka Ichise; Executive Producers, Roy Lee, Doug Davison, Joe Drake, Nathan Kahane, Carsten Lorenz; Director, Takashi Shimizu; Screenplay, Stephen Susco; Based on the film *Jo-On: The Grudge* written and directed by Takashi Shimizu; Co-Producers, Michael Kirk, Aubrey Henderson, Shintaro Shimosawa; Photography, Hideo Yamamoto; Designer, Iwao Saito; Costumes, Shawn Holly Cookson; Editor, Jeff Bettancourt; Music, Christopher Young; Casting, Nancy Nayor Battino, Kelly Wagner; a Sam Raimi presentation of a Ghost House Pictures production; Dolby; Deluxe color; Rated PG-13; 92 minutes; Release date: October 22, 2004

Sarah Michelle Gellar, Ted Raimi

Jason Behr, Sarah Michelle Gellar

Cast
Karen **Sarah Michelle Gellar**
Doug **Jason Behr**
Matthew **William Mapother**
Jennifer **Clea DuVall**
Susan **KaDee Strickland**
Emma **Grace Zabriskie**
Peter **Bill Pullman**
Maria **Rosa Blasi**
Alex **Ted Raimi**
Nakagawa **Ryo Ishibashi**
Yoko **Yoko Maki**
Toshio **Yuya Ozeki**
Kayako **Takako Fuji**
Takeo **Takashi Matsuyama**
Igarashi **Hiroshi Matsunaga**
Suzuki **Hajime Okayama**

and Yoshiyuki Morishita (Guard), Kazuyuki Tsumura (Peter's Co-Worker), Jotaro Kitamura, Taigi Kobayashi (Policemen), Junko Koizumi (Mother), Nana Koizumi (Daughter), Yoichi Okamura (Restaurant Manager)

An American exchange student studying social work in Japan agrees to tend to an elderly woman, only to discover that the old lady's home is possessed by a supernatural horror bent on death.

KaDee Strickland

Takako Fuji   PHOTOS COURTESY OF COLUMBIA

Nicole Kidman

Danny Huston, Nicole Kidman, Peter Stormare

Danny Huston, Nicole Kidman PHOTOS COURTESY OF MIRAMAX

BIRTH

(MIRAMAX) Producers, Jean-Louis Piel, Nick Morris, Lizie Gower; Executive Producers, Kerry Orent, Mark Ordesky, Xavier Marchand; Director, Jonathan Glazer; Screenplay, Jean-Claude Carriere, Milo Addica, Jonathan Glazer; Photography, Harris Savides; Designer, Kevin Thompson; Costumes, John Dunn; Music, Alexandre Desplat; Editors, Sam Sneade, Claus Wehlisch; Associate Producer, Kate Myers; Casting, Avy Kaufman; an Academy production released in association with Fine Line Features; Dolby; Technicolor; Rated R; 100 minutes; Release date: October 29, 2004

Cameron Bright, Lauren Bacall

Cast
Anna **Nicole Kidman**
Young Sean **Cameron Bright**
Joseph **Danny Huston**
Eleanor **Lauren Bacall**
Laura **Alison Elliott**
Bob **Arliss Howard**
Sean **Michael Desautels**
Clara **Anne Heche**
Clifford **Peter Stormare**
Mr. Conte **Ted Levine**
Mrs. Conte **Cara Seymour**

and Scott Johnsen (Caterer), Joe M. Chalmers (Sinclair), Novella Nelson (Lee), Zoe Caldwell (Mrs. Hill), Charles Goff (Mr. Drummond), Sheila Smith (Mrs. Drummond), Milo Addica (Jimmy), Mary Catherine Wright (Young Woman), Elizabeth Greenberg (Teacher), Tessa Auberjonois (Woman in Lobby), Michael Joseph Cortese, Jr. (Patrick, Mini-Bike Driver), John Robert Tramutola (Stevie), Jordan Lage (Peter), Margot Jewers (Real Estate Agent), Matthew Giffuni, Ian Hoffberg, Laura Fallon (Runners), John Juback (Man in Lobby), Kavita R. Mangroo (Woman at Counter), Alexandra K. Salo (Woman at Party), Hollis Jones, Libby Skala (Bridesmaids), Bruce Bennetis (Wedding Photographer), Gregory Smith (Photographer), T. Ryder Smith (Waiter), Ed Bogdanowicz, Jerry Fuentes (Cops), Gregory Dunn (Secretary), Lisa Barnes (Clara's Neighbor)

Ten years after her first husband's death, Anna prepares to remarry, only to be confronted by a ten-year-old boy who shows up at her Upper East Side apartment claiming to be her late husband.

Leigh Warnell

Michael Emerson, Monica Potter

Ned Bellamy, Danny Glover PHOTOS COURTESY OF LIONS GATE

SAW

(LIONS GATE) Producers, Oren Koules, Mark Burg, Gregg Hoffman; Executive Producer, Stacey Testro; Co-Producers, Daniel Jason Heffner, Richard H. Prince; Director, James Wan; Screenplay, Leigh Warnell, James Wan; Photography, David Armstrong; Designer, Julie Berghoff; Costumes, Jennifer Soulages; Music, Charlie Clouser; Editor, Kevin Greutert; Casting, Amy Lippens; Dolby; Color; Rated R; 102 minutes; Release date: October 29, 2004

Cary Elwes

Cast

Dr. Lawrence Gordon **Cary Elwes**
Det. David Tapp **Danny Glover**
Allison Gordon **Monica Potter**
Zep Hindle **Michael Emerson**
Jigsaw **Tobin Bell**
Det. Steven Sing **Ken Leung**
Diana Gordon **Makenzie Vega**
Amanda **Shawnee Smith**
Brett **Benito Martinez**
Kerry **Dina Meyer**
Adam **Leigh Warnell**
Captive **Ned Bellamy**
Mark **Paul Gutrecht**
Carla **Alexandra Chun**
Neighbor **Avner Garbi**
Paul **Mike Butters**

Two men are horrified to find themselves chained on opposite sides of a bathroom with a dead body on the floor between them.

Sharon Warren, C.J. Sanders

C.J. Sanders, Robert Wisdom

RAY

(UNIVERSAL) Producers, Howard Baldwin, Karen Baldwin, Taylor Hackford, Stuart Benjamin; Executive Producers, William J. Immerman, Jamie Rucker King; Co-Producers, Ray Charles Robinson Jr., Alise Benjamin, Nick Morton; Director, Taylor Hackford; Screenplay, James L. White; Story, Taylor Hackford, James L. White; Photography, Pawel Edelman; Designer, Stephen Altman; Costumes, Sharen Davis; Music, Craig Armstrong; Music Supervisor, Curt Sobel; Original and New Recordings, Ray Charles; Casting, Nancy Klopper; a Bristol Bay Prods. presentation of an Anvil Films production in association with Baldwin Entertainment; Dolby; Technicolor; Rated PG-13; 153 minutes; Release date: October 29, 2004

Jamie Foxx

Renee Wilson, Regina King, Kimberly Ardison PHOTOS COURTESY OF UNIVERSAL

Clifton Powell, Jamie Foxx

Jamie Foxx, Kerry Washington

Cast

Ray Charles **Jamie Foxx**
Della Bea Robinson **Kerry Washington**
Margie Hendricks **Regina King**
Jeff Brown **Clifton Powell**
Joe Adams **Harry Lennix**
Fathead Newman **Bokeem Woodbine**
Mary Ann Fisher **Aunjanue Ellis**
Aretha Robinson **Sharon Warren**
Young Ray Robinson **C.J. Sanders**
Ahmet Ertegun **Curtis Armstrong**
Jerry Wexler **Richard Schiff**
Quincy Jones **Larenz Tate**
Gossie McKee **Terrence Dashon Howard**
Milt Shaw **David Krumholtz**
Wilbur Brassfield **Wendell Pierce**
Lowell Fulson **Chris Thomas King**
Jimmy **Thomas Jefferson Byrd**
Tom Dowd **Rick Gomez**
Marlene **Denise Dowse**
Oberon **Warwick Davis**
Dr. Hacker **Patrick Bauchau**
Jack Lauderdale **Robert Wisdom**
Sam Clark **Kurt Fuller**

Himself **Julian Bond**
Ethel McRae **Kimberly Ardison**
Pat Lyle **Renee Wilson**
Mr. Pitt **Willie Metcalf**
Bus Driver **Mike Pniewski**
Young George Robinson **Terrone Bell**
Til **Richard A. Smith**
Billy Ray **Gary Grubbs**
Eula **Carol Sutton**

and Bill Breaux, Alex Van, Jeffrey Galpin, Michael Arata (Cops), Roland "Bob" Harris (Jesse Stone), Tom Clark (Alan Freed), Afemo Omilami (Angry Husband), Elisabeth Omilami (Angry Wife), Vernel Bagneris (Dancin' Al), Fahnlohnee Harris (Trudy Daniels), Michael Travis Stone (Robert), Eric O'Neal, Jr. (Ray Charles, Jr., 5-6 yrs.), Tequan Richmond (Ray Charles, Jr., 9-10 yrs.), Matthew Benjamin (Musician in Billy Ray's), John Swasey, James Huston (Customs Agents), Marc Lynn (Downbeat Reporter), Kyle Scott Jackson (King Bee), Todd J. Smith (Student Reporter), Rutherford "Rudy" Cravens (White Promoter), Darnell Williams (Fast Girl), Jedda Jones (Mercedes), Estella Denson (Lady in Rain)

The true story of how Ray Charles overcame racism and the loss of sight to become one of the great singer-musicians of the Twentieth Century.

2004 Academy Award-winner for Best Actor (Jamie Foxx) and Sound. This film received additional nominations for picture, director, costume design, and editing.

Kerry Washington

Richard Schiff, Curtis Armstrong

ALFIE

(PARAMOUNT) Producers/Screenplay, Charles Shyer, Elaine Pope; Based on the film by Bill Naughton, from his play; Executive Producers, Diana Phillips, Sean Daniels; Director, Charles Shyer; Photography, Ashley Rowe; Designer, Sophie Becker; Costumes, Beatrix Aruna Pasztor; Music, Mick Jagger, Dave Stewart, John Powell; Original Songs Performed by Mick Jagger, Dave Stewart; Editor, Padraic McKinley; Casting, Mindy Marin; a Charles Shyer production; Dolby; Deluxe color; Rated R; 106 minutes; Release date: November 5, 2004

Jane Krakowski, Jude Law

Jude Law PHOTOS COURTESY OF PARAMOUNT

Sienna Miller, Jude Law

Jude Law, Nia Long

Jude Law, Susan Sarandon

Cast

Alfie Elkins **Jude Law**
Julie **Marisa Tomei**
Marlon **Omar Epps**
Lonette **Nia Long**
Dorie **Jane Krakowski**
Nikki **Sienna Miller**
Liz **Susan Sarandon**
Lu Schnitman **Renee Taylor**
Phil **Jeff Harding**
Terry **Kevin Rahm**
Max **Max Morris**
Wing **Gedde Watanabe**
Mrs. Wing **Jo Yang**
Carol **Tara Summers**
Felix **Sam Vincenti**
Uta **Katherine LaNasa**
Bitter Girl **Claudette Mink**
Tonya **Anouska de Georgiou**
Chyna **Anastasia Griffith**
Dr. Miranda Kulp **Jefferson Mays**
Pretty Teacher **Debroah Lynn-Shyer**
Waiting Room Nurse **Veronica Clifford**
Mrs. Liberman **Sondra James**
Joe **Dick Latessa**
Wes **Graydon Carter**
Waldorf Doorman **Steven Morphew**
Bright Young Things **Finlay Robertson, Edward Hogg,
  Martha Cope, Ben Jackson**
New Year's Eve Singer **Charlotte Moore**
and Cosima Shaw (New Year's Eve Stunner), Marjan Neshat (Traffic Cop), Gil Williams (Elvis, the Doorman), Saidah Arrika Ekulona (Gilda, the Receptionist), Stephen Gaghan (Adam), Paul Brooke (Flower Shop Proprietor)

Jude Law, Dick Latessa

Marisa Tomei, Jude Law

Alfie Elkins, a swinging, philosophizing womanizer, tells of his many conquests and setbacks in his seemingly carefree life of bedding as many beautiful women as he can. Remake of the 1966 Paramount film that starred Michael Caine, Shelley Winters, Jane Asher, Julia Foster, and Millicent Martin.

Omar Epps, Jude Law

The Polar Express

THE POLAR EXPRESS

(WARNER BROS.) Producers, Steve Starkey, Robert Zemecis, Gary Goetzman, William Teitler; Executive Producers, Tom Hanks, Jack Rapke, Chris Van Allsburg; Director, Robert Zemeckis; Screenplay, Robert Zemeckis, William Broyles Jr.; Based on the book by Chris Van Allsburg; Photography, Don Burgess, Robert Presley; Designers, Rick Carter, Dong Chiang; Costumes, Joanna Johnston; Music, Alan Silvestri; Original Songs, Glen Ballard, Alan Silvestri; Choreographer, John Caffara; Senior Visual Effects Supervisors, Ken Ralston, Jerome Chen; Visual Effects Producer, Craig Sost; Digital Producer, Chris June; Animation Supervisor, David Schaub; Digital Effects Supervisors, Rob Bredow, Mark Lambert, Alberto Menache, Sean Phillips; Casting, Victoria Burrows, Scot Boland; a Castle Rock Entertainment presentation in association with Shangri-La Entertainment of a Playtone, Image Movers/Golden Mean production; Dolby; Widescreen; Technicolor; Rated G; 100 minutes; Release date: November 10, 2004

Cast
Hero Boy/Father/Conductor/Hobo/
  Scrooge/Santa **Tom Hanks**
Smokey/Steamer **Michael Jeter**
Hero Girl **Nona Gaye**
Lonely Boy **Peter Scolari**
Know-It-All **Eddie Deezen**
Elf General **Charles Fleischer**
Elf Lieutenant/Elf Singer **Steven Tyler**
Sister Sarah/Mother **Leslie Zemeckis**
Voice of Hero Boy **Daryl Sabara**
Voice of Smokey and Steamer **Andre Sogliuzzo**
Voice of Lonely Boy **Jimmy Bennett**
Voice of Sister Sarah **Isabella Peregrina**

and Brendan King, Andy Pellick (Pastry Chefs), Josh Eli, Mark Mendonca, Rolandas Hendricks, Mark Goodman, Jon Scott, Gregory Cast, Sean Scott, Gordon Hart (Waiters), Chris Coppola (Toothless Boy/Elf), Julene Renee (Red Head Girl/Elf), Phil Fondacaro, Debbie Lee Carrington, Mark Povinelli, Ed Gale (Elves), Dante Pastula (Little Boy), Eric Newton, Aidan O'Shea, Aaron Hendry, Kevin C. Carr, Bee Jay Joyer, Jena Carpenter, Karine Mauffrey, Beth Carpenter, Bill Forchion, Devin Henderson, Savig Ben-Binyamin (Acrobatic Elves)

Know-It-All

Santa, Hero Boy, Conductor

Hero Boy

On Christmas Eve a little boy awakens to find a massive train waiting to take him to the North Pole.

This film received Oscar nominations for original song ("Believe"), sound, and sound editing.

The Polar Express

Steamer

Conductor

Hero Boy, Lonely Boy, Hero Girl

Hobo, Hero Boy

The North Pole PHOTOS COURTESY OF WARNER BROS.

Hero Girl, Hero Boy, Lonely Boy

Liam Neeson

KINSEY

(FOX SEARCHLIGHT) Producer, Gail Mutrux; Executive Producers, Michael Kuhn, Francis Ford Coppola, Bobby Rock, Kirk D'Amico; Co-Producer, Richard Guay; Director/Screenplay, Bill Condon; Photography, Frederick Elmes; Designer, Richard Sherman; Costumes, Bruce Finlayson; Music, Carter Burwell; Editor, Virginia Kate; Casting, Douglas Aibel, Cindy Tolan; Presented in association with Qwerty Films of a N1 European Film Produktions/American Zoetrope/Pretty Pictures production; Dolby; J-D-C Scope; Deluxe color; Rated R; 118 minutes; Release date: November 12, 2004

Laura Linney, Liam Neeson

Liam Neeson

Dagmara Dominczyk, Timothy Hutton, Julianne Nicholson, Peter Sarsgaard, Heather Goldenhersh, Chris O'Donnell

Liam Neeson, Laura Linney

Peter Sarsgaard, Liam Neeson, Laura Linney

Cast

Alfred Kinsey	**Liam Neeson**
Clara McMillen Kinsey	**Laura Linney**
Wardell Pomeroy	**Chris O'Donnell**
Clyde Martin	**Peter Sarsgaard**
Paul Gebhard	**Timothy Hutton**
Alfred Seguine Kinsey	**John Lithgow**
Thurman Rice	**Tim Curry**
Herman Wells	**Oliver Platt**
Alan Gregg	**Dylan Baker**
Alice Martin	**Julianne Nicholson**
Kenneth Braun	**William Sadler**
Martha Pomeroy	**Heather Goldenhersh**
Huntington Hartford	**John McMartin**
Sara Kinsey	**Veronica Cartwright**
Barbara Merkle	**Kathleen Chalfant**
Agnes Gebhard	**Dagmara Dominczyk**
Final Interview Subject	**Lynn Redgrave**
Young Man in Gay Bar	**Harley Cross**
Staff Secretary	**Susan Blommaert**
Kinsey at 19	**Benjamin Walker**
Kinsey at 14	**Matthew Fahey**
Kinsey at 10	**Will Denton**
Ben	**John Krasinski**
Emily	**Arden Myrin**
Rep B. Carroll Reece	**Romulus Linney**
Mrs. Spaulding	**Katharine Houghton**
Robert Kinsey	**David Harbour**
Mildred Kinsey	**Judith J.K. Polson**
Anne Kinsey	**Leigh Spofford**
Joan Kinsey	**Jenna Gavigan**
Bruce Kinsey	**Thomas Luke MacFarlane**
Kenneth Hand	**Mike Thurslic**
Grocer	**Jarlath Conroy**
Dr. Thomas Lattimore	**Bill Buell**
Gall Wasp Class Coed	**Michele Federer**

and Alvin Keith (Black Student), Amy Wilson (Marriage Class Coed), Maryelenn Owens (Assistant Professor), Roderick Hill (Clerical Worker), Peg Small (Retired Teacher), Don Sparks (Middle-aged Businessman), Joe Zaloom (Janitor), Kate Reinders, Mara Hobel, Lindsay Schmidt, Jason Patrick Sands, Marcel Simoneau, Bobby Steggert, Johnny Pruitt, Randy Redd (Students), John Epperson (Effete Man in Gay Bar), Jefferson Mays (Effete Man's Friend), Mark Mineart (Slavic Man), Martin Murphy (Bartender), Kate Jennings Grant (Marjorie Hartford), Barry Del Sherman, Fred Burrell (IU Reporters), Michael Arkin, Daniel Ziskie, Tuck Milligan (NYC Reporters), Edwin McDonough (Mr. Morrissey), John Ellison Conlee (Bookstore Clerk), Arthur French (Sharecropper), Chandler Williams (Prison Inmate), Jaime Roman Tirelli (Hispanic Man), Draper Shreeve (Ballet Teacher), Philip Kushner (Bellhop), Joe Badalucco (Radio Repairman), Henrietta Mantooth (Poet), Doris Smith (Old Woman), Reno (Male Impersonator), Pascale Armand (Young Black Woman), Sean Skelton (Staff Photographer), Steven Edward Hart (Reverend), Clifford David (Professor Smithson), Richard Preshong (University Guide)

The true story of how biology professor Alfred Kinsey's study of human sexuality led to his controversial 1948 publication *Sexual Behavior in the Human Male*, paving the way for a more open and thorough understanding of sex.

This film received an Oscar nomination for supporting actress (Linney).

Timothy Hutton, Peter Sarsgaard, Liam Neeson

Liam Neeson, Laura Linney PHOTO COURTESY OF FOX SEARCHLIGHT

FINDING NEVERLAND

(MIRAMAX) Producers, Richard N. Gladstein, Nellie Bellflower; Executive Producers, Bob Weinstein, Harvey Weinstein, Michelle Sy, Gary Binkow, Neal Israel; Director, Marc Forster; Screenplay, David Magee, based on the play *The Man Who Was Peter Pan* by Allan Knee; Photography, Roberto Schaefer; Designer, Gemma Jackson; Costumes, Alexandra Byrne; Music, Jan A.P. Kaczmarek; Editor, Matt Chesse; Co-Producer, Michael Dreyer; Special Effects Supervisor, Kevin Tod Haug; Associate Producer, Tracey Becker; Casting, Kate Dowd; a Film Colony production; U.S.-British; Dolby; Super 35 Widescreen; Deluxe color; Rated PG; 106 minutes; Release date: November 12, 2004

Julie Christie, Joe Prospero, Nick Roud, Freddie Highmore, Luke Spill, Kate Winslet, Johnny Depp

Cast

Sir James Matthew Barrie **Johnny Depp**
Sylvia Llewelyn Davies **Kate Winslet**
Emma du Maurier **Julie Christie**
Mary Ansell Barrie **Radha Mitchell**
Charles Frohman **Dustin Hoffman**
Peter Llewelyn Davies **Freddie Highmore**
Jack Llewelyn Davies **Joe Prospero**
George Llewelyn Davies **Nick Roud**
Michael Llewelyn Davies **Luke Spill**
Sir Arthur Conan Doyle **Ian Hart**
Peter Pan **Kelly Macdonald**
Mrs. Jaspers, Usher **Mackenzie Crook**
Mrs. Snow **Eileen Essel**
Mr. Snow **Jimmy Gardner**
Gilbert Cannan **Oliver Fox**
Nana/Mr. Reilly **Angus Barnett**
Smee **Toby Jones**
Wendy **Kate Maberly**
John **Matt Green**
Michael **Catrin Rhys**
Hook/Lord Carlton **Tim Potter**
Mrs. Darling **Jane Booker**
Stage Manager **Paul Whitehouse**
Sarah **Catherine Cusack**
Emma **Kali Peacock**
Cottage Doctor **Robert Oates**
Hospital Doctor **Nicholas Pritchard**
Doctor Brighton **Jonathan Cullen**

Johnny Depp, Freddie Highmore

and Raymond Waring (Stage Worker), Jack Birmingham, Charlotte Birmingham, Cora Harrison, Sacha Janes, Chelsea Carpenter, Keely Jane, Luciano Cusack, Stella King, Serafina Cusack, Jake Roche, Claudia Davidson, Molly Whitehouse, Noah Harrison, Sophie Whitehouse, Eden Harrison (Orphans), Laura Duguids, Sevan Stephan, Rosie Ede, Richard Braine, Tobias Menzies (Theatre Patrons), Tony Way (Set Mover), Murray McArthur (Stagehand)

The true story of how author James M. Barrie's friendship with the widowed Sylvia Llewelyn Davies and her four boys led to him writing his most enduring work, *Peter Pan*.

2004 Academy Award winner for Best Original Score. This film received additional nominations for picture, actor (Johnny Depp), adapted screenplay, art direction, costume design, and editing

Johnny Depp, Freddie Highmore

Kate Winslet, Johnny Depp

Johnny Depp, Dustin Hoffman

Nick Roud, Joe Prospero, Kate Winslet, Johnny Depp

Freddie Highmore, Joe Prospero, Johnny Depp, Nick Roud, Kate Winslet, Luke Spill

Johnny Depp, Kate Winslet   PHOTOS COURTESY OF MIRAMAX

AFTER THE SUNSET

(NEW LINE CINEMA) Producers, Tripp Vinson, Jay Stern, Beau Flynn; Executive Producers, Patrick Palmer, Toby Emmerich, Kent Alterman; Director, Brett Ratner; Screenplay, Paul Zbyszewski, Craig Rosen; Story, Paul Zbyszewski; Photography, Dante Spinotti; Designer, Geoffrey Kirkland; Costumes, Rita Ryack; Music, Lalo Schifrin; Music Supervisors, Gary Calamar, Thomas Golubic; Casting, Victoria Thomas; a Firm Films/Contrafilm and Rat Entertainment production; Dolby; Widescreen; Deluxe color; Rated PG-13; 97 minutes; Release date: November 12, 2004

Pierce Brosnan

Cast

Max Burdett **Pierce Brosnan**
Lola Cirillo **Salma Hayek**
Stan Lloyd **Woody Harrelson**
Henri Mooré **Don Cheadle**
Sophie **Naomie Harris**
Rowdy Fan **Chris Penn**
Agent Stafford **Mykelti Wiliamson**
Zacharias **Obba Babatunde**
Jean-Paul **Russell Hornsby**
Agnet Kowalski **Rex Linn**
Luc **Troy Garity**
Lakers FBI Agents **Robert Curtis Brown, Mark Moses**
FBI Driver **Michael Bowen**

and Tony Ledard (Referee), Karl Malone, Shaquille O'Neal, Gary Payton, Dyan Cannon, Phil Jackson, Edward Norton (Themselves), Andrew Fiscella (Popcorn Victim), Gianni Russo (Clippers Fan), Jeff Garlin (Ron), Lisa Thornhill (Gail), Kate Walsh (Sheila), Tom McGowan (Ed), Joel McKinnon Miller (Wendell), Rachael Harris (June), Shakara Ledard, Audrey Quock (Masseuses), David Reivers (Bahamian Cop), Kamal Marayati (Ship Entrance Security), Gillian Vigman (Exhibit Guide), Noémie Lenoir, Omyhra Mota, Oluchi Onweagba (Mooré's Girls), Alan Dale (Security Chief), Kirk B.R. Woller (Security Guard), Donald Miller (Radio Voice), Leshay Tomlinson (Receptionist), Anthony Reynolds (Evening Shift Guard), Paul Benedict (Night Shift Guard), Ted Detwiler, Chad Gabriel, Keith Sweitzer, Rodney O'Neal McKnight (Bathroom Boys), Frank Bruynbroek (Ship's Steward)

Pierce Brosnan, Salma Hayek

Omyhra Mota, Don Chaedle, Noémie Lenoir

FBI Agent Stan Lloyd tracks thief Max Burdett to the Bahamas, where Max hopes to make one last score by stealing a Napoleon diamond from a massive cruise ship.

Pierce Brosnan, Woody Harrelson PHOTO COURTESY OF NEW LINE CINEMA

Nicolas Cage, Harvey Keitel

Stewart Finlay-McLennan, Jon Voight, Sean Bean

Nicolas Cage

NATIONAL TREASURE

(WALT DISNEY PICTURES) Producers, Jerry Bruckheimer, Jon Turteltaub; Executive Producers, Mike Stenson, Chad Oman, Christina Steinberg, Barry Waldman, Oren Aviv, Charles Segars; Director, Jon Turteltaub; Screenplay, Jim Kouf, Cormac Wibberley, Marianne Wibberley; Story, Jim Kouf, Oren Aviv, Charles Segars; Photography, Caleb Deschanel; Designer, Norris Spencer; Costumes, Judianna Makovsky; Music, Trevor Rabin; Music Supervisor, Bob Badami; Editor, William Goldenberg; Associate Producers, Benjamin Melniker, Michael E. Uslan, Pat Sandston; Casting, Avy Kaufman; Stunts, George Marshall Ruge; Presented in association with Jerry Bruckheimer Films; Distrubted by Buena Vista; Dolby; Super 35 Widescreen; Technicolor; Rated PG; 131 minutes; Release date: November 19, 2004

Cast
Benjamin Franklin Gates **Nicolas Cage**
Dr. Abigail Chase **Diane Kruger**
Riley Poole **Justin Bartha**
Ian Howe **Sean Bean**
Patrick Gates **Jon Voight**
Agent Sadusky **Harvey Keitel**
John Adams Gates **Christopher Plummer**
Shaw **David Dylan Fisher**
Powell **Stewart Finaly-McLennan**
Shippen **Oleg Taktarov**
Phil **Stephen Pope**
Agent Dawes **Annie Parisse**
Agent Johnson **Mark Pellegrino**
Agent Colfax **Erik King**
Dr. Stan Herbert **Don McManus**
Guard Woodruff **Ron Canada**
Young Ben Gates **Hunter Gomez**
Rebecca **Deborah Yates**

and Arabella Field (Abigail's Secretary), Sharon Wilkins (Butcher Lady), Alexandra Balahoutis (Clerk), Dior Raye (Gift Store Clerk), Yves Michel-Beneche (Museum Kid), Jason Earles (Thomas Gates), Terrence Currier (Charles Carroll), Rod McLachlan (Independence Hall Guide), Elizabeth Greenberg (Liberty Bell Guide), Jody Halse (Franklin Institute Guard), Liam Noble (Franklin Institute Security), Joshua Biton (Technician), Fern D. Baguidy, Jr. (Gala Guard), Thomas Q. Morris (Janitor), Antony Alda (Guard Ferguson), John Travis (Guard Mike)

In order to locate the long coveted Knights Templar Treasure, Ben Gates realizes he must steal the Declaration of Independence, on the back of which lies the final clue to the treasure's whereabouts.

Justin Bartha, Diane Kruger PHOTO COURTESY OF WALT DISNEY PICTURES

THE SPONGEBOB SQUAREPANTS MOVIE

(PARAMOUNT) Producers, Stephen Hillenburg, Julia Pistor; Executive Producers, Albie Hecht, Gina Shay, Derek Drymon; Director, Stephen Hillenburg; Screenplay/Storyboards, Derek Drymon, Tim Hill, Stephen Hillenburg, Kent Osborne, Aaron Springer, Paul Tibbitt; Based ona a story and the series created by Stephen Hillenburg; Sequence Directors, Derek Drymon, Mark Osborne; Photography, Jerzy Zielinski; Production Designer, Nick Jennings; Executive Music Producer, Karyn Rachtman; Music, Gregor Narholz; Editor, Lynn Hobson; Supervising Animation Director, Alan Smart; Lead Storyboard Artist, Serhm Cohen; Animation Directors, Dong Kun Won, Yu Mun Jeong, Hoon Choi, Hee Man Yang, Sang Kyun Shin; Line Producer, Aaron Parry; Associate Producer, Aaron Parry; a Nickelodeon Movies production, in association with United Plankton Pictures; Dolby; Deluxe color; Rated PG; 88 minutes; Release date: November 19, 2004

Patrick, SpongeBob, Dennis the Hitman

Voice Cast

SpongeBob SquarePants/Narrator/
  Clay/Tough Fish #2/Twin #2/
  Houston Voice **Tom Kenny**
Mr. Krabs **Clancy Brown**
Squidward/Fish #4 **Roger Bumpass**
Patrick Starfish/Fish #2/Chum Customer/
  Local Fish **Bill Fagerbakke**
Plankton/Fish #7/Attendant #2 (Lloyd) **Doug Lawrence**
Karen (The Computer Wife)/Old Lady **Jill Talley**
Sandy **Carolyn Lawrence**
Mrs. Puff **Mary Jo Catlett**
King Neptune **Jeffrey Tambor**
Mindy the Mermaid **Scarlett Johansson**
Dennis the Hitman **Alec Baldwin**

and David Hasselhoff (Himself), Kristopher Logan (Squinty the Pirate), D.P. Fitzgerald (Bonesy the Pirate), Cole McKay (Scruffy the Pirate), Dylan Haggerty (Stitches the Pirate), Bart McCarthy (Captain Bart the Pirate), Henry Kingi (Inky the Pirate), Randolph Jones (Tiny the Pirate), Paul Zies (Upper Deck the Pirate), Gerard Greisbaum (Fingers the Pirate), Aaron Hendry (Tangles the Pirate/Cyclops Diver), Maxie Santillan (Gummy the Pirate), Peter DeYoung (Leatherbeard the Pirate), Gino Montesinos (Tango the Pirate), John Siciliano (Pokey the Pirate), David Stifel (Cookie the Pirate), Alex Baker (Martin the Pirate), Robin Russell (Sniffy the Pirate),

Mindy, SpongeBob, Patrick

Tommy Schooler (Salty the Pirate), Ben Wilson (Stovepipe the Pirate), Jose Zelay (Dooby the Pirate), Mageina Tovah (Usher), Chris Cummins, Toddy Duffey (Concession Guys), Dee Bradley Baker (Man Cop/Phil/Perch Perkins/Waiter/Attendant #1/Thug #1/Coughing Fish/Twin #1/Frog Fish/Monster/Freed Fish/Sandals), Sirena Irwin (Reporter Driver/Ice Cream Lady), Lori Alan (Pearl), Tom Wilson (Fish #3/Tough Fish #1—Victor), Carlos Alazraqui (Squire/Goofy Goober Announcer/Thief), Joshua Seth (Prisoner), Tim Blaney (Singing Goofy Goober), Derek Drymon (The Screamer/Voice of Fisherman), Aaron Springer (Laughing Bubble), Neil Ross (Voice of the Cyclops), Stephen Hillenburg (Voice of the Parrot), Michael Patrick Bell (Fisherman)

SpongeBob and Patrick try to find King Neptune's crown, which has been stolen by the evil Plankton.

Patrick, Spongebob, David Hasselhoff PHOTOS COURTESY OF PARAMOUNT

CHRISTMAS WITH THE KRANKS

(COLUMBIA) Producers, Chris Columbus, Mark Radcliffe, Michael Barnathan; Executive Producers, Charles Newirth, Bruce A. Block; Director, Joe Roth; Screenplay, Chris Columbus; Based on the novel *Skipping Christmas* by John Grisham; Photography, Don Burgess; Designer, Garreth Stover; Costumes, Susie DeSanto; Music, John Debney; Music Supervision, Little Steven; Editor, Nick Moore; Co-Producer, Allegra Clegg; Casting, Margery Simkin; a Revolution Studios presentation of a 1492 Pictures production; Dolby; Panavision; Deluxe color; Rated PG-13; 98 minutes; Release date: November 24, 2004

Jamie Lee Curtis

Cast

Luther Krank **Tim Allen**
Nora Krank **Jamie Lee Curtis**
Vic Frohmeyer **Dan Aykroyd**
Walt Scheel **M. Emmet Walsh**
Bev Scheel **Elizabeth Franz**
Spike Frohmeyer **Erik Per Sullivan**
Officer Salino **Cheech Marin**
Officer Treen **Jake Busey**

and Austin Pendleton (Umbrella Santa/Marty), Tom Poston (Father Zabriskie), Julie Gonzalo (Blair Krank), René Lavan (Enrique DeCardenal), Caroline Rhea (Candi), Felicity Huffman (Merry), Patrick Breen (Aubie), John Short (Ned Becker), Bonita Friedericy (Jude Becker), David Hornsby (Randy Becker), Kevin Chamberlin (Mr. Scanlon), Lyndon Smith (Randy Scanlon), Ryan Pfening (Gus Scanlon), Mark Christopher Lawrence (Wes Trogdon), Rachel L. Smith (Trish Trogdon), Vernée Watson-Johnson (Dox), Arden Myrin (Daisy), Jan Hoag (Choir Director), Joe Guzaldo (Burglar), David L. Lander (Tanning Intruder), Kim Rhodes, Patrick O'Connor (Office Staff), Doug Cox, Matt Walsh (Neighbors), Andrew Daly (Husband), Dawn Didawick (Shopper), Cary Thompson (Manager), Julia Roth (Cashier), Taylor Block, Eryan Nicole Gonsalves, Chelsea Broussard (Schoolgirls), Paul Taylor (Fireman), J.P. Romano (Mailman)

Jamie Lee Curtis, Tim Allen, René Lavan, Julie Gonzalo

When their daughter decides to come home for the holidays, the Kranks change their plans to go on vacation, and instead stay home to do up Christmas in a big way.

Austin Pendleton, Tom Poston, Patrick Breen, Dan Aykroyd, Cheech Marin, Jake Busey

Tim Allen, Austin Pendleton PHOTOS COURTESY OF COLUMBIA

Clive Owen, Natalie Portman

Julia Roberts PHOTOS COURTESY OF COLUMBIA

CLOSER

(COLUMBIA) Producers, Mike Nichols, John Calley, Cary Brokaw; Executive Producers, Scott Rudin, Celia Costas, Robert Fox; Director, Mike Nichols; Screenplay, Patrick Marber, based on his play; Photography, Stephen Goldblatt; Designer, Tim Hatley; Costumes, Ann Roth; Editors, John Bloom, Antonia Van Drimmelen; Co-Producer, Michael Haley; Presented in association with Inside Track; Dolby; Color; Rated R; 104 minutes; Release date: December 3, 2004

Jude Law, Natalie Portman

Natalie Portman

Cast
Anna **Julia Roberts**
Dan **Jude Law**
Alice **Natalie Portman**
Larry **Clive Owen**
Taxi Driver **Nick Hobbs**
Customs Officer **Colin Stinton**

Natalie Portman, Clive Owen

A chance run-in between Dan and Alice leads to a relationship which is jeopardized by his increasing interest in Anna, and by Anna's lover Larry's interest in Alice.

This film received Oscar nominations for supporting actor (Owen) and supporting actress (Portman).

Clive Owen, Natalie Portman, Julia Roberts, Jude Law

Jude Law, Julia Roberts

Julia Roberts, Clive Owen

Julia Roberts, Jude Law

Clive Owen

BLADE: TRINITY

(NEW LINE CINEMA) Producers, Peter Frankfurt, Wesley Snipes, David S. Goyer, Lynn Harris; Executive Producers, Toby Emmerich, Stan Lee, Avi Arad; Co-Producer, Art Schaefer; Director/Screenplay, David S. Goyer; Based on the character created for Marvel Comics by Marv Wolfman & Gene Colan; Photography, Gabriel Beristain; Designer, Chris Gorak; Costumes, Laura Jean Shannon; Music, Ramin Djawadi, The RZA; Music Supervisor, George Drakoulias; Editors, Howard E. Smith, Conrad Smart; Visual Effects Supervisor, Joe Bauer; Casting, Ronnie Yeskel, Coreen Mayrs, Heike Brandstatter; an Amen Ra Films production in association with Imaginary Forces; Dolby; Super 35 Widescreen; Deluxe color; Rated R; 113 minutes; Release date: December 8, 2004

Jessica Biel, Wesley Snipes, Ryan Reynolds

Cast

Blade **Wesley Snipes**
Whistler **Kris Kristofferson**
Drake **Dominic Purcell**
Abigail Whistler **Jessica Biel**
Hannibal King **Ryan Reynolds**
Danica Talos **Parker Posey**
Chief Martin Vreede **Mark Berry**
Dr. Edgar Vance **John Michael Higgins**
Asher Talos **Callum Keith Rennie**
Jarko Grimwood **Triple H**
Wolfe **Paul Anthony**
Virago **Francoise Yip**
Wilson Hale **Michael Anthony Rawlins**
Ray Cumberland **James Remar**
Sommerfield **Natasha Lyonne**

and Haili Page (Zoe), Patton Oswalt (Hedges), Ron Selmour (Dex), Christopher Heyerdahl (Caulder), Eric Bogosian (Bentley Tittle), Scott Heindl (Gedge), John Ashker (Campbell), Clay Cullen (Stone), Steven McMichael (Denlinger), Paul Wu (Ellingson), Kimani Ray Smith (Doh), Darren McGuire (Edmond), Shannon Powell (Bystander), Jill Krop (Reporter), Jordan Hoffart (Squid), Kett Kurton (Dingo), Cascy Beddow (Flick), Simon Pidgeon (Proof), Michael St. John Smith (FBI Agent), Stephen Spender, Kwesi Ameyaw (Agents), Alex Rae (Goth Guy Wannabe), Eric Cerra (Goth Vixen Wannabe), Garvin Cross (Hoop), Raymond Sammel, John Ulmer, Justin Sain (Security Guards), Daryl Scheelar (Doctor), Camille Martinez (Hysterical Mother), Michelle Stoll (Vance's Assistant), Dawn Mander (Biomedica Technician)

Parker Posey, Dominic Purcell

Vampire hunter Blade reluctantly teams up with a group of human hunters to stop the resurrected Drake and his horde of undead acolytes. Third in the New Line series, following *Blade* (1998) and *Blade II* (2002), with Snipes and Kristofferson repeating their roles.

Jessica Biel PHOTOS COURTESY OF NEW LINE CINEMA

OCEAN'S TWELVE

(WARNER BROS.) Producer, Jerry Weintraub; Executive Producers, John Hardy, Susan Ekins, Bruce Berman; Director, Steven Soderbergh; Screenplay, George Nolfi; Based on characters created by George Clayton Johnson, Jack Golden Russell; Photography, Peter Andrews; Designer, Philip Messina; Costumes, Milena Canonero; Editor, Stephen Mirrione; Music, David Holmes; Co-Producers, Frederic W. Brost, Gregory Jacobs; Casting, Debra Zane; Dolby; Panavision; Technicolor; Rated PG-13; 125 minutes; Release date: December 10, 2004

Bernie Mac, Carl Reiner

Catherine Zeta-Jones, Robbie Coltrane

Cast

Danny Ocean **George Clooney**
Rusty Ryan **Brad Pitt**
Linus Caldwell **Matt Damon**
Isabel Lahiri **Catherine Zeta-Jones**
Terry Benedict **Andy Garcia**
Basher Tarr **Don Cheadle**
Frank Catton **Bernie Mac**
Virgil Malloy **Casey Affleck**
Turk Malloy **Scott Caan**
Francois Toulour **Vincent Cassel**
Livingston Dell **Eddie Jamison**
Yen **Shaobo Qin**
Saul Bloom **Carl Reiner**
Reuben Tishkoff **Elliott Gould**
Matsui **Robbie Coltrane**
Roman Nagel **Eddie Izzard**
"Molly Star"/Mrs. Caldwell **Cherry Jones**
Van der Woude **Jeroen Krabbe**
Tess Ocean **Julia Roberts**

and Jared Harris (Basher's Engineer), Ed Kross (Bank Officer), Don Tiffany (House Painter), Anne Jacques (Shop Owner), David Sontag, Larry Sontag (Plainclothes Goons), Dina Connolly (Virgil's Fiancee), Nelson Peltz (Partygoer), Mini Anden (Supermodel), Jennifer Liu, Leah Zhang (Mani-pedi Women), Craig Susser (Men's Club Waiter), James Schneider (Club Heckler), Nerissa Tedesco (Palm Reader), Michelle Hines (Assistant Manager), Michael Van Der Heijden (Funeral Priest), Johan Widerberg (Johan), Jeroen Willems (Paul), Chris Tates (Paul's Partner), Michael Delano (Casino Manager), David Lindsay (Arsenal Bus Driver), Al Faris (Frank's Jail Mate), Candice Azzara (Saul's Lady), Youma Diakite, Andrea

Buhl, Sylvia Kwon, Francesca Lancini, Raquel Faria, Elena Potapova, Jessie Bell, Anne-Solenne Hatte, Denny Mendez (Toulour Women), Jerry Weintraub (American Businessman), Martina Stella (Nagel's Assistant), Mattia Sbragia (Commissario Giordano), Carlo Antonazzo (Security Advisor), Mingming Gao (Chinese Mother), Amelie Kahn-Ackerman (Chinese Daughter), Luciano Miele (Hotel Manager), Antonio De Matteo (Hotel Employee), Ana Caterina Morariu (Bruce Willis' Companion), Adriano Giannini (Museum Director), Giulio Magnolia (Photographer), Dennis Di Angelo (Photographer's Assistant), Scott L. Schwartz (Bruiser), Gisela Volodi (Toulour's Butler), Mathieu Simonet (Backpack Kid), Karl A. Brown, Marc Bodnar (Train Security), Albert Finney (LeMarc), Topher Grace, Bruce Willis (Themselves)

Julia Roberts, George Clooney

Casino owner Terry Benedict informs Danny Ocean and his team that they have two weeks to replace the $160 million they stole from him, prompting Ocean and his gang to try to steal a valuable Faberge Egg from a Rome art museum. Sequel to the 2001 film *Ocean's Eleven* (WB), with most principals repeating their roles.

Brad Pitt, Matt Damon

Waris Ahluwalia, Michael Gambon, Anjelica Huston, Noah Taylor, Bud Cort, Bill Murray, Matthew Gray Gubler, Seu Jorge, Jeff Goldblum, Cate Blanchett, Willem Dafoe PHOTO COURTESY OF TOUCHSTONE

THE LIFE AQUATIC WITH STEVE ZISSOU

(TOUCHSTONE) Producers, Wes Anderson, Barry Mendel, Scott Rudin; Executive Producers, Rudd Simmons; Director, Wes Anderson; Screenplay, Wes Anderson, Noah Baumbach; Co-Producer, Enzo Sisti; Photography, Robert Yeoman; Designer, Mark Friedberg; Costumes, Milena Canonero; Editor, David Moritz; Music, Mark Mothersbaugh; Music Supervisor, Randall Poster; Animation, Henry Selick; Visual Effects Supervisor, Jeremy Dawson; Casting, Douglas Aibel; Dolby; Panavision; Technicolor; Rated R; 119 minutes; Release date: December 10, 2004

Cast

Steve Zissou **Bill Murray**
Ned Plimpton (Kingsley Zissou) **Owen Wilson**
Jane Winslett-Richardson **Cate Blanchett**
Eleanor Zissou **Anjelica Huston**
Klaus Daimler **Willem Dafoe**
Alistair Hennessey **Jeff Goldblum**
Oseary Drakoulias **Michael Gambon**
Vladimir Wolodarsky **Noah Taylor**
Bill Ubell **Bud Cort**
Pelé dos Santos **Seu Jorge**
Anne-Marie Sakowitz **Robyn Cohen**
Vikram Ray **Waris Ahluwalia**
Bobby Ogata **Niels Koizumi**
Renzo Pietro **Pawel Wdowczak**
Intern #1 **Matthew Gray Gubler**
Esteban du Plantier **Seymour Cassel**

and Antonio Monda (Festival Director), Isabella Blow (Antonia Cook), James Hamilton (Festival Photographer), Melanie Green (Mandeeza), Nazzareno "Neno" Piana (Elderly Man), Rudd Simmons (Man in Yellow Suit), Leonardo Giovannelli (Werner), Henry S.F. Cooper, Jr. (Talk Show Host), Pietro Ragusa (Academic), Tony Shafrazi (Larry Amin), Noah Baumbach (Phillip), Eric Chase Anderson, Robert Wilson, Don McKinnon (Air Kentucky Pilots), Alessio Santini, Paolo Sirignani, Andrew Weisell, Niccolò Senni, Andrea Guerra, Christiano Irrera, Vincenzo Recchia, Marco Ciarlitto (University of North Alaska Interns), Stefano Maria Ortolani (Italian Man in Audience), Sylvie Genin (French Woman in Audience), Jacques-Henri Lartigue (Lord Mandrake), Muzius Gordon Dietzmann (Javier), Gangyuan Xu (Cedric), Robin Scott (Hugo), Guglielmo Casciaro (Carl), Alessandro de Angelis, Andrea Bertone, Andriy Kachur, Roberto Salvi, Stefano Masciolini (Hennessey Sailors), Robert Sommer, Anna Orso, Ettore Conti (Party Guests), Robert Graham (Venezuelan General), Hal Yamanouchi (Chief Pirate), Conrado Mendoza Dolor, Eduardo Bautista Grantuza, Simeon Maragigak Agelion, Walter Cajapao Caspao, Honorato Ilao Reyes, Roderick Magbay, Demetreo Castillo, Thomas Carwgal de la Peña, Edwarren Batungon, Levi Mickael de Ramon, Aries Corales, Aries Dolor Ilagon, Joseph de los Reyes, Dennis Rayos Martinez, Tatyo Yamanouchi, Wait Tung Wong, Ging Fang Zhu (Pirates), Francis Dokyi (Water Taxi Driver), Begni Bok Dong (Young Ogata), Daniel Acon, Alexander Hamilton (Former Team Zissou, Antarctica), Leica (Cody)

Down on his luck oceanographer Steve Zissou sets out to track down the rare shark that devoured his partner, accompanied by a young man who claims to be his illegitimate son.

SPANGLISH

(COLUMBIA) Producers, James L. Brooks, Richard Sakai, Julie Ansell; Executive Producers, Joan Bradshaw, Christy Haubegger; Director/Screenplay, James L. Brooks; Photography, John Seale; Designer, Ida Random; Costumes, Shay Cunliffe, Louise Mingenbach; Music, Hans Zimmer; Editor, Richard Marks; Co-Producers, Aldric La'auli Porter, Francine Maisler, Richard Marks; Casting, Mary Vernieu; a Gracie Films production; Dolby; Deluxe color; Rated PG-13; 130 minutes; Release date: December 17, 2004

Cast

John Clasky **Adam Sandler**
Deborah Clasky **Téa Leoni**
Flor **Paz Vega**
Evelyn **Cloris Leachman**
Cristina **Shelbie Bruce**
Bernice **Sarah Steele**
Georgie **Ian Hyland**
Cristina (6 yrs. old) **Victoria Luna**
Monica **Cecilia Suarez**
Flor's Husband **Ricardo Molina**
Luz **Brenda Canela**
14 Year-Old Boy **Eddy Martin**
Hostess at Fancy Restaurant **Nicole Nieth**
Businessmen **Jamie Kaler, James Lancaster**
Pietro **Phil Rosenthal**
Gwen **Angela Goethals**
Victor—Maitre D' **Sean Smith**
Alex **Jonathan Hernandez**
Mike—Realtor **Thomas Haden Church**

and Freddy Soto (Manuel—Hispanic Man), Wendy Braun, Nichole Hiltz (Yuppie Girls), Eric Schaeffer (Rabid Sports Fan), Aimee Garcia (Narrator), Jean Gaskill (Arlene—School Director), Spencer Locke, Sarah Hyland (Sleepover Friends), Andrew Sikking, Albert Melera (Chefs), Liz Carey (Hostess at John's Restaurant), Anastasia C. Ford, Yasmeen Azizian, Daizy Cruz, Kristha Sazo (Girls on Balcony), Morgan Ward, Cheryl Ward (Coffee Patrons), Chris Stone (UPS Guy)

Adam Sandler, Paz Vega

Seeking a better life for herself and her daughter, native Mexican Flor comes to Los Angeles to work as the maid for a well-to-do chef and his self-absorbed wife.

Sarah Steele, Adam Sandler

Paz Vega, Téa Leoni PHOTOS COURTESY OF COLUMBIA

Cloris Leachman, Téa Leoni

Jim Carrey, Meryl Streep

Jim Carrey, Billy Connolly PHOTOS COURTESY OF PARAMOUNT/DREAMWORKS

Kara/Shelby Hoffman, Emily Browning, Liam Aiken

LEMONY SNICKET'S A SERIES OF UNFORTUNATE EVENTS

(PARAMOUNT/DREAMWORKS) Producers, Laurie MacDonald, Walter F. Parkes, Jim Van Wyck; Director, Brad Silbering; Screenplay, Robert Gordon; Based on the books *The Bad Beginning, The Reptile Room,* and *The Wide Window* by Lemony Snicket (Daniel Handler); Executive Producers, Scott Rudin, Barry Sonnenfeld, Julia Pistor, Albie Hecht; Photography, Emmanuel Lubezki; Designer, Rick Heinrichs; Costumes, Colleen Atwood; Editor, Michael Kahn; Music, Thomas Newman; Co-Producers, Minor Childers, Scott Aversano; Associate Producer, Linda Hill; Visual Effects Supervisor, Stefen Fangmeier; Casting, Avy Kaufman; a Parkes/MacDonald production, a Nickelodeon Movies production; Dolby; Deluxe color; Rated PG; 108 minutes; Release date: December 17, 2004

Cast

Count Olaf **Jim Carrey**
Klaus Beaudelaire **Liam Aiken**
Violet Beaudelaire **Emily Browning**
Sunny Beaudelaire **Kara Hoffman, Shelby Hoffman**
Lemony Snicket **Jude Law**
Mr. Poe **Timothy Spall**
Justice Strauss **Catherine O'Hara**
Uncle Monty **Billy Connolly**
Aunt Josephine **Meryl Streep**
Bald Man **Luis Guzman**
Hook-Handed Man **Jamie Harris**
Person of Indeterminate Gender **Craig Ferguson**
White Faced Women **Jennifer Coolidge, Jane Adams**
Constable **Cedric the Entertainer**
Grocery Clerk **Robert Clendenin**
Gruff Grocer **Lenny Clarke**
Judge **Fred Gallo**
Gustav **John Dexter**
Mrs. Poe **Deborah Theaker**
Captain Sam **Wayne Flemming**
Critic **Dustin Hoffman**

Kara/Shelby Hoffman, Emily Browning, Liam Aiken

After their parents perish in a fire, the Beaudelaire children are left in the care of the bizarre Count Olaf, who hopes to eliminate them in order to gain their inheritance.

2004 Academy Award winner for Best Makeup. This film received additional nominations for art direction, costumes, and music score.

Jim Carrey, Jane Adams, Jennifer Coolidge, Jamie Harris

Kara/Shelby Hoffman, Liam Aiken

Jim Carrey

Timothy Spall, Cedric the Entertainer

Liam Aiken, Kara/Shelby Hoffman, Emily Browning

Jennifer Coolidge, Jane Adams, Catherine O'Hara, Jim Carrey

Alan Alda

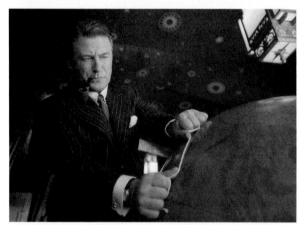

Alec Baldwin

Jude Law, Cate Blanchett

Leonardo DiCaprio

Leonardo DiCaprio, Gwen Stefani PHOTOS COURTESY OF MIRAMAX/WARNER BROS.

THE AVIATOR

(MIRAMAX/WARNER BROS.) Producers, Michael Mann, Sandy Climan, Graham King, Charles Evans Jr.; Executive Producer, Chris Brigham; Director, Martin Scorsese; Screenplay, John Logan; Photography, Robert Richardson; Designer, Dante Ferretti; Costumes, Sandy Powell; Music, Howard Shore; Editor, Thelma Schoonmaker; Special Effects Supervisor, R. Bruce Steinheimer; Second Unit Director, Rob Legato; Stunts, Doug Coleman, Jean Frenette; Aerial Coordinator, Craig Hosking; Casting, Lucie Robitaille; a Forward Pass/Initial Entertainment Group production; Dolby; Panavision; Color; Rated PG-13; 170 minutes; Release date: December 17, 2004

Leonardo DiCaprio   Kelli Garner

John C. Reilly, Leonardo DiCaprio

Cast

Howard Hughes **Leonardo DiCaprio**
Katharine Hepburn **Cate Blanchett**
Ava Gardner **Kate Beckinsale**
Noah Dietrich **John C. Reilly**
Juan Trippe **Alec Baldwin**
Sen. Ralph Owen Brewster **Alan Alda**
Professor Fitz **Ian Holm**
Jack Frye **Danny Huston**
Jean Harlow **Gwen Stefani**
Errol Flynn **Jude Law**
Johnny Meyer **Adam Scott**
Glenn Odekirk **Matt Ross**
Faith Domergue **Kelli Garner**
Mrs. Hepburn **Frances Conroy**

and Brent Spiner (Robert Gross), Stanley DeSantis (Louis B. Mayer), Edward Herrmann (Joseph Breen), Willem Dafoe (Roland Sweet), Kenneth Walsh (Dr. Hepburn), J.C. Mackenzie (Ludlow), Jacob Davich (Howard Hughes, 9 yrs. old), Amy Sloan (Howard's Mother), Sam Hennings (Hell's Angels Stunt Coordinator), Joe Chrest (Hell's Angels Director of Photography), Rufus Wainwright, Loudon Wainwright III, Martha Wainwright (Cocoanut Grove Vocalists), Harry Standjofski (Crony of Louis B. Mayer), Vince Giordano (Cocoanut Grove Bandleader), Josie Maran (Cigarette Girl), Justin Shilton (Hell's Angels Pilot), Arthur Holden (Radio Announcer), Raymond Ducasse (Roscoe Turner), Joseph P. Reidy (Aide to Howard), Stephane Demers (Maitre d'), Yves Jacques (Waiter), Jason Cavalier (Cocoanut Grove Patron), Chris Ufland (Engineer), Al Dubois, John Koensgen (Pan Am Executives), Alan Toy (Man on Crutches), Sebastian Tillinger (Timer), Francesca Scorsese, Charlotte Scott (Little Girls), James Bradford (Uncle Willy), Joe Cobden, Linda Smith (Guests), Ralan Fawcett (Chairman MPA), Jordan St. James (Hughes' Aide at Censor Hearing), David Purdham (Emcee), Kevin O'Rourke (Spencer Tracy), Lisa Bronwyn Moore (Noah's Wife), Emma Campbell (Jack Frye's Wife, Helen), Vincent Laresca (Jorge), Matt Holland (Hughes' Staff Person), Dennis St. John (Nick the Custodian), Keith Campbell (Marine), Al Vandercruys (Doctor), James Rae (FBI Agent), Kathleen McAuliffe (Brewster's Maid), Nellie Sciutto (Secretary), Terry Haig (Another Senator), Joseph McNamara (Himself, Voice), Vladimir Kuznetsov Smith, Mark Akeson, Jason Pollard (Caretakers), Michael-John Wolfe (Cary Grant), Martin Scorsese (Hell's Angel's Projectionist, Voice)

The true story of eccentric billionaire Howard Hughes' determination to make movies on his own terms and his obsession to create the ultimate airplane.

2004 Academy Award-winner for Best Supporting Actress (Cate Blanchett), Art Direction, Cinematography, Costume Design, and Editing. This film received additional nominations for picture, actor (Leonardo DiCaprio), supporting actor (Alan Alda), director, original screenplay, and sound.

Leonardo DiCaprio, Kate Beckinsale

IMAGINARY HEROES

(SONY CLASSICS) Producers, Illana Diamant, Art Linson, Gina Resnick, Denise Shaw, Frank Hubner; Executive Producers, Moshe Diamant, Rudy Cohen, Jan Fantl; Director/Screenplay, Dan Harris; Photography, Tim Orr; Designer, Rick Butler; Costumes, Michael Wilkinson; Music, Deborah Lurie, John Ottoman; Editor, James Lyons; Casting, Jennifer Euston, Meghan Rafferty, Ellen Lewis; Dolby; Super 35 Widescreen; Color; Rated R; 112 minutes; Release date: December 17, 2004

Sigourney Weaver

Sigourney Weaver, Emile Hirsch

Cast

Sandy Travis **Sigourney Weaver**
Tim Travis **Emile Hirsch**
Ben Travis **Jeff Daniels**
Penny Travis **Michelle Williams**
Matt Travis **Kip Pardue**
Marge Dwyer **Deirdre O'Connell**
Kyle Dwyer **Ryan Donowho**
Steph Connors **Suzanne Santo**
Vern **Jay Paulson**
Jack Johnson **Luke Robertson**
Mitchell Goldstein **Lee Wilkof**
Dr. Monte **Terry Beaver**
Shelly Chan **Sara Tanaka**

and Ned Benson (Undercover Hippie), Larry Fessenden (Store Clerk), Ryan Patrick Bachand (Sid), Lori Yeghiayan (Veteran Home Receptionist), Marcia DeBonis (Nurse Lindy), Heidi Newhart (Angela), Ari Graynor (Jenny), Erin Fritch (Emily Slaff), Wayne Kasserman (Robert), Brett Tabisel (Matthew Carey), Henry Strozier (Dr. Davis), Stephen Rowe (Emergency Room Doctor), John Rue (Hal), Sylvia Kauders (Hattie), Jen Jones (Sophie), Lee Brock, Barbara Gulan (Inappropriate Soccer Moms), Adam LeFevre (Bob Clyde), Bruce Norris (Mr. Barnes), Justin Bond (Kiki), Kenny Mellman (Herb), Nicole Tubiola (Tabitha), Fran McGee (Martha), Michael Lawson (Manny), Alberto Vasquez (Manuel), Tonye Patano (Voice of Mean Teacher)

Emile Hirsch, Ryan Donowho

Kip Pardue

The already shaky relationships within the Travis family begin to unravel further after the unexpected death of their older son.

Sigourney Weaver, Jeff Daniels PHOTOS COURTESY OF SONY CLASSICS

FLIGHT OF THE PHOENIX

(20TH CENTURY FOX) Producers, John Davis, William Aldrich, Wyck Godfrey, T. Alex Blum; Executive Producer, Ric Kidney; Director, John Moore; Screenplay, Scott Frank, Edward Burns; Based on a screenplay for *The Flight of the Phoenix* by Lukas Heller from the novel by Elleston Trevor; Photography, Brendan Galvin; Designer, Patrick Lumb; Costumes, George L. Little; Music, Marco Beltrami; Editor, Don Zimmerman; Aerial Photographer, David B. Nowell; Casting, Deborah Aquila, Tricia Wood; an Aldrich Group production/Davis Entertainment Company production; Dolby; Panavision; Deluxe color; Rated PG-13; 113 minutes; Release date: December 17, 2004

Jacob Vargas, Giovanni Ribisi, Miranda Otto, Hugh Laurie, Scott Michael Campbell, Kevork Malikyan, Dennis Quaid, Tyrese Gibbon, Kirk Jones, Tony Curran

Giovanni Ribisi (foreground)

Cast

Frank Towns **Dennis Quaid**
AJ **Tyrese Gibson**
Elliott **Giovanni Ribisi**
Kelly **Miranda Otto**
Rodney **Tony Curran**
Jeremy **Kirk Jones**
Sammi **Jacob Vargas**
Ian **Hugh Laurie**
Liddle **Scott Michael Campbell**
Rady **Kevork Malikyan**
Davis **Jared Padalecki**
Dr. Gerber **Paul Ditchfield**
Newman **Martin "Mako" Hindy**

Miranda Otto, Dennis Quaid

Kirk Jones, Tony Curran

and Bob Brown (Kyle), Anthony Wong (Lead Smuggler), Yi-Ding Wang, Kee-Yick Cheng, Vernon Lehmann (Smugglers)

After a cargo plane crash lands in the Gobi Desert, one of the passengers comes up with the seemingly outrageous idea of building a smaller plane from the wreckage. Remake of the 1965 20th Century Fox film *The Flight of the Phoenix* which starred James Stewart, Richard Attenborough, Hardy Kruger, and Peter Finch. One of the producers of this version, William Aldrich (son of director Robert Aldrich), made an appearance in the first picture.

Scott Michael Campbell, Tyrese Gibbon, Dennis Quaid, Miranda Otto, Tony Curran, Kirk Jones, Hugh Laurie PHOTOS COURTESY OF 20TH CENTURY FOX

Blythe Danner, Ben Stiller, Dustin Hoffman, Barbra Streisand, Teri Polo, Robert De Niro

Blythe Danner, Teri Polo, Robert De Niro, Dustin Hoffman, Barbra Streisand, Ben Stiller

Dustin Hoffman, Robert De Niro PHOTOS COURTESY OF UNIVERSAL/ DREAMWORKS

Robert De Niro, Barbra Streisand

MEET THE FOCKERS

(UNIVERSAL/DREAMWORKS) Producers, Jane Rosenthal, Robert De Niro, Jay Roach; Executive Producers, Amy Sayres, Nancy Tenenbaum; Director, Jay Roach; Screenplay, Jim Herzfeld, John Hamburg; Story, Jim Herzfeld, Marc Hyman; Photography, John Schwartzman; Designer, Rusty Smith; Costumes, Carol Ramsey; Editors, Jon Poll, Lee Haxall; Co-Producer, Jon Poll; Associate Producer, Larry Stuckey; Music, Randy Newman; Original Songs Written and Performed by Randy Newman; Casting, Francine Maisler; a Tribeca/Everyman Pictures production; Dolby; Color; Rated PG-13; 115 minutes; Release date: December 22, 2004

Cast

Jack Byrnes **Robert De Niro**
Gaylord "Greg" Focker **Ben Stiller**
Bernie Focker **Dustin Hoffman**
Roz Focker **Barbra Streisand**
Dina Byrnes **Blythe Danner**
Pam Byrnes **Teri Polo**
Kevin Rawley **Owen Wilson**
Little Jack **Spencer Pickren, Bradley Pickren**
Isabel **Alanna Ubach**
Jorge Villalobos **Ray Santiago**
Officer Le Flore **Tim Blake Nelson**
Judge Ira **Shelley Berman**
Flight Attendant **Kali Rocha**
Airline Clerk **Dorie Barton**

and Jack Plotnick (Rent a Car Agent), Wayne Thomas Yorke (Airport Security Guard), B.J. Hansen (B.J.), J.P. Manoux (Local Cop), Myra Turley (Admitting Nurse), Vahe Bejan, Kathleen Gati (Immigrants), Angelo Tifee (Businessman), Kyle T. McNamee (Undercover Waiter), Cedric Yarbrough (Prison Guard), Max Hoffman (Woody Focker), Benjamin Trueblood (Newborn Baby), Roberto Garcia (Waiter), Bruno Coon (Strolling Minstrel/Band Member), Rock Deadrick, David Sutton (Wedding Band), Linda O'Neil, Bernadette Perez, Tiffany Turner (Girls on Bus)

Greg Focker reluctantly brings his potential in-laws to meet his unconventional parents. Sequel to the 2000 film *Meet the Parents* (Universal/DreamWorks) with De Niro, Stiller, Danner, Polo, and Wilson repeating their roles.

THE WOODSMAN

(NEWMARKET) Producer, Lee Daniels; Executive Producers, Damon Dash, Kevin Bacon, Brook Lenfest, Dawn Lenfest; Director, Nicole Kassell; Screenplay, Nicole Kassell, Steven Fechter; Based on the play by Steven Fechter; Co-Executive Producer, Marvet Britto; Co-Producers, Lisa Cortes, Valerie Hoffman, Dave Robinson; Photography, Xavier Perez Grobet; Designer, Stephen Beatrice; Costumes, Frank Fleming; Music, Nathan Larson; Editors, Brian A. Kates, Lisa Fruchtman; Casting, Billy Hopkins, Suzanne Smith, Kerry Barden, Mark Bennett; a Dash Films, Lee Daniels Entertainment production; Dolby; Technicolor; Rated R; 87 minutes; Release date: December 24, 2004

Kevin Bacon, Kyra Sedgwick

Kevin Bacon

Cast

Walter **Kevin Bacon**
Bob **David Alan Grier**
Mary-Kay **Eve**
Vicki **Kyra Sedgwick**
Carlos **Benjamin Bratt**
Pedro **Carlos Leon**
Rosen **Michael Shannon**
Candy **Kevin Rice**
Sgt. Lucas **Mos Def**
Robin **Hannah Pilkes**
Annette **Jessica Nagle**

and Liam Daniels (Boy at Playground), Joey Hazinsky (Cherub), Clara Infinity Daniels (Little Girl on Bus), Ashley C. Coombs (Girl on Bus), Floraine Maniscioux (Girl in Mall), Aunt Dot (Saleswoman), Spencer Ross (Voice of Sportscaster), Nicole Gibson (Girl with Red Ball)

Having served 12 years in prison for molesting a child, Walter now hopes to go about his life in peace and solitude, only to find his past haunting him.

Mos Def

Kevin Bacon, Benjamin Bratt PHOTOS COURTESY OF NEWMARKET

FAT ALBERT

(20TH CENTURY FOX) Producer, John Davis; Executive Producers, William H. Cosby, Jr., Camille O. Cosby; Director, Joel Zwick; Screenplay, William H. Cosby, Jr., Charles Kipps; Photography, Paul Elliott; Designer, Nina Ruscio; Costumes, Francine Jamison-Tanchuck; Music, Richard Gibbs; Music Supervisor, Dave Jordan; Co-Producer, Jeffrey Stott; Choreographer, Fatima Robinson; Animation Supervisor, Chris Bailey; Key Makeup Artists, Beverly Jo Pryor; Casting, Chemin Sylvia Bernard, Monica Swann; Dolby; Super 35 Widescreen, Deluxe color; Rated PG; 93 minutes; Release date: December 25, 2004

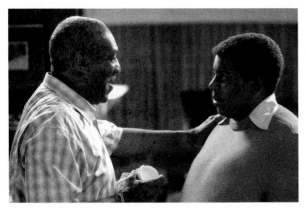

Bill Cosby, Kenan Thompson

Cast

Fat Albert **Kenan Thompson**
Doris **Kyla Pratt**
Rudy **Shedrack Anderson III**
Mushmouth **Jermaine Williams**
Bill **Keith D. Robinson**
Bucky **Alphonso McAuley**
Old Weird Harold **Aaron A. Frazier**
Dumb Donald **Marques B. Houston**
Lauri **Dania Ramirez**
Reggie **Omari Grandberry**
Arthur **J. Mack Slaughter, Jr.**
Coach Gillespi **Rick Overton**
Heather **Keri Lynn Pratt**
Becky **Alice Greczyn**

and Derek "Mr. Bentley" Watkins (Salesman), Jeff Leaf (Basketball Player), Cody Fleetwood (Kid), Annie Abbott (Mrs. Forchick), Nick Zano (Camera Salesman), Jeanne Chinn, Jennifer Kingsley (Women), Alyssa Shafer (Little Girl), Dylan Cash (Emmitt), Damon Elliot (DJ), Jeff Harlan (Dad), Raven-Symone (Danielle V.O.), Jeremy Suarez (Russell V.O.), Earl Billings (Mr. Mudfoot V.O.), Catero Alain Colbert (Lead Teen V.O.), Charles Duckworth, Ben Diskin, Josh Uhler (Teens V.O.), Bill Ratner (Announcer V.O.), Aaron Carter (Teen), Bill Cosby (Himself)

Dania Ramirez, Kenan Thompson

Jermaine Williams (center)

Fat Albert and his friends jump out of the television set into the real world in order to help Doris. Based on the characters created by Bill Cosby and their television spinoffs, *Fat Albert and the Cosby Kids* and *The New Fat Albert Show*.

Kenan Thompson, Aaron Carter PHOTOS COURTESY OF 20TH CENTURY FOX

Sean Penn, Naomi Watts

Sean Penn

Don Cheadle PHOTOS COURTESY OF NEW LINE CINEMA

THE ASSASSINATION OF RICHARD NIXON

(NEW LINE CINEMA) Producers, Alfonso Cuaron, Jorge Vergara; Executive Producers, Arnaud Duteil, Avran Butch Kaplan, Kevin Kennedy, Frida Torresblanco, Alexander Payne, Leonardo DiCaprio, Joana Vicente, Jason Kliot; Director, Niels Mueller; Screenplay, Niels Mueller, Kevin Kennedy; Photography, Emmanuel Lubezki; Designer, Lester Cohen; Costumes, Aggie Guerard Rodgers; Music, Steven Stern; Editor, Jay Cassidy; Line Producer, Debra Grieco; Co-Producers, John Limotte, Doug Bernheim; Casting, Mali Finn; an Anhelo production in association with Appain Way; U.S.-Mexican; Dolby; Deluxe color; Rated R; 105 minutes; Release date: December 29, 2004

Sean Penn

Cast

Samuel J. Bicke **Sean Penn**
Marie Andersen Bicke **Naomi Watts**
Bonny Simmons **Don Cheadle**
Jack Jones **Jack Thompson**
Martin Jones **Brad Henke**
Tom Ford **Nick Searcy**
Julius Bicke **Michael Wincott**
Harold Mann **Mykelti Williamson**
Mae Simmons **April Grace**
Receptionist **Lily Knight**
Sammy Jr. **Jared Dorrance**
Ellen **Jenna Milton**
Julie **Mariah Massa**
Marie's Mother **Eileen Ryan**
Joey Simmons **Derek Greene**

and Joe Marinelli (Mel Samuels), Robert Kenneth Cooper (Irate Driver), Tracy Lynn Middendorf (Businesswoman), Kenneth White, Brett Rickaby, James Morrison Reese, Frank Brown Jr., James C. Carraway, Jay Jacobus (Customers), J.C. Mackenzie (Co-Pilot), Kathryn Howell (Hostage), Denise Balthorp Cassidy (Bank Teller), Gary Mack (Security Man), Melissa Saltzman (Boarding Agent)

As one aspect of his life after another falls apart before his eyes, increasingly unhinged salesman Samuel Bicke begins plotting an attack on President Nixon.

A LOVE SONG FOR BOBBY LONG

(LIONS GATE) Producers, Bob Yari, R. Paul Miller, David Lancaster; Executive Producers, Brad Krevoy, Randall Emmett, George Furla; Director/Screenplay, Shainee Gabel; Inspired by the novel *Off East Magazine St.* by Ronald Everett Capp; Photography, Elliot Davis; Designer, Sharon Lomofsky; Costumes, Jill Ohanneson; Music, Nathan Larson; Music Supervisor, Jim Black; Editors, Lee Percy, Lisa Fruchtman; Line Producer, Betsy Mackey; Associate Producers, Linda Favila, Anson Downes; Casting, Amanda Mackey Johnson, Cathy Sandrich; a Columbia TriStar, El Camino Pictures presentation of a Crossroad Films, Bob Yari production; Dolby; Color; Rated R; 119 minutes; Release date: December 29, 2004

Scarlett Johansson

Cast

Bobby Long **John Travolta**
Pursy Will **Scarlett Johansson**
Lawson Pines **Gabriel Macht**
Georgianna **Deborah Kara Unger**
Cecil **Dane Rhodes**
Junior **David Jensen**
Lee **Clayne Crawford**
Earl **Sonny Shroyer**
Ray **Walter Breaux**
Ruthie **Carol Sutton**
Sean **Warren Blosjo**
Tiny **Bernard Johnson**

and Gina "Ginger" Bernal (Waitress), Douglas Griffin, Earl Maddox, Steve Maye (Men), Don Brady, Will Barnett (Old Men), Patrick McCullough (Streetcar Boy), Leanne Cochran (Streetcar Girl), Nick Loren (Merchant)

Following the death of her estranged mother 18-year-old Pursy Will arrives in New Orleans to find that the dilapidated house she inherited is to be shared with alcoholic former college professor Bobby Long and his protege Lawson Pines.

Scarlett Johansson, John Travolta, Gabriel Macht

Gabriel Macht, John Travolta

Gabriel Macht, Scarlett Johansson, John Travolta PHOTOS COURTESY OF LIONS GATE

IN GOOD COMPANY

(UNIVERSAL) Producers, Paul Weitz, Chris Weitz; Executive Producers, Rodney Liber, Andrew Miano; Director/Screenplay, Paul Weitz; Photography, Remi Adefarasin; Designer, William Arnold; Costumes, Molly Maginnis; Editor, Myron Kerstein; Music, Stephen Trask; Co-Producer, Kerry Kohansky; Associate Producers, Matt Eddy, Lawrence Pressman; Casting, Joseph Middleton; a Depth of Field production; Dolby; Technicolor; Rated PG-13; 109 minutes; Release date: December 29, 2004

Topher Grace, Dennis Quaid

Marg Helgenberger, Dennis Quaid, Topher Grace

Cast

Dan Foreman **Dennis Quaid**
Carter Duryea **Topher Grace**
Alex Foreman **Scarlett Johansson**
Ann Foreman **Marg Helgenberger**
Morty **David Paymer**
Steckle **Clark Gregg**
Eugene Kalb **Philip Baker Hall**
Kimberly **Selma Blair**
Corwin **Frankie Faison**
Enrique Colon **Ty Burrell**
Lou **Kevin Chapman**
Alicia **Amy Aquino**
Jana **Zena Grey**

Topher Grace, Scarlett Johansson

51-year-old ad salesman Dan Foreman is disgusted when a corporate shakeup puts 26-year-old Carter Duryea in the position of being his new boss.

and Colleen Camp (Receptionist), Lauren Tom (Obstetrician), Ron Bottitta (Porsche Dealer), Jon Collin (Waiter), Shishir Kurup (Maitre D'), Tim Edward Rhoze (Theo), Enrique Castillo (Hector), John Cho (Petey), Chris Ausnit (Young Executive),Francesca P. Roberts (Loan Officer), Gregory North (Lawyer),Gregory Hinton, Todd Lyon, Thomas J. Dooley (Moving Men), Robin Kirksey (Basketball Ringer), Kate Ellis (Maya—Roommate), Nick Schutt (Carter's Assistant), John Kepley, Mobin Khan (Salesmen), Jeanne Kort (Saleswoman), Dean A. Parker (Mike), Richard Hotson, Shar Washington (Fired Employees), Rebecca Hedrick (Teddy K's Assistant), Miguel Arteta (Globecom Technician), Sam Tippe (Kid at Party), Roma Torre (Anchorwoman), Andre Cablayan, Dante Powell (Legally Dedd), Malcolm McDowell (Teddy K)

Topher Grace, Clark Gregg PHOTOS COURTESY OF UNIVERSAL

CHASING LIBERTY

(WARNER BROS.) Producers, David Parfitt, Broderick Johnson, Andrwe A. Kosove; Executive Producer, Wayne Rice; Director, Andy Cadiff; Screenplay, Derek Guiley, David Schneiderman; Photography, Ashley Rowe; Designer, Martin Childs; Costumes, Rosie Hackett; Music, Christian Henson; Editor, Jon Gregory; Co-Producers, Kira Davis, Steven P. Wegner, Peter Moravec; Casting, Lisa Beach, Sarah Katzman, Priscilla John; an Alcon Entertainment presentation of a Trademark Films production; Dolby; Arriflex Widescreen; Technicolor; Rated PG-13; 110 minutes; Release date: January 9, 2004. Cast: Mandy Moore (Anna Foster), Matthew Goode (Ben Calder), Jeremy Piven (Agent Alan Weiss), Annabella Sciorra (Agent Cynthia Morales), Caroline Goodall (First Lady Michelle Foster), Mark Harmon (President James Foster), Stark Sands (Grant Hillman), Tony Jayawardena (White House Guard), Briony Glassco (Photo Mother), Lily Tello, Tyla Barnfield (Photo Daughters), Sam Ellis (Phil), Terence Maynard (Harper), Lewis Hancock (Press Secretary), Garrick Hagon (Secretary of State), Zac Benoir (Chairman of the Joint Cheifs of Staff), Jan Goodman (National Security Advisor), Robert Ashe (Chief of Staff), Beatrice Rosen (Gabrielle), The Roots (Themselves), Lucie Liskova (Drunk Girl in Club), Brian Caspe (Agent in Club), Marek Vasut (Drunk Man in Bar), Frantisek Cerny, Milan Cmife, Pavel Karlik (Maquis de Sade Band), Joel Sugerman (Onlooker at the River), Petr Meissel (Man at Train Station), Martin Hancock (McGruff), Maurizio Dal Corso (Italian Waiter), Joseph Long (Eugenio), Miriam Margolyes (Maria), Jan Vosmik, Jan Filipenksy (Farmer's Sons), Jan Kuzelka (Farmer), Nial Iskhakov (Austrian Child), Adrian Bouchet (Gus Gus), Petr Vanek, David Maj (Gen-Xers), Jeremy Healy (Himself), Dusan Fager, Dennison Betram (Partiers), Zdenek Hamouz (Weiss' New Partner)

Mandy Moore, Matthew Goode in *Chasing Liberty*

Annabella Sciorra, Jeremy Piven in *Chasing Liberty* PHOTOS COURTESY OF WARNER BROS.

Michael Imperioli, Eddie Griffin, Anthony Andersen in *My Daddy's Baby* PHOTO COURTESY OF MIRAMAX

MY BABY'S DADDY

(MIRAMAX) Producers, Happy Walters, Eddie Griffin, Matthew Weaver; Executive Producers, Petere Safran, Karen Koch, Bob Weinstein, Harvey Weinstein, Jeremy Kramer; Director, Cheryl Dunye; Screenplay, Eddie Griffin, Damon "Coke" Daniels, Brent Goldberg, David T. Wagner; Photography, Glen MacPherson; Designer, Andrea Stanley; Costumes, Gersha Phillips; Music, Richard Gibbs; Editor, Andy Blumenthal; Co-Producers, Damon "Coke" Daniels, Scott Nemes; Co-Executive Producer, Laura Rister; Casting, Joseph Middleton, Barbara Fiorentino; an Immortal Entertainment production in association with Heartland Prods.; Dolby; Color; Rated PG-13; 86 minutes; Release date: January 9, 2004. Cast: Eddie Griffin (Lonnie), Anthony Anderson (G), Michael Imperioli (Dominic), Method Man (No Good), John Amos (Uncle Virgil), Paula Jai Parker (Rolonda), Bai Ling (Xi Xi), Marsha Thomason (Brandy), Joanna Bacalso (Nia), Amy Sedaris (Annabelle), Tiny Lister (Drive By), Dee Freeman (Peaches), Dennis Akiyama (Cha Ching), Bobb'e J. Thompson (Tupac), Randy Sklar, Jason Sklar (Brotha Stylz), Naomi Gaskin (Venus), Fred Lee (Grandpa Bling Bling), Wynne Pon (Grandma Fung-Yu), Mung Ling Tsui (Sing Sing), Chalant Phifer (Big Swoll), Russell Peters (Obstetrician), Young Dre the Truth (Rapper), Jeanettea Antonio (Bartender), Jordan Madley (Hot Latina), Kardinall Offishall (M.C.), Scott Thompson (Cashier), Quancetia (Woman Shopper #1), Jude Coffey (Cashier #2), Nichie Mee (Nia's Client), Brian Ho (Dang Ling), Jason Burke (Little Swoll), Rudy Webb (Minister), Sal Scozzari (Customer), Isaiah Hooper (Hip-Hop Kid), Daya Vaidya (Dancer/Singer), Lara Vaidya (Background Dancer), Barrington Bignall, Raphael Brown, Daniel Goan, Kojenwa Moitt (Basketball Players), Kira Clavell (Young Woman)

THE HOME TEACHERS

(HAELSTORM) Producer, Dave Hunter; Executive Producer/Director, Kurt Hale; Screenplay, Kurt Hale, John E. Moyer; Photography, Ryan Little; Editor, Wynn Hougaard; Dolby; Color; Rated PG; 82 minutes; Release date: January 9, 2004. Cast: Danny Allen (Billy Bob), Jim Bennett (Pat Mori), Michael Birkeland (Greg), Jeff Birk (Nelson), Emerson Brian (Jenny Blazer), Jimmy Chunga (Phat Cop),

Richard J. Clifford (Johnny Joe), Alex Darrow, Stephanie Darrow (Mori Kids), Paul Eagleston (Day-Dream Reporter), Debbie Ellis (Sister Cooper), Merrily Evans (Sunbeam Teacher), Anna K. Findlay (Lady Cop), Michael Flynn (Karl), Jentri Harding (Josie Blazer), Melanie Harding (LaVon Mori), Jil Hunter (Valiant Teacher), Nan Hunter (Herself), Wally Joyner (Donald Terry), Chad Long (Funeral Director), Gary Ludlow (Dead Guy), John E. Moyer (President Mason), Tayva Patch (Sissy), Peter Pilling (Ice Cream Man), Ryan Radebaugh (Disin Terry), Fay Richins, Frank Richins (Hostages), Melissa Blazer (Elizabeth Sands), Dave Sullivan (Trucker), Daryn Tufts (Joel), Shannon Tuttle (Jani Blazer), Annette Wright (Bonnie Terry)

TORQUE

(WARNER BROS.) Producers, Neal H. Moritz, Brad Luff; Executive Producers, Mike Rachmil, Graham Burke, Bruce Berman; Director, Joseph Kahn; Screenplay, Matt Johnson; Photography, Peter Levy; Designer, Peter J. Hampton; Costumes, Elisabetta Beraldo; Music, Trevor Rabin; Editors, Howard E. Smith, David Blackburn; Co-Producer, Greg Tharp; Visual Effects Supervisor, Eric Durst; Casting, Sarah Halley Finn, Randi Hiller; a Neal H. Moritz production, presented in association with Village Roadshow Pictures; Dolby; Color; Rated PG-13; 81 minutes; Release date: January 16, 2004. Cast: Martin Henderson (Cary Ford), Ice Cube (Trey Wallace), Monet Mazur (Shane), Adam Scott (McPherson), Matt Schulze (Henry), Jaime Pressly (China), Jay Hernandez (Dalton), Will Yun Lee (Val), Justina Machado (Henderson), John Doe (Sheriff Barnes), John Ashker (Yellow Car Driver), Max Beesley (Luther), Dane Cook (Neal Luff), Gichi Gamba (Nomo), Lance Gilbert (18 Wheeler Driver), Faizon Love (Sonny), Hayden McFarland (Kid), Christina Milian (Nina), Kinga Philipps (Neal's Girlfriend), Nichole Mercedes Robinson (Mikisha), Harry Shelley (Officer Frank), Tina Shelley (Reporter), Fredro Starr (Junior), Eddie Steeples (Rasan), Scott Waugh (Red Car Driver), Tony Wilde (Young Dude), Jim Cody Williams (Earl), Jerry Winsett (Farmer)

Jay Hernandez, Martin Henderson, Will Yun Lee in *Torque* PHOTO COURTESY OF WARNER BROS.

CUBA: ISLAND OF MUSIC

(INDEPENDENT) Producers, Gary Keys, Brendan Ward; Director, Gary Keys; Editors, David Himmelstein, Dora Soltani; Color; Not rated; 80 minutes; Release date: January 16, 2004. Documentary on Cuba's music heritage; featuring Gary Keys, Bill Taylor.

Empathy PHOTOS COURTESY OF INDEPENDENT

EMPATHY

(INDEPENDENT) Producers, Amie Siegel, Mark Rance; Director/Screenplay/Editor, Amie Siegel; Photography, Mark Rance; Color; Not rated; 92 minutes; Release date: January 21, 2004. Documentary on the connection between therapists and their patients, with Dr. David Solomon, Aria Knee, Phyllis Baldino, Gigi Buffington, Kerry Cox, Patricia Donegan, Steve Ford, Neal Gantz, John Hiler, Robert McCray, Lily Mojekwu, Catherine O'Connor, Tom Palazzolo, Alix Pearlstein, Maria Silverman, Tracy Thorpe, Stephanie Vogt.

MADE-UP

(RIVERBEND ENTERTAINMENT) Producers, Brooke Adams, Lynne Adams, Mark Donadio; Executive Producer, George W. Fifield, Robert S. Weiner; Director, Tony Shalhoub; Screenplay, Lynne Adams; Photography, Gary Henoch; Designer, Mirian Feldman; Costumes, Lisa Lesniak; Music, Michael Wolff; Editor, Michael Matzdorff; Sister Films; Color; Rated PG-13; 96 minutes; Release date: January 23, 2004. Cast: Brooke Adams (Elizabeth James Tivey), Lynne Adams (Kate James), Eva Amurri (Sara Tivey), Kalen Conover (Chris), Light Eternity (Molly Avrums), Jim Issa (Eli), Lance Krall (Simon), Tony Shalhoub (Max Hires), Gary Sinise (Duncan Tivey)

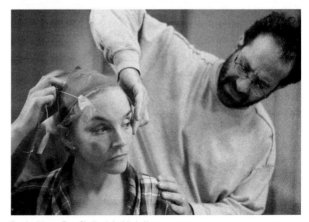

Brooks Adams, Tony Shalhoub in *Made-Up* PHOTO COURTESY OF RIVERBEND ENTERTAINMENT

WOOLY BOYS

(MAC) Producer, Robert Schwartz; Executive Producers, Buffie Stone, Maggie Soboil, Patty Hedeen, Ken Pomersberger; Director, Leszek Burzynski; Screenplay, Max Enscoe, Annie de Young, George "Buck" Flower, Ed Hansen, Glen Stephens; Photography, William Wages; Designer, Stephen Storer; Costumes, Hala Bahmet, Helen Bahmet; Music, Hummie Mann; Editors, Stephen E. Rivkin, Andrew S. Eisen; Casting, Concetta Di Matteo, Carolyn Long; Color; Rated PG; 99 minutes; Release date: January 23, 2004. Cast: Peter Fonda (Stoney), Kris Kristofferson (Shuck), Joseph Mazzello (Charles), Keith Carradine (Hank Dawson), Robin Dearden (Kate), Jad Mager (Billy Spratt), Adam Stradlin (Owen Spratt), Gregory Sporleder (Orville Spratt), Rosanna DeSoto (Martinez), Michael Booth (Agent Colins), Mychael T. Rambo (Hearse Driver), Mark Benninghoffen (Ben), Marquetta Senters (Nurse), Wayne A. Evenson (Carlson), Lana Schwab (Verla), Pamela Walker (Hospital Receptionist), Stephen Pelinski (Doctor Price), Rodney Dimmer, Daniel Rodrigo (FBI Agents), James Cada (Mr. McKormick), Vincent Damahe Benson (Big Bob), Frances F. Ford (Woman in Bowling Alley), Sheila Schafer (Lady in Diner), Brian Brady, John Gream (Troopers), Guapo (Dakota)

EAT THIS NEW YORK

(ARROW) Producers/Directors, Kate Novack, Andrew Rossi; Screenplay: Kate Novack; Photography/Editor, Andrew Rossi; Music, Stephen O'Reilly, Matt Anthony; Color; Not rated; 80 minutes; Release date: January 30, 2004. Documentary on the efforts of two Minneapolis men to open a successful restaurant in New York City.

Eat This New York PHOTOS COURTESY OF ARROW

MOTOCROSS KIDS

(TAG FILMS) Producers, Jonathan Bogner, Steve Austin; Executive Producers, Greg McDonald, Louis J. Pearlman; Director, Richard Gabai; Screenplay, Michael Gannon; Photography, Theo Angell; Designer, Amy R. Strong; Music, Boris Zelkin, Deeji Mincey; Editor, Brett Hedlund; Color; Rated PG; 90 minutes; Release date: January 30, 2004. Cast: Bobby Preston (Skeeter), Brandon Alexander (Street Thug), Jerry Asher (Pirate/Biker), Alan Austin (Callie Reed), Jim Berthiaume (Vester), Gary Busey (Viper), Aimee-Lynn Chadwick (Sports Announcer), Wayne Dalglish (Spike), Phyllis Diller (Lou), Dan Haggerty (Bear Madigan), Todd Holland (Snake), Josh Hutcherson (TJ), Lorenzo Lamas (Evan Reed), Evan Marriott (Mongo), Alexa Nikolas (Katie), Rick Overton (Red Beard)

CATCH THAT KID

(20TH CENTURY FOX) Producer, Andrew Lazar; Executive Producers, Damien Saccani, James Dodson, Mikkel Bondesen; Director, Bart Freundlich; Screenplay, Michael Brandt, Derek Haas; Based on the film *Klatretøsen* written by Nikolaj Arcel, Hans Fabian Wullenweber, Erlend Loe; Photography, Julio Macat; Designer, Tom Meyer; Costumes, Salvador Perez; Editor, Stuart Levy; Co-Producer, Gym Hinderer, Jeff Graup; Music, George S. Clinton; Executive Music Producers, Darren Higman, Laura Z. Wasserman; Casting, Donna Isaacson,

Max Thieriot, Corbin Bleu, Kristen Stewart in *Catch that Kid* PHOTO COURTESY OF 20TH CENTURY FOX

Douglas Aibel; Stunts, Gary Paul; a Fox 2000 Pictures presentation in association with Mediastream III of a Mad Chance/Nimbus Film production; Dolby; Deluxe color; Rated PG; 91 minutes; Release date: February 8, 2004. Cast: Kristen Stewart (Maddy Phillips), Corbin Bleu (Austin), Max Thieriot (Gus), Jennifer Beals (Molly Phillips), Sam Robards (Tom Phillips), John Carroll Lynch (Mr. Hartmann), James Le Gros (Ferrell), Michael Des Barres (Brisbane), Stark Sands (Brad), Lennie Loftin (Flagler), Francois Giroday (Nuffaut), Christine Estabrook (Sharon), Kevin G. Schmidt (Skip), Audrey Wasilewski (Nurse), Meagen Fay (Doctor), Lucy Butler (Brisbane's Assistant), Elizabeth Decker (Brisbane's Secretary), Grant Hayden Scott, Shane Avery Scott (Max), Dawn A.F. Lewis (Blonde), Marcus Hester (Gate Guard), Robert Harvey (Detective), Todd M. Hofacker, Claudia DiFolco, Patrick Stinson, Jerry Penacoli, Maria T. Quiban (Reporters), Kane Ritchotte (Kid Two), Franklin Dennis Jones (Enforcer), Linus Merwin (Kid #3), Kristen Kerr, Chelsea Bond (Moms), Gianina Sbardellati (Racer), Daniel Dotterer (Boy)

PERFECT OPPOSITES

(MAC RELEASING) a.k.a. *A Piece of My Heart;* Producers, Matt Cooper, Lori Miller; Executive Producer, David Cooper; Director, Matt Cooper; Screenplay, Matt Cooper, Stewart J. Zully; Photography, Bernd Heinl; Designer, Franco-Giacomo Carbone; Costumes, Susan Matheson; Music, Brian Tyler; Editors, Jane Kurson, Luis Colina; Casting, Barbara Fiorentino; Color; Rated PG-13; 91 minutes; Release date: February 6, 2004. Cast: Martin Henderson (Drew), Piper Perabo

(Julia), Jennifer Tilly (Elyse Steinberg), Kathleen Wilhoite (Terri), Nichole Hiltz (Celeste), Artie Lange (Lenny Steinberg), Glen Badyna (Ice Cream Attendant), Jason Winer (Danny), Joe Pantoliano (Louis Carbonelli), Jenny Leone (Aubrey), Andrew Keegan (Trey), Aaron Paul (Monty Brant), Cheryl Reeves (Katie), Mark Ryan (Nigel), Caden St. Clair (Robbie), Al White (Dr. Barrett), Stewart J. Zully (Gary)

HIDING AND SEEKING: FAITH AND TOLERANCE AFTER THE HOLOCAUST

(FIRST RUN) Producers/Directors, Menachem Daum, Oren Rudavsky; Photography, Oren Rudavsky; Music, John Zorn; Editor, Zelda Greenstein; Co-Producer, Martin Dornbaum; a Menachem Daum and Oren Rudavsky production in association with Independent Television Sericdes; Color, DV; Not rated; 93 minutes; Release date: February 6, 2004. Documentary in which filmmaker Menachem Daum takes his Talmudic sons on a journey to Poland to teach them tolerance.

THE LOST SKELETON OF CADAVRA

(TRISTAR) Producer, F. Miguel Valenti; Executive Producer, Lars Perksin; Director/Screenplay, Larry Blamire; Photography, Kevin Jones; Editor, Bill Bryn Russell; a Fragmighty, Transom Films, Valenti Entertainment production; Black and white/color; Rated PG; 90 minutes; Release date: February 6, 2004. Cast: Fay Masterson (Betty Armstrong), Andrew Parks (Kro-Bar), Susan McConnell (Lattis), Brian Howe (Dr. Roger Fleming), Jennifer Blaire (Animala), Larry Blamire (Dr. Paul Armstrong), Dan Conroy (Ranger Brad), Robert Deveau (The Farmer), Darren Reed (The Mutant)

HIGHWAYMEN

(NEW LINE CINEMA) Producers, Mike Marcus, Carroll Kemp, Brad Jenkel, Avi Lerner; Executive Producers, Tim Van Rellim, Toby Emmerich, Lynn Harris, Dave Brewington, Trevor Shrot; Director, Robert Harmon; Screenplay, Craig Mitchell, Hans Bauer; Photography, Rene Ohashi; Designer, Paul Austerberry; Costumes, Luis Sequeira; Special Effects Coordinator, Laird McMurray; Dolby; Deluxe color; Rated R; 80 minutes; Release date: February 13, 2004. Cast: Jim Caviezel (James "Rennie" Cray), Rhona Mitra (Molly Poole), Frankie Faison (Will Macklin), Colm Feore (James Fargo), Andrea Roth (Alex Farrow), Gordon Currie

Jim Caviezel in *Highwaymen* PHOTOS COURTESY OF NEW LINE CINEMA

(Ray Boone), Toby Proctor (Rookie), James Kee (Trauma Counselor), Guylaine St. Onge (Olivia Cray), Joe Pingue (Long Hair Mechanic), Maritn Roach (Dective), Ron Bell (Semi Driver), Paul Rutledge (Pickup Driver), Kelly Jones (Pickup Passenger), Bryan Renfro (SUV Driver)

Hiding and Seeking PHOTO COURTESY OF FIRST RUN

Brian Howe in *The Lost Skeleton of Cadavra* PHOTO COURTESY OF TRISTAR

LOVE OBJECT

(VITAGRAPH) Producers, Kathleen Haase, Lawrence Levy; Executive Producers, Edward R. Pressman, Alessandro Camon, John Schmidt; Director/Screenplay, Robert Parigi; Photography, Sidney Sidell; Designer, Trae King; Costumes, Victoria Auth; Music, Nicholas Pike; Editor, Troy Takaki; Casting, Cathy Sandrich Gelfond, Amanda Mackey Johnson, Sig De Miguel, Wendy Weidman; Color; Rated R; 88 minutes; Release date: February 13, 2004. Cast: Desmond Harrington (Kenneth Winslow), Melissa Sagemiller (Lisa Bellmer), Udo Kier (Radley), Rip Torn (Novak), Robert Bagnell (Martin), Brad Henke (Dotson), John Cassini (Jason), Camille Guaty (Counter Girl), Michael Pena (Ramirez), Edie Mirman (Saleswoman), Lyle Kanouse (Stan), Ellen Greene (Typing Supervisor), Opal Anchel (Doris), John Joseph Burns (Porn Clark), Bryan Crump (Mysterious Delivery Guy)

LOST BOYS OF SUDAN

(SHADOW) Producers/Directors, Megan Mylan, Jon Shenk; Photography, Jon Shenk; Editors, Kim Roberts, Mark Becker; an Actual Films and Principe presentation; Color; Not rated; 87 minuts; Release date: February 18, 2004. Documentary on two Sudanese refugees coping with living in Texas, with Peter Kon Dut, Santino Majok Chuor.

Peter Dut in *Lost Boys of Sudan* PHOTO COURTESY OF SHADOW

Charles S. Dutton, Meg Ryan, Omar Epps in *Against the Ropes*

Tony Shalhoub, Meg Ryan, Juan Hernandez in *Against the Ropes* PHOTOS COURTESY OF PARAMOUNT

AGAINST THE ROPES

(PARAMOUNT) Producers, Robert W. Cort, David Madden; Executive Producers, Steven Roffer, Jonathan Pillot, Scarlett Lacey; Director, Charles S. Dutton; Screenplay, Cheryl Edwards; Photography, Jack Green; Designer, Sandra Kybartas; Costumes, Ruth Carter; Music, Michael Kamen; Editor, Eric L. Beason; Associate Producer, Jackie Kallen; Stunt Coordinator/Boxing Choreographer, Roy T. Anderson; Casting, Avy Kaufman; a Cort/Madden production in association with W2 Filmprokutions and Vertriebs and MMP Este Filmproduktions; Dolby; Super 35 Widescreen; Deluxe color; Rated PG-13; 111 minutes; Release date: February 20, 2004. Cast: Meg Ryan (Jackie Kallen), Omar Epps (Luther Shaw), Charles S. Dutton (Felix Reynolds), Tony Shalhoub (Sam LaRocca), Tim

Daly (Gavin Reese), Joe Cortese (Irvin Abel), Kerry Washington (Renee), Sean Bell (Ray Kallen), Dean McDermott (Pete Kallen), Skye McCole Bartusiak (Little Jackie), Juan Hernandez (Pedro Hernandez), Holt McCallany (Dorsett), Tory Kittles (Devon Green), Gene Mack (Kevin Keyes), Beau Starr (Corcoran), Jared Durand (Young Crisco), Diego Fuentes (Car Attendant), Angelo Tucci (Rex), Reg Dreger (Lonnie), Arturo Fresolone (Hernandez's Manager), James Jardine, Michael Buffer (Ring Announcer), Big Daddy Wayne (Stormy), Merwin Mondesir (Street Crony), Doug Lennox (Barrel Chested Man), Hayley Verlyn (Beauty with LaRocca), Moses Myarko (Mouketendi), Aidan Devine (Crisco), Joel Harris (Mathias), Michael Rhoades (Mathias' Manager), Bruce Gooch (Pawn Shop Clerk), Arnold Pinnock, Nevin Pajkic (Heavyweights), Adrianne Keshock (Jenny), Dov Tiefenbach (Organic Clerk), Jackie Kallen (Reporter), Mike Kraft (Jacobs), John Christopher Terry (USA Today Reporter), Tamara Hickey (Megan the Reporter), Karen Robinson (Kimberly Insurance), Noah Danby (LaRocca Henchman), Rocky Zolnierczyk (Sands Fight Referee), Tracey Waterhouse (Receptionist), Neil Crone (HBO Commentator), Ray Marsh (Final Fight Referee), Jeff Ironi (Security Guard), Jean Daigle (Montage Promoter), Carlos Varela, Jr. (Hernandez' Trainer), Jason Jones (Ticket Guy), Shawn Lawrence (Philadelphia Flight Offical), Howard Green (Sands), Julian Scott (Ray Kallen's Sparring Partner), Remo DiCarlo (Buffalo Opponent), Everton McEwan (Luther's Sparring Partner), Eric Reynolds, Egerton Marcus (Hopeful Fighters), Nick Alachiotis (Luther's Trainer), Syd Vanderpool (Luther's Tampa Opponent), Suchart Yodkerepauprai (Rugged Boxer), Hector Perez (Hernandez' Sparring Partner), Rogue Johnson, Paul Lawrie, Donovan Bouhcer, Martin Van Zanten, Edwin Deleon, Chad Keens-Douglas, Michael Amos, Anthony Ferri, Joseph Richardson, Everol Carty, Derek Bujalski (Montage Opponents), Micheal Dion (DJ at Strip Club), Adrian Teodorescu (Referee), Alwin Mascoll (Interviewed Boxer), Peter Wylie (Miami Referee), Dave Dunbar (Philadelphia Referee)

CLIFFORD'S REALLY BIG MOVIE

(WARNER BROS.) Producer, Deborah Forte; Co-Producers, Jef Kaminsky, Martha Atwater; Director, Robert Ramirez; Screenplay, Rhett Reese, Robert Ramirez; Based on the Scholastic book series *Clifford* written by Norman Bridwell; Editor, Monte Bramer; Music, Jody Gray; Songs, Jody Gray, David Steven Cohen; Character Design, Phil Mendez; Casting, Mary Hidalgo; a Scholastic Entertainment Film in association with Big Red Dog Prods.; Dolby; Technicolor;

Rated G; 73 minutes; Release date: February 20, 2004. VOICE Cast: John Ritter (Clifford), Wayne Brady (Shackelford), Grey Delisle (Emily Elizabeth/Mrs. Howard), Jenna Elfman (Dorothy), John Goodman (George Wolfsbottom), Jess Harnell (Dirk), Kel Mitchell (T-Bone), Judge Reinhold (Larry), Kath Soucie (Jetta/Madison), Cree Summer (Cleo), Wilmer Valderrama (Rodrigo), Earl Boen (Mr. Bleakman), Cam Clarke (Hr. Howard/Marcus), Teresa Ganzel (Liza), Ernie Hudson (P.T.), Nick Jameson (Sheriff Lewis), Oren Williams (Charley)

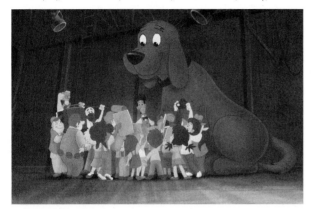

Clifford's Really Big Movie PHOTO COURTESY OF WARNER BROS.

CARLOS CASTANEDA: ENGIMA OF A SORCERER

(INDICAN) Producer/Director/Screenplay/Editor, Ralph Torjan; Executive Producers, Dana Marcoux, Dan Genetti, Pamela Weir-Quiton; Music, Robert Feldman, Ralph Torjan; a Sirius Bandits presentation; Color; Not rated; 91 minutes; Release date: February 27, 2004. Documentary on Carlos Castaneda's teachings on non-ordinary reality, with Amy Wallace, Andra, Richard DeMille, Corey Donovan, Robert J. Feldman, Ron Goldstein, Valerie Kadium, Monica Martinez, Daniel C. Noel, Robert Moss, Victor Sanchez, Melissa Ward, Felix Wolf.

CONFESSIONS OF A BURNING MAN

(WINDLINE) Producers/Directors, Paul Burnett, Ursu Lee; Photography, Jeffrey Chu, Unsu Lee; Music, Paulo Manuelle, Graham Shrimpton; Costumes, Sally Sparks; Editor, Robbie Proctor; Hotbed Media; Color; Not rated; 83 minutes; Release date: February 27, 2004. Documentary on the annual art festival in the Nevada Black Rock Desert in which a huge wooden effigy is burned, with Kevin Epps, Anna Getty, Samantha Weaver, Michael Winaker.

DIRTY DANCING: HAVANA NIGHTS

(LIONS GATE/MIRAMAX) Producers, Lawrence Bender, Sarah Green; Executive Producers, Bob Osher, Meryl Poster, Jennifer Berman, Amir Malin, Rachel Cohen; Director, Guy Ferland; Screenplay, Boaz Yakin, Victoria Arch; Story, Kate Gunzinger, Peter Sagal; Photography, Anthony Richmond; Designer, Hugo Luczyc-Wyhowski; Costumes, Isis Mussenden; Music, Heitor Pereira; Executive Music Producer, Budd Carr; Choreographer, JoAnn Jansen; Casting, Mindy Marin; an Artisan Entertinment, Miramax Films presentation; Dolby; Deuxe color; Rated PG-13; 86 minutes; Release date: February 27, 2004. Cast: Diego

Romola Garai, Diego Luna in *Dirty Dancing: Havana Nights*

Luna (Javier Suarez), Romola Garai (Katey Miller), Sela Ward (Jeannie Miller), John Slattery (Bert Miller), Jonathan Jackson (James Phelps), January Jones (Eve), Mika Boorem (Susie Miller), Rene Lavan (Carlos Suarez), Mya Harrison (Lola Martinez), Polly Cusumano (Polly), Chris Engen (Stephn), Tommy Kavelin (Senor Alonso), Wilmer Cordero (Teacher), Charlie Rodriguez (Grandpa Suarez), Donato Poveda (Troubador), Marisol Padilla Sanchez (Yolanda), Shawn Kane (Country Club Singer), Richard E. Lange (Chaperone), David Rittenhouse (Country Club M.C.), Heather Headley (Rosa Negra Singer), Debbie Castaneda (Girl in Club), Luis Gonzaga (Arturo), Ricardo Alvarez (Miguel), Cesar Detres (Raoul), Yessenia Benavides (Esmerelda), Patrick Swayze (Dance Class Instructor), JoAnn Jansen (Dance Instructor's Partner), Modeso Lacen (Ramon), Alia Maria Alvarez (Chabe Suarez), Angelica Aragon (Alma Suarez), Diego Alvarez (Rafael Suarez), Mary Porster (Mrs. Phelps), Lawrence Duffy (Mr. Phelps), Jerry D. Medina (Palace Singer), Ángel "Cucco" Peña (Julio Daviel), Guillermo de Cun (Palace M.C.), Freddi de Arcé (General Ramirez), Yvonne Caro Caro (Check-In Lady), Matt Birman (Officer in Kitchen), Robert Hoffman (Hoffman), Claudia Salinas (Palace Dancer)

Jonathan Jackson in *Dirty Dancing: Havana Nights* PHOTOS COURTESY OF LIONS GATE/MIRAMAX

RISK/REWARD

(ORGANIC) Producers/Directors, Elizabeth Holder, Xan Parker; Executive Producers, Dori Berinstein, Nicolette Donen, Peter Gilbert; Photography, Cynthia Wade; Music, Mj Mynarski; Editor, Rachel Kittner; Roland Park Pictures; Color; DV; Not rated; 88 minutes; Release date: February 27, 2004. Documentary on the high ranking women who work on Wall Street, with Louise Jones, Carol Warner Wlike, Kimberley Euston, Umber Ahmad.

BROKEN LIZARD'S CLUB DREAD

(FOX SEARCHLIGHT) Producer, Richard Perello; Executive Producers, Lance Hool, Peter E. Lengyel; Director, Jay Chandrasekhar; Screenplay, Broken Lizard; Photography, Lawrence Sher; Designer, Benjamin Conable; Costumes, Melissa Bruning; Music, Nathan Barr; Music Supervisors, Christopher Covert, Barry Cole; Co-Producer, Conrad Hool; Casting, John Papsidera; a Cataland Films production; Dolby; Super 35 Widescreen; Deluxe color; Rated R; 103 minutes; Release date: February 27, 2004. Cast: Bill Paxton (Coconut Pete), Jay Chandasekhar (Putnam Livingston), Kevin Heffernan (Lars), Steve Lemme (Juan Castillo), Paul Soter (Dave), Erik Stolhanske (Sam), Brittany Daniel (Jenny), MC Gainey (Hank), Jordan Ladd (Penelope), Lindsay Price (Yu), Michael Weaver (Roy), Nat Faxon (Manny), Samm Levine (Dirk), Dan Montgomery, Jr. (Rolo), Elena Lyons (Stacy), Tanja Reichert (Kellie), Michael Yurchak (Burke), Richard Perello (Cliff), Julio Bekhór (Carlos), Greg Cipes (Trevor), Ryan Falkner (Marcel), Fabiana Ferre, Paola Hinojos (Go-Go Girls), Veronica Segura (Zoe), Jessica Moreno (Fiona), Heather M. Pemble (Amy Aerobics), Benjamin Digby (Dr. Wick), Jose Cruz, Luis Banderas (Busboys), Claudia Palacios (Buccaneer Waitress)

GREENDALE

(SHAKEY PICTURES) Producers, Neil Young, L.A. Johnson; Executive Producer, Elliot Rabinowitz; Director, Bernard Shakey (Neil Young); Screenplay/Photography/Music, Neil Young; Editor, Toshi Onuki; Dolby; Color; Not rated; 87 minutes; Release date: February 27, 2004. Cast: Sarah White (Sun Green), Eric Johnson (Jed Green/Devil), Ben Keith (Grandpa Green), Erik Markegard (Earth Brown), Elizabeth Keith (Grandma Green), Pegi Young (Edith Green), James Mazzeo (Earl Green), Paul Supplee (Officer Carmichael), Sydney Stephan (Widow), Echobrain (Imitator), Bernard Shakey/Neil Young (Wayne Newton)

Dr. Gilda Carle, David Maynard, Joshua Coleman, Scott Ryan in *Games People Play*

GAMES PEOPLE PLAY: NEW YORK

(FABILUCE/ARTISTIC LICENSE) Producers, James Ronald Whitney, Neil Stephens; Executive Producers, Richard Reichgut, J. David Luce; Director/Screenplay/Editor, James Roland Whitney; Photography, Neil Stephens; Music, Tom Thomsen; Designers, Michael Reichgut, Philip Friedman; Choreographer, Daniel Catanach; a Fire Island Films production; Color; Not rated; 100 minutes; Release date: March 12, 2004. Cast: Joshua Coleman, Sarah Smith, Scott Ryan, Dani Marco, David Maynard, Elisha Imani Wilson, Dr. Gilda Carle, Jim Caruso, James Ronald Whitney.

Cast of *Games People Play* PHOTOS COURTESY OF FABILUCE/ARTISTIC LICENSE

MAESTRO

(SANCTUARY/SONY) Producers, Edmar Flores, Jamal J. Dorsett, Kervyn Marks; Director/Screenplay, Josell Ramos; Music, Antonio Ocasio, Michael X. Cole, Jepthe Guillaume; from Artrution Productions; Color; Not rated; 89 minutes; Release date: March 12, 2004. Documentary on the underground dance club scene of the 80s focusing on three New York City clubs: the Loft, Paradise Garage, and the Gallery, with Larry Levan, David Mancuso, Frankie Knuckles, Nicky Siano, Francis Grasso, Francois K., "Little" Louie Vega, Danny Tenaglia, Tony Humphries, John Jellybean Benitez, Danny Krivit, Joaquin Joe Claussell, Richard Long, Alex Rosner, Keith Haring, Derrick May, Robert Clivilles, Jose Padilla, Sven Vath, Patricia Field, Kenny "Dope" Gonzalez.

AGENT CODY BANKS: DESTINATION LONDON

(MGM) Producers, Guy Oseary, David C. Glasser, Bob Yari, David Nicksay, Dylan Sellers; Executive Producers, Danny Gold, Michael Jackman, Andreas Klein, Mark Morgan, Madonna, Jason Alexander, Jennifer Birchfield-Eick, Kerry David; Director, Kevin Allen; Screenplay, Don Rhymer; Story, Harald Zwart, Dylan Sellers, Don Rhymer; Based on the characters created by Jeffrey Jurgensen; Photography, Denis Crossan; Designer, Richard Holland; Costumes, Steven Noble; Music, Mark Thomas; Music Supervisor, Julianne Jordan; Editor, Andrew MacRitchie; Co-Producer, Robert Meyer Burnett; Casting, John Papsidera, Daniel Hubbard (U.K.); a Bob Yari, Maverick Films, Dylan Sellers production; Dolby; Panavision; Color; Rated PG; 99 minutes; Release date: March 12, 2004. Cast: Frankie Muniz (Cody Banks), Anthony Anderson (Derek), Hannah Spearritt (Emily), Cynthia Stevenson (Mrs. Banks), Daniel Roebuck (Mr. Banks),

Frankie Muniz, Anthony Anderson in *Agent Cody Banks: Destination London*   PHOTO COURTESY OF MGM

Anna Chancellor (Jo Kenworth), Keith Allen (Diaz), James Faulkner (Kenworth), David Kelly (Trival), Santiago Segura (Santiago), Connor Widdows (Alex Banks), Keith David (C.I.A. Director), Rod Silvers (Kumar), Jack Stanley (Ryan), Joshua Brody (Bender), Sarah McNicholas (Marisa), Philip Pedersen (Bender's Mate), Paul Kaye (Neville), Harry Burton (Westminster Headmaster), Julian Firth (Isambard Jerkalot), Martyn Ellis (Welsh Security Guard), Damien Hirst (Arty Farty Security Guard), Mark Williams (Inspector Crescent), James Dreyfus (Gordon), Patti Love (Woman), Henry Miller (Moped Man), Masato Kamo (Japanese Tourist), Sam Douglas (U.S. President), Westminster International Youth Orchestra: Alfie Allen (Berkhamp on Double Bass), Leilah Isaac (Sabeen on Bassoon), Keiron Nelson (Habu on French Horn), Theora Toumazi (Sonya on Violin), Keshini Sukhram (Violinist), Atim Laber (Celist), Carly Minsky (Oboist), Chris Bodell (Brass Player), Javkhaa Chuluunbaatar (Harpsichordist), Sammy Razack (Percussion)

Linda Cardellini, Sarah Michelle Gellar, Freddie Prinze Jr. in *Scooby Doo 2*
PHOTO COURTESY OF WARNER BROS.

SCUMROCK

(INDEPENDENT) Producers, Jon Moritsugu, Andrea Sperling; Director, Jon Moritsugu; Screenplay, Jon Moritsugu, Amy Davis; Photography, Amy Davis; Music, Lance Hahn; Color; Not rated; 79 minutes; Release date: March 17, 2004. Amy Davis (Roxxy), James Duval (Drew), Lance Hahn (Asian Dude), Kyp Malone (Miles)

DIVAN

(ZEITGEIST) Producer/Director, Pearl Gluck; Screenplay, Pearl Gluck, Susan Korda; Photography, William Tyler Smith; Music, Frank London; from Divan Productions; U.S.-Hungarian-Israeli-Ukranian; Color; Not rated; 90 minutes; Release date: March 17, 2004. Documentary in which the filmmaker searches for a couch once owned by her great-great-grandfather.

SCOOBY-DOO 2: MONSTERS UNLEASHED

(WARNER BROS.) Producers, Charles Roven, Richard Suckle; Executive Producers, Brent O'Connor, Kelley Smith-Wait, Joseph Barbera; Director, Raja Gosnell; Screenplay, James Gunn; Based on characters created by Hanna-Barbera Productions; Photography, Oliver Wood; Designer, Bill Boes; Costumes, Leesa Evans; Music, David Newman; Editor, Kent Beyda; Visual Effects Supervisor, Peter Crosman; Co-Producers, James Gunn, Alan G. Glazer; Casting, Mary Vernieu; 2nd Unit/Stunts, Andrew Armstrong; a Mosaic Media Group production; Dolby; Technicolor; Rated PG; 91 minutes; Release date: March 26, 2004. Cast: Freddie Prinze, Jr. (Fred), Sarah Michelle Gellar (Daphne), Matthew Lillard (Shaggy), Linda Cardellini (Velma), Seth Green (Patrick), Peter Boyle (Old Man Wickles), Tim Blake Nelson (Jacobo), Alicia Silverstone (Heather), Neil Fanning (Scooby-Doo Voice), Pat O'Brien, Tazmanian Devil, Ruben Studdard (Themselves), Bill Meilen (Chauffeur), Zahf Paroo (Ned), Christopher Gauthier, Peter New (Daphne's Tattooed Fans), Morgan Brayton, Lisa Ann Beley, Tara Fynn (Mullet Nerdettes), Joe MacLeod, Brandon Jay McLaren, Aaron Ydenberg (Skater Dudes), Lou Bollo, John Ulmer (Flashback Security Guards), Bradley Gosnell, Calum Worthy (Kids on Bikes), Brenna O'Brien (Buttercup Scout), Mark Burgess, Kwesi Ameyaw (Men in Suite), Ted Kozma, Darrell Izeard (Museum Guards), Stephen E. Miller (C.L. Magnus), Karin Konoval (Aggie Wilkins), Paul Jamieson (Scared Man), Andrew McIlroy, Colin Foo (Investors), Andrew Jackson (Man in Car), Nazanin Afshin-Jam (Shaggy Chick), Cascy Beddow (Young Shaggy), Emily Tennant (Young Daphne), Ryan Vrba (Young Fred), Lauren Kennedy (Young Velma), Jeff Tanner (Harry Lang), Alan C. Peterson, Dan Joffre (Faux Ghost Patrons), Richard Dietl (Pickle Man/Faux Ghost Patron), Bill Mondy (Vomit Reporter), Kimani Ray Smith, Catherine Lough Haggquist, Ingrid Torrance, Tiffani Timms (Reporters), Scott McNeil (Evil Masked Figure), Kevin Durand (Black Knight Ghost), C. Ernst Harth (Miner 49er), Christopher R. Supton (Zombie)

THIS OLD CUB

(EMERGING PICTURES) Producers, Jeff Santo, Tim Comstock; Director, Jeff Santo; Photography, Terry Pratt, Garett Griffin, Hollywood Heard; Editor, Christopher Cibelli; Narrator, Joe Mantegna; Color; Not rated; 86 minutes; Release date: March 26, 2004. Documentary in which filmmaker traces his father, Ron Santo's, battle with diabetes and his efforts to be inducted into the Baseball Hall of Fame; with Ron Santo, Dennis Franz, Joe Mantegna, Bill Murray, William L. Petersen, Gary Sinise.

David Arquette in *Never Die Alone*

Reagan Gomez-Preston, DMX in *Never Die Alone* PHOTOS COURTESY OF FOX SEARCHLIGHT

NEVER DIE ALONE

(FOX SEARCHLIGHT) Producers, Earl Simmons (DMX), Alessandro Camon; Executive Producers, Edward R. Pressman, Cameron Casey, Dion Fearon, Marc Gerald; Rudy "Kato" Rangel, John Schmidt; Director, Ernest Dickerson; Screenplay, James Gibson; Based on the novel by Donald Goines; Photography, Matthew Libatique; Designer, Christiaan Wagener; Costumes, Marie France; Music, Damon "Grease" Blackmon, George Duke; Casting, Robi Reed-Humes; Dolby; Super 35 Widescreen; Color; Rated R; 88 minutes; Release date: March 26, 2004. Cast: DMX (King David), Michael Ealy (Michael), Drew Sidora (Ella), Antwon Tanner (Blue), Robby Robinson (Main in Apartment), Luenell Campbell (Jasper), David Arquette (Paul), Clifton Powell (Moon), Wealthy Linn Gener (Asian Girl), Jeff Sanders (Sentry Guard #1), Tommy "Tiny" Lister (Rockie), Shaikra Vanise (Co-Worker), Big Daddy Wayne (Red), Damion Poitier (Alvin), Eric Payne (Orderly), L.K. "Peak" Winbush (Airport Security), Jay Lynch (Earl), D-Taylor Murphy (Parking Attendant), Aisha Tyler (Nancy), Jennifer Sky (Janet), El Rosenblatt (Director), Scott Casperson (A.D.), Mark Kubr (Pretty Boy Actor), Reagan Gomez-Preston (Juanita), Rachelle Drummnod (Twin #1), Larry McCoy (Henchman), Wajid (Cabbie), Michele Shay (Juanita's Mother), Keesha Sharp (Edna), Xavier Simmons (Young Mike), Roderick "Lexx" Stevens (Mugger), Jay Lynch (Earl), Art Evans (Mr. Waters), Henry Gibson (Funeral Director)

MAYOR OF THE SUNSET STRIP

(FIRST LOOK) Producers, Tommy Perna, Greg Little, Christopher Paul Carter; Executive Producer, Donald Zuckerman; Director/Screenplay, George Hickenlooper; Photography, Kramer Morgenthau, Igor Meglic; Music, Anthony Marinelli; Editor, Julie Janata; a Caldera Productions, Kino-Eye American, Perna Productions, Question Mark Productions presentation; Dolby; Color; Rated R; 94

Cher, Rodney Bigenheimer in *Mayor of the Sunset Strip* PHOTOS COURTESY OF FIRST LOOK

minutes; Release date: April 2, 2004. Documentary on 60s radio dj and music groupie Rodney Bingenheimer; featuring Rodney Bigenheimer, Tori Amos, Beck, Sonny Bono, David Bowie, Leo Baudy, Clem Burke, Exene Cervenka, Cher, Alic Cooper, Elvis Costello, Cheri Currie, Michael Des Barres, Pamela Des Barres, John Doe, India Dupre, Corey Feldman, Kim Fowley, Liam Gallagh, Leigh Gorman, Green Day, Deborah Harry, George Hickenlooper, Mick Jagger, Joan Jett, Davy Jones, Kato Kaelin, Lance Loud, Courtney Love, Ray Manzarek, Johnny Marr, Chris Martin, Paul McCartney, Mackenzie Phillips, Poe, Joey Ramone, Keanu Reeves, Paul Reubens, Linda Ronstadt, David Lee Roth, Brooke Shields, Nancy Sinatra, Phil Spector, Gwen Stefani, Chris Stein, Pete Townshend, Ronald Vaughan, Brian Wilson, Lisa Worden, Neil Young, Rob Zombie.

Michelle Agnew, Joe Pascual, Anne Betancourt in *The Gatekeeper* PHOTOS COURTESY OF ABRAMORAMA

THE GATEKEEPER

(ABRAMORAMA) Producers, John Carlos Frey, Jack Lorenz; Director/Screenplay, John Carlos Frey; Photography, Kris Denton; Designer, Daren Janes; Costumes, Julie Reeder; Music, Carlo Giacco; Editor, Jacek Kropinski; Casting, Patrick Rush, Alyson Silverberg; from Gatekeeper Productions; Color; Rated R; 103 minutes; Release date: April 2, 2004. Cast: John Carlos Frey (Adam Fields), Michelle Agnew (Eva Ramirez), Anne Betancourt (Lenora), Joel Brooks (Vance Johnson), Joe Pascual (Jose), Kai Lennox (Peter Randolph), J. Patrick McCormack (Jack Green), Tricia O'Kelley (Jennifer McGregory), Juan Eduardo Gonzalez (Drug Boss), Juan R. Gonzalez (Carlos), Rudy Quintanilla (Jorge Munuz), Rob Roy (FBI Agent #2)

Kai Lennox, John Carlos Frey, Joel Brooks in *The Gatekeeper*

MARATHON

(ALPHAVILLE FILMS) Director, Amir Naderi; Photography, Michael Simmonds; Editors, Amir Naderi, Donal O'Ceilleachair; Color; Not rated; 74 minutes; Release date: April 2, 2004. Cast: Sara Paul (Gretchen), Rebecca Nelson (Gretchen's Mom)

THE WHOLE TEN YARDS

(WARNER BROS.) Producers, Elie Samaha, Arnold Rifkin, David Willis, Allan Kaufman; Executive Producers, Andrew Stevens, Tracee Stanley, David Bergstein, Oliver Hengst; Director, Howard Deutch; Screenplay, George Gallo; Story, Mitchell Kapner, based on his characters; Photography, Neil Roach; Designer, Virginia Randolph-Weaver; Costumes, Rudy Dillon; Line Producer, Andrew Sugerman; Co-Producers, Joseph Merhi, James Holt; Music, John Debney; Associate Producers, Ernst-August Schnieder, Wolfgang Schamburg; A Franchise Pictures presentation of a Cheyenne Enterprises production in association with MHF Zweite Academy Film; U.S.-German; Dolby; Color; Rated PG-13; 99 minutes; Release date: April 9, 2004. Cast: Bruce Willis (Jimmy), Matthew Perry (Oz), Amanda Peet (Jill), Kevin Pollak (Lazlo), Natasha Henstridge (Cynthia), Frank Collison (Strabo), Johnny Messner (Zevo), Silas Weir Mitchell (Yermo), Tasha Smith (Julie), Elisa Gallay (Anya), Tallulah Belle Willis (Buttercup Scout), Johnny Williams (Vito), George Zapata, Carlo Zapata (Guys in Trunk), McNally Sagal (Maitre D'), Carl Ciarfalio, Doc Duhame, Buck MacDancer, Monte Perlin, Ian Quinn, Brad Orrison (Goons), Ned Bellamy (Man in Diner), Emmett Shoemaker (Son), Lou Beatty, Jr. (Bus Driver), Lily Kravets, Jessica Flaherty, Caitlin Morrison (Birthday Guests), Barry Thompson (Kiosk Vendor), Amy Peitz (Waitress), Franck Pesce, Robert Rusler (Policemen), Irene Lopez (Mexican Woman), Julie Lott (Bar Patron)

Christian Taylor (left) in *Showboy* PHOTOS COURTESY OF REGENT

SHOWBOY

(REGENT) Producer, Jason Buchtel; Executive Producer, Pam Tarr; Directors, Lindy Heymann, Christian Taylor; Screenplay, Lindy Heymann, Christian Taylor, Jason Buchtel; Photography, Joaquin Baca-Asay; Music, Daniele Luppi; Editor, Kant Pan; a Fite Films, Squeak Pictures production; Color; Not rated; 93 minutes; Release date: April 9, 2004. Cast: Christian Taylor (Writer), Lindy Heymann (Director), Marilyn Milgrom (Voice of London Producer), Joe Daley (Roomate), Erich Miller (Showboy), Jason Buchtel (Vegas Producer), Aaron Porter (Dance Instructor), Adrian Armas (Model), Billy Sameth (Close Friend), Lauren Ambrose, Alan Ball, Alan Connell, Frances Conroy, Siegfried Fischbacher, Whoopi Goldberg, Rachel Griffiths, Michael C. Hall, Roy Horn, Peter Kruase, Freddy Rodriguez, Jeremy Sisto (Themselves)

Matthew Perry, Bruce Willis in *The Whole Ten Yards* PHOTOS COURTESY OF WARNER BROS.

THIS SO-CALLED DISASTER: SAM SHEPARD DIRECTS THE LATE HENRY MOSS

(IFC FILMS) Producers, Callum Greene, Anthony Katagas; Executive Producer, Holly Becker; Director, Michael Almereyda; Photography, Michael McDonough; Editor, Kate Williams; an IFC, Keep Your Head production; Color; Rated R; 89 minutes; Release date: April 21, 2004. Behind-the-scenes documentary on the 2000 San Francisco stage production of Sam Shepard's play *The Late Henry Moss*; featuring Sean Penn, Nick Nolte, Cheech Marin, Sheila Tousey, T-Bone Burnett, Sam Shepard, James Gammon, Woody Harrleson.

Sean Penn, Woody Harrelson in *This So-Called Disaster*

Nick Nolte in *This So-Called Disaster* PHOTOS COURTESY OF IFC FILMS

MC5*: A TRUE TESTIMONIAL

(AVATAR FILMS) Producer, Laurel Legler; Executive Producers, Howard Thompson, Jim Roehm; Director/Editor, David C. Thomas; Screenplay, David C. Thomas, Laurel Legler; Photography, Anthony Allen; a Future/Now Films Inc. production; Color; Not rated; 120 minutes; Release date: April 23, 2004. Documentary on the punk rock group MC5, featuring Michael Davis, Wayne Kramer, Fred "Sonic" Smith, Dennis Thompson, Rob Tyner (MC5).

Michael Pitt in *Rhinoceros Eyes* PHOTOS COURTESY OF MAD STONE FILMS

RHINOCEROS EYES

(MADSTONE FILMS) Producers, Tom Gruenberg, Eva Kolodner; Executive Producer, Chip Seelig; Director/Screenplay, Aaron Woodley; Photography, David Greene; Designer, Karen Wilson; Costumes, Denise Cronenberg; Music, John Cale, E.C. Woodley; Editors, Robert Crossman, Julie Carr; Casting, John Buchan, Jenny Lewis, Katia Smith; a Directors Program production; Dolby; Color; Rated R; 92 minutes; Release date: April 23, 2004. Cast: Michael Pitt (Chep), Paige Turco (Fran), Gale Harold (Det. Phil Barbara), Matt Servitto (Bundy), James Allodi (Hamish), Jackie Burroughs (Mrs. Walnut), Nadia Litz (Ann), Victor Ermanis (Sweets), Boy Banks (Hospital Orderly), Carrie Clayton (Betty Bumcakes), Michael Charles Cole (Boom Operator), Neil Crone (Security Guard), Robert Crossman (Naked Man), Reginald Doresa (Mr. Walnut), Alexis Dziena (Bird Girl), Daniel Fathers (Producer), Jennifer Gould (Melissa, Movie Actress), David Greene (DP), Richard Hirschfield (Corpse), Costa Kamateros (Gorilla), Anthony Lemke (Dick, Movie Actor), James Mainprize (Peter Morgan), Glen Peloso (Hooker), Judy Sinclair (Woman in Hospital), Lorraine Sinclair (Waitress), Peter Van Dam (Actor), Aaron Woodley (Director)

MC5 in *MC5** PHOTOS COURTESY OF AVATAR FILMS

THE AGRONOMIST

(THINKFILM) Producers, Jonathan Demme, Peter Saraf, Bevin McNamara; Executive Producer, David Wolff; Director, Jonathan Demme; Photography, Aboudja, Jonathan Demme, Peter Saraf, Bevin McNamara; Music, Wyclef Jean, Jerry "Wonda" Duplessis; Editors, Lizi Gelber, Bevin McNamara; Archival Research, Kati Meister; Associate Producers, Edwidge Danticat, Lizi Gelber; a Clinica Estetico presentation; U.S.-Haiti; Duart Color/Black and white, DV; Not rated; 90 minutes; Release date: April 23, 2004. Documentary on Jean Dominique, the Haitian radio personality who campaigned for democracy for his country, with Jean Dominique, Michele Montas, Raoul Labuchin, J.J. Dominique, Aboudja.

Marlee Matlin in *What the #$*! Do We (K)now!?* PHOTO COURTESY OF ROADSIDE ATTRACTIONS/SAMUEL GOLDWYN

WHAT THE #$*! DO WE (K)NOW!?

(ROADSIDE ATTRACTIONS/SAMUEL GOLDWYN) Producers, Betsy Chasse, William Arntz; Directors, Betsy Chasse, William Arntz, Mark Vicente; Screenplay, Betsy Chasse, William Arntz, Matthew Hoffman; Photography, Mark Vicente, David Bridges; Designer, Nava; Costumes, Ronald Leamon; Music, Christopher Franke, Michael Whalen; Editor, Jonathan P. Shaw; Visual Effects, David M. Blume, Evan Jacobs; a Lord of the Wind production; Black and white/Fotokem color; Not rated; 108 minutes; Release date: April 23, 2004. Cast: Marlee Matlin (Amanda), Elaine Hendrix (Jennifer), Barry Newman (Frank), Robert Bailey, Jr. (Reggie), John Ross Bowie (Elliot), Armin Shimerman (Man in Sunway), Robert Blanche (Bob), Davied Albert, Amit Goswami, John Hagelin, Candace Perth, Ramtha, Jeffrey Satinover, William Tiller, Fred Alan Wolf (Themselves), Marsha Clark (Voices), James Langston Drake (Groom), Dawnn Pavlonnis, Mercedes Rose, Sherilyn Lawson (Bridesmaids), Eric Newsome (Voice Over Animated Characters), Leslie Taylor (Bride's Sister), Tin D. Tran (Guy), Tara Walker (Girl at Train Station), Evan Jacobs (Priest in Flashback)

JUSTICE

(RED ANARCHIST) Producers, Amelia Dallis, Amy R. Baird; Director/Screenplay, Evan Oppenheimer; Photography, Luke Geissbuhler; Designer, Beth Kuhn; Costumes, Dona Mandel; Music, Nenad Bach; Editor, Allison Eve Zell; Casting, Felicia Fasano, Mary Vernieu; Color; Not rated; 80 minutes; Release date: April 28, 2004. Cast: Erik Palladino (Drew Pettite), Catherine Kellner (Mara Seaver), Daphne Rubin-Vega (Roberta), Ajay Naidu (Mohammed), Marisa Ryan (Julia), Michael Jai White (Tre), Tom Guiry (The Red Anarchist), Joelle Carter

(Monique), David Patrick Kelly (Marty), Michael Ealy (Woody), Leo Fitzpatrick (The Egg Machine), Larry Pine (The Legend), Alan Cox (Palm Sunday), Helena Lewis (Helena), Daniel Cantor (Terrrence the Ugly American), Gloria Irizarry (Luiza), Firdous Bamji (Samir Khan), Monique Guesnon (Day-Old Bagel Lady), Tim Kang (Bodega Owner), Scott Miller (Cigarette Man), Waleed Zuaiter (Pretzel Vendor), Shoshannah Stern, Jim Wallick (Patrons), Emory Van Cleve (Big Guy), Evan Oppenheimer (He Got Next), Martin Schepelern (Cute Guy in Park)

BOBBY JONES, STROKE OF GENIUS

(FILM FOUNDRY) Producers, Kim Dawson, Tim Moore, John Shepherd; Executive Producers, Dave Ross, Rick Eldridge; Co-Executive Producers, Gregg Galloway, Jim Van Eerden, Tom Crow; Director, Rowdy Herrington; Screenplay, Rowdy Herrington, Tony DePaul, Bill Pryor; Story, Rowdy Herrington, Kim Dawson; Photography, Tom Stern; Designer, Bruce Miller; Costumes, Beverly Safier; Music, James Horner; Editor, Pasquale Buba; Casting, Beverly Holoway; a Bobby Jones Film presentation in association with Dean River Prods. of a Life(n) production; Dolby; Super 35 Widescreen; Color; Rated PG; 126 minutes; Release date: April 30, 2004. Cast: Jim Caviezel (Bobby Jones), Claire Forlani (Mary Malone Jones), Jeremy Northam (Walter Hagen), Malcolm McDowell (O.B. Keeler), Connie Ray (Clara Jones), Brett Rice (Big Bob), Dan Albright (Grandfather Jones), Paul Freeman (Angus), Hilton McCrae (Jimmy Maiden), Aidan Quinn (Harry Vardon), Devon Gearhart (Bobby, age 8), Thomas "Bubba" Lewis (Bobby, age 14), Alistair Begg (Stewart Maiden), Elizabeth Omilami (Camilla), Brian F. Durkin (Perry Adair), John Shepherd (Bob Woodruff), Happy LaShelle (Nell Woodruff), Allen O'Reilly (Grantland Rice), Larry Thompson (John Malone), Tim Ware (George Adair), David Van Horn (Young Perry), Rand Hopkins (Major Cohen), Tom Arcuragi (Ralph Reed), Stephanie Sparks (Alexa Stirling), Erin Smith (Young Alexa), Larry Mayran (Judge Broyles), Kasey Leigh, Neely Glenn (Saucy Co-eds), Matthew Cornwell (Chum), Ted Hurt Huckabee (Rathskeller Drunk), Richard Dobkin (Emory Law Professor), Chris Pierce (Henpecked Husband), Virginia Hopkins (Househunting Wife), Ted Manson (Elderly Law Client), Andrew Masset (Dr. Howard), Pierre Brulatour (Dr. Applegate), Mike Pniewski (Mr. Mullen), Amerjit Deu (Hagen's Chauffeur), Mitch Dean (Inwood Runner), Michael Andrew (Singer), Julie Moore (Woman at Party), Brian Bremer (Well Wisher Autograph Seeker), Mary Jean Feton (Well Wisher at Reception), Dave Roberts (Sportswriter), Jim Harley (Constable O'Brien), Angie Fox (Gardner's Girlfriend), Eleanor Seigler (Perry's Date), Justice Leak (Guy on Street), Richard "John" Lackey III (Baby Bob Jones III), Kelsey Walter (Daughter Clara Jones), Aint Misbehavin (Barbershop Quartet), Robert Pralgo, Frank Hoyt Taylor, Phillip DeVona, David Dwyer, Patrick Cusick, Kevin Stillwell, Jamie Moore, Scott Oliver, Mark Russell Gray, Geoff McKnight (Reporters), Mark Burton (Red), Bob Seel (Billy McAfee), John Kohler (Milt Saul), Kenny Alfonso (Eben Byers), Roy McCrerey (Robert Gardner), Matthew Lanter (Bobby Jones' Caddy), Amanda Best (Elaine Rosenthal), Clark Jarrett (Chick Evans), Gary Gershoff (Davey Herron), John Curran (Bob Cruikshank), Woody Taft (Jess Sweetzer), Robert Duncan (1926 U.S. Open Opponent), John Grzesinski (Roger Wethered), Rudi "Daniel" David (Interlachen Golfer), Kevin Downes (Gene Homans), Bruce McKinnon (11st Merion Starter), Wilbur Fitzgerald (Megaphone Official), Shaun Stuart (1921 British Open Starter), Tommy Cresswell (1926 U.S. Open Official), Rodney Mull (USGA Official), Rick Rueckert (Worchester Official), Bob Harter (Seniro Worchester Official), Alan McGregor (St. Andrew's Starter—1930), Kelly McCormick (Hoylake Steward), Rhoda Griffis (Woman Hit in Leg), John Fitzgerald Page (Program Holder)

Rebecca Romijn-Stamos, Cameron Bright, Greg Kinnear in *Godsend*

GODSEND

(LIONS GATE) Producers, Cathy Schulman, Sean O'Keefe, Marc Butan; Executive Producers, Todd Wagner, Mark Cuban, Jon Feltheimer, Mark Canton, Michael Paseornek, Michael Burns, Eric Kopeloff; Co-Producers, Steve Mitchell, Mark Bomback; Director, Nick Hamm; Screenplay, Mark Bomback; Photography, Kramer Morgenthau; Designer, Doug Kraner; Costumes, Suzanne McCabe; Music, Brian Tyler; Editors, Steve Mirkovich, Niven Howie; Casting, Sarah Halley Finn, Randi Hiller; presented in association with 2929 Entertainment; Dolby; Super 35 Widescreen; Deluxe color; Rated PG-13; 102 minutes; Release date: April 30, 2004. Cast: Greg Kinnear (Paul Duncan), Rebecca Romijn-Stamos (Jessie Duncan), Robert De Niro (Richard Wells), Cameron Bright (Adam Duncan), Merwin Mondesir (Maurice, Young Thug), Sava Drayton (Young Thug #2), Jake Simons (Dan Sandler), Edie Inksetter (Footlocker Cashier), Raoul Bhaneja (Samir Miklat), Jenny Levine (Sandra Shaw), Thomas Chambers (Jordan Shaw), Munro Chambers (Max Shaw), Jeff Christensen (Hal Shaw), Deborah Odell (Tanya), Jordan Scherer (Roy Hazen), Ingrid Veninger (Mrs. Farr), Al Bernstein (Godsend Receptionist), Tracey Hoyt (Delivery Nurse), Leslie Ann Coles (Patricia Cafe Owner), Chris Burtton (Dr. Lieber), Marcia Bennett (Principal Hersch), Mari Trainor (Godsend Nurse), Ann Holloway (File Clerk), Zoie Palmer (Susan Pierce), Janet Bailey (Cora Williams), Devon Bostick (Zachary Clark Wells), Matthew Peart, Andrews Chalmers, Sara Tough, Claire Sheasgreen, Melanie Tonello (St. Pius Students), Matt Robinson (High School Student), David Rehder (Mr. Baker), Nancy Hochman (Mrs. Baker)

Robert De Niro in *Godsend* PHOTOS COURTESY OF LIONS GATE

PEOPLE SAY I'M CRAZY

(PALO ALTO PICTURES) Producers, Katie Cadigan, Ira Wohl; Directors, John Cadigan, Katie Cadigan; Photography, John Cadigan, Laura C. Murray, Katie Cadigan; Editor, Laura C. Murray; Music, Evelyn Glennie; an HBO Cinemax production; Color; Not rated; 84 minutes; Release date: April 30, 2004. Documentary on John Cadigan's efforts to overcome schizophrenia.

Ashley Olsen, Mary-Kate Olsen in *New York Minute* PHOTO COURTESY OF WARNER BROS.

NEW YORK MINUTE

(WARNER BROS.) Producers, Denise Di Novi, Robert Thorne, Mary-Kate Olsen, Ashley Olsen; Director, Dennie Gordon; Screenplay, Emily Fox, Adam Cooper, Bill Collage; Story, Emily Fox; Executive Producer, Alsion Greenspan; Photography, Greg Gardiner; Designer, Michael Carlin; Costumes, Christopher Kargadon; Editors, Michael Jablow, Roderick Davis; Music, George S. Clinton; Music Supervisor, John Houlihan; Co-Producers, Christine Sacani, Jill Zimmerman; Casting, Marci Liroff; a Dualstar Productions/Di Novi Pictures production; Dolby; Deluxe color; Rated PG; 91 minutes; Release date: May 7, 2004. Cast: Ashley Olsen (Jane Ryan), Mary-Kate Olsen (Roxy Ryan), Eugene Levy (Max Lomax), Andy Richter (Bennie Bang), Riley Smith (Jim, the Bike Messenger), Jared Padalecki (Trey Lipton), Dr. Drew Pinsky (Dr. Ryan), Darrell Hammond (Hudson McGill), Andrea Martin (Senator Anne Lipton), Alannah Ong (Ma Bang), Mary Bond Davis (Big Shirl), Bob Saget (Himself), Jack Osbourne (Justin), Joey Klein (Truant at Pool), Neil Crone (Officer Strauss), Jonathan Wilson (Train Conductor), Boy Banks (Ticket Window Guy), Silver Kim (Asian Guy with Chip), Conrad Bergshneider, Robert Williams (Feds), Domenic Cuzzocrea (Homeless Guy), Suresh John (Deli Clerk), Kent Staines (Doorman), Jon Benjamin (I Love NY Vendor), Frank Bonsangue (Con Ed Supervisor), Jo Chim (Ma Bang's Assistant), Lindsay Leese (Customer at Ma Bang's), Pierre Bouvier, Chuck Comeau, Seabstien LeFebvre, David Desrosiers, Jeff Stinco (Simple Plan), Alison Northcott (Video Shoot Groupie), Balazs Koos (Video Shoot Announcer), Trip Phoenix, Philip Drube (Old School Record Execs), Kenny Robinson (Head Security), Todd William Schroeder (Massive Security Guard), Colin Penson (Security Guard), Damon D'Oliveira (News Broadcaster), Eric Woolfe (Male Nurse), Warren Belle (Mickey the Cab Driver), Arnold Pinnock (Big Shirl's Male Beautician), Tasha Ricketts, Stephanie Samuels, Marsha Williams, Wendy Adeliyi (Big Shirl's Beauticians), Donna-Marie Christie, Jamila

Fleming, Shakira Harper, Lurline Lucas, Faustina Owusu-Ansah (House of Bling Customers), John Hemphill (Tim Brooger), Kathy Laskey (Steffi Brooger), Garen Boyajian (Manjhur), Jazz Mann (Auditorium T.A.), Maggie Butterfield (Auditorium Moderator), Gala, Krissy (Reinaldo), Frank Welker (Reinald Vocal Effects)

SUPERSTAR IN A HOUSEDRESS

(HIGHBERGER MEDIA) Producer/Director/Screenplay/Photography/Editor, Craig Highberger; Executive Producer, Andrew La Barbera; Music, Paul Serrato; Dolby; Color; Not rated; 95 minutes; Release date: May 7, 2004. Documentary on Andy Warhol factory member, playwright and drag performer Jackie Curtis; featuring Paul Ambrose, Michael André, Penny Arcade, Michael Arian, Gretchen Berg, Styles Caldwell, Lee Black Childers, Joe Dallesandro, Laura de Coppet, Alexis Del Lago, Harvey Fierstein, Joe Franklin, Robert Heide, Don Herron, Rev. Timothy Holder, Agosto Machado, Sasha McCaffrey, Taylor Mead, Sylvia Miles, Jack Mitchell, Paul Morrissey, Michael Musto, Joey Preston, Rose Royalle, Paul Serrato, Ellen Stewart, Lily Tomlin, John Vaccaro, Steven Watson, Holly Woodlawn.

Jackie Curtis in *Superstar in a Housedress* PHOTO COURTESY OF HIGHBERGER MEDIA

OFF THE LIP

(HANNOVER HOUSE) Producer, Robert Mickelson; Executive Producer, Paula Mazur, Karen Lauder, Marcus Ticotin; Director, Robert Mickelson; Screenplay, Shem Bitterman; Story, Shem Bitterman, Robert Mickelson; Photography, Joey Forsyte; Music, Andrew Gross; Editor, Peregrine Beckman; Casting, Cathy Henderson, Dori Zuckerman; an Abandon Pictures, Film Farm production; Dolby; Color; Rated R; 87 minutes; Release date: May 7, 2004. Cast: Marguerite Moreau (Kat Shutte), Mackenzie Astin (Brad), Adam Scott (David), Mark Fite (Lenser), Davis Rasche (Dr. Martin Shutte), Jim Turner (Boner), Rick Overton (McReady), Peter Mackenzie (Rick), Matty Liu (Boner's Sidekick), Adam Hatley (Brian), Simone Vannucci (Vito), Manny Carabello (Che), Faid Issa (Mee), Puanani Mahoe (Hawaiian Spiritualist), Rush Randle (Crash), Sierra Emory, Brian Talma (Windsurfers), Lucy Chambers (Commune Girl), Robert Lee (Hotel Manager), J.C. Palmore (FBI Agent), Moku, Maka (Hawaiian Thugs), Matthew Beisner (New Ager), Lazaro Quilon (Apologetic Surfer), Paul Hamai (Frank), Sam Ireland (Mad Boyfriend), Katie Kabler (Waitress), Todd Ganzagan (Cop), John Rippy (Bartender), Tony Spear (Dead Head), Allan Mendez (Cowboy), Hulali Brede (Hula Dancer), Robert Brede (Beach Tourist), Steve Madewell (Pilot), Scott Jacobson (Mama's Waiter), Dave "Gruber" Allen (Pupule), Diane Robin (Mrs. Shutte)

Jay Mohr, Julianne Nicholson in *Seeing Other People* PHOTO COURTESY OF LANTERN LANE ENTERTAINMENT

SEEING OTHER PEOPLE

(LANTERN LANE ENTERTAINMENT) Producer, Gavin Polone; Executive Producers, Dan Kaplow, Vivian Cannon, Maya Forbes; Director, Wallace Wolodarsky; Screenplay, Wallace Wolodarsky, Maya Forbes; Photography, Mark Doering-Powell; Designer, Dan Butts; Costumes, Jacqueline Saint Anne; Music, Alan Elliott; Editor, Stewart Schill; Casting, Karen Meisels; a Pariah Entertainment Group production; Dolby; Color; Rated R; 90 minutes; Release date: May 7, 2004. Cast: Jay Mohr (Ed), Julianne Nicholson (Alice), Lauren Graham (Claire), Bryan Cranston (Peter), Josh Charles (Lou), Andy Richter (Carl), Matthew Davis (Donald), Jonathan Davis (Ricky), Jill Ritchie (Sandy), Helen Slater (Penelope), Niki J. Crawford (Venita), Dylan McLaughlin (Jake), Lew Schneider (Marty), Shanna Moakler (Kasey), Mike Faiola (Tim), Nicole Marie Lenz (Miranda), Sheeri Rappaport (Naomi), Chay Santini (Diane), Tom Paul Wilson (Dicey Character), Mitch Morris (Doug), Mimi Rogers (Elise), Rachel Shelley (Lauren), John Riggi (Maitre d'), Wally Wolodarsky (Salesman), Alex Borstein (Tracy), Liz Phair (Yoga Teacher), Mike Elling (Seth), Gavin Feek (Dicey Bystander), Alison Flierl (Party Girl)

Mackenzie Astin, Marguerite Moreau, Adam Scott in *Off the Lip* PHOTO COURTESY OF HANNOVER HOUSE

James Marsden in *The 24th Day* PHOTO COURTESY OF SCREEN MEDIA

THE 24TH DAY

(SCREEN MEDIA) Producer, Nick Stagliano; Director/Screenplay, Tony Piccirillo, based on his play; Executive Producer, Liliana Lovell; Line Producer, Lynn Appelle; Photography, J. Alan Hostetter; Designer, Norman Dodge; Costumes, Leonard Pollack; Music, Kevin Manthei; Editors, Aaron Mackoff, Robert Larkin; Casting, Diane Heery, Mike Lemon; from Nazz Productions; Dolby; Color; Rated R; 92 minutes; Release date: May 14, 2004. Cast: James Marsden (Dan), Scott Speedman (Tom), Soffa Vergara (Isabella), Barry Papick (Mr. Lerner), Charlie Corrado, Jarvis W. George (Officers), Scott Roman (Bartender), Jeffrey Frost (Dan's Assistant), Jona Harvey (Marla), Thea Chaloner (Wife), Brian Campbell (Blondie), Nadia Axakorwsky (Studio Executive)

A SLIPPING-DOWN LIFE

(LIONS GATE) Producer, Richard Raddon; Executive Producers, Derinda Dallas, Robin Lieberman; Director/Screenplay, Toni Kalem; Based on the novel by Ann Tyler; Photography, Michael F. Barrow; Designer, Russell J. Smith; Costumes, Francine LeCoultre; Music, Peter Himmelman; Editor, Hughes Winborne;

Guy Pearce, Lili Taylor in *A Slipping Down Life* PHOTOS COURTESY OF LIONS GATE

Casting, Beth Sepko; a DVC Entertainment, PFG Entertainment production; Dolby; Color; Rated R; 111 minutes; Release date: May 14, 2004. Cast: Lili Taylor (Evie Decker), Guy Pearce (Drumstings Casey), Irma P. Hall (Clotelia), John Hawkes (David Elliot), Veronica Cartwright (Mrs. Casey), Marshall Bell (Mr. Casey), Shawnee Smith (Faye-Jean Lindsay), Sara Rue (Violet), Bruno Kirby (Kiddie Arcades Manager), Tom Bower (Mr. Decker), Jo Ann Farabee (Woman at Salon), Harv Morgan (Dick St. Clair), Jason Russell Waller, Lew Temple (Audience Members), Jason Kavalewitz, Jeff McMillioan, Brian Stack, Kevin Stack (Young Sexband), Billy Harvey (Sloppy Eddie), Mike Hynes, Michael Ramos, Eric Tatuaka (Crotch Crickets), Jamie Dickerson (Redhead Girl), Tony Frank (Zack), James Harrell (Doctor), Clea DuVall (Nurse), Keith McDermott (Paul Ogle), Topher Glenn (Drum's Brother), Dan Bennett (Pharmacist), Mike Keller (Young Guitar Player), Johnny Goudie (Jesse), Floyd Freeman (Old Black Man on Mouth Harp), Vincent Prendergast III (Twin Brother #1), Kirk Watson (Pharmacy Patron)

Gabrielle Union, Jamie Foxx in *Breakin' All the Rules* PHOTO COURTESY OF SCREEN GEMS

BREAKIN' ALL THE RULES

(SCREEN GEMS) Producer, Lisa Turnell; Executive Producer, Paddy Cullen; Director/Screenplay, Daniel Taplitz; Photography, David Hennings; Designer, Jerry Fleming; Costumes, Isis Mussenden; Music, Marcus Miller; Music Supervisor, Peter Coquillard; Editor, Robert Frazen; Casting, Kim Davis Wagner, Justine Baddeley; a Lisa Turnell production; Dolby; Super 35 Widescreen; Deluxe color; Rated PG-13; 85 minutes; Release date: May 14, 2004. Cast: Jamie Foxx (Quincy Watson), Gabrielle Union (Nicky Callas), Morris Chestnut (Evan Fields), Peter MacNicol (Philip Gascon), Jennifer Esposito (Rita Monroe), Bianca Lawson (Helen Sharp), Jill Ritchie (Amy), Samantha Nagel (Sandra, Executive Assistant), Grace Chan (Secretary), Danny Comden (Sam), Octavia L. Spencer (Stylist), Heather Headley (Herself), Patrick Cranshaw (Mr. Lynch), Tate Taylor (Attendant), Bob Stephenson (Ticket Master), Gerald Emerick (TV Host), Amie Petersen (Girl), Faune Chambers (The Betty), Mario Carter, Ambrose Maond Clayton, Trae Ireland (Men at Party), Trina Johnson (Woman at Party), Clyde Sherman (Man at Bar)

WITH ALL DELIBERATE SPEED

(DISCOVERY DOCS) Producer/Director, Peter Gilbert; Executive Producers, Steve Rosenbaum, Don Baer, Billy Campbell, Steve Carlis; Screenplay, Natahn Antila; Photography, Peter Gilbert, Joe Arcidiacono, Andy Lemon, Richard Oakes,

William Rexer; a Camera Planet production; Color; Not rated; 110 minutes; Release date: May 14, 2004. Documentary on the landmark Brown vs. Board of Education decision; featuring Julian Bond, Rev. Joe Delaine, Barbara Johns, Vernon Jordan, Thurgood Marshall Jr., E. Barrett Prettyman.

Jonathan Tucker, Rachael Leigh Cook in *Stateside* PHOTOS COURTESY OF LIONS GATE

STATESIDE

(SAMUEL GOLDWYN FILMS) Producerss, Robert Greenhut, Reverge Anselmo; Executive Producers, Eberhard Kayser, Michele Berk; Co-Producer, Bonnie Hlinomaz; Director/Screenplay, Reverge Anselmo; Photography, Adam Holender; Designer, Michael Shaw; Costumes, Cynthia Flynt; Music, Joel McNeely; Editor, Suzy Elmiger; Casting, Todd Thaler, Jonathan Strauss; a Seven Hills Pictures presentation in association with Cinealpha; Dolby; Panavision; Technicolor; Rated R; 97 minutes; Release date: May 21, 2004. Cast: Rachael Leigh Cook (Dori Lawrence), Jonathan Tucker (Mark Deloach), Agnes Bruckner (Sue Dubois), Val Kilmer (Staff Sgt. Skeer), Joe Mantegna (Gil Deloach), Carrie Fisher (Mrs Dubois), Diane Venora (Mrs Hengen), Ed Begley Jr. (Father Concoff), Michael Goduti (Gregory Tripodi), Daniel Franzese (Danny Tripodi), Paul Le Mat (Dori's Internist), Bridget Barkan (Francine), Billy Lush (Nando), Brian Geraghty (Chris), Joanne Pankow (Sister Olga), Rob Zapple, George DiCenzo (Detectives), Shon Blotzer (Michael), Rachelle Carson (Karen, St. Anthony's Nurse), Sal Ruffino (Cop), Lou Criscuolo (Mr. Tripodi), Abbey Fogt (Emerald Isle Blonde Girl), Johnny Alonso, Robert Rogan, Timmy Sherrill (Lunar Fringe), Zena Grey (Gina Deloach), David Holcomb (Silvio), Marcus Hester (Pink Wig Man), Andre Vippolis (Ricky, Dori's Agent), Rasool K'Han (Hjaveral County Nurse), David Walton (John Pelusso), Rick Warner (Atty O'Dwyer), Mick McGovern (Bailiff), Patrick Walker, Damian Pitts, Stuart Greer, David Stillinger (Drill Instructors), Scott D. Carson (Series Commander), Michael Perry, Earnest Hunte. Reverge Anselmo (Recruits), Marion Boggs (Berta), Peter Jurasik (Hector Pelusso), Caryn Greenhut (Jenny), Chris Helton (Swoop Driver), Robert Trevelier (CIA Agent), Rick Forrester (Lieutenant), Richard Kyle Ladeau (Armorer), Tony Hale (Dori's Uncle Donny), Terry Paul (Morehead City Colonel), Brenden Donovan, Ryan Sweeney (Recruits, Platoon 1021), Robert Greenhut (Director of Irish Play), Penny Marshall (Lt. Chevetone)

STAR SPANGLED TO DEATH

(BIG COMMOTION PICTURES) Director/Screenplay/Editor, Ken Jacobs; Black and white/color; Not rated; 402 minutes; Release date: May 21, 2004. Cast: Jack Smith (The Spirit Not of Life But of Living), Jerry Sims (Suffering), Gib Taylor, Bill Carpenter (The Two Evils), Cecilia Swan (Misplaced Charity), Ken Jacobs (Oscar Friendly/Ringmaster/Janitor)

UNION SQUARE

(ALLIANCE INTL.) Producer, Lillian Miranda; Executive Producer/Director/Photography/Editor, Stephen J. Szklarski; Screenplay, Lillian Miranda, Stephen J. Szklarski; Music, The Lewis Elderlane Experience, Lars Alive; Color, DV; Not rated; 92 minutes; Release date: May 28, 2004. Documentary on the homeless junkies of Manhattan's Union Square, featuring Cheyenne, Mark, Stealth, Ron, James, Mike, Danny, Lock.

Method Man, Sofia Vergara in *Soul Plane* PHOTO COURTESY OF MGM

SOUL PLANE

(MGM) Producers, David Scott Rubin, Jessy Terrero; Executive Producers, Paul Hall, Bo Zenga; Director, Jessy Terrero; Screenplay, Bo Zenga, Chuck Wilson; Photography, Jonathan Sela; Desginer, Robb Buono; Costumes, Shawn Barton; Music, The RZA; Music Supervisor, Melodee Sutton; Editor, Michael R. Miller; Casting, Sheila Jaffe, Georgianne Walken, Ulysses Terrero; Dolby; Deluxe color; Rated R; 86 minutes; Release date: May 28, 2004. Cast: Tom Arnold (Mr. Hunkee), Kevin Hart (Nashawn), Method Man (Muggsy), Snoop Dogg (Captain Mack), K.D. Aubert (Giselle), Godfrey (Gaeman), Brian Hooks (DJ), D.L. Hughley (Johnny), Arielle Kebbel (Heather Hunkee), Mo'nique (Jamiqua), Ryan Pinkston (Billy Hunkee), Missi Pyle (Barbara), Sommore (Cherry), Sofia Vergara (Blanca), Gary Anthony Williams (Flame), John Witherspoon (Blind Man), Loni Love (Shaniece), Stephen Keys (Riggs), Angell Conwell (Tamika), Robert Isaac Lee (Judge Pong), Charles Walker (Jury Foreman), Brent Strickland, Laura Rogers (Reporters), Brian Mulligan (Boarding Agent), Stacey Travis, Donna Cooper, Elisha Wilson (Flight Attendants), Nancy Gibbs (Worldwide Air Woman), Kendall Carly Browne (Ticket Agent, Worldwide Air), Dwayne Adway (Jerome), Terry Crews (Thug, Flight Attendant), Chris Robinson, Big Boy, Karl Malone, Big Sam, Lil' Jon, D Roc, Kaine, La La (Themselves), Chemin Martinez, Lanisha Cole (Bartenders), Bob Morrisey (Carter Seersucker), Crystal Mattison (Sexy Flight Attendant), Francine Dee (Chinese Stripper), Vanessa Ordonez (Latin Stripper), Sandy Carter, Lauren Reau (Strippers), Jeris Lee Poindexter (Giselle's Father), Don Wilson (Business Man), Double Trouble (Dre)

Martin Landau in *Wake*

WAKE

(NEWMARKET/ECHELON) Producer, Susan Landau Finch; Executive Producers, Michael C. Donaldson, Margaret Rockwell; Director/Screenplay, Henry LeRoy Finch; Photography, Patrick Kelly; Designer, Eric Matheson; Costumes, Suszana Megyesi; Music, Chris Anderson, Henry LeRoy Finch; Editor, Gus Carpenter; Casting, Susan Landau Finch; Color, HD; Not rated; 92 minutes; Release date: May 28, 2004. Cast: Blake Gibbons (Raymond Riven), Gale Harold (Kyle Riven), John Winthrop Philbrick (Jack Riven), Dihlon McManne (Sebastian Riven), Martin Landau (Older Sebastian Raven), Muriel Kenderdine (Mother), Dusty Paik (April), Rainer Judd (Dusty), Robert Witham (Police Officer), Judy Griffith, Charles Kozlosky (Bartenders), Melissa Henderson, Marta Kozlosky, Eric Matheson, John Ring, Roger Van Deusen, Randy Visser (Billy Budd's Bar Patrons)

Gale Harold in *Wake* PHOTOS COURTESY OF NEWMARKET/ECHELON

BUKOWSKI: BORN INTO THIS

(MAGNOLIA) Co-Producers, Diane Markow, John McCormick; Director, John Dullaghan; Photography, Matt Mindlin, Art Simon; Music, James Stemple; Editor, Victor Livingston; Color; Not rated; 130 minutes; Release date: June 4, 2004. Documentary on cult writer Charles Bukowski; featuring Bono, John Bryan, Linda Lee Bukowski, Marina Bukowski, Michael Cano, Neeli Cherkovski, Joyce Fante, FrancEye, Taylor Hackford, John Martin, Mike Meloan, Jack Micheline, Pam "Cupcakes" Miller, Dom Muto, William Packard, Sean Penn, Steve Richmond, Barbet Schroeder, Harry Dean Stanton, Tom Waits, Carl Weissner, Liza Williams.

FRANKIE AND JOHNNY ARE MARRIED

(IFC FILMS) Supervising Producer, Matt Grayson; Line Producer, Alice West; Director/Screenplay, Michael Pressman; Photography, Jacek Laskus; Designer, Lauren Hersholt-Nole; Costumes, Van Broughton Ramsey; Music, Don Peake; Editors, Michael Rafferty, Jeff Freeman; Casting, Jeffery Passero; from Curb Entertainment; Dolby; Color; Rated R; 95 minutes; Release date: June 11, 2004. Cast: Lou Antonio, Kathy Baker, Lisa Chess, Hector Elizondo, Steven Glick, David E. Kelley, Jerry Levine, Debra Magit, Leslie Moonves, Jeffery Passero, Mandy Patinkin, Brooks Pressman, Michael Pressman, Barry Primus, Alan Rosenberg, Nina Tassler, Alice West (Themselves), Jillian Armenante (Cynthia), Nicole Gomez Fisher (2nd A.D.), Elizabeth Hayden (Casting Assistant), Ann Hearn (Constance), Lanre Idewu (Paramedic), Linda Klein ("Chicago Hope" Paramedic), Ken Lerner (Rob the Production Manager), Debra Magit (Mother), Vahan Moosekian (Man on Street), Morgan Nagler (Sally), Natalia Nogulich (Theatre Patron), James Oliver (Billy), Maury Sterling (Roger), Stephen Tobolowsky (Murray Mintz)

Charles Bukowski in *Bukowski*

Charles Bukowski in *Bukowski* PHOTOS COURTESY OF MAGNOLIA

Michael Pressman, Lisa Chess in *Frankie and Johnny Are Married* PHOTO COURTESY OF IFC FILMS

WORD WARS

(SEVENTH ART RELEASING) Producer, Eric Chaikin; Director, Eric Chaikin, Julian Petrillo; Executive Producers, Vivian Schiller, Udy Epstein; Photography, Laela Kilbourn; Music, Thor Madsen; Editor, Conor O'Neill; Dolby; Color; Not rated; 80 minutes; Release date: June 11, 2004. Documentary on scrabble fanatics; featuring Joe Edley, Stefan Fatsis, Matt Graham, Marlon Hill, Joel Sherman.

Todd Verow, Dustin Schell in *Anonymous* PHOTO COURTESY OF BANGOR FILMS/ JIM DWYER

ANONYMOUS

(BANGOR FILMS) Producer/Director/Screenplay, Todd Verow; Executive Producer/Music, Jim Dwyer; Editors, Todd Verow, Jim Dwyer; Color; Not rated; 82 minutes; Release date: June 16, 2004. Cast: Todd Verow (Todd), Dustin Schell (John), Jason Bailey (Ben), Lee Kohler (Mr. Kohl), Sophia Lamar (Linda), Florian Sachisthal (Roger)

Marlon Hill in *Word Wars* PHOTO COURTESY OF SEVENTH ART RELEASING

GRAND THEFT PARSONS

(SWIPE FILMS) Producer, Frank Mannion; Executive Producers, Matt Candel, Jess Itzler, Zygi Kamasa, Brad Zipper; Line Producer, Pierre Lorillard; Director, David Caffrey; Screenplay, Jeremy Drysdale; Photography, Robert Hayes; Designer, Bryce Elric Holthousen; Costumes, Sophie Carbonell; Music, Richard G. Mitchell; Editors, Alan Roberts, Mary Finlay; Casting, Sarah Halley Finn, Randi Hiller; a Morty-Stevie G Productions, Redbus Pictures production; Dolby; Color; Rated PG-13; 88 minutes; Release date: June 18, 2004. Cast: Johnny Knoxville (Phil Kaufman), Christina Applegate (Barbara Mansfield), Michael Shannon (Larry Oster-Berg), Robert Forster (Stanley Parsons), Marley Shelton (Susie), Gabriel Macht (Gram Parsons), Mike Shawver (Barney), Jamie McShane (Radio Announcer), Danielle Sapia (Girl at Joshua Tree Inn), Robert Alan Beuth (Reporter), Sara Arrington (Crying Girl), Scott Adsit (Music Expert), Mary Pat Gleason (Nurses), David Caffrey (TV Interviewer), Wesley Mann (Doctor), Jim Cody Williams (Truck Drivre), Kay E. Kuter (Undertaker), Brian Nahas (Bank Manager), Simone Hammond (Check-in Girl), Betsy Rosenfeld (Girl in Line), Jonathan Slavin (Mortuary Clerk), Mike Randleman (P.J. Gambrell), Karen Teliha (Official), Rich Reilly, Carol Kaufman (Plane Passengers), Clint Culp (Uniform Cop), Betty Carvalho (Melon Lady), Paul Goebel (Gas Station Attendant), Michael Gregory (Motorcycle Cop), Tom McCleister (Polyonax Place Barman), Dylan Bruno (Traffic Cop), Phil Kaufman (Handcuffed Felon)

Michael Shannon, Marley Shelton, Johnny Knoxville in *Grand Theft Parsons*
PHOTO COURTESY OF SWIPE FILMS

THE HUNTING OF THE PRESIDENT

(REGENT RELEASING) Producer, Douglas Jackson; Directors/Screenplay, Nickolas Perry, Harry Thomason; Based on the book by Joe Conason, Gene Lyons; Photography, Jim Roberson; Music, Bruce Miller; Editor, Nickolas Perry; Narrator, Morgan Freeman; Dolby; Color/black and white; Not rated; 90 minutes; Release date: June 18, 2004. Documentary on the organized campaign to discredit President Bill Clinton; featuring Paul Begala, Sidney Blumenthal, David Brock, John Camp, James Carville, Larry Case, Joe Conason, Andrew Cooper, Jerry Falwell, Howard Kurtz, Gene Lyons, Susan McDougal, Dan Moldea, Claudia Riley, Betsy Wright.

HOWARD ZINN: YOU CAN'T BE NEUTRAL ON A MOVING TRAIN

(FIRST RUN FEATURES) Producers/Directors, Deb Ellis, Denis Mueller; Photography, Judy Hoffman; Music, Richard Martinez; Editor, Deb Ellis; Narrator, Matt Damon; Color/black and white; Not rated; 78 minutes; Release date: June 18, 2004. Documentary on historian, author, and activist Howard Zinn.

SAINTS AND SINNERS

(AVATAR FILMS) Producer/Director/Screenplay, Abigail Honor; Photography, Van Vizinberg; Music, Michael Picton; a Persona Films production; Dolby; Color; Not rated; 80 minutes; Release date: June 18, 2004. Documentary on how two gay men wish to marry in accordance with the sacrament of the Catholic church.

Vincent Maniscalco, Edward DeBonis in *Saints and Sinners* PHOTO COURTESY OF AVATAR FILMS

GHOSTLIGHT

(LOT 47 FILMS) Producers, Penny Fearon, Richard Move; Executive Producer, Christopher Herrmann; Director, Christopher Herrmann; Screenplay, Richard Move, Christopher Herrmann, Penny Fearon; Photography, Tsuyoshi Kimoto; Designer, Christopher Boyd; Costumes, Pilar Limosner; Music, John Califra; Editors, James Lyons, Matt Absher; Casting, Cyndy Fujikawa; from Mannic Productions; Dolby; Color; Not rated; 80 minutes; Release date: June 23, 2004. Cast: Richard Move (Martha Graham), Ann Magnuson (Barbara Rosen), Earnest Abuba (Isamu Moguchi), Rob Besserer (Erick Hawkins), Jennifer Binford, Amy Piantaggini (Aphrodites), Maryette Charlton (Helen Keller), David Ilku (Ron),

James Carville in *The Hunting of the President* PHOTO COURTESY OF REGENT RELEASING

Donna Coney Island (Liza Minnelli), Flotilla DeBarge (Central Park Drag Queen), Eric Kastel (James), Isaac Mizrahi (Alex), Kevin Kean Murphy (Halston), Kittson O'Neill (Linda), Gita Reddy (Barbara's Receptionist), Clark Render (Andy Warhol), Deborah Harry, Mark Morris (Themselves), Deborah Goodman, Rebecca Jung, Sandra Kaufman, Leslie Myers, Carla Rigon, Blakeley White-McGuire (The Furies), Lisa Dalton, Amy Day, Kerry Elmore, Connie Fleming, Reid Hutchins, Clete Larkey, Eli McAfee, Tomoko Muneto, Carrie Oleson, Tres Bien Pollard (Dancers)

AMERICA'S HEART & SOUL

(WALT DISNEY PICTURES) Producer/Director/Photography, Louis Schwartzberg; Executive Producer, Jake Eberts; Editors, Brian Funck, Tom McGah, Jeff Werner; Associate Producers, Jan Ross, Vincent Ueber; Music, Joel McNeely; Original Theme Song: "The World Don't Bother Me None" written and performed by John Mellencamp; a Blacklight Films production; Dolby; Fotokem color; Rated PG; 84 minutes; Release date: July 2, 2004. Documentary on the interesting lives of seemingly average Americans; featuring George Woodard (Dairy Farmer, Waterbury, VT), Charles Jimmie, Sr. (Tlingit Indian Elder; Klukwan, AK), The Vasquez Brothers (Salsa Dancers; Los Angeles), Frank & Dave Pino (Rock Band; Waltham, MA), John "Yac" Yacobellis (Bike Messenger, NYC), Patty Wagstaff (Aerobatic Flyer; St. Augustine, FL), Paul Stone (Explosive Art; Creede, CO), Ed Holt (Wine Grower; Santa Maria, CA), Weirton Steelworkers (Weirton, WV), Rev. Cecil Williams, Janice Mirkitani (Glide Church; San Francisco), David

George Woodard in *America's Heart & Soul*

Krakauer (Klezmer Clarinetist; NYC), James Andrews & Trombone Shorty (Jazz Musicians; New Orleans), Mark & Ann Savoy (Cajun Musicians; Eunice, LA), Dan Klennert (Junk Art; Elbe, WA), Michael Bennett (Olympic Boxer; Chicago), Erik Weihenmayer (Blind Climber; Ouray, CO), Mosie Burks (Gospel Singer; Jackson, MS), Ace Barnes & James Tuppin (Oil Well Fire Fighters; Livinston, TX), Ben Cohen (Founder, Ben & Jerry's; Willston, VT), Minny Yancy (Rug Weaver; Berea, KY), Roudy Roudebush (Horse Wrangler; Telluride, CO), Rick & Dick Hoyt (Boston Marathon; Boston), Amelia Rudolph (Founder, Bandaloop Cliff Dancers; Muir Beach, CA)

Roudy Roudebush in *America's Heart & Soul* PHOTOS COURTESY OF WALT DISNEY PICTURES

METALLICA: SOME KIND OF MONSTER

(IFC FILMS) Producers/Director, Joe Berlinger, Bruce Sinofsky; Executive Producers, Joe Berlinger, Jon Kamen, Frank Scherma; Photography, Robert Richman, Wolfgang Held; Music, Metallica; Editors, Doug Abel, M. Watanabe Milmore, David Zieff; a Third Eye Motion Picture Company production; Dolby; Color; Not rated; 141 minutes; Release date: July 9, 2004. Documentary on Metallica as they recorded their album *St. Anger*; featuring James Hetfield, Lars Ulrich, Kirk Hammett, Bob Rock, Eric Avery, Joe Berlinger, Dan Braun, Cliff Burnstein, Stefan Chirazi, Dylan Donkin, Eric Forstadt, Gio Gasparetti, Mikes Gillies, Lani Hammett, Zach Harmon, Eric Helmkamp, Cali Tee Hetfield, Castor Virgil Hetfield, Francesca Hetfield, Pepper Keenan, Danny Lohner, Peter Mensch, Dave Mustaine, Jason Newsted, Peter Paterno, Twiggy Ramirez, Scott Reeder, Marc Reiter, Brian Sagrafena, Skylar Satenstein, Bruce Sinofsky, Niclas Swanlund, Phil Towle, Robert Trujillo, Myles Ulrich, Torben Ulrich, Steve Wiig, Chris Wyse.

SLEEPOVER

(MGM) Producers, Charles Weinstock, Bob Cooper; Director, Joe Nussbaum; Screenplay, Elisa Bell; Photography, James L. Carter; Designer, Stephen McCabe; Costumes, Pamela Withers Chilton; Music, Deborah Lurie; Music Supervisor, Elliot Lurie; Editor, Craig P. Herring; Executive Producer, Jeremiah Samuels; Co-Producer, Karen Lunder; Casting, Mary Gail Artz, Barbara Cohen; a Landscape Entertainment production in association with Weinstock Productions; Dolby; Deluxe color; Rated PG; 89 minutes; Release date: July 9, 2004. Cast: Alex Vega (Julie), Mika Boorem (Hannah), Jane Lynch (Gabby), Sam Huntington (Ren), Sara Paxton (Staci), Brie Larson (Liz), Scout Taylor-Compton

(Farrah), Douglas Smith (Gregg), Katija Pevec (Molly), Steve Carell (Sherman), Jeff Garlin (Jay), Kallie Flynn Childress (Yancy), Eileen Boylan (Jenna), Evan Peters (Russell), Hunter Parrish (Lance), Shane Hunter (Miles), Sean Faris (Steve), Ryan Slattery (Peter), Thad Luckinbill (Todd), Brett Wagner (Bouncer), John "Scoot" McNairy (DJ at Club), Johnny Sneed (Mr. Corrado), Courtnee Draper (Girl at Dance), Ursula Whittaker (Attractive Woman), Brooklyn L. McLinn (Bartender), Timothy Dowling (Mr. Chilton), Alice Greczyn (Linda), Colleen Wainwright (Scarf Woman), Summer Glau (Ticket Girl), Max van Ville (Skater Dude), Mageina Tovah (Girl on Phone), Alison Martin (Gabby's Friend)

AFRAID OF EVERYTHING

(MODULAR PICTURES) Producers, David Barker, Chris Hoover; Director/Screenplay, David Barker; Photography, Deborah Eve Lewis; Designer, Bernhard Blythe; Music, Stewart Wallace; Editors, David Barker, Jeff Groth; a Florida Films, Locus Solus Entertainment production; Black and white; Not rated; 80 minutes; Release date: July 9, 2004. Cast: Nathalie Richard (Anne), Sarah Adler (Iris), Daniel Aukin (Donnie), Tom Bigelow, Birgit Christiansen, Edmee Doroszlai, David Higginbotham, Graham Leggat, Olivier Le Vacon, Lynnette Lo (Party Guests)

Phil Towle (standing), Metallica in *Metallica* PHOTOS COURTESY OF IFC FILMS

Scout Taylor-Compton, Alexa Vega, Mika Boorem, Kallie Flynn Childress in *Sleepover* PHOTO COURTESY OF MGM

Jacqueline Bisset in *Swing*

Jacqueline Bisset, Jonathan Winters in *Swing* PHOTOS COURTESY OF DOMINION INTERNATIONAL

SWING

(DOMINION INTERNATIONAL) Producer, Ken Patton; Executive Producers, John Harvey, Mary Keil; Director, Martin Guigi; Screenplay, Mary Keil; Photography, Massimo Zeri; Designer, Don De Fina; Costumes, Jennifer Power, Marianna Astrom-De Fina; Music, Gennaro Cannelora; Editor, Charles B. Weber; from Crazy Dreams Entertainment; Color; Rated PG-13; 98 minutes; Release date: July 9, 2004. Cast: Constance Brenneman (Tina), Innis Casey (Anthony Verdi), Tom Skerritt (George Verdi), Jacqueline Bisset (Christine/Mrs. DeLuca), Jonathan Winters (Uncle Bill), Nell Carter (Grace), Dahlia Waingort (Valerie), Adam Tomei (Mac), Mindy Cohn (Martha), Anne Stark-Robinson (Tina's Mother), Albert Werriweather (Funeral Home Director), Chet Reynold (Radio Announcer), Jim Hanks (Club Jimbo, Maitre D'), Tedd Zzenia (Club Jimbo, Bartender), Kim Venaas (Club Jimbo, Bandleader), Esther Mamet (Josephine Wall), Timothy Roman Rodriguez (Tina's Dance Partner), Archie Drury (Joe Verdi), Barry Bostwick (Freddie), Amy Hutto (Flavor of the Week), Martin Durante (Sal), Emily Dean (Sales Associate), Ana Guigui (Pam), Johnny Bones (Pianist in Nursing Home), Sumalee Montano (Carol), Ken Patton (Pete), H.A.P.I. (Master of Ceremonies), Timothy Heinrich (Jason), Connie Mattson (Angry Customer)

Freestyle PHOTO COURTESY OF PALM PICTURES

LET'S GET FRANK

(RANDOM PRODUCTIONS) Co-Producer, Yvonne Anderson; Director/Narrator, Bart Everly; Music, The Angel; Editor, David Dawkins; Color; Not rated; 75 minutes; Release date: July 14, 1004. Documentary on Congressman Barney Frank as he pursues the 1998 Clinton impeachment proceedings.

PLANET EARTH: DREAMS

(START HERE FILMS) Executive Producer, Dave McWater; Director/Photography/Editor, D.J. Mendel; Screenplay, Richard Foreman; Music, Cynthia J. Hopkins; Dolby; Color; Not rated; 85 minutes; Release date: July 14, 2004. Cast: Cynthia J. Hopkins (Agatha), Tim Donovan, Jr. (Maurice), Ryan Holsopple (Dr. Wanton), Nathan Phillips (Psychiatrist), Timothy McGree (Dr. Hunnicut), Fred Neumann, Frederick Neumann (God-Men), Lisa Hickman (Lad L.), Justine Priestley (Dr. Wanda), Josh Stark, Salvatore Interlandi (Bar Guys), Jay Bavaro (Hot Dog Joe), Joseph Bavaro (Hot Dog Fantasy Delivery Boy), Olivia Cashman (Little Girl), Margaret Rose Champagne (Cocktail Waitress), Jim Illi (Phil), Shauna Kelly (Hot Dog Gal), Russ Russo (Space Couch Man)

Shauna Kelly, Jay Bavaro in *Planet Earth* PHOTO COURTESY OF START HERE FILMS

FREESTYLE: THE ART OF RHYME

(PALM PICTURES) Producer, Henry Alex Rubin; Executive Producers, Tiare White, Brad Abramson, Michael Hirschorn, Shelly Tatro; Director, Kevin Fitzgerald; Photography, Daniel Kozman, Todd Hickey; Music, Darkleaf, Freestyle Fellowship, Omid, DJ Organic; Editors, Rachel Ramist, Isaac Solotaroff, Paul Devlin; a Bowery Films, Organic Films, Center for Hip-Hop Education and VH1 Television production; Black and white/color; Not rated; 74 minutes; Release date: July 16, 2004. Documentary on freestyle rapping; featuring Planet Asia, Bahamadia, Black Thought, Bobitto, Akim Funk Buddah, Eluard Burt, Cut Chemist, Darkleaf, Mos Def, Kirby Dominant, Freestyle Fellowship, Lord Finesse, Craig G, Ghostface Killah, Talib Kweli, The Last Poets, Crazy Legs, Living Legends, The Lyricist Lounge, Medusa, Pharoahe Monch, Otherwize, ?uestlove, Boots Riley, Divine Styler, Supernatural, Sway, Wordsworth.

Emmy Rossum in *Nola* PHOTOS COURTESY OF GOLDWYN FILMS/FIREWORKS

MAKE A WISH

(OPEN CIRCLE PRODS.) Producer/Screenplay, Lauren Johnson; Director, Sharon Ferranti; Photography, Jessica Gallant; Designer, Michael Fitzgerald; Music, Jay Ferranti; Color; Not rated; 96 minutes; Release date: July 21, 2004. Cast: Moynan King (Susan), Hollace Starr (Dawn), Lava Alapai (Chloe), Virginia Baeta (Monica), Susan Durham (Brandt), Melenie Freedom Flynn (Linda), Bob Peterson (Zeke), Amanda Spain (Andrea), Nora Stein (Michelle), Eric Vichi (Steve), Neil Wilson (CK McFarland)

NOLA

(GOLDWYN FILMS/FIREWORKS) Producers, Rachel Peters, Jill Footlick; Director/Screenplay, Alan Hruska; Photography, Horacio Marquinez; Designer, Sharon Lomofsky; Costumes, Melissa Toth; Music, Edmund Choi; Editor, Peter C. Frank; Casting, Alison E. McBryde, Lina Todd; from Archer Entertainment; Color; Rated PG-13; 97 minutes; Release date: July 24, 2004. Cast: Emmy Rossum (Nola), Mary McDonnell (Margaret Langworthy), Steven Bauer (Leo), James Badge Dale (Ben), Thom Christopher (Niles), Michael Cavadias (Wendy), Joe Ambrose (Homeless Man), Lou Cantres (Marshal), Sam Coppola (Gus), Taj Crown (Van Vendor), Janis Dardaris (Nola's Mother), Robert Kabakoff (Reporter), Adam LeFevre (Sam), LeDonna Mabry (Leo's Secretary), Dominica

Marcus (Slick), Lynne Matthew (Judge Belfray), Bernie McInerney (Prof. Cummings), Michael Medeiros (Flanders), Stephanie Mnookin (Classified Ad Rep), Al Nazemian (Young East Indian Man), Sasha Peters (Dog), Larry Pine (Max), James Ransone (Neo-Gothboy), Matt Servitto (Nola's Stepfather), Timothy Owen Waldrip (Clerk), Jerry Walsh (Bailiff), Damian Young (Maitre D')

Mark Lloyd in *Orwell Rolls in His Grave* PHOTOS COURTESY OF SAG HARBOR-BASEMENT PICTURES

ORWELL ROLLS IN HIS GRAVE

(SAG HARBOR-BASEMENT PICTURES) Producer/Director/Screenplay/Editor, Robert Kane Pappas; Photography, Robert Kane Pappas, Alan Hostetter; from Sky Island Films; Color; Not rated; 84 minutes; Release date: July 24, 2004. Documentary on the corporate control of the media; featuring Charles Lewis, Robert McChesney, Mark Crispin Miller, Bernie Sanders, Danny Schechter, Vincent Bugliosi, Jeff Cohen, Dennis Kucinich, Mark Lloyd, Michael Moore, Greg Palast, Helen Thomas.

INESCAPABLE

(ATTA GIRL PRODS.) Producer, Valerie Pichney; Director/Screenplay/Editor, Helen Lesnick; Photography, Jessica Gallant; Color; Not rated; 82 minutes; Release date: July 28, 2004. Cast: Katie Alden (Beth), Natalie Anderson (Jessie), Athena Demos (Chloe), Tanna Frederick (Susan)

Inescapable PHOTO COURTESY OF ATTA GIRL PRODUCTIONS

Los Angeles Plays Itself PHOTO COURTESY OF SUBMARINE ENTERTAINMENT

LOS ANGELES PLAYS ITSELF

(SUBMARINE ENTERTAINMENT) Producer/Director/Screenplay, Thom Andersen; Photography, Deborah Stratman; Editor, Yoo Seung-Hyun; Color, DV; Not rated; 169 minutes; Release date: July 28, 2004. Documentary on the use of Los Angeles for a backdrop or setting as seen in many films.

Soren Fulton, Brady Corbet, Vanessa Anne Hudgens in *Thunderbirds* PHOTO COURTESY OF UNIVERSAL

THUNDERBIRDS

(UNIVERSAL) Producers, Tim Bevan, Eric Fellner, Mark Huffam; Executive Producers, Debra Hayward, Liza Chasin; Director, Jonathan Frakes; Screenplay, William Osborne, Michael McCullers; Story, Peter Hewitt, William Osborne; Based on the television series created by Gerry Anderson; Photography, Brendan Galvin; Designer, John Beard; Costumes, Marit Allen; Music, Hans Zimmer; Editor, Martin Walsh; Visual Effects Supervisors, Mark Nelmes, Mike McGee; Casting, Mary Selway; a StudioCanal presentation of a Working Title production; Dolby; Color; Rated PG; 95 minutes; Release date: July 30, 2004. Cast: Bill Paxton (Jeff Tracy), Anthony Edwards (Brains), Sophia Myles (Lady Penelope), Ben Kingsley (The Hood), Brad Corbet (Alan Tracy), Soren Fulton (Fermat), Vanessa Anne-Hudgens (Tin-Tin), Ron Cook (Parker), Philip Winchester (Scott Tracy), Lex Shrapnel (John Tracy), Dominic Colenso (Virgil Tracy), Ben Torgersen (Gordon Tracy), Rose Keegan (Transom), Deobia Oparei (Mullion), Deborah Weston (Teacher), Lou Hirsch (Headmaster), Alex Barringer (Excited Kid), Demetri Goritsas (News Anchor), Genie Francis (Lisa Lowe), Kyle Herbert (Know It All Kid), Johannes Zadrozny (Panhead), Nicola Walker (Panhead's Mother), Harvey Virdi (Onaha), Bhasker Patel (Kyrano), Stewart Howson (Engineer), Mark Nelmes (Ice Cream Man), Julian Spencer (Henchman), Andy Smart (Henchman/Oil Rig Worker).

OUTFOXED: RUPERT MURDOCH'S WAR ON JOURNALISM

(CINEMA LIBRE) Producer/Director, Robert Greenwald; Photography, Will Miller, Luke Riffle, James Curry, Bob Sullivan, Glen Pearcy, Richard Perez; Music, Nicholas O'Toole; Editors, Douglas Cheek, Jovan Bell, Erin Kelly, Hannah Williams, Monica Kowalski, Jane Pia Abramowitz, Chris M. Gordon; Narrator, Douglas Cheek; from Carolina Productions, MoveOn.Org; Color; Not rated; 78 minutes; Release date: August 6, 2004. Documentary questioning Fox News Channel's "fair and balanced" credo of news coverage; feauring Eric Alterman, David Brock, Jeff Cohen, Walter Cronkite, Av Westin.

SAINTS AND SOLDIERS

(EXCEL ENTERTAINMENT) Producers, Ryan Little, Adam Abel; Executive Producer, Charles Chan; Director/Photography, Ryan Little; Screenplay, Geoffrey Panos, Matt Whitaker; Designer, Steven A. Lee; Music, Bart Hendrickson, J Bateman; Editor, Wynn Hougaard; Casting, Jennifer Buster; Color; Rated PG-13; 90 minutes; Release date: August 6, 2004. Cast: Corbin Allred (Cpl. Nathan "Deacon" Greer), Alexander Niver (Steven Gould), Kirby Heyborne (Flight Sgt. Oberon Winley), Lawrence Bagby (Pvt. Shirl Kendrick), Peter Holden (Gordon Gunderson), Ethan Vincent (Rudi), Melinda Renee (Catherine), Ruby Chase O'Neil (Sophie), Jeff Birk (Radio Announcer), Ben Gourley (Sgt. McKinley), Tane Williams (Injured One-Armed Soldier), Randy Beard, Kelly Klindt (German Officers), Curt Dousett, Michael Buster, Lincoln Hoppe, Joel Bishop, Spencer Funk, Sterling Funk (German Soldiers), M. Casey Reeves (Weeping Soldier), Chris Clark (American Soldier #1), Christian Lee, Christian Malzl, Philip Malzl (Conversing Germans), Dawn Graham, Julie Graham, Addy Meldrum, Matthew Meldrum, McKay Meldrum, Kelly Moyle (Ghost Figures), Jason Allred (Peeing German), Michael Tanner, Gavin Bentley (American Foxhole Soldiers), Chris Kendrick (Sgt. Meldrum), Bill Ferguson, Richard J. Clifford (American Medics).

TOM DOWD & THE LANGUAGE OF MUSIC

(PALM PICTURES) Producers, Mark Moormann, Scott Gordon, Mark Hunt; Executive Producer, Juan Carlos Lopez; Director, Mark Moormann; Photography, Patrick Longman; Editors, Mark Moormann, Tino Wohlwend; a Lanuage of Music Films production; Black and white/color; Not rated; 82 minutes; Release date: August 13, 2004. Documentary on Atlantic Records recording engineer Tom Dowd; featuring Tom Dowd, Ray Charles, Eric Clapton, Ornette Coleman, Aretha Franklin.

L.A. TWISTER

(INDICAN) Producers, Sven Pape, Stephen A. Marinaccio II, Anthony Stoppiello; Director, Sven Pape; Screenplay, Geoffrey Saville-Read; Photography, Patrice Lucien Cochet; Designer, Hans Pfleiderer; Costumes, Rachel Sage; Music, Steven Gutheinz; Editors, Sven Pape, John Refoua; Casting, Lisa London, Catherine Stroud; a Snowdog Films production; Dolby; Color; Not rated; 92 minutes; Release date: August 13, 2004. Cast: Zack Ward (Lenny), Tony Daly (Ethan), Jennifer Aspen (Mindy), Susan Blakely (Vivian), Sarah Thompson (Cindy), Manouschka Guerrier (Terry), Wendy Worthington (Marilyn), Amy Hathaway (Lynn), Lenny Citrano (Jimmy), Nigel Thatch (Leroy), Kathleen McClellan (Bambi), Colleen Camp (Judith), Ray Proscia (Editor), Denice Duff (Francesca), Lorin Eric Salm (The Mime), Ken Davitian (Walter), David Beeler (Petruchio/Minister), Scott Leet (Jack Farrell), Bob Amaral (Allcock), David O'Donnell (1st AD), Branton Boxer (Poolman), Nate Barlow (Mugger/Convenience Store Attendant), Scott Adsit (Technician), Brian Nahas (Lynn's Husband), Rod Tate (Bartender), Ben DiGregorio (Car Salesman), Nick Loren (New Owner), Amandah Reyne, Eric Meyersfield, Tyler Bizzell, Christopher May, Bianca Muller (Audtioners), Kim C. Pape (Baby), Jamie Isaac Conde (Teenager), Stephen A. Marinaccio II (Doorman), Gary Weinberg (Gardener), Gina Marie Young (Hooker)

END OF THE CENTURY

(MAGNOLIA) Producers, Jim Fields, Michael Gramaglia, Rosemary Quigley; Executive Producers, Diana Holtzberg, Andrew J. Hurwitz, Jan Rofekamp; Directors, Jim Fields, Michael Gramaglia; Photography, Jim Fields, Michael Gramaglia, David Bowles, John Gramaglia, Peter Hawkins; Editors, Jim Fields, John Gramaglia; a Chinagraph, Gugat Films production; Color/Black and white; Not rated; 110 minutes; Release date: August 20, 2004. Documentary on The Ramones; featuring Johnny Ramone, Dee Dee Ramone, Tommy Ramone, Joey Ramone, Marky Ramone, Ritchie Ramone, C.J. Ramone, Roberta Bayley, Rodney Bingenheimer, Clem Burke, Jayne County, Danny Fields, Lars Frederiksen, John Frusciante, Kirk Hammett, Debbie Harry, Anthony Kiedis, Walter Lure, Glen Matlock, Legs McNeil, Thurston Moore, Rick Rubin, Captain Sensible, Chris Stein, Seymour Stein, Joe Strummer, Eddie Vedder, Rob Zombie

BENJI OFF THE LEASH!

(MULBERRY SQUARE) Producers, Joe Camp, Margaret Loesch; Executive Producers, Jack Lewis, Phoebe Lewis, Jim Ritchie, Sherman Muths Jr., Sherman Muths III, Roy C. Williams; Director/Screenplay, Joe Camp; Photography, Don Reddy; Designer, Eric Weller; Costumes, Glenn Ralston; Music, Anthony DiLorenzo; Editor, Dava Whisenant; Casting, Cate Praggastis, Judie McKee; a Benji Returns production in association with Mulberry Square Prods.; Dolby; Color; Rated PG; 99 minutes; Release date: August 20, 2004. Cast: Nick Whitaker (Colby Hatchett), Nate Bynum (Sheriff Ozzie), Chris Kendrick (Mr. Hatchett), Randall Newsome (Livingston), Duane Stephens (Sheldon), Christy Summerhays (Claire), Carleton Bluford (Dudley), Neal Barth (Zachariah Finch), Melinda Haynes (Miriam), Kathleen Camp (Nancy/Merlin/Newscaster #4), Jeff Olson (Paul), Donnie Madison (Lincoln Hoppe), Joey Miyashima (Vat), Scott Wilkinson (Movie Producer), Margaret Loesch, Dave Whisenant, Joe Camp (Newscasters)

The Ramones in *End of the Century*

End of the Century PHOTOS COURTESY OF MAGNOLIA

UNCOVERED: THE WAR OF IRAQ

(CINEMA LIBRE) Co-Producers, Robert Greenwald, Devin Smith, Kathryn McArdle, Philippe Diaz; Director, Robert Greenwald; Music, Mars Lasar, Brad Chiet, Jim Ervin; Editors, Kimberly Ray, Chris M. Gordon; Color; Not rated; 87 minutes; Release date: August 20, 2004. Documentary on the Bush Administration's decision to invade Iraq; featuring David Albright, Robert Baer, Milton Bearden, Rand Beers, Bill Christison, David Corn, Philip Coyle, John Dean, Patrick Eddington, Chas Freeman, Graham Fuller, David Kay, John Brady Kiesling, Karen Kwiatowski, Patrick Lang, David MacMichael, Ray McGovern, Scott Ritter, Clare Short, Stansfield Turner, Henry Waxman, Thomas E. White, Joe Wilson, Mary Ann Wright, Peter Zimmerman.

BRIGHT LEAVES

(FIRST RUN FEATURES) . Producer/Director/Screenplay/Photography, Ross iMcElwee; Editors, Ross McElwee, Mark Meato; a Homemade Movies, WGBH Boston, Channel 4 Television production; US.-U.K.; Color; Not rated; 107 minutes; Release date: August 25, 2004. Documentary on the harmful effects of the tobacco industry; featuring Ross McElwee, Patricia Neal, Charleeen Swansea

Ross McElwee in *Bright Leaves* PHOTO COURTESY OF FIRST RUN FEATURES

THE FOURTH WORLD WAR

(BIG NOISE FILMS) Producers/Photography/Editors, Rick Rowley, Jacqueline Soohen; Director, Rick Rowley; Color; Not rated; 78 minutes; Release date: August 26, 2004. Documentary on a global resistance group, "The Fourth World War."

SUSPECT ZERO

(PARAMOUNT) Producers, Paula Wagner, E. Elias Merhige, Gaye Hirsch; Executive Producers, Jonathan Sanger, Moritz Borman, Guy East, Nigel Sinclair, Tom Rosenberg, Gary Lucchesi; Director, E. Elias Merhige; Screenplay, Zak Penn, Billy Ray; Story, Zak Penn; Photography, Michael Chapman; Designer, Ida Random; Costumes, Mary Claire Hannan; Music, Clint Mansell; Editors, John Gilroy, Roebrt K. Lambert; Co-Producers, Lester Berman, Darrren Miller; Casting, Deborah Aquila, Tricia Wood; a C/W Production, presented in association with Intermedia Films and Lakeshore Entertainment; Dolby; Deluxe color; Rated R; 99 minutes; Release date: August 27, 2004. Cast: Aaron Eckhart (Thomas Mackelway), Ben Kingsley (Benjamin O'Ryan), Carrie-Anne Moss (Fran Kulok), Harry Lennix (Rick Charleton), Kevin Chamberlin (Harold Speck), Julian Reyes (Highway Patrolman), Keith Campbell (Raymond Starkey), Chloe Russell (Loretta), Ellen Blake (Dolly), William B. Johnson (Mel), Jerry Gardner (Sheriff Harry Dylan), Daniel Patrick Moriarty (Bud Granger), Curtis Plagge (Jumbo), Nicole Dehuff (Katie Potter), William Mapother (Bill Grieves), Donn Owens (FBI Agent), Brady Coleman (Dyson), Frank Collison (Piper), Catherine Haun (Joan Speck), Lea Franklin (Mother), Angelina C. Torres (Neighbor Lady), David Ode (Bartender), David House (Truth or Consequences Cop), Miguel Zapata (Charlie), Jane Goold (Kathleen), Boots Sutherland (Vic), Benjamin Petry (Little Boy), Jenny Cleveland (Little Boy's Mother), Buddy Joe Hooker (Suspect Zero), Kent Kirkpatrick (Cora), Dorsey Ray (Project Director), Michael Chapman, Marya Beauvais (Prosecutors), Letta E. Gorder (Reporter), Ed Dames (Icarus Trainer), Aaron Donahue (Remote Viewer), Kevin Skousen (Icarus Agent), Ceclia L. Webb, Hope Bell (Gospel Singers)

Aaron Eckhart, Ben Kingsley in *Suspect Zero*

ANACONDAS:
THE HUNT FOR THE BLOOD ORCHID

(SCREEN GEMS) Producer, Verna Harrah; Executive Producer, Jacobus Rose; Director, Dwight Little; Screenplay, John Claflin, Daniel Zelman, Michael Miner, Ed Neumeier; Story, Hans Bauer, Jim Cash, Jack Epps Jr.; Photography, Stephen E. Windon; Designer, Bryce Perrin; Costumes, Terry Ryan; Music, Nerida Tyson-Chew; Editors, Marcus D'Arcy, Marc Warner; Visual Effects Supervisor, Dale Duguid; Visual Effects, Photon VFX; Casting, Justine Baddeley, Kim Davis-Wagner; Dolby; Arriflex Widescreen; Deluxe color; Rated PG-13; 96 minutes; Release date: August 27, 2004. Cast: Johnny Messner (Bill Johnson), KaDee Strickland (Sam Rogers), Matthew Marsden (Dr. Jack Byron), Eugene Byrd (Cole Burris), Salli Richardson-Whitfield (Gail Stern), Nicholas Gonzalez (Dr. Ben Douglas), Karl Yune (Tran), Dennis Arndt (CEO), Morris Chestnut (Gordon Mitchell), Andy Anderson (John Livingston), Nicholas Hope (Christina Van Dyke), Peter Curtin (Lawyer), Khoa Do (Lead Lopak Hunter), Aireti (Lopak Hunter), Andre Tandjung (Bartender)

Carrie-Anne Moss, Aaron Eckhart in *Suspect Zero* PHOTOS COURTESY OF PARAMOUNT

THE BROWN BUNNY

(WELLSPRING) Producer/Director/Screenplay/Photography/Editor/Designer/Costumes/Casting, Vincent Gallo; a Kinetique Inc., Wild Bunch, Vincent Gallo production; Dolby; Color; Not rated; 92 minutes; Release date: August 27, 2004. Cast: Vincent Gallo (Bud Clay), Chloë Sevigny (Daisy), Cheryl Tiegs (Lilly), Elizabeth Blake (Rose), Anna Vareschi (Violet), Mary Morasky (Mrs. Lemon)

BUSH'S BRAIN

(TARTAN USA) Producers/Directors, Joseph Mealey, Michael Shoob; Based on the book by Wayne Slater and James C. Moore; Photography, Joseph Mealey; Music, Michelle Shocked, David Friedman; Editor, Tom Siiter; Narrator, Jacques Vroom; a BeBe Films Inc. produciton; Color; Rated PG-13; 80 minutes; Release date: August 27, 2004. Documentary on President George W. Bush's adviser, Karl Rove; featuring Cathy Bonner, Bruce Buchanan, Max Cleland, Shirley Cuff, Robert Edgeworth, Kent Hance, Bill Israel, Molly Ivins, Richard Leiby, Wade Lieseke Jr., Susie Lieseke, Ken Luce, Garry Mauro, Chuck McDonald, Dave McNeely, Bill Miller, Mike Moeller, James C. Moore, Jesse Oliver, Tom Pauken, Chelle Lieseke Pokorney, Ross Ramsey, Karl Rove, A.R. Schwartz, Wayne Slater, Glenn Smith, Karl Struble, John Weaver, Joseph Wilson.

Morris Chestnut, KaDee Strickland, Matthew Marsden, Nicholas Gonzalez, Johnny Messner, Salli Richardson, Eugene Byrd, Karl Yune in *Anacondas: The Hunt for the Blood Orchid* PHOTOS COURTESY OF SCREEN GEMS

Nicholas Gonzalez, Karl Yune in *Anacondas: The Hunt for the Blood Orchid*

Chloë Sevigny, Vincent Gallo in *The Brown Bunny*

Vincent Gallo, Chloë Sevigny in *The Brown Bunny* PHOTOS COURTESY OF WELLSPRING

BROTHERS IN ARMS

(FIRST RUN FEATURES) Producer, Iris G. Rossi; Executive Producers, Paul Alexander, Iris G. Rossi, Williams Spear, Nicholas Butterworth; Director, Paul Alexander; Photography/Editor, Elizabeth Haviland James; Music, Michael Bacon; a Gordon Motion Picture Co. presentation; Color/black and white, DV, 16mm; Not rated; 67 minutes; Release date: August 27, 2004. Documentary on presidential candidate John Kerry's experience in Vietnam; featuring John F. Kerry, Rev. David Alston, Del Sandusky, Gene Thorson, Mike Medeiros.

John Kerry (right) in *Brothers In Arms* PHOTO COURTESY OF FIRST RUN FEATURES

CHOOCH

(ARTISTIC LICENSE) Producer, Tami Powers; Executive Producers, The Loglisci Brothers, Steve Caple; Director, J.C. Bari, Rajeev Nirmalakhandan; Screenplay, Lucas Limone; Photography, Jesse Ramirez; Designer, Steve Hansen; Music, Kerry Muzzey; Editor, Maya Stark; a Bacchus Films, Fruitbasket Films production; Dolby; Color; Rated R; 81 minutes; Release date: August 27, 2004. Cast:

Carmine Famiglietti (left) in *Chooch* PHOTO COURTESY OF ARTISTIC LICENSE

John Sialiano (Narrator), Carmine Famiglietti (Dino Condito), Paola Walker (Ladonna), Pete Medina (Sgt. Maj.), Lucille Tomczyk (Dino's Mother), Anthony Pellicci (Dino's Father), Joe "Pepper" Tomczyk (Jubilene's Father), Joe Summa (Jubilene Condito), Kiwi Limone (Kiwi Condito), Nick Cerulli (Sally Boy), Gino Cafarelli (Nicol Rubino), Anthony Barrile (Anthony Rubino), Ed Rossy (Soda Shop Gus), Nicholas Teofanis, Jorge Cuevas (Soda Shop Patrons), Ray "Boom Boom" Mancini (Ball Player), Mike Bocchetti (The Mayor of Bocci Park), John "Malibu" Constantino (Sharky the Umpire), Susan Ann Davis (Jubilene's Girlfriend), Tami Powers (Hook Girl), Stefan Lysenko (Billy De Nino), Gina Nanna (Girl in the Red Shirt), Cindy Passero (Bar Girl), Britney Bunker (Mexican Bartender), Cris Cruz (Corporal), Santino Jimenez (Private), Linda Sandoval (Irma), Valtair Teixeira (Rafael the Chef)

THE COOKOUT

(LIONS GATE) Producers/Story, Queen Latifah, Shakim Compere, Darryl "Latee" French; Executive Producers, Michael Paseornek, John Sacchi, Mike Elliot; Director, Lance Rivera; Screenplay, Laurie B. Tuner, Ramsey Gbelawoe, Jeffrey Brian Holmes; Photography, Tom Houghton; Designer, Anne Stuhler; Costumes, Misa Hilton-Brim; Music, Camara Kambon; Editors, Jeff McEvoy, Patricia Bowers; Casting, Leah Daniels-Butler; a Flavor Unit Films production; Dolby; Deluxe color; Rated PG-13; 88 minutes; Release date: September 3, 2004. Cast: Ja Rule (Bling Bling), Tim Meadows (Uncle Leroy), Jenifer Lewis (Lady Em), Storm P (Todd Anderson), Meagan Good (Brittany), Jonathan Silverman (Wes), Farrah Fawcett (Mrs. Crowley), Frankie Faison (JoJo Anderson), Eve (Becky), Danny Glover (Judge Crowley), Queen Latifah (Security Guard), Gerry Bamman (Butler), Rita Owens (Aunt Nettie), Marci Reed (Ms. Peters), Ruperto Vanderpool (Wheezer), Vincent Pastore (Poo Salesman), Kevin Phillips (Jamal Washington), Reg E. Cathey (Frank Washington), Rita Owens (Nettie Washington), Carl Wright (Grandpa), Jerod Mixon (Willie), Jamal Mixon (Nelson), Denee Busy (Little Dee), Shawn Andrew (Jerome), Godfrey (Jasper), Jesse May (Olivier), Lance Spellerberg (Sven), Peggy Cosgrove (Mrs. Atwater), William Stone Mahoney (Commissioner), Walter Simpson III (A.J.), Wilhelm Lewis (Wayne),

Eve, Storm P in *The Cookout*

Ja Rule in *The Cookout* PHOTOS COURTESY OF LIONS GATE

Antonio Walker (Young Thug), Deep Katdare (Clerk), Thomas James O'Leary, Wendi Williams (Reporters), Sandra Mills Scott (Nurse), Marc Plastrik (Police Chief), Channelle Nazaire (Grade School Becky), Otis K. Best III (Grade School Todd), Ali Wright (Grade School Bling Bling), Rodney Henry (Grade School Wheezer), Alex Avant (Police Officer), Divine Compere (Young Cousin), Hasani Houston (Light Skinned Boy), Julian Douglas, Mekhi Clayton-Smith (Two-Year-Old Baby), D.J. Enuff, Marv Albert, Elton Brand, Baron Davis, Mark Cuban (Themselves), Roxy Noffz (Cookie Girl)

Diane Kruger, Josh Hartnett in *Wicker Park* PHOTOS COURTESY OF MGM

Persons of Interest PHOTO COURTESY OF FIRST RUN/ICARUS

Rose Byrne, Josh Hartnett in *Wicker Park*

WICKER PARK

(MGM) Producers, Andrew Lamal, Marcus Viscidi, Tom Rosenberg, Gary Lucchesi; Executive Producers, Georges Benayoun, Gilles Mimouni, Henry Winterstern, Harley Tannenbaum; Director, Paul McGuigan; Screenplay, Brandon Boyce; Based on the motion picture *L'Appartement,* screenplay by Gilles Mimouni; Photography, Peter Sova; Designer, Richard Bridgland; Costumes, Odette Gadoury; Music, Cliff Martinez; Editor, Andrew Hulme; Casting, Deborah Aquila, Tricia Wood, Andrea Kenyon, Randi Wells; a Lakeshore Entertainment production; Dolby; Panavision; Deluxe color; Rated PG-13; 114 minutes; Release date: September 3, 2004. Cast: Josh Hartnett (Matthew), Rose Byrne (Alex), Matthew Lillard (Luke), Diane Kruger (Lisa), Christopher Cousins (Daniel), Jessica Pare (Rebecca), Vlasta Vrana (Jeweler), Amy Sobol (Ellie), Ted Whittall (Walter), Isabel Dos Santos (Chamber Maid), Joanna Noyes (mary), Kerrilyn Keith (Customer), Mark Camacho (Bartender), Marcel Jeannin (Theater Director), Stefanie Buxton (Ticket Agent), Stanley Hilaire (Stage Manager), Zhenhu Han (Mr. Hong), Lu Ye (Ms. Hsia), Christian Paul (Orsino), Gillian Ferrabee (Robin), Frank Fontaine (Priest), Miranda Handford (Actress Olivia), Benjamin Hatcher (Choreographer), Richard Jutras (Hotel Manager), Kelly Anne Patterson (Mostess), Mary Morter (Old Lady), Erika Rosenbaum, Jessica Schulte (Waitresses), Paul Doucet (Driver), Jamieson Boulanger (Boyfriend), Carrie Colak (Girlfriend), Gordon Masten (Hot Dog Vendor)

PERSONS OF INTEREST

(FIRST RUN/ICARUS) Producers, Alison Maclean, Lawrence Konner, Tobias Perse; Directors, Alison Maclean, Tobias Perse; Photography, Richard Rutkowski; Designer, Debbie DeVilla; a Sundance Institute Documentary Fund production; Color; Not rated; 63 minutes; Release date: September 3, 2004. Documentary on the detention of Muslim-Americans following the terrorist attacks of Sept. 11, 2001.

PAPARAZZI

(20TH CENTURY FOX) Producers, Mel Gibson, Bruce Davey, Stephen McEveety; Executive Producer, Louise Rosner; Director, Paul Abascal; Screenplay, Forrest Smith; Photography, Daryn Okada; Designer, Robb Wilson King; Costumes, Denise Wingate; Music, Brian Tyler; Editor, Robin Russell; Casting, Amanda Mackey Johnson, Cathy Sandrich Gelfond, Wendy Weidman; an Icon Prods. presentation; Dolby; Deluxe color; Rated PG-13; 84 minutes; Release date: September 3, 2004. Cast: Cole Hauser (Bo Laramie), Robin Tunney (Abby Laramie), Dennis Farina (Det. Burton), Daniel Baldwin (Wendell Stokes), Tom Hollander (Leonard Clark), Keivn Gage (Kevin Rosner), Blake Bryan (Zach Laramie), Tom Sizemore (Rex Harper), Andrea Baker (Emily), Jordan Baker (Dr. Kelly), Duane Davis (Reggie), Joe Basile (Police Lab Tech), Lauren Birkell (Allison), Wendy Braun (Bo's Publicist), Kelly Carlson (Kristin), Greg Castro (Policeman), Robert Catrini (Smartass Paparazzi), Larry Cedar (Charlie), Dennis Cockrum (Coroner), Joel Connable, Dean Nolen, Angela Martinez (Reporters), Michael Dempsey (Soccer Coach), Andi Eystad (Sierra), Donal Gibson (Deputy Wilson), David Ury, Noah Harpster (Fans), Tim Halligan (Forensic Investigator), Michael Holden (Bo's Lawyer), Anthony R. Jones (CSI Guy), David Kittles (David), Clyde Kusatsu (Dr. Hanson), Sal Lopez (Mexican Man), Fay Masterson (Marcy), Kathe Mazur (2nd Asst. Dir.), Brian McNamara (Bo's Agent), Robert Lee Neely II (Officer), Leyna Nguyen (Field Reporter), Forry Smith (Deputy Walker),

Tom Sizemore, Cole Hauser in *Paparazzi* PHOTO COURTESY OF 20TH CENTURY FOX

Tim Thomerson (Uniformed Officer), Holly Hindman (Beach Runner), Chris Rock (Pizza Delivery Guy), Mel Gibson (Anger Management Patient), Vince Vaughn, Matthew McConaughey, Giuliana De Pandi, Patrick Stinson (Themselves)

ROCKETS REDGLARE!

(SMALL PLANET PICTURES) Producer, William Murchu; Director, Luis Fernandez de la Reguera; Photography, Luis Fernandez de la Reguera, Mathieu Hagnery; Editors, Mathieu Hagnery, Tamir Diab; a Benzfilm Group, Big Plate Pictures production; Black and white/color; Not rated; 89 minutes; Release date: September 3, 2004. Documentary on eccentric actor and artist Rockets Redglare (Michael Morra); featuring Rockets Redglare, Gary Ray, Willem Dafoe, Matt Dillon, Jim Jarmusch, Steve Buscemi, Julian Schnabel, Nick Zedd, Rene Heras, Elizabeth English, Indian Larry, Alexandre Rockwell, Rachel Amodeo, Donald Baechler, M. Henry Jones, Molly Griffith.

Michael Morra in *Rockets Redglare!* PHOTO COURTESY OF SMALL PLANET PICTURES

VIRGIN

(ARTISTIC LICENSE) Producers, Sarah Schenck, Raye Dowell; Executive Producers, Robin Wright Penn, Mark Weiner; Director/Screenplay, Deborah Kampmeier; Photography, Ben Wolf; Designer, Katherine Mathews; Costumes, Karen Yan; Editor, Jane Ambromowitz; Casting, Jen Rudin; a Full Moon Films production; Color; Rated R; 114 minutes; Release date: September 3, 2004. Cast: Elizabeth Moss (Jessie Reynolds), Robin Wright Penn (Mrs. Reynolds), Daphne Rubin-Vega (Frances), Socorro Santiago (Lorna), Peter Gerety (Mr. Reynolds), Stephanie Gaschet (Katie Reynolds), Sam Riley (Michael), Charles Socarides (Shane), Christopher Wynkoop (Pastor), Robert Berlin (Red), Stephen Brian Jones (Cowboy), Andrew Thaman (Newspaper Manager), Patricia Hernandez (Girl in Diner), Susan Varon (Waitress), Tiffany Evans (Parent), Dolly Williams (Drug Store Cashier), Tom Bruno, P.O. Smith, David Berry (Officers), Braithe Gill, Katharine Basilevsky (Classmates), Leslie Graves (Leslie), Lotte Collins (Rhonda), Robert Lehrer (Crinkled Man), Deborah Carlson (Jewelry Store Clerk), Richard Aldis (Drug Store Manager), Ninon Rogers (Jenne), Nick Cisik, Rory Sheridan, Stuart Sierra, Wes Whitehead (Boys in Hallway/Masked Boys), Hugh Foster (Masked Boy), Lisa Altomare (Hospital Administrator), Lisa Preston (Nurse), Tom Oppenheim (Doctor), Doug LaTessa (Protestor), Curtiss Cook (Security Guard), Peter Flierl (Man in Waiting Room)

A LETTER TO TRUE

(ZEITGEIST) Producer/Director, Bruce Weber; Photography, Evan Estern, Jim Fealy, Shane Sigler, Theo Stanley, Pete Zuccarini; Music, John Leftwich; Editor,

A Letter to True PHOTO COURTESY OF ZEITGEIST

Chad Sipkin; Narrators, Julie Christie, Marianne Faithfull, Bruce Weber; a Just Blue Films Inc., Little Bear production; Dolby; Color/black and white; Not rated; 78 minutes; Release date: September 8, 2004. Documentary in which filmmaker Bruce Weber celebrates his Irish Setter "True," as well as celebrities and their canine companions; featuring Dr. Thomas Sessa, Dr. Gerald Johnson, Marleine Bastein, Tully Jensen, Will Tant, John Martin, Reinaldo Posada, Iedo Ivo Lins Lima, Kelly Ammann, Anthony Auello, Bill Casey, Charles Binyan, Robert Cote, Shannon Defricke, Garrett Griffin, Matthew Lancaster, Justin Paoletti, Paul Smith.

Frederick Weller, Neve Campbell in *When Will I Be Loved* PHOTOS COURTESY OF IFC FILMS

WHEN WILL I BE LOVED

(IFC FILMS) Producer, Ron Rotholz; Executive Producers, Robert Bevan, Keith Hayley, Charlie Savill; Director/Screenplay, James Toback; Photography, Larry McConkey; Designer, Ernestor Solo; Costumes, Luca Mosca; Music, Oli "Power" Grant; Editor, Suzy Elmiger; Casting, Susie Farris; a Little Wing Films/Rotholz Pictures production; Dolby; Panavision; Technicolor; Rated R; 81 minutes; Release date: September 10, 2004. Cast: Neve Campbell (Vera Barrie), Frederick Weller (Ford Welles), Ashley Shelton (Ashley), James Toback (Prof.

Neve Campbell, Dominic Chianese in *When Will I Be Loved*

Neve Campbell, Director James Toback of *When Will I Be Loved*

Hassan Al-Ibarhim Ben Rabinowitz), Alex Feldman (Alexei), Brandon Sommers (Brandon), Olivier "Power" Grant (Power), Mike Tyson, Lori Singer, Damon Dash, Richard Turley (Themselves), James Parris (James), Cara Hamill (Cara), Christina Rotholz (Christina), Bridget Lee Hall (Bridget), Thomas Patti (Michael), Jean-Pierre Vertus (Jean-Pierre), Megan Pepin, Erin Omar, Emily Coker (Girls in Park), Kendria Colford (Kendria), Victor Colletti (Poet), Meredith Ostrom (Meredith), Jamison Ernest (Jamison), Joelle Carter (Sam), Dominic Chianese (Count Tommaso Lupo), Michael Mailer (Michael Burke), Barry Primus (Victor Barrie), Karen Allen (Alexandra Barrie), Saif Tahsir (Banker), Michele Marie (Michele), Luca Mosca (Luca), Jason Pendergraft, Robert Covelman, Storm Chambers (Homicide Detectives)

HIJACKING CATASTROPHE: 9/11, FEAR & THE SELLING OF AMERICAN EMPIRE

(IMMEDIATE PICTURES) Producer, Jeremy Earp; Executive Producer, Sut Jhally; Director, Jeremy Earp; Narrator, Julian Bond; a Media Education Foundation production; Color; Not rated; 68 minutes; Release date: September 10, 2004. Documentary criticizing the Republican Party and the Bush administration; featuring Tariq Ali, Benjamin Barber, Medea Benjamin, Noam Chomsky, Kevin

Danaher, Mark Danner, Shadia Drury, Michael Dyson, Daniel Ellsberg, Michael Franti, Stan Goff, William Hartung, Robert W. Jensen, Chalmers Johnson, Jackson Katz, Michael T. Klare, Lt. Cool. Karen Kwiatowski, Norman Mailer, Zia Mian, Mark Crispin Miller, Scott Ritter, Vandana Shiva, Norman Solomon, Greg Speeter, Fernando Suarez del Solar, Immanuel Wallerstein, Jody Williams, Max Wolff.

EVERGREEN

(EVERGREEN FILMS) Producers, Eva Kolonder, Yael Melamede, Norma Jean Straw, Enid Tihanyi Zentelis; Executive Producers, Bill Pope, Evan R. Bell, Cheryl L. Pope, Gary Sharfin; Director/Screenplay, Enid Zentelis; Photography, Matthew Clark; Designer, Katie Rielly; Music, Pat Pansome, John Stirratt; Editors, Meg Reticker, Julie Carr; Casting, Susan Shopmaker; a Straw Stories, Salty Features, Granny Was an Outlaw production; Color; Rated PG-13; 86 minutes; Release date: September 10, 2004. Cast: Cara Seymour (Kate), Mary Kaye Place (Susan), Noah Fleiss (Chat), Gary Farmer (Jim), Lynn Cohen (Grandmom), Addie Land (Henri), Bruce Davison (Frank), Zach Zulauf (Mark Zakowski)

VLAD

(QUANTUM/ROMAR) Producer, Tony Shawkat; Executive Producers, William J. Booker, Dina Burke, Nick Mandracken, Pamela Vlastas; Director/Screenplay, Michael D. Sellers; Photography, Viorel Sergovici; Designer, Radu Corciova; Costumes, Ioana Corciova; Music, Christopher Field; Editor, Joel Bender; Makeup, Alexis Walker, Mircea Voda; Special Effects, Adrian Popescu; a Basra Entertainment, MediaPro Pictures production; Dolby; Color; Rated R; 98 minutes; Release date: September 10, 2004. Cast: Billy Zane (Adrian), Paul Popowich (Jeff Meyer/Husband), Kam Heskin (Alexa Meyer), Nicholas Irons (Justin/Knight), Brad Dourif (Radescu), Francesco Quinn (Vlad Tepes), Monica Davidescu (Linsey), Iva Hasperger (Ilona), Emil Hostina (Mircea), Guy Siner (Ilie), Mirceau Stoian (Claudia), Andrea Macelaru (Stefana), Alin Panc (Petre), Alexandra Velniciuc (Andrea), Zoltan Butuc (Grandfather), John Rhys-Davies (Narrator), Anca-Ioana Androne (Widow), Adrian Pintea (Iancu de Hunedoara), Claudiu Bleont (Vlad II), Iona Ionescu (Mircea Drakula), Catalin Rotaru (Young Vlad), Cristian Popa (Radu cel Frumos)

Kam Heskin, Billy Zane in *Vlad* PHOTOS COURTESY OF QUANTUM/ROMAR

PARTICLES OF TRUTH

(DADA FILMS) Producers, Jennifer Elster, Lewis Helfer; Director/Screenplay, Jennifer Elster; Photography, Toshiro Yamaguchi; Designer, Cherish Magennis; Editor, Ron Len; Casting, Caroline Sinclair; Color; Rated R; 101 minutes; Release date: September 17, 2004. Cast: Jennifer Elster (Lilli Black), Gale Harold (Morrison Wiley), Susan Floyd (Louise), Larry Pine (Mr. Wiley), Leslie Lyles (Mrs. Wiley), Mark Margolis (Grandpa Black), Richard Wilkinson (Will), Elizabeth Van Meter (Flora), Alan Samulski (Johnny), Michael Laurence (Charles), Victoria Rosen (Child Lilli), Rebecca Wright (Infected Woman), Ray Rosato (Timmy), Gregor Manns (Jimmy), Tom Southern (Reggie), Regina Dreyer-Thomas (Grandman Celantano), Margo Singaliese (Francis), Diane Bearden (Barbara), Amy Casanova (Christina), Amie Tedesco (Tortured Girl), Joyce Feurring (Mrs. Weinstein), Jerome Richards (Mr. Weinstein), Leslie Frohberg (Nurse), Petra Quinones (Cleaning Lady), Jose Hernandez, Jr. (Bouncer), Eric Jones (Gary Coleman), Taj Crown (Gapu), Lauren Bond (Anne Friar), David Ley (Yohan Svenson), John Miller (Robert Kirshenbaum), Keith Thomson (Chuck Brown), John Mondin (Bookstore Cashier), Jennifer Rhodes (Waitress), Jonathan Smit (Gallery Owner)

NATIONAL LAMPOON'S GOLD DIGGERS

(P&A RELEASING) a.k.a. *Lady Killers*; Producers, Don Ashley, Amy Greenspun, Gary Preisler; Executive Producers, Leland Preisler, Charles V. Kinstler, Brian Greenspun; Director/Screenplay, Gary Preisler; Photography, Tom Callaway; Designer, Terrence Foster; Costumes, Ellen Falguiere; Music Supervisor, Jerry Gershman; Editor, Robert Brakey; Casting, Aaron Griffith; a Voyage

Jennifer Elster, Gale Harold in *Particles of Truth* PHOTO COURTESY OF DADA FILMS

Entertainment and Delfino Entertainment presentation of a Don Ashley production; Dolby; Deluxe color; Rated PG-13; 87 minutes; Release date: September 17, 2004. Cast: Will Friedle (Cal Menhoffer), Chris Owen (Lenny Smallwood), Nikki Ziering (Charlene), Louise Lasser (Doris Mundt), Renee Taylor (Betty Mundt), Rudy De Luca (Uncle Walt), Jack Ong (Mr. Woo), J.J. Cole (Minister), Carmen Twillie (Gospel Singer), Gabriel Bologna (Jail Guard), Mary Albee (Woman on Street)

CRUTCH

(ILLUMINAIRE) Producers, Rob Moretti, Michael Anthony, Eric Smith; Director, Rob Moretti; Screenplay, Rob Moretti, Paul Jacks; Photography, Brian Fass; Music, Ben Goldberg; Editors, Rob Moretti, Jennifer Erickson; Casting, Ken Schactman; Dolby; Color; Rated R; 88 minutes; Release date: September 17, 2004. Cast: Robert Bray (Michael), James Earley (Jack), Frankie Faison (Jerry), Eben Gordon (David), Tia Dionne Hodge (Janice), Jennifer Katz (Maryann), Tim Loftus (Zack), Rob Moretti (Kenny), Sylvia Norman (Linda), Laura O'Reilly (Lisa), Juanita Walsh (Katie), Jennifer Laine Williams (Julia)

GEORGES BATAILLE'S STORY OF THE EYE

(ARM/CINEMA 25 PICTURES) Producer/Director, Andrew Repasky McElhinney; Executive Producer, Louis Bluver; Screenplay, Andrew Repasky McElhinney, Dan Buskirk, Melissa Elizabeth Forgione, Les Rek, Sean Timothy Sexton, Courtney Shea, Telly, Bosco Younger; Based on the novel *L'historie de l'oeil* by Georges Bataille; Photography, Dan Buskirk, Bosco Younger, Les Rek; Music, City of Horns, Paul David Bergel; Editor, Charlie Mackie; Color; Not rated; 81 minutes; Release date: September 22, 2004. Cast: Melissa Elizabeth Forgione, Querelle Haynes, Sean Timothy Sexton, Courtney Shea, Claude Barrington White.

THE YES MEN

(UNITED ARTISTS) Producers, Sarah Price, Chris Smith; Director, Sarah Price, Chris Smith, Dan Ollman; Costumes, Sal Salamone; Editor, Dan Ollman; Dolby; Color; Rated R; 83 minutes; Release date: September 24, 2004. Documentary in which two hucksters set up a fictional WTO spokesman and accompanying website; featuring Phil Bayly, Dr. Andreas Bichlbauer, Andy Bichlbaum, Mike Bonanno, Patrick Lichty, Michael Moore, Sal Salamone.

Eben Gordon, Rob Moretti in *Crutch* PHOTO COURTESY OF ILLUMINAIRE

RICK

(VITAGRAPH) Producers, Jim Czarnecki, Ruth Charny, Sofia Sondervan; Executive Producers, Edward R. Pressman, John Schmidt; Director/Editor, Curtiss Clayton; Screenplay, Daniel Handler; Photography, Lisa Rinzler; Costumes, Alysia Raycraft; Music, Ted Recihman, Paul Stoney; from ContentFilm and Ruth Charny productions; Dolby; Color; Rated R; 100 minutes; Release date: September 24, 2004. Cast: Bill Pullman (Rick O'Lette), Aaron Stanford (Duke), Agnes Bruckner (Eve O'Lette), Sandra Oh (Michelle), Dylan Baker (Buck), Emmanuelle Chriqui (Duke's Long-Suffering Wife), Marianne Hagan (Laura), Jerome Preston Bates (Lobby Guard), Jamie Harris (Mick), Paz de la Huerta (Vicki), Marin Rathje (Mrs. O'Lette in Picture), William Ryall (Rick's Doorman), Daniel Handler (Pesky Waiter), Dennis Parlato (Business Talk Anchor), P.J. Brown (Jack Lantern), Haviland Morris (Jane), Todd A. Kovner (Jed), Dan Moran (Timothy the Strange Attendant), Kimberly Anne Thompson (New Receptionist), Vita Haas (Party Girl), Andrew Appel (Ambitious Executive), Susan Porro (Anne Balin), Chris Skoglund (Annoying Executive), Robert Gerard Larkin (Harried Executive), R. Brandon Johnson (Fawning Executive), Brian Faherty (Clowning Executive), Josh Casaubon (Handsome Executive), Robin Goldsmith (Genial Executive)

Eric Schaeffer in *Mind the Gap* PHOTO COURTESY OF SKY ISLAND FILMS

Andy Bichlbaum, Mike Bonanno in *The Yes Men*

MIND THE GAP

(SKY ISLAND FILMS) Producers, Eric Schaeffer, Chip Hourihan, Robert Kravitz, Terence Michael; Executive Producers, Pierre Romain, Noel Ashman; Director/Screenplay, Eric Schaeffer; Photography, Marc Blandori; Designer, Tamar Gadish; Costumes, Tara Grodt; Music, Veigar Margeirsson; a Five Minutes Before the Miracle, Terence Michael production; Dolby; Color; Rated R; 134 minutes; Release date: September 24, 2004. Cast: Alan King (Herb Schweitzer), Elizabeth Reaser (Malissa Zubach), Eric Schaeffer (Sam Blue), Christopehr Kovaleski (Rocky Blue), Charles Parnell (John McCabe), Jill Sobule (Jody Buller), Kim Raver (Vicki Walters), John Heard (Henry Richards), Todd Weeks (Dr. Albertson), Mina Badie (Dana), Deirdre Kingsbury (Mother Zubach), Yolonda Ross (Deniese), Dolores McDougal (Woman on the Street), Stan Berger (Morris), Connie Sheppard (Beth), Eileen Ronaldes (Nancy), Michael Gatson (Priest), Pamela Dunlap (Elsa), Pamela Reid (Mrs. Trouchet), Dajon Matthews Roach (Antwon), Richard J. Miller (Dr. Richards), Marcus A. Charles (David), Malcolm Ali Davis (William), Larry Shagawat (Bobby), Lauren Schnipper (Woman with Dog), Nicholas Kaufmann (Boy on Bicycle), Haley Joel (NYC Pretty Young Girl), Dorthi Fox (Grandma, Soul Food Restaurant), Michael Isaiah Johnson (Davis, Soul Food Restaurant), Vera Farmiga (Allison Lee), Marcia Haufrecht (Sady), Jicky Schnee (Denny), Gerre Samuels (Davey), Lynne Matthew (Mother Hollander), Timothy Moody, Ahmed El Shaikh (Hollander Boys), Michael Caruso (Officer Frank Williams), Bernadette Drayont (Rape Mother), Dannelle Johnson (Rape Daughter), Tara Furcini (Taco Bell Worker), Tom Wooler (Baseball Father), Tommy Beeso (Baseball Son), Dr. Jeffrey Fisher (Dr. Hershey), Roy Farfel (Asshole Honker), David S. Jung (Dr. Chang), Charles Sammarco (Lands Arms Hotel Clerk), Amy Lynn (Car Mail Carrier), Jack Leitenberg (Jack), Neil Bonin (Dr. Abraham), Monique Fowler (Dr. Dubai), Jody Ebert (Jim), Brant Spencer (Paul), Lori Yoffe (Joan), Tara Grodt (Hurry Date Hostess), Christopher McCann (Cab Driver), Karen Shallo (Ester), Bill Weeden (Man Walking Dog), Julio Diaz (Times Square Dancer), Doug Barron (Bizman), R.P.M. (Rapist), John Reidy (Man in Street)

Mike Bonanno, Andy Bichlbaum in *The Yes Men* PHOTOS COURTESY OF UNITED ARTISTS

George Calil in *September Tapes* PHOTO COURTESY OF FIRST LOOK PICTURES

CHISHOLM '72: UNBOUGHT & UNBOSSED

(REALSIDE) Producers, Shola Lynch, Phil Bertelsen; Director, Shola Lynch; Photography, Sandi Sissel; Music, Barry Eastmond; Editors, Samuel D. Pollard, Sikay Tang; Color; Not rated; 76 minutes; Release date: September 24, 2004. Documentary on congresswoman Shirley Chisholm's efforts to run for president in 1972; featuring Shirley Chisholm, Octavia Butler, Ron Dellums.

MOOG

(PLEXIFILM) Producers, Hans Fjellestad, Ryan Page; Executive Producers, Gary Hustwit, Keith York; Director/Editor, Hans Fjellestad; Photography, Elia Lyssy; Music, Various; Color; Not rated; 72 minutes; Release date: September 24, 2004. Documentary on how Robert Moog invented an artifical music machine, the Moog Synthesiser; featuring Robert Moog, Charlie Clouser, Herbert Deutsch, Keith Emerson, Gershon Kingsley, Pamelia Kurstin, DJ Logic, Money Mark, Mix Master Mike, Jean-Jacques Perrey, Walter E. Sear, DJ Spooky, Luke Vibert, Rick Wakeman, Bernie Worrell.

Dig! PHOTO COURTESY OF PALM PICTURES

SEPTEMBER TAPES

(FIRST LOOK PICTURES) Producers, Christian Johnston, Judd Payne, George Calil, Wali Razaqi, Matthew Rhodes; Director, Christian Johnston; Screenplay, Christian Johnston, Christian Van Gregg; Music, Gunnard Doboze; Editors, Darren Mann, Jeffro Brunk, Peter Finestone; a Palisades Pictures, Persistent Entertainment production; Dolby; Color; Rated R; 95 minutes; Release date: September 24, 2004. Cast: George Calil (Don Larson), Wali Razaqi (Wali Zarif), Sunil Sadarangani (Suni), Baba Jon (Rahman), General Dil Agha (Northern Alliance Commander), Dawood Zarif, Zahir Zarif (Gun Dealers), Haroon Hadir, Sher Alai (Interviewees), Sher Agah (Chief of Police), Shaw Mahmood (Guide at Airport), Nagilai (Man at Soccer Game), Ajmal Nasir (Hotel Manager), Zia Khadiri (Money-Store Owner), Sharif Omar, Waleed Aziz, Khalid Anwar (Men at Card Game), Babak Ali (Himself), C.K. Smith (Babak's Commander), Vicky Gaur, Bobby Sharma (Henchmen)

THE CLOUD OF UNKNOWING

(POSSIBLE FILMS) Producer, Hal Hartley; Director/Screenplay/Photography/Music, Richard Sylvarnes; Designer, Biscontini Andy; Costumes, Willis Monica; a True Fiction Pictures production; Color; Not rated; 84 minutes; Release date: September 29, 2004. Cast: Miho Nikaido, D.J. Mendel, Thomas Jay Ryan, Lisa Walter

D.J. Mendel, Miho Nikaido in *The Cloud of Unknowing* PHOTO COURTESY OF POSSIBLE FILMS

DIG!

(PALM PICTURES) Producer/Director/Screenplay/Editor, Ondi Timoner; Photography, Ondi Timoner, David Timoner, Vasco Nunes; an Interloper production; Color; Rated R; 107 minutes; Release date: October 1, 2004. Documentary on the rock bands The Brian Jonestown Massacre and The Dandy Warhols; featuring Anton Newcombe, Courtney Taylor-Taylor, Joel Gion, Matt Hollywood, Peter Holmstrom, Zia McCabe, Brent DeBoer, Eric Hedford, Dean Taylor, The Dandy Warhols, Kristen Kerr.

GOING UPRIVER: THE LONG WAR OF JOHN KERRY

(THINKFILM) Producers, George Butler, Mark Hopkins; Executive Producers, William Samuels, Vincent Roberti, Michael R. Klein, Marc Abrams; Director, George Butler; Screenplay, Joseph Dorman; Based on the book by Douglas Brinkley; Photography, Jules Labarthe, Sandi Sissel; Music, Philip Glass; a White Mountain Films production; Black and white/color; Rated PG-13; 87 minutes; Release date: October 1, 2004. Documentary on Senator John Kerry's naval tour of duty during Vietnam; featuring David Alston, Dan Barbiero, Douglas Brinkley, Harvey Bundy, Max Celeland, Bestor Cram, Chris Gregory, Richard Holbrooke, Bob Kerrey, Joe Klein, Michael Medeiros, Bobby Muller, Thomas Oliphant, James Rassmann, Lenny Rotman, Rusty Sachs, Wade Sanders, Del Sandusky, Neil Sheehan, Fred Short, David Thorne, Tom Vallely, Adam Walinsky.

WOMAN THOU ART LOOSED

(MAGNOLIA) Producer, Reben Cannon; Executive Producer/Screenplay, Stan Foster; Based on the novel by T.D. Jakes; Director, Michael Schultz; Photography, Reinhart "Rayteam" Peschke; Music, Todd Cochran; a T.D. Jakes Ministries production; Dolby; Color; Rated R; 94 minutes; Release date: October 1, 2004. Cast: Kimberly Elise (Michelle Jordan), Loretta Devine (Cassey Jordan), Debbi Morgan (Twana), Michael Boatman (Todd), Clifton Powell (Reggie), Idalis DeLeon (Nicole), Bishop T.D. Jakes (Himself), Sean Blakemore (Pervis), Jordan Moseley (Michelle, Age 6), Philip Daniel Bolden (Todd, Age 8), Destiny Edmond (Michelle, Age 12), J. Karen Thomas (Sheila Stewart), Louisa Abernathy (Elderly Mother), Amy Aquino (Miss Rodgers), Malik Barnhardt (Dupree), Porscha

John Kerry (right) in *Going Upriver* PHOTO COURTESY OF THINKFILM

Coleman (Lil' Bit), Conni Marie Brazelton (Delores), Lanier Edwards (Guard), Ellia English (Prison Official), Mary Evans, Jozella Reed (Diners), Chip Fields-Hurd (Woman in Church), Bergen Williams, LaRita Shelby, Melanie Comarcho (Inmates), Mo (Scootie), Maura Gale (Churchgoer), Ricky Harris (Eli), Kennedy Rue McCullough (Mia), Kymberly Newberry (Worker), Roxanne Reese (Homeless Woman), Chaz Lamar Shepherd (Deacon), Alex Thomas (Roscoe), Dan White (Pimp in Beauty Shop), Damon Butler (Delicious, Makeup Beautician)

Deadline PHOTO COURTESY OF BIG MOUTH PRODUCTIONS

DEADLINE

(BIG MOUTH PRODS.) Producers, Katy Chevigny, Dallas Brennan; Directors, Katy Chevigny, Kirsten Johnson; Photography, Kirsten Johnson; Music, Dan Marocco, Steve Earle, Peter Nashel; Editors, Kate Hirson, Carol Dysinger, Charles Olivier; an Arts Engine production; Color; Not rated; 90 minutes; Release date: October 1, 2004. Documentary on Illinois Governor George Ryan's last minute decision on the fate of death row prisoners; featuring George Ryan, Anthony Amsterdam, Stephen Bright, Donald Cabana, Tom Cross, Gary Gauger, Cornelia Grumman, Lawrence Hayes, Grayland Johnson, Elanie Jones, Robert Jones, David Keaton, Larry Marshall, Steve Mills, Maurice Possley, Donald Scheble, Bryan Stevenson, Scott Turow, Robert Warren.

Debbi Morgan, Kimberly Elise in *Woman Thou Art Loosed* PHOTO COURTESY OF MAGNOLIA

TYING THE KNOT

(ROADSIDE ATTRACTIONS) Producers, Jim de Sève, Kian T. Jong, Stephen Pelletier; Director, Jim de Sève; Photography, Eric Juhola, Jeremy Stulberg; Editors, Jim de Sève, Stephen Pelletier, Constance Rodgers; a 1,049 Films production; Color; Not rated; 81 minutes; Release date: October 1, 2004. Docuemtnary on the debate over same sex marriage in the U.S.

THÉRÈSE:
THE STORY OF SAINT THÉRÈSE OF LISIEUX

(LUKE FILMS) Producer, Brian Shields; Director, Leonardo Defilippis; Screenplay, Patti Defillips, Saint Thérèse of Lisieux; Photography, Lourdes Ambrose; Designer, Andrew Baklinski; Costumes, Judy Newland; Music, Sister Marie Therese Sokol; Editor, Bob Brooks; Casting, Mary Sims; from Saint Luke Productions; Color; Rated PG; 96 minutes; Release date: October 1, 2004. Cast: Leonardo Defilippis (Louis Martin), Lindsay Younce (Thèrèse Martin), Melissa Sumpter (Young Thérèse), Maggie Rose Fleck (Marie Martin), Susan Funk (Sister Anne), Linda Hayden (Pauline Martin), Sybil Johnson (Sister Aimee), Judith Kaplan (Mother Marie de Gonzague), Samantha Kramer (Sister Augustine), Jen Nikolaisen (Celine Martin), Mandy Rimer (Leonie Martin), Mary Magda Schultz (Sister Vincent), Brian Shields (Pranzini)

UNCONSTITUTIONAL

(THE DISINFORMATION COMPANY) Producer/Director/Screenplay, Nonny de la Peña; Executive Producers, Robert Greenwald, Earl Katz, Daniel Raskov; Photography, Bestor Cram, Jennifer Jane; Music, Michael Brook; Editors, Joe Bini, Greg Byers; Color; Not rated; 68 minutes; Release date: October 1, 2004. Documentary on the infringement on certain civil liberties that have taken place since the terrorist attacks of September 11, 2001; featuring Aquil Abdullah, Robert Barr, Azmat Begg, A.J. Brown, Vincent Cannistraro, David Cole, Ryan Coonerty, Kathy Culliton, Peter A. DeFazio, Hanan Hamoui, Mohammed Hamoui, Nadin Hamoui, Rham Hamoui, Safouh Hamoui, James Hanes, Douglas Heller, Ken Kurtis, David Lindorff, Dave Meserve, Maj. Michael Mori, Laura Murphy, Donna Newman, Andrew O'Connor, Barbara Olshansky, Anthony Romero, Jayashri Srikantian, Anne Turner, Mara Verheyden-Hilliard, Thomas B. Wilner.

Oliver James, Hilary Duff in *Raise Your Voice* PHOTO COURTESY OF NEW LINE CINEMA

Tying the Knot PHOTO COURTESY OF ROADSIDE ATTRACTIONS

RAISE YOUR VOICE

(NEW LINE CINEMA) Producers, Anthony Rhulen, A.J. Dix, David Brookwell, Sean McNamara, Sara Risher; Executive Producers, Toby Emmerich, Mark Kaufman, Matt Moore, William Shively, Avram Butch Kaplan; Director, Sean McNamara; Screenplay, Sam Schreiber; Story, Mitch Rotter; Photography, John R. Leonetti; Designer, Joseph T. Garrity; Costumes, Aggie Guerard Rogers; Music, Machine Head; Editor, Jeff W. Canavan; a Filmengine presentation of a Clickflicks/Brookwell McNamara production; Dolby; Fotokem color; Rated PG; 106 minutes; Release date: October 8, 2004. Cast: Hilary Duff (Terri Fletcher), Oliver James (Jay Corgan), David Keith (Simon Fletcher), Rita Wilson (Frances Fletcher), Rebecca DeMornay (Aunt Nina), John Corbett (Mr. Torvald), Jason Ritter (Paul Fletcher), Dana Davis (Denise Gilmore), Johnny Lewis (Engelbert "Kiwi" Wilson), Kat Dennings (Sloane), Lauren C. Mayhew (Robin Childers), Robert Trebor (Mr. Wesson), Carly Reeves (Kelly), James Avery (Mr. Gantry), Steven T. Palmer (Street Drummer), Davida Williams (Lauren), Marshall Manesh (Cabbie), Gibby Brand (Mr. Holcomb), Sean Patrick McNamara (Dr. Mark Farley), Fred Meyers (Matthew), Mitch Rotter (Folk Singer), Seis Cuerdas (Flamenco Guitarists), John Gipson (Saxophone Player), T.J. Thyne (Emcee), Adam Gontier, Neil Sanderson, Brad Walst, Bary Stock (Three Days Grace)

THE HILLSIDE STRANGLER

(TARTAN USA) Producers, Hamish McAlpine, Michael Muscal; Executive Producers, Michael Avery, Alexa Jago, Carol Siller, John Steinfield; Director, Chuck Parello; Screenplay, Chuck Parello, Stephen Johnston; Photography, John Pirozzi; Designer, Gregg Gibbs; Costumes, Niklas J. Palm; Music, Danny Saber;

Editor, Paul Heiman; Casting, Johanna Ray; Dolby; Color; Rated R; 97 minutes; Release date: October 8, 2004. Cast: C. Thomas Howell (Kenneth Bianchi), Nicholas Turturro (Angelo Buono), Allison Lange (Claire Shelton), Marisol Padilla Sanchez (Christina Chavez), Jennifer Kelly Tisdale (Erin), Lin Shaye (Jenny Buono), Kent Masters King (Gabrielle), Aimee Brooks (Felicia Waller), Natasha Melnick (Karyn), Brandin Rackley (Janice Cooley), Roz Witt (Frances Bianchi), Tricia Dickson (Heather Brewer), Kylie Rachel (Peaches), Charles Andre Allen (Herb), Molly Brenner (Matilda Plosonko), Zarah Little (Carrie Plosonko), Kevin Mukherji (Ray Patel), Dianah Avery (Kate Sugar), Cletus Young (Charlie Lloyd), Robbie Peron (Jason Barnes), Genevieve Anderson (Tina Mayfield), Bill Pirman (Gary Danesi), Aaron Behr (Don Forney), Alexander Folk (Officer Alan Romer), Danney Rey (Officer Carlos Arenos), Julia Lee (Lisa Erwin), Kelly Lohman (Sue Radigan), Gregg Gibbs (Officer Mike McHale), Laura Mulrenan (Det. Delia Cervanko), Andre Hotchko (Reporter), Hal Cutler (Guard), Sarah Ann Morris (Sharon Oates), Lisa Lee (Nude Victim), Keva Hargrove (Marie Rudolph), Alexa Jago (Amber Wilken)

BAPTISTS AT OUR BARBECUE

(HALESTONE) Producers, Christian Vuissa, F. Matthew Smith; Director, Christian Vuissa; Screenplay, Christian Vuissa, F. Matthew Smith; Based on the novel by Robert Farrell Smith; Photography, Brandon Christensen; Designer, David Graham; Costumes, Brittney Rodee; Music, Greg Duckwitz; Editor, Ludwig Einklang; Casting, Catrine McGregor; a Blue Crow, Mirror Films production; Color; Rated PG; 92 minutes; Release date: October 8, 2004. Cast: Steve Wayne Anderson (Clark Bender), Bob Bedore (Father), Brooks Bedore (Son), Heather Beers (Charity), K. Bethers (Felicity's Mom), Wayne Brennan (Brother Stolt), Bonnie Burt (Sister Hatch), Michael Anthony Christian (Orvil), Bernie M. Diamond (Fern), Patrick Eugene Donahue (Heber), Jake Patrick Evans (Little Lehi), Jan Broberg Felt (Tartan's Mom), John Foss (Howard), Alex Gerrish (Alex Hatch), Frank Gerrish (Conroy Hatch), Deborah E. Graves (Mrs. Holden), Charles Halford (Rich), Lindsey Haun (Sharon), Tony Larimer (Pastor Stevens), Ryan A. Lucas (Willie), Dan Merkley (Tartan Jones), Micaela Nelligan (Wynona Wingate), Diane Rane (Bronwyn Smith), Oscar Rowland (Earl), Rosemberg Salgado (Mr. Holden), Duane Stephens (Bob), Crystal Stone (Loni), Hillary Straga (Datenapping Woman), Katherine Swigert (TV Reporter), Natalie Wesche (Woman in Distress), Helen White (Sister Theo), Melany Wilkins (Sister Lynn), Rhett Willman (Ian Smith), Nikky Winthers (Wendy Hatch), Mindy B. Young (Sister North)

EULOGY

(ARTISAN) Producers, Steve Haft, Kirk D'Amico, Lucas Foster, Richard Barton Lewis; Director/Screenplay, Michael Clancy; Executive Producers, Shelly Glasser, Bo Hyde, Stefan Jonas, Jonas McCord, Kendall Morgan, Rory Rosegarten; Photography, Michael Chapman; Designer, Dina Lipton; Costumes, Tracy Tynan; Music, George S. Clinton; Editors, Richard Halsey, Ryan Kushner; Casting, Patricia Kerrigan DiCerto, Nancy Nayor; a Myriad Pictures Inc., Haft Entertainment production; Dolby; Color; Rated R; 91 minutes; Release date: October 15, 2004. Cast: Hank Azaria (Daniel Collins), Jesse Bradford (Ryan Carmichael), Zooey Deschanel (Kate Collins), Glenne Headly (Samantha), Famke Janssen (Judy Arnolds), Piper Laurie (Charlotte Collins), Kelly Preston (Lucy Collins), Ray Romano (Skip Collins), Rip Torn (Edmund Collins), Debra Winger (Alice Collins), Curtis Garcia (Fred Collins), Keith Garcia (Ted Collins), Rene

Auberjonois (Parson), Lana Novac (Lace), Allisyn Ashley Arm (Collins Daughter), Denise Dowse (Judge), Paget Brewster (Aunt Lily), John Lafayette (Doctor), Lisa Maris (Louise), Claudette Nevins (Barbara Collins), Mary Schmidtberger (Hostess), Natasha Sheridan (Young Kate), Sara Botsford (Mrs. Carmichael), Vincent Castellanos (Adult Film Actor), Mark Harelik (Burt), Rance Howard (Lance Sommers), Sherman Howard (Funeral Director), Micole Mercurio (Delilah the Neighbor), Alex Moore (Young Daniel), Michael Panes (Adult Film Director), Eric Pierpont (Mr. Carmichael), Brian Posehn (Video Store Clerk), Kevin Ruf (Commerical Dad), Rocco Sisto (District Attorney), Ward Stearns, Jr. (Young Ryan at 11), Brandon Waters (Young Ryan at 5)

Hayden Panettiere, Ryan Kelley in *The Dust Factory* PHOTO COURTESY OF MGM

THE DUST FACTORY

(MGM) Producers, Tani Cohen, Eric Small; Executive Producer, Erika Lockridge; Director/Screenplay, Eric Small; Photography, Stephen M. Katz; Designer, Mimi Gramatky; Costumes, Rita Riggs; Music, Luis Enriquez Bacalov; Editor, Glen Farr; Casting, Mary Jo Slater; a Bahr Prods. production; Dolby; FotoKem color; Rated PG; 99 minutes; Release date: October 15, 2004. Cast: Armin Mueller-Stahl (Grandpa Randolph), Hayden Panettiere (Melanie), Ryan Kelley (Ryan Flynn), Kim Myers (Angie Flynn), George De La Peña (Ringmaster), Michael Angarano (Rocky Mazzelli), Peter Horton (Lionel), Kyle Hansen (Rennie), Ted Roisum (Trapeze Catcher), Ayanna Berkshire-Cruse (Hope), Shuhe (Sorrow), Robert Blanche (Ryan Flynn, Sr.)

Piper Laurie, Glenne Headly, Zooey Deschanel in *Eulogy* PHOTO COURTESY OF ARTISAN

HAIR SHOW

(INNOVATION FILM GROUP) Producers, Nikkole Denson, Jeff Clanagan; Executive Producers, Earvin "Magic" Johnson, Steve Imes, Leslie Small; Director, Leslie Small; Screenplay, Andrea Wiley, Sherri A. McGee, Devon Gregory; Photography, Keith Smith; Designer, Leon King; Costumes, Yolanda Braddy; Music, Kennard Ramsay; Music Supervisor, Robert "Big Bob" Francis; Editor, Suzanne Hines; Casting, Monica Swann; an Urbanworks Entertainment presentation of a Magic Johnson production; Dolby; Deluxe color; Rated PG-13; 108 minutes; Release date: October 15, 2004. Cast: Mo'Nique (Peaches), Kellita Smith (Angela), Gina Torres (Marcella), David Ramsey (Cliff), Taraji Henson (Tiffany), Keiko Agena (Jun Ni), Cee Cee Michaela (Simone), Joe Torry (Brian), Andre Blake (Gianni), Bryce Wilson (Drake), Vivica A. Fox, Roshumba Williams, John Salley (Themselves), Tom "Tiny" Lister, Jr. (Agent Little), Tom Virtue (Agent Scott), Reagan Gomez-Preston (Fiona), James Avery (Seymour Gold), Serena Williams (Agent Ross), Tami Anderson (Zora), Michelle Griffin (Mona), Jamaica Ja Toi (Pierre), Bruce Bruce (Lime Pimp), Giorgi-o (Dark Gable), E-40 (Cabbie), Mari Morrow (Gina), Angela Dixon (Sharina), Jaqueline Fleming (Margo), Melanie Comarcho (Gold Tooth Girl), Don Franklin (Basil), Annie McKnight (Noxema), Sarah Leslie, Susan Leslie (Mothers), Sarah Lilly (Jan), Joyful M'Chelle (Stephanie Cole), Kimberly Moss (Betty), Niecy Nash (Debra), Nicole Pano (Woman Driver), Neferteri Shepherd (Ria), Alex Avant (Police Officer), Admiu Colon (Rasta M.C.), Lanre Idewu (Sexy Jamaican), Miguel Costilliano (CluBouncer), Denise Gillyard (Fashion Show Model), Jason Lombard (Sexy Jamaican Dancer), Anika C. McFall (Upscale Client), John Fitzgerald Page (Corporate Big Wig)

Anthony LaPaglia, Caroleen Feeney, Eric Stolz in *Happy Hour* PHOTO COURTESY OF DAVIS ENTERTAINMENT

RIDING THE BULLET

(INNOVATION FILM GROUP) Producers, Mick Garris, David Lancaster, Greg Malcolm, Joel T. Smith, Vicki Sotheran; Executive Producers, Stephen King, Brad Krevoy, Jan Fantl, Frank Hübner, Jörg Westerkamp; Director/Screenplay, Mick Garris; Based on the novella by Stephen King; Photography, Robert C. New; Designer, Andrew Deskin; Music, Nicholas Pike; Editor, Marshall Harvey; Special Makeup Effects, Howard Berger; Special Effects Coordinator, Andrew Chamberlayne; a Motion Picture Corporation of America, ApolloMedia, Motion Picture Corporation of Europe production; U.S.-German-Canadian; Dolby; Color; Rated R; 98 minutes; Release date: October 15, 2004. Cast: Jonathan Jackson (Alan Parker), David Arquette (George Staub), Cliff Robertson (Farmer), Barbara Hershey (Jean Parker), Erika Christensen (Jessica Hadley), Barry W. Levy (Julian Parker), Jackson Warris (6-Year-Old Alan), Jeff Ballard (12-Year-Old Alan), Peter LaCroix (Mature Alan), Chris Gauthier (Hector Passmore), Robin Nielsen (Archie Howard), Matt Frewer (Mr. Clarkson), Simon Webb (Grim Reaper), Keith Dallas (Orderly), Danielle Dunn-Morris (Mrs. Janey McCurdy), Nicky Katt (Ferris), Mike Shustek, Tony Cuzela, Terry Howson (Cops at Accident), Francis Boyle (Talking Corpse), Tatiana Szalay (Sobbing Wife), Mong Lo (Doctor in Men's Room), Davis Purvis (Mr. Dalrymple), Greg Rogers (Businessman Selling Cadillac), Howard Kaylan (Apple Man), Natalye Vivian (Yvonne Ederle), Mick Garris (Dr. Higgins), Mark McConchie (Dr. Shustek), Cynthia Garris (Nurse Annie Wilkes), Catherine Devine (Art Class Model), Haig Sutherland, Ben Cotton (Rally Students), Norman Krevoy (Hospital Janitor), Cecile Krevoy (Sexy Mute Hospital Nurse)

HAPPY HOUR

(DAVIS ENTERTAINMENT) Producers, Kimberly Shane O'Hara, J. Todd Harris, Eric M. Klein; Executive Producer, John Davis; Director, Mike Bencivenga; Screenplay, Mike Bencivenga, Richard Levine; Photography, Giselle Chamma; Designer, Tema Levine; Costumes, Nancy Brous; Music, Jeffrey M. Taylor; Editors, Robert Landau, Nina Kawasaki; Casting, Eve Battaglia, Penny Ludford; an O'Hara/Klein production; Color; Not rated; 93 minutes; Release date: October 22, 2004. Cast: Anthony LaPaglia (Tulley), Eric Stoltz (Levine), Caroleen Feeney (Natalie), Robert Vaughn (Tulley Sr.), Sandrine Holt (Bonnie), Thomas Sadoski (Scott), Mario Cantone (Geoffrey), Malachy McCourt (Dr. Pitcoff), Michael Mulheren (Kelly), Miriam Sirota (Rachel), Cate Smit (Publicist), Sam Breslin Wright (Chris), Randy Evans (Dave), Michael Minutoli (Bruiser), Sean Conroy (Doorman), Larissa Thurston (Woman in Bar), Michelle Maryk (Woman in Park), Bob O'Brien, Jack Newfield, Pete Hamill, Steve Dunleavy (Themselves), Mary Lee Kortes (Singer, Guitar), Brad Albetta (Bass Guitar), Joey "Pajamas" Chiofalo (Accordion), Phil Kester (Drums)

LIGHTNING IN A BOTTLE

(SONY CLASSICS) Producers, Jack Gulick, Alex Gibney, Margaret Bodde; Executive Producers, Martin Scorsese, Paul G. Allen, Jody Patton; Director, Anoine Fuqua; Photography, Lisa Rinzler; Designer, Tom McPhillips; Music, Steve Jordan; Editor, Bob Eisenhardt, Keith Salmon; a Vulcan/Jigsaw production; Dolby; Color; Rated PG-13; 103 minutes; Release date: October 22, 2004. Documentary of a blues concert recorded at Radio City Music Hall; featuring Aerosmith, Gregg Allman, James Blood Ulmer, Clarence "Gatemouth" Brown, Ruth Brown, Solmon Burke, Natalie Cole, Shemeika Copeland, Bill Cosby, Robert Cray, Chuck D., Dr. John, Honeyboy Edwards, John Fogerty, Macy Gray, Buddy Guy, John Hammond, Levon Helm, India Arie, David Johansen, Larry Johnson, Angelique Kidjo, B.B. King, Chris Thomas King, Alison Krauss, Lazy Lester, Keb' Mo', Mic Nuggette, Odetta, Bonnie Raitt, Vernon Reid, Martin Scorsese, Mavis Staples, Hubert Sumlin, Jimmie Vaughan, Kim Wilson.

FISH WITHOUT A BICYCLE

(NEWMARK/ECHELON) Producer, Scott Seligman, Ronnie Marmo, Robert Rothbard, John Ryan; Director, Brian Austin Green; Screenplay, Jenna Mattison; Photography, Florian Stadler; Designer, Donna Ekins-Kapner; Costumes, Mike Sam; Music, Didier Rachou; Editor, Mathew Smith; Casting, Victoria Rocchi; Color; Rated R; 97 minutes; Release date: October 22, 2004.

Brian Austin Green, Jenna Mattison in *Fish Without a Bicycle* PHOTOS COURTESY OF NEWMARK/ ECHELON

Cast: Jenna Mattison (Julianna Mercer), Brian Austin Green (Ben), Jennifer Blanc (Vicki), Bryan Callen (Michael), Brad Rowe (Danny), Ronnie Maro (Ronnie), Edie McClurg (Greta), Jennifer Sky (Hot Chick), Alex Band (Jag), Stephen Arenholz (Bartender), Ben DiGregorio (Dimitri), Jules Dosik (Tattoo Girl), Adam Hendershott (Drive-Thru Geek), Victoria Rocchi (Annie), Francisco Viana (Strip Club Owner)

Bonnie Raitt, B.B. King in *Lightning in a Bottle* PHOTOS COURTESY OF PAUL BRISSMAN/SONY CLASSIC

SURVIVING CHRISTMAS

(DREAMWORKS) Producers, Jenno Topping, Betty Thomas; Executive Producer, Patricia Whitcher; Director, Mike Mitchell; Screenplay, Deborah Kaplan, Harry Elfont, Jeffrey Ventimilia, Joshua Sternin; Story, Deborah Kaplan, Harry Elfont; Photography, Peter Collister, Tom Priestly, Jr.; Designer, Caroline Hanania; Costumes, Mary Jane Fort; Music, Randy Edelman; Editor, Craig McKay; Casting, Juel Bestrop, Jeanne MCCarthy; a Tall Pictures production, a Live Planet production; Dolby; Color; Rated PG-13; 130 minutes; Release date: October 22, 2004. Cast: Ben Affleck (Drew Latham), James Gandolfini (Tom Valco), Christina Applegate (Alicia Valco), Catherine O'Hara (Christine Valco), Josh Zuckerman (Brian Valco), Bill Macy (Doo-Dah), Jennifer Morrison (Missy Vangilder), Udo Kier (Heinrich), David Selby (Horace Vangilder), Stephanie Faracy (Letitia Vangilder), Stephen Root (Dr. Freeman), Sy Richardson (Doo-Dah Understudy), Tangie Ambrose (Kathryn), John BJ Bryant (Cabbie), Peter Jason (Suit), Phill Lewis (Levine the Lawyer), Tumbleweed (Santa), Kate Hendrickson (Santa's Photographer), Bridgette Ho (Five Year Old), Hailey Noelle Johnson (Little Girl), Sean Marquette (Older Brother), Caitlin Fein, Amanda Fein (Freeman

Twins), Kent Osborne (Marley), Bill Saito (Christmas Past), Michael Patrick Bell (Christmas Present), Amy Halloran (Young Scrooge), Joshua Siegel (Chad), Sonya Eddy (Security Lady), Smalls (Security Man), Ron Karabatsos (Deli Man), Wynn Irwin (Customer), Angela Gacad (Cute Girl at Party), Tom Kenny (Man Wrapping Gift), Joan M. Blair (Lonely Lady), John Carter Brown (Depressed Donator), William Thomas, Jr. (Choir Director), Karen Furno, Linda Kerns, Cynthia Marty, Melanie Taylor, Precious McCall, Anika Noni Rose, David Atkinson, Reynaldo Duran, Michael Kosik (Choir), Jon Simanton, Allison Queal, Kacie Borrowman (Elves)

Christina Applegate in *Surviving Christmas*

CELSIUS 41.11: THE TEMPERATURE AT WHICH THE BRAIN...BEGINS TO DIE

(CITIZEN UNITE) Executive Producers, David Bossie, Craig Haffner; Co-Producers/Screenplay, Lionel Chetwynd, Ted Steinberg; Director, Kevin Knoblock; Editors, Michael Hilton, John Tracy; from Adams County Productions; Color; Rated R; 72 minutes; Release date: October 22, 2004. Documentary that attempts to salvage George W. Bush's tarnished reputation after ordering troops into Iraq; featuring Fredic W. Barnes, Michael Barone, Babara Comstock, Alice Fisher, Mansoor Ijaz, Charles Krauthammer, Michael Ledeen, Michael Medved, Joshua Muravchik, John O'Neill, Bill Sammon, Fred Dalton Thompson, Victoria Toensing.

James Gandolfini, Ben Affleck in *Surviving Christmas* PHOTOS COURTESY OF DREAMWORKS

Joaquin Phoenix, Claire Danes in *It's All About Love* PHOTO COURTESY OF STRAND

FARMINGVILLE

(CAMINO BLUFF) Producers/Directors, Carlos Sandoval, Catherine Tambini; Screenplay, Carlos Sandoval; Photography, Karola Ritter, Catherine Tambini; Music, Steven Schoenberg; Editors, John Bloomgarten, Mary Manhardt; Color; Not rated; 79 minutes; Release date: October 22, 2004. Documentary on the attempted murder of a pair of Mexican laborers in the town of Farmingville, NY.

HOME OF THE BRAVE

(EMERGING PICTURES) Producer/Director, Paola di Florio; Associate Producer, Juliane Crump; Narrator, Stockard Channing; Color; Not rated; 75 minutes; Release date: October 27, 2004. Documentary on murdered civil rights activist Viola Liuzzo.

VOICES OF IRAQ

(MAGNOLIA PICTURES) Producer, Eric Manes; Executive Producer, John Robison; Directors/Photography, The People of Iraq; Music, Euphrates; Editors, Stephen Mark, Martin Kunert, Robin Russell; a Boooya Studios production; U.S.-Iraq; Color; Not rated; 80 minutes; Release date: October 29, 2004. Documentary in which the people of Iraq tell their own story in their own words.

MALEVOLENCE

(ANCHOR BAY) Producer/Director/Screenplay, Stevan Mena; Executive Producer, Alex That; Photography, Tsuyoshi Kimoto; a Magnetic Media Production; Dolby; Color; Not rated; 90 minutes; Release date: October 29, 2004. Cast: Samantha Dark (Samantha Harrison), R. Brandon Johnson (Julian), Heather Magee (Marilyn), Richard Glover (Kurt), Courtney Bertolone (Courtney Harrison), John Richard Ingram (Sheriff Riley), Keith Chambers (Max), Kevin McKelvey (Special Agent William Perkins), Leen Gross (FBI Agent Daley), Pamela Marie Guida (Sally), Mia Lotringer (Girl in Basement), Stevan Mena (Officer at Roadblock), Jay Cohen (17-Year-Old Martin Bristol), David K. Guida II (Six-Year-Old Martin Bristol), Mark Dobil (FBI Agent Parker), Karl Schmidt (Security Guard), Dawn Marie Ivans (Girl at Gas Station), Al Bertolone (Umpire), Meaghan Dempsey (Catcher), Danielle Cunetta (Batter), David DeLong, Anne Erdner, Paul Hoffman, Kristi Massamini, John Shambo, Robbie Bowman, Alan Howse (EMS Workers), David K. Guida (Graham Sutter)

IT'S ALL ABOUT LOVE

(STRAND) Producers, Birgitte Hald; Executive Producers, Paul Webster, Bo Ehrhardt, Peter Aalbaek Jensen, Lars Bredo Rahbek; Director, Thomas Vinterberg; Screenplay, Thomas Vinterberg, Mogens Rukov; Photography, Anthony Dod Mantle; Designer, Ben van Os; Costumes, Ellen Lens; Music, Nikolaj Egelund, Zbigniew Preisner; Editors, Valdis Oksarsdottir; Casting, Joyce Nettles, Gregory Kramer, Ilene Starger; Dolby; Color; Rated R; 104 minutes; Release date: October 29, 2004. Cast: Joaquin Phoenix (John), Claire Danes (Elena), Sean Penn (Marciello), Douglas Henshall (Michael), Alun Armstrong (David), Margo Martindale (Betsy), Mark Strong (Arthur), Geoffrey Hutchings (Mr. Morrison), Harry Ditson (George), Thomas Bo Larsen (Night Porter), Teddy Kempner (Brooklyn Receptionist), Indra Ove (Production Assistant), Georgi Staykov (Bookish Interpreter), Anna Wallander (Young Interpreter), Mariann Rudberg (Old Interpreter), Michael Philip Simpson (Master of Ceremonies), Alexander Sapone (Boy in Street), Giulia Melis (Italian Girl in Street), Norman Fearrington (Hotel Bodyguard), Daniel Okine (Ugandan Man), Martha Siima (Ugandan Girl), Suat Kutlug (Robber in Subway), Julia Forgy Viktrup (Reporter), Sean-Micahel Smith (Pete), Ingemar Persson, Wieslaw Figazc, Ronald Khuse (Chefs), Joanna Nowakowski (Young Elan), Dennis Kemp (Young John), (Manager's Assistants), Meaza Beyene Muhaxhiri, Ines Sebalj (Waitresses)

Ronald Reagan in *In the Face of Evil* PHOTO COURTESY OF AMERICAN VAMTAGE MEDIA

IN THE FACE OF EVIL:
REAGAN'S WAR IN WORD AND DEED

(AMERICAN VAMTAGE MEDIA) Producers, Tim Watkins; Executive Producer, Peter Schweizer; Director, Stephen K. Bannon; Screenplay, Stephen K. Bannon, Julia Jones; Music, Scott Knight; Editor, Jason D. Bloom; a Bannon Films, Leo McWatkins production; Color/black and white; Rated PG-13; 110 minutes; Release date: October 29, 2004. Documentary on Ronald Reagan's crusade.

FADE TO BLACK

(PARAMOUNT CLASSICS) Producers, Bob Ezrin, Rich Kleiman, Justin Wlikes; Executive Producers, Shawn Carter, John Meneilly, Jon Kamen, Frank Scherma; Directors, Pat Paulson, Michael John Warren; Photography, Scott Lochmus, Theron Smith, Paul Bozymowski, Luke McCoubrey; Editors, Jim Helton, Jonah Moran, Ron Pantane, Michael John Warren, Adam Zuckerman; an

@radical.media and Marcy Projects production; Dolby; Color; Rated R; 109 minutes; Release date: November 5, 2004. Documentary capturing a farewell concert for rap emcee Jay-Z at Madison Square Garden; featuring Jay-Z, Memphis Bleek, Mary J. Blige, Foxy Brown, Micahel Buffer, Sean "P. Diddy" Combs, Common, Damon Dash, Missy "Misdemeanor" Elliott, Funkmaster Flex, Freeway, R. Kelly, Ghostface Killah, Beyonce Knowles, Timbaland, Slick Rick, Rick Rubin, Beanie Sigel, Ahmir-Khalib Thompson, Twista, Kayne West, Pharrell Williams.

Beyoncé Knowles, Jay-Z in *Fade to Black* PHOTO COURTESY OF PARAMOUNT CLASSICS

INTOXICATING

(ROGUE ARTS) Producers, Mark David, Tommy Burke, Tony Hewett, Jack Rubio; Executive Producers, Justin Kim, Stu Matz, Tom Pellegrini, Annemarie Curry; Director/Photography, Mark David; Screenplay, Kirk Harris; Story, Kirk Harris, Mark David; Designer, Chuck Dutrow; Costumes, Barbara Pushman; Music, Mark David, William Tabanou; Editors, Mark David, Joyce Brand; a Film Kitchen production; Color; Not rated; 102 minutes; Release date: November 5, 2004. Cast: Kirk Harris (Dr. Dorian Shanley), John Savage (William Shanley), Eric Roberts (Teddy), Camilla Overbye Roos (Anna Michelzewski), Joanne Baron (Dr. Eilene Preminger), D.W. Brown (Dr. Michael Tuuri), Ron Gilbert (Officer John Connor), Allan Rich (Michael Reilly), Laurie Baranyay (Megan Foster), Michael Dalmon (Jerry), Christina Carson (Nurse Amy), Marie Black (Katie), Art Chudabala (William's Doctor), Trevor Hale (Man in Bathroom), Aidan Harris Kuykendall (Dorian as a Child), Tina Kuykendall (Mother Shanley), Honey Lauren (Nurse Amanda Snyder), Camille Solari (Mimi), Chaz Divon Tolbert (Ray)

BROTHER TO BROTHER

(WOLFE RELEASING) Producers, Rodney Evans, Jim McKay, Isen Robbins, Aimee Schoof; Director/Screenplay, Rodney Evans; Photography, Harlan Bosmajian; Designer, Ernesto Solo; Costumes, Sarah Beers; Music, Marc Anthony Thompson; Editor, Sabine Hoffmann; Casting, Ricki Maslar, Vince Liebhart, Tom Alberg; a Miasma Films, C-Hundred Film Corporation, Intrinsic Value Films production; Black and white/color; Not rated; 94 minutes; Release date: November 5, 2004. Cast: Anthony Mackie (Perry), Larry Gilliard Jr. (Marcus), Duane Boutte (Young Bruce), Daniel Sunjata (Langston), Alex Burns (Jim), Ray Ford (Wally), Aunjanue Ellis (Zora), Roger Robinson (Bruce Nugent), Kevin Jackson (Isaiah), Billoah Greene (Rashan), Oni Faidah Lampley (Evelyn), James Martinez (Julio), Lance Reddick (James Baldwin), Chad Coleman (El), Reid Mihalko (Harold), Bradley Cole (Macallister), Michael Duvert (Thug), Tracie Thoms (Mother)

Troy Duffy in *Overnight*

OVERNIGHT

(THINKFILM) Producer, Tony Montana; Directors, Tony Montana, Mark Brian Smith; Music, Jack Livesey, Peter Nashel; Editors, Tony Montana, Mark Brian Smith, Jonathan Nixon; a Black & White, Ether Films production; Black and white/color; Rated R; 115 minutes; Release date: November 10, 2004. Documentary about bartender Troy Duffy's success in selling his screenplay for The Boondock Saints to Hollywood only to see his career stall; featuring Troy Duffy, Jeffrey Baxter, Chris Brinker, Jake Busey, Gordon Clark, Billy Connolly, Jim Crabbe, Willem Dafoe, Vincent D'Onofrio, Marie Duffy, Robert Duffy, Tate Duffy, Taylor Duffy, Tyson Duffy, Cassian Elwes, Sean Patrick Flanery, Jason Flom, John Goodman, Shaun Hill, Ramses Ishak, Jimi Jackson, Ron Jeremy, Matthew Modine, Tony Montana, Jerry O'Connell, Norman Reedus, Paul Reubens, Joel Roman, Mark Brian Smith, Ron St. Germaine, Patrick Swayze, Mark Wahlberg, Sharon Waxman, Harvey Weinstein, Billy Zane, Dave Zerr.

Troy Duffy in *Overnight* PHOTOS COURTESY OF THINKFILM

Duane Boutte, Daniel Sunjata in *Brother to Brother* PHOTO COURTESY OF WOLFE RELEASING

NEW GUY

(SIETE MACHOS FILMS) Producers, Bilge Ebiri, Pavlina Hatoupis; Director/Screenplay, Bilge Ebiri; Photography, Branan Edgens, Charles Moss; Designer, Katherine Mathews; Music, Shane Clark, Erik Ilyayev, Erich Rausch; Editor, Cabot Philbrick; Color; Not rated; 85 minutes; Release date: November 10, 2004. Cast: Kelly Miller (Gregg), Scott James (Jim), Jonathan Uffelman (Justin), Tobi-Lyn Byers (Susan), Johnny Ray (The Janitor), Hank Prehodka (The Boss), Harvey Kaufman (Ralph), Dusty Brown (Ted), Louis Cancelmi (Winston), Kelly McAndrew (Janice), Tracy Tobin (Orientation Speaker), Beverly Lauchner (Waitress), Ed Lovett (Man in Bathroom), Marla Mekjian (Executive Assistant), Jana Mestechy (Lucinda), Jane Napier (Sandra), Robert Pollack (The Faxer), Allan Styer (Boss Across Street), Jeff Swarthout (Boss's Visitor #1)

Kelly Miller in *New Guy*

SEED OF CHUCKY

(ROGUE) Producer, David Kirschner, Corey Sienega; Executive Producer, Guy J. Louthan; Director/Screenplay, Don Mancini; Based on his characters; Photography, Vernon Layton; Designers, Peter James Russell, Cristian Niculescu; Costumes, Oana Paunescu; Music, Pino Donaggio; Editor, Chris Dickens; Animatronic Characters and Effects, Tony Gardner; Chuck, Tiffany and Glen Dolls Created by David Kirschner; a David Kirschner production in association with La Sienega Prods.; Dolby; Deluxe color; Rated R; 86 minutes; Release

Chucky, Jennifer Tilly in *Seed of Chucky* PHOTO COURTESY OF ROGUE

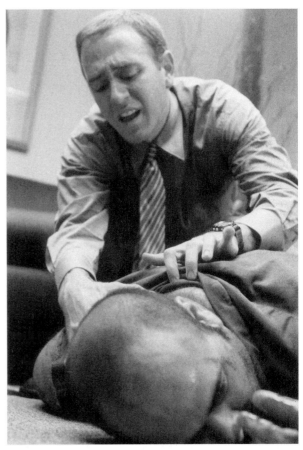

New Guy PHOTOS COURTESY OF SIETE MACHOS FILMS

date: November 12, 2004. Cast: Jennifer Tilly (Herself/Voice of Tiffany), Brad Dourif (Voice of Chucky), Billy Boyd (Voice of Glen and Glenda), Redman, Tony Gardner (Themselves), Hannah Spearritt (Joan), John Waters (Pete Peters), Keith-Lee Castle (Pyschs), Steve Lawton (Stan), Jason Flemyng (Santa), Nicholas Rowe (Lawyer), Stephanie Chambers (Claudia's Mum), Simon James Morgan (Claudia's Dad), Bethany Simons-Danville (Fulvia), Beans El-Balawi (Human Glen), Kristina Kewitt (Human Glenda), Daniel Getzoff (Assistant Director), Nicola Mycroft (Reporter), Guy J. Louthan (Don Mancini), Diana Munteanu (Fan), Anouk Diks (Interviewer), Barnaby Harrison (Laughing Puppeteer), Eliot Mathews, Adi Handac (Cops), Paul Grossman (Little Boy), Nadia Dina Ariqat (Britney)

NOEL

(CONVEX GROUP/NEVERLAND FILMS) Producers, Al Corley, Bart Rosenblatt, Eugene Musso, Zvi Howard Rosenman; Executive Producers, Jonathan Dana, Jeff Arnold, Dan Adler; Director, Chazz Palminteri; Screenplay, David Hubbard; Photography, Russell Carpenter; Designer, Carol Spier; Costumes, Renee April; Music, Alan Menken; Editor, Susan E. Morse; Casting, Billy Hopkins, Suzanne Smith, Kerry Barden, Nadia Rona, Rosina Bucci, Margery Simkin; a Zvi Howard

Rosenman production; Dolby; Panavision; Color; Not rated; 96 minutes; Release date: November 12, 2004. Cast: Penelope Cruz (Nina Vasquez), Susan Sarandon (Rose Harrison), Paul Walker (Mike), Alan Arkin (Artie Venzuela), Marcus Thomas (Jules), Chazz Palminteri (Arizona), David Julian Hirsh (Barton), Chantal Lonergan (Joy), Erika Rosenbaum (Merry), Kim Bubbs (Dr. Matthew Batiste), Ruth Chiang (Nurse Woo), Marcia Bennett (Nurse Stein), Scott Falconbridge (Man in Front Row), Victoria Sanchez (Young Mother), Maurizio Terrazzano (Tom), Gianpaolo Venuta (Young Guy), Joan Barber (Singer), Rob Daly (Paul), Arthur Holden (Pianist), Sonny Marinelli (Dennis), Daniel Sunjata (Marco), Robin Williams (Priest)

MASTER OF THE GAME

(SUNN CLASSIC PICTURES) Producers, Jeff Stolhand, Uygar Aktan, P. Dirk Higdon; Executive Producers, Dennis Hartwig, George S. Shelps; Director, Jeff Stolhand; Screenplay, Uygar Aktan; Photography, Ian Ellis; Designer, Joey Quinlan; Costumes, Stephen M. Chudej; Music, Bryan T. Shaw; Editors, Jeff Stolhand, Andy Cockrum; a Priles Entertainment Inc. production; Color; Rated R; 94 minutes; Release date: November 12, 2004. Cast: Uygar Aktan (3264), Garry Peters (Commander Raster), Steven Prince (Wolfgang), Alex Affolter (Roder), David Stokey (Keppler), Derek Wade (Saperstein), Robert Bassetti (Brickner), Trant Batey (Silverman)

Paul Walker in *Noel*

Penelope Cruz, Susan Sarandon in *Noel* PHOTOS COURTESY OF CONVEX GROUP/NEVERLAND FILMS

YOU SEE ME LAUGHIN'

(MADMAN ENTERTAINMENT) Producer/Director, Mandy Stein; Executive Producers, Tyler Brodie, Hunter Gray, Paul S. Mezey; Editors, Mayin Lo, Josh Melnick; a Journeyman Pictures, Plantain Films productions; Black and white/color; Not rated; 86 minutes; Release date: November 12, 2004. Documentary of the hill country bluesmen of Mississippi's backwoods; featuring R.L. Burnside, Junior Kimbrough, Cedell Davis, T-Model Ford, Asie Payton, Johnny Farmer, Kenny Brown, David Cardwell, Matthew Johnson, Bruce Watson, Bono, Iggy Pop, John "Jojo" Hermann, Jon Spencer, Judah Bauer, Russell Simins.

PAPER CLIPS

(MIRAMAX) Producers, Joe Fab, Robert M. Johnson, Ari Daniel Pinchot; Executive Producers, Harvey Weinstein, Bob Weinstein, Donny Epstein, Yeeshai Gross, Matthew Hiltzik, Elie Landau, Jeffrey Tahler; Directors, Joe Fab, Elliot Berlin; Screenplay, Joe Fab; Photography, Michael Marton; Music, Charlie Barnett; a Johnson Group production in association with Ergo Entertainment; Dolby; Roland House Color; DV-to-25 mm; Not rated; 82 minutes; Release date: November 24, 2004. Documentary in which the children of Whitwell, TN, learn of the Holocaust by collecting 6 million paper clips to represent the 7 million Jews killed by the Nazis; featuring Linda Hooper, Sandra Roberts, Dagmar Schroeder-Hildebrand, Peter Schroeder, David Smith, Bernard Igeilski, Rachel Gleitman, Samuel Sitko, Joe Grabezak, Casey Condra, Cassie Crabtree, Tom Bosley, Sheila Gluck Levine, George Jacobs, Linda Pickett, Dita Smith, Patrick Martin.

THE WORK AND THE GLORY

(EXCEL ENTERTAINMENT) Producer, Scott Swofford; Executive Producer, Larry H. Miller; Director/Screenplay, Russ Holt; Based on the novel The Pillar of Light by Gerald N. Lund; Photography, T.C. Christensen; Designer, John R. Uibel; Costumes, Cathren Warner; Music, Sam Cardon; Editor, Stephen L. Johnson; Casting, Rene Haynes; a Vineyard Productions presentation; Color; Rated PG; 118 minutes; Release date: November 24, 2004. Cast: Sam Hennings (Benjamin Steed), Brenda Strong (Mary Ann Steed), Eric Johnson (Joshua Steed), Alexander Carroll (Nathan Steed), Tiffany Dupont (Lydia McBride), Brighton Hertford (Melissa Steed), Kimberly Varadi (Becca Steed), Colin Ford (Matthew Steed), Kathryn Firago (Hannah McBride), Jim Grimshaw (Josiah McBride), Jonathan Scarfe (Joseph Smith), Sarah Darling (Emma Smith), Edward Albert (Martin Harris), Ryan Wood (Hyrum Smith), Jordan Rose Tarter (Sophronia Smith), Anne Sward (Lucy Mack Smith), Levi Larsen (Samuel Smith), John Woodhouse (Will Murdock), Jonathan Quint (Mark Cooper), Phillip DeVona (David Murdock), Marcus Hester (Caleb Jackson), Emily Podelski (Jessica Roundy), Bill Crabb (Asa Phelps), Annie Abbott (Edith Gates), Wayne Grace, Charles Howerton (Land Agents), Kevin Stillwell (First Man), Bruce C. Taylor (First Member), Sheri Mann Stewart (First Woman), Marc Macaulay (Land Speculator), Stephen Gentry (Second Man), Zane Miller (First Suitor), Joseph Wilkins (Second Members), Tom Turbiville (Teamster), Carey Jones (Third Man), James Van Harper (Wagon Master), Richie Dye (Clinton Roundy), Laura Whyte (Aunt Helen), Terry Haskell (First Troublemaker), Terry Londeree (Parson), Jarron Vosburg (Young Joseph), Thais Albert (Cousin Sabina), Bruce McKinnon (Preacher)

GUERILLA: THE TAKING OF PATTY HEARST

(MAGNOLIA) a.k.a. Neverland: The Rise and Fall of the Symbionese Liberation Army; Producer/Director, Robert Stone; Executive Producers, Mark Samels, Nick Fraser; Photography, Robert Stone, Howard Shack; Music, Gary Lionelli; Editor, Don Kleszy; a Robert Stone production in association with American Experience and the BBC; U.S.-British; Monaco Labs Color; HD Video; Not rated; 89 minutes; Release date: November 26, 2004. Documentary on the terrorist group, the Symbionese Liberation Army, who kidnapped heiress Patty Hearst in 1974; feautinrg Michael Bortin, Tim Findley, Russ Little, John Lester, Dan Grove, Ludlow Kramer.

EASY

(MAGIC LAMP) Producer, Gloria Norris; Executive Producer, James Welling; Director/Screenplay, Jane Weinstock; Photography, Paul Ryan; Designer, Aradhana Seth; Costumes, Mona May; Music, Grant Lee Phillips; Editor, Robert Hoffman; Over Easy Productions; Dolby; Color; Rated R; 99 minutes; Release date: November 26, 2004. Cast: Marguerite Moreau (Jamie Harris), Naveen Andrews (John), Emily Deschanel (Laura), Jordan Garrett (Bobby), Caroline

Patty Hearst in *Guerilla*

Brian F. O'Byrne, Marguerite Moreau in *Easy*

Patty Hearst in *Guerilla* PHOTOS COURTESY OF MAGNOLIA

Goodall (Sandy), Brian F. O'Byrne (Mick), Lanette Ware (Tanya), Anjoa Dias (John's Sister), Nelson Aspen (TV Reporter), Pablo Lewin (Voice of Date), Vanessa Marano (Little Jamie), John Rothman (Dad), Stefanie Sherk (Other Woman), Tom Todoroff (Tom the Vegan), D.B. Woodside (Martin)

I AM DAVID

(LIONS GATE) Producers, Lauren Levine, Clive Parsons, Davina Belling; Director/Screenplay, Paul Feig; Based on the novel by Anne Holm; Photography, Roman Osin; Designer, Giovanni Natalucci; Costumes, Ulivia Pizzetti; Music, Stewart Copeland; Editor, Steven Weisberg; Casting, Pippa Hall; a Walden Media production; Dolby; Color; Rated PG; 90 minutes; Release date: December 3, 2004. Cast: Ben Tibber (David), Jim Caviezel (Johannes), Joan Plowright (Sophie), Hristo Shopov (The Man), Silvia De Santis (Elsa), Paco Reconti (Giovanni), Roberto Attias (Baker), Francesco De Vito (Roberto), Paul Feig, Lucy Russell (Americans), Maria Bonnevie (David's Mother), Viola Carinci (Maria), Marin Jivkov (Cecha), Robert Syulev (Angelo), Alessandro Sperduti (Carlo), Shaila Rubin (Vineyard Owner), Krassimir Kutzuparov (Camp Officer), Elisabetta Bartolomei (Woman at Party), Krassimir Radkov, Diyan Machev (Party Guests), Nikola Rudarov (Store Owner), Enrico Vecchi (Grocer), Dobrin Dossev (Border Guard), Malin Krasteve, Maxim Genchev (Policemen), Ivan Nestorov (Swiss

Marguerite Moreau, Naveen Andrews in *Easy* PHOTOS COURTESY OF MAGIC LAMP

Policeman), Stefan Shteref (Bulgarian Officer), Valery Yordanov (Bulgarian Soldier), Clem Tibber (Young David), Adrian McCourt (David's Father), Panayot Tzanev (Quarry Guard), Nikolai Kipchev (Truck Driver), Paraskeva Djukelova (Young Mother)

STRAIGHT-JACKET

(REGENT/HERE! FILMS) Producer, Michael Warwick; Director/Screenplay, Richard Day; Based on his play; Photography, Michael Pinkey; Designers, Kristen McCarron, Mark Worthington; Music, Stephen Edwards; Editor, Chris Conlee; an SRO Pictures production; Dolby; Color; Not rated; 96 minutes; Release date: December 10, 2004. Cast: Matt Letscher (Guy Stone), Carrie Preston (Sally), Adam Greer (Rick Foster), Veronica Cartwright (Jerry), Victor Raider-Wexler (Saul), Jack Plotnick (Freddie Stevens), Michael Emerson (Victor), George Alan (Waiter), David Burke (Ray Verrine), Ricky Dean Logan, Matt Bushell (Morons), Jennifer Elise Cox (Betty Bright), Shea Curry (Starlet), Tammy Dahlstrom (Tourist), Scott Fishkind (Reporter), John Ganum (Crewman), David Alan Graf (Bailiff), David Jahn (Priest), Chris J. Johnson (Jeff), Butch Klein (Waiter), Tom Lenk (Teddy), Clinton Leupp (Bernice), Chad Lindsey (Mike), Ron Mathews (Salvation Army Man), Adrian Neil (Jeroen), Sam Pancake (Tour Guide), Adrian R'Mante (Hector), Lorna Scott (Louella), Benjamin Sprunger (Trick in Alley), Eric Stonestreet (Labor Organizer), Darlena Tejeiro (Viola), Hamilton von Watts (Clyde, the Bartender), Paul Willson (Coal Executive), Ryun Yu (Bess, the Make-Up Man)

Ben Tibber in *I Am David* PHOTOS COURTESY OF LIONS GATE

In the *Realms of the Unreal* PHOTOS COURTESY OF WELLSPRING

Carrie Preston, Matt Letscher in *Straight-Jacket* PHOTO COURTESY OF REGENT/HERE! FILMS

FABLED

(INDICAN) Producers, Peter Sabat, Rob Bellsey; Executive Producers, Bruce Kirschenbaum, Roy Frumkes; Director/Screenplay/Editor, Ari Kirschenbaum; Photography, Yaron Orbach; Costumes, Terry Matlin; Music, Simple Simon; a Simian Tales production; Black and white/color; Not Rated; 84 minutes; Release date: December 10, 2004. Cast: Desmond Askew (Joseph Fable), Katheryn Winnick (Liz), J. Richey Nash (Alex), Michael Panes (Dr. Roy Frumkes), Coleen Sexton (Lisa from Accounting), Deven May (Jim), Theo Hausen (Brian), Douglas Wert (The Boss), Della Askew (Narrator), William Ryall (Bookman), Adam LeFevre (Pharmacist), Tony Cucci (Bartender), R. Brandon Johnson (James), John O'Connor (Paul), Jim Ireland (Patient), Robert Gerard Larkin (Bar Thug), Susan Porro (Car-Jacked Woman)

SANTA SMOKES

(INDEPENDENT) Directors, Till Schauder, Chris Valentien; Screenplay/Editor, Till Schauder; Photography, Chris Valentien; Music, Roland Baisch, Uwe Schenk; U.S.-German; Color; Not rated; 85 minutes; Release date: December 15, 2004. Cast: Till Terror (Johnny Jones), Kristy Jean Hulslander (Angel), Richard Glover (Jason), Rynel Johnson (Mr. Johnson), Melissa Friedman (Sue)

IN THE REALMS OF THE UNREAL

(WELLSPRING) Producers, Jessica Yu, Susan West; Animation Producer, Kara Vallow; Director/Screenplay/Editor, Jessica Yu; Based on the writings of Henry Darger; Narrator, Dakota Fanning; Photography, Michael Barrow, Tim Bieber, Shan Hagan, Russell Harper; Music, Jeff Beal; a Diorama Films production, presented in association with ITVS; Color; Not rated; 81 minutes; Documentary on janitor, writer, and visionary artist Henry Darger; featuring Mary O'Donnell, Kiyoko Lerner, Mary Rooney, David Berglund, Regina Waters, and the voices of Henry Darger, Larry Pine, Frier McCollister, Wally Wingert, Janice Hong, Ruby McCollister, Paul Robert Langdon.

FOREIGN FILMS
RELEASED IN THE U.S. IN 2004

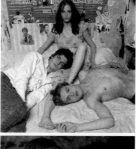

Nicholas Aaron

Joe Simpson

Brendan Mackey PHOTOS COURTESY OF UNIVERSAL

TOUCHING THE VOID

(IFC FILMS) Producer, John Smithson; Executive Producers, Robin Gutch, Charles Furneaux, Paul Trijbits; Director, Kevin Macdonald; Based on the book by Joe Simpson; Photography, Mike Eley; Climbing Photography, Keith Partridge; Art Director/Costumes, Patrick Bill; Music, Alex Heffes; Editor, Justine Wright; Casting, Susie Figgis; a Darlow Smithson production of a Film Four and Film Council presentation in association with Channel 4 and PBS; British; Dolby; Color; Not rated; 107 minutes; American release date: January 23, 2004

Brendan Mackey

Cast
Joe Simpson **Brendan Mackey**
Simon Yates **Nicholas Aaron**
Richard Hawking **Ollie Ryall**
and Joe Simpson, Simon Yates, Richard Hawking (Themselves)

The true story of how Joe Simpson and Simon Yates attempted to climb a treacherous Andes mountain in 1985.

Marina Golbahari

Marina Golbahari

Marina Golbahari

OSAMA

(UNITED ARTISTS) Producers, Siddiq Barmak, Julie LeBrocquy, Julia Fraser; Director/Screenplay/Editor, Siddiq Barmark; Photography, Ebrahim Ghafuri; Designer, Akbar Meshkini; Music, Mohammad Reza Darwishi; a Barmark Film/NHK/LeBrocquy Fraser co-production; Afghani-Japanese-Irish-Dutch, 2003; Color; Rated PG-13; 82 minutes; American release date: February 6, 2004

Cast
"Osama" **Marina Golbahari**
Espandi **Arif Herati**
Mother **Zubaida Sahar**

and Mohamad Nader Khadjeh, Mohamad Haref Harati, Gol Rahman Ghorbandi, Khwanja Nader, Hamida Refah

Because they are forbidden to go outside without a male figure, an Iranian woman tries to pass off her 12-year-old daughter as a boy.

Marina Golbahari. Zubaida Sahar PHOTOS COURTESY OF UNITED ARTISTS

Eva Green, Michael Pitt, Louis Garrel

Eva Green, Michael Pitt (in mirror), Louis Garrel

Louis Garrel, Eva Green, Michael Pitt PHOTOS COURTESY OF FOX SEARCHLIGHT

Michael Pitt, Eva Green

THE DREAMERS

(FOX SEARCHLIGHT) Producer, Jeremy Thomas; Co-Producer, John Bernard; Director, Bernardo Bertolucci; Screenplay, Gilbert Adair, inspired by his novel *The Holy Innocents*; Photography, Fabio Cianchetti; Designer, Jean Rabasse; Costumes, Louise Stjernsward; Music Supervisor, Janice Ginsberg; Editor, Jacopo Quadri; Associate Producers, Hercules Bellville, Peter Watson; Casting, Juliette Menager, Howard Feuer, Lucy Boulting; a HanWay presentation in association with Fox Searchlight, Medusa Film, of a Recorded Picture Co./Peninsular Films/Fiction production; French-Italian-British; Dolby; Color; Rated NC-17; 115 minutes; American release date: February 6, 2004

Cast
Matthew **Michael Pitt**
Isabelle **Eva Green**
Theo **Louis Garrel**
Father **Robin Renucci**
Mother **Anna Chancellor**
Patrick **Florian Cadiou**
Buffs **Jerre Hancisse, Valentin Herlet**
Themselves **Jean-Pierre Kalfon, Jean-Pierre Léaud**
The Usherette **Lola Peploe**
Theo's Girlfriend **Ingy Fillion**

In 1968 Paris an American film enthusiast strikes up a relationship with a sexually adventurous brother and sister.

Louis Garrel, Eva Green, Michael Pitt

GOOD BYE, LENIN!

(SONY CLASSICS) Producer, Stefan Arndt; Director, Wolfgang Becker; Screenplay, Bernd Lichtenberg, Wolfgang Becker; Photography, Martin Kukula; Set Designer, Lothar Holler; Costumes, Aenne Plaumann; Music, Yann Tiersen; Editor, Peter R. Adam; an X Filme Creative Pool (Berlin) production, in association with WDR (Cologne), Arte (Strasbourg); German, 2003; Dolby; Color; Rated R; 119 minutes; American release date: February 27, 2004

Chulpan Khamatova, Daniel Brühl

Cast

Alex Kerner **Daniel Brühl**
Christine Kerner, Alex's Mother **Katrin Sass**
Lara **Chulpan Khamatova**
Ariane Kerner **Maria Simon**
Denis **Florian Lukas**
Rainer **Alexander Beyer**
Robert Kerner, Alex's Father **Burghart Klaussner**
Mrs. Schäfer **Franziska Troegner**
Principal Dr. Klapprath **Michael Gwisdek**
Ganske **Jürgen Holtz**
Mehlert **Jochen Stern**
Sigmund Jähn **Stefan Walz**
Dr. Wagner **Eberhard Kirchberg**
Dr. Mewes **Hans-Uwe Bauer**

and Nico Ledermüller (Alex at 11), Jelena Kratz (Arian at 13), Laureen Hatscher, Felicistas Hatscher (Baby Paula), Martin Brambach, Michael Gerber (Collaborators), Robert Störr (), Philipp Kupfer (Baby Paula), Ernst-Georg Schwill (Taxi Driver), Rainer Werner (Collaborator in Jeans Jacket), Horst-Dieter Stork, Ditmar Bieseke (Grenzers), Hartmut Kuley (NVA Officer), Peter Kurth (X-TV Chief), Arndt Schwering-Sohnrey (Ambulance Driver), Dirk Prinz (Passenger), Jürgen Vogel (Das Kuken), Elke Werner (Salesgirl at HO Market), Regina Ziebach (Gurkenfrau), Wolfgang Stein (Gurkenmann), Mennan Yapo (Salesgirl at Flea Market), Maximilian Brunow (Engineer Sacha), Bojan Keyn (Engineer Niko), Fritz Roth (Coca-Cola Doorman), Armin Dillenberger (Bank Employee), Denys Darahan (Engineer Christian), Bastian Lang (Engineer Frank), Lothar Schlichthar (Fat Man in Pool), Alexander Reed (Wuppertaler), Dr. Ute Michael

Florian Lukas

(Doctor), Svea Timander (Father's New Woman), Hanna Schwamborn (Carla), Rafael Hübner (Thomas), Michael Berge (Party Speaker)

When Alex's socialist mother awakens from a coma eight months after the fall of the Berlin Wall, he attempts to keep her in the dark about the change in the political climate.

Katrin Sass

Maria Simon, Alexander Beyer PHOTOS COURTESY OF SONY CLASSICS

Daniel Brühl, Katrin Sass, Maria Simon

Katrin Sass

Daniel Brühl, Chulpan Khamatova

Chulpan Khamatova, Daniel Brühl

Katrin Sass, Daniel Brühl

Daniel Brühl

Daniel Brühl, Florian Lukas

Isabelle Huppert

Pascal Greggory

LA VIE PROMISE

(EMPIRE) Producer, Éric Névé; Director, Olivier Dahan; Screenplay, Olivier Dahan, Agnès Fustier-Dahan; Photography, Alex Lamarque; Designer, Marco Bardochan; Costumes, Gigi Lepage; Editor, Richard Marizy; Casting, Olivier Carbone; a Bac Films, Canal+, Des Films, France 2 Cinema, La Chauve Soris, Rhône-Alpes Cinéma, Société Française de Production; French, 2002; Dolby; Super 35 Widescreen; Color; Not rated; 93 minutes; American release date: March 4, 2004

Cast

Sylvia **Isabelle Huppert**
Joshua **Pascal Greggory**
Laurence **Maud Forget**
Piotr **André Marcon**
Sandra **Fabienne Babe**
Nurse **Elisabeth Commelin**
Mac **Louis-Do de Lencquesaing**
Stripper **Diana Jones**
Village Woman **Edith Lemerdy**
Waitress **Cylia Malki**
Georges **Rémy Roubakha**
Marie-Jose **Janine Souchon**

A prostitute and her daughter flee from Nice after the latter commits a brutal crime; causing the former to question the path she chose in life.

Isabelle Huppert PHOTOS COURTESY OF EMPIRE

Willem Dafoe, Paul Bettany

Paul Bettany, Gina McKee

Brian Cox, Gina McKee PHOTOS COURTESY OF PARAMOUNT CLASSICS

THE RECKONING

(PARAMOUNT CLASSICS) Producer, Caroline Wood; Executive Producers, Stephen Evans, Angus Finney; Co-Producers, Denise O'Dell, Sarah Halioua; Director, Paul McGuigan; Screenplay, Mark Mills; Based on the book *Morality Play* by Barry Unsworth; Photography, Peter Sova; Designer, Andrew McAlpine; Costumes, Yvonne Blake; Music, Mark Mancina, Adrian Lee; Editor, Andrew Hulme; Associate Producer, Mark Albela; Casting, Jina Jay; a Renaissance Films production in association with Kanzman/MDA Films; British; Dolby; Super 35 Widescreen; Deluxe color; Rated R; 112 minutes; American release date: March 5, 2004

Paul Bettany

Cast

Nicholas **Paul Bettany**
Martin **Willem Dafoe**
Tobias **Brian Cox**
Sarah **Gina McKee**
Simon Damian **Ewen Bremner**
Lord De Guise **Vincent Cassel**
Martha **Elvira Minguez**
Nicholas' Lover **Marián Aguilera**
Jealous Husband **Trevor Steedman**
Stephen **Simon McBurney**
Straw **Tom Hardy**
Springer **George Wells**

and Richard Durden (Town Justice), Mark Benton (Sheriff), Hamish McColl (Innkeeper), Matthew MacFadyen (King's Justice), Luke de Woolfson (Daniel), Niall Buggy (Priest), Julian Barratt (Gravedigger), Luisa Requena Baron (Baker), Pedro Martinez De Dioni (Carpenter), Tom Georgeson (Flint), Smon Pegg (Gaoler), Maria Berganza (Wells' Mother), Rafa Izuzquiza (Wells' Father), Jose Luis Martinez (Man at Play), Valerie Pearson (Woman at Play), James Cosmo (Lambert), Balbino Lacosta (Chamberlain), Heathcote Williams (Undertaker), David Luque (Captain of the Guard)

A priest on the run joins a group of traveling players and suggests that the company perform a play based on a murder trial currently taking place in the village in which they have arrived.

WILBUR WANTS TO KILL HIMSELF

(THINKFILM) Producer, Sisse Graum Olsen; Executive Producer, Peter Aalbaek Jensen; Co-Producer, Gillian Berrie; Director, Lone Scherfig; Screenplay, Anders Thomas Jensen, Lone Scherfig; Photography, Jorgen Johansson; Designer, Jette Lehmann; Music, Joachim Holbeck; Editor, Gerd Tjur; Casting, Des Hamilton; a Zentropa Entertainments6/Wilbur Inc. presentation of a Zentropa Entertainments6, Danish Film Institute, TV2 (Denmark)/Scottish Screen, Glasgow Film Fund (U.K.) production in association with Nordisk Film Biografdistribution, Nordic Film & Television Fund, STV (Sweden), Les Films du Losang (France); Danish-British-Swedish-French, 2003; Color; HD 24P Widescreen; Not rated; 106 minutes; American release date: March 12, 2004

Lisa McKinlay, Jamie Sives

Jamie Sives, Shirley Henderson

Cast

Wilbur **Jamie Sives**
Harbour **Adrian Rawlins**
Alice **Shirley Henderson**
Mary **Lisa McKinlay**
Dr. Horst **Mads Mikkelsen**
Moira **Julia Davis**
Sophie **Susan Vidor**
Taylor **Robert McIntosh**
Ruby **Lorraine McIntosh**
Wayne **Gordon Brown**
Claire **Mhairi Steenbock**

Jamie Sives

and Andrew Townsley (Doctor), Coral Preston (Jenny), Colin McAllister (Supervisor), Owen Gorman (Porter), John Yule (Alan's Father), Anne Marie Timoney (Night Nurse), Martin O'Connor, Elaine Mackenzie Ellis (Suicide Patients), Chun-Wah Tsang (Chinese Waiter), Des Hamilton (Butcher), Jazmin Fraser (Fatima), Rory Elrick (Angus), Lloyd Butler (Thomas), Scott Turner, Connall Henderson, Amber Randell McLean (Children), Olivia Calder (Choma), Samantha McNiven (Morgana)

A frequent would-be suicide moves in with his brother and finds his life being changed by a single mom who visits the siblings' second-hand book shop.

Adrian Rawlins, Shirley Henderson PHOTOS COURTESY OF THINKFILM

INTERMISSION

(IFC FILMS) Producers, Neil Jordan, Stephen Woolley, Alan Moloney; Director, John Crowley; Screenplay, Mark O'Rowe; Photography, Ryszard Lenczewski; Designer, Tom Conroy; Costumes, Lorna Marie Mugan; Music, John Murphy; Editor, Lucia Zucchetti; Casting, Jina Jay; an Irish Film Board, Film Council, IFC Films, Invicta Capital presentation of a Company of Wolves production in association with Parallel Film Prods.; Irish-British; Dolby; Color; HD-to-35mm; Rated R; 102 minutes; American release date: March 19, 2004

Kelly Macdonald

Colm Meaney

Cillian Murphy

Cast

Lehiff **Colin Farrell**
Sally **Shirley Henderson**
Deirdre **Kelly Macdonald**
Jerry Lynch **Colm Meaney**
John **Cillian Murphy**
Maura **Ger Ryan**
Mick **Brían F. O'Byrne**
Sam **Michael McElhatton**
Noeleen **Deirdre O'Kane**

and Kerry Condon (Cafe Waitress), Johnny Thompson (Old Man in Cafe), Emma Bolger (Child with Ice Cream), Deirdre Molloy (Woma in Shopping Mall), Derry Power (Elderly Man on Bus), David Wilmot (Oscar), Owen Roe (Mr. Henderson), Neili Conroy (Helen), John Rogan (Alfred), Tom Farrelly (George), Gerry Moore (Seamus Ruane), Mikel Murfi (Rabbit Man), Tomás O'Sulleabháin (Ben Campion), Pat Laffan (Charlie O'Brien), Rory Keenan (Anthony Lowry), Darragh Kelly (Thomas Downes), Hannah McCabe (Store Assistant), Donagh Deeney (Danny the Busman), Taylor Molloy (Philip), Barbara Bergin (Karen), Tom Jordan Murphy (Brian, Video Store Manager), Conor Lovett (Mr. Leonard), Conleth Hill (Robert), Pascal Scott (Maurice), Norma Sheahan, Cathy Belton, Jeremy Anthony Earls, Catherine Farrell (Students), Laurence Kinlan (Drug Dealer), Patrick Murray (Drug Customer), Conor McDermottroe, Denis Conway (Detectives), Jeff O'Toole (Thomas), Conor Lambert (Nightclub Barman), Simon Delaney (Bill), Ruth McCabe (Celia), Jane Brennan (Mrs. Rooney), David Herlihy (Tony, Security Guard), Michael Hayes (Garda Officer), Stewart Donnan (Cathal), Karl Shiels (Wayne)

A group of disparate working class Dubliners find their lives and actions crossing in unexpected ways.

Shirley Henderson PHOTOS COURTESY OF IFC FILMS

Grégori Derangère, Isabelle Adjani

BON VOYAGE

(SONY CLASSICS) Producers, Michèle Pétin, Laurent Pétin; Director, Jean-Paul Rappeneau; Screenplay, Jean-Paul Rappeneau, Patrick Modiano; Adaptation, Jérôme Tonnerre, Jean-Paul Rappeneau, Gilles Marchand, Julien Rappeneau; Photography, Thierry Arbogast; Designer/Costumes, Catherine Leterrier; Editors, Maryline Monthieux; Music, Gabriel Yared; an ARP production, France 2 Cinéma and France 3 Cinéma presentation of a Canal+ production with the support of La Région Ile de France; French; Dolby; CinemaScope; Color; Rated PG-13; 114 minutes; American release date: March 19, 2004

Cast

Viviane	**Isabelle Adjani**
Beaufort	**Gérard Depardieu**
Camille	**Virginie Ledoyen**
Raoul	**Yvan Attal**
Frédéric	**Grégori Derangère**
Winckler	**Peter Coyote**
Kopolski	**Jean-Marc Stehlé**
Jacqueline de Lusse	**Aurore Clément**
Brémond	**Xavier de Guillebon**
Madame Arbesault	**Edith Scob**
Monsieur Girard	**Michel Vuillermoz**
Andé Arpel	**Nicolas Pignon**
Thierry Arpel	**Nicolas Vaude**
Maurice/Studio Attendant	**Pierre Diot**
The Erudite	**Pierre Laroche**

and Catherine Chevalier (The Erudite's Daughter), Morgane Moré (The Erudite's Granddaughter), Olivier Claverie (Maître Vouriot), Wolfgang Pissors (German Agent), Jacques Pater (Albert de Lusse), Jean Pol Brissart (Hotel Concierge), Vincent Nemeth (The Maître d'), Benjamin Bellecour (Bellhop), Marie-Armelle Deguy (The Socialite), Marie-Christine Orry (The Salesgirl), Serpentine Teyssier (Beaufort's Secretary), Patrick Médioni (The Commissioner), Gary Matthews (English Officer), Benoît Bellal (French Policeman), Christian Drillaud, Michel Dubois, Christian Ruché, Jacques Roehrich, Robert Darmel (Parliament Members), Gérard Collewaert (Session President)

Grégori Derangère, Gérard Depardieu

On the eve of the German occupation of Paris, a disparate group of celebrities, spies, and government officials converge at the Hotel Splendide in Bordeaux.

Peter Coyote, Wolfgang Pissors

Virginie Ledoyen, Jean-Marc Stehlé PHOTOS COURTESY OF SONY CLASSICS

DOGVILLE

(LIONS GATE) Producer, Vibeke Windeløv; Executive Producer, Peter Aalbaek Jensen; Co-Producers, Gillian Berrie, Bettina Brokemper, Anja Grafers, Els Vandervorst; Co-Executive Producers, Lene Borglum, Peter Garde, Lars Johnsson, Marianne Slot; Director/Screenplay, Lars von Trier; Photography, Anthony Dod Mantle; Designer, Peter Grant; Costumes, Manon Rasmussen; Production Design Creative Consultant, Karl Juliusson; Editor, Molly Malene Stensgaard; Casting, Avy Kaufmann, Joyce Nettles; a Zentropa Entertainments8 APS production in association with Isabella Films Intl., Something Else, Memfis Film Intl., Trollhattan Film, Pain Unlimited, Sigma Films/Zoma, Slot Machine Sarl/Liberator 2 Sarl; Danish-Swedish-British-French-German-Dutch, 2003; Dolby; HD 24P Widescreen; Color; Rated R; 177 minutes; American release date: March 26, 2004

Nicole Kidman

Nicole Kidman

Paul Bettany, Nicole Kidman

Cast

Grace **Nicole Kidman**
Gloria **Harriet Andersson**
Ma Ginger **Lauren Bacall**
The Man with the Big Hat **Jean-Marc Barr**
Tom Edison **Paul Bettany**
Mrs. Henson **Blair Brown**
The Big Man **James Caan**
Vera **Patricia Clarkson**
Bill Henson **Jeremy Davies**
Jack McKay **Ben Gazzara**
Tom Edison, Sr. **Philip Baker Hall**
Gangsters **Thom Hoffman, John Randolph Jones**
Martha **Siobhan Fallon Hogan**
Narrator **John Hurt**
Ben **Zeljko Ivanek**
The Man in the Coat **Udo Kier**
Olivia **Cleo King**
Jason **Miles Purinton**
Mr. Henson **Bill Raymond**
Liz Henson **Chloë Sevigny**

and Shauna Shim (June), Stellan Skarsgard (Chuck), Evelina Brinkemo (Athena), Anna Brobeck (Olympia), Tilde Lindgren (Pandora), Evelina Lundqvist (Diana), Helga Olofsson (Dahlia).

A young woman on the run ends up in a seemingly peaceful Rocky Mountain hamlet where she is subjected to all sorts of torment and indignities by the close-knit residents.

Chloë Sevigny PHOTOS COURTESY OF LIONS GATE

Heath Ledger, Orlando Bloom

NED KELLY

(FOCUS) Producers, Lynda House, Nelson Woss; Executive Producers, Tim Bevan, Eric Fellner, Tim White; Co-Producers, Debra Hayward, Liza Chasin; Director, Gregor Jordan; Screenplay, John Michael McDonagh; Based on the novel *Our Sunshine* by Robert Drewe; Photography, Oliver Stapleton; Designer, Steven Jones-Evans; Costumes, Anna Borghesi; Music, Klaus Badelt; Music Supervisor, Nick Angel; Editor, Jon Gregory; Casting, Christine King, Jina Jay; a Universal Pictures/Studio Canal/Working Title Films presentation of an Endymion Films production, in association with WTA; Australian-British, 2003; Dolby; Super 35 Widescreen; Cinevex Color; Rated R; 109 minutes; American release date: March 26, 2004

Cast

Ned Kelly **Heath Ledger**
Joe Byrne **Orlando Bloom**
Julia Cook **Naomi Watts**
Superintendent Francis Hare **Geoffrey Rush**
Mrs. Scott **Rachel Griffiths**
Dan Kelly **Laurence Kinlan**
Steve Hart **Philip Barantini**
Aaron Sherritt **Joel Edgerton**
Fitzpatrick **Kirk Paramore**
Kate Kelly **Kerry Condon**
Grace Kelly **Emily Browning**
Mr. Scott **Geoff Morrell**
Premier Berry **Charles "Bud" Tingwell**

and Saskia Burmeister (Jane Jones), Peter Phelps (Lonigan), Russell Dykstra (Wild Wright), Nick Farnell (Tom Lloyd), Russell Gilbert (Constable Hall), Brooke Harmon (Maggie), Molly McCaffrey (Fanny Shaw), Tim Wright (McIntyre), Nicholas Bell (Richard Cook), Anthony Hayes (Kennedy), Jonathan Hardy (The Great Orlando), Karen Davitt (Anne Jones), Declan Simpson (Johnny Jones), Andrew S. Gilbert (Stanistreet), Jerome Ehlers, Robert Taylor, Warwick Sadler, Morgan Evans (Sherrit Troopers), Warwick Yuen (Chinese Miner), John Muirhead (Rev. Gribble), Bernard Fanning (Irish Singer), Eddy McShortall (Scanlon), Sharlene Yeh (Laundry Girl), Damian Walshe-Howling, John Davidson,

Chris Birt, Peter Forster (Glenrowan Policemen), Peter O'Shea (Reardon), Nick Bourke (Martin Cherry), Christopher Baker (Curnow), Brian Wray (Bracken), Thea Gumbert (Mary Hegarty), Gregan O'Leary (Edward Rogers), Chris Wilson (Odea), Graham Jahne (Whelan), Clayton Jacobson (Sullivan), Cody O'Prey (Young Ned), Tasman Vaughan (Richard Shelton), Greg Saunders (Mr. Shelton), Victoria Eagger (Mrs. Shelton), Peter Young (Red Kelly), Jessica Hall (Girl on Aaron's Knee), Monty Maizels (Greta Old Man), Sarah Pass (Older Barmaid), Alexander Ramsey (James Cook), Samuel Shepherd (Matthew Cook), Dan Bourke, Anthony O'Neill, Paddy O'Neill, Steve Simmonds (Imperial Hotel Musicians), Edward Carisbrooke (Young Cook Stablehand), Erika Felton (Toddler Ellen Kelly), Frank McGree (Greta Policeman), Talia Zucker (Sarah Wicks), Laurie Jensen (Wicks), Jim Howes (Glenrowan Train Doctor), Michael Williams (Glenrowan Train Policeman), Lucy Christopher (Jerilderie Young Woman), Thomas Blackburne (Jerilderie Boy), Jim Russell (Jerilderie Man), Mandy McElhinney (Jerilderie Woman), David Ngoombujarra (Tribesman), John Bolger (Glenrowan Train Priest), Matt Monly (Spitting Farmer), David Miller, Neil Dibbs (Prisoner Warden), Eileen Dibbs (Jerilderie Hostage)

Laurence Kinlan, Orlando Bloom, Philip Barantini, Heath Ledger

Heath Ledger, Naomi Watts PHOTOS COURTESY OF FOCUS

True story of how Irish Catholic farmer Ned Kelly became a folk hero helping the oppressed immigrants in 1800s Australia. Previous film, *Ned Kelly* (UA, 1970) starred Mick Jagger.

SHAOLIN SOCCER

(MIRAMAX) a.k.a. *Siu lam juk kau*; Producer, Kwok-fai Yeung; Director, Stephen Chow; Screenplay, Stephen Chow, Kan-Cheung Tsang; Photography, Pak-huen Kwen, Ting Wo Kwong; Art Director, Kim Hung Ho; Costumes, Yim Man Choy; Music, Lowell Lo, Raymond Wong; Editor, Kit-Wait Kai; a Star Overseas, Universe Entertainment production; Hong Kong, 2001; Dolby; Color; Rated PG; 87 minutes; American release date: April 2, 2004

Stephen Chow (right)

Cast

Sing (Brother #5) **Stephen Chow**
Mui **Vicki Zhao**
Golden Leg Fung **Man Tat Ng**
Hung **Patrick Tse**
Iron Head (Big Brother #1) **Yut Fei Wong**
Dragons Soccer Players **Cecilia Cheung, Karen Mok**
Empty Hand (Brother #4) **Kwok Kuen Chan**
1st Opponent Soccer Player **Vincent Kok**
Weight Vest (Little Brother #6) **Chi Chung Lam**
Hooking Leg (Brother #2) **Chi-Sing Lam**
Girl on the Street **Hui Li**
Iron Shirt **Kai Man Tin**

A soccer player recruits a kung-fu master to help him put together a team to defeat those responsible for his injury.

Stephen Chow (left) PHOTOS COURTESY OF MIRAMAX

Young-soo Oh, Yeo-jin Ha

SPRING, SUMMER, FALL, WINTER...AND SPRING

(SONY CLASSICS) a.k.a. *Bom yeorum gaeul gyeol geurigo bom*; Producer, Lee Seung-jae; Executive Producer, Soma Chung; Co-Producers, Karl Baumgartner, Raimond Goebel, Kim Soheui; Director/Screenplay/Editor, Kim Ki-duk; Photography, Baek Dong-hyeon; Art Director, Oh Sang-man; Costumes, Kim Min-heui; Music, Bark Jee-woong; a Korea Pictures Co. presentation in association with Mirae Asset, Muhan Investment Co., iPictures, Cinesoul, B&B, KBS Media and Filmfoergerung Hamburg, of an LJ Film Co. (South Korea)/Pandora Film Produktion (Germany) production; South Korean-German, 2003; Dolby; Color; Not rated; 102 minutes; American release date: April 2, 2004

Cast

Old Monk **Young-soo Oh**
Adult Monk **Ki-duk Kim**
Young Adult Monk **Young-min Kim**
Boy Monk **Jae-kyeong Seo**
The Girl **Yeo-jin Ha**
Child Monk **Jong-ho Kim**

and Jung-young Kim (The Girl's Mother), Dae-han Ji (Detective Ji), Min Choi (Detective Choi), Ji-a Park (Baby's Mother), Min-Young Song (The Baby)

Four stories taking place throughout the year around a lake on which sits a floating monastery.

Yeo-jin Ha, Jae-kyeong Seo PHOTOS COURTESY OF SONY CLASSICS

I'M NOT SCARED

(MIRAMAX) a.k.a. *Io non ho paura*; Producers, Maurizio Totti, Riccardo Tozzi, Giovanni Stabilini, Marco Chimenz; Executive Producer, Maurizio Totti; Director, Gabriele Salvatores; Screenplay, Niccolo Ammaniti, Francesca Marciano; Based on the novel by Niccolo Ammaniti; Photography, Italo Petriccione; Designer, Giancarlo Basili; Costumes, Patrizia Chericoni, Florence Emir; Music, Pepo Scherman, Ezio Bosso; Editor, Massimo Fiocchi; Casting, Fabio Scamoni, Fabiola Banzi; a Colorado Film, Catteya presentation of a Colorado Film, Cattelya (Italy)/Alquimia Cinema (Spain)/the Producers Films (Not Scared) (U.K.) production in association with Medusa Film; Dolby; Panalight Widescreen; Cinecitta Color; Rated R; 101 minutes; American release date: April 9, 2004

Cast
Anna **Aitana Sanchez Gijon**
Pino **Dino Abbrescia**
Felice **Giorgio Careccia**
Michele **Giuseppe Cristiano**
Filippo **Mattia Di Perro**
Sergio **Diego Abatantuono**
Barbara **Adrianna Conserva**
Teschio **Giulia Matturo**
Salvatore **Stefano Biase**
Remo **Fabio Antonacci**

and Antonella Stefanucci (Assunta), Riccardo Zinna (Pietro), Michele Vasca (Candela), Sausy Sanchez (Filippo's Mother)

A little boy is startled to find another boy hidden in a hole in his Sicilian village.

Giuseppe Cristiano

Giuseppe Cristiano PHOTOS COURTESY OF MIRAMAX

YOUNG ADAM

(SONY CLASSICS) Producer, Jeremy Thomas; Director/Screenplay, David MacKenzie; Based on the novel by Alexander Trocchi; Co-Producers, Alexandra Stone, Nick O'Hagan, Jim Reeve; Associate Producers, Peter Watson, Stephan Mallmann, Gillian Berrie; Photography, Giles Nuttgens; Production Designer, Laurence Dorman; Costumes, Jacqueline Durran; Music, David Byrne; Editor, Colin Monie; Casting, Des Hamilton; a Recorded Picture Company, Hanway, Film Council, Scottish Screen and Sveno Media presentation of a Jeremy Thomas production; British-Scottish-French. 2003; Dolby; Color; Rated NC-17; 98 minutes; American release date: April 16, 2004

Tilda Swinton, Ewan McGregor

Ewan McGregor, Emily Mortimer

Cast
Joe **Ewan McGregor**
Ella **Tilda Swinton**
Les **Peter Mullan**
Cathie **Emily Mortimer**
Jim **Jack McElhone**
Gwen **Therese Bradley**
Daniel Gordon **Ewan Stewart**
Bill **Stuart McQuarrie**
Connie **Pauline Turner**
Bob M'bussi **Alan Cooke**
Sam **Rory McCann**

Peter Mullan, Ewan McGregor

and Ian Hanmore (Freight Supervisor), Andrew Neil (Barman), Arnold Brown (Bowler Hat Man), Meg Fraser (Stall Woman), Stuart Bowman, Wullie Brennan, Rony Bridges, John Kazek, Duncan McHardy, Stewart Porter, Malcom Shields (Black Street Pub Men), Tam Dean Burn (Black Street Barman), Michael Carter (Prosecutor), Struan Rodger (Judge), Matthew Zajac (Forensics Expert), Mhairi Steenbock (Cathie's Flatmate), John Comerford (Jury Foreman), Anne Marie Timoney (Mrs. Gordon), John Yule (Clerk of the Court), Sandy Neilson (Defence Council), Des Hamilton (Witness), Eddie Dahlstrom (Blind Man)

Joe, a young drifter, and his employer come across the corpse of a girl, whose death Joe may know more about than he reveals.

Emily Mortimer, Ewan McGregor PHOTOS COURTESY OF SONY CLASSICS

Miranda Otto

(front) Shirley Henderson, Corin Redgrave

Sophie Stuckey, Goran Visnjic PHOTOS COURTESY OF FIRST LOOK

CLOSE YOUR EYES

(FIRST LOOK) a.k.a. *Hypnotic* and *Doctor Sleep*; Producer, Michelle Camarda; Executive Producers, David M. Thompson, Mike Phillips; Director, Nick Willing; Screenplay, Nick Willing, William Brookfield; Based on the novel *Doctor Sleep* by Madison Smartt Bell; Photography, Peter Sova; Designer, Don Taylor; Costumes, Hazel Pethig; Makeup Effects, Neill R. Gorton; Music, Simon Boswell; Editor, Niven Howie; Casting, Jina Jay, Avy Kaufman; a BBC Films, the Film Consortium presentation in association with the Film Council of a Kismet Film CO. production; British; Dolby; Panavision; Deluxe color; Rated R; 103 minutes; American release date: April 23, 2004

Shirley Henderson, Goran Visnjic

Cast
Dr. Michael Stroker **Goran Visnjic**
Det. Janet Losey **Shirley Henderson**
Clara Strother **Miranda Otto**
Elliot Spruggs **Paddy Considine**
Grace **Claire Rushbrook**
Prof. Catherine Lebourg **Fiona Shaw**
Chief Inspector Clements **Corin Redgrave**
Keith **Josh Richards**
Police Inspector Hilary Ash **Sarah Woodward**
Lebourg's Son **Andrew Woodall**
Martha Strother **Lauren Gabrielle Volpert**
Nursing Home Doctor **John Bett**
Heather **Sophie Stuckey**

and Steve Nye, Joshua McGowan (Young Boys), Angus Wright (Bicycle Man), Tam Dean Burn (Gas Man), Anthony Denham (Police Guard), Howard Lee (Cab Driver), Don McCorkindale (Doorman), John Rogan (Francis Paladine), Andrew French (Police Detective), Gerald Lepkowski (Journalist), Shammi Aulakh (Hotel Desk Clerk), Madison Smartt Bell (Hypnotic Patient), Colin Farrell (Theatre Security Man), Patrick Walton Jr. (Demon in Stomach)

A hypnotist is enlisted to help Scotland Yard catch a serial killer.

LAWS OF ATTRACTION

(NEW LINE CINEMA) Producers, David Bergstein, Beau St. Clair, Julie Durk, David T. Friendly, Marc Turtletaub; Executive Producers, Toby Emmerich, Guy Stodel, Oliver Hengst, Bob Yari, Mark Gordon, Mark Gill, Arthur Lappin, Elie Samaha, Pierce Brosnan, Basil Iwanyk; Director, Peter Howitt; Screenplay, Aline Brosh McKenna, Robert Harling; Story, Aline Brosh McKenna; Co-Producer, Paul Myler; Photography, Adrian Biddle; Designer, Charles J. H. Wood; Costumes, Joan Bergin; Music, Edward Shearmur; Editor, Tony Lawson; Casting, John and Ros Hubbard; a Deep River/Irish Dreamtime production in association with Fern Valley Limited, in association with Stratus Film Company, Intermedia, MHF Zweite Academy Film and Initial Entertainment Group; British-Irish; Dolby; Panavision; Deluxe color; Rated PG-13; 90 minutes; American release date: April 30, 2004

Parker Posey, Pierce Brosnan

Julianne Moore, Pierce Brosnan

Michael Sheen, Julianne Moore

Cast

Daniel Rafferty	**Pierce Brosnan**
Audrey Woods	**Julianne Moore**
Thorne Jamison	**Michael Sheen**
Serena	**Parker Posey**
Sara Miller	**Frances Fisher**
Judge Abramovitz	**Nora Dunn**
Leslie	**Heather Ann Nurnberg**
Ashton Phelps	**Johnny Myers**
Michael Rawson	**Mike Doyle**
Adamo Shandela	**Allan Houston**
TV Host	**Annie Ryan**
Lyman Hersh	**Vincent Marzello**
Waitress	**Sarah James**
Legal TV Reporter	**John Discepolo**
TV Reporter	**Annika Pergament**
Judge Withers	**Marc Turtletaub**
Judge Baker	**Gordan Sterne**
Mary Harrison	**Brette Taylor**
Mr. O'Callaghan	**Brendan Morrissey**
Mrs. Flanagan	**Elva Crowley**

and David Wilmot (Brendan), David Pearse (Pig Farmer), Nuala Kelly (Large Irish Woman), Liz Byrne (Stewardess), David Kelly (Priest/Michael), Peter Balance (Check-in Clerk), Des Fleming (Waiter), James McClatchie (Soloman Steinman), Sarah Gilbert (Gary Gadget's Assistant), Nick Hardin (Man in Bathroom), Brian O'Neill (Limo Driver)

A pair of high powered New York attorneys, pitted against each other on opposite sides of a nasty divorce settlement, find themselves accidentally married after a drunken night at an Irish county festival.

Pierce Brosnan, Frances Fisher PHOTOS COURTESY OF NEW LINE CINEMA

THE SADDEST MUSIC IN THE WORLD

(IFC FILMS) Producer, Niv Fichman, Jody Shapiro; Executive Producers, Atom Egoyan, Daniel Iron; Co-Producer, Phyllis Laing; Director, Guy Maddin; Screenplay, Guy Maddin, George Toles; Based on an original screenplay by Kazuo Ishiguro; Photography, Luc Montpellier; Designer, matthew Davis; Music, Christopher Dedrick; Editor, David Wharnsby; Casting, John Buchan; a Rhombus Media/Buffalo Gal Pictures production in association with Ego Film Arts; Canadian; Black and white/color; Rated R; 99 minutes; American release date: April 30, 2004

Isabella Rosselini, Mark McKinney PHOTOS COURTESY OF IFC FILMS

Cast

Chester Kent **Mark McKinney**
Lady Port-Huntly **Isabella Rossellini**
Narcissa **Maria de Medeiros**
Fyodor **David Fox**
Roderick Kent **Rose McMillan**
Blind Seer **Louis Negin**
Teddy **Darcy Fehr**
Duncan **Claude Dorge**
Mary **Talia Pura**

and Jeff Sutton (Young Chester), Graeme Valentin (Young Roderick), Maggie Nagle (Chester's Mother), Victor Cowie (Man in Bar), Jessica Burleson (Lady's Secretary), Wayne Nicklas (Boardmember), Nancy Drake (American Mother), David Gillies (American Father), Daphne Korol (Widow), Adriana O'Neil (Agnes), Jeff Skinner (Reverend), Craig Aftanas (Old Sleepwalker), Miles Boiselle (Guard), Brock MacGregor (Roderick's Son)

During the Depression beer baroness Lady Port-Huntly announces a competition to find the saddest music in the world, for a cash prize of $25,000.

Julieta Cardinali, Rodrigo Noya

VALENTÍN

(MIRAMAX) Producers, Julio Fernandez, Thierry Forte, Laurens Geels, Massimo Vigliar, Pablo Wisznia; Executive Producer, Eddy de Kroes; Co-Producer, Annemiek van Gorp; Director/Screenplay, Alejandro Agresti; Photography, Jose Luis Cajaraville; Designer, Floris Vos; Costumes, Marisa Urruti; Music, Paul M. van Brugge, Luis Salinas; Editor, Alejandro Brodersohn; a co-production of Castelao Producciones S.A., DMVB Films, First Floor Features, Patagonik Film Group, RWA, Surf Film; Argentine-Dutch-French-Italian-Spanish, 2002; Dolby; Color; Rated PG-13; 86 minutes; American release date: May 7, 2004

Cast

Leticia **Julieta Cardinali**
Abuela **Carmen Maura**
El tio Chiche **Jean Pierre Noher**
Rufo **Mex Urtizberea**
Valentín **Rodrigo Noya**
Father **Alejandro Agresti**
Dr. Galaburri **Carlos Roffé**
Man in Bar **Lorenzo Quinteros**
La Maestra **Marina Glezer**
Roberto **Stéfano Di Gregorio**
El Cura **Fabián Vena**

An eight-year-old boy makes it his mission to bring together his separated parents and save his dysfunctional family.

Rodrigo Noya, Carmen Maura PHOTOS COURTESY OF MIRAMAX

CARANDIRU

(SONY CLASSICS) Producer/Director, Hector Babenco; Screenplay, Victor Nava, Hector Babenco, Fernando Bonassi; Based on the book *Carandiru Station* by Drauzio Varella; Photography, Walter Carvalho; Designer, Clovis Bueno; Costumes, Cristina Camargo; Music, Andre Abujamra; Editor, Mauro Alice; Casting, Vivian Golombeck; an HB Filmes presentation in association with Columbia TriStar do Brasil, Globo Filmes and Br Petrobas; Brazilian, 2003; Dolby; Color; Rated R; 148 minutes; American release date: May 14, 2004

Rodrigo Santoro, Gero Camilo PHOTO COURTESY OF SONY CLASSICS

Cast

Doctor **Luis Carlos Vaesconcelos**
Chico **Milton Gonçalves**
Ebony **Ivan de Almeida**
Dagger **Milhem Cortaz**
Highness **Ailton Graca**
Dalva **Maria Louis Mendonca**
Rosirene **Aida Lerner**
Lady Di **Rodrigo Santoro**
No Way **Gero Camilo**
Herself **Rita Cadillac**

and Lazaro Ramos (Ezequiel), Caio Blat (Deusdete), Wagner Loura (Zico), Julia Ianina (Francineide), Sabrina Greve (Catarina), Floriano Peixoto (Antonio Carlos), Ricardo Blat (Claudiomiro), Vanessa Gerbelli (Celia), Leona Cavalli (Dina), Dionisio Neto (Lula), Antonio Grassi (Warden Pires), Enrique Diaz (Gilson), Robson Nunes (Dada), Andre Ceccato (Beard), Bukassa (Radio Announcer), Sabotage (Fuinha), Gabriel Braga Nunes (Sergio), Walter Breda (Antonio), Jose de Paiva (Charuto), Sergio Loroza (Gordo), Nelson Machado (Carioca), Nill Marcondes (Pimenta), Mauricio Marques (Dalva's Boyfriend), Luis Miranda (Paulo Boca), Marcelo Palmares (Coelho), Silvio Roberto (Baiano), Regis Santos (Mario Cachorro), Drauzio Varella (Himself)

A look inside Sao Pauolo's notorious House of Detention's AIDS-prevention program, as seen through the eyes of an idealistic doctor.

Emmanuelle Béart, Gaspard Ulliel

STRAYED

(WELLSPRING) Producer, Jean-Pierre Ramsay-Levi; Executive Producers, Adam Betteridge, David Rogers; Co-Producers, Michael Cowan, Pierre Héros, Jason Piette; Director, André Téchiné; Screenplay, Gilles Taurand, André Téchiné; Based on the novel *Le Garçon aus Yeux Girls* by Gilles Taurand; Photography, Agnès Godard; Designer, Zé Branco; Costumes, Christian Gasc; Music, Philippe Sarde; Editor, Martine Giordano; Casting, Jacques Grant; co-production of FIT Productions, Spice Factory, and France 2 Cinéma, with the participation of Canal+, Gimages 6, Centre National de la Cinématographie (CNC), Conseil Régional Midi-Pyrénées; French-British, 2003; Dolby; Color; Not rated; 95 minutes; American release date: May 14, 2004

Cast

Odile **Emmanuelle Béart**
Yvan **Gaspard Ulliel**
Philippe **Grégoire Leprince-Ringuet**
Cathy **Clémence Meyer**
Robert **Samuel Labarthe**
Georges **Jean Fornerod**

and Eric Kreikenmayer (Guard), Nicholas Mead (Injured Soldier), Robert Eliott (Young Policeman), Nigel Hollidge (Refugee)

Fleeing Nazi-occupied Paris with her children, a widowed schoolteacher is assisted by a teen boy who teaches the family to survive.

Emmanuelle Béart, Clémence Meyer, Gaspard Ulliel, Grégoire Leprince-Ringuet
PHOTOS COURTESY OF WELLSPRING

TROY

(WARNER BROS.) Producers, Wolfgang Petersen, Diana Rathbun, Colin Wilson; Director, Wolfgang Petersen; Screenplay, David Benioff; Inspired by Homer's *The Iliad*; Photography, Roger Pratt; Designer, Nigel Phelps; Costumes, Bob Ringwood; Music, James Horner; Song: "Remember" by James Horner (music) and Cynthia Weil (lyrics)/performed by Josh Groban with Tanja Tzarovska; Editor, Peter Honess; Co-Producer, Winston Azzopardi; Visual Effects Supervisor, Nick Davis; Second Unit Director/Stunts, Simon Crane; Casting, Lucinda Syson; a Radiant production, in association with Plan B; British-Maltese; Dolby; Super 35 Widescreen; Technicolor; Rated R; 161 minutes; American release date: May 14, 2004

Diane Kruger

Brian Cox, Brendan Gleeson

Rose Byrne

Cast

Achilles **Brad Pitt**
Hector **Eric Bana**
Paris **Orlando Bloom**
Helen **Diane Kruger**
Agamemnon **Brian Cox**
Odysseus **Sean Bean**
King Menelaus **Brendan Gleeson**
King Priam **Peter O'Toole**
Briseis **Rose Byrne**
Andromache **Saffron Burrows**
Thetis **Julie Christie**
Triopas **Julian Glover**
Boagrius **Nathan Jones**
Agamemnon's Officer **Adoni Maropis**
Messenger Boy **Jacob Smith**
Nestor **John Shrapnel**
Polydora **Siri Svegler**
Helen's Handmaiden **Lucie Barat**
Hippasus **Ken Bones**

Brad Pitt PHOTOS COURTESY OF WARNER BROS.

Eric Bana, Orlando Bloom

Old Spartan Fisherman **Manuel Cauchi**
Tecton **Mark Lewis Jones**
Patroclus **Garrett Hedlund**
Glaucus **James Cosmo**
Archeptolemus **Nigel Terry**
Velior **Trevor Eve**
Lysander **Owain Yeoman**
Scamandrius **Luke & Matthew Tal**
Eudorus **Vincent Regan**
Ajax **Tyler Mane**
Aphareus **Louis Dempsey**
Haemon **Joshua Richards**
Singing Women **Desislava Stefanova, Tanja Tzarovska**
Apolloinian Guard **Alex King**
Aeneas **Frankie Fitzgerald**

When Paris spirits the beautiful Helen away from King Menelaus, Agamemnon seizes this opportunity to attack Troy and take control of the Aegean. Previous film versions of the story include *Helen of Troy* (WB, 1956), starring Rosanna Podesta (Helen), Jacques Sernas (Paris), Stanley Baker (Achilles), and Harry Andrews (Hector).

This film received an Oscar nomination for costume design.

Trojan Horse

Tyler Mane

Peter O'Toole, Orlando Bloom

Rose Byrne, Brad Pitt

Garrett Hedlund

LOVE ME IF YOU DARE

(PARAMOUNT CLASSICS) a.k.a. *Jeux d'enfants*; Producer, Christophe Rossignon; Executive Producer, Eve Machuel; Co-Producers, Patrick Quinet, Stephen Quinet; Director, Yann Samuell; Screenplay, Yann Samuell, Jacky Cuckier; Photography, Antoine Roch; Art Director, Jean-Michel Simonet; Costumes, Julie Mauduech; Music, Philippe Rombi; Editor, Andrea Sedlackova; Casting, Gigi Akoka; a Nord-Quest presentation of a Nord-Quest Prod., Studio-Canal, Artemis Prod., France 2 Cinema, M6 Films, Caneo Films (France)/Media Services (Belgium) production; French-Belgian; Dolby; Color; Rated R; 94 minutes; American release date: May 21, 2004

Joséphine Lebas-Joly, Thibault Verhaeghe

Guillaume Canet, Marion Cotillard in *Love Me if You Dare* PHOTOS COURTESY OF PARAMOUNT CLASSICS

Cast

Julien Jeanvier **Guillaume Canet**
Sophie Kowalski **Marion Cotillard**
Julien at 8 years **Thibault Verhaeghe**
Sophie at 8 years **Joséphine Lebas-Joly**
Julien's Mother **Emmanuelle Grönvold**
Julien's Father **Gérard Watkins**
Sergie Nimov Nimovitch **Gilles Lellouche**
Sophie's Sister **Julia Faure**
Christelle Louise Bouchard **Laëtizia Venezia Tarnowska**
Aurélie Miller **Elodie Navarre**

and Nathalie Mattier (Sophie at 80), Robert Willar (Julien at 80), Frédéric Geerts (Igor), Manuela Sanchez (Teacher), Philippe Drecq (School Principal), Luc Bromagne (Priest), Jean-Michel Flagothier (Dorzac), Stéphane Auberghen (Proctor), Isabelle Delval (Clothilde), Emmanuel LeMire, Christophe Rossignon (Doctors), Nathalie Philip (Julien's Nurse), Delphine Aerts (Senior Center Nurse), Isabelle Goethals Carre (Senior Center Director), Mathilde Verkinderen (Charlotte at 8 years), Melchior LeBeaut (Julien at 4 years), Jessica Rinalo, Emmanuel Brunin, Joeffrey Simon, Amandine Courrire, Jessica Vitello (Childern), Michel Angely (Bus Driver), Fernand Kindt (Scrabble Player), Cedric Lombard (Library Student)

Julien and Sophie, life long friends who seem predestined to become lovers, spend their lives challenging one another to accept dares which become increasingly perverse and psychologically damaging.

Jørgen Leth in *The Five Obstructions* PHOTO COURTESY OF KOCH LORBER

THE FIVE OBSTRUCTIONS

(KOCH LORBER) a.k.a. *De Fem Benspaend*; Producer, Carsten Holst; Executive Producers, Pete Aalbaek, Vibeke Windeløv; Directors/Screenplay, Jørgen Leth, Lars Von Trier; Photography, Kim Hattesen, Dan Holmberg; Editors, Camilla Skousen, Morten Højberg; Casting, Marianne Christensen, Magdalena Garcia; Danish-Swiss-Belgian-French; Dolby; Black and white/color; Not rated; 88 minutes; American release date: May 26, 2004

Cast

Speaker/Himself/The Perfect Human **Jørgen Leth**
Himself (Obstructor) **Lars von Trier**
OBSTRUCTION #1—THE PERFECT HUMAN: CUBA
The Perfect Woman **Jacqueline Arenal**
The Perfect Man **Daniel Hernandez Rodriguez**
OBSTRUCTION #3 — THE PERFECT HUMAN: BRUSSELS
The Perfect Woman **Alexandra Vandernoot**
The Perfect Man/Speaker **Patrick Bauchau**
Maid **Marie Dejaer**
Couple **Pascal Perez, Meschell Perez**

Filmmaker Lars von Trier challenges his former teacher, Jørgen Leth, to remake his 1967 short film *The Perfect Human* several times but with a set of restrictions.

THE MOTHER

(SONY CLASSICS) Producer, Kevin Loader; Executive Producers, David M. Thompson, Tracey Scoffield, Angus Finney, Stephen Evans; Director, Roger Michell; Screenplay, Hanif Kureishi; Photography, Alwin Kuchler; Designer, Mark Tildesley; Costumes, Natalie Ward; Music, Jeremy Sams; Editor, Nicolas Gaster; Casting, Mary Selway, Fiona Weir; a BBC Films presentation, in association with Renaissance Films, of a Free Range Films production; British, 2003; Dolby; Color; Rated R; 111 minutes; American release date: May 28, 2004

Daniel Craig, Cathryn Bradshaw

Anne Reid, Daniel Craig

Cast
May **Anne Reid**
Toots **Peter Vaughan**
Helen **Anna Wilson-Jones**
Darren **Daniel Craig**
Au Pair **Danira Govich**
Harry **Harry Michell**
Rosie **Rosie Michell**
Polish Cleaner **Izabella Telezynska**
Bobby **Steven Mackintosh**
Paula **Cathryn Bradshaw**

and Carlo Kureishi, Sachin Kureishi (Jack), Simon Mason (Man in Tate Gallery), Oliver Ford Davies (Bruce), Jonah Coombes (Estate Agent)

Following her husband's sudden death May finds herself unexpectedly having an affair with her daughter Paula's lover, Darren.

Anne Reid, Cathryn Bradshaw

Anne Reid PHOTOS COURTESY OF SONY CLASSICS

The Story of the Weeping Camel

The Story of the Weeping Camel

The Story of the Weeping Camel PHOTOS COURTESY OF THINKFILM

THE CORPORATION

(ZEITGEIST) Producers, Mark Achbar, Bart Simpson; Executive Producer, Mark Achbar; Co-Producers, Cari Green, Nathan Neumer, Tom Shandel; Directors, Mark Achbar, Jennifer Abbott; Screenplay, Joel Bakan, Harold Crooks, Mark Achbar; Based on the book *The Corporation: The Pathological Pursuit of Profit and Power* by Joel Bakan; Photography, Mark Achbar, Rolf Cutts, Jeff Koffman, Kirk Tougas; Music, Leonard J. Paul; Editor, Jennifer Abbott; Archival Researcher, Paula Sawadasky; Narrator, Mikela J. Mikael; a Big Picture Media Corp. production in association with TV Ontario, Vision TV, Knowledge Network, Saskatchewan Communications Network and ACCESS the Education Station; Canadian; Color, Bigital Betacam; Not rated; 145 minutes; American release date: June 4, 2004. Documentary chronicling the history and expanding power of corporations.

With

Jane Akre, Ray Anderson, Joe Badaracco, Maude Barlow, Mark Barry, Elain Bernard, Edwin Black, Carlton Brown, Noam Chomsky, Chris Barrett, Luke McCabe, Peter Drucker, Dr. Samuel Epstein, Andrea Finger, Milton Friedman, Sam Gibara, Richard Grossman, Dr. Robert Hare, Gabriel Herbas, Lucy Hughes, Ira Jackson, Charles Kerngahan, Robert Keyes, Mark Kingwell, Naomi Klein, Tom Kline, Chris Komisarjevsky, Dr. Susan Linn, Robert Monks, Sir Mark Moody-Stuart, Michael Moore, Oscar Olivera, Jonathon Ressler, Jeremy Rifkin, Anita Roddick, Dr. Vandana Shiva, Clay Timon, Michael Walker, Robert Weissman, Steve Wilson, Irving Wladawsky-Berger, Mary Zepernick, Howard Zinn.

The Corporation PHOTO COURTESY OF ZEITGEIST

THE STORY OF THE WEEPING CAMEL

(THINKFILM) a.k.a. *Die Geschichte vom Weinenden Kamel;* Producer, Natalie Lambsdorff; Executive Producer, Tobias N. Siebert; Directors/Screenplay, Byambasuren Davaa, Luigi Falorni; Photography, Luigi Falorni; Music, Marcel Leniz; Editor, Anja Pohl; an HFF Munich production, in association with Bayerischer Rundfunk; German, 2003; Dolby; Color; Not rated; 87 minutes; American release date: June 4, 2004. Documentary on a family of camel herders in Mongolia's Gobi Desert and their efforts to get a mother camel to nurse the baby she's rejected.

This film received an Oscar nomination for documentary, feature.

SEDUCING DR. LEWIS

(WELLSPRING) a.k.a. *La Grande séduction*; Producers, Roger Frappier, Luc Vandal; Director, Jean-Francois Pouliot; Screenplay, Ken Scott; Photography, Allen Smith; Designer, Daniel Hamelin; Costumes, Louise Gagne; Music, Jean-Marie Benoit; Editor, Dominique Fortin; Casting, Lucie Robitaille; a Max Films production; Canadian, 2003; Dolby; Technicolor; Not rated; 108 minutes; American release date: June 16, 2004

David Boutin, Lucie Laurier

Benoît Briere, Raymond Bouchard, Pierre Collin

A small Quebec fishing village is promised a new factory if they are able to entice a full-time physician to live there.

Cast

Germain Lesage **Raymond Bouchard**
Christopher Lewis **David Boutin**
Henri Giroux **Benoit Briere**
Steve Laurin **Bruno Blanchet**
Yvon Brunet **Pierre Collin**
Eve Beauchemin **Lucie Laurier**
Helen Lesage **Rita Lafontaine**
Jeune Germain **Dominic Michon-Dagenais**
Rolland Lesage **Guy-Daniel Tremblay**
Simone Lesage **Nadia Drouin**
Charles Campeau **Roc LaFortune**
Denis Lacoste **Réal Bossé**
Claude Larivée **Guy Villancourt**
Richard Auger **Ken Scott**
Réal Fournier **Jean-Pierre Gonthier**

and Benoît Brière (Henri Giroux), Marc Legault (Marcel Sigouin), Caroline Girard (Lucie Giroux), Betty Jones (Marlène Giroux), Denis Houle (Barman), Claude Gasse (Waiter), Nadia Roswell (Valérie Fournier), Alexandrine Agostini (Francine Fournier), Gilles Pelletier (Alphonse Pinsonneault), Frédéric Desager (Dr. Paul Gosselin), Philippe Daneault (Le Coureur), Marie-France Lambert (Sylvie Auger), Louis-Philippe Dury (Jules Auger), Raphaël Grenier (Jacob Auger), Clémence DesRochers (Clothilde Brunet), Daniel Rousse (Marcel Thibodeau), Caroline Néron (Voix de Brigitte????), Louis Wiriot (Cuisinier), Serge Christianssens (Monsieur Nadeau), Donald Pilon (Monsieur Dupre), Louis Philippe Dandenault (Bertrand Pitt), Manon Gauthier (Mireille Laurin), Véronique Pinette (Chloé Landry), Giséle Trèpanier (Denise Campeau), Nathalie Gascon (Madame Martin), Luc-Martial Dagenais (Avocat)

Raymond Bouchard, David Boutin PHOTOS COURTESY OF WELLSPRING

Jackie Chan, Cécile de France, Steve Coogan

AROUND THE WORLD IN 80 DAYS

(TOUCHSTONE) Producers, Hal Lieberman, Bill Badalato; Executive Producers, Jackie Chan, Willie Chan, Solon So, Alex Schwartz, Phyllis Alia; Co-Producers, Henning Mofenter, Thierry Potok; Director, Frank Coraci; Screenplay, David Titcher, David Benullo, David Goldstein; Based on the novel by Jules Verne; Photography, Phil Meheux; Designer, Perry Andelin Blake; Costumes, Anna Sheppard; Editor, Tom Lewis; Music, Trevor Jones; Visual Effects Producer, Susan Zwerman; Casting, Avy Kaufman; Stunt Choreography, Jackie Chan; Jackie Chan Stunt/Action Coordinator, Chung Chi "Nicky" Li; British-German-Irish; Dolby; Super 35 Widescreen; Color; Rated PG; 116 minutes; American release date: June 16, 2004

Cast

Passpartout (Lau Xing) **Jackie Chan**
Phileas Fogg **Steve Coogan**
Lord Kelvin **Jim Broadbent**
Monique La Roche **Cécile de France**
Inspector Fix **Ewen Bremner**
Lord Kitchener **Ian McNeice**
General Fang **Karen Joy Morris**
Queen Victoria **Kathy Bates**

and Robert Fyfe (Jean Michel), David Ryall (Lord Salisbury), Roger Hammond (Lord Rhodes), Adam Godley (Mr. Sutton), Howard Cooper, Tom Strauss, Kit West (Academy Members), Daniel Hinchcliffe (British Valet), Wolfram Teufel (Belgian Dignitary), Patrick Paroux (French Ticket Clerk), Perry Blake (Vincent van Gogh), Michael Youn (Art Gallery Manager), Eva Ebner (Crazy Lady), Richard Branson (Balloon Man), Macy Gray (Sleeping French Woman), Ben Posener (Angry Engineer), Michael Hoehner (Upset Brakeman), George Inci (Turkish Soldier), Arnold Schwarzenegger (Prince Hapi), Weerathum Wechairuksakul (Gurkha Policeman), Shivesh Ramchandani (Indian Boy), Sirinthorn Ramchandani (Indian Girl), Chris Watkins (British Officer), Kengo Watanabe (Chained Agent), Maggie M. Quigley (Agent), Poon Yin Chi (Lau Xing' Mother), Yotaka Cheukaew (Little

Jing), Sammo Hung (Wong Fei Hung), Parsit Wongrakthai (Man Ting), Teerawat Mulvillai (Fourth Prisoner), Daniel Wu (Bak Mei), Jindarak Satjatepaporn (Village Policeman), Natalie Speri (Stunning Woman), Rob Schneider (San Francisco Hobo), Frank Coraci (Angry Dapper Pedestrian), Luke Wilson (Orville Wright), Owen Wilson (Wilbur Wright), John Keogh (Irish Policeman), Mark Addy (Steamer Captain), John Cleese (Grizzled Sergeant), Will Forte (Young Bobby), Roxanne Borski (Little Girl); Tigers: Wa Chiu Ho (Snake), Wai Ho Yuen (Wu), Wai Luen Tuen (Lung), Ruei Che Chang (Yuen), David Choi Chao (Xing), Hu-Ma Yuan (Crazy Ti), Donald Theerathada (Ho), Tsui-Wei Yin (Yi Yi), Yui Wah Chang, Tung So, Rided Lardpanna, Tat Kwong Chan, Wai Leung Wong, Nattapon Sapaswat, Wai Chung Mak, Chung Kit Li, Gaech Kampakdee, Kwok WL Keung, Tin Hung Yick, Piboon Tailhuan, Anthony Caprio, Haoer Yu, Pradit Seeleum, Kowit Saejoo, Yodying Singpraser, Korawin Pratumsiri, Somchart Kuan-agsorm, Wasin Praipan, Fu Yu Zhang, Pichai Mitari, Nan Zhang, Witchapat Permsaptaweekoon, Wing Fat Chiang (Scorpions)

Eccentric British inventor Phileas Fogg makes a wager with the head of the Royal Academy of Scientists that he can journey around the globe in 80 days. Earlier film of the Verne story starred David Niven (Fogg), Cantinflas (Passepartout), Robert Newton (Fix), and Shirley MacLaine (Princess Aouda), and was released in 1956 by United Artists.

Cécile de France, Steve Coogan, Jackie Chan

Kathy Bates, Jim Broadbent PHOTOS COURTESY OF TOUCHSTONE

I'LL SLEEP WHEN I'M DEAD

(PARAMOUNT CLASSICS) Producers, Michael Kaplan, Michael Corrente; Executive Producer, Roger Marino; Co-Executive Producers, Robert O. Kaplan, Richard E. Johnson, Trisha Van Klaveren; Co-Producer, Marisa Polvino; Director, Mike Hodges; Screenplay, Trevor Preston; Photography, Mike Garfath; Designer, Jon Bunker; Costumes, Evangeline Averre; Music, Simon Fisher Turner; Editor, Paul Carlin; Casting, Leo Davis; a Revere Pictures, Seven Arts presentation of a Will & Co. Prods. production; British-U.S.; Dolby; Technicolor; Rated R; 102 minutes; American release date: June 18, 2004

Cast

Will Graham **Clive Owen**
Helen **Charlotte Rampling**
Davey **Jonathan Rhys-Meyers**
Boad **Malcolm McDowell**
Mickser **Jamie Foreman**
Frank Turner **Ken Stott**
Mrs. Bartz **Sylvia Syms**
Arnie Ryan **Geoff Ball**
Cannibal (Jez) **Desmond Baylis**
Big John **Kirris Riviere**
Al Shaw **Brian Croucher**
Malone **Ross Boatman**
Paulin **Marc O'Shea**

and John Surman (Pathologist), Paul Mohan (Coroner), Damian Dibben (David Myers), Amber Batty (Sheridan), Daisy Beaumont (Stella, Drugs Seeker), Lidija Zovkic (Philippa, Model), Dave Alexander (Little Billy Swan), Lesley Clare O'Neill (Mrs. Turner), Emma Dewhurst (Mrs. Calgani), Francis Magee (Algar, Foreman), Mark Hardy (Calgani), Bruce Byron (Eddy), Jacqueline Defferary (Annie, Waitress), Tim Plester (Hair, Taxi Driver), Noel Clarke (Cyril), Abi Gouhad (Shopkeeper), Peter Sproule (Cyclist), Eric Scruby (Barber), Sophie Jones-Cooper (Hotel Maid)

Will Graham seeks revenge on those responsible for the brutal death of his younger brother.

Charlotte Rampling

Clive Owen

Jonathan Rhys-Meyers PHOTOS COURTESY OF PARAMOUNT CLASSICS

TWO BROTHERS

(UNIVERSAL) Producers, Jean-Jacques Annaud, Jake Eberts; Director/Story, Jean-Jacques Annaud; Screenplay, Alain Godard, Jean-Jacques Annaud; English Dialogue Polished by Julian Fellowes; Photography, Jean-Marie Dreujou; Designer, Pierre Queffelean; Costumes, Pierre-Yves Gayraud; Line Producer, Xavier Castano; Music, Stephen Warbeck; Editor, Noelle Boisson; Tigers Trainer and Director, Thierry Le Portier; Visual Effects, Frederic Moreau; Casting, Francine Maisler, Kathleen Driscoll-Mohler, John and Ros Hubbard, Sophie Blanvillain, Raweeporn Srimonju Jungmeier "Non"; a Pathé presentation of a Pathé Renn Productions/Two Brothers productions, with TF1 Films Production; French-British; Dolby; Panavision; Color; Rated PG; 108 minutes; American release date: June 25, 2004

Tiger cubs in *Two Brothers*

Guy Pearce

Freddie Highmore

Cast

Aidan McRory **Guy Pearce**
Administrator Normandin **Jean-Claude Dreyfus**
Young Raoul **Freddie Highmore**
His Excellency **Oanh Nguyen**
Mrs. Normandin **Philippine Leroy Beaulieu**
Saladin **Moussa Maaskri**
Zerbino **Vincent Scarito**
Naï-Rea **Maï Anh Lê**
The Village Chief **Jaran Phetjareon ("Sitao")**
Miss Paulette **Stephanie Lagarde**
His Execellency's Majordomo **Bernard Flavien**
Sergeant Van Tranh **Annop Vorapanya ("Mu")**
Auctioneer **David Gant**
Verlaine **Teerawat Mulvilai "Ka-Nge"**
Napoléon **Somjin Chimwong "Nen"**
Mrs. Zerbino **Nozha Khouadra**
Dignitary with Goldfish **Pring Sakhorn**
Policeman **Jerry Hoh**

and Juliet Howland (Auction Room Stylish Woman), Caroline Wildi (Auction RooM Companion), Thavirap Tantiwongse (Photographer), Bô Gaulter de Kermoal (Circus Boy), Delphine Kassem (Fleeing Bathing Woman), Alain Fairbairn (Assistant to Auctioneer), Thomas Larget

(Residency Butler), Hy Peahu (Dignitaries' Translator), Luong Ham Chao, Tran Hong, Chea Iem, Ngo Qui Yen (Dignitaries), Mathias Ghiap (Residency Cook), Luong Joan (Residency Servant), Saïd Serrari, Gerard Tan (Circus Boys), Xavier Castano (Butcher), Suban Phuso (Bus Driver), Christophe Cheysson (Newsstand Man)

Two tiger cubs are separated and find their lives taking very different paths.

Guy Pearce, Maï Anh Lê PHOTOS COURTESY OF UNIVERSAL

KING ARTHUR

(TOUCHSTONE) Producer, Jerry Bruckheimer; Executive Producers, Mike Stenson, Chad Oman, Ned Dowd; Director, Antoine Fuqua; Screenplay, David Franzoni; Photography, Slawomir Idziak; Designer, Dan Weil; Costumes, Penny Rose; Editors, Conrad Buff, Jamie Pearson; Music, Hans Zimmer; Special Effects Coordinator, Neil Corbould; Casting, Ronna Kress, Michelle Guish; Stunts, Steve Dent; Irish-British; Dolby; Panavision; Technicolor; Rated PG-13; 126 minutes; American release date: July 7, 2004

Clive Owen, Ivano Marescotti

Til Schweiger, Stellan Skarsgård

Ioan Gruffudd, Keira Knightley, Clive Owen PHOTOS COURTESY OF TOUCHSTONE

Cast

Arthur **Clive Owen**
Lancelot **Ioan Gruffudd**
Tristan **Mads Mikkelsen**
Gawain **Joel Edgerton**
Galahad **Hugh Dancy**
Bors **Ray Winstone**
Guinevere **Keira Knightley**
Merlin **Stephen Dillane**
Cerdic **Stellan Skarsgård**
Cynric **Til Schweiger**
Jols **Sean Gilder**
Horton **Pat Kinevane**
Bishop Germanius **Ivano Marescotti**
Marius Honorius **Ken Stott**
Alecto **Lorenzo de Angelis**

and Stefania Orsola Garello (Fulcinia), Alan Devine (British Scout), Charlie Creed-Miles (Ganis), Johnny Brennan (Lucan), David Murray (Merlin's Lieutenant), Ned Dennehy (Mental Monk), Phelim Drew (Obnoxious Monk), Des Braiden (Third Monk), Malachy McKenna (Cerdic Scout), Brian McGuinness, Patrick Leech (Cerdic Officers), Bosco Hogan (Bishop Decoy), David Wilmot (Woad, Killed by Lancelot), Lochlann O'Mearain (Roman Commander), Paul McGlinchey, Dessie Gallagher (Mercenaries), Maria Gladkowska (Arthur's Mother), Shane Murray-Corcoran (Young Arthur), Daire McCormack (Augustus), Dawn Bradfield (Vanora), Lesley-Ann Shaw (Scottish Village Girl), Joe McKinney (Mangled Saxon), Gerry O'Brien (Woad Advisor), Brian Condon (Cerdic Bodyguard), Donncha Crowley (Monk), Chick Allen (Saxon), Elliot Henderson-Boyle (Young Lancelot), Clive Russell (Lancelot's Father), Stephanie Putson (Lancelot's Mother), Graham McTavish (Roman Officer)

Hoping to return to a peaceful existence in Rome, Arthur is forced to lead his kinghts in a battle to defend Britain against the invading Saxons.

Keira Knightley

TOUCH OF PINK

(SONY CLASSICS) Producers, Jennifer Kawaja, Martin Pope, Julia Sereny; Executive Producer, Charlotte Mickie; Director/Screenplay, Ian Iqbal Rashid; Photography, David Makin; Designer, Gavin Mitchell; Costumes, Joyce Schure; Line Producer, Lena Cordina; an Alliance Atlantis presentation of a Sienna Films, Martin Pope production; Candian-British; Dolby; Color; Rated R; 91 minutes; American release date: July 16, 2004

Kyle MacLachlan, Jimi Mistry

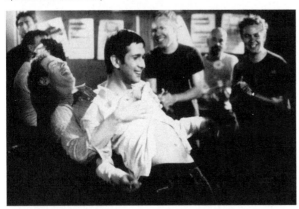

Kristen Holden-Reid, Jimi Mistry

Cast

Alim **Jimi Mistry**
Spirit of Cary Grant **Kyle MacLachlan**
Nuru **Suleka Mathew**
Giles **Kristen Holden-Ried**
Hassan **Brian George**
Dolly **Veena Sood**
Khaled **Raoul Bhaneja**
Delia **Liisa Repo-Martell**
Raymond **Andrew Gillies**

Kristen Holden-Reid, Jimi Mistry

Veena Sood, Suleka Mathew

and Quancetia Hamilton (Airplane Woman), Dean McDermott (Alisdair Keith), Malika Mendez (Sherubai), Barna Moricz (Alex), Sam Moses (Vendor), Sanjay Talwar (Karim), Linda Thorson (Giles' Mother)

When his devout Muslim mother comes to visit him in London, Alim tries to pass off his male lover's sister as his fiancee.

Kristen Holden-Reid, Liisa Repo-Martell PHOTOS COURTESY OF SONY CLASSICS

Meguni Okina in *Ju-On*

JU-ON: THE GRUDGE

(LIONS GATE) Producer, Taka Ichise; Director/Screenplay, Takashi Shimizu; Photography, Tokusho Kikumura; Music, Shiro Sato; Editor, Nobuyuki Takahashi; Visual Effects Supervisor, Hajime Matsumoto; an Oz Co. presentation of a Pioneer LDC Nikkatsu, Oz Co., Xanadeux production, in association with Aozora Investment; Dolby; Color; Rated R; 92 minutes; American release date: July 24, 2004

Cast

Shunsuke Kobayashi **Yûri Yanagi**
Mizuho Tamura **Chiaki Kuriyama**
Yuki **Hitomi Miwa**
Kanna Murakami **Asumi Miwa**
Nakamura **Yoriko Dôguchi**
Kamio **Tarô Suwa**
Manami Kobayashi **Yuue**
Kayako Saeki/Takeo's Wife/
 Toshio's Mother/The Ghost **Takao Fuji**
Takeo Saeki/Kayako's Husband/
 Toshio's Father **Takashi Matsuyama**
Yuji Tooyama **Youji Tanaka**
Noriko Murakami **Yumi Yoshiyuki**

and Denden (Yoshikawa/A Police Detective), Reita Serizawa (Iizuka), Ryôta Koyama (Toshio Saeki/Kayako & Takeo's Son/A Pupil of Shunsuke's), Kazushi Andô (Tsuyoshi Murakami), Yuuko Daike (Kyôko Suzuki/Tasuya's Sister), Makoto Ashikawa (Tasuya Suzuki/Kyôko's Brother/A Realtor), Jun'ichi Kiuchi (Tezuka), Shirô Namiki (A Coroner),

Misa Uehara in *Ju-On* PHOTOS COURTESY OF LIONS GATE

Kahori Fujii (Yoshimi Kitada/Hiroshi's Wife), Hua Rong Weng (Hiroshi Kitada/Yoshimi's Husband), Mayuko Saitô (A Clerk)

A homecare worker arrives to look after the bed-ridden Sachie and finds his house terrorized by the ghosts of a murdered woman and her son. An American remake of this film, *The Grudge* (Columbia) premiered on October 22, 2004.

Tadanobu Asano in *The Blind Swordsman* PHOTOS COURTESY OF MIRAMAX

THE BLIND SWORDSMAN: ZATOICHI

(MIRAMAX) Producers, Masayuki Mori, Tsunehisa Saito; Executive Producer, Cheiko Saito; Co-Producers, Masanori Sanda, Takio Yoshida; Director/Screenplay, Takeshi Kitano; Based on a short story by Kan Shimozawa; Photography, Katsumi Yanagijima; Designer, Norihiro Isoda; Costumes, Kazuko Kurosawa; Music, Keiichi Suzuki; Editors, Takeshi Kitano, Yoshinori Ota; Line Producer, Shinji Komiya; Casting, Takefumi Yoshikawa; a Bandai Visual/Tokyo FM/Dentsu/TV Asahi/Saito Entertainment/Office Kitano production; Japanese, 2003; Dolby; Color; Rated R; 116 minutes; American release date: July 24, 2004

Cast

Zatoichi **Takeshi Beat Kitano**
Hattori, the Bodyguard **Tadanobu Asano**
Aunt Oume **Michiyo Ookusu**
Hattori's Wife **Yui Natsukawa**
Shinkichi **Gadarukanaru Taka**
Osei, the Geisha **Daigoro Tachibana**
Okinu, the Geisha **Yuko Daike**
Ginzo **Ittoku Kishibe**
Ogi **Saburo Ishikura**

and Akira Emoto (Pops, Tavern Owner), Yui Natsukawa (O-Shino, Hattori's Wife), Kohji Miura (Lord Sakai), The Stripes: Hideboh, Ron II, Suji, Noriyasu (Dancing Farmers), Makoto Ashikawa, Edamame Tsumami, Kosuke Ohta, Yoshiyuki Morishita (Carpenters), Naomasa Musaka (Yakuza Boss on the Country Road), Shoken Kunimoto (Rival Swordsman), Daigaku Sekine (Ginzo's Henchman #1), Koji Koike (Boss Funahachi), Koji Kiryu (Dice Dealer at Funahachi's Joint), Taiki Kobayashi (Funahachi's Bodyguard), Ayano Yoshida (Young O-Kinu), Taichi Saotome (Young O-Sei), Kanji Tsuda (Playboy at Home), Ikki Goto, Yoshio Nakamura, Hiroaki Noguchi, Shinichi Nakatsu, Toru Yonezu (Kuchinawa Underlings)

A sightless swordsman agrees to help two geishas who are out to avenge their parents' murder.

INTIMATE STRANGERS

(PARAMOUNT CLASSICS) a.k.a. *Confidences trop intimes*; Producers, Alain Sarde; Executive Producer, Christine Gozlan; Director, Patrice Leconte; Screenplay, Jerome Tonnerre, Patrice Leconte; Photography, Eduardo Serra; Designer, Ivan Maussion; Costumes, Sandrine Kerner; Music, Pascal Esteve; Editor, Joelle Hache; Casting, Catherine Deserbais; an Alain Sarde presentation of an Alain Sarde, France 3 Cinema, Zoulou Films, Assise Prod. production; French; Dolby; Panavision; Color; Rated R; 105 minutes; American release date: July 30, 2004

Fabrice Luchini in *Intimate Strangers*

Cast
Anna **Sandrine Bonnaire**
William **Fabrice Luchini**
Dr. Monnier **Michel Duchaussoy**
Jeanne **Anne Brochet**
Marc **Gilbert Melki**
Luc **Laurent Gamelon**
Mrs. Mulon **Hélène Surgère**
Chatel **Urbain Cancelier**

and Isabelle Petit-Jacques (Dr. Monnier's Secretary), Véronique Kapoyan (Guard), Benoît Pétré (Messenger), Alberto Simono (Mr. Michel), Claude Dereppe (The Customs Client), Aurore Auteuil (The Student Nadokov), Ludovic Berthillot (The Mover), Sabrina Brezzo (The Dance Assistant)

A troubled woman tells her most intimate problems to a financial planner she has mistaken for a psychiatrist.

Sandrine Bonnaire in *Intimate Strangers* PHOTOS COURTESY OF PARAMOUNT CLASSICS

Tim Robbins, Samantha Morton in *Code 46* PHOTO COURTESY OF UNITED ARTISTS

CODE 46

(UNITED ARTISTS) Producer, Andrew Eaton; Executive Producers, Robert Jones, David M. Thompson; Director, Michael Winterbottom; Screenplay, Frank Cottrell Boyce; Photography, Alvin Kuchler, Marcel Zyskind; Designer, Mark Tildesley; Costumes, Natalie Ward; Music, The Free Association; Editor, Peter Christelis; Casting, Wendy Brazington; a Revolution Films production, presented in association with the UK Film Council and BBC Films; British; Dolby; Super 35 Widescreen; Deluxe color; Rated R; 93 minutes; American release date: August 6, 2004

Cast
William **Tim Robbins**
Maria Gonzales **Samantha Morton**
Sylvie **Jennifer Balibar**
Doctor **Essie Davis**
Vendor **Nabil Elouahabi**
Damian Alekan **David Fahm**
William's Boss **Shelley King**
Sphinx Receptionist **Natalie Mendoza**
Check In **Archie Panjabi**
Backland **Om Puri**
Clinic Doctor **Kerry Shale**
Tester **Teo-Wa Vuong**
Hospital Receptionist **Nina Wadia**
Medic **Benedict Wong**

and Togo Igawa (Driver), Sarah Backhouse (Weather Girl), Jonathan Ibbotson (Boxer), Emil Marwa (Mohan), Nina Fog (Wole), Bruno Lastra (Bikku), Christopher Simpson (Paul), Lien Nguyin (Singer in Nightclub), Taro Sherabayani (Jack), Nina Sosanya (Anya), Tuyet Li (Apartment Security), Jennifer Lim (Tester with Couple), Paul Barnes (Man in Corridor), Nabil Massad (Sunglasses Man)

In the near-future, when travel is heavily monitored, an insurance investigator falls dangerously in love with a woman responsible for forging special travel passes.

DANNY DECKCHAIR

(LIONS GATE) Producer, Andrew Mason; Executive Producers, Howard Baldwin, Karen Baldwin, William J. Immerman, Carol Hughes; Co-Producer, Lizzie Bryant; Director/Screenplay, Jeff Balsmeyer; Photography, Martin McGrath; Designer, Kim Buddee; Costumes, Emily Seresin; Music, David Donaldson; Editor, Suresh Ayyar; Special Effects Supervisor, Tad Pride; Casting, Ann Robinson; a Cobalt Media Group-Macquarie Film Corp. presentation of a City Prods. production, in association with Crusader Entertainment, with the support of the NSW Film and TV Office, Australian Film Commission; Australian, 2003; Dolby; Atlab color; Rated PG-13; 90 minutes; American release date: August 11, 2004

Cast
Danny Morgan **Rhys Ifans**
Glenda Lake **Miranda Otto**
Trudy Dunphy **Justine Clarke**
Sandy Upman **Rhys Muldoon**
Sgt. Dave Mackie **Frank Magree**
Jim Craig **Andrew Phelan**
Pete **Andrew Batchelor**
Kate **Jules Sobotta**

and Alan Flower (Ray), Rod Zuanic (Bob), Maggie Dence (Meredith Butcher), Michelle Boyle (Louella), Jane Beddows (Regina), Jeanette Cronin (Maggie Pike), Alex Mann (Sandra Craig), Brian Langsworth, Steven Rassios (Real Estate Agents), Jane Ruggiero (Donna), Gina Bortolin (Helen Costas), Duncan Young (Phil Stubbs), Garrie Scott (Party Shop Assistant), Richard Johnson (Passerby), Dina Gillespie (Kaz), Rod Zuanic (Bob), Ross Perrelli (Young Bobby), Victoria Nucifora (Young Lisa),

Rhys Ifans in *Danny Deckchair* PHOTO COURTESY OF LIONS GATE

Gyton Grantley (Stuey), Amie Mckenna (Tina), Colin Angus (Elderly Neighbor), Andrew Crabbe, Richard Healy, Sean McKenzie, Peter Cook (Reporters), Nadia Townsend (Linda Craig), Peter Fisher (Fire Captain Robbo), Jack Carty (UFO Teenager), Michelle Boyle (Louella), Jane Beddows (Regina Carter), Jasmina Singh, Rajprett Singh, Paviterjeet Singh (Indian Sisters), Lester Morris (Mr. Potts), Nicholas Holland, Marie Patan (In the Morning Presenters), Stephen Holt (Nobbie Furco), Angus King (Darren Kehole), Simon Mills (Old Codger), Karen Pang (Sonya Tims),

Kathryn Dagher (Debby Lleyton), Guy Leslie (Brownie), Nino Alessi (Wazza), Todd Hodgson (Simo), Stephen Hobb (Polesitter), Serge Cockburn (Max Pike), William David Thompson (John Purchie)

Floating over Australia in a deckchair tied to a batch of balloons, Danny Morgan crash lands in the backyard of a lonely policewoman.

Darcy Fehr, Melissa Dionisio in *Cowards Bend the Knee* PHOTO COURTESY OF ZEITGEIST

COWARDS BEND THE KNEE

(ZEITGEIST) Producer, Phillip Monk; Director/Screenplay/Photography, Guy Maddin; Designer, Shawn Connor; Editor, John Gurdebeke; a Power Plant production; Canadian, 2003; Black and white; Not rated; 64 minutes; American release date: August 11, 2004

Cast
Guy Maddin **Darcy Fehr**
Meta **Melissa Dionisio**
Veronica **Amy Stewart**
Liliom **Tara Birthwhistle**
Dr. Fusi **Louis Negin**
Mo Mott **Mike Bell**
Shaky **David Stuart Evans**
Chas **Henry Mogatas**

and Victor Cowie (Maddin, Sr.), Herdis Maddin (Grandma), Marion Martin (Mrs. Maddin), Aurum McBride (Baby), Bernard Lesk (Stickboy), Erin Hershberg, Erika Rintoul, Charlene Van Buekenhout, Sherrill Hershberg, Kathryn Stuart, Lauren Ritz, Rebecca Sandulak, Kirstin Ward, Billy Dee Knight, Erica Smith (Customers), Ricardo Alms, Craig Aftanas, Jim Crawford, Mike Silver, Bob Unger, Mark Yuill, Caelum Vatnsdal, Matt Holm (Hockey Players), Meghan Greenlay, Erin McKenzie (Stylists)

In this silent ode to German Expressionism a man abandons his girlfriend mid-abortion to pursue his new love, a woman obsessed with her dead father.

ALIEN VS. PREDATOR

(20TH CENTURY FOX) Producers, John Davis, Gordon Carroll, David Giler, Walter Hill; Executive Producers, Wyck Godfrey, Thomas M. Hammel, Mike Richardson; Co-Producers, Chris Symes, Matthew Stillman, David Minkowski; DIrector/Screenplay, Paul W.S. Anderson; Story, Paul W.S. Anderson, Dan O'Bannon, Ronald Shusett; Based on the *Alien* characters created by Dan O'Bannon and Ronald Shusett, and the *Predator* characters created by Jim Thomas and John Thomas; Photography, David Johnson; Designer, Richard Bridgland; Costumes, Magali Guidasci; Music, Harald Kloser; Editor, Alexander Berner; Visual Effects Supervisor, John Bruno; Creature Effects Designers/Creators, Alec Gillis, Tom Woodruff, Jr.; Casting, Suzanne M. Smith; a Davis Entertainment/Brandywine production in co-production with Lonlink-Stillking-Kut-Babelsberg in association Inside Track 2LLP; British-Czech-Canadian-German; Dolby; Super 35 Widescreen; Color; Rated PG-13; 100 minutes; Release date: August 13, 2004

Cast

Alexa Woods **Sanaa Lathan**
Sebastian de Rosa **Raoul Bova**
Charles Bishop Weyland **Lance Henriksen**
Graeme Miller **Ewen Bremner**
Maxwell Stafford **Colin Salmon**
Mark Verheiden **Tommy Flanagan**
Joe Connors **Joseph Rye**
Adee Rousseau **Agathe de la Boylaye**
Rusten Quinn **Carsten Norgaard**
Thomas Parks **Sam Troughton**
Stone **Petr Jakl**

Predator, Lance Henriksen

and Pavel Bezdek (Bass), Kieran Bew (Klaus), Carsten Voigt (Mikkel), Jan Filipensky (Boris), Adrian Bouchet (Sven), Andy Lucas (Juan Ramirez), Liz May Brice (Supervisor), Glenn Conroy (Technician), Eoin McCarthy (Karl), KarimaAdebibe (Sacrifical Maiden), Tom Woodruff, Jr. (Grid), Ian Whyte (Scar)

Billionaire Charles Weyland pulls together a team of experts to explore a mysterious pyramid discovered beneath Antarctica where they face deadly opposition from two different kinds of malevolent creatures. This sequel qualifies as the fifth *Alien* film from Fox following *Alien* (1979), *Aliens* (1986), and *Alien 3* (1992), and *Alien Resurrection* (1997), and the third *Predator* film following *Predator* (1987) and *Predator 2:* (1990). Lance Henriksen who appeared in both *Aliens* and *Alien 3* is seen here, albeit as a different character.

Alien, Raoul Bova PHOTOS COURTESY OF 20TH CENTURY FOX

BRIGHT YOUNG THINGS

(THINKFILM) Producers, Gina Carter, Miranda Davis; Executive Producers, Miranda Davis, Andrew Eaton, Michael Winterbottom, Stephen Fry, Chris Auty, Neil Peplow, Jim Reeve, Steve Robbins; Director/Screenplay, Stephen Fry; Based on the novel *Vile Bodies* by Evelyn Waugh; Photography, Henry Braham; Designer, Michael Howells; Costumes, Nic Ede; Music, Anne Dudley; Editor, Alex Mackie; Make-up & Hair Design, Peter King; Casting, Wendy Brazington; a Film Consortium presentation, in association with the U.K. Film Council, Visionview and Icon Film Distribution, of a Revolution Films, Doubting Hall production; British; Dolby; Technicolor; Rated R; 105 minutes; American release date: August 20, 2004

Stephen Campbell Moore, Fenella Woolgar, Emily Mortimer, Michael Sheen

Stephen Campbell Moore, Emily Mortimer

Stephen Campbell Moore, Emily Mortimer

Cast

Nina Blount **Emily Mortimer**
Adam Fenwick-Symes **Stephen Campbell Moore**
Simon Balcairn **James McAvoy**
Miles **Michael Sheen**
Ginger Littlejohn **David Tennant**
Agatha Runcible **Fenella Woolgar**
Lord Monomark **Dan Aykroyd**
The Drunk Major **Jim Broadbent**
King of Anatolia **Simon Callow**
Chief of Customs Officer **Jim Carter**
Mrs. Melrose Ape **Stockard Channing**
Fr. Rothschild **Richard E. Grant**
Lottie Crump **Julia McKenzie**
Colonel Blount **Peter O'Toole**
Gentleman Taking Cocaine **John Mills**
Lady Brown **Imelda Staunton**
Sir James Brown **Bill Paterson**

and Stephen Fry (Chauffeur), Harriet Walter (Lady Metroland), Margaret Tyzack (Lady Throbbing), Nicholas Le Prevost (Lord Metroland), Alec Newman (Tiger La Bouchère), Nigel Planer (Adam's Taxi Driver), Angela Thorne (Kitty), Alex Barclay (Jimmy Vanburgh), Guy Henry (Archie), Simon McBurney (Sneath, Photo-Rat), Bruno Lastra (Basilio), Lisa Dillon (Jane Brown), Arturo Venegas (Alphonse), Ian Hughes (Night Editor), Alan

Peter O'Toole PHOTOS COURTESY OF THINKFILM

Williams (Bockie), Mark Hardy (Angy), Gerard Horan (Race Official), Tony Maudsley (Race Steward), John Mackle (Edwards), Mark Gatiss (Estate Agent), Ivan Marevich (Foreign Dignatory), Rebekah Staton (Imperial Hotel Receptionist), Max MacDonald (Tommy)

Adam Fenwick-Symes, a member of Britian's hedonistic social scene, hopes to raise enough money in order to marry the shallow, status-obsessed Nina.

HERO

(MIRAMAX) a.k.a. *Yingxiong*; Producers, Bill Kong, Zhang Yimou; Executive Producers, Dou Shoufang, Zhang Weipin; Director, Zhang Yimou; Screenplay/Story, Li Feng, Zhang Yimou, Wang Bin; Photography, Christopher Doyle; Designers, Huo Tingxiao, Yi Zhenzhou; Costumes, Emi Wada; Music, Tan Dun; Violin Solos, Itzak Perlman; Editors, Zhai Ru, Angie Lam; Action Director, Tony Ching Siu-tung; Visual Effects Supervisor, Pan Guoyu; a Beijing New Picture Film Co. (China)/Elite Group Enterprises (Hong Kong) production; Chinese-Hong Kong, 2002; Dolby; Super 35 Widescreen; Color; Rated PG-13; 96 minutes; American release date: August 27, 2004

Maggie Cheung

Jet Li

Zhang Ziyi

Cast

Nameless **Jet Li**
Broken Sword **Tony Leung Chiu-wai**
Flying Snow **Maggie Cheung**
Sky **Donnie Yen**
King of Qin **Chen Daoming**
Moon **Zhang Ziyi**
Scholar **Liu Zhong Yuan**
Old Servant **Zheng Tia Yong**
Prime Minister **Yan Qin**
General **Zhang Ya Kun**
Head Eunuch **Ma Wen Hua**
Eunuch **Jin Ming**
Pianist **Xu Kuang Hua**
Musician **Wang Shou Xin**

and Hei Zi, Cao Hua, Li Lei, Xia Bin, Peng Qiang, Liu Jie, Zhang Yi (Qin Guards)

A nameless warrior relates how he stopped various attempts to kill a powerful king who hoped to unite the conflicting municipalities in 3rd century China.

Tony Leung Chiu-wai, Maggie Cheung PHOTOS COURTESY OF MIRAMAX

RED LIGHTS

(WELLSPRING) a.k.a *Feux Rouges*; Producers, Patrick Godeau; Executive Producer, Francoise Galfre; Director, Cedric Kahn; Screenplay, Cedric Kahn, Laurence Ferreira-Barbosa; Based on the novel by Georges Simenon, with Gilles Marchand; Photography, Patrick Marchand; Designer, Francois Abelanet; Costumes, Elizabeth Tavernier, Edwige Morel d'Arleux; Music, Claude Debussy, Arvo Part; Editor, Yann Dedet; an Aleceleo, France 3 Cinema, Gimages, CNC production, in association with participation of Canal+, Cinecinema; French; Dolby; Color; Not rated; 105 minutes; American release date: September 3, 2004

Cast
Antoine Dunan **Jean-Pierre Darroussin**
Helene Dunan **Carole Bouquet**
Man on the Run **Vincent Deniard**
Waitress **Charline Paul**
Inspector Levet **Jean-Pierre Gros**
Young Doctor **Sava Lolov**
Man Yelling into Phone **Igor Skreblin**
Dictor (Voice) **Mylene Demongeot**

On a tense trip to pick up their kids from camp, Antoine loses track of his wife Helene and wonders if she has not become the victim of an escaped criminal.

Jean Pierre Darroussin in *Red Lights*

Carole Bouquet in *Red Lights* PHOTOS COURTESY OF WELLSPRING

MERCI DOCTEUR REY

(REGENT/HERE! FILMS) Producers, Rahila Bootwala, Nathalie Gastaldo; Executive Producer, Ismail Merchant; Director/Screenplay, Andrew Litvack; Photography, Laurent Machuel; Designer, Jacques Bufnoir; Costumes, Pierre-Yves Gayraud; Music, Geoffrey Alexander; Editor, Giles Gardner; Casting, Annette Trumel; a co-production of Eat Your Soup Productions, here! Films, Merchant Ivory Productions; French-U.S., 2002; Dolby; Color; Rated R; 91 minutes; American release date: September 17, 2004

Dianne Wiest, Bulle Ogier in *Merci Docteur Rey*

Cast
Elisabeth Beaumont **Dianne Wiest**
Pénélope **Jane Birkin**
Thomas Beaumont **Stanislas Merhar**
Claude Sabrié **Bulle Ogier**
Murderer **Karim Salah**
Detective **Didier Flamand**
Taxi Driver **Roschdy Zem**
Radio Interviewer **Nathalie Richard**
Rollerboy **Dan Herzberg**
Sybil **Jerry Hall**
Bob **Simon Callow**
Herself **Vanessa Redgrave**
François **Vernon Dobtcheff**

While in Paris with his opera singer mother, closeted Thomas Beaumont answers a personal ad and ends up witnessing a murder.

Stanislas Merhar in *Merci Docteur Rey* PHOTOS COURTESY OF REGENT/HERE! FILMS

HEAD IN THE CLOUDS

(SONY CLASSICS) Producers, Michael Cowan, Bertil Ohlsson, Jonathan Olsberg, Jason Piette, Andre Rouleau, Maxime Remillard; Executive Producers, Julia Palau, Matthew Payne; Co-Producer, Nigel Goldsack; Co-Executive Producers, Julien Remilard, Peter James, James Simpson; Director/Screenplay, John Duigan; Photography, Paul Sarossy; Designer, Jonathan Lee; Costumes, Mario Davignon; Music, Terry Frewer; Editor, Dominique Fortin; Casting, Rosina Bucci, Vera Miller; an Arclight presentation of a Remstar/Spice Factory, Bertil Ohlsson/Dakota/Tusk production in association with Movision; Canadian-British; Dolby; Super 35 Widescreen; Deluxe color; Rated R; 133 minutes; American release date: September 17, 2004

Penelope Cruz, Charlize Theron, Stuart Townsend

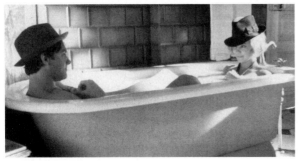

Stuart Townsend, Charlize Theron

Cast

Gilda Bessé **Charlize Theron**
Mia **Penelope Cruz**
Guy **Stuart Townsend**
Maj. Frans Bietrich **Thomas Kretschmann**
Charles Bessé **Steven Berkoff**
Lucien **David LaHaye**

and Karine Vanasse (Lisette), Gabriel Hogan (Julian Elsworth), Peter Crockett (Max), John Jorgenson (Django Reinhardt), Élizabeth Chouvalidzé (Fortune Teller), Jolyane Langlois (Gilda, Age 14), Sophie Desmariais (Élodie), Éloïsa Laflamme-Cervantes (Julie), Ivan Vukov, Sebastian Bailey, Michael Daniel Murphy (Undergraduates), Linda Tomassone (Molly Twelvetrees), Julian Casey (Winston), Lisa Bronwyn Moore (Davina), Frank Fontaine (Unwin), Vanya Rose (Venetia), Amy Sloan (Linda), Sven Eriksson (Centurion), Michèle Chatelet (Elderly Woman), Arthur Holden (Arnold Beck), Paule Ducharme (Simone), Jérôme Tiberghein (Vincent), Lénie Scoffié (Béatrice), Sarah Gravel (Bride), Benjamin Chouinard (Small Boy), Émilie Carrier (Small Girl), Eric Bérard (Stefan Grappelli), Andrew MacKenzie (Joseph Reinhardt), François Rousseau (Baro Ferret), André Farleiros (Roger Grasset), Elisa Sergeant (Bessé's Maid), Cécile Cassel (Céline Bessé), Michel Albert Côté (Taxi Driver), Christopher Freeman (Ferguson), Jérôme Huerta, Carlos Alvear (Nationalist Soldiers), Sonia Auger-Guimont (Photographic Studio Assistant), Heré Desbois (Mailman), Jan Oliver Schroeder (German Soldier, Gardens), Paul-Antoine Taillefer (Michel), Allen Altman (Raul), Mark Antony Krupa (Goltz), Judith Baribeau (Pascale), Armand Laroche (Maitre d', Hotel L'Aiglon), Elizabeth A. Marleau (L'Aiglon Evicted Woman), John Robinson (David Beamish), Harald Winter (German Soldier, Brasserie), Elizabeth Whitmere (W.R.A.C.), Stéphane Boutet (French Officer), Charles Lelaure (French Soldier), Vincent Leclerc (Resistant), Giovanni Sabetta (FFI Man), Stéphane Pasterkamp, Julie Judd (Hairdressers), Annick D'Amours (Annette), Lucien Rémillard (Man at the Barricade), Mélanie Bergeron, Jaladriel Ardacar, Nancy Loof, Mabel Palomino, Sophye Anne Sherer, Martin Tremblay (Ballet Dancers), Michel Langelier (Ballet Teacher), Gilbert Patenaude (Boys Choir's Conductor)

In 1930s Paris Gilda, a free-spirited Bohemian, ends up in a menage à trois with Mia and Guy, both of whom become involved in the plight of the Spanish Republicans.

Charlize Theron, Thomas Kretschmann

Penelope Cruz, Charlize Theron PHOTOS COURTESY OF SONY CLASSICS

COWBOYS & ANGELS

(TLA RELEASING) Producer, Nathalie Lichtenthaler; Executive Producer, James Flynn; Director/Screenplay, David Gleeson; Photography, Volker Tittel; Designer, Jim Furlong; Costumes, Grania Preston; Music, Stephen McKeon; Editor, Andrew Bird; Casting, Gillian Reynolds; a co-production of Wide Eye Films, Peter Stockhaus Filmproduktion, Grosvenor Park Productions; Irish-German-British, 2003; Dolby; Color; Not rated; 89 minutes; American release date: September 17, 2004

Alan Leech, Michael Legge

Alan Leech, Michael Legge

Cast

Shane **Michael Legge**
Vincent Cusack **Alan Leech**
Gemma **Amy Shiels**
Keith **David Murray**
Jerry **Frank Kelly**
Budgie **Colm Coogan**
Frankie **Sean Power**
Bunny **Alvaro Lucchesi**
Richard **Frank Coughlan**
Suit **Nigel Mercier**

Hoping to start a new life in Dublin, Shane finds his staid ways being shaken up by his free-spirited gay roommate, Vincent.

Michael Legge

Amy Shiels, Alan Leech PHOTOS COURTESY OF TLA RELEASING

Chen Shiang-chyi in *Good Bye, Dragon Inn*

GOOD BYE, DRAGON INN

(WELLSPRING) a.k.a. *Bu San*; Producer, Liang Hung-chih; Executive Producer/Director/Screenplay, Tsai Ming-Hang; Photography, Liao Pen-jung; Editor, Chen Sheng-chang; Costumes, Sun Huei-mei; a HomeGreen Films production; Taiwanese, 2003; Dolby; Color; Not rated; 81 minutes; American release date: September 17, 2004

Cast

Projectionist **Lee Kang-sheng**
Ticket Woman **Chen Shiang-chyi**
Japanese Tourist **Mitamura Kiyonobu**
Peanut-Eating Woman **Yang Kuei-Mei**
Themselves **Chun Shih, Miao Tien**

Patrons attend a showing of the film *Dragon Inn* at a run-down Tapei movie theatre on its final night before its closing.

Lee Kang-sheng in *Good Bye, Dragon Inn* PHOTOS COURTESY OF WELLSPRING

ZELARY

(SONY CLASSICS) Producer/Director, Ondrej Trojan; Executive Producer, Milan Kuchynka; Screenplay, Petr Jarchovsky; Based on the novel *Jozova Hanule* by Kveta Legátová; Photography, Asen Sopov; Designer, Milan Bycek; Costumes, Katarina Bielikova; Music, Petr Ostrouchov; Editor, Vladimír Barák; Casting, Ladislav Ondrácek; a co-production of ALEF Film & Media Group, Barrandov Studio, Ceská Film Produktionsgesellschaft GmbH, Total Help Art T.H.A., Österreichischer Rundfunk (ORF); Czech-Russian-German, 2003; Dolby; Color; Rated R; 148 minutes; American release date: September 17, 2004

Anna Geislerová, Ondrej Koval PHOTO COURTESY OF UNIVERSAL

Cast

Eliska/Hana **Anna Geislerová**
Joza **György Cserhalmi**
Lucka **Jaroslava Adamová**
Priest **Miroslav Donutil**
Teacher Tkác **Jaroslav Dusek**
Zena **Iva Bittová**
Richard **Ivan Trojan**
Slávek **Jan Hrufínsky**
Helenka **Anna Vertelárová**
Lipka **Tomás Zatecka**
Michal Kutina **Ondrej Koval**

and Tatiana Vajdová (Anna Kutinová), Frantisek Velecky (Old Kutina), Viera Pavlíková (Old Kutinová), Jurag Hrcka (Vojta Juriga), Imre Boraros (Pavel Juriga), Jana Olhová (Juliska Jurigová), Jan Triska (Old Gorcík), Michal Hofbauer (Young Gorcík), Edita Malovcic (Marie Gorcíková), Reinhard Simonisheck (Dr. Benícek), Gabriela Schmoll (Irca), Zita Kabátová (Old Woman), Svatopluk Benes (Old Man), Jakub Laurych (Young Soldier)

A young medical student, hiding out in a village after fleeing from the Gestapo, agrees to marry the old man who has sheltered her.

Simon Pegg, Nick Frost

Dylan Moran, Kate Ashfield, Simon Pegg, Lucy Davis

Simon Pegg PHOTOS COURTESY OF ROGUE

SHAUN OF THE DEAD

(ROGUE) Producers, Nira Park; Executive Producers, Tim Bevan, Eric Fellner, Natascha Wharton, James Wilson, Alison Owen; Director, Edgar Wright; Screenplay, Simon Pegg, Edgar Wright; Photography, David M. Dunlap; Designer, Marcus Rowland; Costumes, Annie Hardinge; Music, Daniel Mudford, Pete Woodhead; Editor, Chris Dickens; Special Effects Supervisor, Paul Dunn; Zombie Prosthetics Make-up, Stuart Conran; a Universal Pictures Studio Canal and Working Titles Films presentation of a WT2 production, in association with Big Talk Prods.; British; Dolby; Super 35 Widescreen; Color; Rated R; 97 minutes; American release date: September 24, 2004

Cast
Shaun **Simon Pegg**
Liz **Kate Ashfield**
Ed **Nick Frost**
Dianne **Lucy Davis**
David **Dylan Moran**
Mary **Nicola Cunningham**
Pete **Peter Serafinowicz**
Philip **Bill Nighy**
Barbara **Penelope Wilton**
Yvonne **Jessica Stevenson**

and Kier Mills, Matt Jaynes (Clubbers), Gavin Ferguson (Football Kid), Horton Jupiter (Homeless Man), Tim Baggaley (The Usher), Arvind Doshi (Nelson), Rafe Spall (Noel), Sonell Dadral (Danny), Samantha Day (Woman on Trisha), Trisha Goddard, Krishnan Guru-Murthy, Jeremy Thompson, Chris Martin, Jonny Buckland, Keith Chegwin, Carol Barnes, Rob Butler, Vernon Kay (Themselves), David Park (Grace Scientist), Finola Geraghty (Distraught Vox Pop), Robert Fitch (Distressed Man), Sharon Gavin (Florist), Patch Connolly (Pigeon Man), Stuart Powell (Snakehips), Patricia Franklin (Spinster), Steve Emerson (John), Phyllis McMahon (Bernie), Matt Donovan (Hulking Zombie), Christopher Harwood (Grizzled Zombie), Martin Freeman (Declan), Reece Shearsmith (Mark), Tamsin Greig (Maggie), Julia Deaking (Yvonne's Mum), Matt Lucas (Coustin Tom), Nick Ewans (Pyjama Zombie), Alex Lutes (Trisha Zombie)

Underachiever Shaun gets an unexpected chance to show his heroic side when he and his slacker pal Ed attempt to rescue London from a plague of flesh-eating zombies.

The Dead

THE MOTORCYCLE DIARIES

(FOCUS) a.k.a. *Diarios de motocicleta*; Producers, Michael Nozik, Edgard Tenembaum, Karen Tenkoff; Executive Producers, Robert Redford, Paul Webster, Rebecca Yeldham; Co-Producers, Daneil Burman, Diego Dubcovsky; Director, Walter Salles; Screenplay, Jose Rivera; Based on the book *The Motorcycle Diaries* by Ernesto Che Guevara and *With Che Through Latin America* by Alberto Granado; Photography, Eric Gautier; Designer, Carlos Conti; Costumes, Beatriz Di Benedetto; Music, Gustavo Santaolalla; Song: "Al Otro Lado Del Rio" by Jorge Drexler; Editor, Daniel Rezende; Casting, Walter Rippel; a FilmFour presentation of a South Fork Pictures production in association with Tu Vas Voir Prods.; Argentine-U.S.-British-Chilean-Peruvian; Dolby; Color; Super 16-to-35mm; Rated R; 126 minutes; American release date: September 24, 2004

Gael García Bernal

Gael García Bernal

Cast

Ernesto Guevara de la Serna **Gael García Bernal**
Alberto Granado **Rodrigo De la Serna**
Celia de la Serna **Mercedes Morán**
Ernesto Guevara Lynch **Jean-Pierre Moher**
Roberto Guevara **Lucas Oro**
Celita Guevara **Marina Glezer**
Ana María Guevara **Sofita Bertolotto**
Juan Martín Guevara **Franco Solazzi**
Ricardo Diaz Mourelle **Uncle Jorge**

and Sergio Boris, Daniel Kargieman (Young Travelers), Diego Giozri (Rodolfo), Facundo Espinosa (Tomás Granado), Matías Gómez, Diego Treu, Ariel Verdún, Gustavo Mansilla (Kids, Argentina), Mía Maestro (Chichina), Susana Lanteri (Aunt Rosana), Natalia Lobo (La Negra), Maída Andrenacci, Bárbara Lombardo, Dana Frijoli, Valeria Echeverria, Ariel Prieto, Matías Strafe, Nicolas Watson (Chichina's Friends), Carlos Rivkin (Horacio Ferreyra), Elvio Suárez (Uncle Martín), Pablo Viallarrazza (Esteban Aguirre), Lilian Kolinsky (Chichina's Mother), Guillermo Ojeda (Men with Oxen Cart), Oscar Alegre (Don Olate), Fernando Ignacio Llosa (Von Puttkamer), Marta Lubos (Schatzie von Puttkamer), Christian F. Chaparro (Luna), Cristian Arancibia (Tulio), Gabriela Aguilera (Piedad),

Juan Maliqueo (Araucano Father), Samuel Cifuentes (Araucano Son), Constanza B. Majluf, Evelyn Ibarra (Chilean Sisters), Víctor Hugo Ogaz (Young Man, Chile), Fernando Farias (Fire Chief), Maximiliano Toledo (Cataco), César Loperz (Fireman), Pablo Macaya (Janitor), Rosa Curihuentro (Doña Rosa), Erto Pantoja (Mechanic), Vladimir Paredes (Truck Driver), Brandon Cruz (Miner), Vilma V. Verdejo (Miner's Wife), Jaime Azocar (Mine Foreman), María Esther Zamora (Chipi Chipi Band Singer), Pollito Gonzalez, Jorge Lobos, Cuti Aste, Roberto Lindl (Chipi Chipi Band), Gustavo Morales (Félix), Gustavo Bueno (Dr. Hugo Pesce), María Beatriz Abele (Zdenka Pesce), Jonathan Balbis (Luis Pesce), Matías Delgado Rizzi (Tito Pesce), Jorge Rodríguez Paz (Peruvian from Canepa), Jackelyne Vásquez (Luz), Ernesto Cabrejos, Víctor Áangeles, Willy Gutiérrez, Gerald Mayeux, Matías Gomez (Card Players), Jorge Chiarella (Dr. Bresciani), Ricardo Velásquez (Banca), Carolina Infante Sister Margarita), Nidia Bermejo (Young Indian Nurse), Carlos "Caitro" Soto de la Colina (Papa Carlito), Delfina Paredes (Mother Sister Alberto), Nemesio Reyes (Leper from San Pablo), Hernán Herrera (Leper from San Pablo), Antonella Costa (Silvia), Igor Calvo (Dr. Souza Lima), Alberto Granado (Himself), Gustavo Pastorini (Passenger)

Rodrigo De la Serna, Gael García Bernal

The true story of how an eight-month trip through South America in 1952 made young medical student Ernesto Guevara more fully aware of the poverty and hardships of the people.

Rodrigo De la Serna, Gael García Bernal

2004 Academy Award-winner for Best Song ("Al Otro Lado Del Rio"). This film received an additional nomination for adapted screenplay.

Gael García Bernal, Mía Maestro PHOTOS COURTESY OF FOCUS

Gael García Bernal (left)

STAGE BEAUTY

(LIONS GATE) Producers, Robert De Niro, Jane Rosenthal, Hardy Justice; Executive Producers, Richard Eyre, James D. Stern, Amir Malin, Rachel Cohen, Michael Kuhn; Co-Producer, Michael Dreyer; Co-Executive Producers, Jill Tandy, Malcolm Ritchie; Director, Richard Eyre; Screenplay, Jeffrey Hatcher, based on his play *Compleat Female Stage Beauty*; Photography, Andrew Dunn; Designer, Jim Clay; Costumes, Tim Hatley; Music, George Fenton; Editor, Tariq Anwar; Casting, Celestia Fox; a Momentum Pictures, BBC Films, Qwerty Films presentation of a Tribeca production in association with N1 European Filmproduktions, Artisan Entertainment; British-U.S.; Dolby; Panavision; Technicolor; Rated R; 110 minutes; American release date: October 8, 2004

Rupert Everett, Zoe Tapper

Billy Crudup

Billy Crudup, Claire Danes

Cast

Ned Kynaston **Billy Crudup**
Maria **Clare Danes**
King Charles II **Rupert Everett**
Betterton **Tom Wilkinson**
Nell Gwynn **Zoe Tapper**
Sir Charles Sedley **Richard Griffiths**
George Villiars, Duke of Buckingham **Ben Chaplin**
Samuel Pepys **Hugh Bonneville**
Sir Edward Hyde **Edward Fox**
Stage Manager **Derek Hutchinson**
Male Emilia/Dickie **Mark Letheren**
Call Boy **Jack Kempton**
Miss Frayne **Alice Eve**
Lady Meresvale **Fenella Woolgar**

and David Westhead (Harry), Nick Barber (Nick), Stephen Marcus (Thomas Cockerell), Robin Dunn (Butler), Isabella Calthorpe (Lady Jane Bellamy), Andy Merchant, John Street (Thugs), Tom Hollander (Sir Peter Lely), Hermione Gulliford (Mrs. Barry), Clare Higgins (Mistress Revels), Madeleine Worrall (Female Emilia)

The true story of 17th century British actor Ned Kynaston who made a career out of playing women's roles on stage.

Ben Chaplin, Billy Crudup PHOTOS COURTESY OF LIONS GATE

VERA DRAKE

(FINE LINE FEATURES) Producers, Simon Channing Williams, Alain Sarde; Executive Producers, Gail Egan, Robert Jones, Duncan Reid; Co-Producer, Georgina Lowe; Director/Screenplay, Mike Leigh; Photography, Dick Pope; Designer, Eve Stewart; Costumes, Jacqueline Durran; Music, Andrew Dickson; Editor, Jim Clark; Casting, Nina Gold; an Alain Sarde, U.K. Film Council presentation in association with Inside Track of a Thin Man Films; British-French; Dolby; Color; Rated R; 125 minutes; American release date: October 10, 2004

Imelda Staunton

Alex Kelly, Daniel Mays, Imelda Staunton, Phil Davis

Cast
Vera Drake **Imelda Staunton**
Stan **Phil Davis**
Det. Inspector Webster **Peter Wright**
Frank **Adrian Scarborough**
Joyce **Heather Craney**
Sid **Daniel Mays**
Ethel **Alex Kelly**
Susan **Sally Hawkins**
Reg **Eddie Marsan**

and Ruth Sheen (Lily), Helen Coker (WPC Best), Richard Graham (George), Anna Keaveney (Nellie), Lesley Manville (Mrs. Wells), Simon Chandler (Mr. Wells),Sam Troughton (David), Marion Bailey (Mrs. Fowler), Sandra Voe (Vera's Mother), Chris O'Dowd (Sid's Customer), Sinead Matthews (Very Young Woman), Sid Mitchell (Very Young Man), Leo Bill (Ronny), Gerard Monaco (Kenny), Tilly Vosburgh (Mother of Seven), Alan Williams (Sick Husband), Heather Cameron, Billie Cook, Billy Seymour (Children), Nina Fry, Lauren Holden (Dance Hall Girls), Elizabeth Berrington, Emma Amos (Cynical Ladies), Fenella Woolgar (Susan's Confidante), Joanna Griffiths (Peggy), Wendy Nottingham (Ivy), Nick Henson (Private Doctor), Allan Corduner (Psychiatrist), Angie Wallis (Nurse Willoughby), Judith Scott (Sister Beech), Vinette Robinson (Jamaican Girl), Rosie Cavaliero (Married Woman), Lesley Sharp (Jessie Barnes), Liz White (Pamela Barnes), Anthony O'Donnell (Mr. Walsh), Lucy Pleasance (Sister Coombes), Tracy O'Flaherty (Nurse), Peter Wright (Det. Inspector Webster), Martin Savage (Det. Sgt. Vickers), Tom Ellis (Police Constable), Robert Putt (Station Sergeant), Craig Conway (Station Constable), Jake Woof (Ruffian), Vincent Franklin (Mr. Lewis), Michael Gunn (Magistrate),

Imelda Staunton, Phil Davis

Paul Jesson (Magistrate's Clerk), Paul Raffield, Jim Broadbent (Judges), Philip Childs (Prosecution Barrister), Jeffry Wickham (Defense Barrister), Nicholas Jones (Usher), Stephan Dunbar, Angela Curran, Jane Wood (Prisoners), Eileen Davies (Prison Officer)

In early 1950s England, good-hearted housewife Vera Drake secretly performs illegal abortions on the side for underprivileged women.

This film received Oscar nominations for actress (Imelda Staunton), director, and original screenplay.

Imelda Staunton, Phil Davis, Helen Coker PHOTOS COURTESY OF FINE LINE FEATURES

THE FINAL CUT

(LIONS GATE) Producer, Nick Wechsler; Executive Producers, Nancy Paloian-Breznikar, Marco Mehlitz, Michael Ohoven Paseorenk, Guymon Casady; Co-Producers, Eberhard Kayser, William Vince; DIrector/Screenplay, Omar Naim; Photography, Tak Fujimoto; Designer, James Chindlund; Costumes, Monique Prudhomme; Music, Brian Tyler; Editors, Dede Allen, Robert Brakey; Special Effects, Gary Paller; a Lions Gate Entertainment, Cinerenta presentation of an Industry Entertainment, Cinetheta production; Canadian-German; Dolby; Panavision; Deluxe; DV-to-35mm; Rated PG-13; 105 minutes; American release date: October 15, 2004

Cast

Alan Hakman **Robin Williams**
Delila **Mira Sorvino**
Fletcher **Jim Caviezel**
Thelma **Mimi Kuzyk**
Hasan **Thom Bishops**
Michael **Brendan Fletcher**
Simon **Vincent Gale**
Jennifer Bannister **Stephanie Romanov**
Isabel Bannister **Genevieve Buechner**
Young Alan, age 9 **Casey Dubois**
Young Louis Hunt, age 9 **Liam Ranger**

Mira Sorvino, Robin Williams PHOTO COURTESY OF LIONS GATE

and Joely Collins (Legz, the Tattoo Artist), Michael St. John Smith (Charles Bannister), Chris Britton (Jason Monroe), Wanda Cannon (Caroilne Munroe), Chaka White (Pregnant Woman on Bus), Don Ackerman (Tattooed Man), Sarah Deakins (Eliza Monroe), George Gordon (Daniel Monroe), Spencer Achtymichuk (James Monroe, Age 6), Erin Wright (Battered Woman), Miguelito Macario (Rom), Emy Aneke (Security Guard), Stephen Dimopoulos (Uncle Murray), Wendy Noel, Kwesi Ameyaw (Guests), Leanne Adachi (Nathalie), Peter Hall (Adult Louis Hunt), Johnna Wright (Mrs. Hakman), Bart Anderson (Mr. Hakman), Stefan Arngrim (Oliver), Darren Shahlavi (Karim), Blu Mankuma (Zoe Tech Representative), Richard Hendery (Balding Man), Jim Francis (Professor), Jason Diablo (Bobby), Lisa Bunting (Sobbing Woman), Doreen Eby

(Delivery Nurse), Andrew Bramley (Doctor), David James (Dad), Elizabeth Urrea (Patient Parent), Barbara Krebesova (Squabbling Wife), Kolja Liquette (Squabbling Husband), Bryan Elliot (Pregnant Woman's Husband), Ryan Gates (Aging Man), Ian Gschwind (Man), Ellen Kennedy (Woman), Mike Jocelyn (Business Man), Kevin Mundy (Toasting Guy), Katina Robillard (Pretty Woman), Lee Walker, Anne Whitemole (Friends), Darren Hird (Voice of Danny Monroe), W.J. "Bill" Waters (Old Man), Noah Beggs (Protestor), Suzie Stingle (Swing Girl), Rick Pearce (Screeching Car Driver), Carolyn Field (Screeching Car Passenger)

In the future when Zoe chips are implanted in human beings to record their entire life since birth, a "cutter," asked to present an edited film of an executive's life at the man's funeral, begins to question the ethics of his job.

Salimata Traoré, Fatoumata Coulibaly in *Moolaadé* PHOTO COURTESY OF NEW YORKER

MOOLAADÉ

(NEW YORKER) Producer/Director/Screenplay, Ousmane Sembene; Photography, Dominique Gentil; Designer, Joseph Kpobly; Music, Boncana Maïga; Editor, Abdellatif Raïss; a co-production of Ciné-Sud Promotion, Centre Cinematographique Morocian Cinétéléfilms, Direction de la Cinematographie Nationale, Filmi Domireew, Les Films Terre Africaine; Senegal-French-Burkina Faso-Cameroon-Morccocan-Tunisian; Dolby; Color; Not rated; 124 minutes; American release date: October 15, 2004

Cast

Colle Gallo Ardo Sy **Fatoumata Coulibaly**
Hadjatou **Maimouna Hélène Diarra**
Amasatou **Salimata Traoré**
Mercenaire **Dominique Zeïda**
Doyenne des Exciseuses **Mah Compaoré**
Alima Bâ **Aminata Dao**
Mah **Stéphanie Nikiema**
Oumy **Mamissa Sanogo**

A woman in a small West African village risks sheltering some young girls who refuse to participate in the ritual of having their genitals mutilated.

BEING JULIA

(SONY CLASSICS) Proudcer, Robert Lantos; Executive Producers, Mark Millin, Marion Pilowsky, Donald A. Starr, Daniel J.B. Taylor; Co-Producers, Julia Rosenberg, Mark Musselman, Sandra Cunningham, Lajos Ovari; Director, Istvan Szabo; Screenplay, Ronald Harwood; Based on the novel *Theater* by W. Somerset Maugham; Photography, Lajos Koltai; Designer, Luciana Arrighi; Costumes, John Bloomfield; Music, Mychael Danna; Editor, Susan Shipton; Casting, Celestia Fox; a Serendipity Point Films presentation, in association with First Choic Films, Astral Media, Telefilm Canada, Corus Entertainment, Myriad Pictures, ISL Films, Hogarth Prods., Sony Pictures Classics, of a Robert Lantos production; Canadian-British-Hungarian; Dolby; Deluxe color; Rated R; 104 minutes; American release date: October 15, 2004

Annette Bening, Jeremy Irons

Annette Bening, Lucy Punch

Cast

Julia Lambert **Annette Bening**
Michael Gosselyn **Jeremy Irons**
Lord Charles **Bruce Greenwood**
Dolly de Vries **Miriam Margolyes**
Evie **Juliet Stevenson**
Tom Fennel **Shaun Evans**
Avice Crichton **Lucy Punch**
Walter Gibbs **Maury Chaykin**
Grace Dexter **Sheila McCarthy**
Jimmie Langton **Michael Gambon**
Archie Dexter **Leigh Lawson**
Mrs. Lambert **Rosemary Harris**
Aunt Carrie **Rita Tushingham**
Roger Gosselyn **Thomas Sturridge**

and Mari Kiss (Mr. Gosselyn's Secretary), Ronald Markham (Butler), Terry Sachs (Chauffeur), Catherine Charlton (Miss Philips), Max Irons (Curtain Call Boy), Andrew Paton Story Busher, Alison Jiear (Singers), George Lang (Atoine the Maitre D), Michael Culkin (Rupert), Marsha Fitzalan (Florence), Denzal Sinclaire (Singer/Pianist), Julian Richings (Mr. Turnbull), Teresa Churcher (Cynthia), Istvan Komlos (Prompter), Bruce Anderson (Jewellery Shop Assistant), Bryan Burdon (Busker "Chamberlain")

Annette Bening, Shaun Evans

An aging, temperamental actress, worried about the future of her career, has an affair with a young admirer.

This film received an Oscar nomination for actress (Annette Bening).

Michael Gambon, Annette Bening PHOTOS COURTESY OF SONY CLASSICS

John Sharian

Jennifer Jason Leigh

Christian Bale PHOTOS COURTESY OF PARAMOUNT CLASSICS

THE MACHINIST

(PARAMOUNT CLASSICS) Producer, Julio Fernandez; Executive Producers, Antonia Nava, Carlos Fernandez; Director, Brad Anderson; Screenplay, Scott A. Kossar; Photography, Xavi Gimenez; Designer, Alain Bainee; Costumes, Patricia Monne; Music, Roque Banos; Editor, Louis de la Madrid; Casting, Pep Armengol, Wendy Brazington, Sheila Jaffe; a Filmax Entertainment presentation of a Julio Fernandez production of Castelao Prods.; Spanish; Dolby; Widescreen; Color; Rated R; 102 minutes; American release date: October 22, 2004

Aitana Sanchez- Gijon

Cast

Trevor Reznik **Christian Bale**
Stevie **Jennifer Jason Leigh**
Marie **Aitana Sanchez-Gijon**
Ivan **John Sharian**
Miller **Michael Ironside**
Jackson **Larry Gilliard**
Jones **Reg E. Cathey**
Mrs. Shike **Anna Massey**
Nicholas **Matthew Romero Moore**
Supervisor Furman **Robert Long**
Inspector Rogers **Colin Stinton**
Tucker **Craig Stevenson**
Gonazles **Ferran Lahoz**
Evangelisti **Jeremy Xidu**

and Norman Bell (DMV Clerk), Nancy Crane (Waitress), Richard Torrington (Radiologist), Buffy Davis (Marge), Reg Wilson (Bartender), Ramon Camín (Detective), Christopher Hood (Drunk), Marc Aspinall (Inspector Daniels), Guillermo Ayesa (Old Fisherman), Daniel Ceren (Pedestrian), Marta Rubio (Woman in Crowd), Ewan Watson (Man in Crowd), Chike Johnson (Young Policeman), Molly Malcolm (Ticket Agent), Jaume Mimó (Man in Stall), Flora Àlvarez (Woman in Stall)

A troubled machinist who hasn't slept in a year blames his weight loss on unexplained images and messages that seemed to be connected to some terrible secret from his past.

ENDURING LOVE

(PARAMOUNT CLASSICS) Producer, Kevin Loader; Executive Producers, Francois Ivernel, Cameron McCracken, Duncan Reid, Tessa Ross; Director, Roger Michell; Screenplay, Joe Penhall; Based on the novel by Ian McEwan; Photography, Haris Zambarloukos; Designer, John-Paul Kelly; Costumes, Natalie Ward; Music, Jeremy Sams; Editor, Nicolas Gaster; Line Producer, Rosa Romero; Casting, Mary Selway, Fiona Weir; a Pathe Pictures presentation in association with the U.K. Film Council and FilmFour and in association with Inside Track of a Free Range Films production; British; Dolby; Panavision; Deluxe color; Rated R; 97 minutes; American release date: October 29, 2004

Cast

Joe Rose **Daniel Craig**
Jed **Rhys Ifans**
Claire **Samantha Morton**
Robin **Bill Nighy**
Rachel **Susan Lynch**
Mrs. Logan **Helen McCrory**
TV Producer **Andrew Lincoln**
Professor **Corin Redgrave**
Grandfather **Bill Weston**
Boy in Balloon **Jeremy McCurdie**
John Logan **Lee Sheward**
Farmer **Nick Wilkinson**
Spud **Ben Whishaw**
Frank **Justin Salinger**

Rhys Ifans, Daniel Craig

Rhys Ifans

Daniel Craig, Samantha Morton

and Rosanna Michell (Katie Logan), Ella Doyle (Katie Logan's Friend), Félicité Du Jeu (Girl in Logan's Car), Alexandra Aitken (Natasha), Aofie Carroll, Rory Carroll, Sophie Duncan, Susan Duncan (Robin & Rachel's Children), Anna Maxwell Martin (Penny)

After being involved in an unsuccessful attempt to rescue an out of control balloon, Joe Rose finds himself being stalked by one of the other men who tried to help.

Bill Nighy PHOTOS COURTESY OF PARAMOUNT CLASSICS

Fanny Ardant (center)

Joan Plowright

Fanny Ardant, Jeremy Irons

CALLAS FOREVER

(HERE!/REGENT) Producers, Ricccardo Tozzi, Giovannella Zannoni; Executive Producers, Marco Chimenz, Giovanni Stabilini; Line Producers, Pino Butti, Farid Chaouhce, Ricardo García Arrojo; Co-Producers, Andrei Boncea, Fabio Conversi, Olivier Granier, Clive Parsons, Francisco Ramos; Director, Franco Zeffirelli; Screenplay, Martin Sherman, Franco Zeffirelli; Based on an idea by Franco Zeffirelli; Photography, Ennio Guarnieri; Designer, Bruno Cesari; Designer for *Carmen* Sequence, Carlo Centolavigna; Costumes, Annae Annie, Alberto Spiazzi, Karl Lagerfeld, Alessandro Lai; Music, Alessio Vlad; Editor, Sean Barton; Casting, Ilene Starger, Emma Style; a co-production of Medusa Produzione, Catteya, Alquimia Cinema, Galfin, MediaPro Pictures, France 2 Cinema; Italian-French-Spanish-British-Romanian, 2002; Dolby; Color; Rated PG-13; 111 minutes; American release date: November 5, 2004

Cast

Maria Callas	**Fanny Ardant**
Larry Kelly	**Jeremy Irons**
Sarah Keller	**Joan Plowright**
Michael	**Jay Rodan**
Marco	**Gabriel Garko**
Esteban	**Gomez Manuel de Blas**
Scarpia	**Justino Díaz**
Gérard	**Jean Dalric**
Brendan	**Stephen Billington**
Bruna	**Anna Lelio**
Marcello	**Alessandro Bertolucci**
Thierry	**Olivier Galfione**
Escamillo	**Roberto Sanchez**
Ferruccio	**Achille Brugnini**
Eugene	**Eugene Kohn**

and in the *Carmen* scenes: Maria del Mar Rivas (Frasquita), Concha Lopez (Mercedes), Bryan Jardine, Sorin Popa, Bill Avery, Onochi Seietsu (Businessmen), Angel Muñoz, Lucía Real (Featured Dancers); Anna McElhinney, Tara Marie Anderson, Tomi Cristin, Razvan Popa, Barry Mulligan, Florin Piersic, Jr. (Journalists)

At the end of her career Maria Callas is talked into doing a film of *Carmen* in which she would lip sync to her old recordings.

Jay Rodan, Jeremy Irons PHOTOS COURTESY OF HERE!/REGENT FILMS

BRIDGET JONES: THE EDGE OF REASON

(UNIVERSAL/MIRAMAX) Producers, Tim Bevan, Eric Fellner, Jonathan Cavendish; Executive Producers, Debra Hayward, Liza Chasin; Director, Beeban Kidron; Screenplay, Andrew Davies, Helen Fielding, Richard Curtis, Adam Brooks; Based on the novel by Helen Fielding; Line Producer, Bernard Bellew; Photography, Adrian Biddle; Designer, Gemma Jackson; Costumes, Jany Temime; Music, Harry Gregson-Williams; Editor, Greg Hayden; Casting, Michelle Guish; a StudioCanal presentation of a Working Title production; British-U.S.; Dolby; Panavision; Color; Rated PG-13; 108 minutes; American release date: November 12, 2004

Renée Zellweger

Cast

Bridget Jones **Renée Zellweger**
Daniel Cleaver **Hugh Grant**
Mark Darcy **Colin Firth**
Dad **Jim Broadbent**
Mum **Gemma Jones**

and Jacinda Barrett (Rebecca), Sally Phillips (Shazzer), Shirley Henderson (Jude), James Callis (Tom), Jessica Stevenson (Magda), Nell Pearson (Richard Finch), James Faulkner (Uncle Geoffrey), Celia Imrie (Una Alconbury), Campbell Graham (Hamish), Joan Blackham (Shirley), Dominc McHale (Bernard), Donald Douglas (Admiral Darcy), Shirley Dixon (Mrs. Darcy), Alex Fixsen (Cameraman in Aircr Aft), Neil Pearso (Richard Finch), David Cann (Cameraman in Field), Rosalind Halstead (Receptionist), Luis Soto (Mexican Ambassador), Tom Brooke (Production Assistant), Alba Fleming Furlan (Girl in Rome), Lucy Robinson (Janey), David Verrey (Giles Benwick), Mark Tandy (Derek), Stephanie O'Rourke (Sexy P.A.), Jeremy Paxman (Himself), Flaminia Cinque (Scary Corset Lady), Jessica Stevenson (Magda), Trevor Fox (Hairdresser), Alex Jennings (Horatio), Catherine Russell (Camilla), Ian McNeice (Quizmaster), Phillip Gardner (Toastmaster), Wolf Kahler (Commentator), Lilo Baur (Chemist), Hans Flaschberger, Sabina Michael, Paul Humpoletz (Chemist Customers), Joe Caffrey (Homeless Man), Paul Nicholls (Jed), David Auker (Clive, Man on Plane), Patrick Baladi (Steward), Rong Kaomulkadee (Thai Chef), Ting Ting Hu (Thai Prostitute), Michelle Lee (Thai Police Woman), Hon Ping Tang (Thai Jail Guard), Suthas Bhoopongsa (Dudwani), Jason Watkins (Charlie Parker-Knowles), Vee Vimolmal (Phrao), Melissa Ashworth, Pui Fan Lee

Renée Zellweger, Hugh Grant

(Thai Jail Girls), Oliver Chris (Director in Gallery), Sam Hazeldine, Amanda Haberland (Journalists), Neil Dudgeon (Taxi Driver), Peter Gordon (Porter), Sam Beazley (Very Old Man), Simon Andreu Trobat (Mr. Santiago), Arturo Venegas (Mr. Hernandez), Frances Jeater (Miss Gallagher), Christopher Adamson (Man in Corridor), Richard Braine (Vicar)

Bridget Jones begins to wonder if she can sustain her happy relationship with Mark Darcy when she finds herself tempted by her former suitor and ex-boss, Daniel Cleaver. Sequel to the 2001 Miramax-Universal release *Bridget Jones's Diary*, with most of the principals repeating their roles.

Gemma Jones, Renée Zellweger, Jim Broadbent

Renée Zellweger, Colin Firth PHOTOS COURTESY OF UNIVERSAL/MIRAMAX

LA PETITE LILI

(FIRST RUN FEATURES) Executive Producer, Sylvestre Guarino; Co-Producers, Denise Robert, Daniel Lewis; Director, Claude Miller; Screenplay, Claude Miller, Julien Boivent; Based on Anton Chekhov's play *The Seagull* ; Photography, Gerard de Battista; Art Director, Jean-Pierre Kohut Svelko; Costumes, Jacquelie Bouchard; Editor, Veronique Lange; a Les Films de la Boissiere (France)/Cinemaginaire (Canada) production, in association with Les Films Alain Sarde, France 3 Cinema; French-Canadian, 2003; Dolby; Color; Not rated; 104 minutes; American release date: November 12, 2004

Robinson Stevenin, Ludivine Sagnier

Julie Depardieu

Cast

Mado Marceaux **Nicole Garcia**
Brice **Bernard Giraudeau**
Simon Marceaux **Jean-Pierre Marielle**
Lili **Ludivine Sagnier**
Julien Marceaux **Robinson Stevenin**
Jeanne-Marie **Julie Depardieu**
Serge **Yves Jacques**
Leone **Anne Le Ny**
Guy **Marc Betton**
Actor Playing Simon **Michel Piccoli**
Actress Playing Leone **Louise Boisvert**
Julien's Assistant **Charles Senard**

In this modern variation on *The Seagull*, a group of people involved in the film industry gather in Southern Brittany at the house of famous actress Mado Marceaux .

Ludivine Sagnier

Bernard Giraudeau, Nicole Garcia PHOTOS COURTESY OF FIRST RUN FEATURES

Gael García Bernal

Gael García Bernal, Lluís Homar

Gael García Bernal, Javier Cámara

Raúl García Forneiro, Nacho Pérez PHOTOS COURTESY OF SONY CLASSICS

BAD EDUCATION

(SONY CLASSICS) Producer, Agustin Almodóvar; Director/Screenplay, Pedro Almodovar; Photography, Jose Luis Alcaine; Art Director, Antxon Gomez; Music, Alberto Iglesias; Editor, Jose Salcedo; an El Deseo production, in association with TVE, Canal+; Spanish; Dolby; Panavision; Color; Rated NC-17; 104 minutes; American release date: November 19, 2004

Gael García Bernal

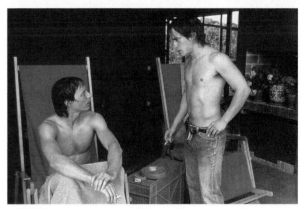

Fele Martínez, Gael García Bernal

Cast

Ángel/Juan/Zahara **Gael García Bernal**
Enrique Goded **Fele Martínez**
Father Manolo **Daniel Giménez Cacho**
Sr. Manuel Berenguer **Lluís Homar**
Paca/Paquito **Javier Cámara**
Mother **Petra Martínez**
Young Ignacio **Nacho Pérez**
Young Enrique **Raúl García Forneiro**
Ignacio **Francisco Boira**

and Juan Fernández (Martín), Alberto Ferreiro (Enrique Serrano), Roberto Hoyas (Camarero), Francisco Maestre (Padre José), Leonor Watling (Mónica), Pedro Almodóvar (Pool Attendant)

A filmmaker, struggling to come up with his next picture, is given a story by his former schoolmate who brings back memories of when the two boys were lovers at the Catholic institution they attended.

Collin Farrell, Jonathan Rhys-Meyers

Rosario Dawson, Colin Farrell

Connor Paolo, Christopher Plummer PHOTOS COURTESY OF WARNER BROS.

ALEXANDER

(WARNER BROS.) Producers, Thomas Schühly, Jon Kilik, Iain Smith, Moritz Borman; Executive Producers, Paul Rassam, Matthias Deyle; Co-Executive Producers, Gianni Nunnari, Fernando Sulichin; Director, Oliver Stone; Screenplay, Christopher Kyle, Laeta Kalogridis; Photography, Rodrigo Prieto; Designer, Jan Roelfs; Costumes, Jenny Beavan; Music, Vangelis; Editors, Tom Nordberg, Yann Herve; Stunts, Gary Powell; Casting, Hopkins Smith & Barden; Visual Effects, The Moving Picture Company; an Intermedia Films presentation of a Moritz Borman production in association with IMF; French-British-Dutch; Dolby; Super 35 Widescreen; Color; Rated R; 175 minutes; American release date: November 24, 2004

Colin Farrell

Cast

Alexander **Colin Farrell**
Olympias **Angelina Jolie**
Philip **Val Kilmer**
Aristotle **Christopher Plummer**
Hephaistion **Jared Leto**
Roxane **Rosario Dawson**
Old Ptolemy **Anthony Hopkins**
Cassander **Jonathan Rhys-Meyers**
Wrestling Trainer **Brian Blessed**
Omen Reader **Tim Pigott-Smith**
Young Alexander **Connor Paolo**
Cleitus **Gary Stretch**
Parmenion **John Kavanagh**
Attalus **Nick Dunning**
Eurydice **Marie Meyer**
Ptolemy **Elliot Cowan**
Philotas **Joseph Morgan**
Antigonous **Ian Beattie**
Nearchus **Denis Conway**
Perdiccas **Neil Jackson**
Crateros **Rory McCann**
Darius **Raz Degan**
Stateira **Annelise Hesme**

and Feodor Atkine (Roxane's Father), David Bedella (Scribe), Jesse Kamm (Child Alexander), Fiona O'Shaughnessy (Nurse), Patrick Carroll (Young Hephaistion), Brian Blessed (Wrestling Trainer), Peter Williamson (Young Nerachus), Morgan Christopher Ferris (Young Cassander), Robert Eearley (Young Ptolemy), Aleczander Gordon (Young Perdiccas), Mick Lally (Horse Seller), Garrett Lombard (Leonatus), Chris Aberdein (Polyperchon),

Val Kilmer, Colin Farrell

Anthony Hopkins

Angelina Jolie, Connor Paolo

Michael Dixon (Campfire Sodier), Erol Sander (Persian Prince), Stéphane Ferrara (Bactrian Commander), Tadhg Murphy (Dying Soldier), Jean Le Duc (Fat Eunuch), Francisco Bosch (Bagoas), Annelise Hesme (Stateira), Tsouli Mohammed (Persian Chamberlain), Toby Kebbell (Pausanius), Laird Macintosh (Greek Officer), Rab Affleck (Attalus' Henchman), Féodor Atkine (Roxane's Father), Harry Kent, Sam Green (Cup Bearers), Bin Bunluerit (Indian King), Jaran Ngamdee (Indian Prince), Brian McGrath (Doctor), Suzanne Bullock, Kate Elouse, Gillian Grueber, Michelle Lukes, Anjali Mehra (Roxane Dancers), Anthony Jean Marie Kurt, Marta Barahona, Monica Zamora, Benny Maslov, Tania Matos, Leighton Morrison, Isaac Mullins, Monica Perego, Matthew Powell (Bagoas Dancers), Max Bollinger (Young Greek Official), Charles Haigh (Aristander), Peter Rnic (Greek Nobleman)

Jared Leto

The story of how Alexander the Great became ruler of Macedonia and conquered much of the known world before dying at the age of 32.

Previous movie on the subject was *Alexander the Great* (UA, 1956) starring Richard Burton, Frederic March, and Claire Bloom.

Colin Farrell

Jean-Pierre Becker, Jérôme Kircher, Clovis Cornillac, Gaspard Ulliel, Denis Lavant, Dominique Bettenfeld

Gaspard Ulliel

Audrey Tautou

Gaspard Ulliel

A VERY LONG ENGAGEMENT

(WARNER INDEPENDENT) Executive Producer, Bill Gerber; Director, Jean-Pierre Jeunet; Story and Adaptation, Jean-Pierre Jeunet, Guillaume Laurant; Dialogue, Guillaume Laurant; Based on the novel by Sebastien Japrisot; Photography, Bruno Delbonnel; Set Designer, Aline Bonetto; Costumes, Madeline Fontaine; Makeup, Nathalie Tissier; Music, Angelo Badalamenti; Editor, Herve Schneid; Casting, Pierre-Jacques Benichou; a 2003 Productions and Warner Bros. Pictures presentation of a production by 2003 Productions, a Warner Bros. France, Tapioca Films and TF1 Films production co-production with the participation of Canal+, with the support of The Centre National de la Cinematographie, the Ile de France Region, The Bretagne Region and the participation of Poitou Charentes Region; French; Dolby; Super 35 Widescreen; Color; Rated R; 133 minutes; American release date: November 26, 2004

Dominique Pinon, Audrey Tautou, Anaïs Durand, Chantal Neuwirth, Ticky Holgado

Audrey Tautou, Albert Dupontel

Audrey Tautou

Marion Cotillard

Cast

Mathilde **Audrey Tautou**
Manech **Gaspard Ulliel**
Lieutenant Esperanza **Jean-Pierre Becker**
Ange Bassignano **Dominique Bettenfeld**
Benoît Notre Dame **Clovis Cornillac**
Tina Lombardi **Marion Cotillard**
Benjamin Gordes **Jean-Pierre Darroussin**
Véronique Passavant **Julie Depardieu**
Commandant Lavrouye **Jean-Claude Dreyfus**
Rovières **André Dussollier**
Germain Pire **Ticky Holgado**
Captain Favourier **Techky Karyo**

Bastoche **Jérôme Kircher**
Six-Sous **Denis Lavant**
Bénédicte **Chantal Neuwirth**
Sylvain **Dominique Pinon**
The Postman **Jean-Paul Rouve**
L'il Louis **Michel Vuillermoz**
Elodie Gordes **Jodie Foster**
Lieutenant Estrangin **Thierry Gibault**
The Cafe Prostitute **Myriam Roustan**
The Murdered Officer **Gilles Masson**
Mariette Notre Dame **Sandrine Rigaud**
The Priest of Milly **Michel Chalmeau**
The Prison Director **Marc Faure**
Jean Descrochelles **Rodolphe Pauly**
Chardolot's Friend **Xavier Maly**
The German Prisoner **Till Bahlmann**

and Tony Gaultier, Louis Marie Audubert (The Gravediggers), Jean Gilles Barbier (The Sergeant), Marc Robert, Pierre Heitz, Philippe Maymat, Eric Debrosse, Mike Gondouin (The Soldiers), Eirc Fraticelli (The Menacing Corsican), Philippe Beautier (The Joker on the Train), Gérald Weingand, Luc Songzoni (The Conned Soldiers), Xavier Berlioz (The Orderly), Frankie Pain (The Madam), Marcel Philippot, Pascale Lievyn (The Bourgeois Couple), Jean-Claude Lecoq (The German Machine Gunner), Rufus (A Breton), Esther Sironneau (The Nurse), Stéphanie Gesnel, Frédérique Bel (The Prostitutes), Alexandre Caumartin, Eric Defosse (The Stretcher Bearers), Gaspar Claus (The Stabbed German), Jean-Philippe Beche (Georges Cornu), Anaïs Durand (Helen Pire)

Following the Great War, Mathilde searches against all odds to find her missing lover who was presumed dead or missing.

This film received Oscar nominations for cinematography and art direction.

André Dussollier, Audrey Tautou

A FOND KISS

(CASTLE HILL) Producer, Rebecca O'Brien; Exeuctive Producer, Ulrich Felsberg; Director, Ken Loach; Screenplay, Paul Laverty; Photography, Barry Ackroyd; Designer, Martin Johnson; Costumes, Carole Miller; Music, George Fenton; Editor, Jonathan Morris; Casting, Kathleen Crawford; a co-production of Bianca Film, Cineart, Glasgow Film Officer, Matador Pictures, Scottish Screen, Sixteen Films Ltd., Tornasol Films; British-Belgian-German-Italian-Spanish; Dolby; Color; Rated R; 104 minutes; American release date: November 26, 2004

Cast

Casim Khan **Atta Yaquib**
Roisin Hanlon **Eva Birthistle**
Sadia Khan **Shamshad Akhtar**
Rukhsana Khan **Ghizala Avan**
Tahara Khan **Shabana Baksh**
Tariq Khan **Ahmad Riaz**
Hammid **Shy Ramsan**

and Gerard Kelly (Parish Priest), John Yule (Headmaster), Gary Lewis (Danny), David McKay (Wee Roddie), Raymond Mearns (Big Roddie), Emma Friel (Annie), Karen Fraser (Elsie), Ruth McGhie (Mary Nolan), Father David Wallace (Father David), Dougie Wallace (Janitor), Jacqueline Bett (Jacqueline), Pasha Bocarie (Amar), Foqia Hayee (Amar's Mother), Abdul Hayee (Amar's Father), Sunna Mirza (Jasmine), Balquees Hassan (Jasmine's Mother), Isabel Johnston (Housekeeper), Tommy McKee (Dog Walker)

A look at the relationship between a second-generation Muslim Pakistani and a Catholic Scottish schoolteacher in Glasgow.

Atta Yaquib, Eva Birthistle

Atta Yaquib, Eva Birthistle PHOTOS COURTESY OF CASTLE HILL

HOUSE OF FLYING DAGGERS

(SONY CLASSICS) a.k.a. *Shi mian mai fu*; Producer, Bill Kong, Zhang Yimou; Executive Producer, Zhang Weiping; Director, Zhang Yimou; Screenplay, Li Feng, Zhang Yimou, Wang Bin; Story, Zhang Yimou, Li Feng, Zhang Wang Bin; Photography, Zhao Xiaoding; Designer, Huo Tingxiao; Costumes, Emi Wada; Music, Shigeru Umebayashi; Editor, Cheng Long; Action Director, Tony Ching Siu-tung; Martial Arts Coordinator, Li Cai; Visual Effects, Animal Ogic Film, Digital Pictures Iloura, Menfond Electronic Art & Computer Design; an Elite Group (2003) Enterprises presentation of an Edko Films (Hong Kong)/Zhang Yimou Studio (China) produciton, in association with Beijing New Picture Film Co., China Film Coproduction Corp.; Hong Kong-Chinese; Dolby; Super 35 Widescreen; Color; Rated PG-13; 119 minutes; American release date: December 3, 2004

Cast

Jin **Takeshi Kaneshiro**
Leo **Andy Lau**
Mei **Zhang Ziyi**
Yee **Song Dandan**

Two police captains go in search of the leader of the rebel group the Flying Daggers and end up battling for the love of his daughter.

This film received an Oscar nomination for cinematography.

Zhang Ziyi

Takeshi Kaneshiro, Zhang Ziyi

Takeshi Kaneshiro, Andy Lau

Takeshi Kaneshiro PHOTOS COURTESY OF SONY CLASSICS

Zhang Ziyi

BEYOND THE SEA

(LIONS GATE) Producers, Andy Paterson, Jan Fanti, Kevin Spacey, Arthur E. Friedman; Director, Kevin Spacey; Screenplay, Kevin Spacey, Lewis Colick; Photography, Eduardo Serra; Designer, Andrew Laws; Costumes, Ruth Myers; Editor, Tgrevor Waite; Make-Up/Hair Design, Peter Swords King; Choreographer, Rob Ashford; Music Producer, Phil Ramone; Executive Producers, Jim Reeve, Steve Robbins, Thierry Potok, Henning Molfenter, Joanne Horowitz, Douglas E. Hansen; Line Producer, Guy Yannahill; Casting, Joanna Colbert, Mary Selway, Fiona Weir, Risa Kes, Jill Green; a Lions Gate Film presentation of an Archer Street/QI Qwuality Intl./Trigger Street production in association with Vision view, Studio Babelsberg Motion Pictures, Endgame Entertainment, Element X and Medienboard Berlin-Brandenburg; British-German; Dolby; Super 35 Widescreen; Color; Rated PG-13; 114 minutes; American release date: December 17, 2004

Kevin Spacey

Bob Hoskins

Kate Bosworth, Kevin Spacey

Cast

Bobby Darin **Kevin Spacey**
Sandra Dee **Kate Bosworth**
Steve Blauner **John Goodman**
Charlie Cassotto Maffia **Bob Hoskins**
Polly Cassotto **Brenda Blethyn**
Mary Duvan **Greta Schacchi**
Nina Cassotto Maffia **Caroline Aaron**
Dick Behrke **Peter Cincotti**

and Michael Byrne (Dr. Andretti), Matt Rippy (David Gershenson), Gary Whelan (Jules Podell), William Ullrich (Little Bobby), Jake Broder (1st Asst. Dir.), Tayfun Bademsoy (Ahmet Ertegun), Tomas Spencer (Delivery Guy), Tom Mannion (Movie Set Reporter), Marcus Brigstocke (Radio Host), Crutis Victor (Dodd Mitchell Cassotto, 11 yrs.), Enrique Alberto Saunders (Dodd Mitchell Cassotto, 6 yrs.), Vinzenz Kiefer (Las Vegas Bellhop), Harvey Friedman (Sandra Dee's Make-up Artist), Andrew James Laws (Director), Torben Liebrecht (1st Trumpet Player), Jeffrey Mittleman (Bass Guitarist), Toni Nissi (Drummer), Clayton Nemrow (Guitarist), Andreas Renell (Ralph Edwards), Mathew Burton (Producer), Natalie O'Hara (Script Supervisor), Sabine Winterfeldt (Costume Designer),

Richie Gibson, Lorenzo Fruzza (Production Assistants), Rene Ifrah (2nd Asst. Dir.), Martin Arno (Sound Mixer), Howard Cooper (Sound Engineer), Joseph Sumner (Sound Asst.), J.J. Straub (Friend of Charlie), Holly Jane Rahlens (Friend of Nina), Cornell Adams (Bobby's World Player), Will Röttgen, Mehmet Yilmez, Tim Williams, Turgay Manduz, Orhan Guner (Bodyguards), Alberto Fortuzzi (Kitchen Waiter), Megan Gay (Nanny), Shaun Lawton (Italian Movie Director), Vittorio Alfieri (Italian Bellhop), Peter Cotton (Safari Club Heckler), Maria Schuster (Heckler's Date), Johnny Challah (Safari Club Drummer), Ricky Watson (Copa Waiter), Amadeus Martin-Reid (George Kirby), Georg Schramm, Sam Douglas (Variety Show Hosts), John Keogh, Joel Kirby, Andy Gatjen, Gabriel Walsh, Andrew Weale, Michael Traynor, Joost Siedhoff (Mourners)

The true story of how Bobby Darin overcame ill health as a child to become a versatile entertainer during his all-too-short lifetime.

William Ullrich, Brenda Blethyn PHOTOS COURTESY OF LIONS GATE

THE KEYS TO THE HOUSE

(LIONS GATE) a.k.a. *Le Chiavi di casa*; Producer, Enzo Porcelli; Co-Producers, Karl Baumgartner, Bruno Pesery; Director, Gianni Amelio; Screenplay, Gianni Amelio, Sandro Petraglia, Stefano Rulli; Photography, Luca Bigazzi; Designer, Giancarlo Basili; Costumes, Piero Tosi, Cristina Francioni; Music, Franco Piersanti; Editor, Simona Paggi; a RAI Cinema/Achab Film/Pola Pandora Film Produktion/Arena Films co-production; Italian-German-French; Dolby; Color; Not rated; 105 minutes; American release date: December 22, 2004

Kim Rossi Stuart, Andrea Rossi

Kim Rossi Stuart, Andrea Rossi

Cast
Gianni **Kim Rossi Stuart**
Paolo **Andrea Rossi**
Nicole **Charlotte Rampling**
Nadine **Alla Faeriovich**
Alberto **Pierfrancesco Favino**
Taxi Driver **Manuel Katzy**
Andreas **Michael Weiss**

and Ingrid Appenroth (Hospital Warden), Dimitri Süsan (Boy Watching TV), Thorsten Schwartz (Male Nurse), Eric Neumann (Playground Boy), Dirk Zippa (Young Man in Wheelchair), Barbara Koster-Chari (Nurse), Anita Bardeleben (Doctor), Ralf Schlesener (Newspaper Seller), Camilla Erblich (Woman on Tramway), Baernd Weikert (Policeman)

Gianni attempts to bond with his 15-year-old mentally handicapped son who has been raised by his mother.

Kim Rossi Stuart, Charlotte Rampling

Kim Rossi Stuart, Andrea Rossi PHOTOS COURTESY OF LIONS GATE

Gerard Butler

Patrick Wilson, Emmy Rossum

Emmy Rossum, Gerard Butler

THE PHANTOM OF THE OPERA

(WARNER BROS.) Producer/Music, Andrew Lloyd Webber; Executive Producers, Austin Shaw, Paul Hitchcock, Louise Goodsill, Ralph Kamp, Jeff Abberley, Julia Blackman, Keith Cousins; Director, Joel Schumacher; Screenplay, Andrew Lloyd Webber, Joel Schumacher; Based on the musical with book by Andrew Lloyd Webber, Richard Stilgoe, originally produced for the stage by Cameron Mackintosh & the Really Useful Group, directed by Harold Prince, from the novel *Le Fantôme de l'Opéra* by Gaston Leroux; Lyrics, Charles Hart; Additional Lyrics, Richard Stilgoe; Music Co-Producer, Nigel Wright; Music Supervisor/Conductor, Simon Lee; Choreographer, Peter Darling; Photography, John Mathieson; Production Designer, Anthony Pratt; Costumes, Alexandra Byrne; Editor, Terry Rawlings; Co-Producer, Eli Richbourg; Visual Effects Supervisor, Nathan McGuinness; a Really Useful Films/Scion Films production, presented in association with Odyssey Entertainment; British; Dolby; Panavision; Color; Rated PG-13; 142 minutes; American release date: December 22, 2004

Cast

The Phantom **Gerard Butler**
Christine Daae **Emmy Rossum**
Raoul de Chagny **Patrick Wilson**
Madame Giry **Miranda Richardson**
André **Simon Callow**
Firmin **Ciaran Hinds**
Buquet **Kevin R. McNally**
Carlotta **Minnie Driver**
Piangi **Victor McGuire**
Reyer **Murray Melvin**
Meg Giry **Jennifer Ellison**
Lefevre **James Fleet**
Carlotta's Maid **Imogen Bain**
Carlotta's Wigmaker **Miles Western**
Carlotta's Seamstress **Judith Paris**
Passirino **Halcro Johnston**
Auctioneer **Paul Brooke**
Porter **Oliver Chopping**
Nun/Nurse **Alison Skilbeck**
Chauffer **Lee Sellers**
Christine's Father **Ramin Karimloo**
Young Phantom **Chris Overton**
Young Christine **Jesika Cannon**
Young Madame Giry **Laura Hounsom**
Ballet Tarts **Lucy Casson, Lorraine Stewart**
Principal Male Dancer **Jose Tirado**
Fops **Jonathan D. Ellis, David Langham**
Confidante **Margaret Preece**

A young chorus girl falls under the spell of the mysterious, deformed phantom who haunts the opera house and wishes for her to become his protege and replace the temperamental Carlotta as the company's star. Previous film versions of the Leroux novel were done in 1925 (Universal, starring Lon Chaney), 1943 (Universal, Claude Rains), 1962 (Hammer-Universal, Herbert Lom), and 1989 (21st Century, Robert Englund).

Emmy Rossum, Jennifer Ellison

Miranda Richardson

Gerard Butler, Emmy Rossum

This film received Oscar nominations for original song ("Learn to Be Lonely"), cinematography, and art direction.

Murray Melvin, Ciaran Hinds, Minnie Driver, Victor McGuire, Simon Callow

Patrick Wilson PHOTOS COURTESY OF WARNER BROS.

Don Cheadle

Sophie Okonedo, Don Cheadle PHOTOS COURTESY OF UNITED ARTISTS/LIONS GATE

HOTEL RWANDA

(UNITED ARTISTS/LIONS GATE) Producers, A. Kitman Ho, Terry George; Executive Producers, Duncan Reid, Sam Bhembe, Roberto Cicutto, Francesco Melzi D'Eril, Hal Sadoff, Martin F. Katz; Director, Terry George; Screenplay, Keir Pearson, Terry George; Photography, Robert Fraisse; Designers, Tony Burrough, Johnny Breedt; Costumes, Ruy Filipe; Editor, Naomi Geraghty; Co-Executive Producers, Bridget Pickering, Luigi Musini; Co-Producers, Bridget Pickering, Luigi Musini; Music, Andrea Guerra, Rupert Gregson-Williams, Afro Celt Sound System; Line Producer, Sally French; a Miracle Pictures/Seamus production produced in association with Inside Track & Mikado Film, co-produced in association with The Industrial Development Corporation of South Africa; British-South African-Italian; Dolby; Super 35 Widescreen, Technicolor; Rated PG-13; 121 minutes; American release date: December 22, 2004

Nick Nolte, Don Cheadle

Cast

Paul Rusesabagina **Don Cheadle**
Tatiana Rusesbagina **Sophie Okonedo**
Jack Daglish **Joaquin Phoenix**
Dube **Desmond Dube**
David **David O'Hara**
Pat Archer **Cara Seymour**
General Bizimungu **Fana Mokoena**
George Rutagunda **Hakeem Kae-Kazim**
Gregoire **Tony Kgoroge**
Elys Rusesabagina **Mosa Kaiser**
Diane Rusesabagina **Mathabo Pieterson**
Roger Rusesabagina **Ofentse Moidselle**
Colonel Oliver **Nick Nolte**
Policeman **Xolani Mali**
Receptionist **Rosie Motene**
Jean Jacques **Neil McCarthy**
Head Chef **Kid Sithole**
Old Guard **Jeremiah Ndlovu**
Odette **Lebo Mashile**
Thomas Mirama **Antonio David Lyons**

Antonio Lyons, Sophie Okonedo, Don Cheadle

and Leleti Khumalo (Fedens), Kgomotso Seitshohlo (Anais), Lerator Mokgotho (Carine), Lennox Mathabathe (Peter), Mothusi Magano (Benedict), Noxolo Maqashalala (Chloe, Prostitute), Thulane Nyembe (Jean Baptiste), Simo Magwaza (Hutu Captain), Miiriam Ngomani (Gregoire's Girlfriend), Harriet Manamela (Alice the Waitress), Roberto Citran (Priest), Mduduzi Mabaso (Hutu Lieutenant), Sonni Cihdiebere, Sibusiso Mholongo (Militiamen),Thomas Kariuki (Xavier), Ashleigh Tobias (Medic)

Cara Seymour, Sophie Okonedo

Don Cheadle

Desmond Dube, Don Cheadle

Sophie Okonedo, Don Cheadle

The true story of how hotel owner Paul Rusesabagina managed to save over 1,200 people from being killed during the genocide crisis in Rwanda in 1994.

This film received Oscar nominations for actor (Don Cheadle), supporting actress Sophie Okonedo, and original screenplay.

Don Cheadle, Nick Nolte

THE CHORUS

(MIRAMAX) a.k.a. *Les Choristes*; Producers, Jacques Perrin, Arthur Cohn, Nicolas Mauvernay; Director, Christophe Barratier; Screenplay, Christophe Barratier, Philippe Lopes-Curval; Inspired by the screenplay to the film *La cauge aux rossignols* by Noel-Noel Rene Wheeler, Geroges Chaperot; Photography, Carlo Varini, Dominique Gentil; Designer, Francois Chauvaud; Costumes, Francoise Guegan; Music, Bruno Coulais; Song: "Look to Your Path (Vois sur ton chemin)" by Bruno Coulais (music) and Christophe Barratier (lyrics); Editor, Yves Deschamps; Casting, Sylvie Brochere; a Jacques Perrin presentation of a Galatee Films, Pathe Renn Prod., France 2 Cinema (France)/Novo Arturo Films, Vega Film (Switzerland) production, in association with Banques Populaires Images 4, with the participation of Canal+; French-Swiss; Dolby; Widescreen; Color; Rated PG-13; 97 minutes; American release date: December 22, 2004

The Chorus

In 1949 France, a new teacher arrives at a harsh disciplinary reform school for boys and hopes to reach his new charges by starting a choir. Remake of the 1947 film *La cage aux rossignols* (*A Cage of Nightingales*).

This film received Oscar nominations for foreign langauge film and original song ("Look to Your Path").

Gérard Jugnot

Cast

Clément Mathieu **Gérard Jugnot**
Rachin **François Berléand**
Chabert **Kad Merad**
Maxence **Jean-Paul Bonnaire**
Violette Morhange **Marie Bunel**
Adult Pierre Morhange **Jacques Perrin**
Adult Pèpinot **Didier Flamand**
Pierre Morhange **Jean-Baptiste Maunier**
Pèpinot **Maxence Perrin**
Mondain **Grégory Gatignol**
Corbin **Thoams Blumental**
Le Querrec **Cyril Bernicot**
Boniface **Simon Fargeot**
Leclerc **Théodul Carré-Cassaigne**
Monsieur Langlois **Philippe Du Janerand**
Countess **Carole Weiss**

and Erick Desmarestz (Doctor Dervaux), Paul Chariéas (Regent), Armen Godel (Medic), Monique Ditisheim (Marie), Steve Gadler (Assistant to Pierre), Fabrice Dubuseset (Carpentier), Marielle Coubaillon (Madame Rachin), Violette Barratier, Lena Chalvon (Rachin's Daughters), Colette Dupanloup (Cook)

Jean Baptiste Maunier

Marie Bunel, Gérard Jugnot PHOTOS COURTESY OF MIRAMAX

WILLIAM SHAKESPEARE'S
THE MERCHANT OF VENICE

(SONY CLASSICS) Producers, Cary Brokaw, Barry Navidi, Jason Piette, Michael Lionello Cowan; Executive Producers, Manfred Wilde, Michael Hammer, Peter James, James Simpson, Alex Marshall, Robert Jones; Co-Producers, Nigel Goldsack, Jimmy de Brabant, Edwige Fenech, Luciano Martino; Co-Executive Producers, Gary Hamilton, Pete Maggi, Julia Verdin; Director/Screenplay, Michael Radford; Based on the play by William Shakespeare; Photography, Benoit Delhomme; Designer, Bruno Rubeo; Costumes, Sammy Sheldon; Music, Jocelyn Pook; Editor, Lucia Zucchetti; Make-up/Hair Designer, Anna Buchanan; Casting, Sharon Howard-Field; a Movision Entertainment, Arclight Films presentation in association with U.K. Film Council, Film Fund Luxembourg, Delux Prods., Immagine e Cinema, Dania Film, Instituto Luce of an Avenue Pictures, Navidi-Wilde Prods., Spice Factory production; British-Italian-U.S.-Luxembourg; Dolby; Super 35 Widescreen; Deluxe color; Rated R; 131 minutes; American release date: December 29, 2004

Lynn Collins, Heather Goldenhersh

Cast
Shylock **Al Pacino**
Antonio **Jeremy Irons**
Bassanio **Joseph Fiennes**
Portia **Lynn Collins**
Jessica **Zuleikha Robinson**
Gratiano **Kris Marshall**
Lorenzo **Charlie Cox**
Nerissa **Heather Goldenhersh**
Lancelot Gobbo **Mackenzie Crook**
Salerio **John Sessions**
Solanio **Gregor Fisher**
Old Gobbo **Ron Cook**
Tubal **Allan Corduner**
The Duke **Anton Rodgers**

and David Harewood (Prince of Morocco), Antonio Gil-Martinez (Aragon), Al Weaver (Stephano),Norbert Konne (Doctor Bellario), Marc Maas (Cush), Jean-Francois Wolff (German Count), Pieter Riemes (English Baron), Stephan Koziak (Soldier), Tom Leick (French Nobleman), Jules Werner (Franciscan Friar), Tony Schiena (Leonardo), Julian Nest (Clerk)

With the intention of revenging his mistreatment moneylender Shylock agrees to advance Antonio 3,000 ducats under the condition that the latter must forfeit his life if he has not returned to payment in three months.

Joseph Fiennes

Jeremy Irons PHOTOS COURTESY OF SONY CLASSICS

Alan Corduner, Al Pacino

Sabrina Seyvecou. Fabrice Deville, Coralie Revel in *Secret Things*
PHOTO COURTESY OF FIRST RUN FEATURES

SECRET THINGS

(FIRST RUN FEATURES) a.k.a. *Choses secrètes*; Producers, Jean-Claude Brisseau, Jean-Francois Geneix; Director/Screenplay, Jean-Claude Brisseau; Photography, Wilfrid Sempé; Costumes/Designer, Maria Luisa Garcia; Music, Julien Civange; a co-production of the Centre National de la Cinematographie, La Sorciere Rouge, Les Aventuriers de l'Image; French; 2002; Dolby; Color; Not rated; 115 minutes; American release date: January 2, 2004. CAST: Coralie Revel (Nathalie), Sabrina Seyvecou (Sandrine), Roger Mirmont (Delacroix), Fabrice Deville (Christophe), Blandine Bury (Charlotte), Olivier Soler (Cadene), Viviane Theophildes (Mme. Mercier), Dorothee Picard (Delacroix's Mother), Pierre Gabaston (Bar Patron), Lisa Heredia (Sandrine's Mother), Arnaud Goujon (Personnnel Manager), Lies Kidji (Young Thief), Patricia Candido Trinca, Lydia Chopart, Michael Couvreur, Boris Le Roy, Aude Breusse (Office Employees), Aurelien Geneix (Man at Party), Alain Couesnon, Bruno Sx (Bouncer), Sylvain Bourguignon (Client), Jean-Claude Brisseau (Sandrine's Father)

Yves Saint Laurent (center) in *Yves Saint Laurent* PHOTO COURTESY OF EMPIRE

YVES SAINT LAURENT: HIS LIFE AND TIMES

(EMPIRE) Producer, Christian Baute; Director/Screenplay, David Teboul; Photography, Philippe Pavans de Ceccatty, Hélène Louvart; Editor, Annette Dutertre; from Movimento Productions; French; 2002; Color; Not rated; 77 min-

utes; American release date: January 7, 2004. Documentary on French fashion designer Yves Saint-Laurent; featuring Yves Saint-Laurent, Pierre Bergé, Edmonde Charles-Roux, Loulou De La Falaise

YVES SAINT LAURENT: 5 AVENUE MARCEAU 75116 PARIS

(EMPIRE) Executive Producers, Christian Baute, Frederic Luzy; Director/Screenplay, David Teboul; Photography, Caroline Champetier; Editors, Martine Giordano, Annette Dutertre; from Movimento Productions; French; 2002; Dolby; Color; Not rated; 85 minutes; American release date: January 7, 2004. Documentary on designer Yves Saint-Laurent's world of fashion; featuring Yves Saint-Laurent, Pierre Bergé, Catherine Deneuve.

AILEEN: LIFE AND DEATH OF A SERIAL KILLER

(LANTERN LANE) Producer, Jo Human; Directors, Nick Broomfield, Joan Churchill; Photography, Joan Churchill; Music, Robert Lane; Editor, Claire Ferguson; a Lafayette Films production; British-U.S.; Color; Rated R; 89 minutes; American release date: January 9, 2004. Documentary on Aileen Wuornos, who was executed in 2002 for the killing of seven men in the state of Florida; featuring Aileen Wuornos, Nick Broomfield.

Yves Saint Laurent in *Yves Saint Laurent* PHOTO COURTESY OF EMPIRE

TOKYO GODFATHERS

(SAMUEL GOLDWYN/DESTINATION) Producer, Masao Maruyama; Executive Producers, Shinichi Kobayashi, Masao Takiyama, Taro Maki; Director/Story, Satoshi Kon; Co-Director, Shogo Furuya; Screenplay, Satoshi Kon, Keiko Nobumotu; Character Designer, Kenichi Konishi; Art Director, Nobutaka Ike; Music, Keiichi Zuzuki; Editor, Takeshi Seyama; a Tokyo Godfathers Committee production, in association with Mad House (Tokyo); Japanese, 2003; Dolby; Color; Rated PG-13; 90 minutes; American release date: January 16, 2004. VOICE CAST: Toru Emari, Yoshiaki Umegaki, Aya Okamoto.

Tokyo Godfathers PHOTO COURTESY OF SAMUEL GOLDWYN/DESTINATION

CRIMSON GOLD

(WELLSPRING) a.k.a. *Talaye sorkh*; Producer/Director/Editor, Jafar Panahi; Screenplay, Abbas Kiarostami; Photography, Hossein Djafarian; Designer, Iraj Raminfar; Music, Peyman Yazdanian; from Jafar Panahi Film Productions; Iranian, 2003; Color; Not rated; 95 minutes; American release date: January 16, 2004. CAST: Hossain Emadeddin (Hussein), Kamyar Sheisi (Ali), Azita Rayeji (The Bride), Shahram Vaziri (The Jeweler), Ehsan Amani (The Man in the Tea House), Pourang Nakhael (The Rich Man), Kaveh Najmabadi (The Seller), Saber Safael (The Soldier)

Azita Rayeji in *Crimson Gold* PHOTO COURTESY OF WELLSPRING

David Gulpilil in *The Tracker* PHOTO COURTESY OF ARTMATTAN

THE TRACKER

(ARTMATTAN) a.k.a. *Endangered*; Producers, Rolf de Heer, Julie Ryan; Director/Screenplay, Rolf de Heer; Exeuctive Producer, Bridget Ikin; Photography, Ian Jones; Music, Rolf de Heer, Graham Tardif; Editor, Tania Nehme; from Vertigo Productions; Australian, 2002; Dolby; Color; Not rated; 90 minutes; American release date: January 16, 2004. CASt: David Gulpilil (The Tracker), Gary Sweet (The Fanatic), Damon Gameau (The Follower), Grant Page (The Veteran), Noel Wilton (Fugitive)

ON THE RUN

(MAGNOLIA) a.k.a. *Cavale*; Producers, Diana Elbaum, Patrick Sobelman; Director/Screenplay, Lucas Belvaux; Photography, Pierre Milon; Designer, Frédèrique Belvaux; Costumes, Cécile Cotton; Music, Riccardo Del Fra; Editor, Ludo Troch; a co-production of Canal+, Centre National de la Cinematographie, Cofimage 12, Entre Chien et Loup, Eurimages, Gimages 5, Matexis Banques Populaires Images 2, Radio Television Belge Francofone (RTBF), Rhône-Alpes Cinéma; French-Belgian, 2002; Dolby; Color; Not rated; 117 minutes; American release date: January 30, 2004. CAST: Lucas Belvaux (Bruno Le Roux), Catherine Frot (Jeanne Rivet), Dominique Blanc (Agnès Manise), Ornella Muti (Cécile Costes), Gilbert Melki (Pascal Manise), Patrick Descamps (Jacquillat), Olivier Darimont (Francis), Alexis Tomassian (Banane), Yves Claessens (Freddy), Christine Henkart (Madame Guiot), Jean-Henri Roger (Neighbor in Burning Apartment), Elie Belvaux (Jeanne's Son), Hervé Livet (Jean-Jean), Eric Vassard (Henchman), Zirek, Thomas Badek, Jean-Philippe Naeder (Secret Agents), Bourlem Guerdjou (Teacher), Hervé Peyrard (ONF Guard)

Blind Shaft PHOTO COURTESY OF KINO

BLIND SHAFT

(KINO) a.k.a. *Mang jing*; Producer/Director/Screenplay, Yang Li; Photography, Yonghong Liu; Art Director, Jun Yang; Music, Yadong Zhang; Editors, Yang Li, Karl Riedl; a Tag Spledour and Films Limited production; Chinese-German-Hong Kong, 2003; Color; Not rated; 92 minutes; American release date: February 4, 2004. CAST: Yi Xiang Li (Song Jinming), Baoqiang Wang (Yuan Fengming), Shuangbao Wang (Tang Zhaoyang), Jing Ai (Xiao Hong), Zhenjiang Bao (First Boss), Sun Wei (Tang Zhaoxia), Jun Zhao (Miss Ma), Yining Wang (Mamasan)

AN AMAZING COUPLE

(MAGNOLIA) a.k.a. *Un couple épatant*; Producer, Patrick Sobelman; Director/Screenplay, Lucas Belvaux; Photography, Pierre Milon; Designer, Frédérique Belvaux; Costumes, Cécile Cotton; Music, Riccardo Del Fra; Editor, Valérie Loiseleux; an Agat Films & Cie, Canal+, Centre National de la Cinematographie, Cofimage 12, Entre Chien et Loup, Eurimages, Gimages 5, Natexis Banques Populaires Images 2, Radio Television Belge Francofone (RTBF), Rhône-Alpes Cinéma; French-Belgian, 2002; Dolby; Color; Rated PG; 97 minutes; American release date: February 6, 2004. CAST: Ornella Muti (Cécile Costes), François Morel (Alain Costes), Valérie Mairesse (Claire), Bernard Mazzinghi (Georges Colinet), Dominique Blanc (Agnès Manise), Gilbert Melki

The Seagull's Laughter PHOTO COURTESY OF THE CINEMA GUILD

(Pascal Manise), Catherine Frot (Jeanne Rivet), Lucas Belvaux (Bruno/Pierre), Raphaële Godin (Louise), Patrick Depeyra (Vincent), Pierre Gérard (Olivier), Jean-Baptiste Montagut (Henri), Vincent Colombe (Rémy), Anne Delol (Nurse), Joss Philopémon (Taxi Driver), Vincent Gardinier (Police Car Driver), Eric Vassard (Thug), Zirek, Thomas Badek (Secret Agents)

Ivan Dobranravov, Vladimir Garin in *The Return* PHOTO COURTESY OF KINO

THE RETURN

(KINO) a.k.a. *Vozvrashcheniye*; Producer, Dmitri Lesnevsky; Executive Producer, Yelena Kovalyova; Director, Andrey Zvyagintsev; Screenplay, Vladimir Moiseyenko, Aleksandr Novototsky; Photography, Mikhail Krichman; Designer, Zhanna Pakhomova; Costumes, Anna Barthuly; Music, Andrei Dergachyov; Editor, Vladimir Mogilevsky; a Ren Film production; Russian, 2003; Dolby; Color; Not rated; 105 minutes; American release date: February 6, 2004. CAST: Vladimir Garin (Andrey), Ivan Dobronravov (Ivan), Konstantin Lavronenko (Father), Natalya Vdovina (Mother), Yelizaveta Aleksandrova (Waitress), Lazar Dubovik (Hooligan), Lyubov Kazakova (Devushka), Galina Petrova (Grandmother), Aleksei Suknovalov (Zavodila), Andrei Sumin (Man at Port)

THE SEAGULL'S LAUGHTER

(THE CINEMA GUILD) a.k.a. *Mávahlátur*; Producer, Kristín Atladóttir; Director/Screenplay, Ágúst Guðmundsson; Based on the novel by Kristin Marja Baldursdóttir; Photography, Peter-Joachim Krause; Designer, Tonie Zetterström; Editor, Henrik D. Moll; a co-production of Archer Street Productions, Isfilm, Hope & Glory Film Productions; Icelandic-German-British, 2001; Dolby; Fujicolor; Not rated; 102 minutes; American release date: February 13, 2004. CAST: Margarét Vilhjálmsdóttir (Freyja), Ugla Egilsdóttir (Agga), Heino Ferch (Björn Theódór), Hilmir Snær Guðnason (Magnús), Kristbjörg Kjeld (Grandma), Edda Björg Eyjólfsdóttir (Dodo), Guðlaug Ólafsdóttir (Ninna), Eyvindur Erlendsson (Granddad), Benedikt Erlingsson (Hilli), Halldóra Geirharðsdóttir (Birna), Jónína Ólafsdóttir (Doctor's Widow), Dilja Mist (Emilía), Charlotte Boving (Mette), Sigurlaug Jónsdóttir (Kidda), Bára Lyngdal (Dísa)

THE CODE

(GOLDWYN) a.k.a. *La Mentale*; Producer, Alain Goldman; Director, Manuel Boursinhac; Screenplay, Manuel Boursinhac, Bibi Naceri; Photography, Kevin Jewison; Designer, Nikos Meletopoulos; Costumes, Marlène Aouat, Claire Gerard-Hirne; Music, Thierry Robin; Editor, Hélène de Luze; Casting, Swan

The Code PHOTO COURTESY OF GOLDWYN

Pham; a co-production of Canal+, Gaumont, Légende Entreprises, TF1 Films Productions; French, 2002; Dolby; Color; Rated R; 116 minutes; American release date: February 13, 2004. CAST: Samuel Le Bihan (Dris), Samy Naceri (Yanis), Clotilde Courau (Nina), Marie Guillard (Lise), Michel Duchaussoy (Fèche), Philippe Nahon (Simon), Francis Renaud (Niglo), Lucien Jean-Baptiste (Foued), Bibi Naceri (Rouquin), David Saracino (Mel), Adrien Saint-Joré (José), Frédéric Pellegeay (Grib), Jean-Pierre Lazzerini (Henry), Stéphane Ferrara (Prosper), Thierry Perkins-Lyautey (Marco), Edith Scot (Mireille), Elisabeth Macocco (Françoise), Mohamed Ahaouari (Djilali), Elisabeth Margoni (Evelyne), Mohamed Damraoui (Omar), Richard Baque (Francis), Rachid Chanana (Malik), Samir Guesmi (Daniel), Marc Samuel (Fakhi), Chloé Mons (Fanfan), Linda Sanchez (Juanita), Nabil Debouze (Hamou), Paco Boublard (Franck), Marc Dubreuil, Ridha Oubrik (Clients), Chantal Garrigues (Lise's Mother), Frédéric Maranber (Sylvain), Françoise Michaud (Child Guardian), Sally Mekki (Femme Fakhi), Jean-Marie Paris (Vigil), Cèdric Delsaux (DJ), Rèmy Roubakha (Taxi Driver), Smaïl Mekki (Syrian), Alexander Koumpan (Romanian), Christine Chansou (Zora), Wanda Naceri (Wanda), Sacha Naceri (Samy)

AFTER THE LIFE

(MAGNOLIA) a.k.a. *Après la vie*; Producers, Patrick Sobelman, Dian Elbaum; Director/Screenplay, Lucas Belvaux; Photography, Pierre Milon; Designer, Frédérique Belvaux; Costumes, Cécile Cotten; Music, Editor, Danielle Anezin; an Agat Films & Cie, Canal+, Centre National de la Cinematographie (CNC), Cofimage 12, Entre Chien et Loup, Eurimages, Gimages 5, Natexis Banques Populaires Images 2, Radio Television Belge Francofone (RTBF), Rhône-Alpes

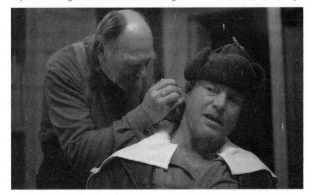

Joachim Calmeyer, Bjørn Floberg in *Kitchen Stories* PHOTO COURTESY OF IFC FILMS

Cinéma; French-Belgian, 2002; Dolby; Color; Not rated; 124 minutes; American release date: February 13, 2004. CAST: Dominique Blanc (Agnès Manise), Gilbert Melki (Pascal Manise), Ornela Muti (Cécile Costes), Catherine Frot (Jeanne Rivet), François Morel (Alain Costes), Lucas Belvaux (Bruno Le Roux), Bernard Mazzinghi (Georges Colinet), Patrick Descamps (Jacquillat), Olivier Darimont (Francis), Alexis Tomassian (Banane), Yves Claessens (Freddy), Pierre Gérard (Olivier), Christine Henkart (Mme. Guiot), Marc Bordure, Sophie Cattani (Cops), Vincent Depeyra (Vincent), Eric Vassard (Henchman), Raphaële Godin (Louise), Jean-Baptiste Montagut (Henri), Vincent Gardinier (Police Car Driver), Zirek, Thomas Basek (Secret Agents), Vincent Colombe (Remy), Bourlem Guerdjou (Teacher)

ABOUNA

(LEISURE TIME FEATURES) a.k.a. *Our Father*; Producer, Guillaume de Seille; Executive Producer, Abderrahmane Sissako; Director/Screenplay, Mahamat-Saleh Haroun; Photography, Abraham Haile Biru; Designer, Laurent Cavero; Costumes, Hassanie Lazinger; Music, Diego Moustapha Ngarade; Editor, Sarah Taouss-Matton; a co-production of Commission Européene, Duo Films, Goi-Goi Productions, Hubert Bals Fund, Ministry of Promotion and Development, Tele-Chad, arte France Cinéma; French-Chad-Dutch, 2002; Dolby; Color; Not rated; 84 minutes; American release date: February 20, 2004. CAST: Ahidjo Mahamat Moussa (Tahir), Hamza Moctar Aguid (Amine), Zara Haroun (Mother), Mounira Khalil (The Mute Girl), Hassan Boulama (Hassan), Diego Moustapha Ngarade (Uncle Adoum), Garba Issa (The Headmaster), Koulsy Lamko (The Father), Ramada Mahamat (The Teacher's Wife), Sossal Mahamat (Teacher's Assistant), Hadje Fatime N'Goua (Doctor), Nouraldine Mahamat Alio (Police Chief), Christophe N'Garoyal (Factory Manager), Haoua Tantine Abakar (Angry Neighbor), Albert Adoum (Fighting Boy)

CRYING LADIES

(UNITEL) Executive Producer, Tony Gloria; Director/Screenplay, Mark Meily; Photography, Lee Meily; Designer, Reji Regalado; Music, Vincent de Jesus; Editor, Danny Anonuevo; Filipino, 2003; Dolby; Color; Not rated; 110 minutes; American release date: February 20, 2004. CAST: Sharon Cuneta (Stella Mate), Hilda Koronel (Rhoda "Aling Doray" Rivera), Angel Aquino (Choleng), Eric Quizon (Wilson Chua), Julio Pacheco (Bong), Ricky Davao (Guido), Shamaine Centenera (Cecile), Johnny Delgado (Priest), Sherry Lara (Mrs. Chua), Raymond Bagatsing (Ipe), Bella Flores (Lost Lady), Edgar Mortiz (Mang Gusting), Bearwin Meily, Winnie Cordero (Game Show Hosts), Gilleth Sandico (Becky), Jemalene Estrada (Giselle), Mark Meily (Fireman)

KITCHEN STORIES

(IFC FILMS) a.k.a. *Salmer fra kjøkkenet*; Producers/Screenplay, Bent Hamer, Jörgen Bergmark; Director, Bent Hamer; Photography, Philip Øgaard; Designer, Billy Johansson; Costumes, Karen Fabritius Gram; Music, Hans Mathisen; Editor, Pål Gengenbach; a co-production of BOB Film Sweden AB, Bulbul Films, Svenska Filminstitutet (SFI); Norwegian-Swedish, 2003; Dolby; Color; Not rated; 95 minutes; American release date: February 20, 2004. CAST: Joachim Calmeyer (Isak Bjornsson), Tomas Norström (Folke Nilsson), Bjørn Floberg (Grant), Reine Brynolfsson (Malmberg), Sverre Anker Ousdal (Dr. Jack Zac. Benjaminsen), Leif Andrée (Dr. Ljungberg), Gard B. Eidsvold (Bakkerman), Lennart Jähkel (Green), Trond Brænne (Ordforer),

BIG ANIMAL

(MILESTONE FILMS) a.k.a. *Duze zwierze*; Producers, Janusz Morgenstern, Slawomire Rogowski; Director, Jerzy Stuhr; Screenplay, Krzysztof Kieslowski; Story, Kazimierz Orlos; Photography, Pawel Edelman; Designer, Monika Sajko-Gradowska; Costumes, Elzbieta Radke; Music, Abel Korzeniowski; Editor, Elzbieta Kurkowska; a production of Telewizja Polska (TVP) S.A.; Polish, 2000; Dolby; Black and white/color; Not rated; 73 minutes; American release date: February 20, 2004. CAST: Jerzy Stuhr (Zygmunt Sawicki), Anna Dymna (Marysia Sawicka), Dominika Bednarczyk, Blazej Wójcik (Bank Clerks), Andrzej Franczyk (Bank Manager), Feliks Szajnert (Drunkard), Zbigniew Kaleta (Photographer), Radoslaw Krzyzowski (Advertising Agent), Stanilsaw Banas (Fire Chief), Piotr Dabrowski, Zbigniew Rola (Firemen), Ewa Worytkiewicz, Malgorzata Zabkowska, Beata Schmischeiner (Councilwomen), Tomasz Schimscheiner (Builder), Zbigniew Kosowski (Stefaniak), Krzysztof Gluchowski (Mayor), Katarzyna Mrózek (Little Girl)

Amos Lavie, Yaël Abecassis in *Alila* PHOTO COURTESY OF KINO

ALILA

(KINO) Producer, Alain Mamou-Mani; Executive Producers, Amos Gitai, Michel Propper; Director, Amos Gitai; Screenplay, Amos Gitai, Marie-Jose Sanselme; Based on the novel by Yehoshua Kenaz; Photography, Renato Berta; Designer, Miguel Markin; Costumes, Laura Dinolesko; Editors, Monica Coleman, Kobi Netanel; from MP Productions; Israeli-French, 2003; Dolby; Color; Not rated; 123 minutes; American release date: February 27, 2004. CAST: Yaël Abecassis (Gabi), Uri Ran Klauzner (Ezra), Hana Laszlo (Mali), Ronit Elkabetz (Ronit), Amos Lavie (Hezi), Lupo Berkowitch (Aviram), Liron Levo (Ilan), Yosef Carmon (Schwartz), Amit Mestechkin (Eyal), Lyn Shiao Zamir (Linda), Keren Mor (Mali), Ilan Appel, Meital Tzadiji (Cops), Carmel Betto (Carmel), Eyal Elhadad (Doorman), Kiang Fang, Hu Hanzhou, Fang Heguo (Chinese Workers), Dalit Kahan (Sharon), Tomer Russo (The Officer), Kobi Zahavi (Kiosk Owner)

JAMES' JOURNEY TO JERUSALEM

(ZEITGEIST) a.k.a. *Massa'ot James Be'eretz Hakodesh*; Producer, Amir Harel; Director, Ran'anan Alexandrowicz; Screenplay, Ran'anan Alexandrowicz, Sami Duenias; Photography, Sharon De Mayo; Art Director, Amir Pick; Costumes, Maya Barsky; Music, Ehud Banai, Noam Halevi, Gil Smetana; Editor, Ron Goldman; from Lama Productions Ltd.; Israeli, 2003; Dolby; Color; Not rated; 87 minutes; American release date: March 5, 2004. CAST: Siyabonga Melongisi Shibe (James), Arieh Elias (Shimi Shabati), Salim Daw (Sallah Shabati), Sandra Schonwald (Rachel), Hugh Masebenza (Skomboze), Florence Bloch (Re'uma), Ya'akov Ronen Morad (Police Officer), Yael Levental (Immigration Officer), David Nabegamabo (Pastor), Pascal I. Newton (Job), Gregory Tal (Feda)

BROKEN WINGS

(SONY CLASSICS) a.k.a. *Knafayim Shvurot*; Producer, Assaf Amir; Executive Producer, Yoav Roeh; Director/Screenplay, Nir Bergman; Photography, Valentin Belonogov; Art Director, Ido Dolev; Costumes, Ada Levin; Music, Avi Belleli; Editor, Einat Glaser-Zarhim; a co-production of the Israeli Film Fund, Norman Productions Ltd., Yes-DBD Satellite Services; Israeli, 2002; Dolby; Color; Rated R; 87 minutes; American release date: March 12, 2004. CAST: Orly Silbersatz Banai (Dafna Ulman), Maya Maron (Maya Ulman), Nitai Gaviratz (Yair Ulman), Vladimir Friedman (Dr. Valentin Goldman), Dana Ivgy (Iris), Danny "Mooki" Niv (Yoram), Daniel Magon (Ido Ulman), Eliana Magon (Bahr Ulman), Yarden Bar-Kochba (Flora, School Counselor), Orit Boger (Teacher), Nimrod Cohen (Gaga), Eitan Green (The Father), Martin Umanski (Video Photographer), Lobo Wizner, Dror Yakar, Eli Zulta (Band Members)

DISTANT

(NEW YORKER) a.k.a. *Uzak*; Producer/Director/Screenplay/Photography, Nuri Bilge Ceylan; Designer, Ebru Yapici; Editor, Ayhan Ergursel; a co-production of NBC Ajans, NBC Film; Turkish, 2002; Dolby; Color; Not rated; 110 minutes; American release date: March 12, 2004. CAST: Muzaffer Özdemir (Mahut), Emin Toprak (Yusuf), Zuhal Gencer Erkaya (Nazan), Nazan Kirilmis (Lover), Feridun Koc (Janitor), Fatma Ceylan (Mother), Ebru Ceylan (Young Girl)

Salim Daw, Arie Elias, Siyabonga Melongisi Shibe in *James' Journey To Jerusalem*
PHOTO COURTESY OF ZEITGEIST

Muzaffer Özdemir in *Distant* PHOTO COURTESY OF NEW YORKER

Elína Hansdóttir in *Nói* PHOTO COURTESY OF PALM PICTURES

NÓI

(PALM PICTURES) a.k.a. *Nói albínói*; Producers, Philippe Bober, Lene Ingemann, Kim Magnusson, Skúli Fr. Malmquist, Thor Sigurjonsson, Thorir Snær Sigurjónsson; Director/Screenplay, Dagur Kári; Photography, Rasmus Videbæk; Designer, Jon Steinar Pagnarsson; Costumes, Tanja Dehmel, Linda B. Arnardóttir; Music, Orri Jonsson, Dagur Kári; a co-production of Zik Zak Kvikmyndir, Essential Filmproduktion GmbH, The Bureau, M&M Productions; Icelandic-German-British-Danish, 2003; Dolby; Color; Rated PG-13; 93 minutes; American release date: March 19, 2004. CAST: Tómas Lemarquis (Nói Kristmundsson), Thröstur Leó Gunnarsson (Kristmundur B. Kristmundsson), Elína Hansdóttir (Íris Óskarsdóttir), Anna Friðriksdóttir (Lína), Hjalti Rögnalvdsson (Óskar Halldórsson), Pétur Einarsson (Priest), Kjartan Bjargmundsson (Gylfi Hákonarson), Greipur Gislason (Dabbi), Ásmundur Ásmudsson (Bartender), Gunnhildur Björk Elíasdóttir (Saleslady), Sveinn Geirsson, Thorgeir Guðmundsson (Policemen)

TWO MEN WENT TO WAR

(INDICAN) Producers, Pat Harding, Ira Trattner; Executive Producers, Amit Barooah, Robert Bevan, Amanda Coombes, Keith Hayley, Charlie Savill; Director, John Henderson; Screenplay, Christopher Villiers, Richard Everett; Based on the book *Amateur Commandos* by Raymond Foxall; Photography, John Ignatius; Designers, Sophie Becher, Steve Carter; Costumes, Jill Taylor; Music, Richard Harvey; Editor, David Yardley; Casting, Sarah Bird; an Ira Trattner

Production; British; Color; Rated PG-13; 109 minutes; American release date: March 26, 2004. CAST: Kenneth Cranham (Sgt. Peter King), Leo Bill (Pvt. Leslie Cutherbertson), Rosanne Lavelle (Emma Fraser), Phyllida Law (Faith), James Fleet (Maj. Bates), Julian Glover (Col. Hatchard), Anthony Valentine (SM Dudley), David Ryall (Winston Churchill), Derek Jacobi (Maj. Merton), Richard Sutton (Pvt. Horrocks), Anthony O'Donnell (Chief Armorer), Paul Bayfield (Mike), Jason Round (Soldier #3), Tim "Nobby" Clarke (Young Sergeant), Nick Miles (Sgt. Mowat), Brian Bosley (Drill Sergeant), Dickon Tolson (Steward), Nick Hussey, Nathan Stevenson (Sentries), Tim McMullan (MP on Train), Barbara Massey (Trolley Lady), Mossie Smith (Mrs. Fraser), Ian Lindsay (Postman), Sara Markland (Daphne), Beth Cordingly (Rose), Erich Redman (German Signals Officer), Sandra Reinton (French Woman), Chris Gudgeon (German Signalman), Stephan Grothgar (German on Train with Driver), Jason Stammers (Stone Throwing German), Richard Everett (German Officer with Dog), Alan Thurston (Military Policeman), Christopher Villiers (Dr. Oliver Holmes), David Curtiz (Interrogator), Charles Oakden (Naval Intelligence Officer), Glen Davies (Corporal)

RAJA

(FILM MOVEMENT) Producers, Bénédicte Bellocq, Souad Lamriki, Margaret Ménégoz; Director/Screenplay, Jacques Doillon; Photography, Hélène Louvart; Costumes, Emma Bellocq; Music, Philippe Sarde; Editor, Gladys Joujou; a co-production of Agora Films, France 3 Cinéma, Les Films du Losange; French-Moroccan; Dolby; Color; Not rated; 112 minutes; American release date: March 26, 2004. CAST: Pascal Greggory (Fred), Najat Benssalem (Raja), Ilham Abdelwahed (Nadira), Hassan Khissal (Youssef), Amhed Akensouss (Ahmed), Oum El Aid It Youss (Oum El Aid), Zineb Ouchita (Zineb), Fatiha Khoulaki (Faitha), Aicha Aarif, Hajiba Firma, Jmiaa Aarif (Jardinieres)

Boubacar Touré, Ali Faka Touré in *I'll Sing For You* PHOTO COURTESY OF FIRST RUN FEATURES

I'LL SING FOR YOU

(FIRST RUN FEATURES) a.k.a. *Je chanterai pour toi*; Producer/Director/Screenplay, Jacques Sarasin; Photography, Stéphan Oriach; Editor, Bearnd Josse; a co-production of the Centre National de la Cinematographie (CNC), Les Productions Faire Bleu; French-Mali, 2001; Black and white/color; Not rated; 76 minutes; American release date: March 26, 2004. CAST: Haruna Harry, Dèmba-Kane Niang, Madieye Niang, Blaise Pascal, Mamadou Sangaré, Malik Sidibé, Ballaké Sissoko, Ali Faka Touré, Boubacar Traoré (Themselves)

RED PERSIMMONS

(CENTRAL MOTION PICTURES CORP.) a.k.a. *Hong shih zi*; Producer, Li-Kong Hsu; Director/Screenplay, T'ung Wang; Photography, Wai-den Yang; Designer, Fu-Hsiung Lee; Taiwanese, 1996; Color; Not rated; 168 minutes; American release date: March 31, 2004. Documentary on the cultivation and harvest of persimmons in Kaminoyama

Red Persimmons PHOTO COURTESY OF CENTRAL MOTION PICTURES CORP.

Rosa Maria Gomez, Juan Carlos Ortuno in *A Thousand Clouds of Peace* PHOTO COURTESY OF STRAND

SON FRÈRE

(STRAND) Producer, Pierre Chevalier; Executive Producer, Joseph Strub; Director, Patrice Chéreau; Screenplay, Patrice Chéreau; Based on the novel by Philippe Besson; Photography, Eric Gautier; Costumes, Caroine de Vivaise; Editor, François Gédigier; a co-production of Azor Films, Centre national de la Cinematographie (CNC), Conseil Général de Loire-Atlantique, Love Streams Productions, arte France Cinéma; French, 2003; Dolby; Color; Not rated; 95 minutes; American release date: April 2, 2004. CAST: Bruno Todeschini (Thomas), Eric Caravaca (Luc), Nathalie Boutefeu (Claire), Maurice Garrel (Old Man), Catherine Ferran (Head Doctor), Antoinette Moya (Mother), Sylvain Jacques (Vincent), Fred Ulysse (Father), Robinson Stévenin (Manuel)

OUTSKIRTS

(FACETS VIDEO) a.k.a. *Okraina*; Producer/Director, Pyotr Lutsik; Executive Producer, Lev Kagno; Screenplay, Pyotr Lutsik, Aleksei Samoryadov; Photography, Nikolai Ivasiv; Designer, Andrei Bessolitsin; Music, Gavriil Popov, Georgi Sviridov; Editor, Svetlana Guralskaya; a co-production of Goskino, Morning of the XXI Century Studio; Russian, 1998; Black and white; Not rated; 95 minutes; American release date: April 2, 2004. CAST: Yuri Dubrovin (Filipp Safronov), Nikolai Olyalin (Kolka Polyuanov), Aleksei Vanin (Vasili Perfilyev), Rimma Markova (Panka's Mother), Viktor Stepanov (The Master), Anatoli Koshcheyev, Viktor Venes (The Lykov Bros), Aleksandr Vdovin (Makhotin), Galina Zolotaryova (Makhotin's Wife), Oleg Mokshantsev (Simavin), Vyacheslav Kulakov (Simavin's Son)

A THOUSAND CLOUDS OF PEACE

(STRAND) a.k.a. *Mil nubes de paz cercan el cielo, amor, jamás acabarás de ser amor*; Producer, Roberto Fiesco; Director/Screenplay, Julián Hernández; Photography, Diego Arizmendi; Designer, Carolina Jiménez; Editors, Jacopo Hernández, Emiliano Arenales Osorio; a co-production of Nubes Cine, Cooperativa Cinematográfica Morelos, Titán Producciones; Mexican, 2003; Black and white; Not rated; 80 minutes; American release date: April 2, 2004. CAST: Salvador Alvarez (Susana), Gloria Andrade (Girl), Llane Fragoso (Mirella), Martha Gómez (Martha), Rosa María Gómez (Mary), Manuel Grapain Zaquelarez (Jorge), Marcos Hernández, Martin Solís (Boys), Salvador Hernández (Antonio), Perla de La Rosa (Anna), Miguel Loaiza (Adrián), Pablo Molina (Andrés), Mario Oliver (Umberto), Juan Carlos Ortuño (Gerardo), Clarisa Rendón (Nadia), Pilar Ruíz (Lola), Juan Carlos Torres (Bruno)

ADORED: DIARY OF A MALE PORN STAR

(WOLFE) a.k.a. *Poco più di un anno fa*; Producers, Samantha Gaetani, Alessandro Tonnini; Director/Screenplay, Marco Filiberti; Photography, Stefano Pancaldi; Designer, Livia Borgognoni; Costumes, Eva Coen; Editor, Valentina Girodo; a co-production of Campinella Productions and Corsaro Productions; Italian, 2003; Color; Not rated; 101 minutes; American release date: April 2, 2004. CAST: Marco Filiberti (Riki Kandinsky/Riccardo Soldani), Urbano Barberini (Federico Soldani), Alessandra Acciai (Juli), Rosalinda Celentano (Luna), Francesca d'Aloja (Charlotte), Erika Blanc (Angela Valle), Claudio Vanni (Claudio Alatri), Luigi Diberti (Rod Lariani, Porn Director), Caterina Guzzanti (Koka), Cosimo Cinieri (Silvio Valle), Giuliana Calandra (Franca Soldani), Franco Oppini (Gigi Ralli), Alberto Alemanno (First), Edoardo Minciotti (Plapla), Massimo Tellini (Guardian at the Movies' Archives)

THE BLONDS

(WOMEN MAKE MOVIES) a.k.a. *Los Rubios*; Producers, Marcelo Cespedes, Barry Ellsworth; Executive Producer, Pablo Wisznia; Director, Albertina Carri; Screenplay, Albertina Carri, Alan Pauls; Photography, Catalina Fernández; Designer, Paola Pelzmajer; Music, Charly García, Gonzalo Córdoba, Ryuichi Sakamoto; Editors, Alejandra Almirón, Catalina Fernández, Carmen Torres; Argentine-U.S., 2003; Dolby; Black and white/color; Not rated; 89 minutes; American release date: April 7, 2004. Documentary following filmmaker Albertina Carri's efforts to locate her missing parents; featuring Analia Couceyro, Albertina Carri, Santiago Giralt, Jesica Suarez, Marcelo Zanelli

THE MIDDLE OF THE WORLD

(FILM MOVEMENT) a.k.a. *O Caminho das Nuvens*; Producers, Bruno Barreto, Lucy Barreto, Angelo Gastal, Luiz Carlos Barreto; Executive Producer, Paula Barreto; Director, Vicente Amorim; Screenplay, David França Mendes; Photography, Gustavo Hadba; Designer, Jean-Louis Leblanc; Music, André Abujamra; Editor, Pedro Amorim; a co-production of Globo Filmes, Luiz Carlos Barreto Produções Cinematográficas, Miravista; Brazilian, 2003; Dolby; Color; Not rated; 85 minutes; American release date: April 9, 2004. CAST: Wagner Moura (Romão), Cláudia Abreu (Rose), Manoel Sebastião Alves Filho (Rodney), Carol Castro (Sereia), Laís Corrêa (Jurema), Cícera Cristina Almino de Lima (Suelena), Cícero Wesley A. Ferreira (Cícero), Claudio Jaborandy (Gideão), Ravi Ramos Lacerda (Antônio), Fábio Lago (Neguiça), Franciolli Luciano (Callado), Sidney Magal (Panamá), Caco Monteiro (Severino), Felipe Newton Silva Rodrigues (Clevis)

TWENTYNINE PALMS

(WELLSPRING) Producers, Rachid Bouchareb, Jean Bréhat; Executive Producer, Muriel Merlin; Director/Screenplay, Bruno Dumont; Photography, Georges Lechaptois; Costumes, Yasmine Abraham; Editor, Dominique Petrot; a co-production of Thoke Moebius Film Company, 3B Productions, The 7th Floor; French-U.S.; Dolby; Color; Not rated; 119 minutes; American release date: April 9, 2004. CAST: Katia Golubeva (Katia), David Wissak (David)

THE TWILIGHT SAMURAI

(EMPIRE) a.k.a. *Tasogare Seibei*; Producers, Hiroshi Fukazawa, Shigehiro Nakagawa, Ichiro Yamamoto; Executive Producers, Tomiyasu Ishikawa, Tetsuo Kan, Tomoo Miyakawa, Toshio Ogiwara, Motoyuki Oka, Nobuyoshi Otani;

Analia Couceyro in *The Blonds* PHOTO COURTESY OF WOMEN MAKE MOVIES

Esther Gorintin in *Since Otar Left* PHOTO COURTESY OF ZEITGEIST

Wagner Moura in *The Middle of the World* PHOTO COURTESY OF FILM MOVEMENT

Katia Golubeva, David Wissak in *TwentyNine Palms* PHOTO COURTESY OF WELLSPRING

Director, Yoji Yamada; Screenplay, Yoji Yamada, Yoshitaka Asam; Based on novels by Shuuhei Fujisawa; Photography, Mutsuo Naganuma; Designer, Mitsuo Degawa; Costumes, Kazuko Kurosawa; Music, Isao Tomita; Editor, Iwao Ishii; a co-production of Hakuhodo Incorporated, Nippon Television Network, Sumitomo Corporation; Japanese, 2002; Dolby; Color; Not rated; 129 minutes; American release date: April 23, 2004. CAST: Hiroyuki Sanada (Seibei Iguchi), Rie Miyazawa (Tomoe Iinuma), Nenji Kobayashi (Choubei Kusaka), Ren Osugi (Toyotarou Kouda), Mitsuru Fukikoshi (Michinojo Iinuma), Hiroshi Kanbe (Naota), Miki Ito (Kayan Iguchi), Erina Hashiguchi (Ito Iguchi), Reiko Kusamura (Iguchi's Mother), Min Tanaka (Zenemon Yogo), Keiko Kishi (Ito), Tetsuro Tamba (Tozaemon Iguchi)

SINCE OTAR LEFT

(ZEITGEIST) a.k.a. *Depuis qu'Otar est parti …*; Producer, Yael Fogiel; Executive Producer (Studio 99), Jana Sardlichvili; Director, Julie Bertucelli; Sceenplay, Julie Bertucceli, Bernard Renucci; Photography, Christophe Pollock; Designer, Emmanuel de Chauvigny; Costumes, Nathalie Raoul; Editor, Emmanuelle Castro; a co-production of arte France Cinema, Entre Chien et Loup, Studio 99 Filmproduktion, Les Films du Poisson, with the participation of Canal+, in collaboration with Radio Television Belge Francofone (RTBF); French-Belgian, 2003; Dolby; Color; Not rated; 103 minutes; American release date: April 30, 2004. CAST: Esther Gorintin (Eka), Nino Khomasuridze (Marina), Dinara Drukarova (Ada), Temour Kalandadze (Tengiz), Roussoudan Bolkvadze (Rusiko), Sacha Sarichvili (Alexi), Douta Skhirtladze (Niko), Abdallah Moundy (Le Berbere), Mzia Eristavi (Dora), Micha Eristavi (Young Dora), Zoura Natrochvili (Voisin), Alexandre Makhorablichvili (Government Official), Jacques Fleury, Frédéric Payen (Businessmen), Irina Toukhoulova (Professor)

BULGARIAN LOVERS

(TLA RELEASING) Producers, Eduardo Campoy, Jesús G. Ciordia, Fernando Guillén Cuervo, Pedro Olea; Executive Producer, Oihana Olea; Director, Eloy de la Iglesia; Screenplay, Eloy de la Iglesia, Antonio Hens, Fernando Guillén Cuervo; Based on the novel by Eduardo Mendicutti; Photography, Néstor Calvo; Designer, Julio Torrecilla; Costumes, Pedro Moreno; Music, Antonio Meliveo; Editor, José Salcedo; a coproduction of Altube Filmeak S.L., CARTEL S.A., Conexión, Televisión Española (TVE); Spanish, 2003; Dolby; Color; Rated R; 101 minutes; American release date: April 30, 2004. CAST: Fernando Guillén Cuervo (Daniel), Dritan Biba (Kyril), Pepón Nieto (Gildo), Roger Pera (Lawyer), Anita Sinkovic (Kalina), Fernando Albizu (Mogambo), Roman Luknár (Simeon), Simón Andreu (Daniel's Father), Julia Martínez (Daniel's Mother), Gracia Olayo (Rosita), Emma Penella (Remedios), Aure Sánchez (Bambi), Alberto Lozano (Taxista), Óscar Iniesta (Emil), Isabel Ampudia, Inés Sajara (Sisters), Alejandro Núñez (Adolescent Kyril), David Pinilla (Tasador)

MORLANG

(FILM MOVEMENT) Producer, Petra Goedings; Executive Producer, San Fu Maltha, Vibeke Windeløv; Director, Tjebbo Penning; Screenplay, Tjebbo Penning, Ruud Schuurman, Matthew Faulk, Mark Skeet; Photography, Han Wennink; Designers, Rikke Jelier, Alfred Schaaf; Costumes, Nanda Korver; Music, Han Otten, Wiebe de Boer; Editor, J.P. Luijsterburg; a Phanta Vision Film III BV production; Dutch, 2001; Dolby; Color; Not rated; 94 minutes; American release date: April 30, 2004. CAST: Paul Freeman (Julius Morlang), Diana Kent (Ellen Morlang), Susan Lynch (Ann Morlang), Eric van der Donk (Wim Giel), Marcel Faber (Robert Jansen), Huib Broos (Peter), Porgy Franssen (Doctor), Joe Gallagher (Policeman), Freida Hand, Paddy O'Connell, Derek Reid (Customs Officers), Maximo Mewe (Spanish Gallery Owner), Nora Mullens, Elvira Out (Nurses), Saskia Rinsma (Heleen), Edward Stelder (Annoying Artist), Robine van der Meer (Spanish Girlfriend)

THE CLAY BIRD

(MILESTONE) a.k.a. *Matir moina*; Producers, Catherine Masud, Marin Karmitz; Executive Producer, Nathalie Kreuther; Director, Tareque Masud; Screenplay, Tareque Masud, Catherine Masud; Photography, Sudheer Palsane; Designer, Sylvain Nahmias; Costumes, Masuda Kazi; Music, Moushumi Bhowmik; Editor, Catherine Masud; a co-production of Audiovision, MK2 Productions; French-Pakistani, 2001; Color; Not rated; 89 minutes; American release date: April 30, 2004. CAST: Nurul Islam Bablu (Anu), Russell Farazi (Rokon), Jayanto Chattopadhyay (Kazi), Rokeya Prachy (Ayesha), Soaeb Islam (Milon), Lameesa R. Reemjheem (Asma), Moin Ahmed (Ibrahim), Md. Moslemuddin (Headmaster), Abdul Karim (Halim Mia), Shah Akam Dewan (Boatman), Golam Mahmud (Shaheen), Pradip Mittra Mithun (Uttam), Auyon Chowdhury (3rd Friend), Masud ali Khan (Khan Bahadur)

OASIS

(LIFESIZE ENTERTAINMENT) Producers, Min-cheul Cho, Jeon Jay, Gye-nam Myeong; Executive Producers, Kaynam Hyung, Sung-min Choi; Director/Screenplay, Chang-dong Lee; Photography, Yeong-taek Choi; Art Director, Jum-hee Shin; Costumes, Sun-young Cha; Music, Jae-jin Lee; Editor, Hyun Kim; a co-production of Dream Venture Capital, East Film Company,

UniKorea Pictures; South Korean, 2002; Dolby; Color; Not rated; 133 minutes; American release date: May 7, 2004. CAST: Kyung-gu Sol (Jong-du Hong), So-ri Moon (Gong-ju Han), Nae-sang Ahn (Jong-Il Hong), Seung-wan Ryoo (Jong-Sae Hong), Kwi-Jung Chu (Jong-Sae's Wife), Jin-gu Kim (Mrs. Hong), Byung-ho Son (Sang-Shik Han), Ga-hyun Yun (Sang-Shik's Wife), Meyong-shin Park (Woman Neighbor), Kyung-geun Park (Woman Neighbor's Husband), Dae-gwan Han, Jin-seob Han (Detectives)

SPRINGTIME IN A SMALL TOWN

(PALM PICTURES) a.k.a. *Xiao cheng zhi chun*; Producers, Bill Kong, Xiaowan Li, Yatming Tang; Director, Zhuangzhuang Tian; Executive Producers, Wouter Barenhrecht, Shaohong Li, Michael J. Werner, Buting Yang; Screenplay, Cheng Ah; Story, Tianji Li; Photography, Mark Li Ping-bing; Designers, Tim Yip Kam-tim, Kuangming Cheng; Costumes, Timmy Yip; Music, Li Zhao; Editor, Jianping Xu; a co-production of Beijing Film Studio, Beijing Rosart Film, China Film Group Corporation, Fortissimo Film Sales, Orly Films, Paradis Films; Chinese-Hong Kong-French-Netherlands, 2002???; Dolby; Color; Rated PG; 116 minutes; American release date: May 14, 2004. CAST: Jingfan Hu (Yuwen), Jun Wu (Dai Liyan), Bai Qing Xin (Zhang Zhichen), Xiao Keng Ye (Lao Huang), Si Si Lu (Dai Xiu)

Paul Freeman, Diana Kent in *Morlang* PHOTO COURTESY OF FILM MOVEMENT

Kyung-gu Sol, So-ri Moon in *Oasis* PHOTO COURTESY OF LIFESIZE ENTERTAINMENT

Jingfan Hu in *Springtime in A Small Town* PHOTO COURTESY OF PALM PICTURES

A DAY WITHOUT A MEXICAN

(TELEVISA CINE) a.k.a. *Un Día sin méxicanos*; Producer, Isaac Artenstein; Director, Sergio Arau; Screenplay, Sergio Arau, Yareli Arizmendi, Sergio Guerrero; Based on the short film *A Day Without a Mexican: Mockumentary* by Yareli Arizmendi and Sergio Guerrero; Photography, Alan Caudillo; Designer, Anthony Rivero Stabley; Costumes, Carlos Brown; Music, Juan Colomer; Editor, Daniel Fort; an Eye on the Ball Films and Jose & Friends Inc. production; Mexican-U.S.-Spanish; Dolby; Color; Rated R; 100 minutes; American release date: May 14, 2004. CAST: Maureen Flannigan (Mary Jo Quintana), Eduardo Palomo (Roberto Quintana), Elpidia Carrillo (Cata), John Getz (Senator Steven Abercrombie III), Bru Miller (George McClaire), Muse Watson (Louis McClaire), Suzanne Friedline (Vicki Martin), Carlos Gomez (Jose Velasquez Diaz), Yareli Arizmendi (Lila Rodriguez), Melinda R. Allen (Ellen Abercrombie), Caroline Aaron (Aunt Gigi), Santiago Guerrero (Bobby Quintana), Sabrina Howard (Lucy Quintana), Tony Abatemarco (Talk Show Host), Frankie Jay Allison (Officer Carr), Fernando Arau, Luis Garcia (Undocumented Workers), Todd Babcock (Nick), Maria Beck (Officer Sanchez), Yennifer Behrens (Suzy), Arell Blanton (Chris), Cassidy Paige Bringas (Tracey/Lucy Abercrombie), Brian Brophy (Barney Montana), Maria Camporredondo Neely (Lila's Mom), Larry Carroll, Suzette Craft, Gwendoline Yeo (Newscasters), Jonathan Fuller (Dean), Joaquin Garrido (Jose Mendoza), Will Greenberg (Jeff Silverman), Raul A. Hinojosa (Abdul Hassan), Charles Kahlenberg (General Hoff), Baron Kelly (Officer Hyland), Shishir Kurup (Alex), Karen Ve Londa (Rapture Informerical Woman), Cyndi Martino (Nurse Jackie), Dori Mizrahi (Unexmployed Actor), Rick Najera (Magician Announcer), Steven Nevius (Sitcom Guy), Christian Parizeau (Little Louis), Ryan Quintana (Border Patrol #1), Salli Saffioti (Kelly), Mary Beth Scherr (Sharon), Leon Singer (Lila's Father), Jason Stuart (Restauranteur), Jossie Thacker (Officer Hyland's Wife), Sylvia Thompson (Parking Officer), Dawn Westlake (Field Reporter), Michael White (TV Host), Ogie Zulueta (Dr. Takeshi)

S21: THE KHMER ROUGE KILLING MACHINE

(FIRST RUN FEATURES) a.k.a. *S-21, la machine de mort Khmère rouge*; Producers, Cati Couteau, Dana Hastier; Executive Producers, Aline Sasson, Liane Willemont; Director/Screenplay, Rithy Panh; Photography, Rithy Panh, Prum Mesa; Music, Marc Marder; Editors, Isabelle Roudy, Marie-Christine Rougerie; a co-production of Institut National de l'Audiovisuel (INA), arte France Cinéma; Cambodian-French, 2003; Color; Not rated; 101 minutes; American release

date: May 19, 2004. Documentary on the genocide prison in Phnom Penh; featuring Khieu "Poey" Ches, Yeay Cheu, Nhiem Ein, Houy Him, Ta Him, Nhieb Ho, Prakk Kahn, Peng Kry, Som Meth, Chum Mey, Vann Nath, Top Pheap, Tcheam Seur, Mak Thim, Sours Thii

MY MOTHER LIKES WOMEN

(NORADOR PRODUCTIONS) a.k.a. *A mi madre le gustan las mujeres*; Producers, Fernando Colomo, Beatrix de la Gándara; Directors/Screenplay, Daniela Fejerman, Inés París; Photography, David Omedes; Music, Juan Bardem; a Fernando Colomo Producciones Cinematograficas S.L. production; Spanish, 2002; Dolby; Color; Not rated; 96 minutes; American release date: May 21, 2004. CAST: Leonor Watling (Elvira), Rosa Maria Sardà (Sofia), María Pujalte (Gimena), Silvia Abascal (Sol), Eliska Sirová (Eliska), Chisco Amado (Miguel), Xabier Elorriaga (Carlos), Álex Angulo (Bernardo), Aitor Mazo (Ernesto), Sergio Otegui (Javier)

Leonor Watling in *My Mother Likes Women* PHOTO COURTESY OF NORADOR PRODUCTIONS

FIRE DANCER

(SILK ROAD PICTURES) Producers, Khaled Wassel, John C. Roche, Nathan C. Powell; Executive Producer, Ghulam Jewayni; Director/Screenplay, Jawed Wassel; Photography, Bud Gardner; Music, John Loeffler; Editors, Jeff Marcello, Lizzie Donahue, Vida Zaher Khadem; from Petunia Productions; Afghanistan-U.S., 2002; Dolby; Color; Not rated; 79 minutes; American release date: June 4, 2004. CAST: Baktash Zaher (Haris), Mariam Weiss (Laila), Yunis Azizi (Rustum), Samira Cameron (Zohra), Omar Arzo (Farhad), Atia Jewayni (Laila's Mother), Freshta Sadeed (Parwanah)

Samara Cameron, Mariam Weiss in *Fire Dancer* PHOTO COURTESY OF SILK ROAD PICTURES

IMELDA

(UNICO ENTERTAINMENT) Associate Producer, Joji Ravina; Producer/Director, Ramona S. Diaz; Photography, Ferne Pearlstein; Music, Bob Aves, Grace Nono; Editor, Leah Marino; a CineDiaz, Unitel Pictures International production; Philippines, 2003; Color; Not rated; 103 minutes; American release date: June 9, 2004. Documentary on former first lady of the Philippines, Imelda Marcos; featuring Imelda Romualdez Marcos, Letty Locsin, Lilly Montejo, Alex Montejo, Francisco Pedrosa, Fe Jimenez, Loreto Ramos, Senator Eva Kalaw, Lorena Almeria, Conrado De Quiros, Carmen Guerrero Nakpil, Josie Vergel De Dios, Katherine Ellison, Ferdinand "Bong Bong" Marcos II, Senator Serge Osmena, Behn Cervantes, Pete Lacaba, Jo-Ann Maglipon, Rudolfo Cuenca, Vicente Paterno, Phil Bronstein, Christian Espiritu, Father James Reuter S.J., Bernice Ocampo, Stephen Bosworth, Richard Holbrooke, Llewelyn White

Imelda Marcos in *Imelda* PHOTO COURTESY OF UNICO ENTERTAINMENT

YOU'LL GET OVER IT

(PICTURE THIS! ENTERTAINMENT) a.k.a. *À cause d'un garçon*; Producers, Christophe Chevallier, Claude Chelli, Hervé Chabalier; Director, Fabrice Cazeneuve; Screenplay, Vincent Molina; Photography, Stephan Massis; Designer, Olivier Raoux; Costumes, Marie-Jose Escolar, Isabelle Vita; Music, Michel Portal; Editor, Jean-Pierre Bloc; Casting, Agathe Hassenforder, Philippe Page; a co-production of Capa Drama, M6 Métropole Télévision; French, 2002; Dolby; Color; Not rated; 90 minutes; American release date: June 18, 2004. CAST: Julien Baumgartner (Vincent), Julia Maraval (Noémie), François Comar (Stéphane), Jérémie Elkaïm (Benjamin), Patrick Bonnel (Bernard, the Father), Christiane Millet (Sylvie), Antoine Michel (Régis, the Brother), Nils Ohlund (Bruno), Bernard Blancan (Swimming Coach), Eric Bonicatto (French Professor), Paco Boublard, Vincent Billouin, Adrien Saint-Joré (Swimming Teammates), Vincent Nemeth (Guidance Counselor), Blandine Pelissier (Guidance Counselor Secretary), Jean-Pierre Becker (Boxing Trainer), Alexandre Carrière, Dimitri Rataud (Men in Marais Bar)

FACING WINDOWS

(SONY CLASSICS) a.k.a. *La Finestra di fronte*; Producers, Tilde Corsi, Gianni Romoli; Director, Ferzan Ozpetek; Screenplay, Ferzan Ozpetek, Gianni Romoli; Photography, Gianfilippo Corticelli; Art Director, Andrea Crisanti; Costumes, Catia Dottori; Music, Andrea Guerra; Editor, Patrizio Marone; a co-production of AFS Film, Clap Filmes, R&C Produzioni, Redwave Films; Italian-British-Turkish-Portuguese, 2003; Dolby; Color; Rated R; 102 minutes; American release date: June 18, 2004. CAST: Giovanna Mezzogiorno (Giovanna), Massimo Girotti (Simone/Davide Veroli), Raoul Bova (Lorenzo), Filippo Nigro (Filippo), Serra Yilmaz (Eminè), Maria Grazia Bon (Sara), Massimo Poggio (Young Davide), Ivan Bacchi (Simone), Olimpa Carlisi (Donna Negozio), Ohame-Brancy Chibuzo (Alessio), Carlo Daniele (Marco), Rosaria De Cicco (Barista), Luciana De Falco (Marilena), Benedetta Gargari (Martina), Enrico Grassi (Vittorio), Serena Habtom Mehari (Microbo), Billo Thiernothian (Giambo)

FATHER AND SON

(WELLSPRING) a.k.a. *Otets i syn*; Producers, Igor Kalyonov, Thomas Kufus; Director, Aleksandr Sokurov; Screenplay, Sergei Potepalov; Photography, Aleksandr Burov; Designer, Natalya Kochergina; a co-production of Isabella Films, Lumen Films, Mikado Film S.r.l., Nikola Film, Zero Film GmbH; Russian-German-Italian-Dutch, 2003; Dolby; Color; Not rated; 82 minutes; American release date: June 18, 2004. CAST: Andrei Shchetinin (Father), Aleksei Nejmyshev (Aleksei, the Son), Aleksandr Razbash (Sasha), Fyodor Lavrov (Fyodor), Marina Zasukhina (Girl)

Julien Baumgartner, Julia Maravel, François Comar in *You'll Get Over It*
PHOTO COURTESY OF PICTURE THIS!

THE INTENDED

(IFC FILMS) Producers, Malene Blenkov, Patricia Kruijer; Executive Producers, Sally Hibbin, Bob Berney; Director, Kristian Levring; Screenplay, Kristian Levring, Janet McTeer; Photography, Jens Schlosser; Designer, Lars Nielsen; Music, Matthew Herbert; Editors, Nicholas Wayman-Harris, Andrew McClelland; Casting, Joyce Nettles; a Parallax Projekt (Innocence) Ltd., Produktionsselskabet, Southeast Asia Film Location Service Sdn. Bhd. Production; British-Danish, 2002; Dolby; Color; Rated R; 110 minutes; American release date: June 25, 2004. CAST: Janet McTeer (Sarah Morris), Olympia Dukakis (Erina), Brenda Fricker (Mrs. Jones), Tony Maudsley (William Jones), JJ Field (Hamish Winslow), David Bradley (The Priest), Philip Jackson (Norton), Robert Pugh (Le Blanc), John Matthew Lau (Judas), Thomas Goh (Jalak), Michael J. Langgi (Ugat)

Aleksei Nejmyshev, Andrei Shchetinin in *Father and Son* PHOTO COURTESY OF WELLSPRING

Oshri Cohen, Aya Koren in *Bonjour Monsieur Shlomi* PHOTO COURTESY OF STRAND

KAENA: THE PROPHECY

(SAMUEL GOLDWYN) a.k.a. *Kaena: La prophétie*; Directors, Chris Delaporte, Pascal Pinon; Screenplay, Chris Delaporte, Tarik Hamdine, Kenneth Oppel; Story, Chris Delaporte, Patrick Daher; Music, Farid Russlan; Editor, Bénédicte Brunet; Lead Character Animator, Brent Paul George; a co-production of Chaman Productions, Studio Canal, TVA International; French-Canadian, 2003; Color; Rated PG-13; 85 minutes; American release date: June 25, 2004. VOICE CAST: Kirsten Dunst (Kaena), Richard Harris (Opaz), Anjelica Huston (Queen of the Selenites), Michael McShane (Assad), Greg Proops (Gommy), Keith David (Preast)

TIME OF THE WOLF

(PALM PICTURES) Producers, Frank Hübner, Andrew Somper, Paco Álvarez; Executive Producers, Martin J. Barab, Alain Bordiec, Georges Campana, Lewis Chesler, Peter Paulich, David Perlmutter, Robert Vaughn, J. David Williams; Director, Rody Pridy; Screenplay, Don French; Photography, Norayr Kasper; Art Director, Kathleen Climie; Costumes, Gersha Phillips; Music, John Scott; Editor, Jeff Warren; Casting, Claudia Smith; a co-production of Animal Tales Productions Inc., Apollo Media, Chesler/Perlmutter Productions Inc.; German-Canadian, 2002; Color; Not rated; 87 minutes; American release date: June 25,

2004. CAST: Burt Reynolds (Archie McGregor), Marthe Keller (Rebecca McGregor), Devin Douglas Drewitz (Aaron), Jason Priestley (Mr. Nelson), John Neville (Preacher), Jamie Kerr (Josh Grossler), Steven Taylor (Freddy McGuire), Charlotte Arnold (Paige McGuire), Anthony Lemke (Alex McKenzie), Fraser McGregor (Arty Bower), J.D. Nicholsen (Old Man Grossler), Shaun MacDonald (Anna MacKenzie), Phil Craig (Merv), Patrick Garrow (Mr. McGuire), Robert King (Ray Ferguson), Robert Bidaman (Sven)

THE ROAD TO LOVE

(ARAB FILM DISTRIBUTION) a.k.a. *Tarik El Hob*; Director, Rémy Lange; Screenplay/Editors, Rémy Lange, Antoine Parlebas; a Les Films de l'Ange production; French, 2001; Color; Not rated; 70 minutes; American release date: June 30, 2004. CAST: Karim Tarek (Karim), Sihem Benamoune (Sihem), Abdellah Taia, Farid Tali (Themselves), Mustapha Khaddar (Mustapha), Mehdi Jouhar (Boy from Social Organization), Roschdy El Glaoui (Exhibitionist/Artist)

BONJOUR MONSIEUR SHLOMI

(STRAND) a.k.a. *Ha-Kochavim Shel Shlomi*; Producer, Eitan Evan; Director/Screenplay, Shemi Zarhin; Photography, Itzik Portal; Art Director, Ariel Glazer; Costumes, Inbal Shuki; Music, Jonathan Bar-Giora; Editor, Einat Glaser-Zarhin; an Eitan Evans, Evanstone production; Israeli, 2003; Dolby; Color; Not rated; 94 minutes; American release date: July 2, 2004. CAST: Oshri Cohen (Shlomi Bar-Dayan), Arieh Elias (Grandfather Bar-Dayan), Esti Zakheim (Rushama Bar-Dayan), Aya Koren (Rona), Yigal Naor (Aviho, The Headmaster), Albert Iluz (Robert Bar-Dayan), Rotem Abuhab (Ziva), Assi Cohen (Sasi), Rotem Nissmo (Tehila), Nisso Keavia (Bagin Yaish), Hillar Sarjon (Tzvia, The Teacher), Gili Biton (Moti), Nissim Dayan (Yehoshua Eldad), Ruti Shukon (Miriam Eldad), Nirit Drori, Yotam Schwimmer, Matan Greenzeit (Haifa Students), Rotem Sabag, Maya Sabag (Abirs), Yakov Berger (Landlord), Yehoshua Yamanuci, Tzadok Hushino (Japanese Soldiers)

THE INHERITANCE

(THE CINEMA GUILD) a.k.a. *Arven*; Producer, Ib Tardini; Executive Producers, Peter Aalbæk Jensen; Director, Per Fly; Screenplay, Per Fly, Mogens Rukov, Kim Leona, Dorte Høeg; Photography, Harald Gunnar Paalgard; Designer, Søren Gam; Music, Halfdan E; Editor, Morten Giese; a Zentropa Entertainments production; Danish-Swedish-Norwegian-British, 2003; Dolby; Color; Not rated; 115 minutes; American release date: July 9, 2004. CAST: Ulrich Thomsen (Christoffer), Lisa Werlinder (Maria), Ghita Nørby (Annelise), Karina Skands (Benedikte), Lars Brygmann (Ulrik), Peter Steen (Niels), Diana Axelsen (Annika), Jesper Christensen (Holger Andresen), Ulf Pilgaard (Aksel), Dick Kaysø (Jens Mønsted), Sarah Juel Werner (Marie-Louise), Linda Myberg (Young Actress), Lucy Andoraison Hansen (Mira), Eric Viala (Frederic Rousseau), Valerie Quent (Rousseau's Wife), Pascal Steffan (Philippe Salliot), Francoise Brustis (Salliot's Wife), Gille Charrier (Patrice), Isabelle Van Moylders (Patrice's Wife), Pia Jondal (Christoffer's Secretary), Magnus Roosmann (Alfred), Thorbjörn Lindström (Jonas), Johannes Kuhnke (Stan the Chef), Erik Olsson (Waiter Martin), Peter Persson (Swedish Hall Porter), Anne-Claire Thiessen (French Cleaning Lady), Claudine Westh (Julie), Gregor Michaj (Man with Headset), Carsten Bjørnlund (Henrik Jansson), Annette Buch Petersen (Petite), Thomas Rode Andersen (Adam, Cook), Oliver Jørck (Aksel, new-born), Oliver Sobol (Aksel, 3 months), Lucas Kornmod Lorentzen (Aksel, ? year), Bruno Suneson (Aksel, 3 years)

ZHOU YU'S TRAIN

(SONY CLASSICS) a.k.a. *Zhou Yu de huo che*; Producers, Sun Zhou, Huang Jianxin, William Kong; Executive Producers, Yang Buting, Zhao Xinxian; Director, Sun Zhou; Screenplay, Sun Zhou, Be Cun, Zhang Mei; Photography, Wang Yu; Designer, Sun Li; Editor, William Chang; Music, Shigeru Umebayashi; a co-production of China Film Co-Production Corporation, China Film Group Corporation, Glory Top Properties, Media Asia Films Ltd., Senjiu Film; Chinese-Hong Kong, 2002; Dolby; Color; Rated PG-13; 97 minutes; American release date: July 16, 2004. CAST: Gong Li (Zhou Yu), Tony Leung Ka Fai (Chen Qing), Sun Honglei (Zhang Qiang)

FREE RADICALS

(KINO) a.k.a. *Böse Zellen*; Producers, Martin Gschlacht, antonin Svoboda; Executive Producer, Bruno Wagner; Director/Screenplay, Barbara Albert; Photography, Martin Gschlacht; Art Director, Katharina Wöppermann; Costumes, Monika Buttinger; Editor, Monika Willi; a co-production of Coop 99, Fama Film AG, zero südwest Gmb H; Austrian-German-Swiss, 2003; Dolby; Color; Not rated; 120 minutes; American release date: July 24, 2004. CAST:

Kathrin Resetarits, Ursula Strauss in *Free Radicals* PHOTO COURTESY OF KINO

Jerry Garcia, Bob Weir in *Festival Express* PHOTO COURTESY OF THINKFILM

Kathrin Resetarits (Manu), Ursula Strauss (Andrea), Georg Friedrich (Andreas), Marion Mitterhammer (Gerlinde), Martin Brambach (Reini), Rupert L. Lehofer (Lukas), Bellinda Akwa-Asare (Sandra), Gabriela Schmoll (Belinda), Christian Ghera (Heinrich), Karl Fischer (Karl), Désiée Ourada (Patricia), Dominik Hartel (Kai), Nicole Skala (Gabi), Deborah Ten Brink (Yvonne), Alfred Worel (Josef), Elisabeth Engstler (Moderatorin), Romana Helcmanovsky (Bini), Sabrina Pochop (Sandy), Angela Kada (Conny), Niko Wlcek (Chris), David Frey (Martin), Jennifer Kramer (Claudia)

DAUGHTERS OF THE SUN

(FACETS THEATRICAL) a.k.a. *Dakhtaran-e khorshid*; Producer, Jahangir Kosari; Director/Screenplay, Maryam Shahriar; Photography, Homayun Payvar; Art Director, Malek Jahan Khazai; Music, Hossein Alizadeh; Editor, Shahrzad Pouya; a Farabi Cinema Foundation production; Iranian, 2000; Color; Not rated; 92 minutes; American release date: July 29, 2004. CAST: Altinay Ghelich Taghani, Soghra Karimi, Zahra Mohammadi, Habib Haddad.

GOZU

(PATHFINDER PICTURES) a.k.a. *Gokudô kyôfu dai-gekijô: Gozu*, \Producers, Harumi Sone, Kana Koido; Director, Takashi Miike; Screenplay, Sakichi Satô; Photography, Kazunari Tanaka; Designer, Akira Ishige; Music, Kôji Endô; Editor, Yasushi Shimamura; a co-production of Klock Worx Co., Rakuei-sha; Japanese, 2003; Color; Rated R; 129 minutes; American release date: July 30, 2004. CAST: Hideki Sone (Minami), Shô Aikawa (Ozaki), Kimika Yoshino (Female Ozaki), Shôhei Hino (Nose), Keiko Tomita (Innkeeper), Harumi Sone (Innkeeper's Brother), Renji Ishibashi (Boss)

FESTIVAL EXPRESS

(THINKFILM) Producers, Gavin Poolman, John D. Trapman; Executive Producers, Ann Carli, Garth Douglas, Willem Poolman; Director, Bob Smeaton; Photography, Peter Biziou, Bob Fiore; Editor, Eamonn Power; an Apollo Films, Peach Tree Films production; British-Dutch, 2003; Dolby; Color; Rated R; 90 minutes; American release date: July 30, 2004. Documentary of a Canadian rock festival train tour; featuring Janis Joplin, The Grateful Dead, The Band, Buddy Guy Blues Band, Delaney & Bonnie & Friends, The Flying Burrito Bros, Ian & Sylvia & The Great Speckled Bird, Mashmakhan, ShaNaNa, Bob Weir, Phil Lesh, Mickey Hart, Rick Danko, Ken Pearson, Richard Bell, John Till, Sylvia Tyson, Jerry Mercer, Kenny Gradney, Eric Andersen, David Dalton, James Cullingham, Rob Bowman, Ken Walker.

PROTEUS

(STRAND) Producers, Anita Lee, Steven Markowitz, Platon Trakoshis; Director, John Greyson; Screenplay, John Greyson, Jack Lewis; Story, Jack Lewis; Photography, Giulio Biccari; Designer, Tom Hannam; Costumes, Grant Carr, Diana Cilliers; Music, Don Pyle, Andrew Zealley; Editor, Roslyn Kalloo; Pluck Productions; Canadian-South African, 2003; Dolby; Color; Not rated; 97 minutes; American release date: July 30, 2004. CAST: Rouxnet Brown (Claas Blank), Shaun Smyth (Virgil Niven), Neil Sandilands (Rijkhaart Jacobz), Kristen Thomson (Kate), Tessa Jubber (Elize), Terry Norton (Betsy), Grant Swanby (Willer), Adrienne Pearce (Tinnie), Brett Goldin (Lourens), A.J. van der Merwe (Settler), Dean Lotz (Governor), Jeroen Kranenburg (Scholz), Johan Jacobs

Neil Sandilands, Rouxnet Brown in *Proteus* PHOTO COURTESY OF STRAND

(Nama Prisoner), Katrina Kaffer (Kaness), Kwanda Malunga (Claas, age 10), Illias Moseko (Claas's Grandfather), Andre Lindveldt (Minstrel), Peter van Heerden (Soldier), Jane Rademeyer (Niven's Wife), Andre Odendaal (Floris), Lola Dollimore (Niven's Daughter), Robin Smith (Munster), Colin le Roux (Hendrik), Andre Rousseau (De Mepesche), Edwin Angless (Hangman)

TASUMA

(ART MATTAN PRODS.) Director, Daniel Sanou Kollo; Music, Cheick Tidiane Seck; Not other credits available; Burkina Faso-French, 2001; Color; Not rated; 90 minutes; American release date: July 30, 2004. CAST: Serge Henri, Aï Keïta, Besani Raoul Khalil, Noufou Papa Ouédraogo, Safiatou Sanou, Sonia Karen Sanou, Stanislas Soré, Mamadou Zerbo

TRANSFIXED

(PICTURE THIS! ENTERTAINMENT) a.k.a. *Mauvais genres*; Producer, Humbert Balsan; Executive Producer, Marie-Astrid Lamboray; Director, Francis Girod; Screenplay, Francis Girod, Philippe Cougrand; Based on the novel by Brigitte Aubert; Photography, Thierry Jault; Designer, Perrine Rulesn; Costumes, Nathalie Leborgne; Music, Alexandre Desplat; Editor, Isabelle Dedieu; a co-production of France 3 Cinema, France Television Images, K2 SA, Le Studio Canal+, Ognon Pictures, RTL, TVI; French-Belgian, 2001; Stereo; Color; Not rated; 105 minutes; American release date: July 30, 2004. CAST: Richard Bohringer (Huysmans), Robinson Stévenin (Bo), Stéphane Metzger (Johnny), William Nadylam (Maeva), Frédéric Pellegeay (Alex), Ginette Garcin (Louisette Vincent), Stéphane de Groot (Pryzuski), Charlie Dupoint (Courtois), Veronica Novak (Elvire), Thibaut Corrion (Marlène), Marcel Dossogne (Professor Ancelin), Micheline Presle (Violette Ancelin)

STANDER

(NEWMARKET) Producers, Hillard Elkins, Martin Katz, Chris Roland, Julia Verdin; Executive Producers, David E. Allen, Izidore Codron, Jan Fantl, Frank Hübner, Steve Markoff, Eric Sandys, Director, Brownsen Hughes; Screenplay, Bima Stagg; Photography, Jess Hall; Designer, Lester Cohen; Costumes, Darion Hing; Music, David Holmes; Editor, Robert Ivison; a co-production of ApolloProMedia, Grosvenor Park Productions, Seven Arts Pictures Limited, The Imaginarium; Canadian-German-South African-British; Dolby; Color; Rated R; 111 minutes; American release date: August 6, 2004. CAST: Thomas Jane (Andre Stander), Ashley Taylor (Deventer), David Patrick O'Hara (Allan Heyl), Dexter Fletcher (Lee McCall), Deborah Kara Unger (Bekkie Stander), Marius Meyers (Gen. Stander), At Botha (Gen. Viljoen), Lionel Newton (Desk Sgt. Smit), Melanie Merle (Sharmaine), Hannes Muller (Jan Wortmann), Shaeleen Tobin (Grace Wortmann), Sean Else (Asst. Det. Ed Janis), Peter Gradner (Allums), Patrick Mynhardt (Judge), Wikus du Toit (Lawyer), Dummond Marais (Prosecutor), Nicole Abel (Young Lady in Bar), Waldemar Schultz (Cop at Accident), Emgee Pretorious (Wedding Judge), James Borthwick (Vorster/Det. Groot), Graham Clarke (Riot General), Andre Stolz (Armourer), Robin Smith (Loudspeaker Colonel), Allan Bevolo, Jacques Gombault (Riot Cops), Anton Dekker (Colonel), Dirk Stoltz (Cop at Slum Apartment), Neels Coetzee (Drunk), Lynn Hooker (Elderly Woman), Iain Paton (Macho Teller), Ben Kruger (Bank Guard), Thomas Ramabu (Sunglasses Hawker), Diaan Lawrenson, Anel Olsson (Bank Tellers), Duncan Lawson (Techie), Paul Luckhoff (Suspect), Cassidy Coombs (Kidnapped Child), Steven Raymond, Chris Steyn (Prisoners), George Moolman (Male Nurse), Andrew Thompson (Farmboy), Val Donald-Bell (Nurse), Moshoeshoe Chabeli (Harold), Ron Smerczak (Wild Coast Cop), Clive Scott (Bank Officer), John Lesley (Old Man), Shafa'ath-Ahmad Kahn (Indian Tailor), Graham Hopkins (Porsche Salesman), Paul Ditchifield (Bank Manager), Chris Buchanan (Lane), Ben Horowitz (Mark Jennings), Charlotte Butler (Marlene Henn), Matt Stern (Celebrity Spotter), Kerry Hiles (Tweaked Customer), Duncan Harling (Airport Cop), Mawongo Tyawa (Zulu), Fats Bookholane (Itano), Paul Slabolespzy (Politico), Justin Strydom (House Dick), Ferdinand Rabie (Barrier Cop), Dan Robbertse, Errol Ballentine (Onlookers), Shane Howarth (Airport Cop), Tessa Jubber (Florida Girl), Gert White, Denton Douglas (Frat Boys), Neil Coppen (Blond God), Tyrone Akal (Mustang Kid), Zaa Nkweta (Black Officer), David Dukas (White Officer)

Dexter Fletcher, Thomas Jane, David Patrick O'Hara in *Stander* PHOTO COURTESY OF NEWMARKET

Marie Brahimi in *The Other World* PHOTO COURTESY OF ARTMATTAN

THE OTHER WORLD

(ARTMATTAN PRODS.) a.k.a. *L'Autre monde*; Director/Screenplay, Merzak Allouache; Music, Gnawa Diffusion; Editor, Sylvie Gadmer; a co-production of Baya Films, Canal+ Horizons, Lancelot Films, We Aime El Djazair, aret France Cinema; Algerian-French, 2001; Dolby; Color; Not rated; 95 minutes; American release date: August 6, 2004. CAST: Marie Brahimi (Yasmine), Karim Bouaiche (Hakim), Nazim Boudjenah (Rachid), Michèle Moretti (Aldjia), Abdelkrim Bahloul (Officer), Boualem Benani (Omar)

LAST LIFE IN THE UNIVERSE

(PALM PICTURES) a.k.a. *Ruang rak noi nid mahasan*; Producers, Wouter Barendrecht, Duangkamol Limcharoen, Nonzee Nimbibutr; Executive Producers, Meileen Choo, Charoen Iamphungporn, Fran Rubel Kuzui, Kaz Kuzui, Michael J. Werner, Arai Yoshikiyo; Director, Pen-Ek Ratanaruang; Screenplay, Pen-Ek Ratanaruang, Prabda Yoon; Photography, Christopher Doyle; Designer, Saksiri Chantarangsri; Costumes, Sombatsara Teerasaroch; Music, Small Room; Editor, Patamanadda Yukol; a co-production of Bohemian Films, Cinemasia; Thai-Japanese, 2003; Dolby; Color; Rated R; 112 minutes; American release date: August 6, 2004. CAST: Tadanobu Asano (Kenji), Sinitta Boonyasak (Noi), Laila Boonyasak (Nid), Yutaka Matsushige (Yukio), Riki Takeuchi (Takashi), Takashi Miike, Yoji Tanaka, Sakichi Satô (Yakuzas), Thiti Rhumorn (Jon), Junko Nakazawa (Librarian), Aikio Anraku (Japanese Housewife), Nortioshi Urano (Salaryman), Phimchanok Nala Dube (Girl in Jon's Apartment), Ampon Rattanawong, Jakrarin Sanitti (Jon's Underlings), Songsith Visunee (Old Man on the Bus), Prayoon Tiancharoengwong (Old Man a the Outdoor Bar), Jakrapan Ruttajak (Security Guard)

BANGRAJAN

(MAGNOLIA) Co-Producer, Nonzee Nimbibutr; Director, Tanit Jitnukul; Screenplay, Tanit Jitnukul, Kongkiat Khomsiri, Patikarn Phejmunee, Buinthin Thuaykaew; Photography, Wichian Ruangwijchayakul; Designer, Buinthin Thuaykaew; Editor, Sunit Atsawinikul; a co-production of BEC-TERO Entertainment, Film Bangkok; Thai, 2000; Dolby; Color; Not rated; 71 minutes; American release date: August 6, 2004. CAST: Jaran Ngamdee (Nai Jun), Winai Kraibutr (Nai In), Theerayut Pratyabamrung (Luang Phor Thammachote), Bin Bunluerit (Nai Thongmen), Bongkoj Khongmalai (E Sa), Chumphorn Thepphithak (Nai Than), Suntharee Maila-or (Taeng-Onn), Phisate Sangsuwan (Nemeao Seehabodee), Theeranit Damrongwinijchai (Mangcha-ngai)

YU-GI-OH!: THE MOVIE

(WARNER BROS.) Producers, Norman J. Grossfeld, Michael Pecerlello; Executive Producer, Alfred R. Kahn; Director, Hatsuki Tsuji; Screenplay, Michael Mercerlello; a co-production of 4 Kids Entertainment, Shueisha, TV Tokyo; Japanese; Dolby; Color; Rated PG; 90 minutes; American release date: August 13, 2004. VOICE CAST: Dan Green (Yugi Moto/Yami Yugi), Eric Stuart (Seto Kaiba), Scottie Ray (Anubis), Wayne Grayson (Joey Wheeler), John Campbell (Tristan Taylor), Tara Jayne (Mokuba Kaiba), Maddie Blaustein (Solomon Moto), Darren Dunstan (Max-A-Million Pegasus), Mike Pollock (Newscaster), Amy Birnbaum (Tea Garnder)

NICOTINA

(ARENAS ENTERTAINMENT) Producers, Laura Imperiale, Martha Sosa Elizondo; Executive Producer, Federico González Compeán, Monica Lozano, Eckehardt Von Damm; Director, Hugo Rodríguez; Screenplay, Martin Salinas; Photography, Marcelo Iaccarino; Art Director, Sandra Cabriada; Costumes, Alejandra Dorantes; Music, Fernando Corona; Editor, Alberto de Toro; Casting, Alejandro Caballero; a co-production of Altavista Films, Arca Difussion, Cacerola Films, Cinecolor, Fondo de Inversion y Estimulos al Cine (FIDECINE), Oberon Films, Televista Cine, Videocine S.A. de C.V., Videocolor; Mexican-Argentine-Spanish; Color; Rated R; 90 minutes; American release date: August 20, 2004. CAST: Diego Luna (Lolo), Marta Belaustegui (Andrea), Lucas Crespi (Nene), Jesús Ochoa (Tomson), Rafael Inclán (Goyo), Rosa Maria Bianchi (Carmen), Daniel Giménez Cacho (Beto), Carmen Madrid (Clara), Norman Sotolongo (Svoboda), Eugenio Montessoro (Carlos), José María Yazpik (Joaquin), Jorge Zárate (Sanchez), Enoc Leaño (Memo)

ALMOST PEACEFUL

(EMPIRE) a.k.a. *Un monde presque paisible*; Producer, Rosalinde Deville; Director, Michel Deville; Screenplay, Michel Deville, Rosalinde Deville; Based on the novel *Quoi de neuf sur la guerre?* By Robert Bober; Photography, André Diot; Designer, Arnaud de Moleron; Costumes, Madeline Fontaine; Music, Giovanni Bottesini; Editor, Andrea Sedlácková; a co-production of Canal+, Centre National de la Cinématographie (CNC), Eléfilm, France 3 Cinéma, France Télévision Images 2, Gimages 6; French, 2002; Dolby; Color; Not rated; 94 minutes; American release date: August 20, 2004. CAST: Simon Abkarian (Albert),

Tabanobu Asano, Sinitta Boonyasak in *Last Life in the Universe* PHOTO COURTESY OF PALM PICTURES

Yugi Moto in *Yu-Gi-Oh!:The Movie* PHOTO COURTESY OF WARNER BROS.

Lucas Crespi, Rafael Inclán in *Nicotina* PHOTO COURTESY OF ARENEAS ENTERTAINMENT

Zabou Breitman (Léa), Vincent Elbaz (Léon), Lubna Azabal (Jacqueline), Denis Podalydès (Charles), Julie Gayet (Mme. Andrée), Malik Zidi (Joseph), Stanislas Merhar (Maurice), Clothilde Courau (Simone), Sylvie Milhaud (Mme. Sarah), Judith D'Aléazzo (Mme. Himmelfarb), François Clavier (Police Commissioner), Hervé Briaux (Proprietor), Pierre Diot (Fascist at Café), Eric Laugérias (Charles' Lawyer), Laurence Masliah (Summer-Camp Director), Stéphane Bientz (Flirtatious Camp Counselor), Bruce Myers (Forest King/Old Tailor), Bernard Ballet (Wasserman), Oksar Bellaïch, Stéphane Bouby, Sylvie Ferro, Adrien Fontanaud, Catherine Giron, Sophie Gourdin, Yannick Guérin, Yaron hazens, Sacha Juaszko, Béatrice Laout, Alexandra Martinez, Meriem Menant, Raphaël Pener, Dominique Pozzetto, Simon Renou, Céline Thiou, Waldemar Wundermann (Children)

ROSENSTRASSE

(SAMUEL GOLDWYN FILMS) Producers, Herbert G. Kloiber, Henrik Meyer, Richard Schöps, Markus Zimmer; Executive Producer, Kerstin Ramcke; Director, Margarethe von Trotta; Screenplay, Margarethe von Trotta, Pamela Katz; Photography, Franz Rath; Designer, Heike Bauersfeld; Costumes, Ursula Eggert; Music, Loek Dikker; Editor, Corina Dietz; Casting, Sabine Schroth; a co-production of Studio Hamburg Letterbox Filmproduktion, Tele-München (TMG), Get Reel Productions; German-Dutch, 2003; Dolby; Color; Rated PG-13; 136 minutes; American release date: August 20, 2004. CAST: Katja Riemann (Lena Fischer, aged 33), Maria Schrader (Hannah Weinstein), Martin Feifel (Fabrian Israel Fischer), Jürgen Vogel (Arthur von Eschenbach), Jutta Lampe (Ruth Weinstein), Doris Schade (Lena Fischer, aged 90), Fedja van Huêt (Luis Marquez), Carola Regnier (Rachel Rosenbauer), Svea Lohde (Ruth Süssman, aged 8), Plien van Bennekom (Marian), Jutta Wachowiak (Frau Goldberg), Romijn Conen (Ben Weinstein), Jan Decleir (Nathan Goldberg), Julia Eggert (Emily), Thekla Reuten (Klara Singer), Lilian Schiffer (Erika), Lena Stolze (Miriam Süssman), Isolde Barth (Fabian's Mother), Fritz Lichtenhahn (Fabian's Father), Carine Crutzen (Erika's Mother), Edwin de Vries (Erika's Father), Nina Kunzendorf (Litzy), Martin Wuttke (Joseph Goebbels), Rainer Strecker (SS Man Schneider), Peter Ender (Policeman Franz), Hans Pete rHallwachs (Father von Eschenbach), Gaby Dohm (Elsa von Eschenbach), Hans Kremer (Weber), Wolfgang Pregler (Müller), Claudia Rieschel (Klara's Colleague), Siemen Rühaak (SS Officer), Heio von Stetten (Von Welz)

IT'S EASIER FOR A CAMEL ...

(NEW YORKER) a.k.a. *Il est plus facile pour un chameau ...* ; Producer, Paulo Branco; Director, Valeria Bruni Tedeschi; Screenplay, Valeria Bruni Tedeschi, Noémie Lvovsky, Agnès de Sacy; Photography, Jeanne Lapoirie; Designer, Emmanuelle Duplay; Costumes, Claire Fraisse; Editor, Anne Weil; Casting, Yann Coridian; a co-production of Gémini Films, Interlinea Films; French-Italian, 2003; Color; Not rated; 110 minutes; American release date: August 20, 2004. CAST: Valeria Bruni Tedeschi (Federica), Chiara Mastroianni (Bianca), Jean-Hugues Anglade (Pierre), Denis Podalydès (Philippe), Marysa Borini (Mother), Roberto Herlitzka (Father), Lambert Wilson (Aurelio), Pasal Bongard (Priest), Nicolas Briançon (Director), Yvan Attal (Man in Park), Emmanuelle Devos (Philippe's Wife), Karine Silla (Céline), Alma Samel (Child Federica), Uta Samel (Child Bianaca), Victor Nebbiolo (Child Aurelio), Helen Sadowska (Dance Teacher), Chloé Mons (Amélie), Hèléne de Saint-Père (Woman in Movie Theater), Pierre-Olivier Mattei (Man in Movie Theater), Laurent Grévill (Doctor), Eva Ionesco (Worker), Gérard Buffart (Concierge), Souzan Chirazi (Lawyer), Roland Romanelli (Accordianist), Magalie Woch (Young Patient)

THIS AIN'T NO HEARTLAND

(INDEPENDENT) Producer/Director/Screenplay/ Photography/Editor, Andreas Horvath; Color, DV-to-35mm; Not rated; 106 minutes; American release date: August 25, 2004. Documentary in which filmmaker Andreas Horvath reveals the ignorance about the war on terrorism while interviewing several people in America's mid-West.

Yvan Attal, Valeria Bruni Tedeschi in *It's Easier for a Camel...* PHOTO COURTESY OF NEW YORKER

MY WIFE MAURICE

(TLA RELEASING) a.k.a. *Ma femme … s'appelle Maurice*; Jean-Marie Poiré, Igor Sekulic; Director, Jean-Marie Poiré; Screenplay, Jean-Marie Poiré, Raffy Shart; Based on the play by Raffy Shart; Photography, Robert Alazraki; Designer, Katia Wyszkop; Costumes, Olivier Bériot; Music, Pierre Charvet, Vincent Prezioso; Editors, Jean-Marie Poiré, Henry Revlou; Casting, Iris Wong; a co-production of Comédie Star, France 2 Cinéma, Seven Pictures, Studio Babelsberg, UFA Babelsberg Gmb H, UFA Fernsehporudktion GmbH; French-German, 2002; Dolby; Color; Not rated; 102 minutes; American release date: August 27, 2004. CAST: Alice Evans (Emmanuelle), Régis Laspalès (Maurice Lappin), Philippe Chevallier (Georges Audefey), Götz Otto (Johnny Zucchini), Anémone (Claire Trouabal), Martin Lamotte (Jean-Bernard Touabal), Virginie Lemoine (Marion Audefey), Guy Marchand (Charles Boisdain), Urbain Cancelier (Poilard), Stéphane Audran (Jacqueline Boisdain), Marco Bonini (Venetian Painter), Jean-Pierre Castaldi (Dealer), Michele Garcia (Pret-a-Poter Saleswoman), Sylvie Joly (Woman), Raphaë Mezrahi (Fashion Type), Paul Belmondo, Benjamin Castaldi (Automobile Salesmen), Danièle Evenou (Baker), Julie Arnold (Commercial), Stefano Antonucci (Concierge)

SUPERBABIES: BABY GENIUSES 2

(TRIUMPH) Producer/Story, Steven Paul; Executive Producer, Frank Hübner; Supervising Producer (Apollo Media), Reinhild Gräber; Director, Bob Clark; Screenplay, Gregory Poppen; Photography, Maher Maleh; Designers, Deren Abram, Ricardo Spinacé; Costumes, Tina Fiorda; Music, Paul Zaza, Helmut Zerlett; Editor, Stan Cole; Casting, Dorothy Koster Paul; a co-production of ApolloMedia, Crystal Sky Communications; German-British-U.S.; Dolby; Color; Rated PG; 88 minutes; American release date: August 27, 2004. CAST: Jon Voight (Bill Biscane/Kane), Scott Baio (Stan Bobbins), Vanessa Angel (Jean Bobbins), Skyler Shaye (Kylie), Justin Chatwin (Zack), Peter Wingfield (Crowe), Gerry Fitzgerald, Leo Fitzgerald, Myles Fitzgerald (Kahuna), Max Iles, Michael Iles (Archie), Jared Scheideman, Jordan Schiedeman (Finkleman), Maia Bastidas, Keana Bastidas (Rosita), Joshua Lockhart, Maxwell Lochkhart (Alex), Anastasia Trovato (Tascha), Shaun Sipos (Brandon), Devin Douglas Drewitz (Peter), Jessica Amlee (Little Greta), Thomas Kretschmann (Roscoe), Alfonso Quijada (Muggles), Shawn MacDonald (Hologram guard), Jy Hariss (Hologram Soda Jerk), Gary Chalk (Police Captain), Alexander Kalugin (Petrov), Barry Greene (Kahuna's Father), Connor Christopher, Jake Smith (Baby Kahuna), Sterling McKay (Boy), Andrew Francis (Ken), Nancy Lilley (Greta), Dagmar

Scott Baio in *Superbabies: Baby Geniuses 2* PHOTO COURTESY OF TRIUMPH

Nicoletta Romanoff in *Remember Me, My Love* PHOTO COURTESY OF IDP DISTRIBUTIONS

Midcap (Reporter), Bobby L. Stewart (Police Sergeant), Stefanie von Pfetten (Jennifer Kraft), Lara Milliken, Reece Thompson (Kids), Rebaecca Reichert (Siska), Gus Lynch (Mr. K), Whoopi Goldberg (Herself), O'Town (Themselves), David Kaye (Voice of Kahuna), Danny McKinnon (Voice of Archie), Melissa Montoya (Voice of Rosita), Rashad Hood (Voice of Alex), Jonathan Singleton (Voice of Finkleman)

REMEMBER ME, MY LOVE

(IDP DISTRIBUTION) a.k.a. *Ricordati di me*; Producer, Domenico Procacci; Director, Gabriele Muccino; Screenplay, Gabriele Muccino, Heidrun Schleef; Photography, Marcello Montarsi; Art Director, Paola Bizzarri; Costumes, Gemma Mascagni; Casting, Francesco Vedovati; Music, Paolo Buonvino; Editor, Claudio Di Mauro; a co-production of Fandango, Medus Produzione, Telepiù, Vice Versa Film; Italian-French, British, 2003; Dolby; Color; Rated R; 125 minutes; American release date: September 3, 2004. CAST: Fabrizio Bentivoglio (Carlo Ristuccia), Laura Morante (Giulia Ristuccia), Nicoletta Romanoff (Valentina Ristuccia), Monica Bellucci (Alessia), Silvio Muccino (Paolo Ristuccia), Gabriele Lavia (Alfredo), Enrico Silvestrin (Stefano Manni), Silvia Cohen (Elena), Alberto Gimignani (Riccardo), Amanda Sandrelli (Louise), Blas Roca-Rey (Matt), Pietro Taricone (Paolo Tucci), Giulia Michelini (Ilaria), Maria Chiara Augenti (Anna Pezzi), Andrea Roncato (Luigi), Stefano Santospago (Andre)

WARRIORS OF HEAVEN AND EARTH

(SONY CLASSICS) a.k.a. *Tian di ying xiong*; Director/Screenplay, He Ping; Photography, Zhoa Fei; Music, A.R. Rahman; a Xian Film Studio production; Chinese-Hong Kong, 2003; Rated R; 114 minutes; American release date: September 3, 2004. CAST: Nakai Kiichi (Lai Xi), Wang Xueqi (Master An), Hasi Bagen (Cao Jian), Vicky Zhao Wei (Wen Zhu), Ho Tao (Ma Gun), Liu Linian (Wu Lao'er), Wang Deshun (Old Diehard), Yeerjiang Mahepushen (Master An's Servant) , Jiang Wen (Captain Zai Li), Zhou Yun (The Monk)

TAE GUK GI: THE BROTHERHOOD OF WAR

(SAMUEL GOLDWYN) a.k.a. *Taegukgi hwinalrimyeo*; Producer, Lee Seong-hun; Director/Screenplay, Kang Je-gyu; Photography, Hong Kyung-Pyo; Music, Lee Dong-jun; Editor, Choi Kyeong-hie; a Kang Je-Kyu Film Co. production; South Korean; Dolby; Color; Rated R; 140 minutes; American release date: September 3, 2004. CAST: Jang Dong-Kun (Jin-tae), Won Bin (Jin-seok), Lee Eun-ju (Young-shin), Choi Min-sik (North Korean Commander)

I HATE SAO PAOLO

(INTUIT FILMS) Producer/Director/Screenplay, Dardo Toledo Barros; Executive Producers, Dardo Toledo Barros, Claudia G. Bischel, Regina Gomes dos Reis, Donald Rabinovitch, Ari Taub; Photography, Carlos "Jay" Yamashita; Designer, Ivan Cesar Teixeira; Music, Pierre Foldes; Editor, Reinaldo C. Vilarino; Brazilian; Color/black and white; Not rated; 90 minutes; American release date: September 8, 2004. CAST: Claudio Fontana (Daniel Mendes Ferraz), Wolney de Assis (Tomas), Regina Temencius (Debora), Alfredo Penteado (Pedro Mirando), Melissa Panzutti (Monica), Celsa Frateschi (Alvaro), Mariana Kupher (Samantha), Daniela Santos (Teresa), Jose Mangoli (Victor), Fortuna Frateschi (Sepharadit Singer), Luiz Bacceli (Jose Augusto), Teresa S. Toledo Barros (Mariana), Dardo Toledo Barros (Cesar), Cristiano Sensi (Danilo)

THE PRIVATE ARCHIVES OF PABLO ESCOBAR

(CINEMA TROPICAL) a.k.a. *Los Archivos privados de Pablo Escobar*; Producers, Yezid Campos, Francoise Nieto; Director, Marc De Beaufort; Screenplay, Alonso Salazar; Photography, Luigi Baquero; Music, Kai, George Pizarro; Editor, Juan Carlos Isaza; Colombian, 2002; Color; Not rated; 70 minutes; American release date: September 9, 2004. Documentary on Pablo Escobar Gaviria, king of Colombia's drug trade.

RECONSTRUCTION

(PALM PICTURES) Producer, Tine Grew Pfeiffer; Director, Christoffer Boe; Screenplay, Christoffer Boe, Mogens Rukov; Photography, Manuel Alberto Claro; Designer, Martin de Thurah; Costumes, Gabi Humnicki; Music, Thomas Knak; Editors, Peter Brandt, Mikkel E.G. Nielsen; Casting, Anja Philip; a co-production of Director's Cut, HR Boe & Co., Nordisk Film, TV2 Danmark; Danish, 2003; Dolby; Color; Rated PG-13; 90 minutes; American release date: September 10, 2004. CAST: Nikolaj Lie Kaas (Alex David), Maria Bonnevie (Simone/Aimee), Krister Henriksson (August Holm), Nicolas Bro (Leo Sand), Helle Fagralid (Nan Sand), Peter Steen (Mel David), Malene Schwartz (Frau Banum), Ida Dwinger (Monica), Mercedes Claro Schelin (Mercedes Sand), Jens Blegaa (Waiter), David Dencik (Bartender), Isabella Miehe-Renard (Journalist)

Nikolaj Lie Kaas, Maria Bonnevie in *Reconstruction* PHOTO COURTESY OF PALM PICTURES

TESTOSTERONE

(STRAND) Producers, David Moreton, Kathryn Riccio; Director, David Moreton; Screenplay, David Moreton, Dennis Hensley; Based on the novel by James Robert Baker; Photography, Ken Kelsch; Designer, Jorge Ferrari; Music, Marco D'Ambrosio; Editors, Roger Schulte, Mallory Gottlieb; a co-production of Blue Streak Films, Cinecolor, Videocolor; Argentine-U.S., 2003; Dolby; Color; Rated R; 105 minutes; American release date: September 10, 2004. CAST: David Sutcliffe (Dean Seagrave), Celina Font (Sofia), Antonio Sabato, Jr. (Pablo Alesandro), Jennifer Coolidge (Louise), Leonardo Brzezicki (Marcos), Sonia Braga (Pablo's Mother), Dario Dukah (Guillermo), Jennifer Elise Cox (Sharon, the Perky Chick), Davenia McFadden (Marnie), Ezequiel Abeijón (Rogelio), Martín Borisenko (Hot Cater Waiter), Barbara Bunge (Bridesmaid), Gustavo Chapa (Cemetery Man), Daniel Di Biase (Taxi Driver), Gabriel Dottavio (Customer), Americo Ferrari (Bald Man), Harry Havilio (Front Desk Man), Wolfram Hoechst (Older Gentleman), Carlos Kaspar, Fabrizio Perez, Alejandro Stulchlik, Claudio Torres (Fat Bad Dudes), Miriam Manfredini (Tourist Mother), Carolina Marcovsky (La Luna Hostess), Luis Mazzeo (Policeman), Hector Pazos (Big Policeman), Luis Sabatini (Salesman), Marcos Woinsky (Mr. Ottenhouse), McCaleb Burnett (Guy in Turtleneck), Julie Fay (Fabulous Gallery Guest), Sergio Gravier (Slight Man)

David Sutcliffe, Leonardo Brzezicki in *Testosterone* PHOTO COURTESY OF STRAND

GHOST IN THE SHELL 2: INNOCENCE

(GO FISH PICTURES) a.k.a. Inosensu: Kôkaku kidôtai; Producers, Mitsuhisa Ishikawa, Toshio Suzuki; Director, Mamoru Oshii; Screenplay, Mamour Oshii; Based on the comic Koukaku-Kidoutai by Masamune Shirô; Photography, Miki Sakuma; Designer, Yohei Taneda; Music, Kenji Kawai; Editors, Sachiko Miki, Chihiro Nakano, Junichi Uematsu; Supervising Animator, Kazuchika Kise; a co-production of Bandai Visual Co. Ltd., Dentsu Inc., Kodansha Ltd., Production I.G.; Japanese; Color; Rated PG-13; 100 minutes; American release date: September 17, 2004. Animated.

INCIDENT AT LOCH NESS

(EDEN ROCK MEDIA) Producers, Werner Herzog, Zak Penn; Executive Producers, Thomas Augsberger, Jay Rifkin; Director, Zak Penn; Screenplay, Werner Herzog, Zak Penn; Photography, John Bailey; Art Directors, Katherine Ferwerda, Caireen Todd; Costumes, Annie Dunn; Music, Henning Lohner; Editors, Howard E. Smith, Abby Schwarzwalder; British; Dolby; Color; Rated PG-13; 94 minutes; American release date: September 17, 2004. WITH: Werner Herzog, Kitana Baker, Gabriel Beristain, Russell Williams, David A. Davidson, Michael Karnow, Robert O'Meara, Zak Penn, Steven Gardner (Crew of Discovery IV), John Bailey, Matthew Nicolay, Tanja Koop, Marty Signore (Crew of Herzog in Wonderland), Elisabeth Beristain, Katherine Ferwerda, Crispin Glover, Jeff Goldblum, Lena Herzog, Ricky Jay, Alexa Lauren, Sophia Penn, Pietro Scalia, Missy Stewart, Jenno Topping, Michele Weiss, David Wilson (Party Guests)

The Take PHOTO COURTESY OF FIRST RUN/ICARUS

THE TAKE

(FIRST RUN/ICARUS) Producers, Avi Lewis, Naomi Lewis, Silva Basmajian; Executive Producer, Laszlo Barna; Photography, Mark Ellam; Music, David Wall; Narrator, Avi Lewis, Naomi Klein; a co-production of Barna-Alper Productions, Klein Lewis Production, with Canadian Brodcasting Corporation (CBC) and the National Film Board of Canada (NFB); Canadian; Color; Not rated; 87 minutes; American release date: September 22, 2004. Documentary in which unexmployed Argentine workers return to their shuttered businesses to re-start them by themselves; featuring Gustavo Cordera, Freddy Espinoza, Nestor Kirchner, Naomi Klein, Avi Lewis, Carlos Menem, Lalo Paret, Anoop Singh, Luis Zanon

INTERNAL AFFAIRS

(MIRAMAX) a.k.a. *Wu Jian dao*; Producer, Andy Lau; Directors, Andrew Lau, Siu Fai Mak; Screenplay, Siu Fai Mak, Felix Chong; Photography, Andrew Lau, Yiu-Fai Lai; Music, Kwong Wing Chan; Art Directors, Wong Ching Ching, Sung Pong Choo; Costumes, Pik Kwan Lee; Editors, Ching Hei Pang, Danny Pang; Action Choreographer, Dion Lam; a Basic Pictures production, presented by Media Asia Films; Hong Kong, 2002; Dolby; Color; Rated R; 101 minutes; American release date: September 24, 2004. CAST: Andy Lau (Lau Kin Ming), Tony Leung Chiu Wai (Chan Wing Yan), Anthony Wong Chau-Sang (SP Wong), Eric Tsang (Sam), Kelly

Andy Lau, Tony Leng Chiu Wai in *Internal Affairs* PHOTO COURTESY OF MIRAMAX

Chen (Dr. lee Sum Yee), Sammi Cheng (Mary), Edison Chen (Young Lau Kin Ming), Shawn Yue (Young Chan Wing Yan), Evla Hsiao (May), Man-chat To (Keung), Ka Tung Lam (Inspector B), Tiny Yip Ng (Sir Inspector Cheung), Dion Lam (Del Piero), Chi Keung Wan (Officer Leung), Hui Kam Fung (Cadet School Principal), Tony Ho (Suspect), Courtney Wu (Stereo Shop Owner), Au Hin Wai (Elephant), Li Tin Cheung (Double 8), Lee Wah Chu (Chief Inspector), Chung Wait Ho, Wong Kam Hung, Leung Ho Kei, Lee Yip Kin, Lee Tze Ming, So Wai Nam, Lai Chi Wai (Sam's Followers), Yuen Waj Ho, Yiu Man Kee, Wong Yin Keung, Mak Wai Kwok, Lam Po Loy, Wong Ch Wang, chen Wing Yee, Kui Mei Yee (CIB Team), Cheung Yuk Sun (Cadet School Instructor), Hui On Tat (Officer Chan), Chaucharew Wichai (Thai Drugdealer), Leung Chiu Yi (May's Daughter)

INCANTATO

(NORTHERN ARTS) a.k.a. *Il Cuore altrove*; Producer, Antonio Avati; Director/Screenplay, Pupi Avati; Photography, Pasquale Rachini; Designer, Simona Migliotti; Costumes, Francesco Crivellini, Mario Carlini; Music, Riz Ortolani; Editor, Amedeo Salfa; a co-production of Palisades Pictures, Duea Film, Rai Cinemafiction; Italian; 2003; Color; Not rated; 107 minutes; American release date: September 24, 2004. CAST: Neri Marcoré (Nello), Giancarlo Giannini (Cesare), Vanessa Incontrada (Angela), Nino D'Angelo (Domenico), Cesare Cremonini (Parroco Santa Lucia), Giulio Bosetti (Dott. Gardini), Angelo Di Loreta (The Monsignore), Anna Longhi (Lina), Sarah Maestri (Grazia), Sandra Milo (Arabella), Edoardo Romano (Prof. Gibertoni), Chiara Sani (Jole), Alfiero Toppetti (Renato)

THE RASPBERRY REICH

(STRAND) Producer, Jürgen Brüning; Director/Screenplay, Bruce La Bruce; Photography, James Carman, Kristian Petersen; Designer, Stefan Dickfeld; Costumes, Ludger Wekenborg; Editor, Jörn Hartmann; a Jürgen Brüning Filmproduktion; German-Canadian; Color; Not rated; 90 minutes; American release date: September 24, 2004. CAST: Susanne Sachsse (Gudrun), Daniel Bätscher (Holger), Andreas Rupprecht (Patrick), Dean Stathis (Andreas), Anton Z. Risan (Clyde), Daniel Fettig (Che), Gerrit (Helmut), Joeffrey (Horst), Ukrike S., Stephan Dilschneider (Neighbors), Sherry Vine (Drag Queen, Stage), Pünktchen (Drag Queen, Door), Sven Reinhard (Policeman), Genesis P-Orridge (TV Personality), Naushad (Muslim), Huseyin Gunus, Alfredo Holz, Claud Matthes, Rafael Caba (Arab Terrorists), Mischka Kral (Diplomat), Marco Volk (Chauffeur)

BLISSFULLY YOURS

(WHY NOT DISTRIBUTION) a.k.a. *Sud sanaeha*; Producers, Eric Chan, Charles de Meaux; Director/Screenplay, Apichatpong Weerasethakul; Photography, Sayombhu Mukdeeprom; Designer, Akekarat Homlaor; Editor, Lee Chatametikool; a co-production of Anna Sanders Films, Kick the Machine, La-ong Dao; Thai-French, 2002; Dolby; Color; Not rated; 125 minutes; American release date: September 24, 2004. CAST: Kanokporn Tongaram (Roong), Min Oo (Min), Jen Jansuda (Orn)

THE WHISPER OF THE WHISTLING WATER

(INDEPENDENT) a.k.a. *C'est le murmure de l'eau qui chant*; Director, Brigitte Cornard; No other credits available; Color; Not rated; 94 minutes; American release date: October 2, 2004. Documentary on artist Louise Bourgeois.

Vanessa Incontrada, Neri Marcoré in *Incantato* PHOTO COURTESY OF NORTHERN ARTS

THE CARD PLAYER

(ANCHOR BAY) Producer/Director, Dario Argento; Executive Producer, Claudio Argento; Screenplay/Story, Dario Argento, Franco Ferrini; Dialogue, Jay Benedict, Phoebe Scholfield; Photography, Benoît Debie; Designer, Marina Pinzutti Ansolini, Antonello Geleng; Costumes, Florence Emir, Patrizia Chericoni; Music, Claudio Simonetti; Editor, Walter Fasano; a co-production of Medusa Produzione, Opera Film Produzione; Italian; Dolby; Color; Not rated; 96 minutes; American release date: October 6, 2004. CAST: Stefania Rocca (Anna Mari), Liam Cunningham (John Brennan), Claudio Santamaria (Carlo Sturni), Antonio Cantafora (Chief Marini), Fiore Argento (Lucia Marini), Silvio Muccino (Remo), Pier Maria Cecchini (Flying Squad Chief), Mia Benedetta (Francesca), Ulisse Minervini (Alvaro), Cosimo Fusco (Berardelli), Claudio Mazzenga (Mario), Adalberto Maria Merli (Chief of Police), Luis Molteni (Medical Examiner), Mario

Opinato (Inspector Morgani), Micaela Pignatelli (Prof. Terzi), Conchita Puglisi (Marta), Gualtiero Scola (Crime Scene Investigator), Giovanni Visentin (Homicide Squad Chief), Jennifer Poli (First Victim, Christine Girdler), Elisabetta Rocchetti (Second Victim), Vera Gemma (Third Victim), Francesco Guzzo, Mistichelli (Anti-Hackers), Franco Vitale (Police Photographer), Emmanuel Bevilacqua (Slot Machine Arcade Owner), Isabella Celani (Doctor), Robert Dawson (Embassy Employee), Elena Falgheri (Teacher), Adriana Fonzi Cruciani (Bunny), Carla Fonzi Cruciani (Bunny's Sister), Robert Madison (Gustavo), Michele Pellegrini (Young Man), Irene Quagliarella (Friend of the Second Victim)

Vodka Lemon PHOTO COURTESY OF NEW YORKER

VODKA LEMON

(NEW YORKER) Executive Producer, Fabrice Guez; Director, Hiner Saleem; Screenplay, Hiner Saleem, Lei Dinety, Pauline Gouzenne; Photography, Christophe Pollock; Designer, Kamal Hamarash; Music, Michel Korb, Roustam Sadoyan; Editor, Dora Mantzoros; a co-production of Dulciné Films, Amka Films Productions S.A., Paradise Films, in association with CINEFACTO, Sintra S.r.l.; French-Italian-Swiss-Armenian, 2003; Dolby; Color; Not rated; 90 minutes; American release date: October 8, 2004. CAST: Romen Avinian (Hamo), Lala Sarkissian (Nina), Ivan Franek (Dilovan), Ruzan Mesropyan (Zine), Zahal Kareilachvili (Giano)

SILENT WATERS

(FIRST RUN FEATURES) a.k.a. *Khamosh Pani: Silent Waters*; Producers, Philippe Avril, Helge Albers; Director, Sabiha Sumar; Screenplay Sabiha Sumar, Paromita Vohra; Photography, Ralph Netzer; Designer, Olivier Meidinger; Costumes, Heike Schultz-Fademrecht; Music, Maden Gopal Singh, Arshad Mahmud, Arjun Sen; Editor, Bettina Böhler; a co-production of Vidhi Films, Flying Moon Filmproduktion, arte; Pakistani-French-German, 2003; Dolby; Color; Not rated; 99 minutes; American release date: October 8, 2004. CAST: Kirron Kher (Ayesha), Aamir Ali Malik (Saleem), Arsad Mahmud (Mahboob), Salman Shahid (Amin), Shilpa Shukla (Zubeida), Sarfaraz Ansari (Rashid), Zaheer Ahmed (Tea Boy), Quratul Ain (Shanno), Abid Ali (Choudhary), Shazim Ashraf (Zubair), Ejaz Baig (Bhatti), Tasleem Bibi (Allabi), Anjum Habibi (Maulana), Navtej Singh Johar (Jaswant), Mubbashir Ali Khan (Laborer), Suhair Fariha Khan (Young Veero), Nadia Malik (Hina), Saba Malik (Courtesan), Taj Mohammad (Village Maulvi), Afaq Mushtaq (Asif), Nisar Quadri (Haji Munnavar), S.A. Rehman (Professor)

ARNA'S CHILDREN

(THINKFILM) Producers, Osnat Tabelsi, Pieter van Huystee; Directors, Danniel Danniel, Juliano Mer Khamis; Photography, Juliano Mer Khamis, Hanna Abu Saada, Uri Steinmetz; Editors, Govert Janse, Obbe Verwer; a co-production of Trabelsi Productions, Pieter van Huystee Film and Television; Israeli-Dutch, 2003; Color; Not rated; 84 minutes; American release date: October 8, 2004. Documentary on Arna Mer Khamis who founded an alternative educational system in Palestine.

THE CHILD I NEVER WAS

(STRAND) a.k.a. *Ein Leben lang kurze Hosen tragen*; Producers, Andrea Hanke, Bettina Scheueren; Director/Screenplay, Kai S. Pieck; Based on the book *Jürgen Bartsch: Opfer und Täter* by Paul Moor and the statements and letters of Jürgen Bartsch; Photography, Egon Werdin; Designer, Bertram Strauss; Costumes, Anne Jendritzko; Music, Kurt Dahlke, Rainer J.G. Uhl; Editor, Ingo Ehrlich; a co-production of MTM West Television & Film GmbH, Westdeutscher Rundfunk (WDR); German, 2002; Black and white/color; Not rated; 83 minutes; American release date: October 8, 2004. CAST: Tobias Schenke (Jürgen Bartsch, Older), Sebastian Urzendowsky (Jürgen Bartsch, Younger), Ulrike Bliefert (Gertrud Bartsch), Walter Gontermann (Gerhard Bartsch), Jürgen Christoph Kamcke (Father Seidlitz), Sebastian Rüger (Young Deacon), Stephan Szasz (Young Priest), Roland Riebeling (Chaplain Herles)

The Child I Never Was PHOTO COURTESY OF STRAND

ANDROMEDIA

(Pathfinder Pictures) a.k.a. *Adorodmedia*; Producers, Takashi Hirano, Kazuya Hamana, Makoto Nakanishi, Toshiaki Nakazawa; Executive Producer, Takashi Kasuga, Morihiro Kodama, Tetsuo Taira, Yasuo Takimoto; Director, Takashi Miike; Screenplay, Kurio Kisaragi; Based on the novel by Kozy Watanabe; Photography, Hideo Yamamoto; Designer, Akira Ishige; Music, Hiromasa Ijichi, Speed, Da Pump; Editor, Yasushi Shimamura; a co-production of Excellent Film, Avex Inc., Sedic International Inc., Tokyo Broadcasting System; Japanese, 1998; Color; Not rated; 109 minutes; American release date: October 8, 2004. CAST: Hiroko Shimabukuo (Mai Hitomi & Ai), Eriko Imai (Yoko), Takako Uehara (Rika), Hitoe Arakaki (Nao), Kenji Harada (Yuu), Ryo Karato (Satoshi Takanaka), Christopher Doyle (Sakkaa), Tomorowo Taguchi (Goda), Issa Hentona (Tooru), Shinobu Miyara (Hiroyuki), Yukinari Tamaki (Kazuma), Ken Okumoto (Daiki)

Jeon Do-yeon , Bae Yong-jun in *Untold Scandal* PHOTO COURTESY OF KINO

UNTOLD SCANDAL

(KINO) a.k.a. *Scandal —Joseon namnyeo sangyeoljisa*; Producer, Oh Jeong-wa; Director, Lee Je-yong; Screenplay, Lee Je-yong, Kim Dae-woo, Kim Heyonjeong; Based on the novel *Les Liaisons Dangereuses* by Choderlos de Laclos; Photography, Kim Byeong-il; Music, Lee Byung-woo; a co-production of CJ Entertainment, Cine Qua Non Films, Shochiku Co.Ltd.; South Korean, 2003; Color; Not rated; 124 minutes; American release date: October 13, 2004. CAST: Lee Mi-suk (Madam Jo), Jeon Do-yeon (Suk), Bae Yong-jun (Jo-won), Jo Hyeonjae (Kwon In-ho), Lee So-yeon (So-ok).

ANATOMY OF HELL

(Tartan) a.k.a. *Anatomie de l'enfer*; Producer, Jean-François Lepetit; Executive Producer, António da Cunha Telles; Director/Screenplay, Catherine Breillat; Based on the novel *Porncratie*; Photography, Yorgos Arvanitis, Susan Gomes, Guillaume Schiffman; Designers, Jean-Marie Milon, Pedro Sá Santos; Costumes, Valérie Guégan, Betty Martins, Catherine Meillan, Sanine Schlumberger; Editor, Pascale Chavance; a co-production of CB Films, Canal+, Centre National de la Cinématographie (CNC), Flach Film, Flach Pyramide International; French, 2003; Dolby; Color; Not rated; 77 minutes; American release date: October 15, 2004. CAST: Amira Casar (The Woman), Rocco Siffredi (The Man), Alexandre Belin, Manuel Taglang (Blow-Job Lovers), Jacques Monge (Man in Bar), Claudio Carvalho (Boy with Bird), Carolina Lopes (Little Girl Playing Doctor), Diego Rodrigues, João Marques, Bruno Fernandes (Little Boys Playing Doctor), Maria Edite Moreeira, Maria João Santos (Pharmacists), Catherine Breillat (Narrator)

SEX IS COMEDY

(IFC FILMS) a.k.a. *Scènes intimes*; Producer, Jean-François Lepetit; Director/Screenplay, Catherine Breillat; Photography, Laurent Machuel; Designer, Frédérique Belvaux; Costumes, Valérie Guégan, Betty Martins; Editor, Pascale Chavance; a CB Films, Canal+, Centre National de la Cinématographie (CNC), Flach Film, France Télévision Images 2, Le Studio Canal+, Studio Images 2, arte France Cinéma production; French-Portuguese; Dolby; Color; Rated R; 92

minutes; American release date: October 20, 2004. CAST: Anne Parillaud (Jeanne), Grégoire Colin (The Actor), Roxane Mesquida (The Actress), Ashley Wanninger (Leo, the First Assistant), Dominique Colladant (Willy), Bart Binnema (Director of Photography), Yves Osmu (The Sound Engineer), Elisabete Piecho (Continuity Girl), Francis Seleck (The Production Manager), Diane Scapa (The Production Designer), Ana Lorena (The Make-Up Artist), Claire Monatte (The Other Make-up Artist), Arnaldo Junior (The Chief Electrician), Elisabete Silva (The Boom Operator), Júlia Fragata (The Set Dresser), Bruno Ramos (The Assistant Camera), Alfredo "Alebé" Ramalho, Rudolfo Santos (Grips), José Cascais (The Property Master)

STELLA STREET

(STRAND) Producer, Ben Swaffer; Executive Producer, John Goldstone; Director, Peter Richardson; Screenplay, Peter Richardson, John Sessions, Phil Cornwell; Photography, Mike Robinson; Designer, Kit Line; Costumes, Diana Moseley; Makeup, Sarita Allison, Lesley Lamont-Fisher; Music/Lounge Songs, Rod Melvin, Dominic Muldowney; Editor, Geoff Hogg; a Stella Street Ltd. Production; British; Dolby; Color; Rated R; 79 minutes; American release date: October 22, 2004. CAST: Phil Cornwell (Nicholson/Caine/Jagger/Bowie /Jimmy/Len/Vince/Nick), John Sessions (Pacino/Mr. Hugget/Pesci/Richards/ Hoffman/Dean), Ronni Ancona (Tara/Madonna/Jerry Hall/Posh Spice /Stephanie), Harry Enfield (Narrator)

POSTMEN IN THE MOUNTAINS

(SHADOW DISTRIBUTION) a.k.a. *Nashan naren nagou*; Producer, Kang Jianmin, Han Sanping; Director, Huo Jianqi; Screenplay, Si Wu; Based on a short story by Peng Jianmin; Photography, Zhao Lei; Designer, Song Jun; Music, Wang Xiaofeng; Editor, Gan Xinrong, Liu Fang; a China Century Entertainment presentation of a Xiaoxiang Film Studio/Beijing Film Studio production; Chinese, 1999; Color; Not rated; 93 minutes; American release date: October 22, 2004. CAST: Teng Lujun (Father), Liu Ye (Son), Gong Yehang (Grandma), Chen Hao (Dong Girl)

800 BULLETS

(TLA RELEASING) a.k.a. *800 balas*; Producer/Director, Álex de la Iglesia; Executive Producer, Juanma Pagazautandua; Screenplay, Álex de la Iglesia, Jorge Guerricaechevarría; Photography, Flavio Martínez Labiano; Art Directors, Biaffra, José Luis Arrizabalaga; Costumes, Paco Delgado; Music, Roque Baños; Editor, Alejandro Lázaro; a co-production of Alan Young Pictures, Canal+

John Sessions, Ronni Ancona in *Stella Street* PHOTO COURTESY OF STRAND

Liu Ye, Teng Lujun in *Postmen in the Mountains* PHOTO COURTESY OF SHADOW DISTRIBUTION

España, Etb (Euskal Telebista), Panico Films, Televisión Española (TVE); Spanish, 2002; Dolby; Color; Rated R; 124 minutes; American release date: October 29, 2004. CAST: Sacho Gracia (Julián Torralba), Ángel de Andrés López (Cheynne), Carmen Maura (Laura), Eusebio Poncela (Scott), Luis Castro (Carlos Torralba), Manuel Tallafé (Manuel), Enrique Martínez (Arrastrao), Luciano Federico (The Undertaker), Eduardo Gómez (Jose Maria, the Hanged Man), Terele Pávez (Rocío), Ramón Barea (Don Mariano), Cesáreo Estébanez (Officer Andrés), Eduardo Antuña (Taxi Driver), Gracia Olayo (Juli), Berta Ojea (Angeles), Yoima Valdés (Sandra), Ane Gabarian (Jacinta), Alfonso Torregrosa (Police Chief), Arantxa Silvestre (Woman in Stagecoach), Juan Viadas (Monitor), Pablo Pinedo (Elias)

Grégoire Colin, Roxane Mesquida in *Sex Is Comedy* PHOTO COURTESY OF IFC FILMS

Sancho Gracia in *800 Bullets* PHOTO COURTESY OF TLA RELEASING

Susana Salazar, Noël Burton in *A Silent Love* PHOTO COURTESY OF ATOPIA

A SILENT LOVE

(ATOPIA) Producer, Pascal Maeder; Director, Federico Hidalgo; Screenplay, Federico Hidalgo, Paulina Robles; Photography, François Dagenais; Designer, Gabriel Tsampalieros; Costumes, Maory Castelo; Editor, Maxime Chalifoux; Canadian-Mexican; Dolby; Color; Not rated; 100 minutes; American release date: October 29, 2004. CAST: Vanessa Bauche (Gladys), Noël Burton (Norman Green), Susana Salazar (Fernanda), Maka Kotto (Andre), Regina Orozco (Ana-Francisca), Carmen Salinas (Georgina), Jorge Zárate (Valdivia), Petre Kosaka (Sushi Chef), Lisette Guertin (Joyce Phelps), Ariadna Álvarez (Lucy), Rosario Zúñiga (Hair Dresser), Paula Jean Hixson (Molly), Li Li (Waitress), Marcus Roberts (Waitress' Boyfriend)

VIOLET PERFUME: NO ONE IS LISTENING

(CASA NOVA FILMS) a.k.a. *Nadie te oye: Perfume de violetas*; Producer/Screenplay, José Buil; Director, Maryse Sistach; Story, José Buil, Maryse Sistach; Photography, Servando Gajá; Art Director, Guadalupe Sánchez; Costumes, Alejandra Dorantes; Music, Annette Fradera; Editors, José Buil, Humberto Hernández; a co-production of Centro de Capacitación Cinematográfica (CCC), Cnca, Filmoteca de la UNAM, Fondo para la Producción Cinematográfica de Calidad, Foprocine, Hubert Bals Fund, Instituto Mexicano de Cinematografia (IMCINE), John Simon Guggenheim Memorial Fundation, Palmera Films, Producciones Tragaluz; Mexican-Dutch; 2001; Dolby; Color; Not rated; 90 minutes; American release date: October 29, 2004. CAST: Ximena Ayala (Yessica), Nancy Gutiérrez (Miriam), Arcelia Ramírez (Alicia), María Rojo (Yessica's Mother), Luis Fernando Peña (Jorge), Gabino Rodgríguez (Héctor), Pablo Delgado (Juan)

BEAR CUB

(TLA RELEASING) a.k.a. *Cachorro*; Producer, Juan Alexander; Executive Producer, José L. García Arrojo; Director, Miguel Albaladejo; Screenplay, Miguel Albaladejo, Salvador García Ruiz; Photography, Alfonso Sanz; Music, Lucio Godoy; Editor, Pablo Blanco; a co-production of Hispanocine Producciones Cinematográficas, Star Line TV Productions; Spanish; Dolby; Color; Rated R; 99 minutes; American release date: November 5, 2004. CAST: José Luis García Pérez (Pedro), David Castillo (Bernardo), Empar Ferrer (Doña Teresa), Elvira Lindo (Violeta), Arno Chevrier (Manuel), Mario Arias (Javi), Josele Román

(Gloria), Diana Cerezo (Lola), Danile Llobregat (Bernardo, 14 Years Old), Juanma Lara (Aitor), Jorge Calvo (Antonio), Josep Tomàs (Juan Carlos), Juanjo Martinez (Iván), Ramón Ramos (Ricardo), Patxi Uribarren (Quique), Isidro Olmo (Ginés), Fernando Albizu (Wald), Javier Martínez (Olmo), Pep Morell (Jorge), Alfonso Torregrosa (Lawyer), Fernando Tejero (Macarrilla), Roberto Hernández (Young Uncle), Fèlix Álvarez (Dani), Cali Caballero (Borja), Jorge Alcázar (Waiter), Montserrat Alcoverro (Palmira), César Díaz (Detective), Melanie Beleña (Dentist Assistant), Ana Albaladejo (Young Professor), Felipe Albaladejo (Manager), Paco Luna (Airport Executive), Daniel Heras (Taxi Driver), Herminia Mendoza (Professor), Manuel Crespo (Employee), Lucía González, Adrián Deacal (Bernardo's Friends), Elena Jiménez, Juan Ramón Deacal (Friends, 14 Years Old), Umesh (Hindu Civil Employee)

BRIGHT FUTURE

(PALM PICTURES) a.k.a. *Akarui mirai*; Producer, Takashi Asai; Executive Producers, Kenji Takahara, Masafumi Odawara, Nobuhiko Sakoh; Director/Screenplay/Editor, Kiyoshi Kurosawa; Photography, Takahide Shibanushi; Designer, Yasuaki Harada; Costumes, Michiko Kitamura; Music, Pacific 231; a Digital Site Corporation, Uplink Co. production; Japanese, 2003; Color; Not rated; 92 minutes; American release date: November 12, 2004. CAST: Jo Odagiri (Yuji Nimura), Tadanobu Asano (Mamoru Arita), Tatsuya Fuji (Shin'ichiro Arita), Takashi Sasano (Mr. Fujiwara), Marumi Shiraishi (Mrs. Fujiwara), Hanawa (Ken Takagi), Yoshiyuki Morishita (Mori), Sayuri Oyamada (Miho Nimura), Ryo (Lawyer), Tetsu Sawaki (Kei)

WHO KILLED BAMBI?

(STRAND) a.k.a. *Qui a tué Bambi?*; Producers, Caroline Benjo, Carole Scotta; Director, Gilles Marchand; Screenplay, Gilles Marchand, Vincent Dietschy; Photography, Pierre Milon; Designer, Laurent Deroo; Costumes, Virginie Montel, Isabelle Pannetier; Music, Alex Beaupain, François Eudes, Lily Margot, Doc Mateo; Editor, Robin Campillo; a co-production of Centre National de la Cinématographie (CNC), Haut et Court, L'Atelier de Production Centre-Val de Loire, La Sofica Sogicinéma, Le Studio Canal+, M6Films, Région Centre, Sofica Sofinergie 5; French, 2003; Color; Not rated; 126 minutes; American release date: November 12, 2004. CAST: Sophie Quinton (Isabelle "Bambi"), Laurent Lucas (Dr. Philipp), Catherine Jacob (Veronique), Yasmine Belmadi (Sami), Michèle Moretti (Mme. Vachon), Valéroe Donzelli (Nathalie), Jean-Claude Jay

Sophie Quinton in *Who Killed Bambi?* PHOTO COURTESY OF STRAND

Jo Odagiri in *Bright Future* PHOTO COURTESY OF PALM PICTURES

(White-Haired Surgeon), Aladin Reibel (Fair-Headed Anaesthetist), Thierry Bosc (General Manager), Luicia Sanchez (Spanish Nurse), Fily Keita (Marion), Sophie Medina (Carole), Joséphine de Meaux (Dumb Nurse), Lucienne Moreau (Lady), Catherine Salvini (Instructor), Jean Dell (Ear, Nose and Throat Specialist), Dorothée Decoene (First Patient), Alexandra Ansidei (Girl with Scoubidou), Lisa Hunyh (Asian Patient), Anne Caillon (Elegant Patient), Françoise Pinkwasser (Surgical Nurse), Dominique Charmet (Patricia)

5 SIDES OF A COIN

(SEVENTH ART RELEASING) Producers/Screenplay, Paul Kell, Jana Ritter; Director/Photography/Editor, Paul Kell; Music, Big Dro, Manifest, Peanutbutterwolf, Son of Mac, Zinndeadly; from The Anomaly Collective; Canadian, 2003; Technicolor; Not rated; 70 minutes; American release date: November 12, 2004. Documentary on the five basic elements of the hip-hop movement; featuring A-Trak, Afrika Bambaataa, The Beat Junkies, The Beatnuts, Bom5, Common, The Crash Crew, Craze, Pee Wee Dance, Dash 167, LeLaSoul, Del, Delta, Dilated Peoples, Son Doobie, Grandmaster Flash, Michael Franti, Frosty Freeze, Miho Hatori, The Herbaliser, Kool Herc, DJ Jazz Jay, Jo-Jo, Jurassic 5, Killa Kela, KRS-One, DJ Krush, Speedy Legs, John Lurie, Biz Markie, Mercedes Ladies, Mix Master Mike, Dan Nakamura, Prince Paul, The Pharcyde, Phase 2, DJ Q-Bert, Quanzilla, Rahzel, Run-D.M.C., Gil Scott-Heron, Scratch Perverts, Skizo, Speedy, DJ Spooky, Lucky Strike, Supernatural, Jeru Tha Damaja, Grand Wizard Theodore, C. Delores Tucker, Imani Wilcox, Elliot Wilson, X-ecutioners

DAYS OF BEING WILD

(KINO) a.k.a. *A Fei jing juen*; Producer, Rover Tang; Executive Producer, Alan Tang; Director/Screenplay, Kar Wai Wong; Photography, Christopher Doyle; Designer, William Chang; Editors, Patrick Tam, Kit-Wai Kai; an In-Gear Film production; Hong Kong, 1991; Dolby; Agfaolor; Not rated; 94 minutes; American release date: November 19, 2004. CAST: Leslie Cheung (Yuddy), Maggie Cheung (Su Lizhen), Andy Lau (Tide), Carina Lau (Leung Fung-Ying), Tik-Wa Poon (Rebecca), Jacky Cheung (Zeb), Danilo Antunes (Rebecca's Lover), Hung Mei-Mei (The Amah), Ling-Hung Ling (Nurse), Tita Munoz (Yuddy's Mother), Alicia Alonzo (Housekeeper), Elena Lim So (Hotel Manageress), Maritoni Fernandez (Hotel Madi), Angela Ponos (Prostitute), Nonong Talbo (Train Conductor), Tony Leung Chiu Wai (Smirk)

YOU I LOVE

(PICTURE THIS) a.k.a. *Ya lyublu tebya*; Producer, Dmitry Troitsky; Directors, Dmitry Troitsky, Olga Stolpovskaja; Screenplay, Olga Stolpovskaja Photography, Aleksandr Simonov; Music, Richardas Norvila; Editors, Oleg Raevsky, Sergey Pluschenko; from Malevich Productions; Russian; Color; Not rated; 83 minutes; American release date: November 19, 2004. CAST: Damir Badmaev (Uloomji), Lyubov Tolkalina (Vera Kirillova), Evgeny Koryakovsky (Timofei Pechorin), Nina Agapova (Elderly Neighbor), Irina Grineva (Make-Up Girl), Anatoly Mankhadykov (Uloomji's Father), Valentina Mankhadykova (Uloomji's Mother), Yuri Sherstnyov (Watch at Zoo), Victor Shevidov (Uncle Vanya), Mihail Tarabukin (Lyolin), Emanuel Michael Vaganda (John), Alexandre Doulerain, Gelb Aleinikov (Senators), Ksenia Balaya (Masha), Yury Askarov (Policeman/Singer)

Lyubov Tolkalina, Evgeny Koryakovsky in *You I Love* PHOTO COURTESY OF PICTURE THIS

BROKEN BRIDGES

(IHC) Producers, Rustam Ibragimbekov, Rafigh Pooya; Director, Rafigh Pooya; Screenplay, Rustam Ibragimbekov, Rafigh Pooya; Iranian; Color; Not rated; 96 minutes; American release date: November 19, 2004. CAST: Rebeccah Bush (Susan), Fatima Ibragimkevoa (Jayran), Peter Reckell (Jeff)

Maggie Cheung in *Days of Being Wild* PHOTO COURTESY OF KINO

FEAR AND TREMBLING

(CINEMA GUILD) a.k.a. *Stupeur et tremblements*; Producer, Alain Sarde; Executive Producer, Christine Gozlan; Director/Screenplay, Alain Corneau; Based on the novel by Amélie Nothomb; Photography, Yves Angelo; Designers, Valérie Leblanc, Philippe Taillefer; Editor, Thierry Derocles; a co-production of Canal+, Divali Films, France 3 Cinema, Les Films Alain Sarde; French-Japanese, 2003; Dolby; Color; Not rated; 107 minutes; American release date: November 19, 2004. CAST: Sylvie Testud (Amélie), Kaori Tsuji (Fubuki), Tarô Suwa (Monsieur Saito), Bison Katayama (Monsieur Omochi), Yasunari Kondo (Monsieur Tenshi), Sokyu Fujita (Monsieur Haneda), Gen Shimaoka (Monsieur Unaji), Heileigh Gomes (Baby Amélie), Eri Sakai (Baby Fubuki)

GO FURTHER

(ABRAMORAMA) Producer/Director, Ron Mann; Executive Producers, Rob Blumenstein, Daniel J. Victor; Screenplay, Solomon Vesta; Photography, Alan Barker, Andrew Black, Robert Fresco, Rob Heydon, Ron Mann; Music, Guido Luciani; Editors, Ryan Feldman, John Sanders, Robert Kennedy; a co-production of Boneyard Entertainment, Cameraplanet Productions, Chum Television, Sphinx Productions; Canadian; Dolby; Color; Not rated; 80 minutes; American release date: November 19, 2004. Documentary in which environmentalists travel around on a bio-fueled bus to show that there are alternative to ecologically destructive habits; featuring Woody Harrelson, Ken Kesey, Tom Ballanco, Jessica Chung, Steve Clark, Sonia Farrell, Michael Franti, Joe Hickey, Anthony Kiedis, Joe Lewis, Renee Loux Underkoffler, Billy Martin, Dave Matthews, John Medeski, Natalie Merchant, Bob Weir, Chris Wood

Woody Harrelson in *Go Further* PHOTO COURTESY OF ABRAMORAMA

NOTRE MUSIQUE

(WELLSPRING) Producers, Alain Sarde, Ruth Waldburger; Director/Screenplay/Editor, Jean-Luc Godard; Photography, Julien Hirsch; Art Director, Anne-Marie Miéville; Casting, Richard Rousseau; a co-production of Avventura Films, Les Films Alain Sarde, Peripheria, France 3 Cinéma, Canal+, Télévision Suisse-Romande (TSR), Vega Film; French-Swiss; Dolby; Color; Not rated; 80 minutes; American release date: November 24, 2004. CAST: Sarah Adler (Judith Lerner), Nade Dieu (Olga Brodsky), Rony Kramer (Ramos Garcia), Simon Eine (Ambassador), Jean-Christophe Bouvet (C. Maillard), George Aguilar, Leticia Gutiérrez (Indians), Aline Schulmann (Spanish Translator), Ferlyn Brass, Jean-Luc Godard, Juan Goytisolo, Mahmoud Darwich, Jean-Paul Curnier, Pierre Bergounioux, Gilles Pecqueux (Themselves)

Kaori Tsuji, Sylvia Testud in *Fear and Trembling* PHOTO COURTESY OF CINEMA GUILD

PURPLE BUTTERFLY

(PALM PICTURES) a.k.a. *Zi hudie*; Producers, Lou Ye, Wei Wang, Zhu Yongde; Director/Screenplay, Lou Ye; Executive Producers, Vincent Maraval, Jean-Louis Piel, Alain de la Mata; Photography, Wang Yu; Designer/Costumes, Liu Weixin; Music, Jorg Lemberg; Editors, Lou Ye, Che Xiaohong; a co-production of Dream Factory, Lou Yi Ltd., Shanghai Film Studios; Chinese-French, 2003; Dolby; Color; Rated R; 127 minutes; American release date: November 26, 2004. CAST: Zhang Ziyi (Cynthia/Ding Hui), Liu Ye (Szeto), Feng Yuanzheng (Xie Ming), Toru Nakamura (Hidehiko Itami), Li Bingbing (Yiling), Kin Ei (Yamamoto)

AMNESIA

(A-FILM DISTRIBUTION) Producers, Frans van Gestel, Jeroen Beker; Director/Screenplay, Martin Koolhaven; Photography, Menno Westendrop; Designer, Floris Vos; Costumes, Maartje Wevers; Music, Fons Merkies; Editor, Job ter Burg; a Motel Films production; Dutch, 2001; Color; Not rated; 90 minutes; American release date: December 1, 2004. CAST: Fedja van Huêt (Alex/Aram), Carice van Houten (Sandra), Theo Maassen (Wouter), Sacha Bulthuis (Mother of Alex and Aram), Cas Enklaar (Eugene), Erik van der Horst (Young Alex/Aram), Eva van der Gucht (Esther), Bert Luppes (The Doctor), Carly Wijs (Woman in Flashback), Hadewych Minis (Girl in Bed), Anniek Pheifer (Doctor's Assistant), Leo van Huêt (Theo)

DESERTED STATION

(FIRST RUN FEATURES) a.k.a. *Istgah-Matrouk* ; Producer/Editor, Hossein Zanbaf; Director, Alireza Raisian; Screenplay, Kambuzia Patrovi; Story, Abbas Kiarostami; Photography, Mohammad Aladpoush; Designer, Mohsen Shah-Ebrahimi; Music, Peyman Yazdanian; a Farabi Cinema Foundation production; Iranian, 2002; Stereo; Color Not rated; 88 minutes; American release date: December 3, 2004. CAST: Leila Hatami (The Wife), Nezam Manouchehri (The Husband), Mehran Rajabi (Feizollah), Mahmoud Pak Neeyat (The Signal Guard)

THE ARYAN COUPLE

(HEMDALE/CELEBRATION) Producers, John Daly, Peter Beale; Director, John Daly; Screenplay, John Daly, Kendrew Lascelles; Photography, Marek Cydorowicz, Sergei Kozlov; Designer, Andrzej Halinski; Music, Igor Khoroshev; Editor, Matthew Booth; a co-production of Atlantic Film and Mairis films; British-U.S.; Dolby; Color; Rated PG-13; 120 minutes; American release date: December 3,

2004. CAST: Martin Landau (Joseph Krauzenberg), Judy Parfitt (Rachel Krauzenberg), Kenny Doughty (Hans Vassman), Caroline Carver (Ingrid Vassman), Danny Webb (Himmler), Christopher Fulford (Edelhein), Steven Mackintosh (Eichmann), Jake Wood (Dresler), Nolan Hemmings (Gerhard), Austen Palmer (Kurt Becher), Tyler Bizzell (Second Sentry), Gretchen Becker (Jolanda), Adrian O'Donnell (Adjutant)

Zhang Ziyi in *Purple Butterfly* PHOTO COURTESY OF PALM PICTURES

AFTER MIDNIGHT

(AVATAR) a.k.a. *Dopo mezzanotte*; Line Producer, Ladis Zanini; Director/Screenplay, Davide Ferrario; Photography, Dante Cecchin; Designer, Francesca Bocca; Music, Daniele Sepe; Editor, Claudio Cormio; Film Commission Torino Piemonte; Multimedia Park; Rossofuoco Productions; Italian; Color; Not rated; 92 minutes; American release date: December 3, 2004. CAST: Giorgio Pasotti (Martino), Francesca Inaudi (Amanda), Fabio Troiano (The Angel of Falchera), Francesca Picozza (Barbara), Silvio Orlando (Narrator), Pietro Eandi (Martino's Grandfather), Andrea Romero (Fast Food Owner), Giampiero Perone (Bruno the Night Watchman), Francesco D'Alessio, Gianni Talia, Andrea Moretti (Members of the Falchera Gang), Gianna Cavalla (The Car Receiver), Claudio Pagano (The Car Receiver's Bodyguard), Maurizio Vaiana (Cousin Mauzirio), Ladis Zanini (The Ballsqueezer), Ivan Negro (Ivan), Lidia Streito Misdim (Indonesian Girl), Alberto Barbera (The Museum Director)

Deserted Station PHOTO COURTESY OF FIRST RUN FEATURES

CONSPIRACY OF SILENCE

(WATCH ENTERTAINMENT) Producer, Davina Stanley; Executive Producers, Amit Barooah, Robert Bevan, Amanda Coombes, Keith Hayley, Stephen Margolis, Charlie Savill; Director/Screenplay, John Deery; Photography, Jason Lehel; Designer, John Ebden; Costumes, Suzanne Cave; Music, Francis Haines, Stephen W. Parsons; Editor, Jamie Trevill; Casting, Susie Bruffin; a Flick Features production; British; Dolby; Color; Not rated; 90 minutes; American release date: December 3, 2004. CAST: Jonathan Forbes (Daniel McLaughlin), Hugh Bonneville (Fr. Jack Dowling), Brenda Fricker (Annie McLaughlin), Sean McGinley (Rector Cathal), Hugh Quarshie (Fr. Joseph Ennis), Jason Barry (David Foley), Paudge Behan (Niall), Sean Boru (Father Murphy), Olivia Caffrey (Liz Foley), Tommy Carey (Sean), Patrick Casey (Father Sweeney), Carmel Cryan (Mrs. McDermott), Catherine Cusack (Mary McLaughlin), Patrick Doyle, Jim Dunne (Senior Umpires), Patrick Duggan (Micky), Christopher Dunne (Fr. Martin Hennessy), James Ellis (Jim O'Brien), Anna Rose Fullen (Martha), Jim Howlin (Team Manager), Jason Kavanagh (Liam), Sinead Keenan (Majella), John Lynch (Fr. Matthew Francis), Edward MacLiam (Fitzpatrick), Owen McDonnell (Noel), Fintan McKeown (Monsignor Thomas), Kevin McMahon (Donal), Brendan McNamara (Declan), Justine Mitchell (Assistant Floor Manager), Ciaran Murtagh (Michael), Jim Norton (Bishop Michael Quinn), Niall O'Brien (John), Christopher O'Dowd (James), Aidan O'Hara (Paul), Lillian Patton (Molly), Sid Rainey (Joe), Phil Roache (Supporter), Fergal Spelman (TV Director), Elaine Symons (Marie), Harry Towb (Father Doherty), Catherine Walker (Sinead), Nuala Walsh (Mrs. McGlynn)

Conspiracy of Silence PHOTO COURTESY OF WATCH ENTERTAINMENT

JESUS, YOU KNOW

(LEISURE TIME FEATURES) a.k.a. *Jesus, Du weisst*; Producers, Anne Baumann, Martin Kraml; Director, Ulrich Seidl; Screenplay, Ulrich Seidl, Veronika Franz; Photography, Jerzy Palacz, Wolfgang Thaler; Editors, Andrea Wagner, Christof Schertenleib; an MMKmedia production; Austrian, 2003; Color; Not rated; 87 minutes; American release date: December 3, 2004. Documentary in which Catholics talk about their interpretations of Jesus; featuring Efriede Ahmad, Waltraute Bartel, Hans-Jürgen Eder, Thomas Grandegger, Thomas Ullram, Angelika Weber, Tanja Müller, Elisabeth Sucham, Heribert Exel, Saleem Ahmad, Ingeborg Heindl, Gottfried Heindl, Michael Welleditsch

Nikolaj Lie Kaas, Mads Mikkelsen in *The Green Butchers* PHOTO COURTESY OF NEWMARKET FILMS

THE GREEN BUTCHERS

(NEWMARKET FILMS) a.k.a. *De Grønne slagtere*; Producers, Kim Magnusson, Tivi Magnusson; Director/Screenplay, Anders Thomas Jensen; Photography, Sebastian Blenkov; Designer, Mia Stengaard; Costumes, Mia Stengaard, Helle Nielsen; Music, Jeppe Kaas; Editor, Anders Villadsen; a co-production of M&M Productions, TV2 Denmark; Danish, 2003; Color; Rated R; 95 minutes; American release date: December 3, 2004. CAST: Line Kruse (Astrid), Nikolaj Lie Kaas (Bjarne/Eigil), Mads Mikkelsen (Svend), Nicolas Bro (Hus Hans), Aksel Erhardtsen (Rev. Villumsen), Bodil Jørgensen (Tina), Ole Thestrip (Holger), Lily Weiding (Ms. Juhl), Camilla Bendix (Egil's Date)

GAME OVER: KASPAROV AND THE MACHINE

(THINKFILM) Producer, Hal Vogel; Executive Producers, Nick Fraser, Eric Michel, Tom Perlmutter, Andre Singer, Andy Thompson, Paul Trijbits; Director, Vikram Jayanti; Photography, Maryse Alberti; Music, Robert Lane; Editor, David G. Hill; a co-production of Alliance Atlantis Communications and the National Film Board of Canada (NFB); Canadian, 2003; Dolby; Color; Rated PG; 90 minutes; American release date: December 3, 2004. Documentary on chess wizard Garry Kasparov's 1997 game against an IBM computer; featuring Garry Kasparov, Joel Benjamin, Michael Greengard, Jeff Kisselhof

Garry Kasparov in *Game Over* PHOTO COURTESY OF THINKFILM

DOLLS

(PALM PICURES) Producers, Takio Yoshida, Masayuki Mori; Director/Screenplay/Editor, Takeshi Kitano; Photography, Katsumi Yanagishima; Designer, Norihiro Isoda; Costumes, Yohjia Yamamoto; Music, Joe Hisaishi; a co-production of Office Kitano, TV Tokyo; Japanese, 2002; Dolby; Color; Not rated; 114 minutes; American release date: December 10, 2004. CAST: Miho Kanno (Sawako), Hidetoshi Nishijima (Matsumoto), Tatsuya Mihashi (Hiro, the Boss), Chieko Matsubara (Ryoko, the Woman in the Park), Kyoko Fukada (Haruna Yamaguchi, the Pop Star), Tsutomu Takeshige (Nukui, the Fan), Kayoko Kishimoto (Haruna's Aunt), Kanji Tsuda (Young Hiro), Yuuko Daike (Young Ryoko), Ren Osugi (Haruna's Manager), Shimadayu Toyotake (Tayu, Puppet Theater Narrator), Kiyosuke Tsuruzawa (Puppet Theater Shamisen Player), Minotaro Yoshida (Puppet of Umegawa the Courtesan), Yoshia (Puppet of Chubei), Shogo Shimizu (Matsumoto's Father), Midori Kanazawa (Matsumoto's Mother), Nao Omori

Miho Kanno, Hidetoshi Nishijima in *Dolls* PHOTO COURTESY OF PALM PICTURES

(Matsumoto's Colleague), Kyoko Yoshizawa (Haruna's Mother), Kazunari Aizawa (The Young Minion), Moro Shioka (Hitman in the Park), Shuhei Saga (The Driver), Al Kitago (Aoki, the Fan), Hawking Aoyama (Son of the Boss's Brother), Yoshitada Ohtsuka (Matsumoto's Friend), Mari Nishio (Sawako's Friend), Sammy Moremore, Jr. (Friend of the Boss's Brother's Son)

A TALKING PICTURE

(KINO) a.k.a. *Un Filme Falado*; Producer, Paulo Branco; Director/Screenplay, Manoel de Oliveira; Photography, Emmanuel Machuel; Designer, Zé Branco; Editor, Valérie Loiseleux; Costumes, Isabel Branco; Gemini Films; Madragoa Filmes; Mikado; Radiotelevisao Portuguesa; Portuguese-French-Italian, 2003; Dolby; Color; Not rated; 96 minutes; American release date: December 10, 2004. CAST: Leonor Silveira (Rosa Maria), Filipa de Almeida (Maria Joana), John Malkovich (Comandante John Walesa), Catherine Deneuve (Delfina), Stefania Sandrelli (Francesca), Irene Papas (Helena), Luís Miguel Cintra (Portueguese Actor), Michel Lubrano di Sbaraglione (Fisherman), François Da Silva (Fisherman's Customer), Nikos Hatzopoulos, Ilias Logothetis (Orthodox Priests), António Ferraiolo (Pompeii Guide), Alparslan Salt (Santa Maria Guide), Ricardo Trepa, David Cardoso (Officials), Júlia Buisel (Delfina's Friend)

Geun-yeong Mun, Jung-ah Yum, Su-jeong Lim in *A Tale of Two Sisters* PHOTO COURTESY OF TARTAN

BANDIDO

(ARCANGELO ENTERTAINMENT) Producers, Roger Christian, Carlos Gallardo, Harald Reichebner; Executive Producers, Raymond Tarabay, J. David Williams; Director, Roger Christian; Screenplay, Ned Kerwin, Scott Duncan; Photography, Kristian Bernier, Mike Southon; Editors, Troy Niemans, Gene Wood, Robin Russell; a coproduction of Global Filmtime, Televisa, Videocine; Mexican-U.S.; Dolby; Color; Rated R; 95 minutes; American release date: December 10, 2004. CAST: Carlos Gallardo (Max Cruz "Bandido"), Edy Arellano (Armas), Michel Bos (CIA Agent), Kim Coates (Beno), Matt Craven (Fletcher), Marintia Escobedo (Scar), Angie Everhart (Natalie), Ana La Salvia (Sofia), Carime Lozano (Rosalia), Manuel Vela (Peña), Ernesto Yáñez (Quintana)

A TALE OF TWO SISTERS

(TARTAN) a.k.a. *Janghwa, Hongryeon*; Director/Screenplay, Ji-woon Kim; Photography, Mo-gae Lee; Art Director, Geun-hyeon Jo; Music, Byung-woo Lee; Editor, Hyeon-mi Lee; b.o.m. Film Productions; Cineclick Asia; i Pictures; Masulpiri Pictures; Muhan Investments; South Korean, 2003; Dolby; Color; Not rated; 115 minutes; American release date: December 17, 2004. Cast: Kap-su Kim (Moo-hyeon), Jung-ah Yum (Eun-joo), Su-jeong Lim (Soo-mi), Geun-yeong Mun (Soo-yeon), Seung-bi Lee (Mi-hee)

Luis Miguel Cintra, Filipa de Almeida, Leonor Silveira in A *Talking Picture* PHOTO COURTESY OF KINO

OPEN MY HEART

(STRAND) a.k.a. *Aprimi il cuore*; Producers, Giada Colagrande, Enrico Agostini, Massimo Cortesi; Director/Story, Giada Colagrande; Screenplay, Giada Colagrande, Francesco Di Pace; Photography, Nicola Vicenti, Luca Coassin; Costumes, Tiziano Musetti, Lucia Gasparrini; Editor, Fabio Nunziata; a Garibaldi production; Italian, 2003; Color; Not rated; 93 minutes; American release date: December 17, 2004. Cast: Giada Colagrande (Caterina), Natalie Cristiani (Maria), Claudio Botosso (Giovanni)

WHORE

(SCREEN MEDIA FILMS) a.k.a. *Yo puta*; Producer, Jose Magan; Director, María Lidón; Screenplay, Isabel Pisano, Adela Ibañez; Photography, Ricardo Aronovich; Designer, Alain Bainée; Music, Javier Navarrete; Editor, Bernat Vilaplana; a Dolores Pictures production; Spanish; Dolby; Color; Rated R; 87 minutes; American release date: December 17, 2004. Cast: Daryl Hannah (Adriana), Denise Richards (Rebecca), Joaquim de Almeida (Pierre), Pierre Woodman, Conrad Son, Dora Venter, Rita Faltoyano, Carol Fonda (Themselves), Africa, Erica, Denisse Valdes (Prostitutes), Charlotte (French Prostitute), Javier (Gigolo)

Anna Paquin, Stephan Enquist in *Darkness* PHOTO COURTESY OF DIMENSION

DARKNESS

(DIMENSION) Producers, Brian Yuzna, Julio Fernádez; Executive Producers, Guy J. Louthan, Carlos Fernández, Bob Weinstein, Harvey Weinstein; Director, Jaume Balagueró; Screenplay, Jaume Balagueró, Fernando de Felipe, Miguel Tejada-Flores; Photography, Xavi Giménez; Designer, Llorenç Miquel; Costumes, Eva Arretxe; Music, Carles Cases; Editor, Luis De La Madrid; a co-production of Castelao Producciones; Dimension Films; Fantastic Factory; Via Digital; Spanish-U.S., 2002; Dolby; Eastmancolor; Rated PG-13; 88 minutes; American release date: December 25, 2004. Cast: Anna Paquin (Regina), Lena Olin (Maria), Iain Glen (Mark), Giancarlo Giannini (Albert Rua), Fele Martínez (Carlos), Stephan Enquist (Paul), Fermi Reixach (Villalobos), Francesc Pagés (Driver, Traffic Jam), Craig Stevenson (Electrician), Paula Fernández, Gemma Lozano (Girls), Xavier Allepuz, Joseph Roberts, Marc Ferrando, Josh Gaeta, Mattew Dixon (Boys), Carlos Castañón, Carles Punyet (Friends), Reg Wilson (Librarian), Ferrán Lahoz (Tax Driver), Pedro Antonio Segura (Patient Traffic Jam), Astrid Fenollar, Lidia Dorado, Clara Manguillot (Old Women)

PROMISING NEW ACTORS OF 2004

Jon Foster (*The Door in the Floor*)

Emily Browning (*Lemony Snicket's A Series of Unfortunate Events, Ned Kelly*)

Freddie Highmore (*Finding Neverland, Two Brothers*)

Bryce Dallas Howard (*The Village*)

Scott Mechlowicz (*Mean Creek, EuroTrip*)

Rachel McAdams (*The Notebook, Mean Girls*)

Stephen Campbell Moore (*Bright Young Things*)

Catalina Sandino Moreno (*Maria Full of Grace*)

Kal Penn (*Harold & Kumar Go to White Castle*)

Emmy Rossum (*Phantom of the Opera, The Day After Tomorrow, Nola*)

Steve Sandvoss (*Latter Days*)

Sharon Warren (*Ray*)

ACADEMY AWARD WINNERS & NOMINEES

Clint Eastwood, Morgan Freeman, Hilary Swank

Clint Eastwood, Hilary Swank

Morgan Freeman PHOTOS COURTESY OF PARAMOUNT

BEST PICTURE
MILLION DOLLAR BABY

(WARNER BROS.) Producers, Clint Eastwood, Albert S. Ruddy, Tom Rosenberg, Paul Haggis; Executive Producers, Gary Lucchesi, Robert Lorenz; Co-Producer, Bobby Moresco; Director/Music, Clint Eastwood; Screenplay, Paul Haggis; Based upon stories in *Rope Burns: Stories from the Corner* by F.X. Toole; Photography, Tom Stern; Designer, Henry Bumstead; Costumes, Deborah Hopper; Editor, Joel Cox; Casting, Phyllis Huffman; a Malpaso production, presented in association with Lakeshore Entertainment; Dolby; Panavision; Technicolor; Rated PG-13; 132 minutes; Release date: December 15, 2004

Cast

Frankie Dunn **Clint Eastwood**
Maggie Fitzgerald **Hilary Swank**
Eddie "Scrap-Iron" Dupris **Morgan Freeman**
Danger Barch **Jay Baruchel**
Big Willie Little **Mike Colter**
Billie "The Blue Bear" **Lucia Rijker**
Father Horvak **Brian O'Byrne**
Shawrelle Berry **Anthony Mackie**
Earline Fitzgerald **Margo Martindale**
Mardell Fitzgerald **Riki Lindhome**
Omar **Michael Peña**
Billie's Manager **Benito Martinez**
Mickey Mack **Bruce MacVittie**
Counterman at Diner **David Powledge**
Cut Man **Joe D'Angerio**
J.D. Fitzgerald **Marcus Chait**
Lawyer **Tom McCleister**
Nurse **Erica Grant**
Pakistani **Naveen**
Little Girl in Truck **Morgan Eastwood**
Paramedic **Jamison Yang**
Rehab Doctor **Ming Lo**
Restaurant Owner **Miguel Perez**
Ring Doctors **Jim Cantafio, Ted Grossman**
Sally Mendoza **Ned Eisenberg**
Second at Vegas Fight **Marco Rodriguez**
Fan in Vegas **Roy Nugent**
Ring Announcer **Don Familton**
Radio Commentator **Mark Thomason**

and Dean Familton, Dr. Louis Moret, V.J. Foster, Jon D. Schorle, Marty Sammon, Steven M. Porter (Refs), Brian T. Finney, Spice Williams-Crosby, Kim Strauss, Rob Maron, Kirsten Berman (Irish Fans), Susan Krebs, Sunshine Chantal, Kim Dannenberg (Rehab Nurses), Eddie Bates (Rehab Resident), Michael Bentt, Bruce Gerard Brown Jr. (Boxers), Jude Ciccolella (Hogan), Kimberly Estrada (Perez), Vladimir Rajcic (Yugoslavian Judge), McKay Stewart (Sparring Boxer), Jaerin Washington (Jamaican Boxer Cornerman)

Clint Eastwood, Hilary Swank

Hoping to make it in the boxing ring, Maggie Fitzgerald comes to veteran train-er Frankie Dunn, begging him to take her on as his first female fighter.

2004 Academy Award-winner for Best Picture, Actress (Hilary Swank), Supporting Actor (Morgan Freeman), and Director. This film received additional nominations for actor (Clint Eastwood), adapted screenplay, and editing.

Anthony Mackie

Morgan Freeman, Clint Eastwood

Hilary Swank

Jay Baruchel, Morgan Freeman

Born Into Brothels

Born Into Brothels

Born Into Brothels PHOTOS COURTESY OF THINKFILM

BEST FEATURE DOCUMENTARY
BORN INTO BROTHELS: CALCUTTA'S RED LIGHT KIDS

(THINKFILM) Producers/Directors/Photography, Ross Kauffman, Zana Briski; Executive Producer, Geralyn White Dreyfous; Co-Executive Producer, Pamela Tanner Boll; Music, John McDowell; Editors, Nancy Baker, Ross Kauffman; Associate Producer, Ellen Peck; a Red Light Films presentation in association with HBO/Cinemax Documentary Prods.; Color, HD; Not rated; 85 minutes; Release date: December 8, 2004. Documentary in which filmmaker Zana Briski tries to help the children of Calcutta's prostitutes by teaching them to use a camera.

BEST FOREIGN LANGUAGE FEATURE
THE SEA INSIDE

(FINE LINE FEATURES) a.k.a. Mar Adentro; Producers, Frenando Bovaira, Alejandro Amenábar; Director, Alejandro Amenábar; Screenplay, Alejandro Amenábar, Mateo Gil; Photography, Javier Aguirresarobe; Line Producer, Emiliano Otegui; Designer, Benjamín Fernández; Music, Alejandro Amenábar, Carlos Núñez; Special Makeup Design, Jo Allen; Wardrobe, Sonia Grande; Casting, Luis San Narciso; a Sogepaq presentation ofa Sogecine, Himenoptero production with the participation of TVE, Canal+; Spanish; Dolby; Super 35 Widescreen; Color; Rated PG-13; 125 minutes; American release date: December 17, 2004

Belén Rueda

Cast

Ramón Sampedro	**Javier Bardem**
Julia	**Belén Rueda**
Rosa	**Lola Dueñas**
Manuela	**Mabel Rivera**
José	**Celso Bugallo**
Gené	**Clara Segura**
Joaquín	**Joan Dalmau**
Germán	**Alberto Giménez**
Javi	**Tamar Novas**
Marc	**Francesc Garrido**
Father Francisco	**José Maria Pou**
Father Andrés	**Alberto Amarilla**
Santiago	**Andrea Occhipinti**
Driver	**Federico Pérez Rey**
Cristian	**Nicolás Fernández Luna**
Samuel	**Raúl Lavisier**

and Xosé Manuel Olveira ("Pico"), César Cambeiro (Judges), Xosé Manuel Esperante, Yolanda Muiños (Journalists), Adolfo Obregón (Executive), José Luis Rodriguez (Presentor), Julio Jordán (Book Binder), Juan Manuel Vidal (Ramón's Friend), Marta Larriade (Girl at the Beach)

Javier Bardem, Belén Rueda

The true story of how paraplegic Ramon Sampredo fought for the right to end his own life.

2004 Academy Award winner for Best Foreign Language Film. This film received an additional nomination for makeup.

Lola Dueñas, Javier Bardem PHOTOS COURTESY OF FINE LINE FEATURES

Violet, Dash

BEST ANIMATED FEATURE
THE INCREDIBLES

(WALT DISNEY PICTURES) Producer, John Walker; Executive Producer, John Lasseter; Director/Screenplay, Brad Bird; Associate Producer, Kori Rae; Music, Michael Giacchino; Story Supervisor, Mark Andrews; Film Editor, Stephen Schaffer; Supervising Technical Director, Rick Sayre; Production Designer, Lou Romano; Character Designers, Tony Fucile, Teddy Newton; Supervising Animators, Tony Fucile, Steven Clay Hunter, Alan Barillaro; Photography, Janet Lucroy, Patrick Lin, Andrew Jimenez; Art Director, Ralph Eggleston; Shading Art Director, Bryn Imagire; Character Supervisor, Bill Wise; Music, Michael Giacchino; Casting, Mary Hidalgo, Kevin Reher, Matthew Jon Beck; a Pixar Animation Studios Film; Dolby; Pixarvision; Technicolor; Rated PG; 115 minutes; Release date: November 5, 2004

Bob Parr, Gilbert Huph

Mirage, Mr. Incredible

Jack Jack, Helen Parr, Violet, Dash, Bob Parr PHOTOS COURTESY OF WALT DISNEY PICTURES

The Incredibles

Voice Cast

Bob Parr/Mr. Incredible **Craig T. Nelson**
Helen Parr/Elastigirl **Holly Hunter**
Lucius Best/Frozone **Samuel L. Jackson**
Syndrome **Jason Lee**
Violet Parr **Sarah Vowell**
Dash Parr **Spencer Fox**
Edna "E" Mode **Brad Bird**
Mirage **Elizabeth Peña**
Gilbert Huph **Wallace Shawn**
The Underminer **John Ratzenberger**
Muriel Hogenson **Jean Sincere**
Bomb Voyage **Dominique Louis**
Newsreel Narrator **Teddy Newton**
Jack Jack Parr **Eli Fucile, Maeve Andrews**
Bernie Kropp **Lou Romano**
Principal **Wayne Canney**
Tony Rydinger **Michael Bird**
Rick Dicker **Bud Kuckey**
Kari **Bret Parker**
Honey **Kimberly Adair Clark**

Bob Parr, Edna "E" Mode

A pair of married superheroes, forced to hide behind civilian identities for fifteen years, find themselves back in action in order to stop a madman bent on destroying the world.

This film received an additional Oscar nomination for original screenplay.

Syndrome

Frozone, Dash

ACADEMY AWARD FOR BEST ACTOR
JAMIE FOXX in *Ray*

ACADEMY AWARD FOR BEST ACTRESS
HILARY SWANK in *Million Dollar Baby*

ACADEMY AWARD FOR BEST SUPPORTING ACTOR
MORGAN FREEMAN in *Million Dollar Baby*

ACADEMY AWARD FOR BEST SUPPORTING ACTRESS
CATE BLANCHETT in *The Aviator*

ACADEMY AWARD NOMINEES FOR BEST ACTOR

Don Cheadle in *Hotel Rwanda*

Leonardo DiCaprio in *The Aviator*

Johnny Depp in *Finding Neverland*

Clint Eastwood in *Million Dollar Baby*

ACADEMY AWARD NOMINEES FOR BEST ACTRESS

Annette Bening in *Being Julia*

Imelda Staunton in *Vera Drake*

Catalina Sandino Moreno in *Maria Full of Grace*

Kate Winslet in *Eternal Sunshine of the Spotless Mind*

ACADEMY AWARD NOMINEES FOR BEST SUPPORTING ACTOR

Alan Alda in *The Aviator*

Jamie Foxx in *Collateral*

Thomas Haden Church in *Sideways*

Clive Owen in *Closer*

ACADEMY AWARD NOMINEES FOR BEST SUPPORTING ACTRESS

Laura Linney in *Kinsey*

Sophie Okonedo in *Hotel Rwanda*

Virginia Madsen in *Sideways*

Natalie Portman in *Closer*

TOP BOX OFFICE STARS & FILMS OF 2004

TOP BOX OFFICE STARS OF 2004

(Clockwise from top left corner)

1. Tom Hanks
2. Tom Cruise
3. Leonardo DiCaprio
4. Nicolas Cage
5. Jim Carrey
6. Denzel Washington
7. Julia Roberts
8. Will Smith
9. Brad Pitt
10. Adam Sandler

TOP 100 BOX OFFICE FILMS OF 2004

1. **Shrek 2** (DW) $435,480,000
2. **Spider-Man 2** (Col) $372,380,000
3. **The Passion of the Christ** (Newmarket) $370,280,000
4. **Meet the Fockers** (Univ/DW) $279,210,000
5. **The Incredibles** (BV) $261,410,000
6. **Harry Potter and the Prisoner of Azkaban** (WB) $249,220,000
7. **The Day After Tomorrow** (20th) $186,720,000
8. **The Bourne Supremacy** (Univ) $175,710,000
9. **National Treasure** (BV) $172,650,000
10. **The Polar Express** (WB) $162,780,000
11. **Shark Tale** (DW) $159,280,000
12. **I, Robot** (20th) $144,620,000
13. **Troy** (WB) $133,230,000
14. **Ocean's Twelve** (WB) $125,410,000
15. **50 First Dates** (Col) $120,400,000
16. **Van Helsing** (Univ) $119,860,000
17. **Lemony Snicket's Series of Unfortunate Events** (Par) $118,640,000
18. **Fahrenheit 9/11** (Lions Gate/IFC) $118,340,000
19. **DodgeBall: A True Underdog Story** (20th) $114,300,000
20. **The Village** (BV) $114,180,000
21. **The Grudge** (Col) $109,910,000
22. **The Aviator** (Mir/WB) $102,620,000
23. **Million Dollar Baby** (WB) $100,440,000
24. **Collateral** (DW/Par) $100,180,000

Shrek, Princess Fiona in *Shrek 2* PHOTO COURTESY OF DREAMWORKS

Tobey Maguire in *Spider-Man 2* PHOTO COURTESY OF COLUMBIA

25. **The Princess Diaries 2: Royal Engagement** (Dis) $94,120,000
26. **Starsky & Hutch** (WB/Mir) $88,210,000
27. **Along Came Polly** (Univ) $87,600,000
28. **Mean Girls** (Para) $86,100,000
29. **The SpongeBob SquarePants Movie** (Para) $85,420,000
30. **Scooby-Doo 2: Monsters Unleashed** (WB) $83,190,000
31. **Anchorman: The Legend of Ron Burgundy** (DW) $81,830,000
32. **The Notebook** (NL) $81,000,000
33. **Alien vs. Predator** (20th) $80,280,000
34. **Man on Fire** (20th) $77,910,000
35. **The Terminal** (DW) $76,870,000
36. **Ray** (Univ) $75,340,000
37. **Garfield** (20th) $75,330,000
38. **Ladder 49** (Touchstone) $74,550,000
39. **Christmas with the Kranks** (Col) $73,710,000
40. **Sideways** (Fox Search) $71,490,000
41. **White Chicks** (Col) $69,150,000
42. **Hidalgo** (Touchstone) $67,250,000
43. **The Forgotten** (Col) $66,510,000
44. **Kill Bill Vol. 2** (Mir) $66,210,000
45. **The Manchurian Candidate** (Para) $65,950,000
46. **Miracle** (BV) $64,350,000
47. **Barbershop 2: Back in Business** (MGM) $62,320,000
48. **Friday Night Lights** (Univ) $61,100,000
49. **The Stepford Wives** (Para/DW) $59,480,000
50. **Without a Paddle** (Para) $58,160,000

Ryan Gosling, Rachel McAdams in *The Notebook* PHOTO COURTESY OF NEW LINE CINEMA

Catherine Zeta-Jones, Kumar Pallana, Tom Hanks in *The Terminal* PHOTO COURTESY OF DREAMWORKS

51. **Dawn of the Dead** (Univ) $57,780,000
52. **The Butterfly Effect** (NL) $57,700,000
53. **Shall We Dance** (Mir) $57,690,000
54. **The Chronicles of Riddick** (Univ) $57,640,000
55. **Saw** (Lions Gate) $54,900,000
56. **13 Going on 30** (Col) $56,100,000
57. **Hellboy** (Col) $55,670,000
58. **Hero** (Mir) $53,490,000
59. **Blade: Trinity** (NL) $52,100,000
60. **King Arthur** (BV) $51,880,000
61. **Finding Neverland** (Mir) $51,660,000
62. **A Cinderella Story** (WB) $51,410,000
63. **The Phantom of the Opera** (WB) $51,200,000
64. **Resident Evil** (Screen Gems) $50,140,000
65. **Home on the Range** (BV) $50,100,000
66. **Fat Albert** (20th) $48,120,000
67. **Secret Window** (Col) $47,100,000
68. **In Good Company** (Univ) $45,550,000
69. **Napoleon Dynamite** (Fox Search) $44,540,000
70. **Spanglish** (Col) $42,100,000
71. **Exorcist: The Beginning** (WB) $41,580,000
72. **Walking Tall** (MGM) $41,250,000
73. **Catwoman** (WB) $40,190,000
74. **Bridget Jones: The Edge of Reason** (Univ/Mir) $40,100,000
75. **You Got Served** (Screen Gems) $39,790,000
76. **The Ladykillers** (BV) $39,100,000
77. **Sky Captain and the World of Tomorrow** (Para) $37,750,000

Jim Carrey, Kate Winslet in *Eternal Sunshine of the Spotless Mind* PHOTO COURTESY OF DREAMWORKS

Luke Mably, Julia Stiles in *The Prince & Me* PHOTO COURTESY OF PARAMOUNT

Adam Sandler in *Spanglish* PHOTO COURTESY OF COLUMBIA

Gwyneth Paltrow, Jude Law in *Sky Captain and the World of Tomorrow*
PHOTO COURTESY OF PARAMOUNT

78. **Raising Helen** (BV) $37,490,000
79. **Taxi** (20th) $36,540,000
80. **Alexander** (WB) $34,270,000
81. **Eternal Sunshine of the Spotless Mind** (Focus) $34,130,000
82. **The Punisher** (Lions Gate) $33,580,000
83. **Closer** (Col) $33,460,000
84. **Team America: World Police** (Para) $32,780,000
85. **Taking Lives** (WB) $32,220,000
86. **Cellular** (NL) $32,100,000
87. **Anacondas: Blood Orchid** (Screen Gems) $31,530,000
88. **Johnson Family Vacation** (Fox Search) $31,210,000
89. **Open Water** (Lions Gate) $29,640,000
90. **Confessions of a Teenage Drama Queen** (BV) $29,180,000
91. **After the Sunset** (NL) $28,320,000
92. **The Prince & Me** (Para) $27,990,000
93. **Garden State** (Fox Search) $26,790,000
94. **Jersey Girl** (Mir) $25,270,000
95. **Twisted** (Para) $25,100,000
96. **Around the World in 80 Days** (BV) $24,100,000
97. **The Life Aquatic with Steve Zissou** (BV) $24,100,000
98. **Hotel Rwanda** (MGM) $23,480,000
99. **Agent Cody Banks: Destination London** (MGM) $23,230,000
100. **Ella Enchanted** (Mir) $22,920,000

BIOGRAPHICAL DATA

Julie Andrews

Alec Baldwin

Roseanne Barr

Angela Bassett

Aames, Willie (William Upton) Los Angeles, CA, July 15, 1960.
Aaron, Caroline Richmond, VA, Aug. 7, 1954. Catholic U.
Abbott, Diahnne NYC, 1945.
Abbott, John London, England, June 5, 1905.
Abraham, F. Murray Pittsburgh, PA, Oct. 24, 1939. U Texas.
Ackland, Joss London, England, Feb. 29, 1928.
Adams, Brooke NYC, Feb. 8, 1949. Dalton.
Adams, Catlin Los Angeles, CA, Oct. 11, 1950.
Adams, Don NYC, Apr. 13, 1923.
Adams, Edie (Elizabeth Edith Enke) Kingston, PA, Apr. 16, 1927. Juilliard, Columbia.
Adams, Jane Washington, DC, Apr. 1, 1965.
Adams, Joey Lauren Little Rock, AR, Jan. 6, 1971.
Adams, Julie (Betty May) Waterloo, IA, Oct. 17, 1926. Little Rock, Jr. College.
Adams, Mason NYC, Feb. 26, 1919. UWi.
Adams, Maud (Maud Wikstrom) Lulea, Sweden, Feb. 12, 1945.
Adjani, Isabelle Germany, June 27, 1955.
Affleck, Ben Berkeley, CA, Aug. 15, 1972.
Affleck, Casey Falmouth, MA, Aug. 12, 1975.
Aghdashloo, Shohreh Tehran, Iran, May 11, 1952.
Agutter, Jenny Taunton, England, Dec. 20, 1952.
Aiello, Danny NYC, June 20, 1933.
Aiken, Liam NYC, Jan. 7, 1990.
Aimee, Anouk (Dreyfus) Paris, France, Apr. 27, 1934. Bauer Therond.
Akers, Karen NYC, Oct. 13, 1945, Hunter College.
Alberghetti, Anna Maria Pesaro, Italy, May 15, 1936.
Albert, Eddie (Eddie Albert Heimberger) Rock Island, IL, Apr. 22, 1908. U of Minn
Albert, Edward Los Angeles, CA, Feb. 20. 1951. UCLA.
Albright, Lola Akron, OH, July 20, 1925.
Alda, Alan NYC, Jan. 28, 1936. Fordham.
Aleandro, Norma Buenos Aires, Argentina, Dec. 6, 1936.
Alejandro, Miguel NYC, Feb. 21, 1958.
Alexander, Jane (Quigley) Boston, MA, Oct. 28, 1939. Sarah Lawrence.
Alexander, Jason (Jay Greenspan) Newark, NJ, Sept. 23, 1959. Boston U.
Alice, Mary Indianola, MS, Dec. 3, 1941.
Allen, Debbie (Deborah) Houston, TX, Jan. 16, 1950. Howard U.

Allen, Joan Rochelle, IL, Aug. 20, 1956. East Illinois U.
Allen, Karen Carrollton, IL, Oct. 5, 1951. U Maryland.
Allen, Nancy NYC, June 24, 1950.
Allen, Tim Denver, CO, June 13, 1953. Western Michigan U.
Allen, Woody (Allan Stewart Konigsberg) Brooklyn, Dec. 1, 1935.
Alley, Kirstie Wichita, KS, Jan. 12, 1955.
Allyson, June (Ella Geisman) Westchester, NY, Oct. 7, 1917.
Alonso, Maria Conchita Cuba, June 29, 1957.
Alt, Carol Queens, NY, Dec. 1, 1960. Hofstra U.
Alvarado, Trini NYC, Jan. 10, 1967.
Ambrose, Lauren New Haven, CT, Feb. 20, 1978.
Amis, Suzy Oklahoma City, OK, Jan. 5, 1958. Actors Studio.
Amos, John Newark, NJ, Dec. 27, 1940. Colorado U.
Anderson, Anthony Los Angeles, CA, Aug. 15, 1970.
Anderson, Gillian Chicago, IL, Aug. 9, 1968. DePaul U.
Anderson, Kevin Waukeegan, IL, Jan. 13, 1960.
Anderson, Loni St. Paul, MN, Aug. 5, 1946.
Anderson, Melissa Sue Berkeley, CA, Sept. 26, 1962.
Anderson, Melody Edmonton, Canada, Dec. 3, 1955. Carlton U.
Anderson, Michael, Jr. London, England, Aug. 6, 1943.
Anderson, Richard Dean Minneapolis, MN, Jan. 23, 1950.
Andersson, Bibi Stockholm, Sweden, Nov. 11, 1935. Royal Dramatic School.
Andes, Keith Ocean City, NJ, July 12, 1920. Temple U., Oxford.
Andress, Ursula Bern, Switzerland, Mar. 19, 1936.
Andrews, Anthony London, England, Dec. 1, 1948.
Andrews, Julie (Julia Elizabeth Wells) Surrey, England, Oct. 1, 1935.
Anglim, Philip San Francisco, CA, Feb. 11, 1953.
Aniston, Jennifer Sherman Oaks, CA, Feb. 11, 1969.
Ann-Margret (Olsson) Valsjobyn, Sweden, Apr. 28, 1941. Northwestern.
Ansara, Michael Lowell, MA, Apr. 15, 1922. Pasadena Playhouse.
Anspach, Susan NYC, Nov. 23, 1945.
Anthony, Lysette London, England, Sept. 26, 1963.
Anthony, Tony Clarksburg, WV, Oct. 16, 1937. Carnegie Tech.
Anton, Susan Yucaipa, CA, Oct. 12, 1950. Bemardino College.
Antonelli, Laura Pola, Italy, Nov. 28, 1941.
Anwar, Gabrielle Lalehaam, England, Feb. 4, 1970.
Applegate, Christina Hollywood, CA, Nov. 25, 1972.

Archer, Anne Los Angeles, CA, Aug. 25, 1947.
Archer, John (Ralph Bowman) Osceola, NB, May 8, 1915. USC.
Ardant, Fanny Monte Carlo, Monaco, Mar 22, 1949.
Arkin, Adam Brooklyn, NY, Aug. 19, 1956.
Arkin, Alan NYC, Mar. 26, 1934. LACC.
Armstrong, Bess Baltimore, MD, Dec. 11, 1953.
Arnaz, Desi, Jr. Los Angeles, CA, Jan. 19, 1953.
Arnaz, Lucie Hollywood, CA, July 17, 1951.
Arness, James (Aurness) Minneapolis, MN, May 26, 1923. Beloit College.
Arquette, David Winchester, VA, Sept. 8, 1971.
Arquette, Patricia NYC, Apr. 8, 1968.
Arquette, Rosanna NYC, Aug. 10, 1959.
Arthur, Beatrice (Frankel) NYC, May 13, 1924. New School.
Asher, Jane London, England, Apr. 5, 1946.
Ashley, Elizabeth (Elizabeth Ann Cole) Ocala, FL, Aug. 30, 1939.
Ashton, John Springfield, MA, Feb. 22, 1948. USC.
Asner, Edward Kansas City, KS, Nov. 15, 1929.
Assante, Armand NYC, Oct. 4, 1949. AADA.
Astin, John Baltimore, MD, Mar. 30, 1930. U Minnesota.
Astin, MacKenzie Los Angeles, CA, May 12, 1973.
Astin, Sean Santa Monica, CA, Feb. 25, 1971.
Atherton, William Orange, CT, July 30, 1947. Carnegie Tech.
Atkins, Christopher Rye, NY, Feb. 21, 1961.
Atkins, Eileen London, England, June 16, 1934.
Atkinson, Rowan England, Jan. 6, 1955. Oxford.
Attenborough, Richard Cambridge, England, Aug. 29, 1923. RADA.
Auberjonois, Rene NYC, June 1, 1940. Carnegie Tech.
Audran, Stephane Versailles, France, Nov. 8, 1932.
Auger, Claudine Paris, France, Apr. 26, 1942. Dramatic Cons.
Aulin, Ewa Stockholm, Sweden, Feb. 14, 1950.
Auteuil, Daniel Alger, Algeria, Jan. 24, 1950.
Avalon, Frankie (Francis Thomas Avallone) Philadelphia, PA, Sept. 18, 1939.
Aykroyd, Dan Ottawa, Canada, July 1, 1952.
Azaria, Hank Forest Hills, NY, Apr. 25, 1964. AADA, Tufts U.
Aznavour, Charles (Varenagh Aznourian) Paris, France, May 22, 1924.
Azzara, Candice Brooklyn, NY, May 18, 1947.

Bacall, Lauren (Betty Perske) NYC, Sept. 16, 1924. AADA.
Bach, Barbara Queens, NY, Aug. 27, 1946.
Bach, Catherine Warren, OH, Mar. 1, 1954.
Backer, Brian NYC, Dec. 5, 1956. Neighborhood Playhouse.
Bacon, Kevin Philadelphia, PA, July 8, 1958.
Bain, Barbara Chicago, IL, Sept. 13, 1934. U Illinois.
Baio, Scott Brooklyn, NY, Sept. 22, 1961.
Baker, Blanche NYC, Dec. 20, 1956.
Baker, Carroll Johnstown, PA, May 28, 1931. St. Petersburg, Jr. College.
Baker, Diane Hollywood, CA, Feb. 25, 1938. USC.
Baker, Dylan Syracuse, NY, Oct. 7, 1959.
Baker, Joe Don Groesbeck, TX, Feb. 12, 1936.
Baker, Kathy Midland, TX, June 8, 1950. UC Berkley.
Bakula, Scott St. Louis, MO, Oct. 9, 1955. Kansas U.
Balaban, Bob Chicago, IL, Aug. 16, 1945. Colgate.
Baldwin, Adam Chicago, IL, Feb. 27, 1962.
Baldwin, Alec Massapequa, NY, Apr. 3, 1958. NYU.

Baldwin, Daniel Massapequa, NY, Oct. 5, 1960.
Baldwin, Stephen Massapequa, NY, May 12, 1966.
Baldwin, William Massapequa, NY, Feb. 21, 1963.
Bale, Christian Pembrokeshire, West Wales, Jan. 30, 1974.
Balk, Fairuza Point Reyes, CA, May 21, 1974.
Ballard, Kaye Cleveland, OH, Nov. 20, 1926.
Bana, Eric Melbourne, Australia, Aug. 9, 1968.
Bancroft, Anne (Anna Maria Italiano) Bronx, NY, Sept. 17, 1931. AADA.
Banderas, Antonio Malaga, Spain, Aug. 10, 1960.
Banerjee, Victor Calcutta, India, Oct. 15, 1946.
Banes, Lisa Chagrin Falls, OH, July 9, 1955. Juilliard.
Baranski, Christine Buffalo, NY, May 2, 1952. Juilliard.
Barbeau, Adrienne Sacramento, CA, June 11, 1945. Foothill College.
Bardem, Javier Gran Canaria, Spain, May 1, 1969.
Bardot, Brigitte Paris, France, Sept. 28, 1934.
Barkin, Ellen Bronx, NY, Apr. 16, 1954. Hunter College.
Barnes, Christopher Daniel Portland, ME, Nov. 7, 1972.
Barr, Jean-Marc Bitburg, Germany, Sept. 27, 1960.
Barr, Roseanne Salt Lake City, UT, Nov. 3, 1952.
Barrault, Jean-Louis Vesinet, France, Sept. 8, 1910.
Barrault, Marie-Christine Paris, France, Mar. 21, 1944.
Barren, Keith Mexborough, England, Aug. 8, 1936. Sheffield Playhouse.
Barrett, Majel (Hudec) Columbus, OH, Feb. 23, 1939. Western Reserve U.
Barrie, Barbara Chicago, IL, May 23, 1931.
Barry, Gene (Eugene Klass) NYC, June 14, 1919.
Barry, Neill NYC, Nov. 29, 1965.
Barrymore, Drew Los Angeles, Feb. 22, 1975.
Baryshnikov, Mikhail Riga, Latvia, Jan. 27, 1948.
Basinger, Kim Athens, GA, Dec. 8, 1953. Neighborhood Playhouse.
Bassett, Angela NYC, Aug. 16, 1958.
Bateman, Jason Rye, NY, Jan. 14, 1969.
Bateman, Justine Rye, NY, Feb. 19, 1966.
Bates, Jeanne San Francisco, CA, May 21, 1918. RADA.
Bates, Kathy Memphis, TN, June 28, 1948. S. Methodist U.
Bauer, Steven (Steven Rocky Echevarria) Havana, Cuba, Dec. 2, 1956. U Miami.
Baxter, Keith South Wales, England, Apr. 29, 1933. RADA.
Baxter, Meredith Los Angeles, CA, June 21, 1947. Interlochen Academy.
Baye, Nathalie Mainevile, France, July 6, 1948.
Beach, Adam Winnipeg, Canada, Nov. 11, 1972.
Beacham, Stephanie Casablanca, Morocco, Feb. 28, 1947.
Beals, Jennifer Chicago, IL, Dec. 19, 1963.
Bean, Orson (Dallas Burrows) Burlington, VT, July 22, 1928.
Bean, Sean Sheffield, Yorkshire, England, Apr. 17, 1958.
Béart, Emmanuelle Gassin, France, Aug. 14, 1965.
Beatty, Ned Louisville, KY, July 6, 1937.
Beatty, Warren Richmond, VA, Mar. 30, 1937.
Beck, John Chicago, IL, Jan. 28, 1943.
Beck, Michael Memphis, TN, Feb. 4, 1949. Millsap College.
Beckinsale, Kate England, July 26, 1974.
Bedelia, Bonnie NYC, Mar. 25, 1946. Hunter College.
Begley, Ed, Jr. NYC, Sept. 16, 1949.
Belafonte, Harry NYC, Mar. 1, 1927.
Bel Geddes, Barbara NYC, Oct. 31, 1922.
Bell, Jamie Billingham, England, Mar. 14, 1988.

Cate Blanchett

Matthew Broderick

Jackie Chan

Patricia Clarkson

Bell, Tom Liverpool, England, Aug. 2, 1933.

Beller, Kathleen NYC, Feb. 10, 1957.

Bellucci, Monica Citta di Castello, Italy, Sept. 30, 1964.

Bellwood, Pamela (King) Scarsdale, NY, June 26, 1951.

Belmondo, Jean Paul Paris, France, Apr. 9, 1933.

Belushi, James Chicago, IL, June 15, 1954.

Belzer, Richard Bridgeport, CT, Aug. 4, 1944.

Benedict, Dirk (Niewoehner) White Sulphur Springs, MT, March 1, 1945. Whitman College.

Benedict, Paul Silver City, NM, Sept. 17, 1938.

Benigni, Roberto Tuscany, Italy, Oct. 27, 1952.

Bening, Annette Topeka, KS, May 29, 1958. San Francisco State U.

Benjamin, Richard NYC, May 22, 1938. Northwestern.

Bennent, David Lausanne, Switzerland, Sept. 9, 1966.

Bennett, Alan Leeds, England, May 9, 1934. Oxford.

Bennett, Bruce (Herman Brix) Tacoma, WA, May 19, 1909. U Washington.

Bennett, Hywel Garnant, South Wales, Apr. 8, 1944.

Benson, Robby Dallas, TX, Jan. 21, 1957.

Bentley, Wes Jonesboro, AR, Sept. 4, 1978.

Berenger, Tom Chicago, IL, May 31, 1950, U Missouri.

Berenson, Marisa NYC, Feb. 15, 1947.

Berg, Peter NYC, March 11, 1964. Malcalester College.

Bergen, Candice Los Angeles, CA, May 9, 1946. U Pennsylvania.

Bergen, Polly Knoxville, TN, July 14, 1930. Compton, Jr. College.

Berger, Helmut Salzburg, Austria, May 29, 1942.

Berger, Senta Vienna, Austria, May 13, 1941. Vienna School of Acting.

Berger, William Austria, Jan. 20, 1928. Columbia.

Bergerac, Jacques Biarritz, France, May 26, 1927. Paris U.

Bergin, Patrick Dublin, Feb. 4, 1951.

Berkley, Elizabeth Detroit, MI, July 28, 1972.

Berkoff, Steven London, England, Aug. 3, 1937.

Berlin, Jeannie Los Angeles, CA, Nov. 1, 1949.

Berlinger, Warren Brooklyn, NY, Aug. 31, 1937. Columbia.

Bernal, Gael García Guadalajara, Mexico, Oct. 30, 1978.

Bernhard, Sandra Flint, MI, June 6, 1955.

Bernsen, Corbin Los Angeles, CA, Sept. 7, 1954. UCLA.

Berri, Claude (Langmann) Paris, France, July 1, 1934.

Berridge, Elizabeth Westchester, NY, May 2, 1962. Strasberg Institute.

Berry, Halle Cleveland, OH, Aug. 14, 1968.

Berry, Ken Moline, IL, Nov. 3, 1933.

Bertinelli, Valerie Wilmington, DE, Apr. 23, 1960.

Best, James Corydon, IN, July 26, 1926.

Bettany, Paul London, England, May 27, 1971.

Bey, Turhan Vienna, Austria, Mar. 30, 1921.

Beymer, Richard Avoca, IA, Feb. 21, 1939.

Bialik, Mayim San Diego, CA, Dec. 12, 1975.

Biehn, Michael Anniston, AL, July 31, 1956.

Biggerstaff, Sean Glasgow, Scotland, Mar. 15, 1983.

Biggs, Jason Pompton Plains, NJ, May 12, 1978.

Bikel, Theodore Vienna, Austria, May 2, 1924. RADA.

Billingsley, Peter NYC, Apr. 16, 1972.

Binoche, Juliette Paris, France, Mar. 9, 1964.

Birch, Thora Los Angeles, CA, Mar. 11, 1982.

Birkin, Jane London, England, Dec. 14, 1947.

Birney, David Washington, DC, Apr. 23, 1939. Dartmouth, UCLA.

Birney, Reed Alexandria, VA, Sept. 11, 1954. Boston U.

Bishop, Joey (Joseph Abraham Gotlieb) Bronx, NY, Feb. 3, 1918.

Bishop, Julie (Jacqueline Wells) Denver, CO, Aug. 30, 1917. Westlake School.

Bishop, Kevin Kent, England, June 18, 1980.

Bisset, Jacqueline Waybridge, England, Sept. 13, 1944.

Black, Jack Edmonton, Alberta, Canada, Apr. 7, 1969.

Black, Karen (Ziegler) Park Ridge, IL, July 1, 1942. Northwestern.

Black, Lucas Speake, AL, Nov. 29, 1982.

Blackman, Honor London, England, Aug. 22, 1926.

Blades, Ruben Panama City, Florida, July 16, 1948. Harvard.

Blair, Betsy (Betsy Boger) NYC, Dec. 11, 1923.

Blair, Janet (Martha Jane Lafferty) Blair, PA, Apr. 23, 1921.

Blair, Linda Westport, CT, Jan. 22, 1959.

Blair, Selma Southfield, MI, June 23, 1972.

Blake, Robert (Michael Gubitosi) Nutley, NJ, Sept. 18, 1933.

Blakely, Susan Frankfurt, Germany, Sept. 7, 1950. U Texas.

Blakley, Ronee Stanley, ID, 1946. Stanford U.

Blanchett, Cate Melbourne, Australia, May 14, 1969.

Bledel, Alexis Houston, TX, Sept. 16, 1981.

Blethyn, Brenda Ramsgate, Kent, England, Feb. 20, 1946.

Bloom, Claire London, England, Feb. 15, 1931. Badminton School.

Bloom, Orlando Canterbury, England, Jan. 13, 1977.

Bloom, Verna Lynn, MA, Aug. 7, 1939. Boston U.

Blount, Lisa Fayettville, AK, July 1, 1957. UArkansas.

Blum, Mark Newark, NJ, May 14, 1950. U Minnesota.

Blyth, Ann Mt. Kisco, NY, Aug. 16, 1928. New Waybum Dramatic School.

Bochner, Hart Toronto, Canada, Oct. 3, 1956. U San Diego.

Bochner, Lloyd Toronto, Canada, July 29, 1924.

Bogosian, Eric Woburn, MA, Apr. 24, 1953. Oberlin College.

Bohringer, Richard Paris, France, Jan. 16, 1941.

Bolkan, Florinda (Florinda Soares Bulcao) Ceara, Brazil, Feb. 15, 1941.

Bologna, Joseph Brooklyn, NY, Dec. 30, 1938. Brown U.

Bond, Derek Glasgow, Scotland, Jan. 26, 1920. Askes School.

Bonet, Lisa San Francisco, CA, Nov. 16, 1967.

Bonham-Carter, Helena London, England, May 26, 1966.

Boone, Pat Jacksonville, FL, June 1, 1934. Columbia U.

Boothe, James Croydon, England, Dec. 19, 1930.

Boothe, Powers Snyder, TX, June 1, 1949. Southern Methodist U.

Borgnine, Ernest (Borgnino) Hamden, CT, Jan. 24, 1917. Randall School.

Bosco, Philip Jersey City, NJ, Sept. 26, 1930. Catholic U.

Bosley, Tom Chicago, IL, Oct. 1, 1927. DePaul U.

Bostwick, Barry San Mateo, CA, Feb. 24, 1945. NYU.

Bottoms, Joseph Santa Barbara, CA, Aug. 30, 1954.

Bottoms, Sam Santa Barbara, CA, Oct. 17, 1955.

Bottoms, Timothy Santa Barbara, CA, Aug. 30, 1951.

Boulting, Ingrid Transvaal, South Africa, 1947.

Boutsikaris, Dennis Newark, NJ, Dec. 21, 1952. Catholic U.

Bowie, David (David Robert Jones) Brixton, South London, England, Jan. 8, 1947.

Bowker, Judi Shawford, England, Apr. 6, 1954.

Boxleitner, Bruce Elgin, IL, May 12, 1950.

Boyd, Billy Glasgow, Scotland, Aug. 28, 1968.

Boyle, Lara Flynn Davenport, IA, Mar. 24, 1970.

Boyle, Peter Philadelphia, PA, Oct. 18, 1933. LaSalle College.

Bracco, Lorraine Brooklyn, NY, Oct. 2, 1949.

Bradford, Jesse Norwalk, CT, May 27, 1979.

Braeden, Eric (Hans Gudegast) Kiel, Germany, Apr. 3, 1942.

Braff, Zach South Orange, NJ, Apr. 6, 1975.

Braga, Sonia Maringa, Brazil, June 8, 1950.

Branagh, Kenneth Belfast, Northern Ireland, Dec. 10, 1960.

Brandauer, Klaus Maria Altaussee, Austria, June 22, 1944.

Brando, Jocelyn San Francisco, CA, Nov. 18, 1919. Lake Forest College, AADA.

Brandon, Clark NYC, Dec. 13, 1958.

Brandon, Michael (Feldman) Brooklyn, NY, Apr. 20, 1945.

Brantley, Betsy Rutherfordton, NC, Sept. 20, 1955. London Central School of Drama.

Bratt, Benjamin San Francisco, CA, Dec. 16, 1963.

Brennan, Eileen Los Angeles, CA, Sept. 3, 1935. AADA.

Brenneman, Amy Glastonbury, CT, June 22, 1964.

Brialy, Jean-Claude Aumale, Algeria, 1933. Strasbourg Cons.

Bridges, Beau Los Angeles, CA, Dec. 9, 1941. UCLA.

Bridges, Jeff Los Angeles, CA, Dec. 4, 1949.

Brimley, Wilford Salt Lake City, UT, Sept. 27, 1934.

Brinkley, Christie Malibu, CA, Feb. 2, 1954.

Britt, May (Maybritt Wilkins) Stockholm, Sweden, Mar. 22, 1936.

Brittany, Morgan (Suzanne Cupito) Los Angeles, CA, Dec. 5, 1950.

Britton, Tony Birmingham, England, June 9, 1924.

Broadbent, Jim Lincoln, England, May 24, 1959.

Broderick, Matthew NYC, Mar. 21, 1962.

Brody, Adrien NYC, Dec. 23, 1976,

Brolin, James Los Angeles, CA, July 18, 1940. UCLA.

Brolin, Josh Los Angeles, CA, Feb. 12, 1968.

Bromfield, John (Farron Bromfield) South Bend, IN, June 11, 1922. St. Mary's College.

Bron, Eleanor Stanmore, England, Mar. 14, 1934.

Brookes, Jacqueline Montclair, NJ, July 24, 1930. RADA.

Brooks, Albert (Einstein) Los Angeles, CA, July 22, 1947.

Brooks, Mel (Melvyn Kaminski) Brooklyn, NY, June 28, 1926.

Brosnan, Pierce County Meath, Ireland. May 16, 1952.

Brown, Blair Washington, DC, Apr. 23, 1947. Pine Manor.

Brown, Bryan Panania, Australia, June 23, 1947.

Brown, Gary (Christian Brando) Hollywood, CA, 1958.

Brown, Georg Stanford Havana, Cuba, June 24, 1943. AMDA.

Brown, James Desdemona, TX, Mar. 22, 1920. Baylor U.

Brown, Jim St. Simons Island, NY, Feb. 17, 1935. Syracuse U.

Browne, Leslie NYC, 1958.

Browne, Roscoe Lee Woodbury, NJ, May 2, 1925.

Bruckner, Agnes Hollywood, CA, Aug. 16, 1985.

Buckley, Betty Big Spring, TX, July 3, 1947. Texas Christian U.

Bujold, Genevieve Montreal, Canada, July 1, 1942.

Bullock, Sandra Arlington, VA, July 26, 1964.

Burghoff, Gary Bristol, CT, May 24, 1943.

Burgi, Richard Montclair, NJ, July 30, 1958.

Burke, Paul New Orleans, July 21, 1926. Pasadena Playhouse.

Burnett, Carol San Antonio, TX, Apr. 26, 1933. UCLA.

Burns, Catherine NYC, Sept. 25, 1945. AADA.

Burns, Edward Valley Stream, NY, Jan. 28, 1969.

Burrows, Darren E. Winfield, KS, Sept. 12, 1966.

Burrows, Saffron London, England, Jan. 1, 1973.

Burstyn, Ellen (Edna Rae Gillhooly) Detroit, MI, Dec. 7, 1932.

Burton, LeVar Los Angeles, CA, Feb. 16, 1958. UCLA.

Buscemi, Steve Brooklyn, NY, Dec. 13, 1957.

Busey, Gary Goose Creek, TX, June 29, 1944.

Busfield, Timothy Lansing, MI, June 12, 1957. East Tennessee State U.

Butler, Gerard Glasgow, Scotland, Nov. 13, 1969.

Buttons, Red (Aaron Chwatt) NYC, Feb. 5, 1919.

Buzzi, Ruth Westerly, RI, July 24, 1936. Pasadena Playhouse.

Bygraves, Max London, England, Oct. 16, 1922. St. Joseph's School.

Bynes, Amanda Thousand Oaks, CA, Apr. 3, 1986.

Byrne, David Dumbarton, Scotland, May 14, 1952.

Byrne, Gabriel Dublin, Ireland, May 12, 1950.

Byrnes, Edd NYC, July 30, 1933.

Caan, James Bronx, NY, Mar. 26,1939.

Caesar, Sid Yonkers, NY, Sept. 8, 1922.

Cage, Nicolas (Coppola) Long Beach, CA, Jan. 7, 1964.

Cain, Dean (Dean Tanaka) Mt. Clemens, MI, July 31, 1966.

Caine, Michael (Maurice Micklewhite) London, England, Mar. 14, 1933.
Caine, Shakira (Baksh) Guyana, Feb. 23, 1947. Indian Trust College.
Callan, Michael (Martin Calinieff) Philadelphia, Nov. 22, 1935.
Callow, Simon London, England, June 15, 1949. Queens U.
Cameron, Kirk Panorama City, CA, Oct. 12, 1970.
Camp, Colleen San Francisco, CA, June 7, 1953.
Campbell, Bill Chicago, IL, July 7, 1959.
Campbell, Glen Delight, AR, Apr. 22, 1935.
Campbell, Neve Guelph, Ontario, Canada, Oct. 3, 1973.
Campbell, Tisha Oklahoma City, OK, Oct. 13, 1968.
Canale, Gianna Maria Reggio Calabria, Italy, Sept. 12, 1927.
Cannon, Dyan (Samille Diane Friesen) Tacoma, WA, Jan. 4, 1937.
Capshaw, Kate Ft. Worth, TX, Nov. 3, 1953. U Misourri.
Cara, Irene NYC, Mar. 18, 1958.
Cardinale, Claudia Tunis, North Africa. Apr. 15, 1939. College Paul Cambon.
Carey, Harry, Jr. Saugus, CA, May 16, 1921. Black Fox Military Academy.
Carey, Philip Hackensack, NJ, July 15, 1925. U Miami.
Cariou, Len Winnipeg, Canada, Sept. 30, 1939.
Carlin, George NYC, May 12, 1938.
Carlyle, Robert Glasgow, Scotland, Apr. 14, 1961.
Carmen, Julie Mt. Vernon, NY, Apr. 4, 1954.
Carmichael, Ian Hull, England, June 18, 1920. Scarborough College.
Carne, Judy (Joyce Botterill) Northampton, England, 1939. Bush-Davis Theatre School.
Caron, Leslie Paris, France, July 1, 1931. Nationall Conservatory, Paris.
Carpenter, Carleton Bennington, VT, July 10, 1926. Northwestern.
Carradine, David Hollywood, CA, Dec. 8, 1936. San Francisco State.
Carradine, Keith San Mateo, CA, Aug. 8, 1950. Colo. State U.
Carradine, Robert San Mateo, CA, Mar. 24, 1954.
Carrel, Dany Tourane, Indochina, Sept. 20, 1936. Marseilles Cons.
Carrera, Barbara Managua, Nicaragua, Dec. 31, 1945.
Carrere, Tia (Althea Janairo) Honolulu, HI, Jan. 2, 1965.
Carrey, Jim Jacksons Point, Ontario, Canada, Jan. 17, 1962.
Carriere, Mathieu Hannover, West Germany, Aug. 2, 1950.
Carroll, Diahann (Johnson) NYC, July 17, 1935. NYU.
Carroll, Pat Shreveport, LA, May 5, 1927. Catholic U.
Carson, John David California, Mar. 6, 1952. Valley College.
Carson, Johnny Corning, IA, Oct. 23, 1925. U of Nebraska.
Carsten, Peter (Ransenthaler) Weissenberg, Bavaria, Apr. 30, 1929. Munich Akademie.
Cartwright, Veronica Bristol, England, Apr 20, 1949.
Caruso, David Forest Hills, NY, Jan. 7, 1956.
Carvey, Dana Missoula, MT, Apr. 2, 1955. San Francisco State U.
Casella, Max Washington D.C, June 6, 1967.
Casey, Bernie Wyco, WV, June 8, 1939.
Cassavetes, Nick NYC, 1959, Syracuse U, AADA.
Cassel, Jean-Pierre Paris, France, Oct. 27, 1932.
Cassel, Seymour Detroit, MI, Jan. 22, 1935.
Cassel, Vincent Paris, France, Nov. 23, 1966.
Cassidy, David NYC, Apr. 12, 1950.
Cassidy, Joanna Camden, NJ, Aug. 2, 1944. Syracuse U.
Cassidy, Patrick Los Angeles, CA, Jan. 4, 1961.
Cates, Phoebe NYC, July 16, 1962.
Cattrall, Kim Liverpool, England, Aug. 21, 1956. AADA.

Caulfield, Maxwell Glasgow, Scotland, Nov. 23, 1959.
Cavani, Liliana Bologna, Italy, Jan. 12, 1937. U Bologna.
Cavett, Dick Gibbon, NE, Nov. 19, 1936.
Caviezel, Jim Mt. Vernon, WA, Sept. 26, 1968.
Cedric the Entertainer (Cedric Kyles) Jefferson City, MO, Apr. 24, 1964.
Chakiris, George Norwood, OH, Sept. 16, 1933.
Chamberlain, Richard Beverly Hills, CA, March 31, 1935. Pomona.
Champion, Marge (Marjorie Belcher) Los Angeles, CA, Sept. 2, 1923.
Chan, Jackie Hong Kong, Apr. 7, 1954.
Channing, Carol Seattle, WA, Jan. 31, 1921. Bennington.
Channing, Stockard (Susan Stockard) NYC, Feb. 13, 1944. Radcliffe.
Chapin, Miles NYC, Dec. 6, 1954. HB Studio.
Chaplin, Ben London, England, July 31, 1970.
Chaplin, Geraldine Santa Monica, CA, July 31, 1944. Royal Ballet.
Chaplin, Sydney Los Angeles, CA, Mar. 31, 1926. Lawrenceville.
Charisse, Cyd (Tula Ellice Finklea) Amarillo, TX, Mar. 3, 1922. Hollywood Professional School.
Charles, Josh Baltimore, MD, Sept. 15, 1971.
Charles, Walter East Strousburg, PA, Apr. 4, 1945. Boston U.
Chase, Chevy (Cornelius Crane Chase) NYC, Oct. 8, 1943.
Chaves, Richard Jacksonville, FL, Oct. 9, 1951. Occidental College.
Chaykin, Maury Canada, July 27, 1954.
Cheadle, Don Kansas City, MO, Nov. 29, 1964.
Chen, Joan (Chen Chung) Shanghai, China, Apr. 26, 1961. Cal State.
Cher (Cherilyn Sarkisian) El Centro, CA, May 20, 1946.
Chiles, Lois Alice, TX, Apr. 15, 1947.
Cho, John Seoul, Korea, June 16, 1972.
Cho, Margaret San Francisco, CA, Dec. 5, 1968.
Chong, Rae Dawn Vancouver, Canada, Feb. 28, 1962.
Chong, Thomas Edmonton, Alberta, Canada, May 24, 1938.
Christensen, Erika Seattle, WA, Aug. 19, 1982.
Christensen, Hayden Vancouver, British Columbia, Apr. 19, 1981.
Christian, Linda (Blanca Rosa Welter) Tampico, Mexico, Nov. 13, 1923.
Christie, Julie Chukua, Assam, India, Apr. 14, 1941.
Christopher, Dennis (Carrelli) Philadelphia, PA, Dec. 2, 1955. Temple U.
Christopher, Jordan Youngstown, OH, Oct. 23, 1940. Kent State.
Church, Thomas Hayden El Paso, TX, June 17, 1961.
Cilento, Diane Queensland, Australia, Oct. 5, 1933. AADA.
Clark, Candy Norman, OK, June 20, 1947.
Clark, Dick Mt. Vernon, NY, Nov. 30, 1929. Syracuse U.
Clark, Matt Washington, DC, Nov. 25, 1936.
Clark, Petula Epsom, England, Nov. 15, 1932.
Clark, Susan Sarnid, Ont., Canada, Mar. 8, 1943. RADA.
Clarkson, Patricia New Orleans, Dec. 29, 1959.
Clay, Andrew Dice (Andrew Silverstein) Brooklyn, NY, Sept. 29, 1957, Kingsborough College.
Clayburgh, Jill NYC, Apr. 30, 1944. Sarah Lawrence.
Cleese, John Weston-Super-Mare, England, Oct. 27, 1939, Cambridge.
Clooney, George Lexington, KY, May 6, 1961.
Close, Glenn Greenwich, CT, Mar. 19, 1947. William & Mary College.
Cody, Kathleen Bronx, NY, Oct. 30, 1953.
Coffey, Scott HI, May 1, 1967.
Cole, George London, England, Apr. 22, 1925.
Coleman, Dabney Austin, TX, Jan. 3, 1932.

George Clooney

Toni Collette

Steve Coogan

John Corbett

Coleman, Gary Zion, IL, Feb. 8, 1968.

Coleman, Jack Easton, PA, Feb. 21, 1958. Duke U.

Colin, Margaret NYC, May 26, 1957.

Collet, Christopher NYC, Mar. 13, 1968. Strasberg Institute.

Collette, Toni Sydney, Australia, Nov. 1, 1972.

Collins, Joan London, England, May 21, 1933. Francis Holland School.

Collins, Pauline Devon, England, Sept. 3, 1940.

Collins, Stephen Des Moines, IA, Oct. 1, 1947. Amherst.

Colon, Miriam Ponce, PR., 1945. UPR.

Coltrane, Robbie Ruthergien, Scotland, Mar. 30, 1950.

Combs, Sean "Puffy" NYC, Nov. 4, 1969.

Comer, Anjanette Dawson, TX, Aug. 7, 1942. Baylor, Texas U.

Conant, Oliver NYC, Nov. 15, 1955. Dalton.

Conaway, Jeff NYC, Oct. 5, 1950. NYU.

Connelly, Jennifer NYC, Dec. 12, 1970.

Connery, Jason London, England, Jan. 11, 1963.

Connery, Sean Edinburgh, Scotland, Aug. 25, 1930.

Connick, Harry, Jr. New Orleans, LA, Sept. 11, 1967.

Connolly, Billy Glasgow, Scotland, Nov. 24, 1942.

Connors, Mike (Krekor Ohanian) Fresno, CA, Aug. 15, 1925. UCLA.

Conrad, Robert (Conrad Robert Falk) Chicago, IL, Mar. 1, 1935. Northwestern.

Constantine, Michael Reading, PA, May 22, 1927.

Conti, Tom Paisley, Scotland, Nov. 22, 1941.

Converse, Frank St. Louis, MO, May 22, 1938. Carnegie Tech.

Conway, Gary Boston, MA, Feb. 4, 1936.

Conway, Kevin NYC, May 29, 1942.

Conway, Tim (Thomas Daniel) Willoughby, OH, Dec. 15, 1933. Bowling Green State.

Coogan, Keith (Keith Mitchell Franklin) Palm Springs, CA, Jan. 13, 1970.

Coogan, Steve Manchester, England, Oct. 14, 1965.

Cook, Rachael Leigh Minneapolis, MN, Oct. 4, 1979.

Coolidge, Jennifer Boston, Aug. 28, 1963.

Cooper, Ben Hartford, CT, Sept. 30, 1930. Columbia U.

Cooper, Chris Kansas City, MO, July 9, 1951. U Misourri.

Cooper, Jackie Los Angeles, CA, Sept. 15, 1921.

Copeland, Joan NYC, June 1, 1922. Brooklyn College, RADA.

Corbett, Gretchen Portland, OR, Aug. 13, 1947. Carnegie Tech.

Corbett, John Wheeling, WV, May 9, 1961.

Corbin, Barry Dawson County, TX, Oct. 16, 1940. Texas Tech. U.

Corcoran, Donna Quincy, MA, Sept. 29, 1942.

Cord, Alex (Viespi) Floral Park, NY, Aug. 3, 1931. NYU, Actors Studio.

Corday, Mara (Marilyn Watts) Santa Monica, CA, Jan. 3, 1932.

Cornthwaite, Robert St. Helens, OR, Apr. 28, 1917. USC.

Corri, Adrienne Glasgow, Scotland, Nov. 13, 1933. RADA.

Cort, Bud (Walter Edward Cox) New Rochelle, NY, Mar. 29, 1950. NYU.

Cortesa, Valentina Milan, Italy, Jan. 1, 1924.

Cosby, Bill Philadelphia, PA, July 12, 1937. Temple U.

Coster, Nicolas London, England, Dec. 3, 1934. Neighborhood Playhouse.

Costner, Kevin Lynwood, CA, Jan. 18, 1955. California State U.

Courtenay, Tom Hull, England, Feb. 25, 1937. RADA.

Courtland, Jerome Knoxville, TN, Dec. 27, 1926.

Cox, Brian Dundee, Scotland, June 1, 1946. LAMDA.

Cox, Courteney Birmingham, AL, June 15, 1964.

Cox, Ronny Cloudcroft, NM, Aug. 23, 1938.

Coyote, Peter (Cohon) NYC, Oct. 10, 1941.

Craig, Daniel Chester, England, 1968.

Craig, Michael Poona, India, Jan. 27, 1929.

Craven, Gemma Dublin, Ireland, June 1, 1950.

Crawford, Michael (Dumbel-Smith) Salisbury, England, Jan. 19, 1942.

Cremer, Bruno Saint-Mande, Val-de-Varne, France, Oct. 6, 1929.

Cristal, Linda (Victoria Moya) Buenos Aires, Argentina, Feb. 25, 1934.

Cromwell, James Los Angeles, CA, Jan. 27, 1940.

Crosby, Denise Hollywood, CA, Nov. 24, 1957.

Crosby, Harry Los Angeles, CA, Aug. 8, 1958.

Crosby, Mary Frances Los Angeles, CA, Sept. 14, 1959.

Cross, Ben London, England, Dec. 16, 1947. RADA.

Cross, Murphy (Mary Jane) Laurelton, MD, June 22, 1950.

Crouse, Lindsay NYC, May 12, 1948. Radcliffe.

Crowe, Russell New Zealand, Apr. 7, 1964.

Crowley, Pat Olyphant, PA, Sept. 17, 1932.

Crudup, Billy Manhasset, NY, July 8, 1968. UNC, Chapel Hill.

Cruise, Tom (T. C. Mapother, IV) July 3, 1962, Syracuse, NY.

Cruz, Penélope (P.C. Sanchez) Madrid, Spain, Apr. 28, 1974.

Bud Cort

Joan Cusack

Judi Dench

Hector Elizondo

Cruz, Wilson Brooklyn, Dec. 27, 1973.
Cryer, Jon NYC, Apr. 16, 1965, RADA.
Crystal, Billy Long Beach, NY, Mar. 14, 1947. Marshall U.
Culkin, Kieran NYC, Sept. 30, 1982.
Culkin, Macaulay NYC, Aug. 26, 1980.
Culkin, Rory NYC, July 21, 1989.
Cullum, John Knoxville, TN, Mar. 2, 1930. U Tennisee.
Cullum, John David NYC, Mar. 1, 1966.
Culp, Robert Oakland, CA, Aug. 16, 1930. U Washington.
Cumming, Alan Perthshire, Scotland, Jan. 27, 1965.
Cummings, Constance Seattle, WA, May 15, 1910.
Cummings, Quinn Hollywood, Aug. 13, 1967.
Cummins, Peggy Prestatyn, North Wales, Dec. 18, 1926. Alexandra School.
Curry, Tim Cheshire, England, Apr. 19, 1946. Birmingham U.
Curtin, Jane Cambridge, MA, Sept. 6, 1947.
Curtis, Jamie Lee Los Angeles, CA, Nov. 22, 1958.
Curtis, Tony (Bernard Schwartz) NYC, June 3, 1924.
Cusack, Joan Evanston, IL, Oct. 11, 1962.
Cusack, John Chicago, IL, June 28, 1966.
Cusack, Sinead Dalkey, Ireland, Feb. 18, 1948.

Dafoe, Willem Appleton, WI, July 22, 1955.
Dahl, Arlene Minneapolis, Aug. 11, 1928. U Minnesota.
Dale, Jim Rothwell, England, Aug. 15, 1935.
Dallesandro, Joe Pensacola, FL, Dec. 31, 1948.
Dalton, Timothy Colwyn Bay, Wales, Mar. 21, 1946. RADA.
Daltrey, Roger London, England, Mar. 1, 1944.
Daly, Tim NYC, Mar. 1, 1956. Bennington College.
Daly, Tyne Madison, WI, Feb. 21, 1947. AMDA.
Damon, Matt Cambridge, MA, Oct. 8, 1970.
Damone, Vic (Vito Farinola) Brooklyn, NY, June 12, 1928.
Dance, Charles Plymouth, England, Oct. 10, 1946.
Danes, Claire New York, NY, Apr. 12, 1979.
D'Angelo, Beverly Columbus, OH, Nov. 15, 1953.
Daniels, Jeff Athens, GA, Feb. 19, 1955. Central Michigan U.
Daniels, William Brooklyn, NY, Mar. 31, 1927. Northwestern.
Danner, Blythe Philadelphia, PA, Feb. 3, 1944. Bard College.

Danning, Sybil (Sybille Johanna Danninger) Vienna, Austria, May 4, 1949.
Danson, Ted San Diego, CA, Dec. 29, 1947. Stanford, Carnegie Tech.
Dante, Michael (Ralph Vitti) Stamford, CT, 1935. U Miami.
Danza, Tony Brooklyn, NY, Apr. 21, 1951. U Dubuque.
D'arbanville-Quinn, Patti NYC, May 25, 1951.
Darby, Kim (Deborah Zerby) North Hollywood, CA, July 8, 1948.
Darcel, Denise (Denise Billecard) Paris, France, Sept. 8, 1925. U Dijon.
Darren, James Philadelphia, PA, June 8, 1936. Stella Adler School.
Darrieux, Danielle Bordeaux, France, May 1, 1917. Lycee LaTour.
Davenport, Nigel Cambridge, England, May 23, 1928. Trinity College.
David, Keith NYC, June 4, 1954. Juilliard.
Davidovich, Lolita Toronto, Ontario, Canada, July 15, 1961.
Davidson, Jaye Riverside, CA, 1968.
Davidson, John Pittsburgh, Dec. 13, 1941. Denison U.
Davies, Jeremy (Boring) Rockford, IA, Oct. 28, 1969.
Davis, Clifton Chicago, IL, Oct. 4, 1945. Oakwood College.
Davis, Geena Wareham, MA, Jan. 21, 1957.
Davis, Hope Tenafly, NJ, Mar. 23, 1964.
Davis, Judy Perth, Australia, Apr. 23, 1955.
Davis, Mac Lubbock, TX, Jan. 21,1942.
Davis, Nancy (Anne Frances Robbins) NYC, July 6, 1921. Smith College.
Davis, Ossie Cogdell, GA, Dec. 18, 1917. Howard U.
Davis, Sammi Kidderminster, Worcestershire, England, June 21, 1964.
Davison, Bruce Philadelphia, PA, June 28, 1946.
Dawber, Pam Detroit, MI, Oct. 18, 1954.
Day, Doris (Doris Kappelhoff) Cincinnati, Apr. 3, 1924.
Day, Laraine (Johnson) Roosevelt, UT, Oct. 13, 1917.
Day-Lewis, Daniel London, England, Apr. 29, 1957. Bristol Old Vic.
Dayan, Assi Israel, Nov. 23, 1945. U Jerusalem.
Deakins, Lucy NYC, 1971.
Dean, Jimmy Plainview, TX, Aug. 10, 1928.
Dean, Loren Las Vegas, NV, July 31, 1969.
DeCarlo, Yvonne (Peggy Yvonne Middleton) Vancouver, BC, Canada, Sept. 1, 1922. Vancouver School of Drama.
Dee, Joey (Joseph Di Nicola) Passaic, NJ, June 11, 1940. Patterson State College.
Dee, Ruby Cleveland, OH, Oct. 27, 1924. Hunter College.
Dee, Sandra (Alexandra Zuck) Bayonne, NJ, Apr. 23, 1942.

DeGeneres, Ellen New Orleans, LA, Jan. 26, 1958.
DeHaven, Gloria Los Angeles, CA, July 23, 1923.
DeHavilland, Olivia Tokyo, Japan, July 1, 1916. Notre Dame Convent School.
Delair, Suzy (Suzanne Delaire) Paris, France, Dec. 31, 1916.
Delany, Dana NYC, March 13, 1956. Wesleyan U.
Delon, Alain Sceaux, France, Nov. 8, 1935.
Delorme, Daniele Paris, France, Oct. 9, 1926. Sorbonne.
Delpy, Julie Paris. Dec, 21, 1969.
Del Toro, Benicio Santurce, Puerto Rico, Feb. 19, 1967.
DeLuise, Dom Brooklyn, NY, Aug. 1, 1933. Tufts College.
DeLuise, Peter NYC, Nov. 6, 1966.
Demongeot, Mylene Nice, France, Sept. 29, 1938.
DeMornay, Rebecca Los Angeles, CA, Aug. 29, 1962. Strasberg Institute.
Dempsey, Patrick Lewiston, ME, Jan. 13, 1966.
DeMunn, Jeffrey Buffalo, NY, Apr. 25, 1947. Union College.
Dench, Judi York, England, Dec. 9, 1934.
Deneuve, Catherine Paris, France, Oct. 22, 1943.
De Niro, Robert NYC, Aug. 17, 1943. Stella Adler.
Dennehy, Brian Bridgeport, CT, Jul. 9, 1938. Columbia.
Denver, Bob New Rochelle, NY, Jan. 9, 1935.
Depardieu, Gérard Chateauroux, France, Dec. 27, 1948.
Depp, Johnny Owensboro, KY, June 9, 1963.
Derek, Bo (Mary Cathleen Collins) Long Beach, CA, Nov. 20, 1956.
Dern, Bruce Chicago, IL, June 4, 1936. UPA.
Dern, Laura Los Angeles, CA, Feb. 10, 1967.
DeSalvo, Anne Philadelphia, PA, Apr. 3, 1949.
Deschanel, Zooey Los Angeles, CA, Jan. 17, 1980.
Devane, William Albany, NY, Sept. 5, 1939.
DeVito, Danny Asbury Park, NJ, Nov. 17, 1944.
Dey, Susan Pekin, IL, Dec. 10, 1953.
DeYoung, Cliff Los Angeles, CA, Feb. 12, 1945. California State U.
Diamond, Neil NYC, Jan. 24, 1941. NYU.
Diaz, Cameron Long Beach, CA, Aug. 30, 1972.
DiCaprio, Leonardo Hollywood, CA, Nov. 11, 1974.
Dickinson, Angie (Angeline Brown) Kulm, ND, Sept. 30, 1932. Glendale College.
Diesel, Vin (Mark Vincent) NYC, July 18, 1967.
Diggs, Taye (Scott Diggs) Rochester, NY, Jan. 2, 1972.
Diller, Phyllis (Driver) Lima, OH, July 17, 1917. Bluffton College.
Dillman, Bradford San Francisco, CA, Apr. 14, 1930. Yale.
Dillon, Kevin Mamaroneck, NY, Aug. 19, 1965.
Dillon, Matt Larchmont, NY, Feb. 18, 1964. AADA.
Dillon, Melinda Hope, AR, Oct. 13, 1939. Goodman Theatre School.
Dixon, Donna Alexandria, VA, July 20, 1957.
Dobson, Kevin NYC, Mar. 18, 1944.
Dobson, Tamara Baltimore, MD, May 14, 1947. Maryland Institute of Art.
Doherty, Shannen Memphis, TN, Apr. 12, 1971.
Dolan, Michael Oklahoma City, OK, June 21, 1965.
Donat, Peter Nova Scotia, Canada, Jan. 20, 1928. Yale.
Donnelly, Donal Bradford, England, July 6, 1931.
D'Onofrio, Vincent Brooklyn, NY, June 30, 1959.
Donohoe, Amanda London, England, June 29 1962.
Donovan, Martin Reseda, CA, Aug. 19, 1957.
Donovan, Tate NYC, Sept. 25, 1963.

Doohan, James Vancouver, British Columbia, Mar. 3, 1920. Neighborhood Playhouse.
Dooley, Paul Parkersburg WV, Feb. 22, 1928. U WV.
Dorff, Stephen Atlanta, GA, July 29, 1973.
Doug, Doug E. (Douglas Bourne) Brooklyn, NY, Jan. 7, 1970.
Douglas, Donna (Dorothy Bourgeois) Baywood, LA, Sept. 26, 1935.
Douglas, Illeana MA, July 25, 1965.
Douglas, Kirk (Issur Danielovitch) Amsterdam, NY, Dec. 9, 1916. St. Lawrence U.
Douglas, Michael New Brunswick, NJ, Sept. 25, 1944. U California.
Douglass, Robyn Sendai, Japan, June 21, 1953. UC Davis.
Dourif, Brad Huntington, WV, Mar. 18, 1950. Marshall U.
Down, Lesley-Anne London, England, Mar. 17, 1954.
Downey, Robert, Jr. NYC, Apr. 4, 1965.
Drake, Betsy Paris, France, Sept. 11, 1923.
Drescher, Fran Queens, NY, Sept. 30, 1957.
Dreyfuss, Richard Brooklyn, NY, Oct. 19, 1947.
Drillinger, Brian Brooklyn, NY, June 27, 1960. SUNY/Purchase.
Driver, Minnie (Amelia Driver) London, England, Jan. 31, 1971.
Duchovny, David NYC, Aug. 7, 1960. Yale.
Dudikoff, Michael Torrance, CA, Oct. 8, 1954.
Duff, Hilary Houston, TX, Sept. 28, 1987.
Dugan, Dennis Wheaton, IL, Sept. 5, 1946.
Dukakis, Olympia Lowell, MA, June 20, 1931.
Duke, Bill Poughkeepsie, NY, Feb. 26, 1943. NYU.
Duke, Patty (Anna Marie) NYC, Dec. 14, 1946.
Dullea, Keir Cleveland, NJ, May 30, 1936. San Francisco State College.
Dunaway, Faye Bascom, FL, Jan. 14, 1941, Florida U.
Duncan, Sandy Henderson, TX, Feb. 20, 1946. Len Morris College.
Dunne, Griffin NYC, June 8, 1955. Neighborhood Playhouse.
Dunst, Kirsten Point Pleasant, NJ, Apr. 30, 1982.
Duperey, Anny Paris, France, June 28, 1947.
Durbin, Deanna (Edna) Winnipeg, Canada, Dec. 4, 1921.
Durning, Charles S. Highland Falls, NY, Feb. 28, 1923. NYU.
Dushku, Eliza Boston, Dec. 30, 1980.
Dussollier, André Annecy, France, Feb. 17, 1946.
Dutton, Charles Baltimore, MD, Jan. 30, 1951. Yale.
DuVall, Clea Los Angeles, CA, Sept. 25, 1977.
Duvall, Robert San Diego, CA, Jan. 5, 1931. Principia College.
Duvall, Shelley Houston, TX, July 7, 1949.
Dysart, Richard Brighton, ME, Mar. 30, 1929.
Dzundza, George Rosenheim, Germany, July 19, 1945.

Easton, Robert Milwaukee, WI, Nov. 23, 1930. U Texas.
Eastwood, Clint San Francisco, CA, May 31, 1931. LACC.
Eaton, Shirley London, England, 1937. Aida Foster School.
Eckemyr, Agneta Karlsborg, Sweden, July 2. Actors Studio.
Eckhart, Aaron Santa Clara, CA, Mar. 12, 1968.
Edelman, Gregg Chicago, IL, Sept. 12, 1958. Northwestern.
Eden, Barbara (Huffman) Tucson, AZ, Aug. 23, 1934.
Edwards, Anthony Santa Barbara, CA, July 19, 1962. RADA.
Edwards, Luke Nevada City, CA, Mar. 24, 1980.
Eggar, Samantha London, England, Mar. 5, 1939.
Eichhorn, Lisa Reading, PA, Feb. 4, 1952. Queens Ont. U RADA.

Eikenberry, Jill New Haven, CT, Jan. 21, 1947.
Eilber, Janet Detroit, MI, July 27, 1951. Juilliard.
Ekberg, Anita Malmo, Sweden, Sept. 29, 1931.
Ekland, Britt Stockholm, Sweden, Oct. 6, 1942.
Eldard, Ron Long Island, NY, Feb. 20, 1965.
Elfman, Jenna (Jennifer Mary Batula) Los Angeles, CA, Sept. 30, 1971.
Elizondo, Hector NYC, Dec. 22, 1936.
Elliott, Alison San Francisco, CA, May 19, 1970.
Elliott, Chris NYC, May 31, 1960.
Elliott, Patricia Gunnison, CO, July 21, 1942. UColorado.
Elliott, Sam Sacramento, CA, Aug. 9, 1944. U Oregon.
Elwes, Cary London, England, Oct. 26, 1962.
Ely, Ron (Ronald Pierce) Hereford, TX, June 21, 1938.
Embry, Ethan (Ethan Randall) Huntington Beach, CA, June 13, 1978.
Englund, Robert Glendale, CA, June 6, 1949.
Epps, Omar Brooklyn, NY, July 23, 1973.
Erbe, Kathryn Newton, MA, July 2, 1966.
Erdman, Richard Enid, OK, June 1, 1925.
Ericson, John Dusseldorf, Germany, Sept. 25, 1926. AADA.
Ermey, R. Lee (Ronald) Emporia, KS, Mar. 24, 1944.
Esmond, Carl (Willy Eichberger) Vienna, June 14, 1906. U Vienna.
Esposito, Giancarlo Copenhagen, Denmark, Apr. 26, 1958.
Estevez, Emilio NYC, May 12, 1962.
Estrada, Erik NYC, Mar. 16, 1949.
Evans, Chris Sudbury, MA, June 13, 1981.
Evans, Josh NYC, Jan. 16, 1971.
Evans, Linda (Evanstad) Hartford, CT, Nov. 18, 1942.
Everett, Chad (Ray Cramton) South Bend, IN, June 11, 1936.
Everett, Rupert Norfolk, England, May 29, 1959.
Evigan, Greg South Amboy, NJ, Oct. 14, 1953.

Fabares, Shelley Los Angeles, CA, Jan. 19, 1944.
Fabian (Fabian Forte) Philadelphia, Feb. 6, 1943.
Fabray, Nanette (Ruby Nanette Fabares) San Diego, Oct. 27, 1920.
Fahey, Jeff Olean, NY, Nov. 29, 1956.
Fairchild, Morgan (Patsy McClenny) Dallas, TX, Feb. 3, 1950. UCLA.
Falco, Edie Brooklyn, NY, July 5, 1963.
Falk, Peter NYC, Sept. 16, 1927. New School.
Fallon, Jimmy Brooklyn, NY, Sept. 19, 1974.
Fanning, Dakota Conyers, GA, Feb. 23, 1994.
Farentino, James Brooklyn, NY, Feb. 24, 1938. AADA.
Fargas, Antonio Bronx, NY, Aug. 14, 1946.
Farina, Dennis Chicago, IL, Feb. 29, 1944.
Farina, Sandy (Sandra Feldman) Newark, NJ, 1955.
Farr, Felicia Westchester, NY, Oct. 4. 1932. Penn State College.
Farrell, Colin Castleknock, Ireland, Mar. 31, 1976.
Farrow, Mia (Maria) Los Angeles, CA, Feb. 9, 1945.
Faulkner, Graham London, England, Sept. 26, 1947. Webber-Douglas.
Favreau, Jon Queens, NY, Oct. 16, 1966.
Fawcett, Farrah Corpus Christie, TX, Feb. 2, 1947. Texas U.
Feinstein, Alan NYC, Sept. 8, 1941.
Feldman, Corey Encino, CA, July 16, 1971.
Feldon, Barbara (Hall) Pittsburgh, Mar. 12, 1941. Carnegie Tech.
Feldshuh, Tovah NYC, Dec. 27, 1953, Sarah Lawrence College.

Fellows, Edith Boston, MA, May 20, 1923.
Fenn, Sherilyn Detroit, MI, Feb. 1, 1965.
Ferrell, Conchata Charleston, WV, Mar. 28, 1943. Marshall U.
Ferrell, Will Irvine, CA, July 16, 1968.
Ferrer, Mel Elbeton, NJ, Aug. 25, 1912. Princeton U.
Ferrer, Miguel Santa Monica, CA, Feb. 7, 1954.
Ferrera, America Los Angeles, CA, Apr. 18, 1984.
Ferris, Barbara London, England, July 27, 1942.
Fledler, John Plateville, WI, Feb. 3, 1925.
Field, Sally Pasadena, CA, Nov. 6, 1946.
Field, Shirley-Anne London, England, June 27, 1938.
Field, Todd (William Todd Field) Pomona, CA, Feb. 24, 1964.
Fiennes, Joseph Salisbury, Wiltshire, England, May 27, 1970.
Fiennes, Ralph Suffolk, England, Dec. 22, 1962. RADA.
Fierstein, Harvey Brooklyn, NY, June 6, 1954. Pratt Institute.
Finch, Jon Caterham, England, Mar. 2, 1941.
Finlay, Frank Farnworth, England, Aug. 6, 1926.
Finney, Albert Salford, Lancashire, England, May 9, 1936. RADA.
Fiorentino, Linda Philadelphia, PA, Mar. 9, 1960.
Firth, Colin Grayshott, Hampshire, England, Sept. 10, 1960.
Firth, Peter Bradford, England, Oct. 27, 1953.
Fishburne, Laurence Augusta, GA, July 30, 1961.
Fisher, Carrie Los Angeles, CA, Oct. 21, 1956. London Central School of Drama.
Fisher, Eddie Philadelphia, PA, Aug. 10, 1928.
Fisher, Frances Milford-on-the-Sea, England, May 11, 1952.
Fitzgerald, Geraldine Dublin, Ireland, Nov. 24, 1914. Dublin Art School.
Fitzgerald, Tara London, England, Sept. 17, 1968.
Flagg, Fannie Birmingham, AL, Sept. 21, 1944. U Alabama.
Flanagan, Fionnula Dublin, Dec. 10, 1941.
Flannery, Susan Jersey City, NJ, July 31, 1943.
Fleming, Rhonda (Marilyn Louis) Los Angeles, CA, Aug. 10, 1922.
Flemyng, Robert Liverpool, England, Jan. 3, 1912. Haileybury College.
Fletcher, Louise Birmingham, AL, July 22 1934.
Flockhart, Calista Stockton, IL, Nov. 11, Rutgers U.
Foch, Nina Leyden, Holland, Apr. 20, 1924.
Foley, Dave Toronto, Canada, Jan. 4, 1963.
Follows, Megan Toronto, Canada, Mar. 14, 1968.
Fonda, Bridget Los Angeles, CA, Jan. 27, 1964.
Fonda, Jane NYC, Dec. 21, 1937. Vassar.
Fonda, Peter NYC, Feb. 23, 1939. U Omaha.
Fontaine, Joan Tokyo, Japan, Oct. 22, 1917.
Foote, Hallie NYC, 1953. U New Hampshire.
Ford, Glenn (Gwyllyn Samuel Newton Ford) Quebec, Canada, May 1, 1916.
Ford, Harrison Chicago, IL, July 13, 1942. Ripon College.
Forest, Mark (Lou Degni) Brooklyn, NY, Jan. 1933.
Forlani, Claire London, England, July 1, 1972.
Forrest, Frederic Waxahachie, TX, Dec. 23, 1936.
Forrest, Steve Huntsville, TX, Sept. 29, 1924. UCLA.
Forslund, Connie San Diego, CA, June 19, 1950. NYU.
Forster, Robert (Foster, Jr.) Rochester, NY, July 13, 1941. Rochester U.
Forsythe, John (Freund) Penn's Grove, NJ, Jan. 29, 1918.
Forsythe, William Brooklyn, NY, June 7, 1955.
Fossey, Brigitte Tourcoing, France, Mar. 11, 1947.
Foster, Ben Boston, MA, Oct. 29, 1980.

Calista Flockhart

Michael Gambon

Jeff Goldblum

Anne Hathaway

Foster, Jodie (Ariane Munker) Bronx, NY, Nov. 19, 1962. Yale.
Foster, Meg Reading, PA, May 14, 1948.
Fox, Edward London, England, Apr. 13, 1937. RADA.
Fox, James London, England, May 19, 1939.
Fox, Michael J. Vancouver, British Columbia, June 9, 1961.
Fox, Vivica A. Indianapolis, July 30, 1964.
Foxworth, Robert Houston, TX, Nov. 1, 1941. Carnegie Tech.
Foxx, Jamie Terrell, TX, Dec. 13, 1967.
Frain, James Leeds, England, Mar. 14, 1969.
Frakes, Jonathan Bethlehem, PA, Aug. 19, 1952. Harvard.
Franciosa, Anthony (Papaleo) NYC, Oct. 25, 1928.
Francis, Anne Ossining, NY, Sept. 16, 1932.
Francis, Arlene (Arlene Kazanjian) Boston, Oct. 20, 1908. Finch School.
Francis, Connie (Constance Franconero) Newark, NJ, Dec. 12, 1938.
Francks, Don Vancouver, Canada, Feb. 28, 1932.
Franklin, Pamela Tokyo, Feb. 4, 1950.
Franz, Arthur Perth Amboy, NJ, Feb. 29, 1920. Blue Ridge College.
Franz, Dennis Chicago, IL, Oct. 28, 1944.
Fraser, Brendan Indianapolis, IN, Dec. 3, 1968.
Frazier, Sheila NYC, Nov. 13, 1948.
Frechette, Peter Warwick, RI, Oct. 1956. U Rhoad Island.
Freeman, Al, Jr. San Antonio, TX, Mar. 21, 1934. CCLA.
Freeman, Mona Baltimore, MD, June 9, 1926.
Freeman, Morgan Memphis, TN, June 1, 1937. LACC.
Frewer, Matt Washington, DC, Jan. 4, 1958, Old Vic.
Fricker, Brenda Dublin, Ireland, Feb. 17, 1945.
Friels, Colin Glasgow, Scotland, Sept. 25, 1952.
Fry, Stephen Hampstead, London, England, Aug. 24, 1957.
Fuller, Penny Durham, NC, 1940. Northwestern.
Funicello, Annette Utica, NY, Oct. 22, 1942.
Furlong, Edward Glendale, CA, Aug. 2, 1977.
Furneaux, Yvonne Lille, France, May 11, 1928. Oxford U.

Gable, John Clark Los Angeles, CA, Mar. 20, 1961. Santa Monica College.
Gabor, Zsa Zsa (Sari Gabor) Budapest, Hungary, Feb. 6, 1918.
Gail, Max Derfoil, MI, Apr. 5, 1943.
Gaines, Boyd Atlanta, GA, May 11, 1953. Juilliard.

Galecki, Johnny Bree, Belgium, Apr. 30, 1975.
Gallagher, Peter NYC, Aug. 19, 1955. Tufts U.
Galligan, Zach NYC, Feb. 14, 1963. Columbia U.
Gallo, Vincent Buffalo, NY, Apr. 11, 1961.
Gam, Rita Pittsburgh, PA, Apr. 2, 1928.
Gamble, Mason Chicago, IL, Jan. 16, 1986.
Gambon, Michael Dublin, Ireland, Oct. 19, 1940.
Gandolfini, James Westwood, NJ, Sept. 18, 1961.
Ganz, Bruno Zurich, Switzerland, Mar. 22, 1941.
Garber, Victor Montreal, Canada, Mar. 16, 1949.
Garcia, Adam Wahroonga, New So. Wales, Australia, June 1, 1973.
Garcia, Andy Havana, Cuba, Apr. 12, 1956. FlaInt.
Garfield, Allen (Allen Goorwitz) Newark, NJ, Nov. 22, 1939. Actors Studio.
Garfunkel, Art NYC, Nov. 5, 1941.
Garland, Beverly Santa Cruz, CA, Oct. 17, 1926. Glendale College.
Garner, James (James Baumgarner) Norman, OK, Apr. 7, 1928. Okla U.
Garner, Jennifer Houston, TX, Apr. 17, 1972.
Garofalo, Janeane Newton, NJ, Sept. 28, 1964.
Garr, Teri Lakewood, OH, Dec. 11, 1949.
Garrett, Betty St. Joseph, MO, May 23, 1919. Annie Wright Seminary.
Garrison, Sean NYC, Oct. 19, 1937.
Gary, Lorraine NYC, Aug. 16, 1937.
Gavin, John Los Angeles, CA, Apr. 8, 1935. Stanford U.
Gaylord, Mitch Van Nuys, CA, Mar. 10, 1961. UCLA.
Gaynor, Mitzi (Francesca Marlene Von Gerber) Chicago, IL, Sept. 4, 1930.
Gazzara, Ben NYC, Aug. 28, 1930. Actors Studio.
Geary, Anthony Coalsville, UT, May 29, 1947. U Utah.
Gedrick, Jason Chicago, IL, Feb. 7, 1965. Drake U.
Geeson, Judy Arundel, England, Sept. 10, 1948. Corona.
Gellar, Sarah Michelle NYC, Apr. 14, 1977.
Geoffreys, Stephen (Miller) Cincinnati, OH, Nov. 22, 1959. NYU.
George, Susan West London, England, England, July 26, 1950.
Gerard, Gil Little Rock, AR, Jan. 23, 1940.
Gere, Richard Philadelphia, PA, Aug. 29, 1949. U Mass.
Gerroll, Daniel London, England, Oct. 16, 1951. Central.
Gershon, Gina Los Angeles, CA, June 10, 1962.
Gertz, Jami Chicago, IL, Oct. 28, 1965.

Getty, Balthazar Los Angeles, CA, Jan. 22, 1975.
Getty, Estelle NYC, July 25, 1923. New School.
Gholson, Julie Birmingham, AL, June 4, 1958.
Ghostley, Alice Eve, MO, Aug. 14, 1926. Oklahoma U.
Giamatti, Paul NYC, June 6, 1967.
Giannini, Giancarlo Spezia, Italy, Aug. 1, 1942. Rome Academy of Drama.
Gibb, Cynthia Bennington, VT, Dec. 14, 1963.
Gibson, Henry Germantown, PA, Sept. 21, 1935.
Gibson, Mel Peekskill, NY, Jan. 3, 1956. NIDA.
Gibson, Thomas Charleston, SC, July 3, 1962.
Gift, Roland Birmingham, England, May 28 1962.
Gilbert, Melissa Los Angeles, CA, May 8, 1964.
Giles, Nancy NYC, July 17, 1960, Oberlin College.
Gillette, Anita Baltimore, MD, Aug. 16, 1938.
Gilliam, Terry Minneapolis, MN, Nov. 22, 1940.
Gillis, Ann (Alma O'Connor) Little Rock, AR, Feb. 12, 1927.
Ginty, Robert NYC, Nov. 14, 1948. Yale.
Girardot, Annie Paris, France, Oct. 25, 1931.
Gish, Annabeth Albuquerque, NM, Mar. 13, 1971. Duke U.
Givens, Robin NYC, Nov. 27, 1964.
Glaser, Paul Michael Boston, MA, Mar. 25, 1943. Boston U.
Glass, Ron Evansville, IN, July 10, 1945.
Gleason, Joanna Winnipeg, Canada, June 2, 1950. UCLA.
Gleason, Paul Jersey City, NJ, May 4, 1944.
Gleeson, Brendan Belfast, Nov. 9, 1955.
Glenn, Scott Pittsburgh, PA, Jan. 26, 1942. William and Mary College.
Glover, Crispin NYC, Sept 20, 1964.
Glover, Danny San Francisco, CA, July 22, 1947. San Francisco State U.
Glover, John Kingston, NY, Aug. 7, 1944.
Glynn, Carlin Cleveland, Oh, Feb. 19, 1940. Actors Studio.
Goldberg, Whoopi (Caryn Johnson) NYC, Nov. 13, 1949.
Goldblum, Jeff Pittsburgh, PA, Oct. 22, 1952. Neighborhood Playhouse.
Golden, Annie Brooklyn, NY, Oct. 19, 1951.
Goldstein, Jenette Beverly Hills, CA, Feb. 4, 1960.
Goldthwait, Bob Syracuse, NY, May 1, 1962.
Goldwyn, Tony Los Angeles, CA, May 20, 1960. LAMDA.
Golino, Valeria Naples, Italy, Oct. 22, 1966.
Gonzales-Gonzalez, Pedro Aguilares, TX, Dec. 21, 1926.
Gonzalez, Cordelia Aug. 11, 1958, San Juan, PR. UPR.
Goodall, Caroline London, England, Nov. 13, 1959. Bristol U.
Gooding, Cuba, Jr. Bronx, N.Y., Jan. 2, 1968.
Goodman, Dody Columbus, OH, Oct. 28, 1915.
Goodman, John St. Louis, MO, June 20, 1952.
Gordon, Keith NYC, Feb. 3, 1961.
Gordon-Levitt, Joseph Los Angeles, CA, Feb. 17, 1981.
Gorshin, Frank Pittsburgh, PA, Apr. 5, 1933.
Gortner, Marjoe Long Beach, CA, Jan. 14, 1944.
Gosling, Ryan London, Ontario, Nov. 12, 1980.
Goss, Luke London, England, Sept. 28, 1968.
Gossett, Louis, Jr. Brooklyn, NY, May 27, 1936. NYU.
Gould, Elliott (Goldstein) Brooklyn, NY, Aug. 29, 1938. Columbia U.
Gould, Harold Schenectady, NY, Dec. 10, 1923. Cornell.
Gould, Jason NYC, Dec. 29, 1966.
Goulet, Robert Lawrence, MA, Nov. 26, 1933. Edmonton.

Grace, Topher NYC, July 12, 1978.
Graf, David Lancaster, OH, Apr. 16, 1950. Ohio State U.
Graff, Todd NYC, Oct. 22, 1959. SUNY/ Purchase.
Graham, Heather Milwaukee, WI, Jan. 29, 1970.
Granger, Farley San Jose, CA, July 1, 1925.
Grant, David Marshall Westport, CT, June 21, 1955. Yale.
Grant, Hugh London, England, Sept. 9, 1960. Oxford.
Grant, Kathryn (Olive Grandstaff) Houston, TX, Nov. 25, 1933. UCLA.
Grant, Lee NYC, Oct. 31, 1927. Juilliard.
Grant, Richard E Mbabane, Swaziland, May 5, 1957. Cape Town U.
Graves, Peter (Aurness) Minneapolis, Mar. 18, 1926. U Minnesota.
Graves, Rupert Weston-Super-Mare, England, June 30, 1963.
Gray, Coleen (Doris Jensen) Staplehurst, NB, Oct. 23, 1922. Hamline.
Gray, Linda Santa Monica, CA, Sept. 12, 1940.
Grayson, Kathryn (Zelma Hedrick) Winston-Salem, NC, Feb. 9, 1922.
Green, Kerri Fort Lee, NJ, Jan. 14, 1967. Vassar.
Green, Seth Philadelphia, PA, Feb. 8, 1974.
Greene, Ellen NYC, Feb. 22, 1950. Ryder College.
Greene, Graham Six Nations Reserve, Ontario, June 22, 1952.
Greenwood, Bruce Quebec, Canada, Aug. 12, 1956.
Greer, Michael Galesburg, IL, Apr. 20, 1943.
Greist, Kim Stamford, CT, May 12, 1958.
Grey, Jennifer NYC, Mar. 26, 1960.
Grey, Joel (Katz) Cleveland, OH, Apr. 11, 1932.
Grieco, Richard Watertown, NY, Mar. 23, 1965.
Grier, David Alan Detroit, MI, June 30, 1955. Yale.
Grier, Pam Winston-Salem, NC, May 26, 1949.
Griffin, Eddie Kansas City, MO, July 15, 1968.
Griffith, Andy Mt. Airy, NC, June 1, 1926. U North Carolina.
Griffith, Melanie NYC, Aug. 9, 1957. Pierce Collge.
Griffith, Thomas Ian Hartford, CT, Mar. 18, 1962.
Griffiths, Rachel Melbourne, Australia, 1968.
Griffiths, Richard Tornaby-on-Tees, England, July 31, 1947.
Grimes, Gary San Francisco, June 2, 1955.
Grimes, Scott Lowell, MA, July 9, 1971.
Grimes, Tammy Lynn, MA, Jan. 30, 1934. Stephens College.
Grizzard, George Roanoke Rapids, NC, Apr. 1, 1928. U North Carolina.
Grodin, Charles Pittsburgh, PA, Apr. 21, 1935.
Groh, David NYC, May 21, 1939. Brown U, LAMDA.
Gross, Mary Chicago, IL, Mar. 25, 1953.
Gross, Michael Chicago, IL, June 21, 1947.
Gruffud, Ioan Cardiff, Wales, Oct. 6, 1973.
Guest, Christopher NYC, Feb. 5, 1948.
Guest, Lance Saratoga, CA, July 21, 1960. UCLA.
Guillaume, Robert (Williams) St. Louis, MO, Nov. 30, 1937.
Guiry, Thomas Trenton, NJ, Oct. 12, 1981.
Gulager, Clu Holdenville, OK, Nov. 16 1928.
Guttenberg, Steve Massapequa, NY, Aug. 24, 1958. UCLA.
Guy, Jasmine Boston, Mar. 10, 1964.
Gyllenhaal, Jake Los Angeles, CA, Dec. 19, 1980.
Gyllenhaal, Maggie Los Angeles, CA, Nov. 16, 1977.

Haas, Lukas West Hollywood, CA, Apr. 16, 1976.
Hack, Shelley Greenwich, CT, July 6, 1952.

Hackman, Gene San Bernardino, CA, Jan. 30, 1930.
Hagerty, Julie Cincinnati, OH, June 15, 1955. Juilliard.
Hagman, Larry (Hageman) Weatherford, TX, Sept. 21, 1931. Bard.
Haid, Charles San Francisco, June 2, 1943. Carnegie Tech.
Haim, Corey Toronto, Canada, Dec. 23, 1972.
Hale, Barbara DeKalb, IL, Apr. 18, 1922. Chicago Academy of Fine Arts.
Haley, Jackie Earle Northridge, CA, July 14, 1961.
Hall, Albert Boothton, AL, Nov. 10, 1937. Columbia.
Hall, Anthony Michael Boston, MA, Apr. 14, 1968.
Hall, Arsenio Cleveland, OH, Feb. 12, 1959.
Hamel, Veronica Philadelphia, PA, Nov. 20, 1943.
Hamill, Mark Oakland, CA, Sept. 25, 1952. LACC.
Hamilton, George Memphis, TN, Aug. 12, 1939. Hackley.
Hamilton, Linda Salisbury, MD, Sept. 26, 1956.
Hamlin, Harry Pasadena, CA, Oct. 30, 1951.
Hampshire, Susan London, England, May 12, 1941.
Hampton, James Oklahoma City, OK, July 9, 1936. Northern Texas State U.
Han, Maggie Providence, RI, 1959.
Handler, Evan NYC, Jan. 10, 1961. Juillard.
Hanks, Colin Sacramento, CA, Nov. 24, 1977.
Hanks, Tom Concord, CA, Jul. 9, 1956. California State U.
Hannah, Daryl Chicago, IL, Dec. 3, 1960. UCLA.
Hannah, Page Chicago, IL, Apr. 13, 1964.
Harden, Marcia Gay LaJolla, CA, Aug. 14, 1959.
Hardin, Ty (Orison Whipple Hungerford, II) NYC, June 1, 1930.
Harewood, Dorian Dayton, OH, Aug. 6, 1950. U Cinncinatti.
Harmon, Mark Los Angeles, CA, Sept. 2, 1951. UCLA.
Harper, Jessica Chicago, IL, Oct. 10, 1949.
Harper, Tess Mammoth Spring, AK, 1952. South Western Misourri State.
Harper, Valerie Suffern, NY, Aug. 22, 1940.
Harrelson, Woody Midland, TX, July 23, 1961. Hanover College.
Harrington, Pat NYC, Aug. 13, 1929. Fordham U.
Harris, Barbara (Sandra Markowitz) Evanston, IL, July 25, 1935.
Harris, Ed Tenafly, NJ, Nov. 28, 1950. Columbia.
Harris, Jared UK, Aug. 24, 1961.
Harris, Julie Grosse Point, MI, Dec. 2, 1925. Yale Drama School.
Harris, Mel (Mary Ellen) Bethlehem, PA, 1957. Columbia.
Harris, Neil Patrick Albuquerque, NM, June 15, 1973.
Harris, Rosemary Ashby, England, Sept. 19, 1930. RADA.
Harrison, Gregory Catalina Island, CA, May 31, 1950. Actors Studio.
Harrison, Noel London, England, Jan. 29, 1936.
Harrold, Kathryn Tazewell, VA, Aug. 2, 1950. Mills College.
Harry, Deborah Miami, IL, July 1, 1945.
Hart, Ian Liverpool, England, Oct. 8, 1964.
Hart, Roxanne Trenton, NJ, July 27, 1952. Princeton.
Hartley, Mariette NYC, June 21, 1941.
Hartman, David Pawtucket, RI, May 19, 1935. Duke U.
Hartnett, Josh San Francisco, July 21, 1978.
Hassett, Marilyn Los Angeles, CA, Dec. 17, 1947.
Hatcher, Teri Sunnyvale, CA, Dec. 8, 1964.
Hathaway, Anne Brooklyn, Nov. 12, 1982.
Hatosy, Shawn Fredrick, MD, Dec. 29, 1975.
Hauer, Rutger Amsterdam, Holland, Jan. 23, 1944.
Hauser, Cole Santa Barbara, CA, Mar. 22, 1975.

Hasuer, Wings (Gerald Dwight Hauser) Hollywood, CA, Dec. 12, 1947.
Haver, June Rock Island, IL, June 10, 1926.
Havoc, June (Hovick) Seattle, WA, Nov. 8, 1916.
Hawke, Ethan Austin, TX, Nov. 6, 1970.
Hawn, Goldie Washington, DC, Nov. 21, 1945.
Hayek, Salma Coatzacoalcos, Veracruz, Mexico, Sept. 2, 1968.
Hayes, Isaac Covington, TN, Aug. 20, 1942.
Hays, Robert Bethesda, MD, July 24, 1947. South Dakota State College.
Haysbert, Dennis San Mateo, CA, June 2, 1954.
Headly, Glenne New London, CT, Mar. 13, 1955. AmCollege.
Heald, Anthony New Rochelle, NY, Aug. 25, 1944. Michigan State U.
Heard, John Washington, DC, Mar. 7, 1946. Clark U.
Heatherton, Joey NYC, Sept. 14, 1944.
Heche, Anne Aurora, OH, May 25, 1969.
Hedaya, Dan Brooklyn, NY, July 24, 1940.
Heder, Jon Fort Collins, CO, Oct. 26, 1977.
Hedison, David Providence, RI, May 20, 1929. Brown U.
Hedren, Tippi (Natalie) Lafayette, MN, Jan. 19, 1931.
Hegyes, Robert Metuchen, NJ, May 7, 1951.
Helmond, Katherine Galveston, TX, July 5, 1934.
Hemingway, Mariel Ketchum, ID, Nov. 22, 1961.
Hemsley, Sherman Philadelphia, PA, Feb. 1, 1938.
Henderson, Florence Dale, IN, Feb. 14, 1934.
Hendry, Gloria Winter Have, FL, Mar. 3, 1949.
Henner, Marilu Chicago, IL, Apr. 6, 1952.
Henriksen, Lance NYC, May 5, 1940.
Henry, Buck (Henry Zuckerman) NYC, Dec. 9, 1930. Dartmouth.
Henry, Justin Rye, NY, May 25, 1971.
Henstridge, Natasha Springdale, Newfoundland, Canada, Aug. 15, 1974.
Herrmann, Edward Washington, DC, July 21, 1943. Bucknell, LAMDA.
Hershey, Barbara (Herzstein) Hollywood, CA, Feb. 5, 1948.
Hesseman, Howard Lebanon, OR, Feb. 27, 1940.
Heston, Charlton Evanston, IL, Oct. 4, 1922. Northwestern.
Hewitt, Jennifer Love Waco, TX, Feb. 21, 1979.
Hewitt, Martin Claremont, CA, Feb. 19, 1958. AADA.
Heywood, Anne (Violet Pretty) Birmingham, England, Dec. 11, 1932.
Hickman, Darryl Hollywood, CA, July 28, 1933. Loyola U.
Hickman, Dwayne Los Angeles, CA, May 18, 1934. Loyola U.
Hicks, Catherine NYC, Aug. 6, 1951. Notre Dame.
Higgins, Anthony (Corlan) Cork City, Ireland, May 9, 1947. Birmingham Dramatic Arts.
Higgins, Michael Brooklyn, NY, Jan. 20, 1921. AmThWing.
Hill, Arthur Saskatchewan, Canada, Aug. 1, 1922. U Brit. College.
Hill, Bernard Manchester, England, Dec. 17, 1944.
Hill, Steven Seattle, WA, Feb. 24, 1922. U Wash.
Hill, Terrence (Mario Girotti) Venice, Italy, Mar. 29, 1941. U Rome.
Hillerman, John Denison, TX, Dec. 20, 1932.
Hinds, Ciaran Belfast, Northern Ireland, Feb. 9, 1953.
Hines, Gregory NYC, Feb. 14, 1946.
Hingle, Pat Denver, CO, July 19, 1923. Tex. U.
Hirsch, Emile Topanga Canyon, CA, Mar. 13, 1985.
Hirsch, Judd NYC, Mar. 15, 1935. AADA.
Hobel, Mara NYC, June 18, 1971.
Hodge, Patricia Lincolnshire, England, Sept. 29, 1946. LAMDA.

Buck Henry

Kate Hudson

Anjelica Huston

Ray Liotta

Hoffman, Dustin Los Angeles, CA, Aug. 8, 1937. Pasadena Playhouse.
Hoffman, Philip Seymour Fairport, NY, July 23, 1967.
Hogan, Jonathan Chicago, IL, June 13, 1951.
Hogan, Paul Lightning Ridge, Australia, Oct. 8, 1939.
Holbrook, Hal (Harold) Cleveland, OH, Feb. 17, 1925. Denison.
Holliman, Earl Tennessa Swamp, Delhi, LA, Sept. 11, 1928. UCLA.
Holm, Celeste NYC, Apr. 29, 1919.
Holm, Ian Ilford, Essex, England, Sept. 12, 1931. RADA.
Holmes, Katie Toledo, OH, Dec. 18, 1978.
Homeier, Skip (George Vincent Homeier) Chicago, IL, Oct. 5, 1930. UCLA.
Hooks, Robert Washington, DC, Apr. 18, 1937. Temple.
Hopkins, Anthony Port Talbot, So. Wales, Dec. 31, 1937. RADA.
Hopper, Dennis Dodge City, KS, May 17, 1936.
Horne, Lena Brooklyn, NY, June 30, 1917.
Horrocks, Jane Rossendale Valley, England, Jan. 18, 1964.
Horsley, Lee Muleshoe, TX, May 15, 1955.
Horton, Robert Los Angeles, CA, July 29, 1924. UCLA.
Hoskins, Bob Bury St. Edmunds, England, Oct. 26, 1942.
Houghton, Katharine Hartford, CT, Mar. 10, 1945. Sarah Lawrence.
Hounsou, Djimon Benin, West Africa, Apr. 24, 1964.
Houser, Jerry Los Angeles, CA, July 14, 1952. Valley, Jr. College.
Howard, Arliss Independence, MO, 1955. Columbia College.
Howard, Ken El Centro, CA, Mar. 28, 1944. Yale.
Howard, Ron Duncan, OK, Mar. 1, 1954. USC.
Howell, C. Thomas Los Angeles, CA, Dec. 7, 1966.
Howells, Ursula London, England, Sept. 17, 1922.
Howes, Sally Ann London, England, July 20, 1930.
Howland, Beth Boston, MA, May 28, 1941.
Hubley, Season NYC, May 14, 1951.
Huddleston, David Vinton, VA, Sept. 17, 1930.
Hudson, Ernie Benton Harbor, MI, Dec. 17, 1945.
Hudson, Kate Los Angeles, CA, Apr. 19, 1979.
Hughes, Barnard Bedford Hills, NY, July 16, 1915. Manhattan College.
Hughes, Kathleen (Betty von Gerkan) Hollywood, CA, Nov. 14, 1928. UCLA.
Hulce, Tom Plymouth, MI, Dec. 6, 1953. North Carolina School of Arts.
Hunnicut, Gayle Ft. Worth, TX, Feb. 6, 1943. UCLA.
Hunt, Helen Los Angeles, CA, June 15, 1963.

Hunt, Linda Morristown, NJ, Apr. 1945. Goodman Theatre.
Hunt, Marsha Chicago, IL, Oct. 17, 1917.
Hunter, Holly Atlanta, GA, Mar. 20, 1958. Carnegie-Mellon.
Hunter, Tab (Arthur Gelien) NYC, July 11, 1931.
Huppert, Isabelle Paris, France, Mar. 16, 1955.
Hurley, Elizabeth Hampshire, England, June 10, 1965.
Hurt, John Lincolnshire, England, Jan. 22, 1940.
Hurt, Mary Beth (Supinger) Marshalltown, IA, Sept. 26, 1948. NYU.
Hurt, William Washington, DC, Mar. 20, 1950. Tufts, Juilliard.
Hussey, Ruth Providence, RI, Oct. 30, 1917. U Michigan.
Huston, Anjelica Santa Monica, CA, July 9, 1951.
Huston, Danny Rome, May 14, 1962.
Hutton, Betty (Betty Thornberg) Battle Creek, MI, Feb. 26, 1921.
Hutton, Lauren (Mary) Charleston, SC, Nov. 17, 1943. Newcomb College.
Hutton, Timothy Malibu, CA, Aug. 16, 1960.
Hyer, Martha Fort Worth, TX, Aug. 10, 1924. Northwestern.

Ice Cube (O'Shea Jackson) Los Angeles, CA, June 15, 1969.
Idle, Eric South Shields, Durham, England, Mar. 29, 1943. Cambridge.
Ifans, Rhys Ruthin, Wales, July 22, 1968.
Ingels, Marty Brooklyn, NY, Mar. 9, 1936.
Ireland, Kathy Santa Barbara, CA, Mar. 8, 1963.
Irons, Jeremy Cowes, England, Sept. 19, 1948. Old Vic.
Ironside, Michael Toronto, Canada, Feb. 12, 1950.
Irving, Amy Palo Alto, CA, Sept. 10, 1953. LADA.
Irwin, Bill Santa Monica, CA, Apr. 11, 1950.
Isaak, Chris Stockton, CA, June 26, 1956. U of Pacific.
Ivanek, Zeljko Lujubljana, Yugoslavia, Aug. 15, 1957. Yale, LAMDA.
Ivey, Judith El Paso, TX, Sept. 4, 1951.
Izzard, Eddie Aden, Yemen, Feb. 7, 1962.

Jackson, Anne Alleghany, PA, Sept. 3, 1926. Neighborhood Playhouse.
Jackson, Glenda Hoylake, Cheshire, England, May 9, 1936. RADA.
Jackson, Janet Gary, IN, May 16, 1966.
Jackson, Kate Birmingham, AL, Oct. 29, 1948. AADA.
Jackson, Michael Gary, IN, Aug. 29, 1958.
Jackson, Samuel L. Atlanta, Dec. 21, 1948.

Jackson, Victoria Miami, FL, Aug. 2, 1958.
Jacobi, Derek Leytonstone, London, England, Oct. 22, 1938. Cambridge.
Jacobi, Lou Toronto, Canada, Dec. 28, 1913.
Jacobs, Lawrence-Hilton Virgin Islands, Sept. 14, 1953.
Jacoby, Scott Chicago, IL, Nov. 19, 1956.
Jagger, Mick Dartford, Kent, England, July 26, 1943.
James, Clifton NYC, May 29, 1921. Oregon U.
Jane, Thomas Baltimore, MD, Jan. 29, 1969.
Janney, Allison Dayton, OH, Nov. 20, 1960. RADA.
Jarman, Claude, Jr. Nashville, TN, Sept. 27, 1934.
Jason, Rick NYC, May 21, 1926. AADA.
Jean, Gloria (Gloria Jean Schoonover) Buffalo, NY, Apr. 14, 1927.
Jeffreys, Anne (Carmichael) Goldsboro, NC, Jan. 26, 1923. Anderson College.
Jeffries, Lionel London, England, June 10, 1926. RADA.
Jergens, Adele Brooklyn, NY, Nov. 26, 1922.
Jillian, Ann (Nauseda) Cambridge, MA, Jan. 29, 1951.
Johansen, David Staten Island, NY, Jan. 9, 1950.
Johansson, Scarlett NYC, Nov. 22, 1984.
John, Elton (Reginald Dwight) Middlesex, England, Mar. 25, 1947. RAM.
Johns, Glynis Durban, S. Africa, Oct. 5, 1923.
Johnson, Don Galena, MO, Dec. 15, 1950. U Kansas.
Johnson, Page Welch, WV, Aug. 25, 1930. Ithaca.
Johnson, Rafer Hillsboro, TX, Aug. 18, 1935. UCLA.
Johnson, Richard Essex, England, July 30, 1927. RADA.
Johnson, Robin Brooklyn, NY, May 29, 1964.
Johnson, Van Newport, RI, Aug. 28, 1916.
Jolie, Angelina (Angelina Jolie Voight) Los Angeles, CA, June 4, 1975.
Jones, Cherry Paris, TN, Nov. 21, 1956.
Jones, Christopher Jackson, TN, Aug. 18, 1941. Actors Studio.
Jones, Dean Decatur, AL, Jan. 25, 1931. Actors Studio.
Jones, Grace Spanishtown, Jamaica, May 19, 1952.
Jones, Jack Bel-Air, CA, Jan. 14, 1938.
Jones, James Earl Arkabutla, MS, Jan. 17, 1931. U Michigan
Jones, Jeffrey Buffalo, NY, Sept. 28, 1947. LAMDA.
Jones, Jennifer (Phyllis Isley) Tulsa, OK, Mar. 2, 1919. AADA.
Jones, L.Q. (Justice Ellis McQueen) Aug 19, 1927.
Jones, Orlando Mobile, AL, Apr. 10, 1968.
Jones, Sam J. Chicago, IL, Aug. 12, 1954.
Jones, Shirley Smithton, PA, March 31, 1934.
Jones, Terry Colwyn Bay, Wales, Feb. 1, 1942.
Jones, Tommy Lee San Saba, TX, Sept. 15, 1946. Harvard.
Jourdan, Louis Marseilles, France, June 19, 1920.
Jovovich, Milla Kiev, Ukraine, Dec. 17, 1975.
Joy, Robert Montreal, Canada, Aug. 17, 1951. Oxford.
Judd, Ashley Los Angeles, CA, Apr. 19, 1968.

Kaczmarek, Jane Milwaukee, WI, Dec. 21, 1955.
Kane, Carol Cleveland, OH, June 18, 1952.
Kaplan, Marvin Brooklyn, NY, Jan. 24, 1924.
Kapoor, Shashi Calcutta, India, Mar. 18, 1938.
Kaprisky, Valerie (Cheres) Paris, France, Aug. 19, 1962.
Karras, Alex Gary, IN, July 15, 1935.
Kartheiser, Vincent Minneapolis, MN, May 5, 1979.

Karyo, Tcheky Istanbul, Oct. 4, 1953.
Kassovitz, Mathieu Paris, France Aug. 3, 1967.
Katt, William Los Angeles, CA, Feb. 16, 1955.
Kattan, Chris Mt. Baldy, CA, Oct. 19, 1970.
Kaufmann, Christine Lansdorf, Graz, Austria, Jan. 11, 1945.
Kavner, Julie Burbank, CA, Sept. 7, 1951. UCLA.
Kazan, Lainie (Levine) Brooklyn, NY, May 15, 1942.
Kazurinsky, Tim Johnstown, PA, March 3, 1950.
Keach, Stacy Savannah, GA, June 2, 1941. U California, Yale.
Keaton, Diane (Hall) Los Angeles, CA, Jan. 5, 1946. Neighborhood Playhouse.
Keaton, Michael Coraopolis, PA, Sept. 9, 1951. Kent State U.
Keegan, Andrew Los Angeles, CA, Jan. 29, 1979.
Keener, Catherine Miami, FL, Mar. 26, 1960.
Keeslar, Matt Grand Rapids, MI, Oct. 15, 1972.
Keitel, Harvey Brooklyn, NY, May 13, 1939.
Keith, David Knoxville, TN, May 8, 1954. U Tennessee.
Keller, Marthe Basel, Switzerland, 1945. Munich Stanislavsky School.
Kellerman, Sally Long Beach, CA, June 2, 1936. Actors Studio West.
Kelly, Moira Queens, NY, Mar. 6, 1968.
Kemp, Jeremy (Wacker) Chesterfield, England, Feb. 3, 1935. Central School.
Kennedy, George NYC, Feb. 18, 1925.
Kennedy, Leon Isaac Cleveland, OH, 1949.
Kensit, Patsy London, England, Mar. 4, 1968.
Kerr, Deborah Helensburg, Scotland, Sept. 30, 1921. Smale Ballet School.
Kerr, John NYC, Nov. 15, 1931. Harvard, Columbia.
Kerwin, Brian Chicago, IL, Oct. 25, 1949.
Keyes, Evelyn Port Arthur, TX, Nov. 20, 1919.
Kidder, Margot Yellow Knife, Canada, Oct. 17, 1948. U British Columbia.
Kidman, Nicole Hawaii, June 20, 1967.
Kiel, Richard Detroit, MI, Sept. 13, 1939.
Kier, Udo Koeln, Germany, Oct. 14, 1944.
Kilmer, Val Los Angeles, CA, Dec. 31, 1959. Juilliard.
Kincaid, Aron (Norman Neale Williams, III) Los Angeles, CA, June 15, 1943. UCLA.
King, Perry Alliance, OH, Apr. 30, 1948. Yale.
Kingsley, Ben (Krishna Bhanji) Snaiton, Yorkshire, England, Dec. 31, 1943.
Kinnear, Greg Logansport, IN, June 17, 1963.
Kinski, Nastassja Berlin, Germany, Jan. 24, 1960.
Kirby, Bruno NYC, Apr. 28, 1949.
Kirk, Tommy Louisville, KY, Dec. 10 1941.
Kirkland, Sally NYC, Oct. 31, 1944. Actors Studio.
Kitt, Eartha North, SC, Jan. 26, 1928.
Klein, Chris Hinsdale, IL, March 14, 1979.
Klein, Robert NYC, Feb. 8, 1942. Alfred U.
Kline, Kevin St. Louis, MO, Oct. 24, 1947. Juilliard.
Klugman, Jack Philadelphia, PA, Apr. 27, 1922. Carnegie Tech.
Knight, Michael E. Princeton, NJ, May 7, 1959.
Knight, Shirley Goessel, KS, July 5, 1937. Wichita U.
Knox, Elyse Hartford, CT, Dec. 14, 1917. Traphagen School.
Knoxville, Johnny (Phillip John Clapp) Knoxville, TN, March 11, 1971.
Koenig, Walter Chicago, IL, Sept. 14, 1936. UCLA.
Kohner, Susan Los Angeles, CA, Nov. 11, 1936. U California.
Korman, Harvey Chicago, IL, Feb. 15, 1927. Goodman.

Korsmo, Charlie Minneapolis, MN, July, 20, 1978.
Koteas, Elias Montreal, Quebec, Canada, 1961. AADA.
Kotto, Yaphet NYC, Nov. 15, 1937.
Kozak, Harley Jane Wilkes-Barre, PA, Jan. 28, 1957. NYU.
Krabbe, Jeroen Amsterdam, The Netherlands, Dec. 5, 1944.
Kretschmann, Thomas Dessau, East Germany, Sept. 8, 1962.
Kreuger, Kurt St. Moritz, Switzerland, July 23, 1917. U London.
Krige, Alice Upington, South Africa, June 28, 1955.
Kristel, Sylvia Amsterdam, The Netherlands, Sept. 28, 1952.
Kristofferson, Kris Brownsville, TX, June 22, 1936. Pomona College.
Kruger, Hardy Berlin, Germany, April 12, 1928.
Krumholtz, David NYC, May 15, 1978.
Kudrow, Lisa Encino, CA, July 30, 1963.
Kurtz, Swoosie Omaha, NE, Sept. 6, 1944.
Kutcher, Ashton (Christopher Ashton Kutcher.) Cedar Rapids, IA, Feb. 7, 1978.
Kwan, Nancy Hong Kong, May 19, 1939. Royal Ballet.

LaBelle, Patti Philadelphia, PA, May 24, 1944.
LaBeouf, Shia Los Angeles, CA, June 11, 1986.
Lacy, Jerry Sioux City, IA, Mar. 27, 1936. LACC.
Ladd, Cheryl (Stoppelmoor) Huron, SD. July 12, 1951.
Ladd, Diane (Ladner) Meridian, MS, Nov. 29, 1932. Tulane U.
Lahti, Christine Detroit, MI, Apr. 4, 1950. U Michigan.
Lake, Ricki NYC, Sept. 21, 1968.
Lamas, Lorenzo Los Angeles, CA, Jan. 28, 1958.
Lambert, Christopher NYC, Mar. 29, 1958.
Landau, Martin Brooklyn, NY, June 20, 1931. Actors Studio.
Landrum, Teri Enid, OK, 1960.
Lane, Abbe Brooklyn, NY, Dec. 14, 1935.
Lane, Diane NYC, Jan. 22, 1963.
Lane, Nathan Jersey City, NJ, Feb. 3, 1956.
Lang, Stephen NYC, July 11, 1952. Swarthmore College.
Lange, Jessica Cloquet, MN, Apr. 20, 1949. U Minnesota
Langella, Frank Bayonne, NJ, Jan. 1, 1940. Syracuse U.
Lansbury, Angela London, England, Oct. 16, 1925. London Academy of Music.
LaPaglia, Anthony Adelaide, Australia. Jan 31, 1959.
Larroquette, John New Orleans, LA, Nov. 25, 1947.
Lasser, Louise NYC, Apr. 11, 1939. Brandeis U.
Lathan, Sanaa NYC, Sept. 19, 1971.
Latifah, Queen (Dana Owens) East Orange, NJ, 1970.
Laughlin, John Memphis, TN, Apr. 3.
Laughlin, Tom Minneapolis, MN, 1938.
Lauper, Cyndi Astoria, Queens, NYC, June 20, 1953.
Laure, Carole Montreal, Canada, Aug. 5, 1951.
Laurie, Hugh Oxford, England, June 11, 1959.
Laurie, Piper (Rosetta Jacobs) Detroit, MI, Jan. 22, 1932.
Lauter, Ed Long Beach, NY, Oct. 30, 1940.
Lavin, Linda Portland, ME, Oct. 15 1939.
Law, John Phillip Hollywood, CA, Sept. 7, 1937. Neighborhood Playhouse, U Hawaii.
Law, Jude Lewisham, England, Dec. 29, 1972.
Lawrence, Barbara Carnegie, OK, Feb. 24, 1930. UCLA.
Lawrence, Carol (Laraia) Melrose Park, IL, Sept. 5, 1935.
Lawrence, Martin Frankfurt, Germany, Apr. 16, 1965.

Lawrence, Vicki Inglewood, CA, Mar. 26, 1949.
Lawson, Leigh Atherston, England, July 21, 1945. RADA.
Leachman, Cloris Des Moines, IA, Apr. 30, 1930. Northwestern.
Leary, Denis Boston, MA, Aug. 18, 1957.
Léaud, Jean-Pierre Paris, France, May 5, 1944.
LeBlanc, Matt Newton, MA, July 25, 1967.
Ledger, Heath Perth, Australia, Apr. 4, 1979.
Lee, Christopher London, England, May 27, 1922. Wellington College.
Lee, Jason Huntington Beach, CA, Apr. 25, 1970.
Lee, Mark Sydney, Australia, 1958.
Lee, Michele (Dusiak) Los Angeles, CA, June 24, 1942. LACC.
Lee, Sheryl Augsburg, Germany, Arp. 22, 1967.
Lee, Spike (Shelton Lee) Atlanta, GA, Mar. 20, 1957.
Legge, Michael Newry, Northern Ireland, 1978.
Legros, James Minneapolis, MN, Apr. 27, 1962.
Leguizamo, John Columbia, July 22, 1965. NYU.
Leibman, Ron NYC, Oct. 11, 1937. Ohio Wesleyan.
Leigh, Jennifer Jason Los Angeles, CA, Feb. 5, 1962.
Le Mat, Paul Rahway, NJ, Sept. 22, 1945.
Lemmon, Chris Los Angeles, CA, Jan. 22, 1954.
Leno, Jay New Rochelle, NY, Apr. 28, 1950. Emerson College.
Lenz, Kay Los Angeles, CA, Mar. 4, 1953.
Lenz, Rick Springfield, IL, Nov. 21, 1939. U Michigan.
Leonard, Robert Sean Westwood, NJ, Feb. 28, 1969.
Leoni, Téa (Elizabeth Téa Pantaleoni) NYC, Feb. 25, 1966.
Lerner, Michael Brooklyn, NY, June 22, 1941.
Leslie, Joan (Joan Brodell) Detroit, MI, Jan. 26, 1925. St. Benedict's.
Lester, Mark Oxford, England, July 11, 1958.
Leto, Jared Bossier City, LA, Dec. 26, 1971.
Levels, Calvin Cleveland. OH, Sept. 30, 1954. CCC.
Levin, Rachel (Rachel Chagall) NYC, Nov. 24, 1954. Goddard College.
Levine, Jerry New Brunswick, NJ, Mar. 12, 1957, Boston U.
Levy, Eugene Hamilton, Canada, Dec. 17, 1946. McMaster U.
Lewis, Charlotte London, England, Aug. 7, 1967.
Lewis, Geoffrey San Diego, CA, Jan. 1, 1935.
Lewis, Jerry (Joseph Levitch) Newark, NJ, Mar. 16, 1926.
Lewis, Juliette Los Angeles CA, June 21, 1973.
Li, Jet Beijing, China, Apr. 26, 1963.
Ligon, Tom New Orleans, LA, Sept. 10, 1945.
Lillard, Matthew Lansing, MI, Jan. 24, 1970.
Lincoln, Abbey (Anna Marie Woolridge) Chicago, IL, Aug. 6, 1930.
Linden, Hal Bronx, NY, Mar. 20, 1931. City College of NY.
Lindo, Delroy London, England, Nov. 18, 1952.
Lindsay, Robert Ilketson, Derbyshire, England, Dec. 13, 1951, RADA.
Linn-Baker, Mark St. Louis, MO, June 17, 1954. Yale.
Linney, Laura New York, NY, Feb. 5, 1964.
Liotta, Ray Newark, NJ, Dec. 18, 1955. U Miami.
Lisi, Virna Rome, Italy, Nov. 8, 1937.
Lithgow, John Rochester, NY, Oct. 19, 1945. Harvard.
Liu, Lucy Queens, NY, Dec. 2, 1967.
Livingston, Ron Cedar Rapids, IA, June 5, 1968.
LL Cool J (James Todd Smith) Queens, NY, Jan. 14, 1968.
Lloyd, Christopher Stamford, CT, Oct. 22, 1938.
Lloyd, Emily London, England, Sept. 29, 1970.

Lindsay Lohan

Bernie Mac

Kyle MacLachlan

Edie McClurg

Locke, Sondra Shelbyville, TN, May, 28, 1947.
Lockhart, June NYC, June 25, 1925. Westlake School.
Lockwood, Gary Van Nuys, CA, Feb. 21, 1937.
Loggia, Robert Staten Island, NY, Jan. 3, 1930. U Mo.
Lohan, Lindsay NYC, July 2, 1986.
Lohman, Alison Palm Springs, CA, Sept. 18, 1979.
Lollobrigida, Gina Subiaco, Italy, July 4, 1927. Rome Academy of Fine Arts.
Lom, Herbert Prague, Czechoslovakia, Jan. 9, 1917. Prague U.
Lomez, Celine Montreal, Canada, May 11, 1953.
Lone, John Hong Kong, Oct 13, 1952. AADA.
Long, Justin Fairfield, CT, June 2, 1978.
Long, Nia Brooklyn, NY, Oct. 30, 1970.
Long, Shelley Ft. Wayne, IN, Aug. 23, 1949. Northwestern.
Lopez, Jennifer Bronx, NY, July 24, 1970.
Lopez, Perry NYC, July 22, 1931. NYU.
Lords, Tracy (Nora Louise Kuzma) Steubenville, OH, May 7, 1968.
Loren, Sophia (Sophia Scicolone) Rome, Italy, Sept. 20, 1934.
Louis-Dreyfus, Julia NYC, Jan. 13, 1961.
Louise, Tina (Blacker) NYC, Feb. 11, 1934, Miami U.
Love, Courtney (Love Michelle Harrison) San Francisco, CA, July 9, 1965.
Lovett, Lyle Klein, TX, Nov. 1, 1957.
Lovitz, Jon Tarzana, CA, July 21, 1957.
Lowe, Chad Dayton, OH, Jan. 15, 1968.
Lowe, Rob Charlottesville, VA, Mar. 17, 1964.
Löwitsch, Klaus Berlin, Germany, Apr. 8, 1936, Vienna Academy.
Lucas, Josh Little Rock, AR, June 20, 1971.
Lucas, Lisa Arizona, 1961.
Luckinbill, Laurence Fort Smith, AK, Nov. 21, 1934.
Luft, Lorna Los Angeles, CA, Nov. 21, 1952.
Luke, Derek Jersey City, NJ, Apr. 24, 1974.
Lulu (Marie Lawrie) Glasgow, Scotland, Nov. 3, 1948.
Luna, Barbara NYC, Mar. 2, 1939.
Luna, Diego Mexico City, Dec. 29, 1979.
Lundgren, Dolph Stockolm, Sweden, Nov. 3, 1959. Royal Inst.
LuPone, Patti Northport, NY, Apr. 21, 1949, Juilliard.
Lydon, James Harrington Park, NJ, May 30, 1923.
Lynch, Kelly Minneapolis, MN, Jan. 31, 1959.

Lynley, Carol (Jones) NYC, Feb. 13, 1942.
Lyon, Sue Davenport, IA, July 10, 1946.
Lyonne, Natasha (Braunstein) NYC, Apr. 4, 1979.

Mac, Bernie (Bernard Jeffrey McCollough) Chicago, IL, Oct. 5, 1958.
MacArthur, James Los Angeles, CA, Dec. 8, 1937. Harvard.
Macchio, Ralph Huntington, NY, Nov. 4, 1961.
MacCorkindale, Simon Cambridge, England, Feb. 12, 1953.
Macdonald, Kelly Glasgow, Scotland, Feb. 23, 1976.
MacDowell, Andie (Rose Anderson MacDowell) Gaffney, SC, Apr. 21, 1958.
MacFadyen, Angus Scotland, Oct. 21, 1963.
MacGinnis, Niall Dublin, Ireland, Mar. 29, 1913. Dublin U.
MacGraw, Ali NYC, Apr. 1, 1938. Wellesley.
MacLachlan, Kyle Yakima, WA, Feb. 22, 1959. U Wa.
MacLaine, Shirley (Beaty) Richmond, VA, Apr. 24, 1934.
MacLeod, Gavin Mt. Kisco, NY, Feb. 28, 1931.
MacNaughton, Robert NYC, Dec. 19, 1966.
Macnee, Patrick London, England, Feb. 1922.
MacNicol, Peter Dallas, TX, Apr. 10, 1954. U Mn.
MacPherson, Elle Sydney, Australia, 1965.
MacVittie, Bruce Providence, RI, Oct. 14, 1956. Boston U.
Macy, W. H. (William) Miami, FL, Mar. 13, 1950. Goddard College.
Madigan, Amy Chicago, IL, Sept. 11, 1950. Marquette U.
Madonna (Madonna Louise Veronica Cicone) Bay City, MI, Aug. 16, 1958. U Mi.
Madsen, Michael Chicago, IL, Sept. 25, 1958.
Madsen, Virginia Winnetka, IL, Sept. 11, 1963.
Magnuson, Ann Charleston, WV, Jan. 4, 1956.
Maguire, Tobey Santa Monica, CA, June 27, 1975.
Maharis, George Astoria, NY, Sept. 1, 1928. Actors Studio.
Mahoney, John Manchester, England, June 20, 1940, W U III.
Mailer, Stephen NYC, Mar. 10, 1966. NYU.
Majors, Lee Wyandotte, MI, Apr. 23, 1940. E. Ky. State College.
Makepeace, Chris Toronto, Canada, Apr. 22, 1964.
Mako (Mako Iwamatsu) Kobe, Japan, Dec. 10, 1933. Pratt.
Malden, Karl (Mladen Sekulovich) Gary, IN, Mar. 22, 1914.
Malkovich, John Christopher, IL, Dec. 9, 1953, Il State U.

Ewan McGregor

Helen Mirren

Julianne Moore

Tim Blake Nelson

Malone, Dorothy Chicago, IL, Jan. 30, 1925.

Malone, Jena Lake Tahoe, NV, Nov. 21, 1984.

Mann, Terrence KY, 1945. NC School Arts.

Manoff, Dinah NYC, Jan. 25, 1958. Cal Arts.

Mantegna, Joe Chicago, IL, Nov. 13, 1947. Goodman Theatre.

Manz, Linda NYC, 1961.

Marais, Jean Cherbourg, France, Dec. 11, 1913. St. Germain.

Marceau, Sophie (Maupu) Paris, France, Nov. 17, 1966.

Marcovicci, Andrea NYC, Nov. 18, 1948.

Margulies, Julianna Spring Valley, NY, June 8, 1966.

Marin, Cheech (Richard) Los Angeles, CA, July 13, 1946.

Marin, Jacques Paris, France, Sept. 9, 1919. Conservatoire National.

Marinaro, Ed NYC, Mar. 31, 1950. Cornell.

Mars, Kenneth Chicago, IL, Apr. 14, 1936.

Marsden, James Stillwater, OK, Sept. 18, 1973.

Marsh, Jean London, England, July 1, 1934.

Marshall, Ken NYC, June 27, 1950. Juilliard.

Marshall, Penny Bronx, NY, Oct. 15, 1942. UN. Mex.

Martin, Andrea Portland, ME, Jan. 15, 1947.

Martin, Dick Battle Creek, MI Jan. 30, 1923.

Martin, George N. NYC, Aug. 15, 1929.

Martin, Millicent Romford, England, June 8, 1934.

Martin, Pamela Sue Westport, CT, Jan. 15, 1953.

Martin, Steve Waco, TX, Aug. 14, 1945. UCLA.

Martin, Tony (Alfred Norris) Oakland, CA, Dec. 25, 1913. St. Mary's College.

Martinez, Olivier Paris, France, Jan. 12, 1966.

Mason, Marsha St. Louis, MO, Apr. 3, 1942. Webster College.

Massen, Osa Copenhagen, Denmark, Jan. 13, 1916.

Masters, Ben Corvallis, OR, May 6, 1947. U Or.

Masterson, Mary Stuart Los Angeles, CA, June 28, 1966, NYU.

Masterson, Peter Angleton, TX, June 1, 1934. Rice U.

Mastrantonio, Mary Elizabeth Chicago, IL, Nov. 17, 1958. U Il.

Masur, Richard NYC, Nov. 20, 1948.

Matheson, Tim Glendale, CA, Dec. 31, 1947. Cal State.

Mathis, Samantha NYC, May 12, 1970.

Matlin, Marlee Morton Grove, IL, Aug. 24, 1965.

Matthews, Brian Philadelphia, PA, Jan. 24. 1953. St. Olaf.

May, Elaine (Berlin) Philadelphia, PA, Apr. 21, 1932.

Mayo, Virginia (Virginia Clara Jones) St. Louis, MO, Nov. 30, 1920.

Mayron, Melanie Philadelphia, PA, Oct. 20, 1952. AADA.

Mazursky, Paul Brooklyn, NY, Apr. 25, 1930. Bklyn College.

Mazzello, Joseph Rhinebeck, NY, Sept. 21, 1983.

McAdams, Rachel London, Ontario, Oct. 7, 1976.

McAvoy, James Glasgow, Scotland, 1979.

McCallum, David Scotland, Sept. 19, 1933. Chapman College.

McCarthy, Andrew NYC, Nov. 29, 1962, NYU.

McCarthy, Kevin Seattle, WA, Feb. 15, 1914. Minn. U.

McCartney, Paul Liverpool, England, June 18, 1942.

McClanahan, Rue Healdton, OK, Feb. 21, 1934.

McClure, Marc San Mateo, CA, Mar. 31, 1957.

McClurg, Edie Kansas City, MO, July 23, 1950.

McCormack, Catherine Alton, Hampshire, England, Jan. 1, 1972.

McCowen, Alec Tunbridge Wells, England, May 26, 1925. RADA.

McCrane, Paul Philadelphia, PA, Jan. 19. 1961.

McCrary, Darius Walnut, CA, May 1, 1976.

McDermott, Dylan Waterbury, CT, Oct. 26, 1962. Neighborhood Playhouse.

McDonald, Christopher NYC, Feb. 15, 1955.

McDonnell, Mary Wilkes Barre, PA, Apr. 28, 1952.

McDonough, Neal Dorchester, MA, Feb. 13, 1966.

McDormand, Frances Illinois, June 23, 1957.

McDowell, Malcolm (Taylor) Leeds, England, June 19, 1943. LAMDA.

McElhone, Natascha (Natasha Taylor) London, England, Mar. 23, 1971.

McEnery, Peter Walsall, England, Feb. 21, 1940.

McEntire, Reba McAlester, OK, Mar. 28, 1955. Southeastern St. U.

McGavin, Darren Spokane, WA, May 7, 1922. College of Pacific.

McGill, Everett Miami Beach, FL, Oct. 21, 1945.

McGillis, Kelly Newport Beach, CA, July 9, 1957. Juilliard.

McGinley, John C. NYC, Aug. 3, 1959. NYU.

McGoohan, Patrick NYC, Mar. 19, 1928.

McGovern, Elizabeth Evanston, IL. July 18, 1961. Juilliard.

McGovern, Maureen Youngstown, OH, July 27, 1949.

McGregor, Ewan Perth, Scotland, March 31, 1971.

McGuire, Biff New Haven, CT, Oct. 25. 1926. Mass. State College.

McHattie, Stephen Antigonish, NS, Feb. 3. Acadia U AADA.

McKean, Michael NYC, Oct. 17, 1947.
McKee, Lonette Detroit, MI, July 22, 1955.
McKellen, Ian Burnley, England, May 25, 1939.
McKenna, Virginia London, England, June 7, 1931.
McKeon, Doug Pompton Plains, NJ, June 10, 1966.
McKuen, Rod Oakland, CA, Apr. 29, 1933.
McLerie, Allyn Ann Grand Mere, Canada, Dec. 1, 1926.
McMahon, Ed Detroit, MI, Mar. 6, 1923.
McNair, Barbara Chicago, IL, Mar. 4, 1939. UCLA.
McNamara, William Dallas, TX, Mar. 31, 1965.
McNichol, Kristy Los Angeles, CA, Sept. 11, 1962.
McQueen, Armelia North Carolina, Jan. 6, 1952. Bklyn Consv.
McQueen, Chad Los Angeles, CA, Dec. 28, 1960. Actors Studio.
McRaney, Gerald Collins, MS, Aug. 19, 1948.
McShane, Ian Blackburn, England, Sept. 29, 1942. RADA.
McTeer, Janet York, England, May 8, 1961.
Meadows, Jayne (formerly Jayne Cotter) Wuchang, China, Sept. 27, 1924. St. Margaret's.
Meaney, Colm Dublin, May 30, 1953.
Meara, Anne Brooklyn, NY, Sept. 20, 1929.
Meat Loaf (Marvin Lee Aday) Dallas, TX, Sept. 27, 1947.
Medwin, Michael London, England, 1925. Instut Fischer.
Mekka, Eddie Worcester, MA, June 14, 1952. Boston Cons.
Melato, Mariangela Milan, Italy, Sept. 18, 1941. Milan Theatre Acad.
Meredith, Lee (Judi Lee Sauls) Oct. 22, 1947. AADA.
Merkerson, S. Epatha Saganaw, MI, Nov. 28, 1952. Wayne St. Univ.
Merrill, Dina (Nedinia Hutton) NYC, Dec. 29, 1925. AADA.
Messing, Debra Brooklyn, NY, Aug. 15, 1968.
Metcalf, Laurie Edwardsville, IL, June 16, 1955. Il St. U.
Metzler, Jim Oneonda, NY, June 23, 1955. Dartmouth.
Meyer, Breckin Minneapolis, May 7, 1974.
Michell, Keith Adelaide, Australia, Dec. 1, 1926.
Midler, Bette Honolulu, HI, Dec. 1, 1945.
Milano, Alyssa Brooklyn, NY, Dec. 19, 1972.
Miles, Joanna Nice, France, Mar. 6, 1940.
Miles, Sarah Ingatestone, England, Dec. 31, 1941. RADA.
Miles, Sylvia NYC, Sept. 9, 1934. Actors Studio.
Miles, Vera (Ralston) Boise City, OK, Aug. 23, 1929. UCLA.
Miller, Barry Los Angeles, CA, Feb. 6, 1958.
Miller, Dick NYC, Dec. 25, 1928.
Miller, Jonny Lee Surrey, England, Nov. 15, 1972.
Miller, Linda NYC, Sept. 16, 1942. Catholic U.
Miller, Penelope Ann Santa Monica, CA, Jan. 13, 1964.
Miller, Rebecca Roxbury, CT, 1962. Yale.
Mills, Donna Chicago, IL, Dec. 11, 1945. Ull.
Mills, Hayley London, England, Apr. 18, 1946. Elmhurst School.
Mills, John Suffolk, England, Feb. 22, 1908.
Mills, Juliet London, England, Nov. 21, 1941.
Milner, Martin Detroit, MI, Dec. 28, 1931.
Mimieux, Yvette Los Angeles, CA, Jan. 8, 1941. Hollywood High.
Minnelli, Liza Los Angeles, CA, Mar. 19, 1946.
Miou-Miou (Sylvette Henry) Paris, France, Feb. 22, 1950.
Mirren, Helen (Ilynea Mironoff) London, England, July 26, 1946.
Mistry, Jimi Scarborough, England, 1973.

Mitchell, James Sacramento, CA, Feb. 29, 1920. LACC.
Mitchell, John Cameron El Paso, TX, Apr. 21, 1963. Northwestern.
Mitchum, James Los Angeles, CA, May 8, 1941.
Modine, Matthew Loma Linda, CA, Mar. 22, 1959.
Moffat, Donald Plymouth, England, Dec. 26, 1930. RADA.
Moffett, D. W. Highland Park, IL, Oct. 26, 1954. Stanford U.
Mohr, Jay New Jersey, Aug. 23, 1971.
Mokae, Zakes Johannesburg, So. Africa, Aug. 5, 1935. RADA.
Molina, Alfred London, England, May 24, 1953. Guildhall.
Moll, Richard Pasadena, CA, Jan. 13, 1943.
Monaghan, Dominic Berlin, Dec. 8, 1976.
Monk, Debra Middletown, OH, Feb. 27, 1949.
Montalban, Ricardo Mexico City, Nov. 25, 1920.
Montenegro, Fernada (Arlete Pinheiro) Rio de Janiero, Brazil, 1929.
Montgomery, Belinda Winnipeg, Canada, July 23, 1950.
Moody, Ron London, England, Jan. 8, 1924. London U.
Moor, Bill Toledo, OH, July 13, 1931. Northwestern.
Moore, Constance Sioux City, IA, Jan. 18, 1919.
Moore, Demi (Guines) Roswell, NM, Nov. 11, 1962.
Moore, Dick Los Angeles, CA, Sept. 12, 1925.
Moore, Julianne (Julie Anne Smith) Fayetteville, NC, Dec. 30, 1960.
Moore, Kieron County Cork, Ireland, 1925. St. Mary's College.
Moore, Mandy Nashua, NH, Apr. 10, 1984.
Moore, Mary Tyler Brooklyn, NY, Dec. 29, 1936.
Moore, Roger London, England, Oct. 14, 1927. RADA.
Moore, Terry (Helen Koford) Los Angeles, CA, Jan. 7, 1929.
Morales, Esai Brooklyn, NY, Oct. 1, 1962.
Moranis, Rick Toronto, Canada, Apr. 18, 1954.
Moreau, Jeanne Paris, France, Jan. 23, 1928.
Moreno, Catalina Sandino Bogota, Colombia, Apr. 19, 1981.
Moreno, Rita (Rosita Alverio) Humacao, P.R., Dec. 11, 1931.
Morgan, Harry (Henry) (Harry Bratsburg) Detroit, Apr. 10, 1915. U Chicago.
Morgan, Michele (Simone Roussel) Paris, France, Feb. 29, 1920. Paris Dramatic School.
Moriarty, Cathy Bronx, NY, Nov. 29, 1960.
Moriarty, Michael Detroit, MI, Apr. 5, 1941. Dartmouth.
Morison, Patricia NYC, Mar. 19, 1915.
Morita, Noriyuki "Pat" Isleton, CA, June 28, 1932.
Morris, Garrett New Orleans, LA, Feb. 1, 1937.
Morris, Howard NYC, Sept. 4, 1919. NYU.
Morrow, Rob New Rochelle, NY, Sept. 21, 1962.
Morse, David Hamilton, MA, Oct. 11, 1953.
Morse, Robert Newton, MA, May 18, 1931.
Mortensen, Viggo New York, NY, Oct. 20, 1958.
Morton, Joe NYC, Oct. 18, 1947. Hofstra U.
Morton, Samantha Nottingham, England, May 13, 1977.
Mos Def (Dante Beze) Brooklyn, Dec. 11, 1973.
Moses, William Los Angeles, CA, Nov. 17, 1959.
Moss, Carrie-Anne Vancouver, BC, Canada, Aug. 21, 1967.
Mostel, Josh NYC, Dec. 21, 1946. Brandeis U.
Mouchet, Catherine Paris, France, 1959. Ntl. Consv.
Moynahan, Bridget Binghamton, NY, Sept. 21, 1972.
Mueller-Stahl, Armin Tilsit, East Prussia, Dec. 17, 1930.
Muldaur, Diana NYC, Aug. 19, 1938. Sweet Briar College.

Mulgrew, Kate Dubuque, IA, Apr. 29, 1955. NYU.
Mulhern, Matt Philadelphia, PA, July 21, 1960. Rutgers U.
Mull, Martin N. Ridgefield, OH, Aug. 18, 1941. RI School of Design.
Mulroney, Dermot Alexandria, VA, Oct. 31, 1963. Northwestern.
Mumy, Bill (Charles William Mumy, Jr.) San Gabriel, CA, Feb. 1, 1954.
Muniz, Frankie Ridgewood, NJ, Dec. 5, 1985.
Murphy, Brittany Atlanta, GA, Nov. 10, 1977.
Murphy, Cillian Douglas, Ireland, March 13, 1974.
Murphy, Donna Queens, NY, March 7, 1958.
Murphy, Eddie Brooklyn, NY, Apr. 3, 1961.
Murphy, Michael Los Angeles, CA, May 5, 1938. U Az.
Murray, Bill Wilmette, IL, Sept. 21, 1950. Regis College.
Murray, Don Hollywood, CA, July 31, 1929.
Musante, Tony Bridgeport, CT, June 30, 1936. Oberlin College.
Myers, Mike Scarborough, Canada, May 25, 1963.

Nabors, Jim Sylacauga, GA, June 12, 1932.
Nader, Michael Los Angeles, CA, 1945.
Namath, Joe Beaver Falls, PA, May 31, 1943. U Ala.
Naughton, David Hartford, CT, Feb. 13, 1951.
Naughton, James Middletown, CT, Dec. 6, 1945.
Neal, Patricia Packard, KY, Jan. 20, 1926. Northwestern.
Neeson, Liam Ballymena, Northern Ireland, June 7, 1952.
Neff, Hildegarde (Hildegard Knef) Ulm, Germany, Dec. 28, 1925. Berlin Art Acad.
Neill, Sam No. Ireland, Sept. 14, 1947. U Canterbury.
Nelligan, Kate London, Ontario, Mar. 16, 1951. U Toronto.
Nelson, Barry (Robert Nielsen) Oakland, CA, Apr. 16, 1920.
Nelson, Craig T. Spokane, WA, Apr. 4, 1946.
Nelson, David NYC, Oct. 24, 1936. USC.
Nelson, Judd Portland, ME, Nov. 28, 1959, Haverford College.
Nelson, Lori (Dixie Kay Nelson) Santa Fe, NM, Aug. 15, 1933.
Nelson, Tim Blake Tulsa, OK, 1964.
Nelson, Tracy Santa Monica, CA, Oct. 25, 1963.
Nelson, Willie Abbott, TX, Apr. 30, 1933.
Nemec, Corin Little Rock, AK, Nov. 5, 1971.
Nero, Franco (Francisco Spartanero) Parma, Italy, Nov. 23, 1941.
Nesmith, Michael Houston, TX, Dec. 30, 1942.
Nettleton, Lois Oak Park, IL, 1931. Actors Studio.
Neuwirth, Bebe Princeton, NJ, Dec. 31, 1958.
Newhart, Bob Chicago, IL, Sept. 5, 1929. Loyola U.
Newman, Barry Boston, MA, Nov. 7, 1938. Brandeis U.
Newman, Laraine Los Angeles, CA, Mar. 2, 1952.
Newman, Nanette Northampton, England, 1934.
Newman, Paul Cleveland, OH, Jan. 26, 1925. Yale.
Newmar, Julie (Newmeyer) Los Angeles, CA, Aug. 16, 1933.
Newton, Thandie Zambia, Nov. 16, 1972.
Newton-John, Olivia Cambridge, England, Sept. 26, 1948.
Nguyen, Dustin Saigon, Vietnam, Sept. 17, 1962.
Nicholas, Denise Detroit, MI, July 12, 1945.
Nicholas, Paul Peterborough, Cambridge, England, Dec. 3, 1945.
Nichols, Nichelle Robbins, IL, Dec. 28, 1933.
Nicholson, Jack Neptune, NJ, Apr. 22, 1937.
Nickerson, Denise NYC, Apr. 1, 1959.

Nicol, Alex Ossining, NY, Jan. 20, 1919. Actors Studio.
Nielsen, Brigitte Denmark, July 15, 1963.
Nielsen, Connie Elling, Denmark, July 3, 1965.
Nielsen, Leslie Regina, Saskatchewan, Canada, Feb. 11, 1926. Neighborhood Playhouse.
Nighy, Bill Caterham, England, 1949.
Nimoy, Leonard Boston, MA, Mar. 26, 1931. Boston College, Antioch College.
Nixon, Cynthia NYC, Apr. 9, 1966. Columbia U.
Noble, James Dallas, TX, Mar. 5, 1922, SMU.
Noiret, Philippe Lille, France, Oct. 1, 1930.
Nolan, Kathleen St. Louis, MO, Sept. 27, 1933. Neighborhood Playhouse.
Nolte, Nick Omaha, NE, Feb. 8, 1940. Pasadena City College.
Norris, Bruce Houston, TX, May 16, 1960. Northwestern.
Norris, Christopher NYC, Oct. 7, 1943. Lincoln Square Acad.
Norris, Chuck (Carlos Ray) Ryan, OK, Mar. 10, 1940.
North, Heather Pasadena, CA, Dec. 13, 1950. Actors Workshop.
North, Sheree (Dawn Bethel) Los Angeles. Jan. 17, 1933. Hollywood High.
Northam, Jeremy Cambridge, Eng., Dec. 1, 1961.
Norton, Edward Boston, MA, Aug. 18, 1969.
Norton, Ken Jacksonville, Il, Aug. 9, 1945.
Noseworthy, Jack Lynn, MA, Dec. 21, 1969.
Nouri, Michael Washington, DC, Dec. 9, 1945.
Novak, Kim (Marilyn Novak) Chicago, IL, Feb. 13, 1933. LACC.
Novello, Don Ashtabula, OH, Jan. 1, 1943. U Dayton.
Nuyen, France (Vannga) Marseilles, France, July 31, 1939. Beaux Arts School.

O'Brian, Hugh (Hugh J. Krampe) Rochester, NY. Apr. 19, 1928. Cincinnati U.
O'Brien, Clay Ray, AZ, May 6, 1961.
O'Brien, Margaret (Angela Maxine O'Brien) Los Angeles, CA, Jan. 15, 1937.
O'Connell, Jerry (Jeremiah O'Connell) New York, NY, Feb. 17, 1974.
O'Connor, Carroll Bronx, NY, Aug. 2, 1924. Dublin National U.
O'Connor, Glynnis NYC, Nov. 19, 1955. NYSU.
O'Donnell, Chris Winetka, IL, June 27, 1970.
O'Donnell, Rosie Commack, NY, March 21, 1961.
Oh, Sandra Nepean, Ontario, Nov. 30, 1970.
O'Hara, Catherine Toronto, Canada, Mar. 4, 1954.
O'Hara, Maureen (Maureen Fitzsimons) Dublin, Ireland, Aug. 17, 1920.
O'Herlihy, Dan Wexford, Ireland, May 1, 1919. National U.
O'Keefe, Michael Larchmont, NY, Apr. 24, 1955. NYU, AADA.
Okonedo, Sophie London, England, Jan. 1, 1969.
Oldman, Gary New Cross, South London, England, Mar. 21, 1958.
Olin, Ken Chicago, IL, July 30, 1954. U Pa.
Olin, Lena Stockholm, Sweden, Mar. 22, 1955.
Olmos, Edward James Los Angeles, CA, Feb. 24, 1947. CSLA.
O'Loughlin, Gerald S. NYC, Dec. 23, 1921. U Rochester.
Olson, James Evanston, IL, Oct. 8, 1930.
Olson, Nancy Milwaukee, WI, July 14, 1928. UCLA.
Olyphant, Timothy HI, May 20, 1968.
O'Neal, Griffin Los Angeles, CA, 1965.
O'Neal, Ryan Los Angeles, CA, Apr. 20, 1941.
O'Neal, Tatum Los Angeles, CA, Nov. 5, 1963.
O'Neil, Tricia Shreveport, LA, Mar. 11, 1945. Baylor U.
O'Neill, Ed Youngstown, OH, Apr. 12, 1946.

O'Neill, Jennifer Rio de Janeiro, Feb. 20, 1949. Neighborhood Playhouse.
Ontkean, Michael Vancouver, B.C., Canada, Jan. 24, 1946.
O'Quinn, Terry Newbury, MI, July 15, 1952.
Ormond, Julia Epsom, England, Jan. 4, 1965.
O'Shea, Milo Dublin, Ireland, June 2, 1926.
Osment, Haley Joel Los Angeles, CA, Apr. 10, 1988.
O'Toole, Annette (Toole) Houston, TX, Apr. 1, 1953. UCLA.
O'Toole, Peter Connemara, Ireland, Aug. 2, 1932. RADA.
Overall, Park Nashville, TN, Mar. 15, 1957. Tusculum College.
Owen, Clive Keresley, England, Oct. 3, 1964.
Oz, Frank (Oznowicz) Hereford, England, May 25, 1944.

Pacino, Al NYC, Apr. 25, 1940.
Pacula, Joanna Tamaszow Lubelski, Poland, Jan. 2, 1957. Polish Natl. Theatre Sch.
Paget, Debra (Debralee Griffin) Denver, Aug. 19, 1933.
Paige, Janis (Donna Mae Jaden) Tacoma, WA, Sept. 16, 1922.
Palance, Jack (Walter Palanuik) Lattimer, PA, Feb. 18, 1920. U NC.
Palin, Michael Sheffield, Yorkshire, England, May 5, 1943, Oxford.
Palmer, Betsy East Chicago, IN, Nov. 1, 1926. DePaul U.
Palmer, Gregg (Palmer Lee) San Francisco, Jan. 25, 1927. U Utah.
Palminteri, Chazz (Calogero Lorenzo Palminteri) New York, NY, May 15, 1952.
Paltrow, Gwyneth Los Angeles, CA, Sept. 28, 1973.
Pampanini, Silvana Rome, Sept. 25, 1925.
Panebianco, Richard NYC, 1971.
Pankin, Stuart Philadelphia, Apr. 8, 1946.
Pantoliano, Joe Jersey City, NJ, Sept. 12, 1954.
Papas, Irene Chiliomodion, Greece, Mar. 9, 1929.
Paquin, Anna Winnipeg, Manitoba, Canada, July, 24, 1982.
Pare, Michael Brooklyn, NY, Oct. 9, 1959.
Parker, Corey NYC, July 8, 1965. NYU.
Parker, Eleanor Cedarville, OH, June 26, 1922. Pasadena Playhouse.
Parker, Fess Fort Worth, TX, Aug. 16, 1925. USC.
Parker, Jameson Baltimore, MD, Nov. 18, 1947. Beloit College.
Parker, Jean (Mae Green) Deer Lodge, MT, Aug. 11, 1912.
Parker, Mary-Louise Ft. Jackson, SC, Aug. 2, 1964. Bard College.
Parker, Nathaniel London, England, May 18, 1962.
Parker, Sarah Jessica Nelsonville, OH, Mar. 25, 1965.
Parker, Trey Auburn, AL, May 30, 1972.
Parkins, Barbara Vancouver, Canada, May 22, 1943.
Parks, Michael Corona, CA, Apr. 4, 1938.
Parsons, Estelle Lynn, MA, Nov. 20, 1927. Boston U.
Parton, Dolly Sevierville, TN, Jan. 19, 1946.
Patinkin, Mandy Chicago, IL, Nov. 30, 1952. Juilliard.
Patric, Jason NYC, June 17, 1966.
Patrick, Robert Marietta, GA, Nov. 5, 1958.
Patterson, Lee Vancouver, Canada, Mar. 31, 1929. Ontario College.
Patton, Will Charleston, SC, June 14, 1954.
Paulik, Johan Prague, Czech., 1975.
Paulson, Sarah Tampa, FL, Dec. 17, 1975.
Pavan, Marisa (Marisa Pierangeli) Cagliari, Sardinia, June 19, 1932. Torquado Tasso College.
Paxton, Bill Fort Worth, TX, May. 17, 1955.

Paymer, David Long Island, NY, Aug. 30, 1954.
Pays, Amanda Berkshire, England, June 6, 1959.
Peach, Mary Durban, South Africa, Oct. 20, 1934.
Pearce, Guy Ely, England, Oct. 5, 1967.
Pearson, Beatrice Dennison, TX, July 27, 1920.
Peet, Amanda NYC, Jan. 11, 1972.
Peña, Elizabeth Cuba, Sept. 23, 1961.
Pendleton, Austin Warren, OH, Mar. 27, 1940. Yale.
Penhall, Bruce Balboa, CA, Aug. 17, 1960.
Penn, Chris Los Angeles, CA, June 10, 1962.
Penn, Kal Montclair, NJ, Apr. 23, 1977.
Penn, Robin Wright Dallas, TX, Apr. 8, 1966.
Penn, Sean Burbank, CA, Aug. 17, 1960.
Pepper, Barry Campbell River, BC, Canada, Apr. 4, 1970.
Perabo, Piper Toms River, NJ, Oct. 31, 1976.
Perez, Jose NYC, 1940.
Perez, Rosie Brooklyn, NY, Sept. 6, 1964.
Perkins, Elizabeth Queens, NY, Nov. 18, 1960. Goodman School.
Perkins, Millie Passaic, NJ, May 12, 1938.
Perlman, Rhea Brooklyn, NY, Mar. 31, 1948.
Perlman, Ron NYC, Apr. 13, 1950. U Mn.
Perreau, Gigi (Ghislaine) Los Angeles, CA, Feb. 6, 1941.
Perrine, Valerie Galveston, TX, Sept. 3, 1943. U Ariz.
Perry, Luke (Coy Luther Perry, III) Fredricktown, OH, Oct. 11, 1966.
Pesci, Joe Newark, NJ. Feb. 9, 1943.
Pescow, Donna Brooklyn, NY, Mar. 24, 1954.
Peters, Bernadette (Lazzara) Jamaica, NY, Feb. 28, 1948.
Peters, Brock NYC, July 2, 1927. CCNY.
Petersen, Paul Glendale, CA, Sept. 23, 1945. Valley College.
Petersen, William Chicago, IL, Feb. 21, 1953.
Peterson, Cassandra Colorado Springs, CO, Sept. 17, 1951.
Pettet, Joanna London, England, Nov. 16, 1944. Neighborhood Playhouse.
Petty, Lori Chattanooga, TN, Mar. 23, 1963.
Pfeiffer, Michelle Santa Ana, CA, Apr. 29, 1958.
Phifer, Mekhi NYC, Dec. 12, 1975.
Phillippe, Ryan (Matthew Phillippe) New Castle, DE, Sept. 10, 1975.
Phillips, Lou Diamond Phillipines, Feb. 17, 1962, U Tx.
Phillips, MacKenzie Alexandria, VA, Nov. 10, 1959.
Phillips, Michelle (Holly Gilliam) Long Beach, CA, June 4, 1944.
Phillips, Sian Bettws, Wales, May 14, 1934. U Wales.
Phoenix, Joaquin Puerto Rico, Oct. 28, 1974.
Picardo, Robert Philadelphia, PA, Oct. 27, 1953. Yale.
Picerni, Paul NYC, Dec. 1, 1922. Loyola U.
Pidgeon, Rebecca Cambridge, MA, 1963.
Pierce, David Hyde Saratoga Springs, NY, Apr. 3, 1959.
Pigott-Smith, Tim Rugby, England, May 13, 1946.
Pinchot, Bronson NYC, May 20, 1959. Yale.
Pine, Phillip Hanford, CA, July 16, 1920. Actors' Lab.
Piscopo, Joe Passaic, NJ, June 17, 1951.
Pisier, Marie-France Vietnam, May 10, 1944. U Paris.
Pitillo, Maria Mahwah, NJ, 1965.
Pitt, Brad (William Bradley Pitt) Shawnee, OK, Dec. 18, 1963.
Pitt, Michael West Orange, NJ, Apr. 10, 1981.
Piven, Jeremy NYC, July 26, 1965.

Robert Patrick

Randy Quaid

John Rhys-Davies

Kurt Russell

Place, Mary Kay Tulsa OK, Sept. 23, 1947. U Tulsa.
Platt, Oliver Windsor, Ontario, Can., Oct. 10, 1960.
Playten, Alice NYC, Aug. 28, 1947. NYU.
Pleshette, Suzanne NYC, Jan. 31, 1937. Syracuse U.
Plimpton, Martha NYC, Nov. 16, 1970.
Plowright, Joan Scunthorpe, Brigg, Lincolnshire, England, Oct. 28, 1929. Old Vic.
Plumb, Eve Burbank, CA, Apr. 29, 1958.
Plummer, Amanda NYC, Mar. 23, 1957. Middlebury College.
Plummer, Christopher Toronto, Canada, Dec. 13, 1927.
Podesta, Rossana Tripoli, June 20, 1934.
Poitier, Sidney Miami, FL, Feb. 27, 1927.
Polanski, Roman Paris, France, Aug. 18, 1933.
Polito, Jon Philadelphia, PA, Dec. 29, 1950. Villanova U.
Polito, Lina Naples, Italy, Aug. 11, 1954.
Pollack, Sydney South Bend, IN, July 1, 1934.
Pollak, Kevin San Francisco, CA, Oct. 30, 1958.
Pollan, Tracy NYC, June 22, 1960.
Pollard, Michael J. Passaic, NJ, May 30, 1939.
Polley, Sarah Toronto, Ontario, Canada, Jan. 8, 1979.
Portman, Natalie Jerusalem, June 9, 1981.
Posey, Parker Baltimore, MD, Nov. 8, 1968.
Postlethwaite, Pete London, England, Feb. 7, 1945.
Potente, Franka Dulmen, Germany, July 22, 1974.
Potter, Monica Cleveland, OH, June 30, 1971.
Potts, Annie Nashville, TN, Oct. 28, 1952. Stephens College.
Powell, Jane (Suzanne Burce) Portland, OR, Apr. 1, 1928.
Powell, Robert Salford, England, June 1, 1944. Manchester U.
Power, Taryn Los Angeles, CA, Sept. 13, 1953.
Power, Tyrone, IV Los Angeles, CA, Jan. 22, 1959.
Powers, Mala (Mary Ellen) San Francisco, CA, Dec. 29, 1921. UCLA.
Powers, Stefanie (Federkiewicz) Hollywood, CA, Oct. 12, 1942.
Prentiss, Paula (Paula Ragusa) San Antonio, TX, Mar. 4, 1939. Northwestern.
Presle, Micheline (Micheline Chassagne) Paris, France, Aug. 22, 1922. Rouleau Drama School.
Presley, Priscilla Brooklyn, NY, May 24, 1945.

Presnell, Harve Modesto, CA, Sept. 14, 1933. USC.
Preston, Kelly Honolulu, HI, Oct. 13, 1962. USC.
Preston, William Columbia, PA, Aug. 26, 1921. Pa State U.
Price, Lonny NYC, Mar. 9, 1959. Juilliard.
Priestley, Jason Vancouver, Canada, Aug, 28, 1969.
Primus, Barry NYC, Feb. 16, 1938. CCNY.
Prince (P. Rogers Nelson) Minneapolis, MN, June 7, 1958.
Principal, Victoria Fukuoka, Japan, Jan. 3, 1945. Dade, Jr. College.
Prinze, Freddie, Jr., Los Angeles, CA, March 8, 1976.
Prochnow, Jurgen Berlin, June 10, 1941.
Prosky, Robert Philadelphia, PA, Dec. 13, 1930.
Proval, David Brooklyn, NY, May 20, 1942.
Provine, Dorothy Deadwood, SD, Jan. 20, 1937. U Wash.
Pryce, Jonathan Wales, UK, June 1, 1947, RADA.
Pryor, Richard Peoria, IL, Dec. 1, 1940.
Pullman, Bill Delphi, NY, Dec. 17, 1954. SUNY/Oneonta, U Mass.
Purcell, Lee Cherry Point, NC, June 15, 1947. Stephens.
Purdom, Edmund Welwyn Garden City, England, Dec. 19, 1924. St. Ignatius College.

Quaid, Dennis Houston, TX, Apr. 9, 1954.
Quaid, Randy Houston, TX, Oct. 1, 1950. U Houston.
Qualls, DJ (Donald Joseph) Nashville, TN, June 12, 1978.
Quinlan, Kathleen Mill Valley, CA, Nov. 19, 1954.
Quinn, Aidan Chicago, IL, Mar. 8, 1959.

Radcliffe, Daniel London, England, July 23, 1989.
Raffin, Deborah Los Angeles, CA, Mar. 13, 1953. Valley College.
Ragsdale, William El Dorado, AK, Jan. 19, 1961. Hendrix College.
Railsback, Steve Dallas, TX, 1948.
Rainer, Luise Vienna, Austria, Jan. 12, 1910.
Ramis, Harold Chicago, IL, Nov. 21, 1944. Washington U.
Rampling, Charlotte Surmer, England, Feb. 5, 1946. U Madrid.
Ramsey, Logan Long Beach, CA, Mar. 21, 1921. St. Joseph.
Randell, Ron Sydney, Australia, Oct. 8, 1920. St. Mary's College.
Rapaport, Michael March 20, 1970.
Rapp, Anthony Chicago, Oct. 26, 1971.

Rasche, David St. Louis, MO, Aug. 7, 1944.
Rea, Stephen Belfast, Northern Ireland, Oct. 31, 1949.
Reason, Rex Berlin, Germany, Nov. 30, 1928. Pasadena Playhouse.
Reddy, Helen Melbourne, Australia, Oct. 25, 1942.
Redford, Robert Santa Monica, CA, Aug. 18, 1937. AADA.
Redgrave, Corin London, England, July 16, 1939.
Redgrave, Lynn London, England, Mar. 8, 1943.
Redgrave, Vanessa London, England, Jan. 30, 1937.
Redman, Joyce County Mayo, Ireland, 1919. RADA.
Reed, Pamela Tacoma, WA, Apr. 2, 1949.
Reems, Harry (Herbert Streicher) Bronx, NY, 1947. U Pittsburgh.
Rees, Roger Aberystwyth, Wales, May 5, 1944.
Reese, Della Detroit, MI, July 6, 1932.
Reeves, Keanu Beiruit, Lebanon, Sept. 2, 1964.
Regehr, Duncan Lethbridge, Canada, Oct. 5, 1952.
Reid, Elliott NYC, Jan. 16, 1920.
Reid, Tara Wyckoff, NJ, Nov. 8, 1975.
Reid, Tim Norfolk, VA, Dec, 19, 1944.
Reilly, Charles Nelson NYC, Jan. 13, 1931. U Ct.
Reilly, John C. Chicago, IL, May 24, 1965.
Reiner, Carl NYC, Mar. 20, 1922. Georgetown.
Reiner, Rob NYC, Mar. 6, 1947. UCLA.
Reinhold, Judge (Edward Ernest, Jr.) Wilmington, DE, May 21, 1957. NC
Reinking, Ann Seattle, WA, Nov. 10, 1949.
Reiser, Paul NYC, Mar. 30, 1957.
Remar, James Boston, MA, Dec. 31, 1953. Neighborhood Playhouse.
Renfro, Brad Knoxville, TN, July 25, 1982.
Reno, Jean (Juan Moreno) Casablanca, Morocco, July 30, 1948.
Reubens, Paul (Paul Reubenfeld) Peekskill, NY, Aug. 27, 1952.
Revill, Clive Wellington, NZ, Apr. 18, 1930.
Rey, Antonia Havana, Cuba, Oct. 12, 1927.
Reynolds, Burt Waycross, GA, Feb. 11, 1935. Fla. State U.
Reynolds, Debbie (Mary Frances Reynolds) El Paso, TX, Apr. 1, 1932.
Rhames, Ving (Irving Rhames) NYC, May 12, 1959.
Rhoades, Barbara Poughkeepsie, NY, Mar. 23, 1947.
Rhodes, Cynthia Nashville, TN, Nov. 21, 1956.
Rhys, Paul Neath, Wales, Dec. 19, 1963.
Rhys-Davies, John Salisbury, England, May 5, 1944.
Rhys-Meyers, Jonathan Cork, Ireland, July 27, 1977.
Ribisi, Giovanni Los Angeles, CA, Dec. 17, 1974.
Ricci, Christina Santa Monica, CA, Feb. 12, 1980.
Richard, Cliff (Harry Webb) India, Oct. 14, 1940.
Richards, Denise Downers Grove, IL, Feb. 17, 1972.
Richards, Michael Culver City, CA, July 14, 1949.
Richardson, Joely London, England, Jan. 9, 1965.
Richardson, Miranda Southport, England, Mar. 3, 1958.
Richardson, Natasha London, England, May 11, 1963.
Rickles, Don NYC, May 8, 1926. AADA.
Rickman, Alan Hammersmith, England, Feb. 21, 1946.
Riegert, Peter NYC, Apr. 11, 1947. U Buffalo.
Rifkin, Ron NYC, Oct. 31, 1939.
Rigg, Diana Doncaster, England, July 20, 1938. RADA.
Ringwald, Molly Rosewood, CA, Feb. 16, 1968.
Ritter, John Burbank, CA, Sept. 17, 1948. US. Cal.

Rivers, Joan (Molinsky) Brooklyn, NY, NY, June 8, 1933.
Roache, Linus Manchester, England, 1964.
Robards, Sam NYC, Dec. 16, 1963.
Robbins, Tim NYC, Oct. 16, 1958. UCLA.
Roberts, Eric Biloxi, MS, Apr. 18, 1956. RADA.
Roberts, Julia Atlanta, GA, Oct. 28, 1967.
Roberts, Ralph Salisbury, NC, Aug. 17, 1922. UNC.
Roberts, Tanya (Leigh) Bronx, NY, Oct. 15, 1954.
Roberts, Tony NYC, Oct. 22, 1939. Northwestern.
Robertson, Cliff La Jolla, CA, Sept. 9, 1925. Antioch College.
Robertson, Dale Oklahoma City, July 14, 1923.
Robinson, Chris West Palm Beach, FL, Nov. 5, 1938. LACC.
Robinson, Jay NYC, Apr. 14, 1930.
Robinson, Roger Seattle, WA, May 2, 1940. USC.
Rochefort, Jean Paris, France, 1930.
Rock, Chris Brooklyn, NY, Feb. 7, 1966.
Rock, The (Dwayne Johnson) Hayward, CA, May 2, 1972.
Rockwell, Sam Daly City, CA, Nov. 5, 1968.
Rodriguez, Michelle Bexar County, TX, July 12, 1978.
Rogers, Mimi Coral Gables, FL, Jan. 27, 1956.
Rogers, Wayne Birmingham, AL, Apr. 7, 1933. Princeton.
Romijn-Stamos, Rebecca Berkeley, CA, Nov. 6, 1972.
Ronstadt, Linda Tucson, AZ, July 15, 1946.
Rooker, Michael Jasper, AL, Apr. 6, 1955.
Rooney, Mickey (Joe Yule, Jr.) Brooklyn, NY, Sept. 23, 1920.
Rose, Reva Chicago, IL, July 30, 1940. Goodman.
Ross, Diana Detroit, MI, Mar. 26, 1944.
Ross, Justin Brooklyn, NY, Dec. 15, 1954.
Ross, Katharine Hollywood, Jan. 29, 1943. Santa Rosa College.
Rossellini, Isabella Rome, June 18, 1952.
Rossovich, Rick Palo Alto, CA, Aug. 28, 1957.
Rossum, Emmy NYC, Sept. 12, 1986.
Roth, Tim London, England, May 14, 1961.
Roundtree, Richard New Rochelle, NY, Sept. 7, 1942. Southern Il.
Rourke, Mickey (Philip Andre Rourke, Jr.) Schenectady, NY, Sept. 16, 1956.
Rowe, Nicholas London, England, Nov. 22, 1966, Eton.
Rowlands, Gena Cambria, WI, June 19, 1934.
Rubin, Andrew New Bedford, MA, June 22, 1946. AADA.
Rubinek, Saul Fohrenwold, Germany, July 2, 1948.
Rubinstein, John Los Angeles, CA, Dec. 8, 1946. UCLA.
Ruck, Alan Cleveland, OH, July 1, 1960.
Rucker, Bo Tampa, FL, Aug. 17, 1948.
Rudd, Paul Boston, MA, May 15, 1940.
Rudd, Paul Passaic, NJ, Apr. 6, 1969.
Rudner, Rita Miami, FL, Sept. 17, 1955.
Ruehl, Mercedes Queens, NY, Feb. 28, 1948.
Ruffalo, Mark Kenosha, WI, Nov. 22, 1967.
Rule, Janice Cincinnati, OH, Aug. 15, 1931.
Rupert, Michael Denver, CO, Oct. 23, 1951. Pasadena Playhouse.
Rush, Barbara Denver, CO, Jan. 4, 1927. U Calif.
Rush, Geoffrey Toowoomba, Queensland, Australia, July 6, 1951. U of Queensland.
Russell, Jane Bemidji, MI, June 21, 1921. Max Reinhardt School.
Russell, Kurt Springfield, MA, Mar. 17, 1951.

Russell, Theresa (Paup) San Diego, CA, Mar. 20, 1957.
Russo, James NYC, Apr. 23, 1953.
Russo, Rene Burbank, CA, Feb. 17, 1954.
Rutherford, Ann Toronto, Canada, Nov. 2, 1920.
Ryan, John P. NYC, July 30, 1936. CCNY.
Ryan, Meg Fairfield, CT, Nov. 19, 1961. NYU.
Ryan, Tim (Meineslschmidt) Staten Island, NY, 1958. Rutgers U.
Ryder, Winona (Horowitz) Winona, MN, Oct. 29, 1971.

Sacchi, Robert Bronx, NY, 1941. NYU.
Sägebrecht, Marianne Starnberg, Bavaria, Aug. 27, 1945.
Saint, Eva Marie Newark, NJ, July 4, 1924. Bowling Green State U.
Saint James, Susan (Suzie Jane Miller) Los Angeles, CA, Aug. 14, 1946. Conn. College.
St. John, Betta Hawthorne, CA, Nov. 26, 1929.
St. John, Jill (Jill Oppenheim) Los Angeles, CA, Aug. 19, 1940.
Sala, John Los Angeles, CA, Oct. 5, 1962.
Saldana, Theresa Brooklyn, NY, Aug. 20, 1954.
Salinger, Matt Windsor, VT, Feb. 13, 1960. Princeton, Columbia.
Salt, Jennifer Los Angeles, CA, Sept. 4, 1944. Sarah Lawrence College.
Samms, Emma London, England, Aug. 28, 1960.
San Giacomo, Laura Orange, NJ, Nov. 14, 1961.
Sanders, Jay O. Austin, TX, Apr. 16, 1953.
Sandler, Adam Bronx, NY, Sept. 9, 1966. NYU.
Sands, Julian Yorkshire, England, Jan 15, 1958.
Sands, Tommy Chicago, IL, Aug. 27, 1937.
San Juan, Olga NYC, Mar. 16, 1927.
Sara, Mia (Sarapocciello) Brooklyn, NY, June 19, 1967.
Sarandon, Chris Beckley, WV, July 24, 1942. U WVa., Catholic U.
Sarandon, Susan (Tomalin) NYC, Oct. 4, 1946. Catholic U.
Sarrazin, Michael Quebec City, Canada, May 22, 1940.
Sarsgaard, Peter Scott Air Force Base, Illinois, Mar. 7, 1971.
Savage, Fred Highland Park, IL, July 9, 1976.
Savage, John (Youngs) Long Island, NY, Aug. 25, 1949. AADA.
Saviola, Camille Bronx, NY, July 16, 1950.
Savoy, Teresa Ann London, England, July 18, 1955.
Sawa, Devon Vancouver, BC, Canada, Sept. 7, 1978.
Saxon, John (Carmen Orrico) Brooklyn, NY, Aug. 5, 1935.
Sbarge, Raphael NYC, Feb. 12, 1964.
Scacchi, Greta Milan, Italy, Feb. 18, 1960.
Scalia, Jack Brooklyn, NY, Nov. 10, 1951.
Scarwid, Diana Savannah, GA, Aug. 27, 1955, AADA. Pace U.
Scheider, Roy Orange, NJ, Nov. 10, 1932. Franklin-Marshall.
Scheine, Raynor Emporia, VA, Nov. 10. Va Commonwealth U.
Schell, Maria Vienna, Jan. 15, 1926.
Schell, Maximilian Vienna, Dec. 8, 1930.
Schlatter, Charlie Englewood, NJ, May 1, 1966. Ithaca College.
Schneider, John Mt. Kisco, NY, Apr. 8, 1960.
Schneider, Maria Paris, France, Mar. 27, 1952.
Schreiber, Liev San Francisco, CA, Oct. 4, 1967.
Schroder, Rick Staten Island, NY, Apr. 13, 1970.
Schuck, John Boston, MA, Feb. 4, 1940.
Schultz, Dwight Milwaukee, WI, Nov. 10, 1938. Marquette U.
Schwartzman, Jason Los Angeles, CA, June 26, 1980.

Schwarzenegger, Arnold Austria, July 30, 1947.
Schwimmer, David Queens, NY, Nov. 12, 1966.
Schygulla, Hanna Katlowitz, Germany, Dec. 25, 1943.
Sciorra, Annabella NYC, Mar. 24, 1964.
Scofield, Paul Hurstpierpoint, England, Jan. 21, 1922. London Mask Theatre School.
Scoggins, Tracy Galveston, TX, Nov. 13, 1959.
Scolari, Peter Scarsdale, NY, Sept. 12, 1956. NYCC.
Scott, Campbell South Salem, NY, July 19, 1962. Lawrence.
Scott, Debralee Elizabeth, NJ, Apr. 2, 1953.
Scott, Gordon (Gordon M. Werschkul) Portland, OR, Aug. 3, 1927. Oregon U.
Scott, Lizabeth (Emma Matso) Scranton, PA, Sept. 29, 1922.
Scott, Seann William Cottage Grove, MN, Oct. 3, 1976.
Scott Thomas, Kristin Redruth, Cornwall, Eng., May 24, 1960.
Seagal, Steven Detroit, MI, Apr. 10, 1951.
Sears, Heather London, England, Sept. 28, 1935.
Sedgwick, Kyra NYC, Aug. 19, 1965. USC.
Segal, George NYC, Feb. 13, 1934. Columbia.
Selby, David Morganstown, WV, Feb. 5, 1941. U WV.
Sellars, Elizabeth Glasgow, Scotland, May 6, 1923.
Selleck, Tom Detroit, MI, Jan. 29, 1945. US Cal.
Serbedzija, Rade Bunic, Yugoslavia, July 27, 1946.
Sernas, Jacques Lithuania, July 30, 1925.
Serrault, Michel Brunoy, France. Jan. 24, 1928. Paris Consv.
Seth, Roshan New Delhi, India. Aug. 17, 1942.
Sevigny, Chloe Springfield, MA, Nov. 18, 1974.
Sewell, Rufus Twickenham, England, Oct. 29, 1967.
Seymour, Jane (Joyce Frankenberg) Hillingdon, England, Feb. 15, 1952.
Shalhoub, Tony Green Bay, WI, Oct. 9, 1953.
Shandling, Garry Chicago, IL, Nov. 29, 1949.
Sharif, Omar (Michel Shalhoub) Alexandria, Egypt, Apr. 10, 1932. Victoria College.
Shatner, William Montreal, Canada, Mar. 22, 1931. McGill U.
Shaver, Helen St. Thomas, Ontario, Canada, Feb. 24, 1951.
Shaw, Fiona Cork, Ireland, July 10, 1955. RADA.
Shaw, Stan Chicago, IL, 1952.
Shawn, Wallace NYC, Nov. 12, 1943. Harvard.
Shea, John North Conway, NH, Apr. 14, 1949. Bates, Yale.
Shearer, Harry Los Angeles, CA, Dec. 23, 1943. UCLA.
Shearer, Moira Dunfermline, Scotland, Jan. 17, 1926. London Theatre School.
Sheedy, Ally NYC, June 13, 1962. USC.
Sheen, Charlie (Carlos Irwin Estevez) Santa Monica, CA, Sept. 3, 1965.
Sheen, Martin (Ramon Estevez) Dayton, OH, Aug. 3, 1940.
Sheffer, Craig York, PA, Apr. 23, 1960. E. Stroudsberg U.
Sheffield, John Pasadena, CA, Apr. 11, 1931. UCLA.
Shelley, Carol London, England, England, Aug. 16, 1939.
Shepard, Sam (Rogers) Ft. Sheridan, IL, Nov. 5, 1943.
Shepherd, Cybill Memphis, TN, Feb. 18, 1950. Hunter, NYU.
Sher, Antony England, June 14, 1949.
Sheridan, Jamey Pasadena, CA, July 12, 1951.
Shields, Brooke NYC, May 31, 1965.
Shire, Talia Lake Success, NY, Apr. 25, 1946. Yale.
Short, Martin Toronto, Canada, Mar. 26, 1950. McMaster U.

Shue, Elisabeth S. Orange, NJ, Oct. 6, 1963. Harvard.
Siemaszko, Casey Chicago, IL, March 17, 1961.
Sikking, James B. Los Angeles, CA, Mar. 5, 1934.
Silva, Henry Brooklyn, NY, 1928.
Silver, Ron NYC, July 2, 1946. SUNY.
Silverman, Jonathan Los Angeles, CA, Aug. 5, 1966. USC.
Silverstone, Alicia San Francisco, CA, Oct. 4, 1976.
Silverstone, Ben London, England, Apr. 9, 1979.
Simmons, Jean London, England, Jan. 31, 1929. Aida Foster School.
Simon, Paul Newark. NJ, Nov. 5, 1942.
Simon, Simone Bethune, France, Apr. 23, 1910.
Simpson, O. J. (Orenthal James) San Francisco, CA, July 9, 1947. UCLA.
Sinbad (David Adkins) Benton Harbor, MI, Nov. 10, 1956.
Sinclair, John (Gianluigi Loffredo) Rome, Italy, 1946.
Sinden, Donald Plymouth, England, Oct. 9, 1923. Webber-Douglas.
Singer, Lori Corpus Christi, TX, May 6, 1962. Juilliard.
Sinise, Gary Chicago, Mar. 17. 1955.
Sizemore, Tom Detroit, MI, Sept. 29, 1964.
Skarsgård, Stellan Gothenburg, Vastergotland, Sweden, June 13, 1951.
Skerritt, Tom Detroit, MI, Aug. 25, 1933. Wayne State U.
Skye, Ione (Leitch) London, England, Sept. 4, 1971.
Slater, Christian NYC, Aug. 18, 1969.
Slater, Helen NYC, Dec. 15, 1965.
Smart, Amy Topanga Canyon, CA, Mar. 26, 1976.
Smith, Charles Martin Los Angeles, CA, Oct. 30, 1953. Cal State U.
Smith, Jaclyn Houston, TX, Oct. 26, 1947.
Smith, Jada Pinkett Baltimore, MD, Sept. 18, 1971.
Smith, Kerr Exton, PA, Mar. 9, 1972.
Smith, Kevin Red Bank, NJ, Aug. 2, 1970.
Smith, Kurtwood New Lisbon, WI, Jul. 3, 1942.
Smith, Lane Memphis, TN, Apr. 29, 1936.
Smith, Lewis Chattanooga, TN, 1958. Actors Studio.
Smith, Lois Topeka, KS, Nov. 3, 1930. U Wash.
Smith, Maggie Ilford, England, Dec. 28, 1934.
Smith, Roger South Gate, CA, Dec. 18, 1932. U Ariz.
Smith, Will Philadelphia, PA, Sept. 25, 1968.
Smithers, William Richmond, VA, July 10, 1927. Catholic U.
Smits, Jimmy Brooklyn, NY, July 9, 1955. Cornell U.
Snipes, Wesley NYC, July 31, 1963. SUNY/Purchase.
Snoop Dogg (Calvin Broadus) Long Beach, CA, Oct. 20, 1971.
Sobieksi, Leelee (Liliane Sobieski) NYC, June 10, 1982.
Solomon, Bruce NYC, 1944. U Miami, Wayne State U.
Somers, Suzanne (Mahoney) San Bruno, CA, Oct. 16, 1946. Lone Mt. College.
Sommer, Elke (Schletz) Berlin, Germany, Nov. 5, 1940.
Sommer, Josef Greifswald, Germany, June 26, 1934.
Sordi, Alberto Rome, Italy, June 15, 1920.
Sorvino, Mira Tenafly, NJ, Sept. 28, 1967.
Sorvino, Paul NYC, Apr. 13, 1939. AMDA.
Soto, Talisa (Miriam Soto) Brooklyn, NY, Mar. 27, 1967.
Soul, David Chicago, IL, Aug. 28, 1943.
Spacek, Sissy Quitman, TX, Dec. 25, 1949. Actors Studio.
Spacey, Kevin So. Orange, NJ, July 26, 1959. Juilliard.
Spade, David Birmingham, MS, July 22, 1964.

Spader, James Buzzards Bay, MA, Feb. 7, 1960.
Spall, Timothy London, England, Feb. 27, 1957.
Spano, Vincent Brooklyn, NY, Oct. 18, 1962.
Spenser, Jeremy London, England, July 16, 1937.
Spinella, Stephen Naples, Italy, Oct. 11, 1956. NYU.
Springfield, Rick (Richard Spring Thorpe) Sydney, Australia, Aug. 23, 1949.
Stadlen, Lewis J. Brooklyn, NY, Mar. 7, 1947. Neighborhood Playhouse.
Stahl, Nick Dallas, TX, Dec. 5, 1979.
Stallone, Frank NYC, July 30, 1950.
Stallone, Sylvester NYC, July 6, 1946. U Miami.
Stamp, Terence London, England, July 23, 1939.
Stanford, Aaron Westford, MA, Dec. 18, 1977.
Stang, Arnold Chelsea, MA, Sept. 28, 1925.
Stanton, Harry Dean Lexington, KY, July 14, 1926.
Stapleton, Jean NYC, Jan. 19, 1923.
Stapleton, Maureen Troy, NY, June 21, 1925.
Starr, Ringo (Richard Starkey) Liverpool, England, July 7, 1940.
Staunton, Imelda UK, Jan. 9, 1956.
Steele, Barbara England, Dec. 29, 1937.
Steele, Tommy London, England, Dec. 17, 1936.
Steenburgen, Mary Newport, AR, Feb. 8, 1953. Neighborhood Playhouse.
Sterling, Robert (William Sterling Hart) Newcastle, PA, Nov. 13, 1917. U Pittsburgh.
Stern, Daniel Bethesda, MD, Aug. 28, 1957.
Sternhagen, Frances Washington, DC, Jan. 13, 1932.
Stevens, Andrew Memphis, TN, June 10, 1955.
Stevens, Connie (Concetta Ann Ingolia) Brooklyn, NY, Aug. 8, 1938. Hollywood Professional School.
Stevens, Fisher Chicago, IL, Nov. 27, 1963. NYU.
Stevens, Stella (Estelle Eggleston) Hot Coffee, MS, Oct. 1, 1936.
Stevenson, Juliet Essex, England, Oct. 30, 1956.
Stevenson, Parker Philadelphia, PA, June 4, 1953. Princeton.
Stewart, Alexandra Montreal, Canada, June 10, 1939. Louvre.
Stewart, Elaine (Elsy Steinberg) Montclair, NJ, May 31, 1929.
Stewart, French (Milton French Stewart) Albuquerque, NM, Feb. 20, 1964.
Stewart, Jon (Jonathan Stewart Liebowitz) Trenton, NJ, Nov. 28, 1962.
Stewart, Martha (Martha Haworth) Bardwell, KY, Oct. 7, 1922.
Stewart, Patrick Mirfield, England, July 13, 1940.
Stiers, David Ogden Peoria, IL, Oct. 31, 1942.
Stiles, Julia NYC, Mar. 28, 1981.
Stiller, Ben NYC, Nov. 30, 1965.
Stiller, Jerry NYC, June 8, 1931.
Sting (Gordon Matthew Sumner) Wallsend, England, Oct. 2, 1951.
Stockwell, Dean Hollywood, Mar. 5, 1935.
Stockwell, John (John Samuels, IV) Galveston, TX, Mar. 25, 1961. Harvard.
Stoltz, Eric Whittier, CA, Sept. 30, 1961. USC.
Stone, Dee Wallace (Deanna Bowers) Kansas City, MO, Dec. 14, 1948. UKS.
Storm, Gale (Josephine Cottle) Bloomington, TX, Apr. 5, 1922.
Stowe, Madeleine Eagle Rock, CA, Aug. 18, 1958.
Strassman, Marcia New Jersey, Apr. 28, 1948.
Strathairn, David San Francisco, Jan. 26, 1949.
Strauss, Peter NYC, Feb. 20, 1947.
Streep, Meryl (Mary Louise) Summit, NJ, June 22, 1949 Vassar, Yale.
Streisand, Barbra Brooklyn, NY, Apr. 24, 1942.

David Ogden Stiers   Jerry Stiller   Tilda Swinton   Jay Thomas

Stritch, Elaine Detroit, MI, Feb. 2, 1925. Drama Workshop.
Stroud, Don Honolulu, HI, Sept. 1, 1937.
Struthers, Sally Portland, OR, July 28, 1948. Pasadena Playhouse.
Studi, Wes (Wesley Studie) Nofire Hollow, OK, Dec. 17, 1947.
Summer, Donna (LaDonna Gaines) Boston, MA, Dec. 31, 1948.
Sutherland, Donald St. John, New Brunswick, Canada, July 17, 1935. U Toronto.
Sutherland, Kiefer Los Angeles, CA, Dec. 18, 1966.
Suvari, Mena Newport, RI, Feb. 9, 1979.
Svenson, Bo Goreborg, Sweden, Feb. 13, 1941. UCLA.
Swank, Hilary Bellingham, WA, July 30, 1974.
Swayze, Patrick Houston, TX, Aug. 18, 1952.
Sweeney, D. B. (Daniel Bernard Sweeney) Shoreham, NY, Nov. 14, 1961.
Swinton, Tilda London, England, Nov. 5, 1960.
Swit, Loretta Passaic, NJ, Nov. 4, 1937, AADA.
Sylvester, William Oakland, CA, Jan. 31, 1922. RADA.
Symonds, Robert Bistow, AK, Dec. 1, 1926. TexU.
Syms, Sylvia London, England, June 1, 1934. Convent School.
Szarabajka, Keith Oak Park, IL, Dec. 2, 1952. U Chicago.

T, Mr. (Lawrence Tero) Chicago, IL, May 21, 1952.
Tabori, Kristoffer (Siegel) Los Angeles, CA, Aug. 4, 1952.
Takei, George Los Angeles, CA, Apr. 20, 1939. UCLA.
Talbot, Nita NYC, Aug. 8, 1930. Irvine Studio School.
Tamblyn, Russ Los Angeles, CA, Dec. 30, 1934.
Tambor, Jeffrey San Francisco, CA, July 8, 1944.
Tarantino, Quentin Knoxville, TN, Mar. 27, 1963.
Tate, Larenz Chicago, IL, Sept. 8, 1975.
Tautou, Audrey Beaumont, France, Aug. 9, 1978.
Taylor, Elizabeth London, England, Feb. 27, 1932. Byron House School.
Taylor, Lili Glencoe, IL, Feb. 20, 1967.
Taylor, Noah London, England, Sept. 4, 1969.
Taylor, Renee NYC, Mar. 19, 1935.
Taylor, Rod (Robert) Sydney, Australia, Jan. 11, 1929.
Taylor-Young, Leigh Washington, DC, Jan. 25, 1945. Northwestern.
Teefy, Maureen Minneapolis, MN, Oct. 26, 1953, Juilliard.
Temple, Shirley Santa Monica, CA, Apr. 23, 1927.

Tennant, Victoria London, England, Sept. 30, 1950.
Tenney, Jon Princeton, NJ, Dec. 16, 1961.
Terzieff, Laurent Paris, France, June 25, 1935.
Tewes, Lauren Braddock, PA, Oct. 26, 1954.
Thacker, Russ Washington, DC, June 23, 1946. Montgomery College.
Thaxter, Phyllis Portland, ME, Nov. 20, 1921. St. Genevieve.
Thelen, Jodi St. Cloud, MN, 1963.
Theron, Charlize Benoni, So. Africa, Aug. 7, 1975.
Thewlis, David Blackpool, Eng., 1963.
Thomas, Henry San Antonio, TX, Sept. 8, 1971.
Thomas, Jay New Orleans, July 12, 1948.
Thomas, Jonathan Taylor (Weiss) Bethlehem, PA, Sept. 8, 1981.
Thomas, Marlo (Margaret) Detroit, Nov. 21, 1938. USC.
Thomas, Philip Michael Columbus, OH, May 26, 1949. Oakwood College.
Thomas, Richard NYC, June 13, 1951. Columbia.
Thompson, Emma London, England, Apr. 15, 1959. Cambridge.
Thompson, Fred Dalton Sheffield, AL, Aug. 19, 1942.
Thompson, Jack (John Payne) Sydney, Australia, Aug. 31, 1940.
Thompson, Lea Rochester, MN, May 31, 1961.
Thompson, Rex NYC, Dec. 14, 1942.
Thompson, Sada Des Moines, IA, Sept. 27, 1929. Carnegie Tech.
Thornton, Billy Bob Hot Spring, AR, Aug. 4, 1955.
Thorson, Linda Toronto, Canada, June 18, 1947. RADA.
Thurman, Uma Boston, MA, Apr. 29, 1970.
Ticotin, Rachel Bronx, NY, Nov. 1, 1958.
Tierney, Lawrence Brooklyn, NY, Mar. 15, 1919. Manhattan College.
Tiffin, Pamela (Wonso) Oklahoma City, OK, Oct. 13, 1942.
Tighe, Kevin Los Angeles, CA, Aug. 13, 1944.
Tilly, Jennifer Los Angeles, CA, Sept. 16, 1958.
Tilly, Meg Texada, Canada, Feb. 14, 1960.
Tobolowsky, Stephen Dallas, TX, May 30, 1951. Southern Methodist U.
Todd, Beverly Chicago, IL, July 1, 1946.
Todd, Richard Dublin, Ireland, June 11, 1919. Shrewsbury School.
Tolkan, James Calumet, MI, June 20, 1931.
Tomei, Marisa Brooklyn, NY, Dec. 4, 1964. NYU.
Tomlin, Lily Detroit, MI, Sept. 1, 1939. Wayne State U.
Topol (Chaim Topol) Tel-Aviv, Israel, Sept. 9, 1935.

Torn, Rip Temple, TX, Feb. 6, 1931. UTex.
Torres, Liz NYC, Sept. 27, 1947. NYU.
Totter, Audrey Joliet, IL, Dec. 20, 1918.
Towsend, Robert Chicago, IL, Feb. 6, 1957.
Townsend, Stuart Dublin, Ireland, Dec. 15, 1972.
Travanti, Daniel J. Kenosha, WI, Mar. 7, 1940.
Travis, Nancy Astoria, NY, Sept. 21, 1961.
Travolta, Joey Englewood, NJ, Oct. 14, 1950.
Travolta, John Englewood, NJ, Feb. 18, 1954.
Trintignant, Jean-Louis Pont-St. Esprit, France, Dec. 11, 1930. DullinBalachova Drama School.
Tripplehorn, Jeanne Tulsa, OK, June 10, 1963.
Tsopei, Corinna Athens, Greece, June 21, 1944.
Tubb, Barry Snyder, TX, 1963. Am Consv Th.
Tucci, Stanley Katonah, NY, Jan. 11, 1960.
Tucker, Chris Decatur, GA, Aug. 31, 1972.
Tucker, Jonathan Boston, May 31, 1982.
Tucker, Michael Baltimore, MD, Feb. 6, 1944.
Tune, Tommy Wichita Falls, TX, Feb. 28, 1939.
Tunney, Robin Chicago, June 19, 1972.
Turner, Janine (Gauntt) Lincoln, NE, Dec. 6, 1963.
Turner, Kathleen Springfield, MO, June 19, 1954. U Md.
Turner, Tina (Anna Mae Bullock) Nutbush, TN, Nov. 26, 1938.
Turturro, John Brooklyn, NY, Feb. 28, 1957. Yale.
Tushingham, Rita Liverpool, England, Mar. 14, 1940.
Twiggy (Lesley Hornby) London, England, Sept. 19, 1949.
Twomey, Anne Boston, MA, June 7, 1951. Temple U.
Tyler, Beverly (Beverly Jean Saul) Scranton, PA, July 5, 1928.
Tyler, Liv Portland, ME, July 1, 1977.
Tyrrell, Susan San Francisco, Mar. 18, 1945.
Tyson, Cathy Liverpool, England, June 12, 1965. Royal Shake. Co.
Tyson, Cicely NYC, Dec. 19, 1933. NYU.

Uggams, Leslie NYC, May 25, 1943. Juilliard.
Ullman, Tracey Slough, England, Dec. 30, 1959.
Ullmann, Liv Tokyo, Dec. 10, 1938. Webber-Douglas Acad.
Ulrich, Skeet (Bryan Ray Ulrich) North Carolina, Jan. 20, 1969.
Umeki, Miyoshi Otaru, Hokaido, Japan, Apr. 3, 1929.
Underwood, Blair Tacoma, WA, Aug. 25, 1964. Carnegie-Mellon U.
Unger, Deborah Kara Victoria, British Columbia, May 12, 1966.
Union, Gabrielle Omaha, NE, Oct. 29, 1973.

Vaccaro, Brenda Brooklyn, NY, Nov. 18, 1939. Neighborhood Playhouse.
Valli, Alida Pola, Italy, May 31, 1921. Academy of Drama.
Van Ark, Joan NYC, June 16, 1943. Yale.
Van Damme, Jean-Claude (J-C Vorenberg) Brussels, Belgium, Apr. 1, 1960.
Van De Ven, Monique Zeeland, Netherlands, July 28, 1952.
Van Der Beek, James Chesire, CT, March 8, 1977.
Van Devere, Trish (Patricia Dressel) Englewood Cliffs, NJ, Mar. 9, 1945. Ohio Wesleyan.
Van Dien, Casper Ridgefield, NJ, Dec. 18, 1968.
Van Doren, Mamie (Joan Lucile Olander) Rowena SD, Feb. 6, 1933.
Van Dyke, Dick West Plains, MO, Dec. 13, 1925.
Vanity (Denise Katrina Smith) Niagara, Ont., Can, Jan. 4, 1959.

Van Pallandt, Nina Copenhagen, Denmark, July 15, 1932.
Van Patten, Dick NYC, Dec. 9, 1928.
Van Patten, Joyce NYC, Mar. 9, 1934.
Van Peebles, Mario NYC, Jan. 15, 1958. Columbia U.
Van Peebles, Melvin Chicago, IL, Aug. 21, 1932.
Vance, Courtney B. Detroit, MI, Mar. 12, 1960.
Vardalos, Nia Winnipeg, Manitoba, Can., Sept. 24, 1962.
Vaughn, Robert NYC, Nov. 22, 1932. USC.
Vaughn, Vince Minneapolis, MN, Mar. 28, 1970.
Vega, Isela Hermosillo, Mexico, Nov. 5, 1940.
Veljohnson, Reginald NYC, Aug. 16, 1952.
Vennera, Chick Herkimer, NY, Mar. 27, 1952. Pasadena Playhouse.
Venora, Diane Hartford, CT, 1952. Juilliard.
Vereen, Ben Miami, FL, Oct. 10, 1946.
Vernon, John Montreal, Canada, Feb. 24, 1932.
Victor, James (Lincoln Rafael Peralta Diaz) Santiago, D.R., July 27, 1939. Haaren HS/NYC.
Vincent, Jan-Michael Denver, CO, July 15, 1944. Ventura.
Violet, Ultra (Isabelle Collin-Dufresne) Grenoble, France, Sept. 6, 1935.
Visnjic, Goran Sibenik, Yugoslavia, Sept. 9, 1972.
Vitale, Milly Rome, Italy, July 16, 1928. Lycee Chateaubriand.
Vohs, Joan St. Albans, NY, July 30, 1931.
Voight, Jon Yonkers, NY, Dec. 29, 1938. Catholic U.
Von Bargen, Daniel Cincinnati, OH, June 5, 1950. Purdue.
Von Dohlen, Lenny Augusta, GA, Dec. 22, 1958. U Tex.
Von Sydow, Max Lund, Sweden, July 10, 1929. Royal Drama Theatre.

Wagner, Lindsay Los Angeles, CA, June 22. 1949.
Wagner, Natasha Gregson Los Angeles, CA, Sept. 29, 1970.
Wagner, Robert Detroit, Feb. 10, 1930.
Wahl, Ken Chicago, IL, Feb. 14, 1953.
Waite, Genevieve South Africa, 1949.
Waite, Ralph White Plains, NY, June 22, 1929. Yale.
Waits, Tom Pomona, CA, Dec. 7, 1949.
Walken, Christopher Astoria, NY, Mar. 31, 1943. Hofstra.
Walker, Clint Hartford, IL, May 30, 1927. USC.
Walker, Paul Glendale, CA, Sept. 12, 1973.
Wallach, Eli Brooklyn, NY, Dec. 7, 1915. CCNY, U Tex.
Wallach, Roberta NYC, Aug. 2, 1955.
Wallis, Shani London, England, Apr. 5, 1941.
Walsh, M. Emmet Ogdensburg, NY, Mar. 22, 1935. Clarkson College, AADA.
Walter, Jessica Brooklyn, NY, Jan. 31, 1944 Neighborhood Playhouse.
Walter, Tracey Jersey City, NJ, Nov. 25, 1942.
Walters, Julie London, England, Feb. 22, 1950.
Walton, Emma London, England, Nov. 1962. Brown U.
Wanamaker, Zoë NYC, May 13, 1949.
Ward, Burt (Gervis) Los Angeles, CA, July 6, 1945.
Ward, Fred San Diego, CA, Dec. 30, 1942.
Ward, Rachel London, England, Sept. 12, 1957.
Ward, Sela Meridian, MS, July 11, 1956.
Ward, Simon London, England, Oct. 19, 1941.
Warden, Jack (Lebzelter) Newark, NJ, Sept. 18, 1920.
Warner, David Manchester, England, July 29, 1941. RADA.
Warner, Malcolm-Jamal Jersey City, NJ, Aug. 18, 1970.

Warren, Jennifer NYC, Aug. 12, 1941. U Wisc.
Warren, Lesley Ann NYC, Aug. 16, 1946.
Warren, Michael South Bend, IN, Mar. 5, 1946. UCLA.
Warrick, Ruth St. Joseph, MO, June 29, 1915. U Mo.
Washington, Denzel Mt. Vernon, NY, Dec. 28, 1954. Fordham.
Washington, Kerry Bronx, Jan. 31, 1977.
Wasson, Craig Ontario, OR, Mar. 15, 1954. U Ore.
Watanabe, Ken Koide, Japan, Oct. 21, 1959.
Waterston, Sam Cambridge, MA, Nov. 15, 1940. Yale.
Watson, Emily London, England, Jan. 14, 1967.
Watson, Emma Oxford, England, Apr. 15, 1990.
Watts, Naomi Shoreham, England, Sept. 28, 1968.
Wayans, Damon NYC, Sept. 4, 1960.
Wayans, Keenen Ivory NYC, June 8, 1958. Tuskegee Inst.
Wayans, Marlon NYC, July 23, 1972.
Wayans, Shawn NYC, Jan. 19, 1971.
Wayne, Patrick Los Angeles, CA, July 15, 1939. Loyola.
Weathers, Carl New Orleans, LA, Jan. 14, 1948. Long Beach CC.
Weaver, Dennis Joplin, MO, June 4, 1924. U Okla.
Weaver, Fritz Pittsburgh, PA, Jan. 19, 1926.
Weaver, Sigourney (Susan) NYC, Oct. 8, 1949. Stanford, Yale.
Weaving, Hugo Nigeria, Apr. 4, 1960. NIDA.
Weber, Steven Queens, NY, March 4, 1961.
Wedgeworth, Ann Abilene, TX, Jan. 21, 1935. U Tex.
Weisz, Rachel London, England, Mar. 7, 1971.
Welch, Raquel (Tejada) Chicago, IL, Sept. 5, 1940.
Weld, Tuesday (Susan) NYC, Aug. 27, 1943. Hollywood Professional School.
Weldon, Joan San Francisco, Aug. 5, 1933. San Francisco Conservatory.
Weller, Peter Stevens Point, WI, June 24, 1947. Am. Th. Wing.
Welling, Tom NYC, Apr. 26, 1977.
Wendt, George Chicago, IL, Oct. 17, 1948.
West, Adam (William Anderson) Walla Walla, WA, Sept. 19, 1929.
West, Dominic Sheffield, England, Oct. 15, 1969.
West, Shane Baton Rouge, LA, June 10, 1978.
Westfeldt, Jennifer Guilford, CT, Feb. 2, 1971.
Wettig, Patricia Cincinatti, OH, Dec. 4, 1951. Temple U.
Whaley, Frank Syracuse, NY, July 20, 1963. SUNY/Albany.
Whalley-Kilmer, Joanne Manchester, England, Aug. 25, 1964.
Wheaton, Wil Burbank, CA, July 29, 1972.
Whitaker, Forest Longview, TX, July 15, 1961.
Whitaker, Johnny Van Nuys, CA, Dec. 13, 1959.
White, Betty Oak Park, IL, Jan. 17, 1922.
White, Charles Perth Amboy, NJ, Aug. 29, 1920. Rutgers U.
Whitelaw, Billie Coventry, England, June 6, 1932.
Whitman, Stuart San Francisco, Feb. 1, 1929. CCLA.
Whitmore, James White Plains, NY, Oct. 1, 1921. Yale.
Whitney, Grace Lee Detroit, MI, Apr. 1, 1930.
Whitton, Margaret Philadelphia, PA, Nov. 30, 1950.
Widdoes, Kathleen Wilmington, DE, Mar. 21, 1939.
Widmark, Richard Sunrise, MN, Dec. 26, 1914. Lake Forest.
Wiest, Dianne Kansas City, MO, Mar. 28, 1948. U Md.
Wilby, James Burma, Feb. 20, 1958.
Wilcox, Colin Highlands, NC, Feb. 4, 1937. U Tenn.
Wilder, Gene (Jerome Silberman) Milwaukee, WI, June 11, 1935. Uiowa.

Wilkinson, Tom Leeds, England, Dec. 12, 1948. U of Kent.
Willard, Fred Shaker Heights, OH, Sept. 18, 1939.
Williams, Billy Dee NYC, Apr. 6, 1937.
Williams, Cara (Bernice Kamiat) Brooklyn, NY, June 29, 1925.
Williams, Cindy Van Nuys, CA, Aug. 22, 1947. KACC.
Williams, Clarence, III NYC, Aug. 21, 1939.
Williams, Esther Los Angeles, CA, Aug. 8, 1921.
Williams, Jobeth Houston, TX, Dec 6, 1948. Brown U.
Williams, Michelle Kalispell, MT, Sept. 9, 1980.
Williams, Olivia London, England, Jan. 1, 1968.
Williams, Paul Omaha, NE, Sept. 19, 1940.
Williams, Robin Chicago, IL, July 21, 1951. Juilliard.
Williams, Treat (Richard) Rowayton, CT, Dec. 1, 1951.
Williams, Vanessa L. Tarrytown, NY, Mar. 18, 1963.
Williamson, Fred Gary, IN, Mar. 5, 1938. Northwestern.
Williamson, Nicol Hamilton, Scotland, Sept. 14, 1938.
Willis, Bruce Penns Grove, NJ, Mar. 19, 1955.
Willison, Walter Monterey Park, CA, June 24, 1947.
Wilson, Demond NYC, Oct. 13, 1946. Hunter College.
Wilson, Elizabeth Grand Rapids, MI, Apr. 4, 1925.
Wilson, Lambert Neuilly-sur-Seine, France, Aug. 3, 1958.
Wilson, Luke Dallas, TX, Sept. 21, 1971.
Wilson, Owen Dallas, TX, Nov. 18, 1968.
Wilson, Patrick Norfolk, VA, July 3, 1973.
Wilson, Scott Atlanta, GA, Mar. 29, 1942.
Wincott, Jeff Toronto, Canada, May 8, 1957.
Wincott, Michael Toronto, Canada, Jan. 6, 1959. Juilliard.
Windom, William NYC, Sept. 28, 1923. Williams College.
Winfrey, Oprah Kosciusko, MS, Jan. 29, 1954. Tn State U.
Winger, Debra Cleveland, OH, May 17, 1955. Cal State.
Winkler, Henry NYC, Oct. 30, 1945. Yale.
Winn, Kitty Washington, D.C., Feb, 21, 1944. Boston U.
Winningham, Mare Phoenix, AZ, May 6, 1959.
Winslet, Kate Reading, England, Oct. 5, 1975.
Winslow, Michael Spokane, WA, Sept. 6, 1960.
Winter, Alex London, England, July 17, 1965. NYU.
Winters, Jonathan Dayton, OH, Nov. 11, 1925. Kenyon College.
Winters, Shelley (Shirley Schrift) St. Louis, Aug. 18, 1922. Wayne U.
Withers, Googie Karachi, India, Mar. 12, 1917. Italia Conti.
Withers, Jane Atlanta, GA, Apr. 12, 1926.
Witherspoon, Reese (Laura Jean Reese Witherspoon) Nashville, TN, Mar. 22, 1976.
Wolf, Scott Newton, MA, June 4, 1968.
Wong, B.D. San Francisco, Oct. 24,1962.
Wong, Russell Troy, NY, Mar. 1, 1963. Santa Monica College.
Wood, Elijah Cedar Rapids, IA, Jan 28, 1981.
Wood, Evan Rachel Raleigh, NC, Sept. 7, 1987.
Woodard, Alfre Tulsa, OK, Nov. 2, 1953. Boston U.
Woodlawn, Holly (Harold Ajzenberg) Juana Diaz, PR, 1947.
Woods, James Vernal, UT, Apr. 18, 1947. MIT.
Woodward, Edward Croyden, Surrey, England, June 1, 1930.
Woodward, Joanne Thomasville, GA, Feb. 27, 1930. Neighborhood Playhouse.
Woronov, Mary Brooklyn, NY, Dec. 8, 1946. Cornell.

Jennifer Tilly

Sigourney Weaver

Kate Winslet

Catherine Zeta-Jones

Wright, Amy Chicago, IL, Apr. 15, 1950.
Wright, Max Detroit, MI, Aug. 2, 1943. Wayne State U.
Wright, Teresa NYC, Oct. 27, 1918.
Wuhl, Robert Union City, NJ, Oct. 9, 1951. U Houston.
Wyatt, Jane NYC, Aug. 10, 1910. Barnard College.
Wyle, Noah Los Angeles, CA, June 2, 1971.
Wyman, Jane (Sarah Jane Fulks) St. Joseph, MO, Jan. 4, 1914.
Wymore, Patrice Miltonvale, KS, Dec. 17, 1926.
Wynn, May (Donna Lee Hickey) NYC, Jan. 8, 1930.
Wynter, Dana (Dagmar) London, England, June 8. 1927. Rhodes U.

York, Michael Fulmer, England, Mar. 27, 1942. Oxford.
York, Susannah London, England, Jan. 9, 1941. RADA.
Young, Alan (Angus) North Shield, England, Nov. 19, 1919.

Young, Burt Queens, NY, Apr. 30, 1940.
Young, Chris Chambersburg, PA, Apr. 28, 1971.
Young, Sean Louisville, KY, Nov. 20, 1959. Interlochen.
Yulin, Harris Los Angeles, CA, Nov. 5, 1937.
Yun-Fat, Chow Lamma Island, Hong Kong, May 18, 1955.

Zacharias, Ann Stockholm, Sweden, Sept. 19, 1956.
Zadora, Pia Hoboken, NJ, May 4, 1954.
Zahn, Steve Marshall, MN, Nov. 13, 1968.
Zellweger, Renée Katy, TX, Apr. 25, 1969.
Zerbe, Anthony Long Beach, CA, May 20, 1939.
Zeta-Jones, Catherine Swansea, Wales, Sept. 25, 1969.
Zimbalist, Efrem, Jr. NYC, Nov. 30, 1918. Yale.
Zuniga, Daphne Berkeley, CA, Oct. 28, 1963. UCLA

OBITUARIES

2004

Acquanetta (Burnu Acquanetta), 83, Wyoming-born model-turned-actress died on Aug. 16, 2004 in Ahwatukee, AZ. She had been suffering from Alzheimer's disease. She could be seen in such kitschy pictures as *Arabian Nights, Captive Wild Woman, Jungle Woman, Tarzan and the Leopard Woman,* and *The Son of Monte Cristo.* She is survived by four sons from her second marriage.

Carl Anderson, 58, Virginia-born actor, best known for playing Judas in the 1973 musical *Jesus Christ Superstar,* died of leukemia on February 23, 2004 in Los Angeles. His few other movies include *The Color Purple.* No reported survivors.

Victor Argo (Victor Jiménez), 69, Bronx-born character actor died of lung cancer in Manhattan on April 6, 2004. His credits include *Mean Streets, Taxi Driver, The Rose, Desperately Seeking Susan, The Last Temptation of Christ, Crimes and Misdemeanors, King of New York, Smoke, Ghost Dog: The Way of the Samurai, Angel Eyes, Don't Say a Word,* and *The Yards.* Survived by two sisters.

John Drew Barrymore, 72, Los Angeles-born actor died on Nov. 29, 2004 in Los Angeles. His movies include *Quebec, While the City Sleeps, High School Confidential, Night of the Quarter Moon, The Night They Killed Rasputin, The Trojan Horse, Pontius Pilate,* and *The Clones.* The son of actors John Barrymore and Dolores Costello, he is survived by his daughter, actress Drew Barrymore.

Jackson Beck, 92, New York City-born radio announcer-actor, who hosted such series as *Superman,* died at his Manhattan home on July 28, 2004. He could be heard in such motion pictures as *Take the Money and Run, Cry Uncle, Power,* and *Radio Days.* Survived by his stepson.

Elmer Bernstein, 82, New York City-born composer, who earned an Academy Award for scoring *Thoroughly Modern Millie,* died on Aug. 18, 2004 at his home in Ojai, CA. He received additional Oscar nominations for *The Man with the Golden Arm, The Magnificent Seven, Summer and Smoke,* the title song from *Walk on the Wild Side, To Kill a Mockingbird, Return of the Seven, Hawaii* (and for the song "My Wishing Doll"), the title song from *True Grit,* the song "Wherever Love Takes Me" from *Gold, Trading Places, The Age of Innocence,* and *Far from Heaven,* as well as scoring such other movies as *The Ten Commandments* (1956), *Sweet Smell of Success, Cape Fear, The Great Escape, National Lampoon's Animal House, Stripes, Ghostbusters,* and *My Left Foot.* He is survived by his second wife; two sons, two daughters, and five grandchildren.

Marlon Brando, 80, Omaha-born screen, stage and television actor, perhaps the most trend-setting and brilliantly eccentric performer of his generation, who earned Academy Awards for his performances in *On the Waterfront* and *The Godfather* (an award which he refused), died in Los Angeles of pulmonary fibrosis on July 1, 2004. He received additional Oscar nominations for *A Streetcar Named Desire* (recreating his star-making Broadway role), *Viva Zapata!, Julius Caesar, Sayonara, Last Tango in Paris,* and *A Dry White Season.* His other theatrical motion pictures are *The Men* (his debut, in 1950), *The Wild One, Desiree, Guys and Dolls, The Teahouse of the August Moon, The Young Lions, The Fugitive Kind, One-Eyed Jacks* (which he also directed), *Mutiny on the Bounty* (1962), *The Ugly American, Bedtime Story, Morituri, The Chase, The Appaloosa, A Countess from Hong Kong, Reflections in a Golden Eye, Candy, The Night of the Following Day, Burn!, The Nightcomers, The Missouri Breaks, Superman, Apocalypse Now, The Formula, The Freshman, Christopher Columbus: The Discovery, Don Juan DeMarco, The Island of Dr. Moreau,* and *The Score.* He also appeared in the unreleased *The Brave* and the direct-to-video title *Free Money.* He is survived by several children.

Lyndon Brook, 77, British actor-writer died on Jan. 9, 2004 in London. His films include *The Purple Plain, The Spanish Gardener, Song without End* (as Richard Wagner), *The Longest Day,* and *Plenty.* He was the son of actor Clive Brook.

Larry Buchanan, 71, Texas born low budget filmmaker died on Dec. 2, 2004 in Tucson, AZ, of complications from a collapsed lung. His theatrical directorial credits include *Swamp Rose, A Bullet for Pretty Boy,* and *Goodbye Norma Jean.* Survived by his wife of 52 years, a daughter, and three sons.

Virginia Capers (Eliza Virginia Capers), 78, South Carolina-born screen, stage and television actress, who won a Tony Award in 1974 for her role in the musical *Raisin,* died on May 6, 2004 in Los Angeles, of complications from pneumonia. Her movies include *The Lost Man, The Great White Hope, Big Jake, Trouble Man, The North Avenue Irregulars, Ferris Bueller's Day Off, Howard the Duck,* and *What's Love Got to Do With It.* She is survived by her son and a brother.

Ray Charles (Ray Charles Robinson), 73, Georgia-born pianist-singer, who became one of the great entertainers of the 20th century with his soulful recordings of such songs as "I Got a Woman," "What I Say," and "Hit the Road, Jack," died of complications of liver disease on June 10, 2004 at his home in Beverly Hills, CA. He also made appearances in such movies as *Swingin' Along, The Big T.N.T. Show, The Blues Brothers, Love Affair* (1994), and *Spy Hard.* Survived by his twelve children.

Tim Choate, 49, Dallas-born screen, stage, and television actor was killed in a motorcycle accident on Sept. 24, 2004 in Los Angeles. Among his movies were *The Europeans, Jane Austen in Manhattan, Blow Out, Ghost Story, Soapdish, Jefferson in Paris,* and *Pearl Harbor.* Survived by his wife, a son, his mother, his father, and a sister.

Cy Coleman (Seymour Kaufman), 75, Bronx-born composer of such notable songs as "Witchcraft" and "Hey, Look Me Over," died on Nov. 18, 2004 in New York City. In addition to writing songs for several Broadway musicals including *Sweet Charity, I Love My Wife, On the 20th Century,* and *City of Angels,* he wrote the scores for such pictures as *Father Goose, The Art of Love, Garbo Talks,* and *Family Business.* He is survived by his wife and daughter.

Robert F. Colesberry, 57, Philadelphia-born producer, who earned an Oscar nomination for the 1988 film *Mississippi Burning,* died in Manhattan of complications from heart surgery on Feb. 9, 2004. His other credits include *After Hours, Come See the Paradise, Billy Bathgate* (in which he also acted), *The Devil's Own,* and *Race With the Devil.* On television he earned an Emmy as executive producer of the mini-series *The Corner* and was a co-creator and actor on the HBO series *The Wire.* He is survived by his wife, Karen L. Thorson, a fellow-producer on *The Wire,* and two sisters.

Phillip Crosby, 68, actor-singer, son of entertainer Bing Crosby, died of a heart attack on Jan. 13, 2004 at his home in Los Angeles. He appeared on screen in *Duffy's Tavern, Out of This World, Robin and the 7 Hoods,* and *None But the Brave.* His twin brother, Dennis, committed suicide in 1991. Survivors include his four children.

Marlon Brando

Rodney Dangerfield

Frances Dee

Virginia Grey

Rodney Dangerfield (Jacob Cohen), 82, New York City-born stand-up comedian-actor, known for his catch phrase "I don't get no respect," died on Oct. 5, 2004 in Los Angeles of complications from heart surgery. He was seen in such movies as *The Projectionist* and *Caddyshack*, while starring in and writing *Easy Money*, *Back to School*, *Rover Dangerfield* (also producer and storyboard artist), *Ladybugs*, *Meet Wally Sparks*, *My 5 Wives*, and *The 4th Tenor*. Survived by his wife and two children from a previous marriage.

Philippe De Broca, 71, Paris-born director-writer-actor, best known for the cult comedy *King of Hearts*, died of cancer in Neuilly-sur-Seine on Nov. 26, 2004. His other credits as director include *The Seven Deadly Sins*, *That Man from Rio* (for which he earned an Oscar nomination for contributing to the screenplay), *The Devil by the Tail*, and *Dear Inspector*. He is survived by his wife and two children.

Frances Dee, 96, Los Angeles-born actress, who appeared in such movies as *Little Women* (1933, as Meg) and *If I Were King*, died on March 6, 2004 in Norwalk, CT, after suffering a stroke three weeks earlier. After doing extra work she acted in such movies as *Playboy of Paris*, *An American Tragedy*, *June Moon*, *If I Had a Million*, *The Night of June 13th*, *King of the Jungle*, *The Silver Cord* (marking her first appearance opposite Joel McCrea, whom she married in 1933), *Of Human Bondage* (1934), *Becky Sharp*, *Come and Get It*, *Wells Fargo*, *Souls at Sea*, *So Ends Our Night*, *I Walked With a Zombie*, *Happy Land*, *The Private Affairs of Bel Ami*, *Mister Scoutmaster*, and her last, *Gypsy Colt*, in 1954. McCrea died in 1990. She is survived by three sons, including former actor Jody McCrea, six grandchildren, and two great-grandchildren.

Irina Demick, 67, French actress, a protégé of Fox studio head Darryl F. Zanuck, died on Oct. 8, 2004 in Indianapolis. For 20th Century-Fox she was seen in such 1960s films as *The Longest Day*, *The Visit*, *Up from the Beach*, *Those Magnificent Men in Their Flying Machines*, and *Prudence and the Pill*.

Carlo Dipalma, 79, Italian cinematographer died on July 9, 2004 in Rome. His credits include *Divorce Italian Style*, *Blowup*, *The Appointment*, *Hannah and Her Sisters*, *Radio Days*, *Alice*, *Bullets Over Broadway*, *Mighty Aphrodite*, and *Everyone Says I Love You*. Survived by his wife and a daughter.

Eric Douglas, 46, Los Angeles-born performer, youngest son of actor Kirk Douglas, was found dead at a Manhattan apartment building on July 7, 2004. Cause of death was unknown. He was seen in such movies as *A Gunfight*, *The Flamingo Kid*, *Tomboy*, and *The Golden Child*. Other survivors include his mother, his brother, and two stepbrothers, one of whom is actor Michael Douglas.

Doris Dowling, 81, actress of the 1940s died on June 18, 2004 in Los Angeles of unspecified causes. Among her films were *And Now Tomorrow*, *The Lost Weekend*, *The Blue Dahlia*, *Bitter Rice*, and Orson Welles' version of *Othello*. Survived by her third husband.

Fred Ebb, 76, New York City-born lyricist, known for his collaboration with John Kander on such musicals as Cabaret and Chicago, died of a heart attack on September 11, 2004 in New York. He and Kander also wrote original material for such movies as *Cabaret*, *Funny Lady* (earning an Oscar nomination for the song "How Lucky Can You Get?"), *A Matter of Time*, *New York New York*, *Stepping Out*, and *Chicago* (Oscar nomination for "I Move On"). Survived by six nieces and nephews.

Sam Edwards, 89, Georgia-born screen, radio and television character actor, died of a heart attack on July 28, 2004 in Durango, CO. Among his movie credits are *East Side Kids*, *Twelve O'Clock High*, *Operation Pacific*, *Revolt in the Big House*, *Hello Dolly!*, *Suppose They Gave a War and Nobody Came*, *Scandalous John*, and *Escape from Witch Mountain*. Survivors include his stepson.

Carl Esmond, 96, Viennese character actor died on December 4, 2004 in Brentwood, CA. His American film credits include *The Dawn Patrol* (1938), *Seven Sweethearts*, *The Story of Dr. Wassell*, *Ministry of Fear*, *Without Love*, *Walk a Crooked Mile*, and *From the Earth to the Moon* (as Jules Verne). His wife survives him.

Tommy Farrell, 82, Hollywood-born screen and television actor, who played Corporal Thad Carson on the series "The Adventures of Rin Tin Tin," died on May 9, 2004 in Woodland Hills, CA, of natural causes. His films include *Duchess of Idaho*, *At War with the Army*, *The Strip*, *Colorado Ambush*, *Meet Danny Wilson*, *Wyoming Roundup*, *North by Northwest*, *Kissin' Cousins*, and *A Guide for the Married Man*. His mother was actress Glenda Farrell. He is survived by his wife, a son, three daughters, and three grandchildren.

George "Buck" Flower, 66, Oregon-born character actor died of undisclosed causes on June 18, 2004. He was seen in such movies as *The Daring Dobermans*, *Adventures of the Wilderness Family*, *A Small Town in Texas*, *The Fog (1980)*, *Butterfly*, *Starman*, *Back to the Future*, and *Pumpkinhead*.

Brian Gibson, 59, British film and television director, best known for the 1993 Tina Turner biopic *What's Love Got to Do With It*, died in London on Jan. 4, 2004, of bone cancer. His other films as director include *Breaking Glass* (which he also wrote), *The Juror*, and *Still Crazy*, while he served as executive producer on *Frida*. Survived by his second wife, two daughters from his first marriage, his mother, his sister, and a niece and a nephew.

Nelson Gidding, 84, New York City-born screenwriter, who earned an Oscar nomination for *I Want to Live!*, died of congestive heart failure on May 2, 2004 in Santa Monica, CA. Among his other credits are *The Helen Morgan Story*, *Onionhead*, *Odds Against Tomorrow*, *Lisa* (The Inspector), *Nine Hours to Rama*, *The Haunting*, *The Andromeda Strain*, and *The Hindenburg*. He is survived by his second wife, a son and a grandson.

Jerry Goldsmith, 75, Pasadena-born film composer, who received an Oscar for his score for The Omen, died of cancer on July 21, 2004 in Beverly Hills, CA. He received additional Oscar nominations for *Freud*, *A Patch of Blue*, *The Sand Pebbles*, *Planet of the Apes* (1968), *Patton*, *Papillon*, *Chinatown*, *The Wind and the Lion*, for the song "Ave Satani" from *The Omen*, *The Boys from Brazil*, *Star Trek: The Motion Picture*, *Poltergeist*, *Under Fire*, *Hoosiers*, *Basic Instinct*, *L.A. Confidential*, and *Mulan*. Survived by his wife, two sons, three daughters, six grandchildren, and a great-grandchild.

Spalding Gray, 62, Rhode Island-born actor and monologist, best known for such one-man works as *Swimming to Cambodia* and *Monster in a Box*, both of which were filmed, was found dead in New York's East River on March 7, 2004. He had been reported missing since January 10th and had suffered from severe depression. He acted in such movies as *The Killing Fields*, *True Stories*, *Clara's Heart*, *Beaches*, *Straight Talk*, *King of the Hill*, *Twenty Bucks*, *The Paper*, *Bliss*, and *Kate & Leopold*. He is survived by his wife, two sons, a stepdaughter, and two brothers.

Virginia Grey, 87, Los Angeles-born motion picture and television actress, died on July 31, 2004 in Los Angeles. Starting as a child actress in the 1927 film *Uncle Tom's Cabin*, she continued in films for the next forty-some years, appearing in such pictures as *The Great Ziegfeld*, *Idiot's Delight*, *The Hardys Ride High*, *Another Thin Man*, *The Women*, *The Captain is a Lady*, *Hullabaloo*, *Washington Melodrama*, *Blonde Inspiration*, *The Big Store*, *Whistling in the Dark*, *Mr. and Mrs. North*, *Tarzan's New York Adventure*, *Grand Central Muder*, *Stage Door Canteen*, *Sweet Rosie O'Grady*, *Flame of the Barbary Coast*, *Swamp Fire*, *Unconquered*, *So This is New York*, *Mexican Hayride*, *Jungle Jim*, *Bullfighter and the Lady*, *Target Earth*, *All That Heaven Allows*, *The Rose Tattoo*, *Jeanne Eagles*, *Portrait in Black*, *The Naked Kiss*, *Madame X* (1966), and *Airport*. Survived by her sister, two nieces, and two nephews.

Helmut Griem, 72, Hamburg-born screen actor, best known for playing Maximilian in the Oscar-winning musical *Cabaret*, died on Nov. 19, 2004 in Munich, Germany. His other credits include *The Damned*, *The Mackenzie Break*, *Ludwig*, *Voyage of the Damned*, and *Sergeant Steiner*.

Uta Hagen, 84, German-born actress, best known for her numerous stage roles, including her Tony Award-winning performances in the original productions of *The Country Girl* and *Who's Afraid of Virginia Woolf?*, died at her Manhattan home on January 14, 2004. She appeared in only three theatrical motion pictures, *The Other*, *The Boys from Brazil*, and *Reversal of Fortune*. Survived by her daughter from her marriage to actor Jose Ferrer. She later wed actor-teacher Herbert Berghof (in 1957) and remained wed to him until his death in 1990.

Dorothy Hart, 82, Cleveland-born screen and television actress died on July 11, 2004 in Asheville, NC. Her brief five year career in films included such credits as T*he Gunfighters*, *Down to Earth*, *The Naked City*, *The Countess of Monte Cristo*, and *Lone Shark*. She is survived by her son, three grandchildren, and her sister.

Elroy "Crazylegs" Hirsch, 80, Wisconsin-born football player, former receiver for the Los Angeles Rams, died on Jan. 28, 2004 in Madison, WI, of natural causes. In 1953 he portrayed himself in the bio-film *Crazylegs*, followed by acting roles in two movies, *Unchained* and *Zero Hour!* Survived by his wife, son, and a daughter.

Jane Hoffman, 93, Seattle-born screen, stage and television actress died on. July 26, 2004 in Woodland Hills, CA. Her film credits include *Ladybug Ladybug*, *They Might Be Giants*, *Up the Sandbox*, *The Day of the Locust*, *Tattoo*, *Batteries Not Included*, *In & Out*, and *Deconstructing Harry*. She is survived by a son and two granddaughters.

Martin Jurow, 92, New York City-born motion picture producer, responsible for such films as *Breakfast at Tiffany's* and *The Pink Panther*, died on February 12, 2004 in Dallas, TX, after suffering from Parkinson's disease. His other credits include *The Hanging Tree*, *The Fugitive Kind*, *Soldier in the Rain*, *The Great Race*, and *Terms of Endearment*, on which he served as a co-producer. Survivors include his wife, a daughter, and a grandson.

Fred Karlin, 67, Chicago-born composer, who won an Academy Award for co-writing the song "For All We Know" from the film *Lovers and Other Strangers*, died of cancer on March 26, 2004 in Culver City, CA. He received additional nominations for his score for *The Baby Maker* and the song "Come Follow, Follow Me," from *The Little Ark*. His other movie scores include *Up the Down Staircase*, *Westworld*, *Zandy's Bride*, and *Leadbelly*. Survived by his wife, a brother, a son, two daughters, and four grandchildren.

Howard Keel, 85, Illinois born-singer actor, star of such classic MGM musicals as *Show Boat*, *Kiss Me Kate*, and *Seven Brides for Seven Brothers*, died on Nov. 7, 2004 in Palm Desert, CA, of colon cancer. Following his American debut playing Frank Butler in the 1950 film of *Annie Get Your Gun*, he was seen in such other films as *Pagan Love Song*, *Three Guys Named Mike*, *Texas Carnival*, *Callaway Went Thataway*, *Lovely to Look At*, *Ride Vaquero*, *Calamity Jane*, *Rose Marie* (1954), *Jupiter's Darling*, *Kismet* (1955), *The Big Fisherman*, *Armored Command*, *The Day of the Trifids*, and *The War Wagon*. He is survived by his third wife, four children, and ten grandchildren.

Ed Kemmer, 84, Pennsylvania-born screen and television actor, best know for playing Commander Buzz Corry on the early sci-fi children's series *Space Patrol*, died in New York City on Nov. 9, 2004 after suffering a stroke. He appeared in such films as *Behind the High Wall*, *Too Much Too Soon*, *The Hot Angel*, *Hong Kong Confidential*, and *Earth vs. the Spider*.

Lincoln Kilpatrick, 72, St. Louis-born screen and television character actor died of lung cancer on May 18, 2004 in Los Angeles. Among his film credits are *Madigan*, *A Lovely Way to Die*, *Brother John*, *The Omega Man*, *Soylent Green*, and *Uptown Saturday Night*.

Alan King (Irwin Alan Kniberg), 76, Brooklyn-born comedian, actor, and producer, died of cancer in Manhattan on May 9, 2004. He appeared in such movies as *Hit the Deck, Miracle in the Rain, The Helen Morgan Story, Bye Bye Braverman, The Anderson Tapes, Just Tell Me What You Want, Author Author, Memories of Me, Night and the City* (1992), *Casino*, and *Sunshine State*. Survived by his wife of 57 years, two sons, a daughter, and seven grandchildren.

Anna Lee (Joan Boniface Winnifrith), 91, British screen and television actress, who appeared in two Oscar winners for Best Picture, *How Green Was My Valley* and *The Sound of Music*, died of pneumonia on May 14, 2004 at her Los Angeles home. Her other movies include *King Solomon's Mines* (1937), *My Life with Caroline, Flying Tigers, Commandos Strike at Dawn, Flesh and Fantasy, Forever and a Day, The Ghost and Mrs. Muir, Fort Apache, The Last Hurrah, The Horse Soldiers, The Man Who Shot Liberty Valance, What Ever Happened to Baby Jane?, 7 Women*, and *Star!* From 1978 to 2003 she played the role of Lila Quartermaine on the soap opera *General Hospital* and its spin-off, *Port Charles*. She is survived by two sons and two daughters from her first two marriages (the first being to director Robert Stevenson), a sister, seven grandchildren, and two great-grandchildren.

Robert Lees, 91, screenwriter responsible for such Abbott and Costello comedies as *Hold That Ghost* and *Abbott and Costello Meet Frankenstein*, was decapitated by an intruder in his Los Angeles home on June 14, 2004. Among his other credits are *The Invisible Woman, Hit the Ice, Crazy House, The Wistful Widow of Wagon Gap, Abbott and Costello Meet the Invisible Man*, and *Jumping Jacks*. Survivors include his companion of twenty years.

Janet Leigh (Jeanette Helen Morrison), 77, California-born screen and television actress, best remembered for her Oscar-nominated role as the terrified victim stabbed to the death in the shower in Alfred Hitchcock's *Psycho*, died of vasculitis on October 3, 2004 in Beverly Hills. Her other motion pictures include *The Romance of Rosy Ridge* (debut, 1947), *Hills of Home, Words and Music, Act of Violence, Little Women* (1949), *Holiday Affair, Angels in the Outfield* (1951), *Two Tickets to Broadway, Scaramouche, Fearless Fagin, The Naked Spur, Houdini, Prince Valiant, Living it Up, The Black Shield of Falworth, Pete Kelly's Blues, My Sister Eileen* (1955), *Jet Pilot, Touch of Evil, The Vikings, Who Was That Lady?, Pepe, The Manchurian Candidate* (1962), *Bye Bye Birdie, Wives and Lovers, Harper, An American Dream, Grand Slam, Hello Down There, Night of the Lepus, Boardwalk*, and *The Fog* (1980). She is survived by her fourth husband and two daughter from her marriage to actor Tony Curtis, one of whom is actress Jamie Lee Curtis.

Lu Leonard, 77, Long Island-born character actress died on May 14, 2004 in Woodland Hills, CA, of heart failure. She could be seen in such movies as *Annie, Starman, Micki + Maude, You Can't Hurry Love, Kuffs*, and *Made in America*. No survivors.

Robert Lewin, 84, New York City-born writer-producer, who received an Oscar nomination for his first film script, *The Bold and the Brave*, died of lung cancer on Aug. 28, 2004 in Santa Monica, CA. His only other theatrical credit was writing, directing, and producing the independent feature *Third of a Man*. The rest of his work was done on television, where he earned an Emmy nomination as producer of the series *The Paper Chase*. Survived by two daughters, a son, a sister, and four grandchildren.

Alfred Lynch, 72, British film, stage, and television actor, who played Tranio in the 1967 film of *The Taming of the Shrew*, died of cancer on Dec. 16, 2003. His other movies include *On the Fiddle* (Operation Snafu), *The Password is Courage, 55 Days at Peking, The Hill, The Sea Gull, Loophole*, and *The Krays*.

Nino Manfredi (Saturnino Manfredi), 83, Italian film actor, perhaps best known in America for starring in the film *Bread and Chocolate*, died on June 4, 2003 in Rome, following a stroke. His other credits include *The Last Judgment, Torture Me but Kill Me with Kisses, Le Bambole* (The Dolls), T*he Conspirators, Treasure of San Gennaro, Between Miracles*, and *We All Loved Each Other So Much*. He is survived by his wife and three children.

Irene Manning (Inez Harvout), 91, Cincinnati-born stage and screen actress-singer died of congestive heart failure on May 28, 2004 at her home in San Carlos, CA. Her films include *The Old Corral* (her debut, billed as Hope Manning), *The Big Shot, Yankee Doodle Dandy* (as Fay Templeton, singing "So Long, Mary"), *The Desert Song* (1943), *Shine on Harvest Moon, Make Your Own Bed*, and *The Doughgirls*. She is survived by two stepdaughters, three stepsons, and five grandchildren.

Trudy Marshall, 82, Brooklyn-born actress died of lung cancer in Century City, CA, on May 23, 2004. Among her film credits are *The Sullivans, The Dancing Masters, The Purple Heart, The Dolly Sisters, Dragonwyck, The Fuller Brush Man, Shamrock Hill*, and *Full of Life*.

Portland Mason, 55, Los Angeles-born child actress, the offspring of actors James and Pamela Mason, died on May 10, 2004 in Santa Monica, CA. Her handful of movies include *The Man in the Grey Flannel Suit, Bigger Than Life*, and *Cry Terror!*, the last two starring her father. Survived by her husband.

Frank Maxwell, 87, New York City-born character actor died of complications from heart disease on Aug. 4, 2004 in Santa Monica, CA. He was seen in such pictures as *Lonelyhearts, Ada, By Love Possessed, The Intruder, The Haunted Palace, The Wild Angels, Madame X* (1966), and *Mr. Majestyk*. He was president of AFTRA from 1984 to 1989 and was a regular on the daytime serial *General Hospital* for twelve years. Survivors include his daughter and a step-daughter.

Billy May, 87, Pittsburgh-born musical arranger and composer, best known for his collaborations with Frank Sinatra, died at this home in San Juan Capistrano, CA, on Jan. 22, 2004. He wrote scores for such films as *Sergeants 3, Tony Rome, The Secret Life of an American Wife*, and *The Front Page* (1974). Survived by his wife, 4 daughters, and his brother.

Mercedes McCambridge (Charlotte Mercedes Agnes McCambridge), 87, Illinois-born screen, stage, and television character actress, who won an Academy Award for her motion picture debut, *All the King's Men*, died of natural causes on March 2, 2004 in San Diego. Her other films include *Inside Straight, Johnny Guitar, Giant* (Oscar nomination), *A Farewell to Arms* (1957), *Touch of Evil, Cimarron* (1960), *Angel Baby, The Exorcist* (as the voice of the demon), and *Thieves*. There were no survivors.

Robert Merrill, 87, Brooklyn-born baritone who became one of the Metropolitan Opera's best known singers, died on Oct. 23, 2004 in New York. He also appeared in the movies *Senorita from the West, Aaron Slick from Punkin Crick*, and *Anger Management*. Survivors include his wife, son and daughter.

Howard Keel

Janet Leigh

Mercedes McCambridge

Ann Miller

Russ Meyer, 82, Oakland-born director, known for such low-budget sexploitation films as *Faster, Pussycat! Kill! Kill!* and *Vixens*, died of complications of pneumonia on September 18, 2004 at his home in the Hollywood Hills. Among his other pictures are *The Immortal Mr. Teas, Fanny Hill, Mudhoney, Cherry, Harry & Raquel, Beyond the Valley of the Dolls, The Seven Minutes, Up!*, and *Supervixens*. No reported survivors.

Ann Miller (Johnnie Lucille Ann Collier), approximately 81, Texas-born dancer-actress-singer, one of the screen's great tap dancers, who helped make such musicals as *Easter Parade, On the Town*, and *Kiss Me Kate* among the best of the MGM output, died of lung cancer on January 22, 2004 in Los Angeles. Following her 1934 debut in *Anne of Green Gables*, she was seen in such movies as *The Devil on Horseback, New Faces of 1937, Stage Door, Having Wonderful Time, You Can't Take It With You, Room Service, Too Many Girls, Melody Ranch, Priorities on Parade, Reveille with Beverly, What's Buzzin' Cousin?, Eadie Was a Lady, Eve Knew Her Apples, The Kissing Bandit, Watch the Birdie, Texas Carnival, Lovely to Look At, Small Town Girl* (1953), *Deep in My Heart, Hit the Deck, The Great American Pastime, Won Ton Ton the Dog Who Saved Hollywood*, and *Mulholland Dr.* There were no survivors.

Betty Miller, 79, Boston-born screen, stage and television actress died on May 3, 2004 in Manhattan after a long illness. Although principally known for her stage work she could be seen in such movies as *The Pope of Greenwich Village, A League of Their Own, Angie*, and *Bringing Out the Dead*. Survived by her son.

Sidney Miller, 87, Pennsylvania-born actor-composer-director, died of Parkinson's disease on January 10, 2004 in Los Angeles. Starting as a teenager he appeared in such movies as *Three on a Match, The Mayor of Hell, Wild Boys of the Road, Boys Town, Andy Hardy Gets Spring Fever, Babes in Arms, Girl Crazy*, and *Yours, Mine & Ours*. He later became a busy television director. Survivors include his son, actor Barry Miller.

Jan Miner, 86, Boston-born screen, stage, and television actress, who played Sally Marr, the mother of comedian Lenny Bruce, in the 1974 Oscar-nominated film *Lenny*, died on February 15, 2004 in Bethel, CT. She had been in failing health for many years. Her other movies include *The Swimmer, Willie & Phil*, and *Mermaids*. She was probably best known for her 27-year stint as Madge the Manicurist on a series of commercials for Palmolive dishwashing liquid. Her husband of 35-years, actor Richard Merrell, died in 1988. She is survived by her brother.

Richard Ney, 87, New York City-born motion picture actor, best known for playing the eldest son, Vin, in the Oscar-winning film *Mrs. Miniver*, died of heart disease on July 18, 2004 in Pasadena, CA. His other movies include *The War Against Mrs. Hadley, The Late George Apley, Joan of Arc, The Fan* (1949), *The Lovable Cheat, Babes in Bagdad, Midnight Lace*, and *The Premature Burial*. He retired from show business in the 1960s to become an investment advisor and author. Previously married (1943-45) to his Mrs. Miniver co-star Greer Garson, he is survived by his third wife and a stepdaughter.

Ron O'Neal, 66, New York-born screen, stage, and television actor, best known for his starring role as Harlem drug dealer Youngblood Priest in the 1972 film *Superfly*, died of pancreatic cancer on January 14, 2004 in Los Angeles. His other credits include *Move, Superfly T.N.T., The Master Gunfighter, When a Stranger Calls, The Final Countdown, Red Dawn, Hero and the Terror*, and *Original Gangstas*. Survived by his wife.

Jerry Orbach, 69, Bronx-born screen, stage and television actor, who won a Tony Award for the musical *Promises Promises* and created the role of El Gallo in the original production of *The Fantasticks*, died on Dec. 28, 2004 in New York following a long battle with prostate cancer. His movies include *The Gang That Couldn't Shoot Straight, Prince of the City, Dirty Dancing, Crimes and Misdemeanors, Beauty and the Beast* (voice of Lumiere), *Toy Soldiers* (1991), *Straight Talk, Universal Soldier*, and *Mr. Saturday Night*. On television he starred on the long-running series *Law and Order*. Survived by his wife and two sons.

Jack Paar, 85, Ohio-born television personality, who became famous for hosting *The Tonight Show* and *The Jack Paar Show*, died at his home in Greenwich, CT, on Jan. 27, 2004. Prior to his television career he could be seen in a handful of movies including *Walk Softly, Stranger, Love Nest*, and *Down Among the Sheltering Palms*. Survived by his wife, a daughter, and a grandson.

Hildy Parks, 78, Washington D.C.-born actress-turned-writer-producer, died of complications from a stroke on Oct. 7, 2004 in Englewood, NJ. As an actress she could be seen in such pictures as *The Night Holds Terror, Fail-Safe*, and *The Group*. She later wrote several Tony Awards telecasts, also serving as producer with her husband, Alexander H. Cohen (who died in 2000). Survived by two sons and a daughter.

Robert Pastorelli, 49, New Jersey-born screen and television character actor was found dead of a heroin overdose on March 8, 2004 at his Hollywood Hills home. Best known to television audiences for his role as house painter Eldin on the series *Murphy Brown*, he was also seen in such motion pictures as *Outrageous Fortune, Dances with Wolves, Striking Distance, Michael, A Simple Wish, Heist*, and *Be Cool*, released posthumously. Survived by his daughter.

Albert Paulsen (Paulson), 78, Ecuador-born American character actor, who won an Emmy Award in 1964 for the presentation of *One Day in the Life of Ivan Denisovich*, died of natural causes in Los Angeles on April 25, 2004. His movie credits include *All Fall Down, The Manchurian Candidate* (1962), *Che, The Laughing Policeman*, and *The Next Man*. Survivors include his brother.

Maria Perschy, 66, Austrian actress died of cancer on Dec. 3, 2004 in Wien, Austria. Her movies include *Freud, Man's Favorite Sport?, 633 Squadron, Treasure of Pancho Villa, 99 Women*, and *Murders in the Rue Morgue* (1971).

Daniel Petrie, 83, Nova Scotia-born film and television director, whose credits include *A Raisin in the Sun* and *Fort Apache: The Bronx*, died of cancer on Aug. 22, 2004 at his home in Los Angeles. Among his other theatrical features are *The Bramble Bush, The Spy with a Cold Nose, The Neptune Factor, Buster and Billie, Lifeguard, Resurrection, The Bay Boy* (which he also wrote), *Square Dance, Rocket Gibraltar*, and *Lassie*. On television he won Emmy Awards for the films *Eleanor and Franklin* and *Eleanor and Franklin: The White House Years*. He is survived by his wife; two sons, Daniel Jr. and Donald, both of whom are directors; and two daughters.

Bernard Punsly, 80, New York City-born actor, the last surviving member of the original "Dead End" kids, died on Jan. 20, 2004 in Los Angeles. He made his debut playing "Milty" in the 1937 film *Dead End*, repeating his role from the original Broadway production. He went on to appear with the other "Dead End Kids" in such pictures as *Crime School, Angels With Dirty Faces, Hell's Kitchen, The Angels Wash Their Faces, Junior G-Men*, and *Mug Town*. He left the acting profession to become a physician. Survived by his wife and son.

Frances Rafferty, 81, Iowa-born actress of the 1940s died on Apr. 18, 2004 in Paso Robles, CA. Her credits include *The War Against Mrs. Hadley, Dr. Gillespie's Criminal Case, Thousands Cheer, Girl Crazy, Dragon Seed, Mrs. Parkington, Abbott and Costello in Hollywood*, and *Bad Bascomb*. Survived by her husband and two children.

David Raksin, 92, Philadelphia-born motion picture composer, who earned Oscar nominations for his scores for *Forever Amber* and *Separate Tables*, died on Aug. 9, 2004 in Van Nuys, CA, of heart failure. In addition to his famous theme from the 1944 *Laura*, his many other credits include *The Secret Life of Walter Mitty, Force of Evil, The Bad and the Beautiful, Pat and Mike, Carrie* (1952), *Suddenly, Al Capone, Too Late Blues*, and *Two Weeks in Another Town*. Survived by a son, a daughter, and three grandchildren.

Tony Randall (Leonard Rosenberg), 84, Oklahoma-born screen, stage and television actor, who appeared in such hit comedies as *Pillow Talk* and *Lover Come Back*, died on May 17, 20004 in Manhattan, of complications from a long illness. His other films include *Oh Men! Oh Women!* (his debut, in 1957), *Will Success Spoil Rock Hunter?, No Down Payment, The Adventures of Huckleberry Finn* (as the King), *Let's Make Love, Boys' Night Out, Island of Love, The Brass Bottle, 7 Faces of Dr. Lao, Send Me No Flowers, Fluffy, The Alphabet Murders* (as Hercule Poirot), *Hello Down There, Everything You Always Wanted to Know About Sex* But Were Afraid to Ask, Foolin' Around, Fatal Instinct*, and *Down

with Love*. On television he won an Emmy Award for the sitcom adaptation of *The Odd Couple*. He is survived by his second wife and their two children.

John Randolph (Emanuel Cohen), 88, New York City-born character actor, who returned to acting in his fifties after being blacklisted for several years, died on Feb. 24, 2004 at his Hollywood home. He was seen in such movies as *Seconds, Pretty Poison, Gaily Gaily, There Was a Crooked Man …, Little Murders, Serpico, Earthquake, King Kong* (1976), *Frances, Prizzi's Honor, The Wizard of Loneliness*, and *You've Got Mail*. In 1987 he won a Tony Award for *Broadway Bound*. Survived by two children, a granddaughter, and a brother.

Ronald Reagan, 93, Illinois-born former motion picture and television actor who left show business behind to become governor of California and then 40th President of the United States, died on June 5, 2004 at his Los Angeles home of pneumonia after a ten year battle with Alzheimer's disease. His motion picture credits include *Hollywood Hotel, Boy Meets Girl, Brother Rat, Dark Victory, Hell's Kitchen, The Angels Wash Their Faces, Knute Rockne: All-American, Santa Fe Trail, Nine Lives Are Not Enough, King's Row, This is the Army, That Hagen Girl, The Voice of the Turtle, John Loves Mary, Night Unto Night, It's a Great Feeling, The Hasty Heart, Storm Warning, Bedtime for Bonzo, She's Working Her Way Through College, The Winning Team, Tropic Zone, Cattle Queen of Montana, Hellcats of the Navy*, and his last, *The Killers*, in 1964. Survivors include his wife, former actress Nancy Davis, their two children, and his adopted son from his first marriage to actress Jane Wyman.

Christopher Reeve, 52, New York City-born actor, best known for his starring role as the Man of Steel in the 1978 film *Superman*, died on October 10, 2004 in Mount Kisco, NY, of a heart attack. His other movie credits include three *Superman* sequels, *Somewhere in Time, Deathtrap, The Bostonians, Street Smart, Switching Channels, Noises Off, The Remains of the Day, Speechless*, and *Village of the Damned (*1995). He was paralyzed after a horse riding accident in 1995. He is survived by his wife, his parents, a brother, and three children.

Eugene Roche, 75, Boston-born screen, stage and television character actor died of a heart attack on July 28, 2004 in Encino, CA. Among his films are *Splendor in the Grass, They Might Be Giants, Slaughterhouse-Five, Mr. Ricco, The Late Show, Corvette Summer, Foul Play, Oh God You Devil*, and *Executive Decision*. He is survived by his wife and nine children.

Max Rosenberg, 89, New York-born producer died on June 14, 2004 in Los Angeles. Among his credits were *Rock Rock Rock, The Curse of Frankenstein, Horror Hotel* (City of the Dead), *Ring-a-Ding Rhythm* (It's Trad Dad), *Dr. Terror's House of Horrors, The Deadly Bees, Torture Garden, The Mind of Mr. Soames, Tales from the Crypt*, and *At the Earth's Core*. Survived by his companion; his two daughters; and three grandchildren.

Peggy Ryan, 80, Long Beach-born actress-dancer, known for her starring vehicles with Donald O'Connor in the 1940s, died of complications from two strokes on Oct. 30, 2004 in Las Vegas. Her other pictures include T*he Grapes of Wrath, What's Cookin'?, Private Buckaroo, When Johnny Comes Marching Home, Mister Big, Chip Off the Old Block, The Merry Monahans, Babes on Swing Street, Patrick the Great, Shamrock Hill, There's a Girl in My Heart*, and *All Ashore*, the last three featuring her second husband, dancer Ray McDonald. In later years she was known for playing Jenny Sherman on the hit series *Hawaii Five-O*. Survived by her daughter, a son, and five grandchildren.

Tony Randall

John Randolph

Ronald Reagan

Christopher Reeve

Isabel Sanford, 86, New York City-born screen, stage and television actress, best known for her Emmy-winning portrayal of Louise Jefferson on the long-running series *The Jeffersons*, died in Los Angeles of natural causes on July 9, 2004. She could also be seen in such motion pictures as *Guess Who's Coming to Dinner*, *Pendulum*, *The Comic*, *The New Centurions*, *Lady Sings the Blues*, *Up the Sandbox*, *Love at First Bite*, *Original Gangstas*, and *Jane Austen's Mafia!* Survived by her daughter, two sons, seven grandchildren, and six great-grandchildren.

Artie Shaw (Arthur Jacob Arshawsky), 94, New York City-born clarinet-player and big band leader, perhaps most famous for his recording of "Begin the Beguine," died on Dec. 30, 2004. He appeared as himself in the films *Dancing Co-Ed* and *Second Chorus*, and pretty much retired from show business in the 1950s. His eight marriages, all of which ended in divorce, include those to actresses Lana Turner, Ava Gardner, Doris Dowling, and Evelyn Keyes.

Carrie Snodgress, 57, Illinois-born screen and television actress, who received an Oscar nomination for her performance in the 1970 film *Diary of a Mad Housewife*, died in Los Angeles on April 1, 2004 of heart failure while awaiting a liver transplant. Her other movie credits include *Rabbit Run*, *The Fury*, *A Night in Heaven*, *Pale Rider*, *Blue Sky*, *White Man's Burden*, *Wild Things*, and *Bartleby* (2002). Survived by her son with musician Neil Young.

Ray Stark, 89, Chicago-born motion picture producer, whose films *Funny Girl* and *The Goodbye Girl* earned him Oscar nominations for Best Picture, died of on January 14, 2004 in Los Angeles. His many other movies include *The World of Suzie Wong*, *The Night of the Iguana*, *Reflections in a Golden Eye*, *The Owl and the Pussycat*, *Fat City*, *The Way We Were*, *The Sunshine Boys*, *Murder by Death*, *California Suite*, *The Electric Horseman*, *Chapter Two*, *Seems Like Old Times*, *Somewhere in Time*, *Annie*, *Brighton Beach Memoirs*, *Biloxi Blues*, *Steel Magnolias*, and *Lost in Yonkers*. Survived by a daughter and granddaughter.

Jan Sterling (Jane Sterling Adriance), 82, New York City-born actress, who earned an Oscar nomination for the film *The High and the Mighty*, died on March 26, 2004 in Woodland Hills, CA, following a series of strokes. Following her 1948 debut in *Johnny Belinda*, she was seen in such pictures as *Caged*, *Union Station*, *The Mating Season*, *Ace in the Hole*, *Rhubarb*, *Sky Full of Moon*, *Pony Express*, *The Human Jungle*, *Women's Prison*, *Female on the Beach*, *The Harder They Fall*, *Slaughter on Tenth Avneue*, *High School Confidential*, *Kathy*

O, *The Incident*, *The Angry Breed*, and *First Monday in October*. The widow of actor Paul Douglas (who died in 1959), she later lived with actor Sam Wanamaker, until his death in 1993. No reported survivors.

Frank Thomas, 92, Santa Monica-born animator, one of Walt Disney's famed "nine old men," died of a cerebral hemorrhage on Sept. 8, 2004 in La Canada Flintridge, CA. He helped to animate such noted Disney features as *Pinocchio*, *Bambi*, *Cinderella*, *Alice in Wonderland*, *Peter Pan*, *Lady and the Tramp*, *Sleeping Beauty*, *One Hundred and One Dalmatians*, *The Sword in the Stone*, *Robin Hood*, and *The Fox and the Hound*. He is survived by his wife of 58 years, their children and grandchildren.

Ingrid Thulin, 77, Swedish actress, acclaimed for her roles in such Ingmar Bergman films as *Wild Strawberries* and *Cries and Whispers*, died of cancer on Jan. 7, 2004 in Stockholm. Among her other motion pictures are *The Magician*, *The Four Horsemen of the Apocalypse* (1962), *The Silence*, *Games of Desire*, *La Guerre est Finie* (The War Is Over), *Hour of the Wolf*, *The Damned*, and *Madam Kitty*. Survived by her husband of more than 30 years, Harry Schein, co-founder of the Swedish Film Institute.

Sir Peter Ustinov, 82, London-born actor-director-writer, one of Britain's foremost actors of the post-war era, who won Academy Awards for his performances in *Spartacus* and *Topkapi*, died of heart failure on March 28, 2004 near his home in Bursins, Switzerland. Among his many motion picture credits are *One of Our Aircraft is Missing*, *The Way Ahead* (also serving as co-writer), *The True Glory*, *Private Angelo* (also co-director, writer, producer), *Odette*, *The Magic Box*, *Quo Vadis* (Academy Award nomination), *Beau Brummell*, *The Egyptian*, *Lola Montes*, *The Sundowners*, *Romanoff & Juliet* (and director, writer, producer), *Billy Budd* (and director, co-writer, producer), *Lady L* (and director, writer), *The Comedians*, *Blackbeard's Ghost*, *Hot Millions* (and co-writer; Academy Award nomination for screenplay), *Viva Max!*, *Hammersmith is Out!* (and director), *Logan's Run*, *Treasure of Matecumbe*, *Purple Taxi*, *The Last Remake of Beau Geste*, *Death on the Nile* (the first of several appearances as Hercule Poirot), *Charlie Chan and the Curse of the Dragon Queen*, *The Great Muppet Caper*, *Evil Under the Sun*, *Memed*, *My Hawk* (and director, writer); *Lorenzo's Oil*, *Stiff Upper Lips*, *The Bachelor*, and *Luther* (2003). Survived by his third wife, four children, and a grandchild.

Jan Sterling

Sir Peter Ustinov

Paul Winfield

Fay Wray

Dorothy Van Engle (Donessa Dorothy Hollon), 87, actress who appeared in three of pioneering black filmmaker Oscar Micheaux's 1930 films, died on May 10, 2004 in Ocala, FL. Her films were *Harlem After Midnight*, *Murder in Harlem*, and *Swing*. Survived by her two sons, five grandchildren, and three great-grandchildren.

Joe Viterelli, 66, Bronx born character actor, best known for playing Robert De Niro's henchman "Jelly" in the 1999 comedy *Analyze This* and its 2002 sequel, died of complications from heart surgery on Jan. 29, 2004 in Las Vegas. Following his 1990 film debut in *State of Grace*, he was seen in such movies as *Mobsters*, *Ruby*, *The Firm*, *Bullets Over Broadway*, *The Crossing Guard*, *Jane Austen's Mafia!*, *Mickey Blue Eyes*, and *Shallow Hal*. He is survived by his wife and five children.

Noble Willingham, 72, Texas-born character actor died at his Palm Springs, CA home on January 17, 2004. Following his debut in *The Last Picture Show*, he was seen in such movies as *Paper Moon*, *Chinatown*, *Big Bad Mama*, *Norma Rae*, *La Bamba*, *Good Morning Vietnam*, *City Slickers*, *Of Mice and Men* (1992), *The Hudsucker Proxy*, and *Up Close and Personal*. Survivors include his wife and three children.

Beatrice Winde (Beatrice Lucille Williams), 79, Chicago-born screen, stage, and television character actress, died of cancer on Jan. 3, 2004 at her Manhattan home. She could be seen in such motion pictures as *The Taking of Pelham One Two Three*, *Mandingo*, *Rich Kids*, *A Rage in Harlem*, *The Super*, *Jefferson in Paris*, *The Real Blonde*, *Mickey Blue Eyes*, and *The Hurricane* (1999). Survived by two brothers.

Paul Winfield, 62, Los Angeles-born screen, stage, and television actor, who received an Oscar nomination for playing the father in the 1972 film *Sounder*, died of a heart attack on March 7, 2004 in Los Angeles. His other movies include *The Lost Man* (his debut, in 1969), *Brother John*, *Trouble Man*, *Gordon's War*, *Huckleberry Finn* (as Jim), *Conrack*, *Twilight's Last Gleaming*, *Carbon Copy*, *Mike's Murder*, *The Terminator*, *The Serpent and the Rainbow*, *Presumed Innocent*, *Cliffhanger*, *Dennis the Menace*, *Mars Attacks!*, and *Catfish in Black Bean Sauce*. Survived by his sister.

Ralph E. Winters, 94, Toronto-born film editor, who won Academy Awards for his work on *King Solomon's Mines* and *Ben-Hur*, died on Feb. 26, 2004 in Los Angeles of natural causes. He received additional Oscar nominations for *Quo Vadis*, *Seven Brides for Seven Brothers*, *The Great Race*, and *Kotch*. He is survived by his second wife and five daughters.

Iggie Wolfington, 82, Philadelphia-born screen, stage, and theatre character actor, died of natural causes on Sept. 30, 2004 in Studio City, CA. Best known for his Tony-nominated role as Marcellus Washburn in the original production of *The Music Man*, he later appeared in such movies as *Penelope*, *Herbie Rides Again*, *The Strongest Man in the World*, *Telefon*, and 1941. He was the founder of the Hollywood branch of the Actors Fund. Survivors include his wife, actress Lynn Wood.

Fay Wray, 96, Canadian-born screen, stage and television actress, who earned motion picture immortality playing the screaming heroine carried off by the giant ape in the 1933 classic *King Kong*, died at her Manhattan apartment on August 8, 2004. Starting in silent films she went on to appear in such movies as *Wild Horse Stampede*, *The Wedding March*, *Legion of the Condemned*, *The First Kiss*, *The Four Feathers* (1929), *Pointed Heels*, *Thunderbolt*, *The Border Legion*, *Paramount on Parade*, *The Sea God*, *The Texan*, *The Conquering Horde*, *Dirigible*, *The Unholy Garden*, *Doctor X*, *The Most Dangerous Game*, *Mystery of the Wax Museum*, *Ann Carver's Profession*, *One Sunday Afternoon* (1933), *The Bowery*, *The Countess of Monte Cristo*, *Viva Villa!*, *Affairs of Cellini*, *The Richest Girl in the World*, *The Clairvoyant*, *They Met in a Taxi*, *Smashing the Spy Ring*, *Adam Had Four Sons*, *Treasure of the Golden Condor*, *Small Town Girl* (1953), *The Cobweb*, *Queen Bee*, *Hell on Frisco Bay*, *Rock Pretty Baby*, *Tammy and the Bachelor*, and *Summer Love*. Survivors include three children and two grandchildren.

INDEX

A

A-Trak 317
Aalbaek, Pete 248
Áangeles, Víctor 268
Aarif, Aicha 299
Aarif, Jmiaa 299
Aaron, Caroline 27, 122, 286, 303
Aaron, Nicholas 227
Aarons, Bonnie 117
Aarsman, Daniel 53
Abakar, Haoua Tantine 297
Abascal, Paul 207
Abascal, Silvia 303
Abatantuono, Diego 240
Abatemarco, Tony 303
Abberley, Jeff 288
Abbott, Annie 176, 221
Abbott, Jennifer 250
Abbrescia, Dino 240
Abdelwahed, Ilham 299
Abdullah, Aquil 214
Abdulov, Vitalei 104
Abdy, Pamela 108
Abecassis, Yaël 298
Abeijón, Ezequiel 311
Abel, Adam 202
Abel, Doug 199
Abel, Nicole 307
Abelanet, Francois 263
Abele, María Beatriz 268
Aberdein, Chris 281
Aberlin, Betty 51
Abernathy, Louisa 50, 213
Abkarian, Simon 308
Aboudja, 191
Abouna 297
Abraham, Ken 131
Abraham, Marc 48
Abraham, Yasmine 301
Abram, Deren 310

Abramowitz, Jane Pia 202
Abrams, Marc 213
Abrams, Patsy Grady 130
Abramson, Brad 201
Abreu, Cláudia 301
Absher, Matt 198
Abuba, Earnest 198
Abuhab, Rotem 305
Abujamra, André 245, 301
Acciai, Alessandra 300
Achbar, Mark 250
Acheson, James 94
Acheson, Mark 82
Achibald, Gary 112
Achtymichuk, Spencer 272
Ackerman, Don 61, 272
Ackerman, Thomas 99
Ackroyd, Barry 284
Acon, Daniel 166
Acosta, Ana Maria 103
Acquanetta, 381
Adachi, Leanne 272
Adair, Catherine 29
Adair, Gilbert 229
Adair, Sandra 95
Adair-Rios, Mark 27
Adam, Peter R. 230
Adamová, Jaroslava 266
Adams, Brooke 181
Adams, Cornell 286
Adams, Edie 85
Adams, J. 37
Adams, Jane 46, 168, 169
Adams, Keith 62
Adams, Lynne 181
Adams, Steve 67
Adams, T.J. 84
Adams, Tom 84
Adamson, Andrew 74
Adamson, Christopher 277
Adamthwaite, Michael 56

Adamy, Julie 111
Addica, Milo 146
Addison, Tiffany L. 35
Addy, Mark 252
Adefarasin, Remi 179
Adeliyi, Wendy 192
Adelstein, Paul 114, 115
Adjani, Isabelle 236
Adkins, Eric 124
Adler, Dan 220
Adler, Gilbert 43
Adler, Matt 78
Adler, Sarah 199, 318
Adlon, Pamela S. 28
Adored: Diary of a Male Porn Star 300
Adoum, Albert 297
Adsit, Scott 87, 119, 197, 203
Aduramo, Israel 119
Adway, Dwayne 128, 195
Aerosmith, 216
Aerts, Delphine 248
Afraid of Everything 199
Africa 321
Afrika Bambaataa 317
Afro Celt Sound System 290
Afshin-Jam, Nazanin 187
Aftanas, Craig 244, 259
After Midnight 319
After the Life 297
After the Sunset 158, 347
Afterman, Peter 59
Agah, Sher 212
Against the Ropes 184
Agapova, Nina 317
Agbonkpolo, Ayo 68

Agelion, Simeon Maragigak 166
Agena, Keiko 216
Agent Cody Banks: Destination London 186, 347
Agers, Charla 35
Agha, General Dil 212
Agnew, Michelle 189
Agney, Larry 29
Agnone, Frank 141
Agostini, Alexandrine 251
Agostini, Enrico 321
Agresti, Alejandro 244
Agronomist, The 191
Aguid, Hamza Moctar 297
Aguilar, G.A. 134
Aguilar, George 83, 318
Aguilera, Gabriela 268
Aguilera, Marián 233
Aguirre, Ofelia 65
Aguirresarobe, Javier 331
Ahaouari, Mohamed 297
Ahluwalia, Waris 166
Ahmad, Efriede 319
Ahmad, Maher 88, 126
Ahmad, Saleem 319
Ahmad, Umber 186
Ahmed, Moin 302
Ahmed, Zaheer 313
Ahn, Nae-sang 302
Ahue, Terry L. 32
Aibel, Douglas 109, 154, 166, 182
Aiello, Rick 107
Aikawa, Shô 306
Aiken, Liam 18, 168, 169
Aileen: Life and Death of a Serial Killer 294
Ain, Quratul 313
Aint Misbehavin 191
Aireti 204
Aitcheson, Fraser 92

Aitken, Alexandra 275
Aizawa, Kazunari 320
Ajibade, Yemi Goodman 119
Akal, Tyrone 307
Akarui Mirai 316
Akensouss, Amhed 299
Akerman, Malin 112
Akeson, Mark 171
Akhtar, Shamshad 284
Akinshina, Oksana 104
Akiyama, Dennis 180
Akoka, Gigi 248
Akre, Jane 250
Aktan, Uygar 221
Akwa-Asare, Bellinda 306
Akyama, Denis 38
Alacchi, Carl 78, 87
Alachiotis, Nick 184
Aladpoush, Mohammad 318
Alai, Sher 212
Alamo, The 58
Alan, Devon 144
Alan, George 223
Alan, Lori 160
Alapai, Lava 201
Alazraki, Robert 310
Alazraqui, Carlos 160
Albaladejo, Ana 316
Albaladejo, Felipe 316
Albaladejo, Miguel 316
Albe, Paul 107
Albee, Mary 210
Albela, Mark 233
Alberg, Tom 219
Albers, Helge 313
Albert, Barbara 306
Albert, David 191
Albert, Edward 221
Albert, Marv 206
Albert, Thais 221
Alberti, Maryse 118, 320

Baumann, Anne 319
Baumbach, Noah 166
Baumgarten, Alan 88
Baumgartner, Julien 304
Baumgartner, Karl 239, 287
Baur, Lilo 277
Baur, Marc 118
Baute, Christian 294
Bavaro, Jay 200
Bavaro, Joseph 200
Baxter, James 74
Baxter, Jeffrey 219
Baxter, Trevor 124
Bay, Willow 29
Bayfield, Paul 299
Bayley, Roberta 203
Baylis, Desmond 253
Bayly, Phil 210
Baynham, Patrick 92
Bays, Joe 82
Bazely, Paul 121
Be Cun, 306
Beach, Lisa 92, 180
Beal, Bowd J. 89
Beal, Jeff 223
Beale, Peter 318
Beall, Charlie 121
Beall, Richard 125
Beals, Jennifer 182
Bean, Sean 159, 246
Bear Cub 316
Beard, John 202
Beard, Randy 202
Beard, Tom 121
Bearden, Diane 210
Bearden, Milton 203
Béart, Emmanuelle 245
Beasley, John 56
Beasley, William S. 29
Beason, Eric L. 58, 184
Beat Junkies, The 317
Beatnuts, The 317
Beatrice, Stephen 141,175
Beatson, Bert 126
Beattie, Ian 280
Beattie, Stuart 114
Beatty, Lou, Jr. 189
Beaudoin, Sydni 66
Beaulieu, Philippine Leroy 254
Beaumont, Daisy 253
Beaupain, Alex 316
Beautier, Philippe 283
Beauvais, Marya 204
Beauvais-Milon, Garcelle 35
Beavan, Jenny 280
Beaver, Terry 172
Beazley, Sam 277
Beche, Jean-Philippe 283
Becher, Sophie 299
Beck, 188

Beck, Christophe 77, 82, 102, 113, 119, 136
Beck, Jackson 381
Beck, Maria 303
Beck, Matthew Jon 332
Becker, Gretchen 319
Becker, Holly 190
Becker, Jean-Pierre 282, 283, 304
Becker, Judy 108
Becker, Mark 184
Becker, Sophie 150
Becker, Tracey 156
Becker, Wolfgang 230
Beckinsale, Kate 70, 171
Beckman, Claire 100
Beckman, Peregrine 193
Bedard, Brigitte 49
Beddow, Cascy 164, 187
Beddows, Jane 259
Bedella, David 281
Bednarczyk, Dominika 298
Bedore, Bob 215
Bedore, Brooks 215
Bee, Denise 36
Beebe, Dion 114
Beebe, Reda 59, 62
Beeler, David 203
Beers, Heather 215
Beers, Rand 203
Beers, Sarah 103, 219
Beesley, Max 181
Beeso, Tommy 211
Before Sunset 95
Begala, Paul 198
Begg, Alistair 191
Begg, Azmat 214
Beggs, Noah 272
Begler, Michael 54, 76
Begley, Ed, Jr. 195
Behan, Paudge 319
Behr, Aaron 215
Behr, Jason 145
Behrens, Yennifer 303
Beinbrink, Will 122
Being Julia 273
Beisner, Matthew 193
Beitel, Jason 102
Bejan, Vahe 174
Bejarano, Oscar 103
Beker, Jeroen 318
Bekhór, Julio 186
Bel, Frédérique 283
Belaustegui, Marta 308
Belcher, Patricia 123
Beleña, Melanie 316
Beley, Lisa Ann 187
Belin, Alexandre 314
Bell, Art 78
Bell, Elisa 113, 199

Bell, Evan R. 209
Bell, George Anthony 50
Bell, Hilary 31
Bell, Hope 204
Bell, Jamie 144
Bell, Jessie 165
Bell, Jovan 202
Bell, Kristen 45
Bell, Lauren 117
Bell, Madison Smartt 242
Bell, Marshall 194
Bell, Michael Patrick 160, 217
Bell, Mike 259
Bell, Nicholas 238
Bell, Norman 274
Bell, Richard 306
Bell, Rini 87
Bell, Ron 183
Bell, Sean 184
Bell, Terrone 149
Bell, Tobin 147
Bella, Robert 45
Bellaïch, Oksar 309
Bellal, Benoît 236
Bellamy, James 119
Bellamy, Ned 147, 189
Bellange, Tetchena 78
Belle, Warren 192
Bellecour, Benjamin 236
Belleli, Avi 298
Beller, Marty 64
Bellew, Line Bernard 277
Bellflower, Nellie 156
Belli, William 129
Belling, Davina 222
Bello, Maria 44, 125
Bellocq, Bénédicte 299
Bellocq, Emma 299
Bellsey, Rob 223
Bellucci, Monica 40, 107, 310
Bellville, Hercules 229
Belmadi, Yasmine 316
Belmondo, Paul 310
Belonogov, Valentin 298
Belton, Cathy 235
Beltrami, Marco 53, 101, 173
Belugou, Marylou 78
Belvaux, Elie 295
Belvaux, Frédérique 295, 296, 297, 314
Belvaux, Lucas 295, 296, 297
Ben-Binyamin, Savig 152
Benamoune, Sihem 305
Benani, Boualem 308
Benavides, Yessenia 185
Benayoun, Georges 207
Bencivenga, Mike 216
Bendele, George 31
Bender, Chris 30
Bender, Joel 209

Bender, Lawrence 62, 185
Bendinger, Jessica 128
Bendix, Camilla 320
Benedetta, Mia 313
Benedetto, Beatriz Di 268
Benedict, Jay 313
Benedict, Paul 158
Benes, Svatopluk 266
Benevento, Nicholas 27
Benichou, Pierre-Jacques 282
Benigni, Roberto 73
Bening, Annette 273, 339
Benioff, David 246
Benitez, John Jellybean 186
Benjamin, Alise 148
Benjamin, Joel 320
Benjamin, Jon 192
Benjamin, Matthew 149
Benjamin, Medea 209
Benjamin, Stuart 148
Benjaminson, Scott 126
Benji off the Leash! 203
Benjo, Caroline 316
Benn, Te Te 50
Bennent, David 107
Bennetis, Bruce 146
Bennett, Bridget 71
Bennett, Dan 194
Bennett, Eliza 54
Bennett, Jim 180
Bennett, Jimmy 152
Bennett, Jonathan 68, 69
Bennett, Marcia 192, 221
Bennett, Mark 175
Bennett, Michael 199
Bennett, Sonja 33
Benninghoffen, Mark 182
Benoir, Zac 180
Benoit, Jean-Marie 251
Benrubi, Abraham 119
Benson, Alison 72
Benson, Amber 31
Benson, Ashley 66
Benson, Dan 113
Benson, Ned 172
Benson, Phil 51
Benson, Vincent Damahe 182
Benssalem, Najat 299
Bentall, Paul 121
Bentinck, Timothy 121
Bentivoglio, Fabrizio 310
Bentley, Gavin 202
Benton, Mark 233
Bentt, Michael 328
Bentt, Michael A. 114
Benullo, David 252
Beraldo, Elisabetta 181
Beran, Ladislav 53
Beranek, Allen 126
Bérard, Eric 264

Berdan, Brian 32
Beren, Vera 64
Bereuer, Beverley 34
Berg, Alec 37
Berg, Peter 114, 115, 138
Berganza, Maria 233
Berge, Michael 230
Bergé, Pierre 294
Bergel, Paul David 210
Berger, Howard 216
Berger, Peter 82
Berger, Stan 211
Berger, Yakov 305
Bergeron, Bibo 135
Bergeron, Mélanie 264
Berghoff, Julie 147
Bergin, Barbara 235
Bergin, Joan 243
Bergin, Patrick 60
Berglund, David 223
Berglund, Spencer 134
Bergman, Nir 298
Bergmark, Jörgen 297
Bergounioux, Pierre 318
Bergshneider, Conrad 192
Bergstein, David 45, 189, 243
Berinstein, Dori 186
Bériot, Olivier 310
Beristain, Elisabeth 312
Beristain, Gabriel 164, 312
Berk, Michele 195
Berke, Mayne 136
Berkfeldt, Denis 125
Berkoff, Steven 264
Berkowitch, Lupo 298
Berkshire-Cruse, Ayanna 215
Berléand, François 292
Berlin, Elliot 221
Berlin, Robert 208
Berlinger, Joe 199
Berlioz, Xavier 283
Berman, Bruce 49, 106, 165, 181
Berman, Jennifer 140, 185
Berman, Kirsten 328
Berman, Lester 204
Berman, Shelley 174
Bermann, George S. 46
Bermejo, Nidia 268
Bernal, David "Elsewhere" 32
Bernal, Gael García 22, 268, 269, 279
Bernal, Gina "Ginger" 178
Bernard, Chemin Sylvia 176
Bernard, Elain 250
Bernard, Evan 139
Bernard, Jessie 115
Bernard, John 229
Bernardi, David 138
Bernecker, Nadine 119
Berner, Alexander 260